Court of Protection

A user's guide

courtofprotectionhandbook.com

Court of Protection Handbook is supported by courtofprotectionhandbook.com

On the site, you will find:
- links to relevant statutory materials and other guidance that space precluded us from including in the appendices;
- precedent orders covering the most common situations that arise before the court;
- useful (free) web resources; and
- updates on practice and procedure before the Court of Protection. These updates take the form of posts on the site's blog, and also (where relevant) updates cross-referenced to the relevant paragraphs in the book.

Register to receive email updates at www.courtofprotectionhandbook.com

Follow us on Twitter @COPhandbook

Available as an ebook at www.lag.org.uk/ebooks

The purpose of Legal Action Group is to promote equal access to justice for all members of society who are socially, economically or otherwise disadvantaged. To this end, it seeks to improve law and practice, the administration of justice and legal services.

Court of Protection Handbook

A user's guide

SECOND EDITION

Alex Ruck Keene, Kate Edwards,
Professor Anselm Eldergill
and Sophy Miles

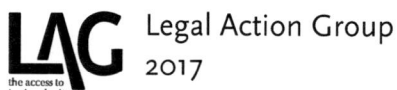

Legal Action Group
2017

This revised first edition published in Great Britain 2017
by LAG Education and Service Trust Limited
National Pro Bono Centre, 48 Chancery Lane, London WC2A 1JF
www.lag.org.uk

© Alex Ruck Keene, Kate Edwards, Professor Anselm Eldergill and Sophy Miles 2017

First edition published 2014
Revised first edition published 2016

While every effort has been made to ensure that the details in this text are correct, readers must be aware that the law changes and that the accuracy of the material cannot be guaranteed and the author and the publisher accept no responsibility for any losses or damage sustained.

The rights of the authors to be identified as authors of this work have been asserted by them in accordance with the Copyright, Designs and Patents Act 1988.

All rights reserved. No part of this publication may be reproduced, stored in a retrieval system or transmitted in any form or by any means, without permission from the publisher.

British Library Cataloguing in Publication Data

a CIP catalogue record for this book is available from the British Library.

Crown copyright material is produced with the permission of the Controller of HMSO and the Queen's Printer for Scotland.

This book has been produced using Forest Stewardship Council (FSC) certified paper. The wood used to produce FSC certified products with a 'Mixed Sources' label comes from FSC certified well-managed forests, controlled sources and/or recycled material.

ISBN 978 1 908407 88 7
E-ISBN 978 1 908407 89 4

Typeset by RefineCatch Limited, Bungay, Suffolk
Printed in Great Britain by Hobbs the Printers, Totton, Hampshire

Foreword to the second edition

by Sir William Charles, Vice-President of the Court of Protection

In their various ways the authors of this Handbook are at the centre of the work done by the Court of Protection and its ad hoc Rules Committee. So are those who are referred to in its preface as contributors. Its second edition, like the first, is therefore based on cutting edge experience of the work of the Court of Protection, its practice and the changes that have been and are being made to its Rules. It follows that the guidance given by this Handbook has an informed and solid foundation.

That guidance is given in language and through a format that is designed to and should assist all users of the Court of Protection and so the subject of proceedings before that court referred to in the legislation as P.

At first and sometimes second sight some of the legislation and processes are complex. I recommend this Handbook as a useful and practical guide to their application and so as a result that helps family, friends, public authorities and the Court to identify and promote what is in P's best interests.

On a more personal note I would like to thank the authors for the work that they have done and continue to do on matters concerning the Court of Protection and so its users. Without them and others who have given up their time to work on the ad hoc Rules Committee and on projects relating to the Court of Protection many of the steps taken with a view to improving its performance would not have been possible.

The product of the work that the authors and others have done relating to what the Court of Protection does, and how it goes about doing it, is admirably captured and explained in this edition of the Handbook.

Sir William Charles
November 2016

Foreword to the first edition
by Sir James Munby, President of the Court of Protection

Once again we are all indebted to the Legal Action Group. Its latest handbook, *Court of Protection Handbook: a user's guide*, handsomely lives up to the well-deserved reputation of its various predecessors.

The Handbook is, as it says, a user's guide. It is a very practical guide, written by those whose expert knowledge of the law and procedure of the Court of Protection is more than matched by their deep understanding, based on experience, of the realities of how the Court of Protection works. Aimed not just at the lawyers who practise in the Court of Protection but also at the increasing number who, whether by choice or otherwise, appear before the Court as litigants in person, the Handbook will, I am sure, be of great benefit to all who use it.

The organisation of the Handbook, explained in the introduction, is clear, sensible and user-friendly. Particularly useful, not least as an important way of explaining what might otherwise appear complex, are the various tables, flow-charts and other diagrams which are such a valuable feature of the Handbook.

The authors are to be congratulated for giving us such a useful and practical work. It should be in the hand of every practitioner and, more particularly, of every lay user of the Court of Protection.

James Munby
30 June 2014

Preface

The Mental Capacity Act (MCA) 2005 is an extraordinarily wide-reaching piece of legislation: any of us at any time could find ourselves incapable of taking decisions about our health, our welfare, or our finances. The Court of Protection, the specialist court established by the MCA 2005 as the ultimate decision-maker in relation to those lacking capacity to take those decisions, is, in consequence a court with a very wide reach.

There are many books which deal with the MCA 2005, and there are also a number of books which deal with the Court of Protection. However, when the first edition was published in 2014, it was the first book to set out to address in detail the practice and processes of the court – across the whole range of its work – in terms aimed not solely at lawyers who are advising those bringing or responding to applications but also to the increasing numbers of people who either by choice or otherwise are involved in proceedings before the Court of Protection without the help of lawyers or specialist advisers. Sufficient has changed in the practice and procedure of the court since the first edition of the book that the time has now come for a second edition.

The book is accompanied by a website: www.courtofprotectionhandbook.com, upon which will be found links to relevant statutory materials and other guidance that space precluded us from including in the appendices, together with updates on practice and procedure before the Court of Protection cross-referenced to the relevant paragraphs in the book. We make more use of the website in this second edition than we did in the first, and all our precedent orders are now to be found there as opposed to within the covers of this book.

This edition of the book (but hopefully only this edition) is hamstrung by the fact that it appears during the life of the Case Management Pilot. This Pilot, explained at paras 4.101–4.103, gives rise to a set of different rules which apply for cases on it. We refer to those rules using the form COPR PrXX, by contrast with COPR rXX for the rules applying outside the Pilot. The Pilot rules (new Parts 1–5 and 15) are to be found at appendix B to this book, together with the 'old' versions of those rules. We hope that by the time of the next edition (as to the timing of which we make no promises) matters will no longer be as cumbersome.

We are very grateful to all those who have contributed their thoughts and expertise at various stages of the two editions of this book's life, and in particular Alastair Pitblado (the Official Solicitor to the Senior Courts), Neil Allen, Romana Canneti, Gordon Ashton OBE, Victoria Butler-Cole, Helen Clift, Penny Cooper, Joan Goulbourn, Janet Ilett, Nicola Mackintosh QC (Hon), Michelle Pratley, Lucy Series, Emma Stacey, Beverley Taylor, Susan Thompson and Aswini Weereratne QC. We are grateful to Floyd Porter and the other partners at Miles and Partners LLP for allowing us to reproduce some of their precedents. We also very grateful to Hilary O'Keefe for undertaking the thankless task of producing what is now appendix C translating the Civil Procedure Rules costs provisions into the COPR, and to Lucy Logan-Green for her assistance in wrestling the text of the second edition into shape. Thanks still remain due to Stephen Knafler QC for his invaluable input at the planning stages of the first edition and his work in pulling together resources.

Special thanks must go to Mark Neary for taking the time to describe a Court of Protection case from the perspective of those most affected by the outcome – his son Steven and himself. We are also very fortunate that Dr Ian Hall was kind enough to contribute a concise account of how to get the best from an expert psychiatric witness, and Lynne Phair to give her perspective as an expert nursing witness. We would also particularly like to thank Esther Pilger, our publisher at Legal Action Group for – yet again – corralling, in her inimitable style, busy practitioners into producing their best work and to translating that work into so user-friendly a format.

We would also like to thank those who have kept the authors going through the darker nights of the soul. Alex thanks, above all, his wife Pieta, for her unswerving support and (very well-feigned) toleration of his disappearing into the ether of the internet at odd hours of the day and night in pursuit of a thought; he would also like to thank Zoë and Benjamin for making it so clear when Daddy has done enough for the day. Kate would like to thank her husband, Stephen Elliott, for his support and encouragement throughout the many hours spent shut away writing. Anselm would like to thank his wife Helen, and his cat Captain Haddock for keeping him company. Sophy would like to thank Guy, Frank and Rebecca for everything including remarkable forbearance.

We state the law as at 1 November 2016.

We welcome feedback, which should be sent to the editors at courtofprotectionhandbook@gmail.com.

Alex Ruck Keene
Kate Edwards
Anselm Eldergill
Sophy Miles
November 2016

Authors

Alex Ruck Keene is a barrister at 39 Essex Chambers. Alex has been recommended as a leading expert in the field of mental capacity law for several years, appearing in cases involving the Mental Capacity Act 2005 at all levels up to and including the Supreme Court. He also writes extensively about mental capacity law and policy, and has contributed to works including *The International Protection of Adults* (2015, Oxford University Press), Jordan's annual *Court of Protection Practice* and the fourth edition of *Assessment of Mental Capacity* (Law Society/BMA 2015). He is an Honorary Research Lecturer at the University of Manchester and a Wellcome Trust Research Fellow at King's College London. He has sat on both the ad hoc committees convened to review the Court of Protection Rules 2007, is a member of the Mental Health and Disability Committees of the Law Societies of both England & Wales and Scotland, and the creator of the website www.mentalcapacitylawandpolicylaw.org.uk. In addition to editing this book, Alex wrote chapters 10, 11 (to which Sophy also contributed), 12, 14, 15, 17, 18, 19 and 22–26 (Sophy contributing to chapter 25).

Kate Edwards is an associate solicitor and professional property and affairs deputy with the Court of Protection team at Slater and Gordon Lawyers. She is a member of STEP (Society of Trusts & Estates Practitioners) and the founder of the Court of Protection Practitioners Association (CoPPA). Kate wrote chapters 7, 8 and 20 and co-wrote, with Sophy, chapter 16.

Professor Anselm Eldergill is a district judge in the Court of Protection and a visiting professor at University College London. Before becoming a judge he was a practising legal aid solicitor specialising in mental health law for over 25 years, and then led the mental health team at Eversheds. He was President of the Mental Health Lawyers Association and of the Institute of Mental Health Act Practitioners, and ranked 1 in Chambers Directory. He is an Alexander Maxwell Scholar and the author of *Mental Health Review Tribunals: Law and Procedure* (Sweet & Maxwell 1997) and articles for journals such as the Princeton University Law Journal, Journal of Forensic Psychiatry and The Guardian. He was chairman of the Mental Health Act Commission's Law and Ethics Committee. Anselm wrote chapters 3–5.

Sophy Miles is a barrister at Doughty Street Chambers. She qualified as a solicitor in 1989 and was a founding partner at Miles and Partners LLP where she led the mental health and capacity team for 16 years. Sophy regularly appears in the Court of Protection and has been involved in significant cases under the inherent jurisdiction including *JE v DE and others* and *Hillingdon v Neary*. She is a fee-paid judge of the First-tier Tribunal (Mental Health). Sophy writes and trains on mental health and mental capacity issues and writes the regular Court of Protection updates in *Legal Action*. She is co-author of LAG's *Mental Heath Tribunal Handbook*. She is a member of the Law Society's Mental Health and Disability Committee. She is an accredited mediator (Regent's University London). Sophy wrote chapters 6, 9, 13 and 21, co-wrote (with Kate) chapters 16, and contributed to chapters 11 and 25.

Contents

Foreword to the second edition   v
Foreword to the first edition   vii
Preface   ix
Authors   xiii
Table of cases   xxiii
Table of statutes   xxxvii
Table of statutory instruments   xliii
Table of European and international conventions and treaties   lvii
Table of codes of practice and practice guidance   lix
Abbreviations   lxi

1 Introduction   1
The scheme of the book   2
Approach   2
Changes from the first edition and the reform of the Court of Protection   4

2 Steven Neary's story   5

3 An overview of the Mental Capacity Act 2005   13
Introduction   16
The Law Commission's work   17
Statutory principles (section 1)   17
Who lacks capacity (sections 2 and 3)   22
Best interests (section 4)   28
Summary – waypoint   35
The statutory mechanisms   36
More about advance decisions   39
More about LPAs   43
More about court orders and deputies   45
More about section 5 ('acts in connection with a person's care or treatment')   52
A general framework   54
Deprivation of liberty   61

xv

Interplay with the MHA 1983   69
Principles of mental health law   76
The future   79

4   **The Court of Protection**   81
Introduction and background   84
Establishment and constitution   84
HMCTS and court administration   87
Where to find the law and guidance   91
Jurisdiction of the Court of Protection   98
The range of applications and orders that may be made   99
Court of Protection procedures   111
Case management   114

5   **Is an application appropriate?**   117
Introduction   118
Maxims and principles   121
Considering the evidence   122
Possible alternative remedies   128

6   **Funding and representation**   157
Being a litigant in person   158
Legal representation   162
Legal aid in the Court of Protection   164

7   **Making an application: property and affairs cases**   181
Introduction   183
Preliminary matters   183
Deputyship applications   190
Deputyship in personal injury award cases   200
Statutory wills and gifting   203
Powers of attorney   206
Jointly owned property and other trustee matters   208
Removal of attorney or deputy   209
Redress   211
Recovery of capacity   212
Death of P   212
Mixed applications   213
Bulk applications   214

8   **Responding to an application and contested applications: property and affairs**   217
Introduction   218
Initial steps   218
Consenting to an application   219

Becoming a party 220
Being removed as a party 221
Contesting an application 222
Contested applications – the Case Management Pilot 223
The stages of the property and affairs pathway 224

9 Making an application: health and welfare cases 229
Introduction 231
Before making an application 231
Types of application 232
The Case Management Pilot 233
How to make an application 235
Completing the forms and supporting information 236
Evidence of capacity 240
Supporting evidence 241
Human rights issues 242
Fees 242
Confidential matters 242
Urgent applications 243
Issue of the proceedings 243
Permission 243
Disputing the court's jurisdiction 244
Service and notification 245
Responding to an application 245
Consenting to an application 246
Becoming a party 246
Contesting an application 246
Being removed as a party 248

10 Interim hearings and interim applications 251
Introduction 252
The jurisdiction of the court to make interim orders and give directions 252
Case management 253
Pilot Practice Direction 4B 261
Making effective use of court time 267
Interim relief and interim hearings 272
Urgent applications 273

11 P, protected parties and children 277
Introduction 279
Participation of P 279
Protected parties 284
Children 287

Litigation friends   288
COPR Pr1.2/COPR r3A representatives   304
Accredited Legal Representatives   308

12 Evidence and disclosure   317
Introduction   318
Evidence   318
Disclosure   356

13 Publicity, privacy and confidentiality   365
Introduction   366
The Administration of Justice Act 1960   367
The approach of the court to reporting restrictions   381

14 Fact-finding   391
Introduction   392
When is fact-finding necessary?   392
Preparing for a fact-finding hearing   396
The determination of contested facts   399
Fact-finding and future risk   403
Fact-finding: consequences   404

15 The final determination of the application   405
Introduction   406
Determining an application without a final hearing   406
Finalising the issues and the evidence; timetabling   408
Skeleton arguments   412
The hearing   412
Judgment   424
Final orders   426
P regains capacity or dies   428
Case study: facilitating participation of 'P' in Court of Protection proceedings   429

16 Costs   433
Introduction   434
The statutory provisions   434
The general rule   436
Departing from the general rule   438
Alternative dispute resolution/mediation – costs consequences   440
Appeals   440
Summary   441

17 Enforcement   443
Introduction   444

The powers of the Court of Protection   445
Committal proceedings   450
Continuing contempt   452

18 Reconsideration and appeals   455
Introduction   456
Reconsideration   456
What can be appealed?   458
Who can appeal?   458
Appellate structure   458
Permission   459
The appellant's notice and skeleton argument   463
The respondent's notice and skeleton argument   465
The position between the grant of permission and the determination of the appeal   468
Determination of appeals   468
Second appeals   471
Appeals to the Court of Appeal and Supreme Court   472

19 Alternative dispute resolution   475
Introduction   476
Code of Practice   476
Court of Protection Rules   477
Case-law   478
The Select Committee   479
Mediation and ADR in practice – types of ADR and how to decide between them   480

20 Office of the Public Guardian   489
Introduction   490
Responsibilities   490
Register of lasting powers of attorney and deputies   491
Searching the registers   493
Supervision   495
Annual reports   495
Court Visitors   496
Investigations   498
Panel deputies   499

21 Deprivation of Liberty applications in the Court of Protection   501
Introduction   502
Challenging deprivations of liberty in care homes and hospitals   504

xix

Applications under MCA 2005 s21A   507
'Re X' applications   521

22   Medical treatment cases   531
Introduction   532
The scope of the court's jurisdiction   532
Serious medical treatment cases: definition   532
Other medical treatment cases   535
Pre-action steps   535
Urgent applications   536
Allocation   537
Case management   537
Declarations   539
Is there really a best interests decision to be taken?   540

23   Safeguarding and the Court of Protection   543
Introduction   544
What is safeguarding?   545
The overlap between safeguarding and the Court of Protection   548
Safeguarding during the currency of Court of Protection proceedings   551
Police involvement   552

24   The Court of Protection and the Administrative Court   555
Introduction   556
The limits of the Court of Protection's jurisdiction   556
Parallel proceedings   558
The approach of the Administrative Court   559

25   Human rights and the Court of Protection   561
Introduction   562
Relying upon the ECHR in the course of proceedings   562
Human Rights Act 1998 declarations and damages   563
Practice points   566
The Convention on the Rights of Persons with Disabilities   566

26   Cross-border matters   571
Introduction   572
What counts as a foreign jurisdiction?   573
The basis of jurisdiction of the Court of Protection   573
Recognition and enforcement of foreign protective measures   574
Foreign lasting powers of attorney   576

27   Instructing experts in Court of Protection cases   579
Introduction   580

Psychiatrists 580
Nurses 583

APPENDICES 587

A **Primary legislation** 589
B **Secondary legislation** 705
C **Civil Procedure Rules costs provisions as applied in the Court of Protection** 805
D **Statements and letters** 815
E **Checklists for best interests assessment, care planning and transition planning** 841
F **Court of Protection fees** 847
G **Useful addresses and resources** 849

Index 855

Table of cases

A (A Child) (Abduction: Contempt), Re [2008] EWCA
    Civ 1138 — 17.15
A (A Child) (Fact-Finding: Speculation), Re [2011]
    EWCA
    Civ 12 — 14.21
A (Court of Protection: Delay and Costs), Re [2014]
    EWCOP 48, [2015] COPLR 1 — 10.19, 15.2
A and C, Re (Equality and Human Rights Commission
    intervening) [2010] EWHC 978 (Fam), [2010]
    COPLR Con Vol 10 — 23.12
A County Council v AB (Participation of P in
    Proceedings) [2016] EWCOP 41 — 12.25, 15.36, 15.73
A County Council v K, D and L [2005] EWHC 144
    (Fam), [2005] 1 FLR 851 — 12.61
A County Council v Mother [2011] EWHC 1804
    (Fam), [2012] 2 FLR 939 — 14.22
A Healthcare NHS Trust v P [2015] EWCOP 15,
    [2015] COPLR 147 — 13.52
A Hospital NHS Trust v CD [2015] EWCOP 74, [2016]
    COPLR 1 — 15.40
A Local Authority v B, F and G [2014] EWCOP B18 — 17.20
A Local Authority v DS [2012] EWHC 1442 (Fam),
    [2012] 1 WLR 3098, [2013] 1 FLR 1429 — 12.72
A Local Authority v HS and others [2013] EWHC 2410
    (COP) — 12.11, 16.20, 23.15
A Local Authority v K [2005] EWHC 144 (Fam), [2005]
    1 FLR 851 — 14.21
A Local Authority v K [2013] EWHC 242 (COP), [2013]
    COPLR 194 — 22.6
A Local Authority v M [2014] EWCOP 33, [2015]
    COPLR 6 — 12.81, 14.21
A Local Authority v S [2009] EWHC 2115 (Fam) — 12.81, 14.21
A Local Authority v SY [2013] EWHC 3485 (COP),
    [2014] COPLR 1 — 9.38
A Local Authority v TZ (No 2) [2014] EWHC 973
    (COP) — 3.127
A London Borough v BB, AM, SB, EL Trust [2011]
    EWHC 2853 (Fam), [2012] COPLR 16 — 23.16
A v A Health Authority and another [2002] Fam 213 — 24.4

xxiv *Court of Protection Handbook / Table of cases*

A, B, and C v X and Z [2012] EWHC 2400 (COP), [2013] COPLR 1	7.85, 11.11
A, Re (a patient) [2016] EWCOP 38	17.21
A, Re (conjoined twins: medical treatment) (No 2) [2001] 1 FLR 267	11.62
A, Re (male sterilisation) [200] 1 FLR 549	14.6
AA v NA (an appeal: fact finding) [2010] EWHC 1282 (Fam), [2010] 2 FLR 1173	14.9
AA, Re [2012] EWHC 4378 (COP)	22.8
AB (A Child) (Temporary Leave to Remove from Jurisdiction: Expert Evidence, Re) [2014] EWHC 2758 (Fam), [2015] 1 FCR 164	6.87
AB (care proceedings: disclosure of medical evidence to police) [2002] EWHC Fam 2198, [2003] 1 FLR 579	12.118
AB (Revocation of Enduring Power of Attorney), Re [2014] EWCOP 12, [2014] WTLR 1303	7.58, 7.111, 7.112
AB v LCC (A Local Authority) and the Care Manager of BCH [2011] EWHC 3151 (COP), [2012] COPLR 314	11.42
AB, Re [2013] EWHC B39 (COP)	7.28
ACCG and another v MN and others [2013] EWHC 3859 (COP)	24.8
AG, Re [2015] EWCOP 78, [2016] COPLR 13	14.5, 23.12
AH v (1) Hertfordshire Partnership NHS Trust, (2) Ealing Primary Care Trust [2011] EWHC 3524 (COP), [2012] COPLR 327	16.20
AHK, AM, AS, FM v Secretary of State for the Home Department [2013] EWHC 1426 (Admin)	12.111
AI v MT (Alternative dispute resolution) [2013] EWHC 100 (Fam), [2013] 2 FLR 371	19.13
Aintree University Hospitals NHS Foundation Trust v DJ [2013] EWCA Civ 65, [2013] 4 All ER 67, (2013) 16 CCLR 554	18.47, 22.7
Aintree University Hospitals NHS Foundation Trust v James [2013] UKSC 67, [2013] COPLR 492, (2013) 16 CCLR 554	3.83, 15.39, 18.1, 18.47, 18.48, 18.49, 22.9, 22.15, 22.20, 22.22
AJ (An Adult) (Deprivation of Liberty: Safeguards), Re [2015] EWCOP 5, [2015] Fam 291, (2015) 18 CCLR 158	11.48, 21.5, 21.22, 21.59, 21.67
An English Local Authority v SW 2014] EWCOP 43, [2015] COPLR 29	26.7
An NHS Trust v DE [2013] EWHC 2562 (Fam), [2013] COPLR 531	25.18, 25.21
An NHS Trust v (1) K, (2) Another Foundation Trust [2012] EWHC 2292 (COP), [2012] COPLR 694	22.18, 22.21

An NHS Trust v D [2012] EWHC 886 (COP), [2012] COPLR 499	11.66, 22.18
An NHS Trust v L, FL, TL [2013] EWHC 4313 (Fam), [2013] COPLR 558	22.24
AN v Lithuania (App No 17280/08, decision of 31 May 2016)	11.4, 11.48, 15.35
ATL v Public Guardian [2015] EWCOP 77	7.67
B (Children), Re [2008] UKHR 35	14.21
B (Disclosure to Other Parties), Re [2001] 2 FLR 1017	12.107
B Borough Council v S [2006] EWHC 2584 (Fam), [2007] 1 FCR 574, (2006) 9 CCLR 596	10.68
B v B [2010] EWHC 453 (Fam), [2012] COPLR 450	11.70
B v B [2010] EWHC 543 (Fam), [2012] COPLR 480	11.67
B, Re (a patient) (Court of Protection: appeal) [2006] 1 WLR 278	18.56
B, Re (care proceedings: appeal) [2013] UKSC 33, [2013] 1 WLR 1911	18.48, 18.49
B, Re (care: expert witnesses) [1996] 1 FLR 667	12.63
B, Re (children: care proceedings: standard of proof) [2008] UKHL 35, [2009] 1 AC 11	14.22, 14.24, 14.28
B, Re (disclosure of material) [1990] 2 FLR 36	12.106
Baker Tilly (a firm) v Makar, [2013] EWHC 759 (QB), [2013] COPLR 245	11.17
Banks v Goodfellow (1870) LR 5 QB 549, [1861-1873] All ER 47	7.85
Beaney, Re [1978] 1 WLR 770, [1978] 2 All ER 595	3.50, 5.42, 5.77, 7.85
Bennett v Compass Group [2002] EWCA Civ 642, [2002] CP Rep 58	11.20
Bishop, Re [1965] Ch 540	5.50
BM, JB v AG [2014] EWCOP B20	7.44
Bovale Ltd v Secretary of State for Communities and Local Government [2009] EWCA Civ 171, [2009] 1 WLR 2274	4.30
Bradbury v Paterson [2014] EWHC 3992 (QB), [2015] COPLR 425	11.40, 11.60
Brocklebank, ex p (1877) 6 Ch D 358	11.70
Buckley, Re [2013] COPLR 39	7.58, 7.61, 7.112
Burnip v Birimingham City Council [2012] EWCA Civ 629, [2013] PTSR 117	25.18
C and D (Children), Re [2010] EWHC 3714 (Fam), [2011] 1 FLR 990	14.22
Calderdale MBC v S and the Legal Services Commission [2004] EWHC 2529 (Fam), [2005] 1 FLR 751	12.66
Carmarthenshire CC v Lewis [2010] EWCA Civ 1567	11.17
CC v KK and STCC [2012] EWHC 2136 (COP), [2012] COPLR 627	11.12, 12.60, 12.61, 12.83, 15.38
Charnock v Rowan [2012] EWCA Civ 2, [2012] CP Rep 18	12.24

Cheshire West and Cheshire Council v P and M [2011] EWHC 1330 (Fam), [2011] COPLR Con Vol 273	12.7, 12.92, 14.1, 14.20
Cheshire West and Chester Council v P (No 2) [2011] EWCA Civ 1333, [2012] COPLR 76	18.57
Cheshire West and Chester Council v P [2014] UKSC 19, [2014] AC 896, (2014) 17 CCLR 5	3.192, 3.193, 11.4, 18.7, 21.3, 21.5, 21.11, 21.56, 25.18
Cheshire West and Chester Council v P [2011] EWCA Civ 1257, [2012] COPLR 37	15.65
City of Sunderland v MM and others [2009] COPLR Con Vol 881	25.6
City of Westminster v FS (unreported, 9 September 2009)	12.65
D (Minors) (Child Abuse: Interviews), Re [1998] 2 FLR 10	5.22
D v An MHS Trust (medical treatment: consent) [2004] 1 FLR 1110	22.8
D, Re (a child) [2014] EWHC 121 (Fam)	15.21
D, Re (costs) [2012] EWHC 886 (COP), [2012] COPLR 499	16.11
D, Re (minors) (adoption reports: confidentiality) [1996] AC 593	12.107
D, Re [2012] EWHC 885 (COP) [2012] COPLR 493	15.5
Daniels v Walker (practice note) [2000] 1 WLR 1382 (Disclosure)	12.90
Day v Harris [2013] COPLR 254	5.50
Days Healthcare UK Ltd (formerly known as Days Medical AIDS Ltd) v Pihsiang Machinery Manufacturing Co Ltd [2006] EWHC 1444 (QB), [2007] CP Rep 1	17.5
Dellow's Will Trusts, Re 1964] 1 WLR 451	5.21, 14.21
DGP Law v DGHP and others [2015] EWCOP 58	7.45
DH NHS Foundation Trust v PS [2010] EWHC 1217 (Fam), [2010] COPLR Con Vol 346	22.21
Director of Public Prosecutions v Kilbourne [1973] AC 729	5.18
DL v A Local Authority [2012] EWCA Civ 253, (2012) 15 CCLR 267	5.84
Dunhill v Burgin (Nos 1 and 2) [2014] UKSC 18, [2013] COPLR 157, (2014) 17 CCLR 203	11.11
Dunn v Durham CC [2012] EWCA Civ 1654 [2013] 1 WLR 2305	12.106, 12.107
E (A Child) (Family Proceedings: Evidence), Re [2016] EWCA Civ 473	12.119
E, Re (Mental health patient) [1984] 1 WLR 320	11.70
E, Re [2014] EWCOP 27	16.10
Egan v Motor Services (Bath) Ltd [2007] EWCA Civ 1002, [2008] 1 All ER 1156	15.61
Elsholz v Germany (App No 25735/94), (2002) 34 EHRR 58, [2000] 2 FLR 486, 13 July 2000	12.76

Enfield LBC v SA and others [2010] EWHC 196 (Admin), [2010] COPLR Con Vol 362	12.23, 12.26, 12.56, 12.92, 14.19, 14.28, 23.21
English v Emery Reimbold and Strick Ltd [2002] EWCA Civ 605, [2002] 1 WLR 2409	18.18
Essex County Council v RF [2015] EWCOP 1	23.16, 25.8
F, Re (adult: court's jurisdiction) [2001] Fam 38	14.5, 14.6
F, Re (mental patient: sterilisation) [1990] 2 AC 1	3.6
F, Re [2009] EWHC B30 (COP), [2009] COPLR Con Vol 390, (2009) 12 CCLR 530	4.97, 9.42, 10.5
FH, Re [2016] EWCOP 14, [2016] COPLR 287	7.46
Fieldman v Markovic [2001] CP Rep 119	18.25
Figgis, Re [1969] 1 Ch 123	5.50
Friendly Trust's Bulk Application, Re [2016] EWCOP 40	7.129, 16.8
G (An Adult) (Costs), Re [2015] EWCA Civ 446, [2015] COPLR 438	16.19
G (An Adult), Re [2014] EWCOP 1361, [2014] COPLR 416	12.7, 12.92, 14.1, 14.20
G v A [2009] EWHC 11 (Fam)	15.61
G v E (by his litigation friend the Official Solicitor) and F [2010] EWHC 3385 (Fam), (2011) 14 CCLR 140, [2010] COPLR Con Vol 454	16.20
G v E (Deputyship and litigation friend) [2010] EWHC 2512 (COP), [2010] COPLR Con Vol 470	3.127, 3.129, 9.2, 19.8
G, Re [2016] EWCOP 37	21.51
G, Re, London Borough of Redbridge v G (by her litigation friend the Official Solicitor), C and F [2014] EWHC 1361 (COP)	8.16
Gillick v West Norfolk and Wisbech AHA [1985] UKHL 7, [1986] 1 AC 112	11.13, 11.22, 11.49, 11.58
GM, Re [2013] COPLR 290	7.58, 7.90, 7.112
Griffin v Griffin [2000] 2 FLR 44, CA	17.5
Guardian News and Media Ltd, Re [2010] UKSC 1, [2010] 2 AC 697	13.66, 13.79
H, Re (a minor and incapacitated person), Baker v H and the Official Solicitor [2009] COPLR Con Vol 606	7.51
H, Re (minors) (sexual abuse: standard of proof) [1995] UKHL 16, [1996] AC 563	5.21, 14.24, 14.25
HA, Re [2012] EWHC 1068 (COP), [2012] COPLR 534	6.65, 6.68, 21.51
Hadkinson v Hadkinson [1952] P 285	17.20
Hale v Tanner [2000] 2 FLR 879	17.15
Halsey v Milton Keynes NHS Trust [2004] EWCA Civ 576, [2004] 1 WLR 3002	19.34
Hammerton v Hammerton [2007] EWCA Civ 248	17.18
Harcourt, Re [2013] COPLR 69	7.109, 7.110
HBCC v LG [2010] EWHC 1527 (Fam)	6.11

HC, Re [2015] EWCOP 29	7.59, 7.64, 7.65
Hillingdon LBC v Neary [2011] EWHC (COP) 1377, [2011] COPLR Con Vol 623	1.2, 2.1, 2.15, 5.54, 8.2, 8.22, 9.4, 9.24, 19.8, 21.22, 23.12
Hillingdon LBC v Neary [2011] EWHC 3522 (COP), [2011] COPLR Con Vol	2.1, 2.3, 2.4, 2.6, 16.20
Hillingdon LBC v Neary [2011] EWHC 413 (COP), [2011] COPLR Con Vol 677	13.65
Hillingdon LBC v WW (Special Educational Needs: Other) [2016] UKUT 253 (AAC)	11.12, 21.27
HL v UK (App No 45508/99) [2004] ECHR 471, (2004) 7 CCLR 498	3.172, 3.196, 21.4
HL, Re (a child) [2013] EWCA Civ 655, [2014] 1 WLR 1160	12.69
HM, Re (vulnerable adult abduction) [2010] EWHC 870 (Fam), [2010] 2 FLR 1057	17.6, 26.7
HNL, Re. See ATL v Public Guardian	
Hollington v Hewthorn and Co Ltd [1943] KB 587	12.18
Hornal v Neuberger Products [1957] 1 QB 247	5.21
I v D [2016] EWCOP 35, [2016] COPLR 432	7.28, 7.89
Iberian Trust Ltd v Founders Trust and Investment Co Ltd [1932] 2 KB 87	17.5
Independent News and Media Ltd v A [2010] EWCA Civ 343	13.64, 14.46
Islington LBC v QR [2014] EWCOP 26, (2014) 17 CCLR 344	11.12
ITW v Z [2009] EWHC 2525 (Fam), (2009) 12 CCLR 635	3.69, 3.70, 3.84
Ivinovic v Croatia (App No 13006/13, decision of 18 September 2014)	11.4
J, Re [2011] COPLR Con Vol 716	7.109
James v Baily Gibson and Co [2002] EWCA Civ 1690	18.25
JE (Jamaica) v Secretary of State for the Home Department [2014] EWCA Civ 14	18.59
JG (a child by her guardian) v LSC, KG, SC, The Law Society and the Secretary of State for Justice [2013] EWHC 804, [2013] 2 FLR 1174	12.66
JG v Lord Chancellor and others [2014] EWCA Civ 656, [2014] 2 FLR 1218	6.86, 12.76
JM (Incapacitated Persons) (Deprivation of Liberty: Appointment of Representatives), Re [2016] EWCOP 15, [2016] COPLR 302	6.69, 11.79, 11.83, 11.90, 11.91, 21.6, 21.56, 21.57
Jolly v Jay [2002] EWCA Civ 277	18.21
Jones, Re [2014] EWCOP 59, [2016] WTLR 661	3.77, 7.88, 15.54
JSC BTA Bank v Mkhtar Abblyzov [2013] EWHC 1979 (Comm)	17.20
JW, Re [2015] EWCOP 82, [2016] COPLR 36	7.44

K v LBX [2012] EWCA Civ 79, [2012] COPLR 411, (2012) 15 CCLR 112	14.4
KD and LD v Havering LBC [2009] COPLR Con Vol 770	10.13
Khanna v Lovell White Durrant [1995] 1 WLR 121	12.36
Kings College NHS Foundation Trust v C and V [2015] EWCOP 80, [2016] COPLR 50	3.61
KK v STCC, See CC v KK and STCC	
KY and DD (without notice applications) [2011] EWHC 1277 (Fam), [2012] 2 FLR 200	10.68
L v L [2006] EWHC 956 (Fam), [2008] 1 FLR 26	19.14
L, Re (a minor) (police investigation: privilege) [1997] AC 16	12.116
L, Re (care assessment: fair trial) [2002] EWHC 1379 (Fam)	12.80
L, Re (Case Management: Wasted Costs) 2016] EWFC B8	16.18, 16.20
L, Re (children) (preliminary finding: power to reverse) [2013] 1 WLR 634	14.29
Lambeth LBC v S, C, V and J (by his guardian), Legal Services Commission (intervening) [2005] EWHC 776 (Fam), [2005] 2 FLR 1171	12.66
Ladd v Marshall [1954 1 WLR 1489	18.46
Lancashire CC v D [2008] EWHC 832 (Fam), [2010] 2 FLR 196	14.22
Lashin v Russia (App No 33117/02, decision of 22 January 2013)	11.4
L-B (Children) (Care Proceedings: Power to Revise Judgment), Re [2013] UKSC 8, [2013] 1 WLR 634	14.29
LBB v JM, BK and CM [2010] COPLR Con Vol 779	12.8, 14.3, 14.4
LBH v GP and MP, unreported, 8 April 2009	23.22
LBL v PB and P [2011] EWHC 502 (COP), [2011] COPLR Con Vol 166	10.41, 19.12, 23.14
LBX v TT [2014] EWCOP 24, [2014] COPLR 561	6.10
Lexus Financial Services (t/a Toyota Financial Services (UK) Plc) v Russell [2008] EWCA Civ 424	14.22
LLBC v TG, JG and KR [2007] EWHC 2640 (Fam), [2009] 1 FLR 414	10.68
Local Authority v Mrs D and another [2013] EWHC B34	9.4
Local Authority X v HI [2016] EWHC 1123 (Fam)	12.109
Loughlin v Singh and others [2013] EWHC 1641 (QB), [2013] COPLR 371	7.12, 7.78, 12.96, 12.98, 12.113, 13.116
M v Press Association [2016] EWCOP 34	13.81
M (Best Interests: Deprivation of Liberty), Re [2013] EWHC 3456 (COP), [2014] COPLR 35	15.40, 15.42, 21.55
M and R (Minors) (Child Abuse: Expert Evidence), Re [1996] 4 All ER 239, [1996] 2 FLR 195	12.60
M, Re (a minor) (disclosure of material) [1990] 2 FLR 36	12.106

M, Re (best interests: deprivation of liberty) [2013] EHWC 3456 (COP), [2014] COPLR 35	11.42
M, Re (sexual abuse allegations: interviewing techniques) [1999] 2 FLR 92	12.60
M, Re [2012] COPLR 430	26.9
M, Re, N v O and P [2013] COPLR 91	7.41, 7.42, 7.43
Mann v Mann [2014] EWHC 537 (Fam)	16.17, 16.20
Mantovanelli v France (App No 21497/93) [1997] 24 EHRR 370	12.80
MASM v Hackney LBC [2015] EWCOP 3, [2015] COPLR 239	17.1, 17.5
Masterman-Lister v Brutton & Co, Masterman-Lister v Jewell and another [2002] EWCA Civ 1889, [2003] 1 WLR 1511	11.11, 11.16, 11.29
MB, Re (Caesarean section) [1997] EWCA Civ 3093, [1997] 2 FLR 426	3.58
Milroy v British Telecommunications Plc 2015] EWHC 532 (QB)	12.25
Milton Keynes Council v RR [2014] EWCOP B19, [2014] EWCOP 34 (costs)	23.16
Mitchell v Alasia [2005] EWHC 11 (QB)	3.45
ML, Re (use of Skype technology) [2013] EWHC 2091 (Fam)	15.57
MM, Re, Local Authority X v MM and KM [2007] EWHC (Fam), [2009] 1 FLR 443	14.26
MN (An Adult) (Court of Protection: Jurisdiction), Re [2015] EWCA Civ 411, [2016] Fam 87, (2015) 18 CCLR 521	4.52, 4.101, 10.19, 15.8, 17.1, 21.51, 21.54, 22.19, 22.25, 23.18, 24.1, 24.4, 24.9, 25.3, 25.5, 26.7, 26.9, 26.11
MN, Re (Recognition and enforcement of foreign protective measures) [2010] EWHC 1926 (Fam), [2010] COPLR Con Vol 893	26.7
Mrs P v Rochdale BC [2016] EWCOP B1	8.10
Mubarak v Mubarak (No 1) [2001] 1 FLR 698	17.15
N (An Adult) (Court of Protection: Jurisdiction), Re. See MN (An Adult) (Court of Protection: Jurisdiction), Re	
Newcastle City Council v WM [2015] EWFC 42, [2016] 2 FLR 184	15.45
Newcastle upon Tyne Hospitals Foundation Trust v LM [2015] EWHC 454 (COP), [2015] 1 FCR 373	11.26, 16.11, 17.5, 22.14
NHS Trust v FG [2014] EWCOP 30, [2015] 1 WLR 1984	13.62, 22.8, 26.7
NHS Trust v Ms T [2004] EWHC 1279 (Fam), (2005) 8 CCLR 38	3.45
NK v VW and others [2012] COPLR 105	9.35

Norfolk CC v PB [2014] EWCOP 14, [2015] COPLR 118	15.31, 15.32
North Yorkshire CC v MAG [2015] EWCOP 64	21.52, 21.53
North Yorkshire CC v MAG [2016] EWCOP 5, [2016] COPLR 346	21.53
Nottinghamshire Healthcare NHS Trust v RC [2014] EWHC 1136 (COP)	22.14
NRA, Re [2015] EWCOP 59, [2015] COPLR 690	6.69, 11.42, 11.47, 11.77, 11.78, 11.79, 12.33, 13.72, 21.6, 21.23, 21.57, 21.61, 21.65, 21.67, 21.67
O-M, GM (and KM) v The Local Authority, LO and EM [2009] EWCA Civ 1405, [2010] 2 FLR 58	12.57
Onassis v Vergottis [1968] 2 Lloyd's Rep 403	14.22
Oxfordshire CC v M [1994] 2 WLR 393	12.117
P (by his litigation friend the Official Solicitor) v Cheshire West and Chester Council. See Cheshire West and Chester Council v P	
P (MIG and MEG), See Surrey County Council v CA, LA, MIG and MEG	
P (Vulnerable adult: deputies) [2010] EWHC 1592 (Fam), (2010) 13 CCLR 610	3.129
P, Re (Abortion) [2013] EWHC 50 (COP), [2013] COPLR 405	22.8
P, Re (Capacity to Tithe Inheritance) [2014] EWHC B14 (COP)	7.85
P, Re [2009] EWHC 163 (COP)	7.88
P, Re [2010] EWHC 1592 (Fam), (2010) 13 CCLR 610	3.127
PA, Re [2015] EWCOP 38, [2016] Fam 47	26.9, 26.11
PAW, Re [2015] EWCOP 57, [2015] WTLR 1785	7.44
PD, Re [2015] EWCOP 48, [2015] COPLR 544	11.90
P v Surrey CC [2015] EWCOP 54, [2015] COPLR 747	21.67
PH v A local authority and others [2011] EWHC 1704 (Fam), [2012] COPLR 128	12.8, 12.62, 12.83, 12.84
Phillips v Symes [2004] EWHC 2330 (Ch), [2005] 1 WLR 2043	12.81
PJS v News Group Newspapers Ltd [2016] UKSC 26, [2016] AC 1081	13.67
PO, Re [2013] EWHC 3932 (COP), [2014] COPLR 62, [2013] WLR (D) 495	9.51, 26.7
Practice Direction (Fam Div: Family Proceedings: Case Management) [1995] 1 WLR 332, [1995] 1 All ER 586	14.19
Practice Guidance (CP: Transparency in the Court of Protection: Publication of Judgments) [2014] EWHC B2 (COP), [2014] 1 WLR 235, [2014] COPLR 78	13.61, 22.18
Prudential Assurance Company v McBains Cooper and others [2000] 1 WLR 2000	15.61

Public Guardian v AW [2014] EWCOP 28, [2014] WTLR 1705	7.58, 7.112
Public Guardian v DA, YS and ES [2015] EWCOP 41, [2015] WTLR 1647	7.58, 7.112
Public Guardian v JM [2014] EWHC B4 (COP)	7.107, 20.42
Public Guardian v PM [2016] EWCOP 25, [2016] COPLR 488	7.111
R (A) v Chief Constable of Kent [2013] EWCA Civ 1706	24.11
R (A Child), Re 2010] EWCA Civ 303	18.43
R (B) v Merton LBC [2003] EWHC 1689 (Admin), [2003] 4 All ER 280	21.67
R (Burke) v General Medical Council [2005] EWCA Civ 1003, [2006] QB 273, (2004) 7 CCLR 609	22.7, 23.12
R (C) v A Local Authority [2011] EWHC 1539 (Admin), [2011] COPLR Con Vol 972	24.6
R (C) v Secretary of State for Justice [2016] UKSC 2, [2016] 1 WLR 444	13.61
R (Chatting) v (1) Viridian Housing (2) Wandsworth LBC [2012] EWHC 3595 (Admin), [2013] COPLR 108	24.9
R (Davis and Davis) v West Sussex County Council [2012] EWHC 2152 (Admin), [2013] PTSR 494	23.15
R (DO) v LBH [2012] EWHC 4044 (Admin)	24.6
R (Faulkner) v Director of Legal Aid Casework [2016] EWHC 717 (Admin), [2016] 2 Costs LR 237	6.79
R (H) v Secretary of State for Health [2005] UKHL 60, [2006] 1 AC 441	21.28
R (Mohammed) v Secretary of State for Defence [2012] EWHC 3454 (Admin)	12.110
R (Moosa) v Legal Services Commission [2013] EWHC 2804 (Admin)	6.49
R (Public Law Project) v Secretary of State for Justice 2016] UKSC 39, [2016] 3 WLR 387	6.29
R (S) v General Teaching Council for England [2013] EWHC 2779 (Admin)	15.61
R (T) v Legal Aid Agency, LBE and others [2013] EWHC 960 (Admin), [2013] Fam Law 805, [2013] 2 FLR 1315	12.71
R (von Brandenburg) v East London and City NHS Trust [2004] 2 AC 280	15.67
R v City of London Magistrates' Court ex p Green [1997] 3 All ER 551	17.5
R v Farooqi (Munir Ahmed) [2013] EWCA Crim 1649	10.11, 15.32
R v Lucas (Lyabode Ruth) [1981] QB 720	14.21
R v Lubemba (Cokesix) [2014] EWCA Crim 2064, [2015] 1 WLR 1579	15.46
R v St Edmundsbury and Ipswich Diocese (Chancellor) ex p White 1948] 1 KB 195, [1947] 2 All ER 170	4.5
Raja v Van Hoogstraten (No 9) [2009] 1 WLR 1143	15.22

Table of cases   xxxiii

RC v CC and X Local Authority [2014] EWHC 131 (COP)	12.104, 12.105, 12.106, 12.107, 12.110
RC, Re (deceased) [2010] COPLR Con Vol 1022	15.71
Redbridge LBC v G [2014] EWCOP 17	23.11
RGS, Re [2012] EWHC 4162 (COP)	11.19, 11.42
RGS, Re [2013] EWHC 1417 (COP)	9.31
Rhesa Shipping Co SA v Edmunds (The Popi M) [1985] 1 WLR 948	14.22
RP v Nottingham City Council and the Official Solicitor (mental capacity of parent) [2008] EWCA Civ 462, (2008) 11 CCLR 316	12.115
RP v UK (App No 38245/08, decision of 9 October 2012), [2013] 1 FLR 744	11.47
RP Z, Re [2016] EWCOP 1	7.49
RR (Costs), Re [2014] EWCOP 34	9.4
RS v LCC [2015] EWCOP 56	12.50
S (A Child) (Identification: Restrictions on Publication), Re [2004] UKHL 47, [2005] 1 AC 593	13.77, 13.78
S and S, Re [2008] COPLR Con Vol 1074	18.8
S, Re (adult's lack of capacity: carer and residence) [2003] EWHC 1909 (Fam), [2003] FLR 1235	3.85, 14.5, 14.6, 14.7, 14.8
S, Re (children) [2007] EWCA Civ 694	18.18
S, Re (ex parte orders) [2001] 1 FLR 308, [2001] 1 WLR 211	10.68
S, Re (hospital patient: court's jurisdiction) [1996] Fam 1, [1995] 1 FLR 1075	17.5
S, Re (vulnerable adult) [2007] 2 FLR 1095	24.4
S, Re [2010] EWHC 2405, [2010] COPLR Con Vol 1112	12.82
SA, Re (vulnerable adult with capacity: marriage) [2005] EWHC 2942 (Fam), [2006] 1 FLR 867	17.5
SA, Re [2010] EWHC 196 (Admin)	5.22, 12.92, 12.99
SA, Re [2010] EWCA Civ 1128	11.17, 17.3
S-B (Children) (Care Proceedings: Standard of Proof), Re [2009] UKSC 17, [2010] 1 AC 678	14.25, 14.29
S v S (Arbitral Award: Approval) [2014] EWHC 7 (Fam), [2014] 1 WLR 2299	19.14
Sandwell and West Birmingham Hospitals NHS Trust v CD [2014] EWCOP 23, [2014] COPLR 650, (2014) 17 CCL Rep 395	10.65
SB, Re (a patient: capacity to consent to termination) [2013] EWHC 1417 (COP), [2013] COPLR 445	11.12, 11.54
S-B, Re (children: care proceedings) [2009] UKSC 17, [2010] 1 AC 678	14.25, 14.29
SBC v PBA and others [2011] EWHC 2580 (Fam), [2011] COPLR Con Vol 1095	3.127
SC v BS and A Local Authority [2012] COPLR 567	12.80, 12.81
SC v LBH [2010] EWHC B29 (COP) (sub nom RC, Re (deceased) [2010] COPLR Con Vol 1022	16.20

Sharma and Judkins v Hunters [2011] EWHC 2546 (COP), [2012] COPLR 166	16.3
Sheffield City Council v E and another [2005] Fam 326	11.12
Shire v Secretary of State for Work and Pensions [2003] EWCA Civ 1465	18.43
Shtukaturov v Russia [2008] ECHR 223, (2008) 11CCLR 440	11.4, 23.12
SK, Re [2012] EWHC 1990 (COP), [2012] COPLR 712	8.12, 8.16, 9.57
SMBC v WMP [2011] EWHC B13 (COP), (2011) 14 CCLR 413, [2011] COPLR Con Vol 1177	12.80
Somerset County Council v MK [2014] EWCOP B25 (damages not quantified), [2015] EWCOP B1 (indemnity costs)	23.16
Southwark LBC v B [1993] 2 FLR 559	17.15
SRK, Re [2016] EWCOP 27, [2016] 3 WLR 867	7.80
Staffordshire CC v K [2016] EWCOP 27, [2016] COPLR 504	21.60
Storck v Germany (61603/00) (2006) 43 EHRR 6	21.1
Surrey County Council v M and others [2013] EWHC 2400 (Fam), [2013] 157 (32) SJLB 31	23.15
Swain v Hillman [2001] 1 All ER 91	18.22
T, Re (a child) [2002] EWCA Civ 1736	18.15
T, Re [2004] EWCA Civ 458, [2005] 2 FLR 838	14.21
TA v AA [2013] EWCA Civ 1661	18.24, 18.54, 18.56
Tajik Aluminium Plant v Hydro Aluminium AS 2005] EWCA Civ 1218, [2006] 1 WLR 767	12.33
Tanfern Ltd v Cameron MacDonald (Practice Note) [2000] 1 WLR 1311	18.22
Terluk v Berezovsky [2011] EWCA Civ 1534	18.46
TG, Re (children) (care proceedings: case management: expert evidence) [2013] EWCA Civ 5, [2013] 1 FLR 1250	12.69, 18.50
Three Rivers (No 6) [2004] UKHL 48, [2005] 1 AC 610	12.117
UF v (1) A Local Authority (2) AS (3) Director of Legal Casework (4) Ministry of Justice [2013] EWHC 4289 (COP), [2014] COPLR 93	6.65, 6.66, 6.67, 9.29, 11.42, 21.25
University College London Hospitals NHS Foundation Trust v G [2016] EWCOP 28	13.81
V, Re [2004] 1 FLR 944	25.5
V v Associated Newspapers Ltd [2016] EWCOP 21, [2016] COPLR 236	13.21, 13.26, 13.49, 13.72
VE, Re [2016] EWCOP 16, [2016] COPLR 406 [2016] 4 WLR 64	11.78, 21.63
W (A Child) (Care Proceedings: Welfare Evaluation: Functions of Local Authority), Re [2013] EWCA Civ 1227, [2014] 2 FLR 431	15.7, 23.18
W v M and others [2011] EWHC 2443 (Fam), [2012] COPLR 222	22.7, 23.18

W v M and S (reporting restriction order) [2011] EWHC 1197 (COP), [2011] COPLR Con Vol 1226	13.52, 13.55, 13.68, 17.5, 22.18
W, Re (ex parte orders) [2000] 2 FLR 927	10.68
Walbrook Trustee (Jersey) Ltd v Fattall [2008] EWCA Civ 427	18.43
Wandsworth Clinical Commissioning Group v IA [2014] EWHC 990 (COP)	12.80
Watt v ABC [2016] EWCOP 2532	7.70
WBC v CP and others [2012] EWHC 1944 (COP) (linked [2011] EWHC 1539 (Admin))	16.20
Webb Resolutions Ltd v JT Ltd [2013] EWHC 509 (TCC), [2013] TCLR 6	10.56
Westminster City Council v Sykes [2014] EWHC B9 (COP), (2014) 17 CCLR 139	3.29, 13.72
Whiting, Re [2013] EWHC B27 (Fam), [2014] COPLR 107	10.62, 17.5, 17.15, 17.19
Windham, Re (1862) 4 De G F & J 53	16.10
Wye Valley NHS Trust v B [2015] EWCOP 60, [2015] COPLR 843	15.39
X (Deprivation of Liberty), Re [2014] EWCOP 25, [2014] COPLR 674, (2014) 17 CCLR 297	3.193, 4.101, 6.69, 21.6, 21.56
X (Deprivation of Liberty), Re [2014] EWCOP 37, (2014) 17 CCLR 464	3.193, 6.69, 21.6, 21.56
X (Deprivation of Liberty), Re [2015] EWCA Civ 599, [2015] COPLR 582	3.194, 6.69, 21.6, 21.56
X and Y v Croatia (App No 5193/90, decision of 3 November 2011)	11.4, 12.83
X and Y, Re (children) [2012] EWCA Civ 1500, [2013] Fam Law 148	10.62, 17.15
Y County Council v ZZ [2013] COPLR 463	11.48
YA (F) v A Local Authority [2010] EWHC 2770, [2010] COPLR Con Vol 1226	25.6
YA v Central and North West London NHS Trust [2015] UKUT 37 (AAC)	11.82, 21.28
Z v Finland (1997) 25 EHRR 371	11.20

Table of statutes

Abortion Act 1967		s2(1)	12.24
s1	22.8	s4	12.24
Access to Health Records Act		s11	12.56
1990	5.84	Commissioner for Older People	
Access to Medical Reports Act		(Wales) Act 2006	5.84
1988	5.84	Communications Act 2003	
Administration of Estates Act 1925		s127	5.84
ss45–47	7.89	Contempt of Court Act	
Administration of Justice Act		s1–4	13.44
1960	13.5	s11	13.44
s12	13.6	s19	13.44
Administration of Justice Act 1969		Courts Act 2003	
s12(2)	18.56	s1(1)(aa)	4.15
Adult Support and Protection		s2(1)	4.17
(Scotland) Act 2007	23.10	s2(5)	4.14
Arbitration Act 1996	19.14	Courts and Criminal Justice Act 2015	
Attachment of Earnings Act 1971		s20	5.84
	17.10	s21	5.84
Care Act 2014	5.84, 11.86,	Courts and Legal Services Act 1990	
	23.2, 23.3, 23.5,	s58	16.5
	23.6, 23.7, 23.10	Criminal Justice and Police Act 2001	
s1(2)(c)	23.5	s42A	5.84
s32	5.70	Data Protection Act	
s42	23.5	1998	5.84, 12.106
s42(2)	23.9	Disability Discrimination Act	
s42(3)	23.6	1995	5.84
Care Standards Act 2000		Domestic Violence, Crime and	
Part 2	12.46	Victims Act 2004	
Children Act 1989	3.96, 5.2, 5.82,	s5	5.84
	12.61, 14.3,	Enduring Powers of Attorney Act	
	14.5, 14.9, 14.19	1985	4.36, 4.79
Part 4	14.19	s4(2)	20.7
s31(2)	14.3, 14.3, 14.21	Environmental Protection Act 1990	
Civil Evidence Act 1972		Part 3	5.84
s3	12.56	Sch 3	5.84
s3(1)	6.87	Equality Act 2010	5.84
Civil Evidence Act		s19	5.84
1995	12.23, 12.56	s26	5.84
s1(2)(a)	12.23	s27	5.84

Equality Act 2010 *continued*		Legal Aid, Sentencing *continued*	
Part 3	5.84	Sch 1 Part 3	6.38
s199	5.50	Legal Services Act 2007	
Family Law Act 1996	5.84		13.23
Fraud Act 2006		s194(3)	16.5
s4	5.77	Local Government Act 1974	
Freedom of Information Act		Part III	5.84
2000	5.84	Part IIIA	5.84
Health Act 2009	5.84	Lunacy Amendment	
Health and Social Care Act 2008		Act 1862	16.10
Part 1 Chapter 2	12.46	Malicious Communications	
Health Service Commissioners Act		Act 1988	5.84
1993	5.84	Mental Capacity	
Health Service Commissioner		Act 2005	**(reproduced in full in appendix A)** 1.2, 1.10, 2.3, 2.6, 2.9, 2.10, 3.1, 3.8, 3.9, 3.14, 3.40, 3.47, 3.64, 3.66, 3.68, 3.88, 3.89, 3.91, 3.93, 3.96, 3.102, 3.114, 3.128, 3.159, 3.162, 3.164, 3.166, 3.168, 3.169, 3.173, 3.184, 3.186, 3.187, 3.188, 3.189, 3.194, 3.195, 3.205, 3.206, 3.208, 3.209, 3.210, 3.211, 3.112, 3.214, 3.217, 3.218, 3.219, 3.220, 3.222, 3.227, 3.231, 3.232, 3.233, 3.234, 4.1, 4.5, 4.26, 4.29, 4.36, 4.37, 4.43, 4.44, 4.65, 5.2, 5.41, 5.77, 5.80, 5.84, 6.6, 6.20, 6.30, 6.34, 6.35, 6.36, 6.45, 7.13, 7.28, 7.39, 7.40, 7.58, 7.93, 7.95, 9.28, 9.35, 10.4, 10.40, 11.21, 11.25, 11.28, 11.43, 11.56, 12.23, 12.55, 12.58, 12.67, 12.80, 12.81, 12.90, 12.92, 12.98, 12.116, 12.118, 13.82, 14.5, 14.9, 14.26, 15.39, 15.65, 16.2, 19.4, 19.15, 20.5, 21.4, 24.1, 24.4, 25.6, 25.16, 25.17, 25.18, 25.19	
(Amendment) Act 1996			
5.84			
Human Fertilisation and Embryology			
Act 1990	4.46		
Human Rights Act			
1998	4.39, 5.84, 9.44, 24.5, 25.6, 25.12, 25.14, 25.14		
s4	4.11, 22.17, 25.6		
s4(5)(f)	25.6		
s6(1)	12.6		
s6(3)	12.6		
s7	25.3		
s7(1)(b)	25.4, 25.5		
s8	25.6		
s8(3)	25.9		
Legal Aid, Sentencing and Punishment of Offenders			
Act 2012	6.25, 6.26, 16.6		
s4	6.25		
s10	6.27		
s25	6.76		
s26	16.6		
s26(1)	16.6		
Sch 1	6.25, 6.27, 6.28, 6.34		
Sch 1 Part 1		Part 1	4.36
para 5	6.34	s1	3.10, 3.147, 4.52, 4.105
Sch 1 Part 1			
para 5(1)	6.34, 6.45	s1(1)	3.10, 11.53
Sch 1 Part 1		s1(2)	3.10, 12.8
para 5(3)	6.36, 6.45	s1(3)	3.10, 25.21
Sch 1 Part 1		s1(4)	3.10
para 5(4)	6.37	s1(5)	3.10, 7.61, 10.19, 11.51, 12.6, 15.7, 24.9
Sch 1 Part 1			
para 9	6.39		

Table of statutes xxxix

Mental Capacity Act 2005 *continued*		Mental Capacity Act 2005 *continued*	
s1(6)	3.10	s5(4)	3.156
s2	3.33, 7.85, 11.11, 11.13	s6(6)	3.137, 3.156
		s6(7)	3.156
s2(1)	21.27	s7	3.136, 5.77
s2(3)	3.39	s7(1)	5.64
s2(3)(b)	11.17	s7(2)	5.64
s2(4)	3.13, 12.8	s8(1)	5.66
s2(5)	4.45, 11.13, 11.51	s9(2)	4.70
		s10	4.70
s2(6)	4.45	s11	3.168
s3	3.33, 3.43, 3.52, 7.85, 11.11, 11.13	s11(7)(a)	3.118, 3.120
		s11(7)(b)	3.120
		s11(7)(c)	3.118
s3(2)	3.53	s11(8)	3.118
s3(3)	3.54	s13(2)	3.118
s3(4)	3.47	s12(2)	4.76, 7.90
s4	3.65, 3.67, 3.71, 3.118, 3.123, 3.138, 3.147, 3.154, 3.162, 3.164, 3.236, 4.52, 4.58, 5.77, 14.4, 25.21	s12(3)	7.90
		s15	3.121, 4.50, 10.5, 11.77, 15.66, 21.4, 21.21, 22.19, 26.6
		s15(1)(a)	17.1
s4(1)	3.66	s15(1)(c)	4.52, 17.1, 22.19, 22.25
s4(2)	3.67		
s4(3)	3.67	s15(2)	4.50
s4(4)	3.67, 15.39	s16	3.122, 3.195, 4.49, 4.52, 4.53, 4.54, 4.55, 5.16, 6.65, 6.69, 11.77, 21.2, 21.4, 21.6, 21.21, 21.52, 21.56, 22.19, 26.6
s4(5)	3.67		
s4(6)	3.67, 11.74, 11.77		
s4(6)(a)	3.104		
s4(7)	3.67		
s4(9)	3.71		
s4(10)	3.67		
s4(11)	3.67		
s4A	21.10	s16(1)	3.122, 4.52, 9.6
s5	3.94, 3.96, 3.97, 3.100, 3.101, 3.136, 3.137, 3.149, 3.153, 3.154, 3.155, 3.156, 3.157, 3.158, 3.159, 3.162, 3.164, 3.168, 3.169, 3.190, 3.191, 5.2, 5.66, 5.67, 5.78, 22.9	s16(2)	4.55, 9.6
		s16(2)(a)	9.15, 21.66, 22.19
		s16(3)	4.52
		s16(4)	3.125, 4.57
		s16(4)(a)	9.6
		s16(4)(b)	9.6
		s16(5)	3.143
		s16(6)	4.58
		s16(7)	4.52
		s16(8)	4.68, 7.106
		s16A	22.17
s5(2)	3.151	s17	5.16
s5(3)	3.149	s17(1)	4.53

Mental Capacity Act 2005 *continued*		Mental Capacity Act 2005 *continued*	
s17(2)	4.53	s21A(5)(a)	21.20
s18	7.84	s21A(5)(b)	21.20
s18(1)	4.54	s21A(6)	6.67, 21.15, 21.20
s18(1)(k)	11.28, 11.43		
s18(2)	4.54	s21A(7)	21.15, 21.20
s18(3)	11.13, 11.51	s22	4.69, 7.98
s19(1)	3.139, 4.59	s22(1)	4.69
s19(1)(b)	7.50, 11.43	s22(2)	4.70
s19(2)	3.141, 4.61	s22(2)(a)	7.99
s19(3)	3.140, 4.60	s22(3)	3.118, 4.71, 7.97, 7.109
s19(4)	3.142, 4.62		
s19(5)	4.63	s22(3)(a)	7.97
s19(7)	4.67, 16.8	s22(3)(b)	7.105
s19(8)	3.145, 4.64	s22(4)	4.72
s19(9)	4.66, 7.51	s22(5)	4.73
s19(9)(b)	20.27, 20.38	s23	4.69, 7.98
s20	3.168, 9.6	s23(1)	4.74
s20(1)	3.146, 3.147	s23(2)(a)	4.74
s20(2)	9.6	s23(2)(b)	4.74
s20(2)(a)	3.147	s23(3)(a)	4.75, 7.100
s20(2)(b)	3.147	s23(3)(b)	4.75
s20(3)	7.102	s23(3)(c)	4.75, 7.100
s20(3)(a)	3.147	s23(3)(d)	4.75, 7.100
s20(3)(b)	3.147	s23(4)	4.76
s20(3)(c)	3.147	s24	3.104, 3.120, 3.156
s20(4)	3.147, 4.71		
s20(5)	3.147, 9.6	s24(1)	3.103
s20(6)	3.146, 3.147	s24(2)	3.106
s20(7)	3.147	s24(3)	3.108
s21A	6.33, 6.62, 6.64, 6.66, 6.74, 9.8, 9.15, 9.28, 11.12, 11.48, 11.91, 11.104, 21.2, 21.4, 21.21, 21.16, 21.19, 21.20, 21.21, 21.22, 21.23, 21.25, 21.27, 21.28, 21.29, 21.31, 21.32, 21.33, 21.36, 21.41, 21.45, 21.51, 21.52, 21.55	s24(4)	3.108
		s25	3.120, 3.156
		s25(2)(b)	3.119
		s25(5)	3.107
		s25(7)	3.120
		s26	3.120, 3.156
		s26(1)	3.105, 3.120, 3.146
		s26(2)	3.110
		s26(3)	3.109
		s26(4)	3.111, 4.77
		s26(5)	3.112, 4.78
		ss27–29	4.44
		s27	4.46, 5.2
		s27(1)	4.46
		s28	4.47, 5.2
s21A(2)	21.21	s29	4.48
s21A(2)(b)	6.65	s29(1)	4.48
s21A(3)(a)	6.65, 21.20, 21.21	s39D	21.22, 21.23, 21.24
s21A(3)(b)	21.20	s44	5.84

Table of statutes

Mental Capacity Act 2005 continued		Mental Capacity Act 2005 continued	
Part 2	4.36	Sch A1	
s45(1)	17.5	paras 68(2)	21.12
s46(2)(c)	4.11	Sch A1	
s47	17.7, 17.19	paras 68(4)	21.12
s47(1)	4.6, 17.5, 17.5, 17.13	Sch A1 paras 68(5)	21.9
s48	4.96, 4.98, 10.1, 10.6, 10.61	Sch A1 paras 69(2)	21.12
s49	4.19, 7.13, 12.3, 12.45, 12.46, 12.47, 12.48, 12.49, 12.50, 12.51, 12.52, 12.53, 12.56, 13.10, 20.37	Sch A1 paras 69(4), (5)	21.12
		Sch A1 para 71(2)	21.12
		Sch A1 para 102	21.13
		Sch A1 para 117	21.14
		Sch A1 para 140	21.24
		Sch A1 Part 8	21.13, 21.15
s49(6)	12.46	Sch 1	4.36
s49(7)	12.46	Sch 1 para 6	7.97
s49(8)	12.46	Sch 1 para 13(3)	7.97
s49(9)	12.46	Sch 1 para 13(4)	7.97
s50	5.2, 9.15, 21.25	Sch 1A	3.174, 4.36
s50(1)(a)	9.15, 9.28	Sch 2	4.36
s50(1)(b)	9.15	Sch 2 para 11	20.14
s50(1)(c)	9.15	Sch 3	4.36, 4.91, 4.93, 26.1, 26.2, 26.4, 26.9
s50(3)	5.2		
s51(2)(j)	17.7		
s52	4.30		
s52(3)	4.30	Sch 3 para 1	26.5, 26.10
s53(4)	18.13	Sch 3 para 4	26.9
s55	16.2	Sch 3 para 5	26.9
s55(3)–(6)	16.3	Sch 3 para 7(1)	26.6
ss57–61	20.1	Sch 3 para 7(2)	26.8
s58(1)	20.4	Sch 3 para 12	26.11
s61	20.31	Sch 3	
s61(2)	7.13, 12.45	para 12(2)(b)	26.12
s61(4)	12.49	Sch 3	
Part 3	4.36	para 13(1), (2)	26.13
s62	3.68	Sch 3 para 14(1)	26.13
s63	4.36	Sch 3 para 16	7.98
s64(1)	3.104	Sch 3 para 20(1)	26.10
s66	4.36	Sch 3 para 20(2)	26.10
Sch A1	3.174, 3.176, 4.36, 4.101, 5.84, 6.62, 6.68, 9.3, 10.34, 21.4, 21.9, 21.13, 21.67	Sch 3 para 22(1)	26.10
		Sch 4	4.36, 4.79, 7.94
		Sch 4 para 2(9)(b)	4.88
		Sch 4 para 3(2)	4.86
Sch A1 para 6	3.181, 21.10	Sch 5	4.36
Sch A1 paras 67	21.10	Sch 6	4.36
Sch A1 paras 67–73	5.84, 21.9	Sch 6 para 6(c)	26.12
		Sch 6 para 10	13.6

Mental Health Act 1983	3.13, 3.96, 3.153, 3.177, 3.179, 3.187, 3.188, 3.205, 3.207, 3.208, 3.210, 3.211, 3.212, 3.218, 3.219, 3.224, 3.231, 3.232, 3.233, 3.234, 5.2, 5.81, 6.38, 6.56, 13.6, 21.19, 21.67, 22.9	Offences Against the Persons Act 1861	5.84
		Parliamentary and Health Service Commissioners Act 1987	5.84
		Parliamentary Commissioner Act 1967	5.84
s2	3.210, 3.216, 3.220, 3.221, 3.225, 3.227, 3.228, 3.229, 3.230, 3.233, 5.84	Police and Criminal Evidence Act 1984	
		s17(1)(e)	5.84
		Prosecution of Offenders Act 1985	12.34
		Protection from Harassment Act 1997	
s3	3.210, 3.213, 3.216, 3.220, 3.221, 3.225, 3.227, 3.228, 3.233, 5.84	s1	5.84
		Public Health Act 1936	
		s83	5.84
		s84	5.84
		s85	5.84
s4	3.210, 3.233, 5.84	s287	5.84
		Public Services Ombudsman (Wales) Act 2005	5.84
s5	3.210		
s5(2)	3.210	Sale of Goods Act 1979	5.65
s5(4)	3.210		
s35	3.210	Senior Courts Act 1981	
ss35–38	3.233	s37	17.5
s44	3.233	s51	16.18
s45A	3.233	s51(6)	16.3
s47	3.233	Sexual Offences Act 2003	5.84
s48	3.233		
s51	3.233	Social Services and Well-being (Wales) Act 2014	5.84, 23.2, 23.3, 23.10
s62	3.229		
s64D	3.231		
s72	11.96		
s73	11.96	s5	23.8
s74	11.96	s50	5.70
s75	11.96	s126	23.8, 23.9
s115	5.84	s127	23.10
s117	7.90	s197	23.8
s127	5.84	Trustee Act 2000	
s135	3.210, 5.84	s4	7.61
s136	3.210, 5.84	Welsh Language Act 1993	15.50
Part IV	3.213, 3.220, 3.224		
Part IVA	3.224	Youth Justice and Criminal Evidence Act 1999	
Part VII	3.1, 4.2		
Mental Health Act 2007	3.9, 3.173, 3.195, 3.222, 3.224, 3.229, 4.36, 21.4	s27	15.45
		s29(2)	15.45

Table of statutory instruments

Care and Support (Direct Payments) (Wales) Regulations 2015 SI No 1815	5.70
Care and Support (Direct Payments) Regulations 2014 SI No 2871	5.70
Civil Legal Aid (Costs) Regulations 2013 SI No 611	16.6
Civil Legal Aid (Financial Resources and Payment for Services) Regulations 2013 SI No 480	6.25, 6.61
reg 5(1)(g)	6.63
reg 5(1)(g)(ii)(aa)	6.65
reg 6	6.70
Civil Legal Aid (Merits Criteria) Regulations 2013 SI No 104	6.25, 6.42
regs 4–5	6.42
reg 7	6.42
reg 8	6.42
reg 11(7)	6.44, 6.47
reg 32	6.44
reg 33	6.46
reg 39	6.48
reg 39(c)	6.49
reg 41	6.51
reg 42	6.52
reg 52	6.54
reg 52(2)	6.54
Civil Legal Aid (Procedure) Regulations 2012 SI No 3098	6.25, 6.73
reg 5	6.32
reg 22	6.73
reg 54(3)	6.88
Civil Legal Aid (Remuneration) (Amendment) Regulations 2013 SI No 2877	6.87
Sch 2	6.81
Civil Legal Aid (Statutory Charge) Regulations 2013 SI No 503	6.25, 6.78
reg 8	6.78
reg 9	6.78
Civil Procedure (Amendment) Rules 2016 SI No 234	17.10

xliii

Civil Procedure Rules 1998 SI No 3132	4.37, 4.123, 8.37, 11.26, 17.8, 18.52, 18.55
Part 3	
Part 8	22.25
Part 21	25.14
r21.4(c)	11.69
Part 31	12.91
r31.1	12.91
r31.4	12.91
Part 40	
PD 40E	15.61
Parts 44–47	App C
r44.2	18.57
r44.2(1)–(8)	
r44.2(3)	18.57
r44.2(3)(a)	18.57
r44.3(3)(a)	18.57
r44.3(4)	18.57
Part 52	18.55
r52.9A	18.57, 18.58
r52.9A(4)	18.59
r52.13(2)	18.52
PD 52A	18.55
PD 52C	18.55
Part 70	17.9
r70.3	17.9, 17.10
PD 70	17.11
Part 71	17.9
Part 72	17.9
Part 73	17.9
Part 83	17.9
Part 84	17.9
Part 89	17.10
Costs in Criminal Cases (General) Regulations 1986 SI No 1335	12.34
Court Funds Rules 2011 SI No 1734	5.77
Court of Protection (Amendment) Rules 2015 SI No 548	7.23, 7.29, 11.1, 11.2, 12.4, 16.4
Court of Protection Rules 2001 SI No 824	4.2
Court of Protection Rules 2007 SI No 1744 **(reproduced in full in appendix B)**	4.110, 8.2, 11.21, 11.23, 11.43, 12.55, 14.19, 16.10
r1.2	7.30
r1.3	10.12
r3	4.104, 4.106, 8.18, 15.45, 19.9, 21.16
r3(3)(c)	12.65

Court of Protection Rules 2007 SI No 1744 *continued*

r3A	4.109, 4.119, 7.30, 9.27, 11.5, 11.6, 11.74, 11.75, 11.76, 11.80, 11.81, 11.82, 11.83, 11.86, 11.92, 11.93, 11.94, 11.98, 11.99, 11.101, 21.62, 21.67, 21.69, 21.70, 21.73
r3A(2)	9.28
r3A(2)(a)	11.7
r3A(2)(b)	11.7, 11.87
r3A(2)(c)	6.45, 6.54, 11.7, 11.74, 11.75, 11.86, 21.6
r3A(2)(d)	11.7, 11.86
r3A(2)(e)	11.7, 11.86
r3A(4)	9.28, 11.10, 11.87
r3A(4)(a)	11.10
r3A(4)(b)	11.10
r3A(5)	11.10
r4	4.107, 6.6, 11.94, 12.5, 16.14, 16.15, 19.9, 21.16
r4(1)	13.47
r4(2)	13.47
r4(2)(d)	16.14
r4(2)(e)	16.14
r4(3)	6.6, 13.47, 16.15
r5	4.111, .9
r5(2)(b)	4.29
Part 3	13.9
r6	11.14, 11.21, 11.84, 11.86, 18.2
r7(2)(a)	18.4
r7A	4.21, 10.14
r9(1)	8.37, 11.26
r9(2)	16.5
r9A	9.8
Part 4	13.4
r11(3)(a)	12.14
r11(7)	11.95, 11.96
r12(4), (5)	18.14
r14	9.24, 12.28
r14(2)(a)	17.12
r15	9.46
r16	13.83
r17(2)	13.85
r17(4)	13.85
r18	12.85, 13.82
r20(1)–(6)	13.84
r21.3(3)	11.26
Part 5	14.1

Court of Protection Rules 2007 SI No 1744 *continued*

r25	11.25, 11.26, 12.5, 12.89, 12.104
r25(2)(d)	10.27
Part 6	7.23
r32	7.23
r33(1)	7.30
r38	7.28
rr39–39H	7.29
Part 7	11.8
r40(3)	7.32
r40(3)	7.32
r46	7.30
r49	7.32
rr50–52	5.2
r51	21.22
r51(1)(a)	9.15
r51(1)(b)	20.40
r51(1)(d)	9.15
r51(2)(a)	7.6, 8.4
r52	8.4
r52(5)	8.14
r53(2)	7.125
r59	9.51
Part 9	7.8, 9.21
r62	9.49
r63(c)(iii)	7.10
r64	9.43
r65	9.49
r66	7.23, 9.53
r66(1)	7.23
r70	7.10, 7.23
r72	7.33, 8.9, 9.56
r72(5)	12.16
r72(6), (8)	7.10, 9.32
r72(8)	8.15
r73	6.49
r73(1)	21.34
r73(1)(b)	8.13, 9.26, 9.58
r73(2)	8.15, 8.17
r73(4)	9.27
r74	18.10, 21.34
r74(2)	8.10
r74(2)(a)	9.27
r74(2)(b)	9.32
r75(1)	8.16
r75(3)	8.17
r75(4)	8.17
r76	8.18
Part 10	10.22
r78(1)	10.22

Court of Protection Rules 2007 SI No 1744 *continued*

r78(2)	10.22, 12.16
r78(5)	10.22
r79	10.22
r79(c)	10.22
r80(1)	10.23
r80(2)	10.23
r80(3)	10.23
r80(4)	10.23
r81	10.70
r82	10.61
r82(1)(a)	17.5
r83	4.11
r83(1)	25.6
r84(1)(a)	9.51
r84(1A)	9.51
r84(3)	18.44
r85	11.25, 12.5, 12.89
r85(4)	10.25
r85(5)	10.25
r85(6)	10.25
r86	4.11
r87	5.2, 9.51, 9.52, 11.56
r87(1)(b)	15.70
r87(2)(b)	11.56
r87A	15.7, 23.18
r87A(2)	15.7
r89	7.54, 9.52, 10.18, 15.6, 18.4, 18.6, 18.8, 18.25, 21.67
r89(2)	18.3
r89(3)(a)	18.3
r89(4)	18.4
r89(6)(a)	18.4
r89(6A)	18.4, 18.5
r89(6B)	18.4, 18.5
r89(6C)	18.4, 18.5
r89(7)	18.6
r89(10)	18.4
Part 13	13.4, 13.7, 13.44
rr90–93	13.4
r91	13.2, 13.45, 13.64
r91(1)	13.45
r91(3)	13.45
r92	13.44, 13.46
r92(2)	22.18
r93(1)(a)	13.45
Part 14	5.18, 12.4
r94(1)	12.12
r94(2)	12.12
r95	12.4

Court of Protection Rules 2007 SI No 1744 *continued*

r95(a)(iii)	15.45
r95(d)	12.24
r95(e)	12.25, 15.36, 15.73
r96(1)	12.14
r96(2)	12.15
r96(3), (4)	12.15
r97(c)	12.16
r98	12.43, 15.53
r99(2)	12.16
r99(3)	12.21
r100	12.17
r101(1), (2)	12.22
r101(3), (4)	12.22
r101(5)	12.22
r102	12.28
r103	12.28
r104	12.42
r105	12.32
r106(1)	12.33
r106(2)	12.33
r106(3)	12.35
r106(4)	12.35
r106(6)(a)	12.34
r106(6)(b)	12.34
r106(7)	12.34
r107	12.31, 12.36, 12.101
r108	12.40
r108(1)	12.39
r108(3)	12.39
r108(4)	12.39
r108(7)	12.39
r111	12.40
r113	12.42
r113(1)	12.40
r113(2), (3)	12.40
r113(4)	12.40
rr115–116	12.42
r117	12.46
r117(2)	12.47
r117(3)(a)	12.46
r117(4)	12.53
r117(5)	12.46
r117(7)	12.46
r118(1)	12.53
r118(2), (3)	12.53
Part 15	12.55, 12.57, 12.58, 12.59
r119(b)	12.47
r120(1)(a)–(b)	12.64
r120(2)	12.64
r121	12.65

Court of Protection Rules 2007 SI No 1744 *continued*

r122	12.47, 12.81
r123(1)	12.65
r125(1)	12.75, 12.86
r125(2)	12.86
r125(2)(d)	12.87
r125(3)	12.86
r125(4)	12.88
r125(5)–(6)	12.87
r125(7)	12.75, 12.88
r126(1)	12.80
r126(2)–(4)	12.82
r126(5)	12.80, 12.116
r128(1)	12.89
r128(2)–(3)	12.89
r128(4)	12.89
r129	12.80
r129(1)	12.80
r130(1)	12.65
r130(2)	12.74
r130(3)	12.78
r131(1)	12.74
r131(2)	12.80
r131(5)	12.49, 12.74
r132	12.91
r133(2)(b)	12.92, 14.19
r133(3)	12.92, 12.101, 14.19
r138	12.102, 12.103
r138(2)	12.103
Part 16	12.91, 12.92, 12.93
r132	12.91
Part 17	11.2, 11.98, 11.100
r140	11.52
r140(1)	11.46, 11.64
r140(1)(a)	11.29, 11.34
r140(1)(b)	11.29, 11.34
r141(1)	4.110
r141(2)	11.14
r141(3), (4)	11.21, 11.49
r141(5)(b)	11.21
r141(5)(c)	11.21
r141(6)	11.14
r142(1)(b)	11.33
r142(1)(c)	11.33, 11.36
r142(2)	11.28
r142(3)(a)	11.29
r142(3)(b)	11.29, 11.31
r142(4)	11.28
r143(1)	11.34
r143(2)	11.34
r143(5)	11.37

Court of Protection Rules 2007 SI No 1744 *continued*

r144	11.62
r144(1)	11.38, 11.53, 11.57, 11.58, 11.60
r144(1)(c)	11.64
r144(2)	11.39, 11.53, 11.61
r144(3)	11.64
r144(4)	11.53
r145A	11.59
r147	11.75, 11.92, 11.93, 11.94
r148	11.92, 11.93
r148(2)	11.75, 11.93
r148A	11.81
r148B(1)	11.82
r148B(2)	11.82
r148B(5)	11.82
r148C	11.75
Part 19	16.4
r155(1)	16.5
r155(2)	16.5
r155(4)	16.5
r156	8.6, 8.11, 8.21, 10.56, 11.69, 11.70, 16.7, 16.10, 16.12
r157	10.56, 11.69, 16.7, 16.10, 16.12, 18.57
r158	16.9
r159	9.4, 10.56, 16.12, 16.15
r160	16.5
r163	11.65
r164	16.8
r165	15.71
r166	8.11, 11.71, 12.81
r167	7.122, 15.71
r169	18.9
Part 20	18.2
r171(2)	18.44
r171A(1)(a)	18.11
r171A(1)(b)	18.11, 18.52
r171A(2)(a), (b)	18.11
r171A(3)	18.9
r171B	18.13
r171B(2)	18.53
r171B(3)	18.52
r172	18.9, 18.24
r172(1)	18.13
r172(2)(b)	18.14
r172(3)	18.23
r172(4)	18.23
r172(5)	18.23
r172(6)	18.24

Table of statutory instruments li

Court of Protection Rules 2007 SI No 1744 *continued*
r172(7)	18.24
r172A	18.13
r173(1)(a), (b)	18.22
r174	18.6
r175(1)	18.16
r175(2)	18.19
r175(2)(a)	18.19, 18.20
r175(2)(b)	18.16
r175(3)	18.32
r175(4)	18.32
r176(1)(a)	18.36
r176(1)(b)	18.35
r176(2)	18.36
r176(4)	18.37
r176(5), (6)	18.39
r178(1)	18.45
r179(1)	18.46
r179(1)(b)	18.46
r179(2)(a)	18.46
r179(2)(b)	18.46
r179(3)	18.48
r179(5)	18.35
Part 21	17.5
r184	17.8
r184(a)	17.9, 17.10
r185	17.12, 17.14
r186	17.12, 17.14
r186(1)	12.28, 17.15
r187	17.12, 17.14, 17.18
r188	17.12, 17.14
r188(2)	17.17
r189	17.12, 17.14
r190	17.12, 17.14
r191	17.12, 17.14
r192(1)	17.7
r192(2)	17.7
r192(3)	17.7
r193	17.19
r194	17.7
r200	7.51
r202	4.91, 4.92, 15.70
PD 2A	11.6, 11.9, 11.76, 11.81, 11.86, 11.98
PD 2A para 3	11.9
PD 2A para 6	11.9
PD 2A para 8	11.75
PD 2A para 12	11.76
PD 3A	4.20, 11.9
PD 3A para 2.1	4.21
PD 3A para 2.2	10.14

Court of Protection Rules 2007 SI No 1744 *continued*

PD 3A para 3	4.22
PD 3B	18.2
PD 3C	16.5
PD 6A	7.23
PD 6B	7.29
PD 7 para 6	7.30
PD 7A para 9	7.32
PD 9A	7.8, 9.21, 9.26, 9.43
PD 9A para 14	9.42
PD 9B	9.32
PD 9B para 4	7.10, 9.32
PD 9B para 7	7.10, 9.32
PD 9B para 10	9.33
PD 9C para 4	7.10, 9.32
PD 9D	4.37, 7.9
PD 9E	4.37, 13.15, 13.44, 13.68, 13.69, 22.2, 22.4, 22.6, 22.7, 22.8, 22.9, 22.11, 22.19
PD 9E paras 3	4.11, 22.4
PD 9E paras 4	4.11
PD 9E para 5	22.4
PD 9E paras 5–7	13.44
PD 9E para 6	22.8
PD 9E para 9	22.10
PD 9E para 11	22.16
PD 9E para 12	22.17
PD 9E para 16	13.44, 22.18
PD 9E para 17	22.19
PD 9E para 18	22.19
PD 9F	7.86
PD 10	10.22
PD 10A	10.22, 10.24, 10.27
PD 10A para 4	10.22
PD 10A para 9	10.23
PD 10A para 11	10.23
PD 10A para 15	10.24
PD 10A para 16	10.24
PD 10A paras 18–21	10.27
PD 10B	9.48, 10.23, 10.64, 10.65, 10.72
PD 10B para 1	10.66
PD 10B para 4	10.65
PD 10B para 5	10.67
PD 10B para 6	10.66, 10.69
PD 10B para 7	10.66, 10.67
PD 10B para 9	10.70
PD 10B para 12	10.72
PD 10B para 13	10.66
PD 10B para 16	10.64

Court of Protection Rules 2007 SI No 1744 *continued*

PD 11A	4.11, 25.10, 25.14
PD 11A paras 1–3	25.10
PD 11A paras 4–8	25.11
PD 11A para 9	25.11
PD 12A	4.11
PD 12B	5.2, 9.51, 15.69, 15.70
PD 12B para 2	9.51
PD 12B paras 5–7	15.70
PD 12B para 8	9.51
PD 13A	13.2, 13.4, 13.7, 13.9, 13.12, 13.32, 13.33, 13.47, 13.61, 13.71
PD 13A para 4	13.47
PD 13A para 6	13.47
PD 13A para 8	13.48
PD 13A para 10	13.49
PD 13A para 11	13.49
PD 13A para 12	13.49
PD 13A paras 13–19	13.50, 13.52
PD 13A para 14	13.50
PD 13A para 15	13.52
PD 13A para 16	13.52
PD 13A para 17	13.52
PD 13A para 18	13.50
PD 13A para 19	13.52
PD 13A para 20	13.52
PD 13A para 21	13.52
PD 13A para 22	13.52
PD 13A para 24	13.53
PD 13A para 25	13.53
PD 13A para 27	13.54, 13.61
PD 13A para 28	13.53, 13.55
PD 13A para 29	13.71
PD 13A para 31	13.9
PD 13A para 33	13.10
PD 13A para 34	13.11, 13.12
PD 13B	10.29, 14.15, 15.12, 15.14, 15.22
PD 13B para 4.2	15.12
PD 13B para 4.3	15.12
PD 13B para 4.4	14.16
PD 13B para 4.5	14.16
PD 13B para 4.6	15.15
PD 13B para 4.7	15.16
PD 13B para 4.8	15.17
PD 13B para 4.9	15.17
PD 13B para 4.10	15.18
PD 13B para 4.11	15.19
PD 13B para 10.1	15.13
PD 14	12.4, 12.29

Court of Protection Rules 2007 SI No 1744 *continued*

PD 14A	12.17, 12.28, 12.42, 15.54, 15.55
PD 14A paras 1–19	12.28
PD 14A paras 20–31	12.18
PD 14A paras 33–50	12.17
PD 14A para 39	12.18
PD 14A para 54	12.31
PD 14B	12.17, 12.41, 12.42
PD 14B paras 1–15	12.41
PD 14B para 9	12.39
PD 14B paras 16–33	12.42
PD 14D	12.34
PD 14D para 3	12.33
PD 14D para 4	12.34
PD 14D para 10	12.34
PD 15A	12.55, 12.65, 12.68, 12.82
PD 15A para 1	12.65
PD 15A paras 3–4	12.57
PD 15A para 6(a)	12.81
PD 15A para 8	12.81
PD 15A para 15	12.82
PD 17A	11.2, 11.21, 11.25
PD 17A para 5	11.28
PD 17A para 7(a)	11.29
PD 17A para 7(b)	11.29
PD 17A para 7(c)	11.29
PD 17A para 8	11.29
PD 17A para 9	11.31
PD 17A para 11	11.32
PD 17A para 13	11.34
PD 17B para 2	11.81
PD 17B para 3	11.75
PD 19A	16.5
PD 19B	16.8
PD 20A	18.2, 18.26, 18.30
PD 20A para 8	18.20
PD 20A para 9	18.20
PD 20A para 10	18.20
PD 20A para 11	18.26
PD 20A para 12	18.30
PD 20A para 14	18.26
PD 20A paras 16, 17	18.26
PD 20A paras 18–21	18.31
PD 20A para 22	18.27
PD 20A para 23	18.27
PD 20A para 24	18.27
PD 20A para 25	18.28
PD 20A para 26	18.29
PD 20A para 28, 29	18.29
PD 20A para 31	18.21, 18.36

Table of statutory instruments lv

Court of Protection Rules 2007 SI No 1744 *continued*
PD 20A para 32	18.34
PD 20A para 33	18.34
PD 20A para 34	18.34
PD 20A para 40	18.40
PD 20A para 41	18.40
PD 20A paras 44–47	18.41
PD 20A para 48	18.42
PD 20A para 49	18.41
PD 20B para 5	18.19
PD 20B	18.2, 18.14, 18.38
PD 20B paras 3.1–3.4	18.12
PD 21A	12.28, 17.12, 17.14
PD 21A para 6	17.12
PD 23B	7.122, 15.68, 15.69, 15.70
PD 23B paras 3, 4	15.70
PD 23B para 5	7.120, 15.68
PD 23B para 6	15.68
PD 23B para 10	15.71
PD 23B para 11	15.71
Family Procedure (Amendment) (No 5) Rules 2012 SI No 3061	12.69
Family Procedure Rules 2010 SI No 2955	4.37, 8.37, 11.23, 12.55, 12.69
r9.14	8.37
r9.17	8.37
r9.17(5)	8.38
r16.6(6)	11.23
r16.6(8)	11.25
Pt 25	12.55, 12.58
r25.1	12.69
PD 16A para 2.1	11.52
Health and Social Care Act 2008 (Regulated Activities) Regulations 2010 SI No 781	5.84
regs 9–24	5.84
Lasting Powers of Attorney, Enduring Powers of Attorney and Public Guardian Regulations 2007 SI No 1253	4.37
reg 31	20.16
reg 32	20.21
reg 32(2)	20.21
reg 37	7.122, 15.71
reg 40	7.122, 15.71
reg 44	20.34
Local Authority Social Services and National Health Services Complaints (England) Regulations 2009 SI No 309	5.84
reg 14	5.84

Mental Capacity (Deprivation of Liberty: Appointment of Relevant Persons Representative) Regulations 2008 SI No 1315	21.24
Mental Health Review Tribunal for Wales Rules 2008 SI No 2705	
r13(5)(b)	11.95
Mental Health Tribunal Rules 1983 SI No 942	4.110
National Health Service (Direct Payments) Regulations 2013 SI No 1617	
reg 5	5.72
reg 6	5.72
Regulatory Reform (Collaboration etc between Ombudsmen) Order 2007 SI No 1889	5.84
Rules of the Supreme Court	4.110
Supreme Court Rules 2009 SI 2009 No 1603	18.56
Pt 7	18.60
Tribunal Procedure (First-tier Tribunal) (Health, Education and Social Care Chamber) Rules 2008 SI No 2699	
r11(7)(b)	11.95

Table of European and international conventions and treaties

Convention on the Jurisdiction, Applicable Law, Recognition, Enforcement and Co-operation in respect of Parental Responsibility and Measures for the Protection of Children	26.9
European Convention on Human Rights	3.172, 4.26, 4.35, 4.39, 4.40, 5.84, 6.26, 12.6, 18.49, 24.5, 25.1, 25.6, 25.10
Art 2	23.4
Art 3	23.4
Art 5	2.1, 3.192, 3.193, 4.40, 4.41, 4.106, 6.66, 6.69, 6.79, 11.4, 11.48, 15.65, 21.1, 21.7, 21.24, 21.52, 21.53, 21.56, 21.57, 21.59, 21.60, 23.4, 25.7, 25.9, 25.17
Art 5(1)	3.169, 3.199, 21.59
Art 5(4)	2.8, 11.48, 21.15, 21.20, 21.23, 21.24
Art 6	6.86, 9.60, 11.4, 12.80, 12.106
Art 8	2.1, 3.199, 4.40, 4.42, 6.57, 6.86, 9.60, 11.4, 12.76, 12.106, 13.49, 13.53, 13.69, 13.77, 14.4, 23.4, 23.12, 23.15, 25.7
Art 8(2)	14.4
Art 10	13.49, 13.53, 13.69, 13.77
Art 14	25.18
Hague Convention on the International Protection of Adults 2000	4.93, 26.2
Art 38	26.15
United National Convention on the Rights of Persons with Disabilities	1.10, 3.236, 15.35, 25.1, 25.15, 25.17, 25.18, 25.19, 25.20, 25.21
Art 12	25.16, 25.17
Art 12(4)	25.17
Art 14	25.17

Table of codes of practice and practice guidance

Codes of Practice

Deprivation of Liberty Safeguards (DOLS) Code of Practice to supplement the main Mental Capacity Act 2005 Code of Practice (2008)	2.1, 3.9, 3.175, 3.232, 3.236, 4.37, 5.11, 11.42, 11.104, 21.4
Mental Capacity Act 2005 Code of Practice (2007)	4.37, 7.58, 9.2, 9.6, 19.4, 19.6, 19.7
paras 4.23–4.25	3.64
para 4.59	11.17
para 5.64	19.4
para 7.21	3.118, 3.132
para 8.38	9.6
Chapter 15	9.2, 19.5
para 15.3	19.5
para 15.6	19.5
para 15.7	19.6
para 15.13	19.7

Practice Guidance

Committal for Contempt of Court (May 2013), Lord Chief Justice and President of the Family Division	6.23
Committal for Contempt of Court (March 2015) Lord Chief Justice's Practice Direction: Committal for Contempt of Court	4.37, 13.56, 17.17
PD 4	13.56
PD 5	13.56
PD 8	13.58
PD 9	13.57
PD 10	13.58
PD 13	13.59
Court of Protection Practice Direction 10AA	21.2, 21.30, 21.31, 31.37
Pt 2	3.193, 21.63

Facilitating the participation of 'P' and vulnerable persons
 in Court of Protection Proceedings (November 2016)   15.44
  para 2   21.31
  para 3   21.31
  para 10   21.37
  para 15   21.38
  para 20   21.38
  para 24   21.43
  para 26   21.39
  para 41   21.69
  para 47   21.71
  para 48   21.72

Court of Protection Practice Direction — Transparency
 Pilot (29 January 2016)   4.113

Guidance on the Remuneration of Expert Witnesses
  para 4.2   6.84
  para 4.5   6.86
  para 4.14   6.84
  para 4.15   6.84

Guide to Allowances under Part V of the Costs in Criminal
 Cases (General) Regulations 1986, 2007
  Annex A   12.34

Lord Chancellor's Guidance under section 4 of Legal Aid,
 Sentencing and Punishment of Offenders Act 2012   6.25, 6.55, 6.59, 6.60
  para 7.14   6.60
  para 7.16   6.60
  para 7.23   6.60
  para 9   6.60
  para 9.5   6.60
  para 9.8   6.60

McKenzie Friends (Civil and Family Courts) (July 2010)
 Lord Neuberger and Sir Nicholas Wall   4.121, 6.10
  para 2   6.10
  para 3   6.10
  para 4   6.10
  para 5   6.10
  para 6   6.10
  para 8   6.10
  para 9   6.10
  para 12   6.10
  para 13   6.10
  paras 18–30   6.10

Transparency in the Court of Protection: publication of
 judgments (January 2014), Sir James Munby   13.1, 22.18

Practice Guidance June 15
  para 2   13.58

Abbreviations

ABE	Achieving best evidence
ACO	Authorised court officer
ADR	Alternative dispute resolution
ALR	Accredited legal representative
AJA 1960	Administration of Justice Act 1960
AMHP	Approved mental health professional
CAFCASS	Children and Family Court Advisory and Support Service
CCG	Clinical commissioning group
CEA 1972	Civil Evidence Act 1972
CEA 1995	Civil Evidence Act 1995
CFO	Court Funds Office
CHC	NHS continuing healthcare
CICA	Criminal Injuries Compensation Authority
CMC	Civil Mediation Council
COPR	Court of Protection Rules 2007 SI No 1744
CQC	Care Quality Commission
CRPD	UN Convention on the Rights of Persons with Disabilities
CSSIW	Care and Social Services Inspectorate Wales
CTO	Community treatment order
DOLS	Deprivation of Liberty Safeguards
DPA 1998	Data Protection Act 1998
ECHR	European Convention on Human Rights
ECtHR	European Court of Human Rights
EPA	Enduring power of attorney
EqA 2010	Equality Act 2010
FNC	NHS-funded nursing care
FPR	Family Procedure Rules 2010 SI No 2955
GMC	General Medical Council
HCPC	Health and Care Professions Council
HMCTS	Her Majesty's Courts and Tribunals Service
HMRC	Her Majesty's Revenue and Customs
IMCA	Independent mental capacity advocate
IMHA	Independent mental health advocate
LAA	Legal Aid Agency
LASPO	Legal Aid, Sentencing and Punishment of Offenders Act 2012
LPA	Lasting power of attorney
LSC	Legal Services Commission
MCA 2005	Mental Capacity Act 2005

MHA 1983	Mental Health Act 1983
MHA 2007	Mental Health Act 2007
MoJ	Ministry of Justice
NAA 1948	National Assistance Act 1948
NMC	Nursing and Midwifery Council
OPG	Office of the Public Guardian
P	The relevant person
PACE 1984	Police and Criminal Evidence Act 1984
PALS	Patient advice and liaison service
PCT	Primary care trust
PD	Practice direction
PGO	Public Guardianship Office
PHA 1997	Protection from Harassment Act 1997
PSU	Personal Support Unit
RPR	Relevant person's representative
RTM	Round table meeting
SRA	Solicitors Regulation Authority
VHCC	Very high costs case

CHAPTER 1
Introduction

1.1   The scheme of the book

1.2   Approach

1.3   Changes from the first edition and the reform of the Court of Protection

The scheme of the book

1.1 The book is divided into four parts.

1.2 In the first section, we set out an overview of the Mental Capacity Act (MCA) 2005 and of the Court of Protection. In order to ensure that the book's focus is where it should be – on the people whose lives are affected by its decisions – this section starts with a chapter written by Mark Neary, the father and carer of Steven Neary, whose story[1] illustrates both the potential for misuse of the MCA 2005 by statutory authorities and the powers of the Court of Protection.

1.3 In the second section, the book proceeds in chronological order through the life of an application (or, to be precise, from the point before an application is even prepared – by asking, first, the often overlooked question of whether it is actually appropriate to bring an application to the Court of Protection). We then trace the process through from the drafting of the application, pre-issue (where relevant), issue, response and then on to any directions hearings necessary before the final determination of the application, before dealing with the questions of costs, enforcement and appeals.

1.4 In a series of – mostly – shorter chapters in the third section, we address a number of specific issues that arise in connection with the Court of Protection's jurisdiction, such as applications in relation to deprivation of liberty and the interaction between the Court of Protection and the Administrative Court.

1.5 The fourth section, the appendices, contain the key statutory materials and guidance, together with samples of important documents such as letters of instruction, as well as useful contact addresses and resources. Precedent orders can be found on the (free) website that accompanies the book: www.courtofprotectionhandbook.com. On the website can also be found links to relevant primary and secondary legislation, practice directions, and other useful resources, as well as blog posts and updates to the text of the work.

Approach

1.6 We need to make four important – linked – points at the outset of the book as to the approach that we have taken.

---

1 Encapsulated in the judgment in *Hillingdon LBC v Neary* [2011] EWHC 1377 (COP), [2011] COPLR Con Vol 623.

1.7 First, while it has deep historical roots, the Court of Protection in its new incarnation with jurisdiction to take decisions not solely in regard to the property and affairs of those without capacity but also in regard to their health and welfare has been in existence only since October 2007, and it is still therefore a comparative newcomer. Its practices and processes are in significant measure still being worked out. This book is, in part, a contribution to the development of those practices and processes, although we have sought to make clear whenever we move beyond description into prescription.

1.8 Second, this book covers the span of the Court of Protection's work. However, only a very small number of applications relating to property and affairs received by the court are contentious; the vast majority are decided 'upon the papers' by either a judge or an authorised court officer. Those sections of the book which relate to the determination of contested applications, and, in particular, to hearings, are inevitably very much focused upon health and welfare applications.

1.9 Third, insofar as the book deals with the determination of health and welfare applications in particular, it does so from a starting point that there is a wealth of valuable guidance to be found from proceedings relating to children (and especially care proceedings). It is vital to emphasise, however, that we are *not* saying that incapacitated adults[2] are to be equated with 'big children'. Very far from it – the law that Court of Protection judges have to apply and the factors to take into account when considering what substantive decision to take upon an application relating to an incapacitated adult are – and should be – very different from the law and factors that apply in relation to a child. However, the forensic processes in both types of proceedings are – we suggest – very similar, and for very good reason: they are above all designed to ensure that, as best as possible, a judge is put in a position to take the decision that it right for a person who is not a protagonist in the proceedings but their subject.[3]

1.10 Fourth and finally, hanging over the entirety of the book is a very large question as to whether the MCA 2005 is compatible with the United Nations Convention on the Rights of Persons with Disabilities. There is a strong argument that the MCA 2005

---

2 The Court of Protection can, of course, take decisions in relation to children of 16 and 17. This jurisdiction is not often invoked. We touch on the position of the children where relevant; see in particular chapter 11.
3 See, in this regard, The Honourable Mr Justice Baker, 'Reforming the Court of Protection: lessons to be learned from the Family Justice Reforms' [2014] 4 *Elder Law Journal* 1, 45–50.

is not, at least in its current form. We summarise the key points in relation to this issue in chapter 25, but note that it is one that is likely to rise further up the agenda as the Committee on the Rights of Persons with Disabilities turns its attention to the position of the UK in 2017.

1.11 It should be noted that the law relating to capacity issues is significantly different in both Northern Ireland and Scotland; this book should not be used as a guide to the principles and practices adopted in those jurisdictions.[4]

1.12 In this book we use 'P' to refer to the person whom it is said lacks capacity to take the material decisions.

Changes from the first edition and the reform of the Court of Protection

1.13 Over and above the updating that is required to incorporate developments in the case-law (such as those relating to the deprivation of liberty saga addressed in chapter 21), much of the book has been substantially rewritten to reflect the fact that the Court of Protection is a very different place to the court it was when we published the first edition in 2014. Not only are the majority of hearings now held in public under the Transparency Pilot (discussed in chapter 13), reforms were introduced in 2015 designed to secure the greater participation of P in proceedings (discussed in chapters 10 and 15), and, most recently, the Case Management Pilot began on 1 September 2016. The Case Management Pilot, which will run until 31 August 2017, is intended to effect a major change in the culture of both practitioners and the judiciary; it also – and not entirely helpfully – means that, for the length of the Pilot, practitioners and the judiciary will need to grapple with overlapping sets of rules. An overview of the Pilot is given in chapter 4 at para 4.101, and chapters 7–15 have been entirely recast to provide a guide through the Pilot.

---

4 Readers are directed, in particular, to chapters 12 and 13 of Ashton et al, *Court of Protection Practice 2016*, Jordans; and also, for a fuller discussion, to Frimston et al, *The International Protection of Adults*, Oxford University Press, 2015.

CHAPTER 2

Steven Neary's story

This chapter is written by Steven Neary's father, Mark Neary

2.1 My experience of the Court of Protection comes through being caught up in the deprivation of liberty safeguards (DOLS). I am the father of Steven Neary, who for nearly the whole of 2010 was held in a positive behaviour unit under four successive DOLS authorisations. When the case eventually came before the Court of Protection in December 2010, Steven was immediately released and allowed to return to his home. The standard authorisation was terminated. At a subsequent hearing in May 2011,[1] the judge found that the local authority had breached Steven's rights under Articles 5 (right to liberty and security) and 8 (right to respect for private and family life) of the European Convention on Human Rights (ECHR) for the whole year, and all four DOLS authorisations had been unlawful.

2.2 In the light of that successful outcome after a truly horrendous year when my family was needlessly torn apart, you'd expect my view of the Court of Protection to be a positive one. And it is, I have nothing negative to report about the experience, although I have concerns about accessing the court in the first place.

2.3 Mr Justice Peter Jackson quoted the Magna Carta in his introduction to his judgment in our case. His reference induced a powerful emotional reaction in me and from commentaries on our case, I know that it resonated with a lot of people. I can see why. Issues that the Court of Protection regularly address usually involve matters of liberty, best interests and the role of the state in the lives of incapacitated people. Steven's case rested heavily on all those things and as

---

1 *Hillingdon LBC v Neary* [2011] EWHC 1377 (COP), [2011] COPLR Con Vol 623. See also *Hillingdon LBC v Neary* [2011] EWHC 3522 (COP) on the question of costs.

I've become more acquainted with the Mental Capacity Act (MCA) 2005, I can see that what was articulated in the Magna Carta is relevant to our lives today. Thank goodness. In Steven's case, the local authority behaved appallingly and a running thread of the judgment is their lack of frankness towards Steven and me. The judge concluded one part of his judgment with the sentence that, had Hillingdon had their way: 'Steven would have faced a life in public care that he did not want and does not need'.[2] Since our case moved into the public domain, I have been approached by many families where what nearly happened to Steven, has actually happened to them. Sadly, more and more people are encountering what Steven and I had to face – challenging state decisions about incapacitated people is seldom successful through internal processes. This is for a number of reasons. First, the family is always outnumbered by large multi-disciplinary teams of professionals. Second, often, the real agendas are withheld from families, making challenge impotent. In our case, the local authority led Steven and me to believe that we were in a 'transition home plan' for six months. Although we were unhappy about the timescale, there did seem to be light at the end of the tunnel. But as Mr Justice Peter Jackson held:

> Between April and July 2010 Hillingdon pursued two inconsistent agendas. The professionals were opposed to Steven returning home, whether or not a final decision had been taken. The agenda so far as Steven and Mr Neary were concerned was a return home under the transition plan. It was only when the transition plan was about to lead to an actual return home that the pursuit of two agendas became unfeasible and the true view of the professionals was disclosed. The records show that the professionals were at times uneasy about this lack of frankness, but it happened nonetheless.[3]

2.4 In August 2010, after (as Mr Justice Peter Jackson put it) 'the cat of Hillingdon's thinking was out of the bag',[4] the local authority promised to refer the disagreement over the DOLS to the court. It should have been a straightforward challenge to a DOLS submission. But it took them two-and-a-half months to make a submission, and when they did, they applied for welfare deputyship. Mr Justice Peter Jackson remarked on the 'extraordinarily wide ranging'[5] orders the court was asked to make, but the DOLS authorisations were not

---

2 [2011] EWHC 3522 (COP) para 28.
3 Para 155(3).
4 Para 155(5).
5 Para 122.

mentioned at all in the local authority's submission. I can't know for sure, but it looks to me like they were hoping to be granted welfare deputyship and then they would have had full control and their DOLS authorisations wouldn't have come under the spotlight. Faced with this sort of conduct, the odds seem very stacked against P or their family.

2.5 Once Hillingdon's real agenda was exposed on 8 July 2010, I knew that the only possible way of challenging their plan to move Steven to a hospital in Wales was through the Court of Protection. In his judgment, Mr Justice Peter Jackson declared that the onus was on the local authority to bring the matter before the court, but throughout the year, I was repeatedly told by Hillingdon that if I disagreed with their plans, it was down to me to instigate proceedings. I know differently now, but at the time I believed them. It is very common, and a deeply unsettling fact for many families, that when their children are 'transitioned' into adult social care services, the parents are effectively side-lined. My twenty years of experience of Steven counted for nothing in the year that Steven was in the unit – in one document, I wasn't even recognised as his next of kin, that role went to his 'care champion' within the unit. So it's not surprising that many families, like me at the time, don't realise they can challenge state decisions, far less know how to go about it. When the DOLS were authorised, I was told that I was Steven's 'relevant person's representative' (RPR) but did not have a clue what that meant in practice. All I knew was that, by this time, I had been attending meetings for four months and had absolutely no say in any of the care planning for Steven's future. My role as Steven's RPR was never fully explained to me. If it had, I would probably have triggered the court process myself much sooner.

2.6 Once the penny dropped in July 2010 that the matter could only be resolved through the Court of Protection, the next big hurdle was accessing the court. I used the Internet to put out a call for help, and someone sent me a list of solicitors who might be prepared to take our case on. It was a dispiriting exercise. Most of the firms I contacted confessed to insufficient knowledge of the Mental Capacity Act to take the case on. The vast majority didn't return my calls. I had a hopeful few days with one firm until they told me that I didn't qualify for legal aid. I didn't know it at the time, but under the DOLS legislation I was automatically entitled to legal aid as Steven's RPR. And that was just me – I had not been told, or considered, that *Steven*, as the person being deprived of his liberty, was entitled to legal aid. That was partly because (as the judge found) they had failed to press for

Steven to be allocated an independent mental capacity advocate (IMCA). This is someone who could have led professional backing for Steven's case and opened up legal doors that had remained firmly closed to me. Even when an independent psychologist reported on the lack of advocacy for Steven or me on 16 August 2010, his report was deliberately suppressed (a fact that the judge described as deplorable[6]) and it took until 29 October for Hillingdon to appoint an IMCA for Steven (coincidentally, the day after they submitted their own court application). When the IMCA came on board, the effect was transformative. Three weeks later we had a solicitor and three weeks after that, we were in court.

2.7 I have told the story of how we eventually got a solicitor many times, and people often think I've exercised some dramatic license in the narrative. A member of the Facebook group I set up is an expert in the DOLS and offered to contact a law firm in Cornwall (bear in mind, we live in west London) who she felt had the necessary experience to take our case on. On the day she contacted him, he happened to be at, of all things, a DOLS conference in London. It was a turgid event and he was prepared to bunk off for the afternoon and travel across London to meet me. Three weeks after this unexpected meeting, we were in court and Steven was released.

2.8 I know that Steven and I were blocked every step of the process by Hillingdon, but there must be a better, quicker way of accessing the Court of Protection. It took from 15 April 2010 (the date the first DOL was authorised) until 26 October 2010 (two weeks before the fourth DOL was authorised) before Steven got an IMCA. It took until 22 November 2010 before we found a solicitor. When it comes to the issue of the liberty of an incapacitated person, I would suggest that this is hardly enabling the detained person 'to have the lawfulness of his detention reviewed speedily by the court' as required by Article 5(4) ECHR. I accept that the main reason for the delay was the approach adopted by Hillingdon, which was severely criticised by the judge, but actually getting through the doors of the Court of Protection for a family member can be extremely difficult without legal representation.

2.9 My apologies if I have laboured the point, but when things get as serious as our case had become, the MCA 2005 only has a value if the people who fall within the scope of it are able to access justice. To have that access either effectively blocked for eleven months or for it

---

6 [2011] EWHC 3522 (COP) para 114.

2.10 Even if it would not help directly with getting to court, it would definitely help if the detained person or their representative was allowed to approach the IMCA service directly, rather than having to rely on the supervisory body who authorised the DOL to refer you for one. To put it bluntly, if the local authority do not want you to have external advocacy from an IMCA, you are not going to get one. As I write this chapter, the House of Lords have just published their recommendations following their review into the MCA 2005.[7] One of their proposals is that P or his representative be given direct access to IMCA services. That can only be good news if the recommendation is taken up.

2.11 On a happier note, at the first hearing in the Court of Protection on 21 December 2010, Steven was represented by the Official Solicitor and I had my own counsel. Mr Justice Mostyn terminated the current DOLS authorisation and allowed Steven home. On Christmas Eve 2010 Steven returned home – 359 days after he walked out of the front door, setting off for three days' respite.

2.12 Of course, the scrutiny didn't end with Steven's return home. Between then and the hearing in February 2011, we had the visits from the two court-appointed experts (one a psychologist; the other a social work expert), plus a further visit from the Official Solicitor. Although things at home had been going very well since Steven's return, I found these visits very anxiety-provoking. Once again, I felt like I was having to prove and to put a case for the most important, fundamental aspects of Steven's life, and if I was unable to present his life properly, the consequences could have been dire. The local authority had not revised its 'care plan', so a move to a hospital in Wales was still a possibility. I felt that if one little thing was misinterpreted, or if the experts did not share the view of Mr Justice Mostyn, then the whole nightmare might start up again. I know that for the Court of Protection to make a thorough, robust decision it needs as much information as possible, but it seems to me that life under the microscope applies more to the learning disabled than any other member of our society, and it's terrifying. I'd had a year of Hillingdon interpreting every aspect of Steven's life negatively. Steven loves engaging in endless conversations about his favourite

---

7 *Mental Capacity Act 2005: post-legislative scrutiny*, Select Committee on the Mental Capacity Act 2005, Report of Session 2013–14, HL Paper 139, published March 2014; available at: www.publications.parliament.uk/pa/ld201314/ldselect/ldmentalcap/139/139.pdf.

things – Mr Bean, Take That, flavours of crisps – but at the unit, these conversations were viewed through a negative, judgmental prism. His love of Mr Bean was seen as obsessive and obstructive to him engaging in more 'acceptable, mature interactions'. The thought that the court-appointed psychologist might share that view scared the hell out of me. Thankfully, he didn't, and when we returned to court in February 2011, the order for Steven to live in his own home was made permanent. The Official Solicitor then pushed for the lawfulness of Hillingdon's actions throughout 2010 to be judged and the judge agreed with him. All of a sudden, the spotlight was off Steven and me. We no longer had to put a good case – that task now fell on Hillingdon.

2.13 Two weeks before the hearing before Mr Justice Peter Jackson at which the lawfulness of Hillingdon's actions were to be examined, we encountered another setback. Because Mr Justice Mostyn had terminated the DOLS authorisation, I was no longer entitled to legal aid. Steven would still be represented by the Official Solicitor, but I lost the team that had been so successful in December 2010 and February 2011. This meant that I had to appear as a litigant in person. Thankfully, the Official Solicitor put together a fabulous case, because it would have been impossible for me on my own to cover all the legal arguments that the case before Mr Justice Peter Jackson was built on.

2.14 Obviously, the most important aspect of the entire case was to get the DOLS authorisations withdrawn and allow Steven to return home, but as events have demonstrated since the case, the importance of having the DOLS legislation and process examined and the actions of the supervisory body looked into has had a major impact across the country in terms of practice. Since 2011, I have regularly been invited to speak at events involving social care, legal and best interests professionals and have seen how our judgment has shaped the way many of these professionals work. I'm not sure the case would have had that impact if it had ended in February 2011 with the termination of the authorisation and the decision to allow Steven to live at home permanently.

2.15 Finally, I am regularly asked about the publicity our case attracted (and still does) and whether it has been in Steven's best interests. In the first instance in 2010, I turned to social media and the wider national media out of desperation. The motivation was to find some guidance and support which must surely have been in Steven's best interests. I was always confident that I was acting in Steven's best interests but approaching the press was quite a dramatic manoeuvre. I was also fairly confident that I could shield Steven from any external situation that he'd find difficult to cope with, as I had done all his life. I knew that I would never put him in a public situation that would cause him anxiety or distress. I can honestly say, as I did in court, that I don't think Steven has been affected at all by the publicity. He continues to live his life in his own idiosyncratic, Steven Neary way. He is interested whenever we appear in the press or on the television, but then gets back to watching Fawlty Towers or whatever he is doing at the time. For me, the most important thing about the court's decision to allow the case to be reported openly is that it has enabled people to engage with a very human story. It's a son and father story. And because son and father were identified as Steven and Mark, the judgment clearly comes alive as a story of two human beings caught in a horrendous situation. When I speak publicly and tell the story, people laugh, cry and rage because they connect with the three-dimensional characters at the heart of the story. I met a judge a few weeks back and he said it was a very 'filmatic' story. I'm not sure that could happen if we were '*SN and MN vs A local authority*'. The learning disabled are a pretty invisible, unacknowledged section of our society and I believe it is important for our stories to be told. I continue to write about our lives because if attitudes are going to change in the future, we have to move away from the mindset that sees people like Steven as not quite human. Steven Neary is a fully rounded human being – SN (or P) is not an object or a case study. And that for me is ample reason to have our case in the public arena and for the push for the Court of Protection to be more open in its reporting of its cases. Mr Justice Peter Jackson's judgment is often referred to as 'landmark judgment'. I am delighted that it is used as a key reference point in social work, legal and best interest assessor training. But more importantly, I am glad that it is in the public domain to help other Stevens and other Marks who suddenly find themselves in the same awful situation we got trapped in, back in 2010. On a weekly basis, I am contacted by people with relatives trapped in care homes or hospitals where either the person or their family want them to live at home. Worryingly, in many cases, there is no DOLS authorisation, so there is no way of challenging the detention. I always suggest people push for a DOLS authorisation as at least that will give them the opportunity to take the matter to court. *Hillingdon v Neary* has given hope to lots of families and I am proud of that. If our experience helps just one person, that can only be a good thing.

CHAPTER 3

An overview of the Mental Capacity Act 2005

3.1	Introduction
3.6	The Law Commission's work
3.10	**Statutory principles (section 1)**
3.12	The presumption of capacity
3.15	Duty to help the person make their own decision where possible
3.20	Unwise decision-making
3.24	Duty to act in the person's best interests
3.31	Duty to consider less restrictive options
3.33	**Who lacks capacity (sections 2 and 3)**
3.40	The incapacity test
	What is meant by 'unable to make a decision'?
3.46	How much information is relevant information
3.52	Capacity to understand the relevant information
3.54	Capacity to retain the relevant information
3.55	Capacity to weigh the relevant information
3.64	Capacity to communicate one's decision
3.65	**Best interests (section 4)**
3.67	Matters to consider
3.72	Best interests and substituted judgment
3.78	Safety, health, care, treatment and liberty

continued

3.80		Wishes, feelings and objectivity
3.87		**Summary – waypoint**
3.90		**The statutory mechanisms**
3.93		Four main mechanisms
3.96		Above and below the line
		Going below the line
3.102		**More about advance decisions**
3.103		An advance decision 'to refuse treatment'
3.105		Effect of advance decisions
3.106		Formalities
3.109		Validity and applicability of advance decisions
3.114		**More about LPAs**
3.119		Interplay between advance decisions and LPAs
3.121		**More about court orders and deputies**
3.126		Personal welfare deputies
3.139		Who may be a deputy
		Two or more deputies
3.143		A deputy's powers and duties
3.146		Interplay between advance decisions and deputyship
3.147		Restrictions on deputies
3.148		Powers of deputies compared with donees and the court
3.149		**More about section 5 ('acts in connection with a person's care or treatment')**
3.159		**A general framework**
3.166		**Deprivation of liberty**
3.176		The six requirements
		The age requirement • The mental health requirement • The mental capacity requirement • The best interests requirement • The no refusals requirement • The eligibility requirement
3.189		The DOLS scheme and the four mechanisms
3.192		The *Cheshire West* and *Re X* cases

3.195 Three murky streams forming one river
3.198 Ten commandments
3.200 Detention and deprivation of liberty

3.205 Interplay with the MHA 1983
3.206 Treating physical disorders
3.208 Treating mental disorders
The scheme set out in the original MCA 2005
3.232 Deprivation of liberty and the MHA 1983

3.234 Principles of mental health law

3.236 The future

Introduction

3.1 The Mental Capacity Act (MCA) 2005 received the royal assent on 7 April 2005. Most of its provisions came into effect on 1 October 2007. Prior to the MCA 2005:
- The Court of Protection only had jurisdiction over an incapacitated person's property and financial affairs. The relevant legal provisions were set out in Part VII of the Mental Health Act (MHA) 1983 and in rules made under that Act.
- Most treatment and care decisions were governed by the common law, in other words by laws and principles set down by judges rather than in legislation.
- The test which the judges formulated was beautifully simple: If the individual had capacity to make their own decision, treatment or care required their consent. If they lacked capacity, the clinician was under a duty to give any treatment or care necessary to preserve their life, health or well-being which was in their best interests.

3.2 The beauty of the scheme was its simplicity and the fact that it was non-prescriptive; it left much to the discretion of those providing the treatment or care. The weakness of the scheme was its simplicity and the fact that it was non-prescriptive; it left much to the discretion of those providing the treatment or care.

3.3 Because of the decision-making discretion given to professionals and family carers, few cases came to court. Only cases which involved especially significant or difficult decisions – such as life-sustaining treatment and sterilisation – tended to be referred.

3.4 As the years went by, many people became concerned by the lack of any structured process for deciding more commonplace personal welfare matters – issues such as where and with whom an incapacitated person should live, how much contact they should have with family members and friends, how to help them to develop their activities and skills, what medication they should receive, and so on.

3.5 Depending on the values, resources and time of family members and professionals, great to little or no care might be taken to establish which decisions the person could make for themselves. Similarly, if incapacitated, the individual might have considerable involvement in decisions about their welfare and future or none at all.

The Law Commission's work

3.6 Much useful work was done by the Law Commission to address these difficult issues. The Commission's fourth programme published in September 1989 noted the view that existing legal mechanisms were 'complicated, inflexible and piecemeal' and stated that the recent House of Lords decision in *Re F*[1] could not provide a comprehensive solution.[2]

3.7 Lady Hale (then Brenda Hoggett) was an important driver of the reform programme, and the Law Commission's Report of 1995[3] which had a draft Bill appended to it was preceded by a number of consultation and discussion papers.

3.8 The Law Commission's proposals were debated and in some respects modified over the following years, eventually emerging as the MCA 2005.

3.9 Subsequently, a number of important insertions to the Act were made by the MHA 2007. In particular, a new scheme for authorising deprivation of liberty under the MCA 2005 was introduced.

Statutory principles (section 1)

3.10 The MCA 2005 starts with a number of fundamental statutory principles which apply, and must be applied, whenever a person does something under the Act.

---

1 Reported as *Re F (mental patient: sterilisation)* [1990] 2 AC 1.
2 Fourth Programme of Law Reform (1989) Law Com NO 185, Item 9; Cm 800.
3 *Mental incapacity (report)* [1995] EWLC 231, 15 January 1995. The report can be downloaded from the BAILII website: www.bailii.org/ew/other/EWLC/1995/231_s.html.

THE STATUTORY PRINCIPLES	
Section 1(1) provides that the following principles apply for the purposes of the Act:	
1	A person must be assumed to have capacity unless it is established that he lacks capacity (MCA 2005 s1(2)).
2	A person is not to be treated as unable to make a decision unless all practicable steps to help him to do so have been taken without success (MCA 2005 s1(3)).
3	A person is not to be treated as unable to make a decision merely because he makes an unwise decision (MCA 2005 s1(4)).
4	An act done, or decision made, under the Act for or on behalf of a person who lacks capacity must be done, or made, in his best interests (MCA 2005 s1(5)).
5	Before the act is done, or the decision is made, regard must be had to whether the purpose for which it is needed can be as effectively achieved in a way that is less restrictive of the person's rights and freedom of action (MCA 2005 s1(6)).

3.11 It is important to emphasise the importance of these principles at the outset, and useful to illustrate one or two of the situations in which they can be significant.

The presumption of capacity

3.12 The first principle is that the relevant person 'must be assumed to have capacity unless it is established that he lacks capacity'.

3.13 The starting point, therefore, is *always* that this person has capacity to make this particular decision for themselves. That remains the legal position until it is established that it is more likely than not that they lack this capacity.[4]

3.14 A fair number of cases brought to the Court of Protection are brought because the evidence is quite finely balanced and there is a dispute about the person's capacity. In such cases, the presumption of capacity may be decisive. In medical practice, for example in an A&E

---

4 MCA 2005 s2(4). In proceedings under the MCA 2005 'or any other enactment, any question whether a person lacks capacity within the meaning of this Act must be decided on the balance of probabilities'. The reference to proceedings under 'any other enactment' is likely to be relevant to certain proceedings taken under the MHA 1983.

setting, it is not uncommon for a doctor when asked about a person's capacity to say that it is 'fifty-fifty'; evidently, the presumption of capacity has not been displaced. And, when it comes to depriving someone of their liberty under the Act, it follows that the presumption that they can make their own decision about whether to not to be in the particular hospital or care home must first be displaced.

Duty to help the person make their own decision where possible

3.15 The second principle is that a person is not to be treated as unable to make the particular decision for themselves unless all practicable steps to help them to do so have been taken without success.

3.16 What is practicable – that is, capable of being put into practice – depends on the circumstances at the time.

3.17 If a person in need of immediate medical treatment is unconscious after a serious motorway accident it will not be practicable before intervening to take any steps to help them make their own decision about the particular medical intervention.

3.18 At the other end of the scale is the situation where it is practicable to assist a person with a learning disability to make their own will. If there is no urgency, the fact that the person lacks capacity to make their own will today is not decisive if with assistance over weeks or months they can develop the necessary understanding. It may be possible to break the relevant information down into a more understandable form, to repeat key points over a number of weeks, to devise helpful visual aids and so on.

3.19 Likewise, an unwell person in hospital who is asked about a return home or a move into residential care may appear to lack capacity to make the decision at this moment. However, with more time to reflect, clearer explanations, and the benefit of discussing the options with family members, trusted friends or an advocate, they may well have capacity to make their own decision.

Unwise decision-making

3.20 The third principle is that 'A person is not to be treated as unable to make a decision merely because he makes an unwise decision'.

3.21 One can rephrase this by saying that a person is not to be treated as being unable to make their own decision merely because the decision they make *or propose making* is considered by some person or persons to be unwise.

3.22 Although a person cannot be found to lack capacity *merely* because their proposed decision is unwise, fairly obviously an unwise or irrational decision may raise significant doubts and so trigger an assessment of their capacity.

3.23 In practice this principle is often in play, particularly when it comes to decisions about whether to remove older people into residential care. There are many older people who prefer to 'take their chances' at home rather than live in a care home, notwithstanding the risk of falls and some physical suffering. Some of them, in common with all generations, will have a stubborn streak, 'unreasonably' refuse good or well-meant advice, or demonstrate a lifelong antipathy to being told what to do. The fact that others think they are being unwise is insufficient. They only lack capacity if their ability to understand, retain and weigh the information relevant to the decision, including the foreseeable benefits and risks of deciding one way or the other, is undermined in some significant way by an impairment or disturbance of their mind or brain. Otherwise, their decision is essentially no different to that of a person who goes mountaineering, hang-gliding or motor racing – risky and the doctor might not do it, arguably unwise, could end unhappily, but they are within their rights.

Duty to act in the person's best interests

3.24 The fourth principle is that, 'An act done, or decision made, under the Act for or on behalf of a person who lacks capacity must be done, or made, in his best interests'.

3.25 This was also part of the old common law test which, it may be recalled, required a clinician, social worker or other professional carer to give the incapacitated person any treatment or care necessary to preserve their life, health or well-being 'which was in their best interests'.

3.26 The final phrase drew attention to the fact that providing treatment or care is not always in a person's best interests. Obvious examples are where further prolonging a terminally ill patient's life would cause them considerable suffering for little benefit, and where a patient's fierce resistance to treatment means that it is not in their best interests to attempt to give it by restraint.

3.27 If a person lacks capacity to make a decision, so that someone else must make it for them, applying the best interests requirement does not mean that other people's interests are always irrelevant and must be given no weight. As an example, almost all parents want their children to be happy and free from worry. The Court of Protection may therefore authorise making a gift from the incapacitated person's funds to a child in need. If the incapacitated person still had capacity to make the gift they would wish to help in this way; and it is in their best interests to do on their behalf that which they themselves would obviously do if they could. Similarly, most people with capacity consider and take into account the wishes, feelings and needs of their spouse or partner when making decisions which affect them. It is in the incapacitated person's best interests to have regard to these historic genuine feelings and values if they can no longer hold or express them.

3.28 The critical error to avoid is an analysis of the person's best interests which disregards or downplays their wishes, feelings, values and beliefs in the perverted belief that critical objectivity is undermined by subjective considerations.

3.29 The law requires objective analysis of a subject not an object. The incapacitated person is the subject. Therefore, it is *their* welfare in the context of *their* wishes, feelings, beliefs and values that is important. This is the principle of beneficence which asserts an obligation to help others further *their* important and legitimate interests, not one's own.[5]

3.30 Why would anyone wish a person to receive care otherwise than in accordance with their wishes if they can be cared for adequately in accordance with their wishes?

Duty to consider less restrictive options

3.31 The fifth principle is that: 'Before the act is done, or the decision is made, regard must be had to whether the purpose for which it is needed can be as effectively achieved in a way that is less restrictive of the person's rights and freedom of action'.

3.32 This principle is sometimes paraphrased as 'one must choose the least restrictive option', which risks being misleading. The 'least restrictive option' of those available may be to do nothing and to neglect the person. That is not what the principle requires. The decision-maker must have regard to whether the necessary purpose or aim (eg treating a severe illness which is causing considerable suffering) can be as effectively achieved in a less restrictive way (eg in a way which is acceptable to the person or more acceptable to them).

---

5 From *Westminster City Council v Sykes* [2014] EWHC B9 (COP), (2014) 17 CCLR 139 at section 10.

Why an act or decision is now needed, and the effectiveness of less restrictive approaches, must be considered.

Who lacks capacity (sections 2 and 3)

3.33 The purpose of the MCA 2005 is to provide a structure and appropriate mechanisms for making a decision on behalf of a fellow citizen who lacks capacity to make their own decision.

3.34 The first consideration therefore is, 'does this person lack capacity?' Does this person lack or now lack the capacity necessary to exercise a citizen's usual constitutional right to make their own decision? Does a decision now need to be made for them, in their best interests?

3.35 This is a matter of constitutional importance for a second reason. Those capable of acting are responsible for their actions and omissions and, being responsible for them, accountable to others. The counterpart of freedom and autonomy is accountability for acts freely and autonomously done.

3.36 The law takes what some people call an 'issue specific' or 'functional' approach to capacity. It assesses a person's ability to make a particular decision at a particular time, not their ability to make decisions generally.

3.37 As has been seen, everyone is assumed to have capacity to make the decision(s) in question unless and until it is established that they lack this capacity, which must be established on the balance of probabilities. Furthermore, a person is not to be treated as lacking capacity to make the decision in question unless all practicable steps to help them to do so have been taken without success.

3.38 A person does not lack capacity simply because they have a mental disorder or disability (sometimes described as a 'status approach' to capacity). Nor are they to be treated as lacking capacity to make the decision(s) in question merely because they propose making a decision which others consider to be unwise (sometimes called an 'outcome approach').

3.39 Furthermore, a lack of capacity cannot be established merely by reference to their age or appearance, a condition of theirs such as mental illness or a learning disability, or an aspect of their behaviour, which might lead others to make unjustified assumptions about their capacity.[6] One needs to be especially careful in the case of those

6 MCA 2005 s2(3).

who may merely be stubborn or eccentric. The correct test of capacity must be applied and lack of capacity be established.[7]

The incapacity test

3.40 For the purposes of the Act, a person lacks capacity in relation to a matter 'if at the material time he is unable to make a decision for himself in relation to the matter because of an impairment of, or a disturbance in the functioning of, the mind or brain'.[8]

3.41 Accordingly, capacity is both:
- *time-specific*, focusing on the particular time when a decision has to be made – so the loss of capacity can be temporary, partial or fluctuating, and
- *decision- or issue-specific*, concentrating on the particular matter to which the decision relates, rather than the ability to make decisions generally – so, someone may lack capacity in relation to one particular matter but not another.

3.42 The fact that a temporary impairment or disturbance of the mind or brain suffices brings within the Act those who are unable to make a decision because of the effects of alcohol or drugs. This is particularly relevant for A&E staff.

What is meant by 'unable to make a decision'?

3.43 This is the 'section 3 test'. For these purposes, a person is unable to make a decision for themselves if they are unable:
- to understand the information relevant to the decision;
- to retain that information;
- to use or weigh that information as part of the process of making the decision; or
- to communicate their decision (whether by talking, using sign language or any other means).

| Understand | → | Retain | → | Use/Weigh | → | Communicate |

3.44 It can be seen that being 'unable to decide' does not literally mean that. Demonstrating incapacity involves establishing that the person's

---

7 See *Court of Protection Practice 2016*, Ashton et al, Jordans, at p110 et seq.
8 It does not matter whether the impairment or disturbance is permanent or temporary.

capacity to make the decision in question is in some way fundamentally compromised by the fact that the functioning of their mind or brain is impaired or disturbed. In other words, because of an impairment or disturbance of their mind or brain they are unable to understand, retain or weigh the information relevant to the decision, or are unable to communicate their decision. A link must be demonstrated.

RELEVANT INFORMATION	THE PERSON IS UNABLE	IMPAIRED OR DISTURBED MIND OR BRAIN
• The decision requires the person to consider relevant information	• To understand it, or • To retain it, or • To use or weigh it, or • To communicate their decisions	• This is because of an impairment or disturbance in the functioning of the mind or brain

3.45 The test is not purely about cognition or capacity to reason. A person may understand the relevant information, be able to retain it, and intellectually able to acknowledge its significance, but be unable to give it weight because of an overwhelming phobia, obsessive thoughts, compulsive behaviour, abnormally impulsive behaviour or some other impairment or disturbance. It is therefore going too far to say that the quality of the decision is irrelevant as long as the person 'understands' what he or she is deciding.[9]

How much information is relevant information

3.46 How much information is relevant – the level and amount of information which the person must be capable of understanding, retaining and weighing in order to have capacity to make the decision – turns on the significance and complexity of the decision in question.

9 As Ashton noted in the 2014 edition of the *Court of Protection Practice*, Jordans (at page 995), 'in *Mitchell v Alasia* [2005] EWHC 11 (QB), Cox J relied on qualities such as impulsiveness and volatility when deciding that the claimant was incapable of managing and administering his own affairs'. Similarly, in *NHS Trust v Ms T* [2004] EWHC 1279 (Fam), (2005) 8 CCLR 38, although there was no problem in respect of Ms T's intellectual capacity, and she was able to acknowledge intellectually that her belief was delusional, her wishes were driven by a delusional belief that any transfusion would only add to the evil circulating within her system.

3.47 The MCA 2005 states that: 'The information relevant to a decision includes information about the reasonably foreseeable consequences of (a) deciding one way or another, or (b) failing to make the decision' (section 3(4)). This therefore is relevant information that needs to be understood, retained, used and weighed in order to have capacity to make the decision.

3.48 Some decisions are relatively insignificant and involve understanding and weighing very little information; other decisions are more complicated or have foreseeable consequences that are more significant.

3.49 Regardless of whether a person has capacity, the aim of all explanations is to simplify matters as far as possible but no further. Once the information relevant to a decision has been communicated in as understandable a way as possible – by breaking it down and using plain language and aids, but without resorting to omitting information which is relevant if more difficult to understand and weigh – one is still left with a spectrum of decisions ranging from those which are simple and require understanding relatively little to those that require understanding and weighing more.

3.50 In the case of a simple and trivial gift, such as giving a small present to a friend, there is not much to it and very little to grasp in order to make a valid gift. By definition, more significant transactions – those where the reasonably foreseeable consequences are more significant for the person concerned – require the capacity to understand and weigh the more significant consequences. Thus, in the old case of *Re Beaney*,[10] where the person was giving her house and only main asset to one of three children at the end of her life instead of by will, and the significance was to disinherit the other two children, the degree of understanding required was as high as that required for a will: the donor had to understand the claims of all potential donees and the extent of the property being disposed of. Unless she understood that, she would be entirely failing to grasp the significance, the essence, of the transaction.

3.51 It follows from the fact that capacity is issue-specific, and partly depends on the nature or complexity of the decisions to be made, that a person may have capacity to make some decisions for themselves (eg capacity to marry) but lack capacity to do other things (eg to make a will). A person may have capacity to bring or defend a small, relatively trivial claim in court, where the nature of the dispute and the issues are simple to understand and weigh, but lack capacity to

10 *Re Beaney* [1978] 1 WLR 770, [1978] 2 All ER 595.

litigate a case where the nature of the dispute or the issues are more significant or complex. Likewise, they may have capacity to consent to a simple medical procedure but not something much more significant.

Capacity to understand the relevant information

3.52 The first of the four parts of the section 3 test concerns the person's capacity 'to understand' the relevant information.

3.53 The Act says that a person is not to be regarded as being unable to understand the information relevant to a decision if they are able to understand an explanation of it given to them in a way that is appropriate to their circumstances (using simple language, visual aids or any other means).[11] A relatively common example of a person being unable to understand the information relevant to a medical treatment decision would be an inability to understand the meaning of even common words, as a result of a very profound brain injury, learning disability or dementia.

Capacity to retain the relevant information

3.54 The fact that a person is able to retain the information relevant to a decision for a short period only does not prevent them from being regarded as able to make the decision.[12] However, by definition, before one can weigh relevant information one must be able to retain it long enough to do so. As an example, even a clear and simple explanation of the information relevant to a treatment decision involves communicating what is wrong (the diagnosis), what is proposed (the treatment), the likely outcome with and without treatment (the prognosis) and any significant treatment risks (adverse effects). If a person understands the diagnosis but has forgotten it by the time the proposed treatment is being explained, they are unable to retain all of the relevant information for long enough to enable them to weigh it and make a decision.

Capacity to weigh the relevant information

3.55 This is the ground which has proved to be the most difficult and controversial in practice.

---

11 MCA 2005 s3(2).
12 MCA 2005 s3(3).

3.56 Even though a person can understand and retain all of the information relevant to a decision, and can communicate their preferred decision, they will still be held to be unable to make the decision if they cannot 'use or weigh' the information as part of the process of making the decision.

3.57 A simple example is that of a person who because of mental illness believes that their consultant psychiatrist is an imposter. The individual can understand and retain the relevant information given to them by the psychiatrist about their diagnosis, the proposed treatment, and so forth. They can also communicate the decision they intend to make. However, because they do not believe the doctor is a doctor, and give no weight at all to what the person says, they cannot 'use or weigh' the information as part of the process of making the decision. Therefore, they will be held to lack capacity to make the decision, on the weighing ground.

3.58 In the old case of *Re MB (Caesarean section)*,[13] MB consented to a Caesarean operation but then refused to be given anaesthesia by injection because she had a phobia of needles. When MB went into labour, the hospital obtained a declaration that it would be lawful to perform any necessary Caesarean upon her because she was incapable of consenting to or refusing treatment.

3.59 In that kind of case, the individual can understand and retain the relevant information about the proposed treatment and the foreseeable consequences of deciding one way or the other, repeat it back word for word and communicate their decision to refuse. That is not the issue. However, as in MB, it may be held that she is unable to use or weigh this information as part of the process of making the decision because her mind is disturbed by a terror of needles. She is petrified. This is so overwhelming as to prevent her from being able to use or weigh the relevant information about the foreseeable consequences of declining the intervention.

3.60 All cases are, of course, fact-specific. The important point is that the weight a person gives to relevant information, and their ability to use it when making the decision, are legally important considerations.

3.61 Some say that as soon as you refuse or discontinue treatment against medical advice you risk being found to lack capacity because it will be said that you have not understood or used the medical information properly, or have given it insufficient weight. That may happen in practice to a degree but it is not a correct statement of the

13 [1997] EWCA Civ 3093, [1997] 2 FLR 426.

law. It has to be demonstrated that the person is *unable* to use or weigh the information given to them and that this inability is *because of* an impairment or disturbance of the mind or brain. A link must be established.[14]

3.62 What is true when it comes to serious medical treatment decisions is that the more autonomy the law sanctions the more deaths there will be. Freedom to make 'unwise' decisions comes at a price in terms of safety, and safety bears a price in terms of freedom. It is not possible to have it both ways.

3.63 It is important to be aware of any temptation to overcome this uncomfortable truth by a misuse of the intellect or evidence. One must not give in to 'the self-interested lie' and construct a contrived incapacity argument in order to release *oneself* from an almost unbearable burden.

Capacity to communicate one's decision

3.64 This applies to people who are unconscious or in a coma and those with the rare condition sometimes known as 'locked-in syndrome', who are conscious but cannot speak or move at all. If a person cannot communicate their decision in any way, the MCA 2005 says they should be treated as if they are unable to make that decision. However, before deciding that this is so, it is necessary to take all practicable steps to help them communicate; for example, one might involve speech and language therapists, specialists in non-verbal communication and other appropriate professionals. Communication by simple muscle movements can show that somebody may have capacity to make a decision.[15]

Best interests (section 4)

3.65 If it is the case that the relevant person is unable to make their own decision, then by definition unless the decision can be postponed someone else must make it for them.

---

14 This point was emphasised strongly in *Kings College NHS Foundation Trust v C and V* [2015] EWCOP 80, [2016] COPLR 50, in which the judge also reviewed and summarised the case-law on the determination of capacity since the Act came into force.

15 See Code of Practice paras 4.23–4.25: www.justice.gov.uk/downloads/ protecting-the-vulnerable/mca/mca-code-practice-0509.pdf.

3.66 The decision made for them must be made in their 'best interests'. The MCA 2005 provides that one must not determine what is in a person's best interests merely on the basis of their age or appearance, or a condition of theirs, or an aspect of their behaviour, which might lead others to make unjustified assumptions about what might be in their best interests.[16]

Matters to consider

3.67 The person making the determination must consider all of the relevant circumstances. Rather unhelpfully, the Act says that 'relevant circumstances' are those which the person determining best interests is aware of and which it would be reasonable to regard as relevant.[17] However, the person making the decision must in particular consider the matters set out in the table on the next page.

3.68 As to the five considerations in the table:

1) The first of them differs from the second guiding principle, which stated that a person is not to be treated as unable to make a decision unless all practicable steps to help them to do so have been taken without success.

   Even if the person cannot *presently* make their own decision (even, for example, with the assistance of family members and simple, clear explanations) and so lacks capacity to decide the matter, one must consider if and when they are likely to have that capacity.

   It may be that with more time to reflect, further treatment, improved health, reduced medication levels, clearer explanations and the benefit of discussing the options with family members, trusted friends or an advocate, they are likely to develop or recover the capacity to decide.

   If so, this must be considered when deciding what is in their best interests. Depending on the urgency, it may be in their best interests to postpone the decision until they can make it for themselves.

2) The second makes a different point to that made by the second guiding principle. The point here is that, if the person cannot make their own decision because all practicable steps to help them to do so have failed, they must still be permitted and encouraged

---

16 MCA 2005 s4(1).
17 MCA 2005 s4(11).

BEST INTERESTS CONSIDERATIONS (MCA 2005 s4)
The person determining what is in the person's best interests must in particular (MCA 2005 s4(2)):

1	Consider whether it is likely that the person will at some time have capacity in relation to the matter in question and, if it appears likely that he will, when that is likely to be (MCA 2005 s4(3)).
2	So far as reasonably practicable, permit and encourage the person to participate, or to improve his ability to participate, as fully as possible in any act done for him and any decision affecting him (MCA 2005 s4(4)).
3	Consider, so far as is reasonably ascertainable, the person's past and present wishes and feelings (and, in particular, any relevant written statement made by him when he had capacity); the beliefs and values that would be likely to influence his decision if he had capacity; and the other factors that he would be likely to consider if he were able to do so (MCA 2005 s4(6)).
4	If it is practicable and appropriate to consult them, take into account the views of the following people: • anyone named by the person as someone to be consulted on the matter in question or on matters of that kind; • anyone engaged in caring for the person or interested in his welfare; • any donee of a lasting power of attorney granted by the person; and • any deputy appointed for the person by the court as to the matters mentioned in paragraph 3 and what would be in the person's best interests (MCA 2005 s4(7)).
5	Not be motivated by a desire to bring about his death where the determination relates to life-sustaining treatment and considering whether the treatment is in the best interests of the person concerned (MCA 2005 s4(5)). ('Life-sustaining treatment' means treatment which in the view of a person providing healthcare for the person concerned is necessary to sustain life: s4(10)).

to participate in the decision-making process and any act done on their behalf. This is, of course, provided that this is reasonably practicable.
3) The third consideration draws attention to five matters:
   i) the person's present wishes and feelings;
   ii) the person's past wishes and feelings;

iii) the beliefs and values that would be likely to influence their decision if they had capacity;
iv) any relevant written statement made by the person when they had capacity (this could be a written statement about the treatment which the person wishes to receive rather than to reject);
v) the other factors that they would be likely to consider if they were able to do so.

4) Provided that it is practicable and appropriate, the fourth consideration imposes a requirement to consult carers, nominated persons and persons appointed under the MCA 2005 about the person's wishes, feelings, beliefs and values, and the factors which they would have been likely to take into account if they still had capacity to make their own decision.

Clearly, family members and non-professional carers will often know much more than the professionals about the person's wishes, feelings, beliefs, values, life goals and views concerning care and treatment. Proper consultation and sharing of information is critical to building up a true picture of the person's best interests.

5) The final listed matter provides that any person determining whether life-sustaining treatment is in the best interests of the person concerned must not be motivated by a desire to bring about their death. This legal requirement ties in with section 62 which states that nothing in the Act constitutes a defence to a charge of manslaughter or murder or is to be read or taken as legalising or authorising assisted suicide.

3.69 None of the listed considerations has automatic precedence.[18] This would be impossible given that the person determining best interests must also consider any other (unlisted) relevant considerations of which he or she is aware.

3.70 The weight to be attached to the various factors depends on the circumstances of the particular individual. A feature or factor which in one person's situation may carry great, possibly even preponderant, weight may in another, superficially similar, case carry much less, or even very little, weight. Sometimes one or more features or factors may be of 'magnetic importance' in influencing or even determining what is in the person's best interests.[19]

---

18 See *ITW v Z* [2009] EWHC 2525 (Fam), (2009) 12 CCLR 635, per Munby J (as he then was) at para 32.
19 *ITW v Z* at para 32.

3.71 The person who determines best interests does not incur any legal liability for their determination simply because a court later comes to a different view. The Act provides that there is sufficient compliance with section 4 if, having complied with the requirements of the section, the person 'reasonably believes' that what they do or decide is in the best interests of the person concerned.[20] Unless one takes a peculiarly authoritarian view, in many situations more than one belief can reasonably be held. It is quite possible that family members and/or members of the multi-disciplinary team may 'reasonably' believe something different.

Best interests and substituted judgment

3.72 To what extent must the aim of the person determining best interests be to identify and make the decision which they believe the person themselves would have made if they had, or still had, capacity to make it?

3.73 'Substituted judgment' is a principle which holds that surrogate decisions should be made by establishing as accurately as possible the decision which the incapacitated person would have made for themselves if they had capacity.

3.74 The Law Commission argued that 'best interests' on the one hand and 'substituted judgment' on the other were not in fact mutually exclusive. It favoured a 'best interests' criterion which contained a strong element of 'substituted judgment'.[21]

3.75 A main reason for rejecting a pure substituted judgment test was not that the views, beliefs and values of an incapacitated person were unimportant but that they are important:

> One of the failings of a pure 'substituted judgment' model is the unhelpful idea that a person who cannot make a decision should be treated as if his or her capacity were perfect and unimpaired, and as if present emotions need not also be considered.[22]

3.76 One must take into account and give weight to the person's present wishes and feelings, and what they now view as important, and not just the values and beliefs which they held when they had capacity, even if more objective.

3.77 Furthermore, as the Commission noted when rejecting a pure substituted judgment approach, if a person has never had capacity

---
20 MCA 2005 s4(9).
21 Law Com No 231 para 3.25.
22 Law Com No 231 para 3.29.

then 'substituted judgment' is impossible and there is no viable alternative to a best interests approach.[23]

Safety, health, care, treatment and liberty

3.78   It must not be assumed that because the decision concerns care or medical treatment that therefore the person's care and medical treatment, and physical safety, are the most important considerations. There will usually be many other competing factors to consider, such as a person's attachment to their home, their privacy and sense of security at home, their attitude towards institutional life and the importance to them of their freedom.

3.79   The importance of individual liberty is of the same fundamental importance to incapacitated people who still have clear wishes and preferences about where and how they live as it is for those who remain able to make capacitous decisions. This desire to determine one's own interests is common to almost all human beings. Society is made up of individuals, and each individual wills certain ends for themselves and their loved ones, and not others, and has distinctive feelings, personal goals, traits, habits and experiences. Because this is so, most individuals wish to determine and develop their own interests and course in life, and their happiness often depends on this. The existence of a private sphere of action, free from public coercion or restraint, is indispensable to that independence which everyone needs to develop their individuality, even where their individuality is diminished, but not extinguished, by illness. It is for this reason that people place such weight on their liberty and right to choose.

Wishes, feelings and objectivity

3.80   The fact that the individual's past and present wishes, feelings, beliefs and values must be considered tells us that this is not a sterile objective test of best interests.

3.81   It is not a case of trying to determine what some hypothetical objective or rational person would decide in this situation when presented with these choices. Nor are we seeking to do anything more sophisticated than impose on the individual an objective and rational analysis based on professional expertise of what they ought sensibly to do in that situation.

---

23 See further in this regard *Re Jones* [2014] EWCOP 59.

3.82 The law requires objective analysis of a subject not an object. The incapacitated person is the subject. Therefore, it is *their* welfare in the context of *their* wishes, feelings, beliefs and values that is important. This is the principle of beneficence which asserts an obligation to help others further *their* important and legitimate interests, not one's own.

3.83 That this is so is emphasised by Lady Hale in the *Aintree* case:[24]

> Finally, insofar as Sir Alan Ward and Arden LJ were suggesting that the test of the patient's wishes and feelings was an objective one, what the reasonable patient would think, again I respectfully disagree. The purpose of the best interests test is to consider matters from the patient's point of view. That is not to say that his wishes must prevail, any more than those of a fully capable patient must prevail. We cannot always have what we want. Nor will it always be possible to ascertain what an incapable patient's wishes are. Even if it is possible to determine what his views were in the past, they might well have changed in the light of the stresses and strains of his current predicament. In this case, the highest it could be put was, as counsel had agreed, that 'It was likely that Mr James would want treatment up to the point where it became hopeless'. But insofar as it is possible to ascertain the patient's wishes and feelings, his beliefs and values or the things which were important to him, it is those which should be taken into account because they are a component in making the choice which is right for him as an individual human being.

3.84 It also emerges from various decisions of the President of the Court of Protection. Naturally, precisely how much weight to give to a person's present wishes and feelings will depend on the particular context and the individual's circumstances. The relevant circumstances will include the degree of their incapacity; the strength and consistency of their views; the possible impact on them of knowing that their wishes and feelings are not being given effect to; the extent to which their wishes and feelings are, or are not, rational, sensible, responsible and pragmatically capable of sensible implementation; and the extent to which their wishes and feelings, if given effect to, can properly be accommodated within the overall assessment of what is in her best interests. However, while the weight to be attached to the person's wishes and feelings will always be case-specific and fact-specific, their wishes and feelings

---

24 *Aintree University Hospitals NHS Foundation Trust v James* [2013] UKSC 67, (2013) 16 CCLR 554 at para 45.

will always be a significant factor to which the court must pay close regard.[25]

3.85 The drawing up of a 'balance sheet' in personal welfare cases, listing the actual and potential advantages and disadvantages of each alternative,[26] should not be a dry accountant's exercise which omits what is personal, but one that includes the 'personal' element of 'personal welfare'.

3.86 Whatever weight is given to the person's wishes and feelings, it is imperative not to reformulate them and claim to know better than they do what they truly wish, feel or will; in other words, not to be an 'aesthetic bully'.[27]

Summary – waypoint

3.87 There is a lot here for a reader new to the subject to grapple with, so it is worth summarising where we have got.

3.88 So far, in general terms, we have looked at three things:

1) the statutory principles to be applied to anything and everything done under the MCA 2005;
2) what we mean by lacking capacity to make a decision for oneself;
3) what we mean by best interests, and how to go about determining what is in a person's best interests.

We have also seen that the decisions which may be made for someone under the Act can relate to their personal welfare or to their property and financial affairs.

3.89 In diagrammatic form, this is where we have reached:

---

25 *ITW v Z* [2009] EWHC 2525 (Fam), (2009) 12 CCLR 635, per Munby J at para 35.
26 *Re S (adult's lack of capacity: carer and residence)* [2003] FLR 1235.
27 Care must be taken not to treat humanity as the raw material upon which the professional imposes her or his creative will, for the last century exposed the dangers of this way of thinking. It is, Berlin suggested, a form of thinking to which the scientist may be especially prone; for if, as Comte believed, scientific method will in due course reveal all truths, then what case is there for freedom of opinion or action, at least as an end in itself, and why should any conduct be tolerated that is not authorised by appropriate experts? See Sir I Berlin, *Four essays on liberty*, OUP, 1969, pp150–151.

```
┌─────────────────────────────────────────────────────────────────┐
│  The circumstances require the person concerned to make a decision │
└─────────────────────────────────────────────────────────────────┘
                                  ↓
┌─────────────────────────────────────────────────────────────────┐
│  Someone is concerned about whether the person has capacity to make │
│                            the decision                          │
└─────────────────────────────────────────────────────────────────┘
                                  ↓
┌─────────────────────────────────────────────────────────────────┐
│  The person's capacity to make the particular decision is assessed: is it the │
│  case that because of an impairment or disturbance of their mind or brain │
│  they are unable to understand, retain or weigh the information relevant to │
│       this decision, or are unable to communicate their decision?│
└─────────────────────────────────────────────────────────────────┘
               ↙                                    ↘
┌──────────────────────────────┐    ┌──────────────────────────────┐
│ If this cannot be established │    │    If this is established on the │
│ on the balance of probabilities,│    │ balance of probabilities then, by │
│ the law regards the person as │    │ definition, if they cannot make the │
│ having capacity to make their │    │ decision for themselves someone │
│ own decision. Who decides? They│    │      must decide for them.   │
│           decide.            │    │                              │
└──────────────────────────────┘    └──────────────────────────────┘
                                                    ↙
┌─────────────────────────────────────────────────────────────────┐
│  The way we do this is by applying the MCA 2005. That is why it exists: it is │
│  an Act which sets out the framework to be used when making a decision for │
│          someone who cannot make their own decision.            │
└─────────────────────────────────────────────────────────────────┘
                                  ↓
┌─────────────────────────────────────────────────────────────────┐
│  When using and applying the Act, a person making a decision for someone │
│  must always act in their best interests, rather than eg in their own interests. │
└─────────────────────────────────────────────────────────────────┘
```

The statutory mechanisms

3.90   That helps but takes matters only so far.

3.91   What does the phrase, 'The way the person does that is by applying the MCA 2005', mean in practice? Are there forms or documents to complete, does an application need to be made to a court, does a decision-maker need to be formally appointed, and so on?

3.92   Put differently, we now know the principles, but what are the mechanisms – the mechanics of getting the job done?

Four main mechanisms

3.93   There are four main decision-making mechanisms, four ways of making decisions under the MCA 2005.

An overview of the Mental Capacity Act 2005

3.94   All of them are relevant to personal welfare decision-making. Only two of them – lasting powers of attorney (LPA) and the Court of Protection – are relevant to financial and property-related matters.

Arrangements made by the person themselves when they had capacity	
1. Advance decisions to refuse treatment	An adult with capacity to do so may make an advance decision to refuse a particular treatment at a later date if they lack capacity at that time to decide whether or not to receive it. Because the decision was made when the person still had capacity, subject to certain exceptions it is binding on clinicians.
2. Lasting powers of attorney (LPA)	An adult with capacity to do so may make an LPA appointing one or more trusted persons to make decisions for them at a later date which they lack capacity to make for themselves.
There are two types of LPA. One is used to authorise the person's chosen attorney(s) to make personal welfare decisions; the other is used to authorise making financial and property-related decisions on the individual's behalf.
(LPAs replaced the old-style enduring powers of attorney (EPAs), which were limited to authorising financial and property-related decisions and could not provide for personal welfare matters. Previously made EPAs continue to have effect but no new ones may be created.)
Arrangements which can be made for them after capacity has been lost	
3. Court orders	The Court of Protection can make the particular decision(s) on the person's behalf or appoint a person called 'a deputy' to make personal welfare and/or financial and property-related decisions for the person as and when they arise.
4. Section 5	MCA 2005 s5 relates only to personal welfare matters and is an exemption from legal liability provision. In general terms, it states that a carer (paid or unpaid) will not be liable for non-negligent care and treatment given to an incapacitated person provided they comply with the conditions set out in section 5.

3.95   It is helpful to say a little more about this overall decision-making structure.

Above and below the line

3.96 The first two mechanisms – the 'above the line' mechanisms in the table above – are things which adults with capacity can do for themselves to plan for the day when they lose capacity:

- As regards personal welfare matters, they can make a decision in advance to refuse a particular treatment or treatments they dislike and/or appoint a person or persons they trust to make future personal welfare decisions for them which they lack the capacity to make.
  From this it can be seen that if a person lacks capacity to make the decision in question the first thing to do is to check whether they made their own arrangements to cater for this situation when they had capacity. If so then, unless their arrangement is invalid or inapplicable for some proper legal reason, apply this mechanism. If not 'go below the line' and – unless there are appropriate ways of dealing with the situation outside the MCA 2005 – make an application to the Court of Protection or rely on the protection afforded by section 5.

- As regards financial and property-related matters, the only mechanism 'above the line' is an LPA for property and financial matters.
  If the person has made an LPA (or previously an old-style EPA) then unless it requires registration, or is invalid or inapplicable for some proper legal reason, this is the appropriate mechanism to use.

- Because only adults (people aged 18 or over) can make these 'above the line' arrangements, necessarily it follows that if the incapacitated person is a child there cannot exist a valid LPA, EPA or advance decision to refuse treatment. In their case it will always be necessary either to go 'below the line' or to seek an alternative to the MCA 2005, such as parental authority or a provision of the Children Act 1989 or MHA 1983.

Going below the line

3.97 If the incapacitated person did not make their own 'above the line' arrangements in anticipation that subsequently they might lack capacity to make this decision, it will be necessary to resort to the two remaining mechanisms, 'below the line':

- As regards financial and property-related matters, the only mechanism 'below the line' is a court application. The usual application is to apply to the court for it to appoint a 'deputy for property and affairs' on the incapacitated person's behalf. The person

appointed, who is often a close relative or a solicitor, is authorised by the court to deputise for the incapacitated person and to make financial and property-related decisions for them, subject to any restrictions in the court order. Because routine financial decisions – for example, paying bills – are needed on a day-to-day or week-to-week basis, this is more practical than going to court each time a financial decision is required.
- As regards personal welfare matters – for example, decisions about providing care or treatment to the individual – there are two options: making an application to court or applying section 5.

3.98 For reasons that may not always be valid, the Court of Protection has sometimes discouraged the appointment of personal welfare deputies.

3.99 An application for a court order should be made if it is in the person's best interests – for example, because the care or treatment is particularly intrusive, there is a significant dispute about what is in the person's best interests or appointing a personal welfare deputy is in the person's best interests.

3.100 In practice, almost all routine care and treatment is provided under the protection of section 5 without a court order or deputy in place. Many routine treatment and care decisions are not opposed by the incapacitated person, their family or paid carers. For example, decisions about bathing and treating an unconscious person or a decision to dress and help feed someone with severe dementia. Other decisions, where there is some difference of opinion, can be resolved by holding a best interests meeting at which the options are discussed and a resolution reached. In all of these cases, what is happening in legal terms is that the care and treatment is being provided in reliance on the last mechanism, section 5, and there will be no application to the Court of Protection for it to authorise the step in question.

3.101 Section 5 does not as such authorise providing any care or treatment; rather, it exempts a person who does provide an incapacitated person with care or treatment from any legal liability, provided they reasonably believe it is in the individual's best interests and the other section 5 conditions are satisfied.

More about advance decisions

3.102 The purpose of this chapter is not to provide an exhaustive statement of the law but to introduce the reader to the basic MCA 2005 principles and structures applicable to Court of Protection work. There are a few points concerning advance decisions which it is useful to know at the outset.

An advance decision 'to refuse treatment'

3.103 MCA 2005 s24(1) provides that an 'advance decision' means a decision made by an adult 'when he has capacity to do so' that if:

(a) at a later time and in such circumstances as he may specify, a specified treatment is proposed to be carried out or continued by a person providing health care for him, and
(b) at that time he lacks capacity to consent to the carrying out or continuation of the treatment,

the specified treatment is not to be carried out or continued.

3.104 From this, it can be seen that:

- An advance decision can only relate to 'treatment' proposed by someone providing health care, not personal care. The term 'treatment' includes 'a diagnostic or other procedure'.[28] The intention presumably is that a person cannot refuse basic personal care which they may require upon becoming incapacitated such as shelter, feeding, drinking, clothing and washing. There is no right to die in squalor.
- Second, a person with capacity may decide in advance what treatment to refuse but not what treatment to receive. A clinician cannot be required to give treatment which they consider is clinically inappropriate.[29]
- Third, on a literal reading, the right is to refuse a particular specified treatment, not to refuse treatment by a specified health care provider or treatment at a specified hospital or place.

Effect of advance decisions

3.105 The effect of a valid advance decision which it is accepted is applicable to the particular treatment is that the incapacitated person is treated as having made the decision with capacity on the future date

---

28 See MCA 2005 s64(1).
29 A person can of course set out in writing in advance what treatment they wish to receive if and when they lack capacity and this must be taken into account when deciding what treatment (if any) is in their best interests: see MCA 2005 s4(6)(a). However, such a statement is not binding in the way that an advance decision made under section 24 is. Since it is not binding, nothing has been decided in advance.

when they would otherwise be given the treatment.[30] In other words, notwithstanding that the person now lacks capacity to consent or to refuse consent to the treatment, it operates as a valid and binding refusal of that treatment.

Formalities

3.106 In terms of the formalities, an advance decision can be expressed 'in layman's terms',[31] provided of course it is sufficiently clear what treatment is being ruled out and the circumstances in which it is not to be given.

3.107 An advance decision to refuse treatment need not be in writing unless it relates to life-sustaining treatment. In this instance, to be applicable it must be in writing and include a statement 'to the effect that it is to apply to that treatment even if life is at risk'. It must then be signed by the relevant person (or by someone in their presence and at their direction) in the presence of a witness who then signs as a witness.[32] These formalities exist because the individual may literally be signing their life away.

3.108 The person concerned may withdraw or alter their advance decision at any time they have capacity to do so,[33] and a withdrawal (including a partial withdrawal) of an advance decision which relates to life-sustaining treatment need not be in writing.[34]

Validity and applicability of advance decisions

3.109 A person does not incur liability for the consequences of withholding or withdrawing a treatment if at the time the person reasonably believes that an advance decision refusing the treatment exists which is 'valid and applicable' to the treatment.[35]

3.110 Conversely, a person is liable in law to the incapacitated person if the person carries out or continues a particular treatment when at the time he or she is satisfied that an advance decision refusing the treatment exists which is 'valid and applicable' to it.[36]

---

30 MCA 2005 s26(1).
31 MCA 2005 s24(2).
32 MCA 2005 s25(5).
33 MCA 2005 s24(3).
34 MCA 2005 s24(4).
35 MCA 2005 s26(3).
36 MCA 2005 s26(2).

3.111 The Court of Protection may make a declaration as to whether an advance decision exists, is valid or is applicable to a particular treatment.[37]

3.112 Nothing in an apparent advance decision stops a person providing life-sustaining treatment, or doing any act that the person reasonably believes to be necessary to prevent a serious deterioration in the person's condition, while a decision as respects any relevant issue is sought from the court.[38]

3.113 In any disputed case, it can be seen that the two key issues are validity and applicability.

Validity	• An advance decision is not binding if it is not valid. • An advance decision is not valid if the person lacked capacity to make it at the time. • An advance decision is not valid if the person withdrew it at any time when s/he had capacity to do so. • An advance decision is not valid if the person has done anything else clearly inconsistent with it remaining their fixed decision.
Applicability	• An advance decision is not binding if it is not applicable to the particular treatment. • An advance decision is not applicable if the person still has capacity to make this particular treatment decision (simply ask them for their decision). • An advance decision is not applicable if the treatment is not the treatment specified in the advance decision. • An advance decision is not applicable if any circumstances specified in the advance decision are absent. • An advance decision is not applicable if there are reasonable grounds for believing that circumstances exist which the person did not anticipate at the time of the advance decision which would have affected their decision. • An advance decision is not applicable to life-sustaining treatment unless it is verified by a statement to the effect that it is to apply to that treatment even if life is at risk, and the decision is in writing, signed and witnessed.

---

37 MCA 2005 s26(4).
38 MCA 2005 s26(5).

More about LPAs

3.114 Although not fully appreciated, the new personal welfare LPA was the 'game-changer' in the MCA 2005.

3.115 The previous common law position in relation to incapacitated persons was that the clinician, social worker or other professional carer was under a duty to give any treatment or care necessary to preserve their life, health or well-being which was in their best interests. In other words, the best interests care or treatment decision was taken by the relevant professional.

3.116 Where a registered LPA is in force, the position now is that there is always someone from whom the relevant professional requires a consent. For as long as the receiver of the proposed care or treatment has capacity, treatment and care requires their consent. If they lack capacity to consent or refuse consent, the professional must go to the person nominated by them to make the decision.

3.117 This represents a considerable shift in the balance of power. Any adult with capacity can now nominate a trusted family member, friend, colleague or professional to make personal welfare decisions for them which they are unable to make in the future, in preference to leaving the best interests determination to the relevant professional.

3.118 The necessary detail is dealt with in the relevant chapters. However, it is probably helpful to emphasise the following points about LPAs at the outset:

- The person who makes the LPA is called the 'donor'. Strictly speaking, a person appointed is a 'donee'. However, in practice most people prefer 'attorney' because it is more natural and was the term used for many years in relation to the old-style EPAs.
- More than one attorney can be appointed but, if more than one, the document creating the LPA must state whether they are only authorised to make decisions jointly or can act alone or jointly ('jointly and severally').
- An LPA is not valid unless and until it has been registered (that is, stamped and entered on a register) by the Public Guardian.
- Completing an LPA is not difficult but involves using the prescribed form, and there are separate forms for the creation of a personal welfare LPA and for the creation of a property and financial affairs LPA.
- An attorney must act in accordance with the statutory principles and best interests requirements in MCA 2005 s4.

- What constitutes a 'personal welfare' decision is not exhaustively defined. However, the range of best interests decisions which may be made by a personal welfare attorney on behalf of an incapacitated person is likely to be extensive. The main Code of Practice suggests that they include decisions about:
  - where the incapacitated person should live and whom they should live with;
  - their day-to-day care, including diet and dress;
  - whom they may have contact with;
  - consenting to or refusing consent to medical examination and treatment;
  - necessary arrangements for medical, dental or optical treatment;
  - community care assessments and the provision of community care services;
  - participation in social activities, leisure activities, education or training;
  - personal correspondence and papers;
  - rights of access to personal information about the donor;
  - complaints about their care or treatment.[39]
- This decision-making authority is subject to the restriction that a donee may only make personal welfare decisions which he or she reasonably believes the donor lacks capacity to make for themselves.[40] Furthermore, a personal welfare donee has no authority to give or to refuse consent to life-sustaining treatment unless the LPA document expressly permits this.[41]
- A donor may revoke the power at any time he or she still has capacity to do so.[42]
- The Court of Protection can revoke an LPA in certain circumstances, for example where a donee has contravened their authority or has behaved in a way which is not in the person's best interests.[43]

Interplay between advance decisions and LPAs

3.119 An advance decision to refuse a particular treatment is not valid if the person later makes an LPA authorising an attorney to decide

---

39 See Code of Practice para 7.21.
40 MCA 2005 s11(7)(a).
41 MCA 2005 s11(7)(c) and (8).
42 MCA 2005 s13(2).
43 MCA 2005 s22(3).

whether or not to consent to the particular treatment in the event they lack capacity to make the decision.[44]

3.120 That restriction aside, the existence of an LPA does not in itself prevent an advance decision from being valid and applicable.[45] Indeed, a valid and applicable advance decision made by a person with capacity after making an LPA prevents their donee from consenting to that treatment. This is because, other than the statutory exception just referred to, a donee's authority is subject to the person's advance decision 'rights' in MCA 2005 ss24–26.[46] Furthermore, a donee may only make those personal welfare decisions which he or she reasonably believes the donor lacks capacity to make[47] and the advance decision has effect as if the refusal of treatment was made with capacity at the time the treatment is proposed.[48]

More about court orders and deputies

3.121 Court orders and deputies are dealt with in greater detail later. However, in brief, MCA 2005 s15 provides that the Court of Protection may make declarations as to:

- whether a person has or lacks capacity to make a decision specified in the declaration;
- whether a person has or lacks capacity to make decisions on such matters as are described in the declaration;
- the lawfulness or otherwise of any act done, or yet to be done, in relation to that person.

3.122 Section 16 applies if a person lacks capacity in relation to a matter or matters concerning their personal welfare or property and affairs.[49] It enables the court by order to make such decisions on their behalf or to appoint a deputy to make the decisions for the person.

3.123 Without prejudice to MCA 2005 s4, the court may make an order or appoint a deputy on such terms as it considers are in the incapacitated person's best interests – and may do so even though no application is before it 'on those terms'.

44 MCA 2005 s25(2)(b).
45 MCA 2005 s25(7).
46 MCA 2005 s11(7)(b).
47 MCA 2005 s11(7)(a).
48 MCA 2005 s26(1).
49 MCA 2005 s16(1).

3.124 Naturally, if the judge can make the decision, it will generally be inappropriate for him or her to authorise someone else to make it.

3.125 Consequently, the Act provides that a decision by the court is to be preferred to the appointment of a deputy to make a decision; and that the powers conferred on the deputy should be as limited in scope and duration 'as is reasonably practicable in the circumstances': see MCA 2005 s16(4).

Personal welfare deputies

3.126 Personal welfare deputy orders are considerably less common than property and affairs deputyships for reasons which seem invalid or inconsistent to some incapacitated people and their families.

3.127 The circumstances in which it is appropriate to appoint a personal welfare deputy are explained in *Re P*,[50] *G v E, Manchester City Council and F*,[51] *SBC v PBA and others*[52] and *A Local Authority v TZ (No 2)*.[53]

3.128 Roderic Wood J observed in *SBC v PBA and others* that the test to be applied when determining whether to appoint a deputy (whether to manage a person's property and affairs or take decisions regarding their health and welfare) is to be derived from the unvarnished words of the MCA 2005. What is in the person's best interests is the governing criterion, as with all other decisions made under the Act.

3.129 As His Lordship noted, nothing in the then two leading cases on the appointment of deputies compelled a different conclusion: *Re P (vulnerable adult: deputies)*[54] and *G v E (deputyship and litigation friend)*.[55]

3.130 Naturally, it will rarely be appropriate for a judge to effectively deputise someone to judge a dispute or make a decision brought before the court for a judicial decision.

3.131 However, sometimes it may well be in a person's best interests to authorise their spouse or life partner, or the parent of a severely learning disabled young adult, to deputise for them in day-to-day personal welfare matters as well as day-to-day property matters.

3.132 That individual will often be best placed to make good quality decisions on the incapacitated person's behalf which best promote

---

50 [2010] EWHC 1592 (Fam), (2010) 13 CCLR 610.
51 [2010] EWHC 2512 (COP).
52 [2011] EWHC 2580 (Fam), [2011] COPLR Con Vol 1095.
53 [2014] EWHC 973 (COP).
54 [2010] EWHC 1592 (Fam), (2010) 13 CCLR 610.
55 [2010] EWHC 2512 (COP).

their interests in connection with community care assessments and services; access to personal information about them; complaints about their care, or treatment; arrangements for dental and optical treatment; GP appointments, medical appointments and examinations; social activities; and day-to-day care, education and training.[56]

3.133 In each of these instances, if the incapacitated person still had capacity they would decide whether or not to consent to proposed treatment or care and it may well be in their best interests that their 'nearest and dearest' now deputises for them in this capacity. The marriage vows are a relevant statement made when the person had capacity. Cohabitation, devotion and mutual commitment over many years are a relevant circumstance.

3.134 One advantage of an approach that takes each case on its merits is that a symmetry emerges from the shadows which is consistent with the ethos of the legislation in enabling a judge to advance the best interests of people who have lost capacity. An individual who still had capacity when the Act came into force was or is able to appoint a trusted person such as a spouse or partner to make future decisions for them which they cannot make. What, though, of the person who lost capacity to appoint their spouse or partner before the Act was in force? As in the case of their property, surely the court has the option of appointing as their deputy the person they would have appointed as their attorney. That is, of course, provided on the evidence that the advantages are real and it is in their best interests.

3.135 On this construction, the argument that property and financial affairs deputyship is somehow always different in kind to personal welfare deputyship is artificial. For many incapacitated people, just as many personal welfare decisions as financial decisions are made for them each week.

3.136 The fact that a person who provides routine care is given legal protection by MCA 2005 s5 does not mean that it is not in their best interests to have a personal welfare deputy any more than the fact that a person who provides necessary goods and services is given legal protection by section 7 means that it is not in their best interests to have a financial deputy. Sections 5 and 7 both exist to ensure that people who are incapacitated do not go without what they need.

3.137 It may be significant that the same subsection (MCA 2005 s6(6)) provides that section 5 does not authorise a person to do an act which conflicts with a decision made by a donee or a deputy, which perhaps

---

56 See Code of Practice para 7.21.

points away from a suggestion that the statutory norm is that donees but not deputies will commonly make personal welfare decisions in preference to reliance on section 5.

3.138 Ultimately, the decision in each case ought to turn on what is in that person's best interests. It would be strange if the statutory framework is that a judge ought not to appoint a personal welfare deputy even if he or she is satisfied that it is in the person's best interests. Where does this leave their wishes and feelings? What of their beliefs and values, and the views expressed by the persons consulted? MCA 2005 s4 says that the judge must have regard to these considerations. The position of a spouse or partner of 50 years' duration or the parent of a brain-damaged child who is having their 18th birthday is not the same as that of a paid carer.

Who may be a deputy

3.139 A deputy must be an adult (aged 18 or over) or, in the case of property and affairs deputyships, a trust corporation.[57]

3.140 A person may not be appointed as a deputy without their consent.[58]

3.141 The court may appoint the holder of a specified office or position as the person's deputy,[59] for example the holder of a particular local authority finance office. This avoids the need for a new order when the current holder of the post moves on and is replaced.

Two or more deputies

3.142 The court may appoint two or more deputies to act jointly, jointly or alone ('severally'), or jointly in respect of some matters and jointly or alone in respect of others.[60]

A deputy's powers and duties

3.143 Subject to certain restrictions dealt with below, the court may confer on a deputy such powers and/or impose on them such duties as it thinks necessary or expedient for giving effect to, or otherwise in connection with, their appointment.[61]

---

57 MCA 2005 s19(1).
58 MCA 2005 s19(3).
59 MCA 2005 s19(2).
60 MCA 2005 s19(4).
61 MCA 2005 s16(5).

3.144 A deputy:
- is appointed to make decisions on the incapacitated person's behalf, not on the court or judge's behalf (in other words, the deputy is deputising for the person concerned, not for the judge or court);
- is to be treated as that person's agent in relation to anything done or decided within the scope of their appointment and in accordance with the Act;[62]
- must act in accordance with the authority conferred by the court.

3.145 With regard to property and affairs deputyships, the court may confer on a deputy powers to:
- take possession or control of all or any specified part of the person's property;
- exercise all or any specified powers in respect of it, including such powers of investment as the court may determine.[63]

Interplay between advance decisions and deputyship

3.146 A personal welfare deputy may not consent to treatment which is prohibited by an advance decision because the authority conferred on a deputy is subject to the provisions of the Act.[64] Furthermore, MCA 2005 s20(1) provides that a deputy does not have power to make a decision for the person if he or she knows or has reasonable grounds for believing that the person has capacity to decide the matter, and the advance decision has effect as if the refusal was made with capacity at the time the treatment is proposed.[65]

Restrictions on deputies

3.147 The Act provides that certain powers may not be conferred on or exercised by a deputy:

---

62 As a general proposition, whatever P has power to do for themselves (eg request a community care assessment) may be done by their agent and, conversely, what a person cannot do for themselves (eg force a doctor to give a particular drug) cannot be done by their agent.
63 MCA 2005 s19(8).
64 MCA 2005 s20(6).
65 MCA 2005 s26(1).

Powers which a deputy does not have	Powers which the court may not give a deputy
With regard to the person's personal welfare	
A deputy does not have power to make a decision in relation to a matter if he or she knows or has reasonable grounds for believing that the person concerned has capacity in relation to that matter (MCA 2005 s20(1)).	The court may not give a deputy power to prohibit a named person from having contact with the incapacitated person (MCA 2005 s20(2)(a)). Power to prohibit such contact is reserved to judges (and personal welfare attorneys).
A deputy may not refuse consent to the carrying out or continuation of life-sustaining treatment in relation to the relevant person (MCA 2005 s20(5)).	The court may not give a deputy power to direct a professional responsible for the relevant person's health care to allow a different professional to take over that responsibility (MCA 2005 s20(2)(b)).
A deputy may not do an act that is intended to restrain the person unless the four conditions set out in MCA 2005 s20(7) are satisfied.	The court may not give a deputy power to make a decision on the relevant person's behalf which is inconsistent with a decision made, within the scope of their authority and in accordance with the Act, by a donee of a lasting power of attorney (MCA 2005 s20(4)).
A deputy is not authorised to deprive the person of their liberty.	
With regard to the person's property and affairs	
A deputy does not have power to make a decision in relation to a matter if he or she knows or has reasonable grounds for believing that the person concerned has capacity in relation to that matter (MCA 2005 s20(1)).	The court may not give a deputy power to make a decision on the relevant person's behalf which is inconsistent with a decision made, within the scope of their authority and in accordance with the Act, by a donee of an LPA (MCA 2005 s20(4)).
	A deputy may not be given powers with respect to the execution of a will for the person concerned (MCA 2005 s20(3)(b)).

continued

An overview of the Mental Capacity Act 2005 51

Powers which a deputy does not have	Powers which the court may not give a deputy
	A deputy may not be given powers with respect to the settlement of any of the person's property, whether for P's benefit or for the benefit of others (MCA 2005 s20(3)(a)).
	A deputy may not be given powers with respect to the exercise of any power (including a power to consent) vested in the person whether beneficially or as trustee or otherwise (MCA 2005 s20(3)(c)).
General limitations imposed by the Act	
The authority conferred on a deputy is subject to the provisions of the Act and, in particular, to MCA 2005 s1 (the principles) and s4 (best interests): MCA 2005 s20(6).	

Powers of deputies compared with donees and the court

3.148 It can be seen that deputies have fewer powers than donees and judges:

	Court	LPA donee	Deputy
Power to refuse life-sustaining treatment	✓	✓	X
Power to give or refuse consent to other forms of treatment and care	✓	✓	✓
Power to restrain P to give care or treatment	✓	✓	✓
Power to prohibit contact with a named person	✓	✓	X
Power to allow another person to take charge of P's treatment	✓	✓(?)	X
Power to deprive P of their liberty	✓	X	X

A donee's powers are subject to any conditions and restrictions in the LPA and any authority to give or refuse life-sustaining treatment is conditional on it being expressly provided for in the LPA. Similarly, a deputy's authority is subject to any duties and conditions specified in the order appointing them. A donee, deputy or judge may not make a decision for a person if they know or reasonably believe that the person has capacity to make their own decision. There may be other qualifications in a particular case such as the existence of an advance decision and the table compares the maximum powers which each decision-maker may possess.

More about section 5 ('acts in connection with a person's care or treatment')

3.149 Everyone is liable to an incapacitated person for criminal acts such as ill-treatment or neglect and for negligent treatment or care. MCA 2005 s5 does not affect these liabilities.[66]

3.150 Instead, it provides that a professional or non-professional carer is regarded as having the person's consent for any treatment or care given to them if five conditions are satisfied.

3.151 Because of this presumed consent, the legal effect is that the carer need not worry that technically he or she may be committing an assault because the person concerned lacks capacity to consent to the operation, treatment or piece of care being provided.[67] Likewise, provided that the conditions are satisfied, the carer is protected even if later it is held that a person who objected to care or treatment did in fact have capacity at the time and a right to refuse it.

3.152 The essential thrust of the provision is that those who care for people without capacity should be protected from legal liability provided that the care is reasonably believed to be in the person's best interests and is performed without negligence.

3.153 Because section 5 is a 'freedom from legal liability' provision, it is of a different kind to those sections of the MHA 1983 which authorise treatment or care without consent but which require applications and medical recommendations to be completed before the power arises.

3.154 There are no statutory forms to complete under section 5, although in non-routine situations it is sensible to keep some kind of written record of the decision. Rather, the section is there to be invoked and relied on as a defence if the carer is later challenged and

---

66 MCA 2005 s5(3).
67 MCA 2005 s5(2). The person who does the act (D) does not incur any liability in relation to the act that he would not have incurred if P had had capacity to consent in relation to the matter, and had consented to D's doing the act.

it is suggested that they are legally liable to the incapacitated person for their act.

THE FIVE SECTION 5 CONDITIONS			
1	The act is one undertaken 'in connection with' another person's care or treatment.	• This embraces nursing, medical and dental treatment, speech and language therapy, psychological interventions, social work, community care and also personal care such as assistance with washing, dressing, personal hygiene and feeding. • The phrase 'in connection with' indicates that section 5 also covers diagnostic examinations and tests, assessment procedures, taking a person to see their doctor, arranging the provision of a care service, etc.	
2	The person doing it takes reasonable steps to establish whether the recipient has capacity.	Unless the carer has given it to the lawyers 'on a plate', they will have taken reasonable steps to establish lack of capacity – which does not necessarily require a capacity assessment – and reasonably believe that the person lacks capacity to make this particular treatment or care decision for themselves.	
3	The person reasonably believes that the recipient lacks capacity.		
4	The person reasonably believes that it will be in their best interests for the act to be done.	• This involves applying the best interests considerations in section 4. • More than one thing can reasonably be believed and the level of protection to a carer is generous to that extent.	
5	If the person uses restraint, he or she reasonably believes *both* that it is necessary to do the act in order to prevent harm to the person and that the act is a proportionate response to the likelihood of their suffering harm and the seriousness of that harm.	• The Act states that for these purposes one person restrains another if he or she a) uses, or threatens to use, force to secure the doing of an act which he or she resists, or b) restricts their liberty of movement, whether or not they resist. • Restricting someone's liberty or using force is always undesirable. If used to give care or treatment, the requirement here is essentially that the care or treatment is necessary and does more good than the restraint does harm; it is the lesser of two evils.	

3.155 When providing care or treatment, it may seem tempting to seek to rely on section 5 in all situations, and thereby to avoid the complexities of advance decisions, LPAs and court orders.

3.156 This would be a mistake. For example, the Act provides that:
- nothing in section 5 affects the operation of sections 24–26 (advance decisions to refuse treatment);[68] and that
- section 5 does not authorise a person to do an act which conflicts with a decision properly made within the scope of his authority by a donee of a lasting power of attorney or a deputy appointed by the court.[69]

3.157 It is not possible therefore simply to leap to section 5 as a way around having to learn the framework. The first step is to consider whether the person made an applicable advance decision or LPA. Only if they did not provide for this situation, or their advance decision or LPA is irrelevant or invalid, does one move on to considering the need for a court application or relying on section 5.

3.158 Furthermore, one cannot reasonably believe that it is in the person's best interests to delay going to court and to continue to provide the care or treatment under section 5 if there is a significant disagreement about whether it is in the person's best interests which cannot be resolved.

A general framework

3.159 It is now possible to set out a framework that is generally applicable to all personal welfare decisions made under the MCA 2005:

---

68 MCA 2005 s5(4).
69 MCA 2005 s6(6). This prohibition does not prevent a person providing life-sustaining treatment, or doing any act which he or she reasonably believes to be necessary to prevent a serious deterioration in P's condition, while a decision as respects any relevant issue is sought from the court: see MCA 2005 s6(7).

	Step	Example
1	The circumstances require a person to make a decision in connection with their own care or treatment	Mr Smith is being examined at hospital and it is apparent that he has a significant heart condition. Treatment is recommended.
2	Someone is concerned about whether this person has capacity to make the decision for themselves	Mr Smith also suffers from quite severe dementia. The doctor is concerned that he appears not to understand the relevant information being conveyed concerning the diagnosis, the treatment which is necessary medically and the prognosis with and without treatment.
3	The person's capacity to make this particular decision for themselves is assessed: Is it the case that because of an impairment or disturbance of their mind or brain they are unable to understand or retain or weigh the information relevant to this decision, or are unable to communicate their decision?	Mr Smith's capacity to make his own decision about whether or not to have the proposed assessment procedures and treatment is assessed.
4	If this cannot be established on the balance of probabilities, the law regards the person as having capacity to make their own decision. Who decides? They decide.	On the evidence, the doctor is satisfied that the presumption of capacity has been rebutted. Because of an impairment of the brain (dementia) Mr Smith is unable to understand, retain and weigh the information relevant to the treatment decision.
	If it is established on the balance of probabilities that the person cannot make the decision for themselves, then (unless it can be postponed) someone will have to make it for them.	

Step		Example
5	The way the person does this is by applying the MCA 2005. It is an Act which sets out a framework to be used when making a decision for someone who lacks the capacity to make their own decision.	The doctor applies the treatment and care framework set out in the MCA 2005. The Act contains four mechanisms in relation to providing a person with care and/or treatment. The person must take each in turn and work out which is applicable.
6	When the relevant person still had capacity to do so, did he or she make a valid advance decision to refuse this particular treatment?	There are caveats, but in general terms if Mr Smith did then this is the relevant mechanism to apply.
7	When the relevant person still had capacity to do so, did he or she make a (registered) LPA which covers care or treatment decisions of this kind?	There are caveats, but in general terms if Mr Smith did then this will be the relevant mechanism to apply. Ask the attorney (donee) whether or not he or she consents to this treatment on Mr Smith's behalf.
8	If there does not appear to be a relevant advance decision or LPA, is this a situation where it is necessary or appropriate as being in the person's best interests to apply for a court order as to whether the care or treatment should be given?	If it is such a situation, apply to the court. If not, then there are only four mechanisms and, since three of them are properly 'not in play', there is only one left. Therefore, the care or treatment can be given under the MCA 2005 if the section 5 conditions are satisfied but not otherwise.
9	Apply MCA 2005 s5 – are the five section 5 conditions satisfied?	(a) Is this something connected with the person's care or treatment? (b) Have reasonable steps been taken to establish whether the person has capacity to make their own decision about whether or not to receive this particular piece of care or treatment? (c) Does the person providing the care or treatment reasonably believe that the other person lacks capacity to decide this?

continued

An overview of the Mental Capacity Act 2005 57

Step	Example
	(d) Does the person reasonably believe that it will be in their best interests to receive this piece of care or treatment (or for an act connected with it to be done)? (e) If restraint is used to provide the care or treatment, does the person reasonably believe that the care or treatment is necessary and does more good than the restraint does harm (see above for the precise criteria)?

3.160 This gives us a fairly clear framework for providing care and/or treatment to an incapacitated person who has a physical health problem such as a heart or liver disorder. Indeed, once one has learned this basic framework, it can be used in relation to all treatment and care decisions, from helping an incapacitated person to dress to a decision to switch off life-support:

Example 1

3.161 P was recently involved in a car accident and has sustained severe brain injury. P's life is being sustained artificially. There is no prospect of recovery. Medical professionals and family members agree that the situation is hopeless and must now consider whether to stop treatment.

3.162 Taking each of the listed steps in turn:
a) The circumstances require P to make a decision about his care or treatment, ie to consent or refuse consent to what is proposed.
b) Someone is concerned that P lacks capacity to make this decision for himself.
c) P's capacity to make this particular decision is assessed.
d) Because of an impairment or disturbance of P's mind or brain, P is unable to understand, retain or weigh the information relevant to the treatment decision or is unable to communicate his decision.
e) Because P cannot make the decision for himself, someone must decide for P. The way this is done is by applying the

MCA 2005 which sets out the framework to be used when making a decision for someone who lacks the capacity to make their own decision.
f) The MCA 2005 contains four mechanisms to consider in turn.
g) If P made a valid advance decision refusing life-sustaining treatment in such circumstances when he had capacity, the general rule is that it must be respected.
h) If P has a registered LPA appointing a trusted person to make decisions for P about life-sustaining treatment in such circumstances, generally that person has the right to decide.
i) If there is no advance decision or LPA which resolves the matter, is this a case where an application to the Court of Protection is necessary or in P's best interests, for a judge to decide whether or not further treatment is hopeless? That would be unusual. Sadly, following serious road traffic accidents, it is not uncommon in intensive care settings for professionals and family members to agree that the situation is now hopeless. A judge would have to decide any application on the evidence and here all of the evidence is consistent and to the same effect. In reality, a court application would simply cause delay and avoidable distress to no benefit.
j) If the first three mechanisms are not applicable, the only one left is MCA 2005 s5.
k) Is this decision something connected with P's care and treatment? Yes.
l) Have reasonable steps been taken to assess P's capacity? Yes.
m) Is it reasonably believed that P lacks capacity to make this decision for himself? Yes.
n) Is it in P's best interests to stop treatment? This is the issue. Address it by considering the best interests requirements and considerations in MCA 2005 s4 ('The person making the determination must consider all the relevant circumstances and, in particular, must . . .').
o) The restraint condition adds little here if stopping treatment is in P's best interests. Insofar as this technically involves the use of a degree of restraint, it is reasonable to believe that this is a necessary and proportionate response.

Example 2

3.163 P has developed very advanced dementia and now lives in a care home. Sadly, he seems to have lost the ability to respond to his environment, to speak and to control movement. He cannot sit without support. He requires a wheelchair, is doubly incontinent and needs help with all personal care. He is being taken to a local park and, because it is raining, needs his footwear changing. A care assistant, Ms Q, puts some boots on before taking him out.

3.164 If this was ever challenged then, taking each of the listed steps in turn:

a) The circumstances require P to make a decision about his care or treatment, ie to consent or refuse consent to what is proposed.

b) Based on their long acquaintance, his care assistant's concern is that he no longer has capacity to make this decision for himself, or indeed even to understand that a change of footwear needs to be considered.

c) P's capacity to make this particular decision is assessed. In reality, the care assistant is not aware that she is assessing P's capacity but, if she was ever asked why she acted as she did, she might say that:
   – she knows P and his needs very well;
   – for some time P has been unable to make his own decisions about what to wear because his cognitive decline is now such that he cannot understand or use relevant verbal or visual information;
   – medical and nursing assessments have confirmed this; and
   – P did not demonstrate any awareness of or response to the suggestion or prompt that his footwear was changed. In other words, because of an impairment or disturbance of P's mind or brain he is unable to understand, retain or weigh the information relevant to the care decision or is unable to communicate his decision.

d) Because P cannot make this care decision for himself, someone must decide for him. The way this is done is by applying the MCA 2005 which sets out the framework to be used when making a decision for someone who lacks the capacity to make their own decision.

e) The Act contains four mechanisms to consider in turn.

f) Any advance decision which P has made will relate only to treatment, not care, and will not be relevant.
g) If there is a registered LPA appointing a trusted person to make care decisions, then P's care must be consistent with any consents and refusals of consent made by his attorney on his behalf in relation to his care plan.
h) This is not a case where an application is going to be made to the Court of Protection for an order permitting the care assistant to change his footwear. If P already has a personal welfare deputy appointed for him by the court then, as with an LPA, his care must be consistent with any consents and refusals of consent made by his deputy in relation to his care plan.
i) If none of the first three mechanisms are applicable, apply MCA 2005 s5.
j) Is this decision something connected with P's care and treatment? Yes.
k) Have reasonable steps been taken to assess P's capacity? Yes. It is not necessary in the circumstances to do a fresh formal capacity assessment.
l) Is it reasonably believed that P lacks capacity to make this decision for himself? Yes.
m) Is it in P's best interests to have this piece of care? Yes. If the care assistant was ever asked to justify the decision, she might say:
   – that P's care plan is devised to promote his best interests;
   – that it includes visits to local places;
   – that P seems to enjoy the outings and there is a health benefit.
   In section 4 terms, it is in P's best interests to give him this piece of care having regard to his known wishes and feelings, the views concerning his best interests of family members and professional carers and other relevant considerations, such as the care plan which addresses his health and welfare needs.
n) The restraint condition adds little here. If changing P's footwear before going out is in his best interests then, insofar as this technically involves a degree of force, it is reasonable to believe that it is a necessary and proportionate response.

3.165 The second example may seem rather artificial, although relatives and care home staff are sometimes involved in disagreements about clothing and dressing. Its main function here is to emphasise that once one has learned the above model it can be used as a framework for any situation, from routine care to intensive care. It is therefore worth considering.

Deprivation of liberty

3.166 To recap, the MCA 2005 in its original form included a fairly clear framework in relation to providing care or treatment to an incapacitated person.

3.167 It did not adequately address the problem that an incapacitated person who did not wish to receive this care or treatment was often not permitted to leave the hospital, care home or other place where it was being given.

3.168 In certain circumstances, MCA 2005 s5 permitted a carer to restrict the person's liberty of movement and to use reasonable and proportionate force in order to give the care or treatment. Likewise, if the individual had a personal welfare donee or deputy appointed for them, that person could authorise such restraints in identical circumstances.[70]

3.169 What no one other than a judge of the Court of Protection could do was to authorise depriving the person of their liberty in order to give them the care or treatment. The authority conferred by section 5, deputyship and an LPA was limited to restrictions of liberty which did not amount to deprivation of liberty:

Restriction of liberty	Deprivation of liberty
Permitted A person restrains another person if s/he (a) uses, or threatens to use, force to secure the doing of an act which s/he resists, or (b) restricts their liberty of movement, whether or not they resist.	**Not permitted** The person doing the act ('D') does more than merely restrain the other person if s/he deprives that person of their liberty within the meaning of Article 5(1) of the European Convention on Human Rights, whether or not D is a public authority

70 MCA 2005 ss11 and 20.

3.170 This was a problem for three reasons:

a) First, if the reality was that many care homes were depriving residents of their liberty, it was not practical for them to obtain a court order authorising this for every such resident. They would soon be bankrupt given the relatively modest fees paid by local authorities and the costs involved in applying for court orders.

b) Second, if the reality was that many incapacitated people were being deprived of their liberty in relatives' homes or in supported living accommodation, it was similarly unrealistic to expect families and housing providers to obtain court orders for each person affected.

c) Third, there was uncertainty as to the dividing-line between restricting someone's liberty of movement (permitted without a court order) and depriving them of their liberty (not permitted without a court order). It was not always clear to care providers where the line was, nor therefore whether it had been crossed and a court order was required.

3.171 Even allowing for some uncertainty, it was obvious that a considerable number of incapacitated hospital patients and care home residents were being deprived of their liberty without any proper legal order or authority permitting it, without the use of clear and explicit criteria, with no proper application process and no adequate form of judicial review.

3.172 In essence, this was what was commonly referred to as the 'Bournewood gap' as a result of a famous case in which the European Court of Human Rights found that this lacuna in English and Welsh law breached the European Convention on Human Rights (ECHR).[71]

3.173 The eventual consequence was that a new scheme was inserted in the MCA 2005 (by the MHA 2007) which enables hospitals and care homes to obtain a legal authority to deprive people of their liberty under the MCA 2005 without having to obtain an order from a court.

3.174 This authority – called a standard authorisation – can be obtained from the relevant local authority (or in Wales, in some cases, the

---

71 *HL v United Kingdom* Application no 45508/99, [2004] ECHR 471 ('the Bournewood case').

National Assembly), with the incapacitated person having a right to apply to court for a review of the authorisation.[72]

3.175 This 'deprivation of liberty safeguards' scheme – known colloquially as the 'DOLS scheme' – commenced operation on 1 April 2009. The detail is set out as necessary in the relevant chapters. However, briefly, it applies only to hospitals and care homes. It seeks to ensure that the relevant person is assessed at least annually by two suitably qualified and independent professionals. They must certify that the care and treatment arrangements made for the incapacitated person are in their best interests, necessary to protect them from harm, proportionate and so forth.

The six requirements

3.176 The new Schedule A1 to the MCA 2005 provides that deprivation of liberty under the scheme requires that six requirements are satisfied: the age, mental health, mental capacity, best interests, no refusals and eligibility requirements.

3.177 The purpose of the requirements is the same as in the case of the 'sectioning criteria' in the MHA 1983, ie to prevent people who do not meet the statutory requirements from being deprived of their liberty.

The age requirement

3.178 The age requirement is simply that the person must be an adult. A child may not be deprived of their liberty under a standard authorisation.

The mental health requirement

3.179 The second requirement is simply that the person suffers from a mental disorder within the meaning of the MHA 1983 (but disregarding the requirement in the 1983 Act sometimes to demonstrate that a learning disability is associated with abnormally aggressive or seriously irresponsible conduct).

---

72 The new authorisations are commonly referred to as 'DOLS orders'. Most of the relevant provisions are set out in two new schedules at the end of the MCA 2005: Schedules A1 and 1A. Even now it is not known publicly who devised the scheme and drafted the schedules, which were not put out to prior consultation.

The mental capacity requirement

3.180 The requirement here is that the person lacks capacity to make their own decision about whether or not to be accommodated in the particular hospital or care home in order to receive the care or treatment in question.

The best interests requirement

3.181 This is really four requirements masquerading as one. It is satisfied only if all of the following conditions are satisfied:

1) the person is being detained in the hospital or care home for the purpose of being given care or treatment in circumstances which amount to a deprivation of their liberty;[73]
2) this is in their best interests;
3) this is necessary in order to prevent harm to them; and
4) their detention in the care home or hospital for the purpose of being given care or treatment in circumstances which amount to a deprivation of their liberty is a proportionate response to the likelihood of them suffering harm, and the seriousness of that harm (if they were not so detained).

3.182 If one or more of the four conditions is not satisfied, the person does not meet the best interests requirement; and, because a standard authorisation may only be given if all six requirements are satisfied in their totality, that person may not be deprived of their liberty under the scheme.

The no refusals requirement

3.183 The essence of this oddly phrased requirement is to ensure that the relevant person does not have in place a valid LPA or advance decision which a standard authorisation would breach.

3.184 Specifically, a person may not be deprived of their liberty in a care home or hospital in order to give them treatment or care which by virtue of their advance decision may not be given to them under the MCA 2005.

---

73 More precisely, they are a 'detained resident'. By MCA 2005 Sch A1 para 6, a 'detained resident' is 'a person detained in a hospital or care home – for the purpose of being given care or treatment – in circumstances which amount to deprivation of the person's liberty'. If this is not the case, then no authorisation is required, because there is no deprivation that requires authorisation.

3.185   Nor may they be deprived of their liberty in order to give them treatment or care which their personal welfare donee under an LPA has refused consent to on their behalf.

3.186   The underlying premise is that one cannot use the MCA 2005 to break the MCA 2005.

The eligibility requirement

3.187   This requirement is concerned with the inter-relationship between the MHA 1983 and the MCA 2005.

3.188   In certain situations where the MHA 1983 is 'in play', detention or compulsory treatment or care takes place under that Act, not the MCA 2005. This requirement is dealt with below, after some relevant provisions of the MHA 1983 have first been considered.

The DOLS scheme and the four mechanisms

3.189   The four care and treatment mechanisms set out in the original MCA 2005, which were explained above, are unaffected by this 'standard authorisation 'DOLs scheme' and are still good law.

3.190   Where a person lacks capacity to consent to treatment or care, their treatment or care is subject to any relevant advance decision, LPA or court order, or is given under the protection of MCA 2005 s5. All that has changed is that if it is necessary and in their best interests to deprive them of their liberty so that this care or treatment can be given, then a standard authorisation is required alongside (or a court order).

3.191   So, for example, a person may be deprived of their liberty at a care home under a standard authorisation in order to give them the care determined to be in their best interests, which in practice most often is provided under the protection of section 5.

The *Cheshire West* and *Re X* cases

3.192   Because the DOLS scheme just described only applies to care homes and hospitals, the absence of a simple equivalent procedure for people deprived of their liberty in other settings such as supported living accommodation or their own homes remained a problem. This gap was considered in the *Cheshire West* case[74] where the Supreme Court found that three incapacitated people were deprived of their liberty in non-care home settings and that they were equally entitled to a proper legal process under Article 5 ECHR.

74 *Cheshire West and Chester Council v P* [2014] UKSC 19, (2014) 17 CCLR 5.

3.193   Following the judgment in *Cheshire West*, a non-statutory 'streamlined procedure' designed to comply with Article 5 was formulated by the President of the Court of Protection, Sir James Munby, in *Re X and others (Deprivation of Liberty)*[75] and *Re X (Deprivation of Liberty) (No 2)*[76] and brought into law as Part 2 of Court of Protection Practice Direction (PD) 10AA.

3.194   Although the President's approach was criticised in some respects by the Court of Appeal in *Re X (Court of Protection Practice)*,[77] the '*Re X* Procedure' remains that to follow where authorisation is required under MCA 2005 for a deprivation of liberty outside hospital or a care home. It involves filing an application form (form COPDOL10) together with certain required information such as a copy of the person's care plan, and paying a fee. If the person affected has not expressed any objection to the care arrangements and application is uncontroversial the judge may authorise the deprivation of liberty 'on the papers', and further identical reviews then take place at least annually.

Three murky streams forming one river

3.195 It can be seen that there are now three different procedures in existence in relation to a deprivation of liberty under MCA 2005:

- As originally enacted, MCA 2005 required an application to a judge under section 16 in all cases where authorisation for a deprivation of liberty was sought. This approach is still used for complicated cases where a deprivation of liberty is but one of a range of issues requiring the court's determination. For example, an application may require the court to determine the relevant person's best interests in relation to deprivation of liberty, residence, family contact, treatment and care.
- There is then the 'DOLS scheme' inserted in the MCA 2005 (by the MHA 2007), which commenced operation on 1 April 2009. This is an administrative procedure which enables a deprivation of liberty in a care home or hospital to be authorised by a local authority, with a right of appeal to a judge of the Court of Protection.
- There is also now a '*Re X* procedure' designed to enable a deprivation of liberty in a setting other than a care home or hospital to be authorised by a judge on the papers in appropriate cases. This is discussed further in chapter 21.

75 [2014] EWCOP 25, [2014] COPLR 674, (2014) 17 CCLR 297.
76 [2014] EWCOP 37, (2014) 17 CCLR 464.
77 [2015] EWCA Civ 599, [2015] COPLR 582.

3.196 The reason for this unsatisfactory piecemeal approach is not hard to discern. Almost twenty years ago the Department of Health strongly opposed the original 'Bournewood' application and, having eventually lost that case, over many years it has fought hard to minimise the impact.

3.197 The Law Commission is now reviewing the deprivation of liberty procedures and a draft Bill containing new procedures is expected at the end of 2016.

Ten commandments

3.198 Deprivation of liberty schemes are intended to be protective schemes. Anyone who is deprived of their liberty – that is, who is under another person's complete and effective control and is not free to leave – is vulnerable to abuse.

3.199 The subject is dealt with in detail in chapter 21. However, at this preliminary stage, the relevant domestic and convention law can be understood as imposing ten commandments:

1) Deprivation of liberty requires that the person has been confined in a particular restricted space 'for a not negligible length of time'. This is the 'objective condition'.
2) In addition, a 'subjective condition' must be met before a person is deprived of their liberty. This is that they have not validly consented to their confinement.
3) However, a person cannot consent to being confined if they lack capacity to consent to it.
4) The distinction between deprivation of liberty and restriction of liberty is one of degree or intensity, not one of nature or substance.
5) The starting-point is the specific situation of the individual concerned. Account must be taken of a whole range of factors arising in the particular case, such as the type, duration, effects and manner of implementation of the measure in question.
6) The critical issue is whether the professionals exercise 'complete and effective control' over the person's care and movements, so that the individual is 'under continuous supervision and control and is not free to leave'.
7) The state's obligations under the convention are engaged if a public authority is directly involved in the detention (it is 'imputable to the state'), but also where the state has breached its positive obligation to protect the person against interferences by private persons.

8) This is because Article 5(1) ECHR imposes a positive obligation on the state to protect the liberty of its citizens. The state is obliged to take measures providing effective protection of vulnerable persons, including reasonable steps to prevent a deprivation of liberty of which the authorities have or ought to have knowledge.

9) It is also essential that the person concerned should have access to a court and the opportunity to be heard in person or, where necessary, through some form of representation. Fundamental procedural safeguards are called for in order to protect the interests of detained persons who, on account of their mental disabilities, are not fully capable of acting for themselves.

10) With regard to persons in need of psychiatric treatment in particular, the state is also under an obligation to secure to its citizens 'their right to physical integrity' under Article 8 ECHR. Private psychiatric institutions, in particular those where persons are held without a court order, need not only a licence, but also competent supervision by the state on a regular basis of whether confinement and medical treatment is justified.

Detention and deprivation of liberty

3.200 A critical thing to understand is that in law there is a distinction between 'detention' and 'deprivation of liberty'. This is counterintuitive because most people use these words interchangeably in everyday conversation.

3.201 At first blush, the first commandment appears to be one of those vague legal statements which are of no use to anyone. However, that is not so.

3.202 In our field of interest, the particular restricted space in which the relevant person is confined will often be a hospital, a part of a hospital such as a ward or A&E department, a police station or a care home. A person who is prevented from leaving hospital for a brief period, say for one hour, until he can be assessed by a doctor is being 'detained' there but is not in fact being 'deprived of his liberty'. This is because his confinement is, in this sense, for a 'negligible length for time'.

3.203 Compare that with the case of an older person in a care home. Their situation for the next hour may be exactly the same: they are not allowed to leave. However, it may be the case that nor will they be allowed to leave tomorrow or next week or next month. Their confinement in a particular restricted space is 'for a not negligible length of time', in which case the objective condition for a deprivation of liberty is met.

3.204 The doctor's action is an emergency measure which does not carry with it any general claim to a right to control the person's liberty of movement; to prevent that person from being 'at liberty'. It is only in the second case that the 'confiner' claims a general power or right to control the person's liberty of movement to the extent that a right to confine is claimed. Unlike me or you, the concrete reality is that their liberty is no longer theirs and is in the hands of another: they do not decide whether and when to leave, where to go, when if at all to return, what they do when they leave, and so on.

Interplay with the MHA 1983

3.205 The final matter to deal with in any overview of the personal welfare provisions is the interplay between the MCA 2005 and the MHA 1983.

Treating physical disorders

3.206 We have seen that it is relatively easy to understand when the MCA 2005 mechanisms apply in the case of care or treatment for a physical disorder such as a heart or liver disorder:

Physical disorders

CAPACITY

CONSENT REQUIRED

NO CAPACITY

APPLY THE MENTAL CAPACITY ACT

3.207 Because the MHA 1983 is only concerned with the treatment of mental disorders, (subject to one small caveat) the legal position of 'sectioned' patients with regard to treating their physical health problems is exactly the same as for everyone else, and is that set out in the diagram above.

Treating mental disorders

3.208 What then is the legal position where the proposed treatment is treatment for a mental disorder? Does the MHA 1983 or the MCA 2005 apply?

3.209 It is easier to understand the position if one considers first the simpler scheme set out in the MCA 2005 as originally enacted, before considering the modifications introduced by subsequent amendments.

The scheme set out in the original MCA 2005

3.210 The simpler scheme set out in the MCA 2005 as originally enacted was as follows:

- The general rule is (and remains) that the MCA 2005 applies whenever you wish to give care or treatment to an incapacitated person outside the terms of the MHA 1983.
- In other words, if the patient's treatment is covered by the terms of the MHA 1983 then that Act applies.
- If their treatment falls outside the MHA 1983 then the MCA 2005 will apply.
- Treatment may fall outside the MHA 1983 because it is treatment for a physical health problem (see above); or it may fall outside because it is treatment for a mental health problem but the MHA 1983 does not authorise giving it without the person's consent.
- In the second case, one then has to see if there is legal authority outside the MHA 1983 to give the treatment without the person's consent, which takes us to the MCA 2005.
- When then is treatment for mental disorder without consent not authorised under the MHA 1983? The simple answer is: when the individual is not subject to a section of that Act which authorises psychiatric treatment without consent.
- As is well-known, if a person has been 'sectioned' under the MHA 1983 the fact that the person is 'under a section' may permit professionals to give them psychiatric treatment without consent. If this is the case then the treatment is authorised under the MHA

An overview of the Mental Capacity Act 2005 71

1983 and it is not necessary to establish whether it is authorised under the MCA 2005.

- However, relatively few sections of the MHA 1983 in fact authorise treating an individual without their consent:

TREATING MENTAL DISORDER WITHOUT CONSENT	
Authorised by the MHA 1983 (or MHA 1983 rules apply)	Not authorised – apply the MCA 2005
Section 2 patients (those liable to be detained in hospital for assessment and any necessary treatment for up to 28 days)	Informal patients (those in hospital and in the community who are not presently subject to a section of the MHA 1983)
Section 3 patients (those liable to be detained in hospital for treatment for up to six or 12 months at a time)	Patients detained under the short-term sections of the MHA 1983 that have a maximum duration of 72 hours or less (ss4, 5(2), 5(4), 135, 136)
Patients subject to a Community Treatment Order	Patients subject to guardianship under the MHA 1983
	Conditionally discharged restricted patients
	Persons remanded to hospital by a criminal court for a report on their mental condition under MHA 1983 s35
	Persons in prison, eg prison medical units

3.211 Naturally, many people find this confusing. When studying the right-hand column, it seems odd to them that a person may be detained or subject to a MHA 1983 'order' – such as short-term detention or guardianship – but their treatment or care be governed by a different Act, the MCA 2005.

3.212 The reason for this relates to the framework of the MHA 1983 and its interplay with the old common law rules which the MCA 2005 replaced. As enacted, the framework constructed by the MHA 1983 was more liberal than much of today's legislation.

3.213 Subject to complying with various procedural safeguards set out in Part IV of the Act, such as obtaining a second-opinion, persons who were liable to be detained in hospital for up to 28 days (section 2) or for up to six months or more (section 3 and its criminal law equivalents) could be treated without their consent. In their case, their compulsory admission was founded on an application made, in most cases, by an independent approved social worker supported by two medical recommendations, one provided by a specialist.

3.214 People who were not considered to be so unwell as to require detention in hospital for those sorts of period were not liable to treatment without their consent under the Act, and therefore could only be so treated in the limited circumstances then permitted by the common law. These are all the people in the right-hand column now covered by the MCA 2005.

3.215 As can be seen from the right-hand column, the vast majority of people with mental health problems fell within this category, because on any given day relatively few people are subject to one of the more Draconian sections in the left-hand column.

3.216 Looking at who is in the right-hand column, the purpose of the holding sections with a maximum duration of 72 hours or less is to enable a person to be assessed, most often with a view to making an application under section 2 or 3. Because they have not yet been detained on the basis of an application supported by two medical recommendations, the MHA 1983 does not authorise their treatment without consent. Any treatment during this period had to be justifiable under common law.

3.217 The MCA 2005 replaced the common law in this area; hence the person is detained under one Act but potentially treatable under another.

3.218 Similarly, the MHA 1983 did not authorise giving treatment without consent to persons on community orders such as guardianship and those who had been conditionally discharged. Only patients who were liable to detention were liable to treatment without consent under the Act; and only then if the person was subject to the longer sections and certain legal formalities were observed. Similarly, therefore, any treatment without consent was given under the common law, which now has been replaced by the MCA 2005.

3.219 In diagrammatic form, therefore, the relationship with the MHA 1983 set out in the MCA 2005 in its original form was as follows:

An overview of the Mental Capacity Act 2005   73

Mental disorders

```
         MENTAL        CAPACITY
         HEALTH ACT    CONSENT
         1983 ss2, 3   REQUIRED
         (treatment
         orders)
                       ↕
                       NO CAPACITY
                       MENTAL CAPACITY
                       ACT 2005
```

3.220 Looking at the diagram, where it was proposed to give a person treatment for mental disorder – antipsychotics, antidepressants, other medication, ECT, etc – that person's situation would come within one of three legal groups, each of which is represented by a segment of the circle:

- If the person was subject to section 2 or one of the treatment orders in the MHA 1983, such as section 3, the rules in (Part IV of) the MHA 1983 applied and, subject to complying with the procedural safeguards set out there, the patient was liable to treatment without their consent.
- If the citizen was not subject to one of those MHA 1983 sections, they retained a citizen's usual rights and were in the same legal position as everyone else. If they had capacity (or, strictly speaking, it could not be established that they lacked it) then treatment required their consent; in short, they could refuse it. If they lacked capacity to make a decision about the treatment then the MCA 2005 applied – unless the patient was 'sectioned' at that point and taken into section 2 of the Act or one of its treatment sections, such as section 3.

3.221 And that is the purpose of the connectors in the diagram. The individual's situation is fluid, not static – the membranes (lines) separating the three segments are permeable and the individual will move across the lines from one segment to another as their mental health and capacity fluctuates, they are sectioned under section 2 or 3 or released from liability to detention under section 2 or 3.

3.222   That was the situation when the MCA 2005 first came into force but it has now been complicated by the MHA 2007.

3.223   There were two main changes to the simpler structure just described.

3.224   First, the MHA 2007 inserted a new 'community treatment order' (CTO) in the MHA 1983. The legal rules governing the treatment of patients on a CTO are set out in Parts 4 and 4A of the MHA 1983. The general rule is that if it is proposed to give treatment for mental disorder to a person on a CTO you apply the legal framework in Parts 4 and 4A of the MHA 1983. Our diagram now becomes:

Mental disorders

[Diagram: A circle divided into four quadrants labelled:
- MHA 1983 CTO
- CAPACITY CONSENT REQUIRED
- MHA 1983 ss2, 3 etc
- NO CAPACITY MCA 2005]

3.225   As can be seen, the individual may now be in one of four groups, and be moving between four groups.

3.226   As with most post-1983 mental health legislation, it is questionable whether the practical benefits justify the extra complexity and the legislation is poorly constructed.

3.227   The second significant change related to ECT. As far as antipsychotic and other medication for mental disorder is concerned, sectioning a person under section 2 or 3 still has the same effect as before: the MHA rules apply, not the MCA 2005. Because, as we have seen, the former permit treatment without consent, from a psychiatrist's point of view this may be a 'trump card' in terms of overcoming a patient's refusal to take prescribed medication. (Once the section comes to an end and the patient reverts to informal status, the same problem may of course represent itself.)

3.228 When it comes to ECT, however, taking a person into one of the treatment sections of the MHA (ss2, 3, etc) no longer necessarily has the effect of 'trumping' or circumventing the protections of the MCA 2005.

3.229 The new ECT rules inserted into the MHA 1983 by the MHA 2007 provide that a section 2 or treatment order patient with capacity cannot be given ECT to which they do not consent unless it can be justified as urgent treatment which is necessary to save their life or immediately necessary to prevent a serious deterioration of their condition.[78]

3.230 Likewise, unless it can be justified as urgent treatment on these terms, an incapacitated section 2 or treatment order patient cannot be given ECT if it would conflict with a relevant advance decision or with a decision made by the Court of Protection, a Court of Protection appointed deputy or a donee appointed under a personal welfare LPA.

3.231 What we see here for the first time is the autonomy provisions in the MCA 2005 starting to infiltrate and cut down the compulsory treatment provisions in the MHA 1983, at least as far as ECT is concerned, and the position is very similar with regard to CTOs.[79]

Deprivation of liberty and the MHA 1983

3.232 Turning to the interplay between the detention provisions in the MHA 1983 and the deprivation of liberty provisions in the MCA 2005, the MHA 1983 only permits detention in a hospital. The standard authorisation scheme in the MCA 2005 applies to hospitals and care homes; and the Court of Protection can also authorise deprivation of liberty in any other location.

3.233 Where a person requires detention in a hospital for psychiatric treatment, the MCA 2005 is not to be used (in preference to the MHA 1983) if the individual falls within any of the following groups:

- People who are currently detained in a hospital under one of the following sections of the MHA 1983: sections 2, 3, 4, 35–38, 44, 45A, 47, 48, 51.
- People who, though not currently detained, are subject to one of these sections or to a CTO, if the care or treatment in question

---

78 For the precise criteria, see MHA 1983 s62.
79 See eg MHA 1983 s64D.

consists wholly or partly of medical treatment for mental disorder in a hospital.
- People who, though not currently detained, are subject to one of these sections, or to a CTO or guardianship, if accommodating them in the hospital or care home under the MCA 2005 would conflict with a requirement imposed on them under their MHA 1983 section.
- People who are subject to guardianship under the MHA 1983, if they object to being accommodated in the particular hospital for the purpose of being given some or all of the proposed medical treatment for their mental disorder (unless they have a donee or deputy who consents to each matter to which they objects).
- People who meet the criteria for being sectioned under section 2 or 3 of the MHA 1983, if they object to being accommodated in the particular hospital for the purpose of being given some or all of the proposed medical treatment for their mental disorder (unless they have a donee or deputy who consents to each matter to which they object).

Principles of mental health law

3.234 That then is the basic relationship between the MCA 2005 and the MHA 1983.

3.235 As a final point, when legislating in this area it is useful to bear the following principles in mind:[80]

1) It is unsatisfactory to seek to determine principles by reason only, without regard for human experience of the world within which principles are formulated and applied. Our value judgments are judgments about experienced objects.

2) There are many reasons to limit state intervention in people's lives: errors in law spread their negative effects throughout the nation as opposed to individual errors that are limited in scope; the damage of erroneous laws affect citizens more than legislators, who are thus less inclined to repeal them; it takes longer to repair the damage done by legislation than the damage done by individuals by their own private choices; because of the constant watch of critics, politicians are less inclined to publicly admit

---

80 A Eldergill, 'Is anyone safe? civil compulsion under the draft Mental Health Bill', *Journal of Mental Health Law*, January 2003.

error and undo the damage done; politicians are more inclined than citizens to make decisions based on political gain and prejudice, rather than principle.[81]

3) The British constitution separates powers, the aim being to keep executive powers in check and under proper scrutiny, and so to secure good government. This is necessary because the 'whole art of government consists in the art of being honest',[82] and 'it is not by the consolidation, or concentration of powers, but by their distribution, that good government is effected'.[83]

4) Promoting liberty, protecting individuals from harm caused by those at liberty, and those not at liberty from abuse by those who are, alleviating suffering, and restoring to health those whose health has declined, are all legitimate objectives, in that they reflect values embraced by virtually all members of our society.[84]

5) We are, however, 'faced with choices between ends equally ultimate, and claims equally absolute, the realisation of some of which must inevitably involve the sacrifice of others'.[85] Whether individuals 'should be allowed certain liberties at all depends on the priority given by society to different values, and the crucial point is the criterion by which it is decided that a particular liberty should or should not be allowed, or that its exercise is in need of restraint'.[86]

6) When enacting mental health legislation, Parliament has generally sought to erect a balanced legal structure that harmonises three things: individual liberty; bringing treatment to bear where treatment is necessary and can be beneficial; and the protection of the public.[87] Those we describe as 'patients' are themselves members of the public, so that the law must seek to ensure that members of the public are not unnecessarily detained, and also that they are protected from those who must necessarily be detained.

81 Benjamin Constant, *Political writings* (Biancamaria Fontana (trans and ed)), Cambridge University Press, 1988.
82 Thomas Jefferson, *Rights of British America, 1774. The writings of Thomas Jefferson, memorial edition* (Lipscomb and Bergh (eds)), Washington DC, 1903–04.
83 *Thomas Jefferson: Autobiography, 1821. The writings of Thomas Jefferson, memorial edition* 1:122.
84 AC Eldergill, *Mental health review tribunals – law and practice*, Sweet & Maxwell, 1997, p45.
85 Berlin, Sir I, *Four essays on liberty*, OUP, 1969, p168.
86 RWM Dias, *Jurisprudence*, Butterworths, 5th edn, 1985, p109.
87 *Hansard*, HC Vol 605 col 276.

7) The use of compulsion has been permitted when significant harm is foreseeable if an individual remains at liberty. Its function is to protect the individual or others from those risks that arise when a person's capacity to judge risks, or to control the behaviour giving rise to them, is impaired by mental disorder.
8) Other risks are, constitutionally, matters for citizens to weigh in their own minds. The purpose of compulsion is not to eliminate that element of risk in human life that is simply part of being free to act and to make choices and decisions. A person who obeys our laws is entitled to place a high premium on their liberty, even to value it more highly than their health. Subject to the stated limits, people are entitled to make what others regard as errors of judgment, and to behave in a manner which a doctor regards as not in their best interests, in the sense that it does not best promote health.
9) This desire to determine one's own interests is common to human beings, and so not to be portrayed as an abuse of liberty. On the one hand stands liberty, a right which Parliament and the law should always favour and guard, on the other licence, a wilful use of liberty to contravene the law, which the law must of necessity always punish.
10) Any power given to one person over another is capable of being abused. No legislative body should be deluded by the integrity of their own purposes, and conclude that unlimited powers will never be abused because they themselves are not disposed to abuse them.[88] Mankind soon learns to make interested uses of every right and power which they possess or may assume.[89]
11) This risk of abuse is multiplied if the individual is not free to escape abuse, is incapacitated or otherwise vulnerable, or their word is not given the same weight as that of others. Children and adults with mental health problems are particularly at risk and the law has usually afforded them special protection.
12) This protection involves imposing legal duties on those with power, conferring legal rights on those in their power, and independent scrutiny of how these powers and duties are exercised. The effectiveness of such schemes depends on whether, and to what extent, they are observed.
13) This is a matter of constitutional importance, for the observance of legal rights and the rule of law are the cornerstones of all

---

88 Thomas Jefferson: *Notes on Virginia Q.XIII*, 1782. Memorial edition, 2:164.
89 Thomas Jefferson: *Notes on Virginia Q.XIII*, 1782. Memorial edition, 2:164.

liberal democracies. The rule of law 'implies the subordination of all authorities, legislative, executive [and] judicial . . . to certain principles which would generally be accepted as characteristic of law, such as the ideas of the fundamental principles of justice, moral principles, fairness and due process. It implies respect for the supreme value and dignity of the individual.'[90]

14) In any legal system, 'it implies limitations on legislative power, safeguards against abuse of executive power, adequate and equal opportunities of access to legal advice and assistance, . . . proper protection of the individual and group rights and liberties, and equality before the law . . . It means more than that the government maintains and enforces law and order, but that the government is, itself, subject to rules of law and cannot itself disregard the law or remake it to suit itself'.[91]

15) In framing these principles and laws, Parliament has sought to be just, justice being 'a firm and continuous desire to render to everyone that which is his due'.[92]

16) When new laws are necessary, they should impose minimum powers, duties and rights; provide mechanisms for enforcing duties and remedies for abuse of powers; be unambiguous, just, in plain English, and as short as possible.

17) Because there is a long record of experimentation in human conduct, cumulative verifications give these principles a well-earned prestige. Lightly to disregard them is the height of foolishness.[93]

The future

3.236 The Law Commission's review of deprivation of liberty (noted at para 3.197 above) will also include proposals for amendments of other parts of the Act. In its provisional proposals, the Law Commission proposed amending section 4 so as to introduce (in essence) a presumption that a person's identifiable wishes and feelings should be followed in the making of any best interests decision.[94] This

90 David M Walker, *The Oxford companion to law*, Clarendon Press, 1980, p1093.
91 David M Walker, *The Oxford companion to law*, p1093.
92 Justinian, Inst, 1, 1.
93 J Dewey, *Human nature and conduct*, Allen & Unwin, 1922.
94 Law Commission, *Mental Capacity and Deprivation of Liberty: A Consultation Paper* (2015), chapter 12, available at: www.lawcom.gov.uk/project/mental-capacity-and-deprivation-of-liberty/.

proposal was suggested, in part, to bring the Act into greater compliance with the UN Convention on the Rights of Persons with Disabilities (discussed further in chapter 25). In its interim statement published in May 2016 following consultation Law Commission also indicated that it was considering qualifying the 'section 5 defence' so as to provide additional procedural safeguards in respect of certain key decisions by public authorities.[95] The Law Commission's draft Bill will be published in March 2017; whether and when legislation will be placed before Parliament to take the Commission's final proposals forward is at the time of writing unknown.

---

95 Law Commission, *Mental Capacity and Deprivation of Liberty: Interim Statement* (May 2016), available at www.lawcom.gov.uk/wp-content/uploads/2016/06/mental_capacity_interim_statement.pdf.

CHAPTER 4

The Court of Protection

4.1	Introduction and background
4.5	Establishment and constitution
4.12	Circuit judges and district judges
4.13	Independence of the judiciary
4.15	HMCTS and court administration
4.20	Authorised court officers
4.23	Workload and number of applications
4.25	The court's budget
4.26	Where to find the law and guidance
4.36	Mental Capacity Act 2005
4.37	Rules, practice directions, practice guidance, regulations and orders, and codes
4.38	Textbooks
4.39	European Convention on Human Rights
4.43	Jurisdiction of the Court of Protection
4.44	Exempt matters to which the MCA 2005 does not apply
	People falling outside the Act
	Family matters falling outside the Act (section 27)
	Mental Health Act matters (section 28)
	Voting rights (section 29)
4.49	The range of applications and orders that may be made

continued

81

4.50 Declarations
4.52 Court orders and decisions under section 16
Section 16 and personal welfare matters • Section 16 and property and financial matters
4.55 Appointing deputies under section 16
Who may be a deputy • Two or more deputies • Appointment of successors • Property and affairs deputyships • Restrictions on deputies • Security, reports and the Public Guardian • Reimbursement and remuneration • Revoking a deputy's appointment
4.69 Powers in relation to LPAs
Determining whether an LPA exists or still exists • Impropriety or failure to act in P's best interests • Powers of court in relation to the operation of lasting powers of attorney • Gifts
4.77 Powers in relation to advance decisions to refuse treatment
4.79 Powers in relation to EPAs
Objections to the registration of an EPA • Powers in connection with a registered EPA • Giving directions concerning the operation of the EPA • Revocation of a registered EPA • Objections to a registered EPA
4.91 Other powers
Applications under COPR r202 • Applications under MCA 2005 Sch 3
4.94 Interim orders where there is reason to believe person lacks capacity

4.100 Court of Protection procedures
4.101 Case Management Pilot
4.104 The overriding objective
4.107 Duty of the parties
4.108 Who are the parties to the proceedings
4.109 Involvement of the person concerned
4.110 Litigation friends

4.111 Case management
4.112 Hearings
4.114 Legal aid
4.115 Personal Support Unit (PSU)

4.116 McKenzie friends and lay representation
McKenzie friends • *Lay representation*
4.122 Appeals
4.123 Enforcement of orders and declarations

Introduction and background

4.1 Prior to the Mental Capacity Act (MCA) 2005 coming into force, the Court of Protection's jurisdiction was limited to dealing with an incapacitated person's property and financial affairs.

4.2 The court was an office of the Supreme Court with a full-time Master and nominated officers. The relevant legal provisions were set out in Part VII of the Mental Health Act (MHA) 1983, supplemented by Court of Protection Rules[1] which regulated its procedures. Appeals from the Master were to the Chancery Division of the High Court.

4.3 Hearings were in London and usually took the form of an inquiry around a conference table rather than a trial. The great advantages were sometimes said to be informality and flexibility, and the perceived disadvantages too much informality and flexibility, in terms of case management, pleadings, advance disclosure and witness statements.

4.4 The Public Guardianship Office (PGO) was responsible for administering the court and it also supervised the affairs of those under the court's jurisdiction.

Establishment and constitution

4.5 The new Court of Protection established by the MCA 2005 is a Superior Court of Record.[2]

4.6 It has 'in connection with its jurisdiction the same powers, rights, privileges and authority as the High Court',[3] for example in relation to witnesses, contempt of court and enforcement.

4.7 Its jurisdiction includes much of the personal welfare and healthcare jurisdiction previously exercised by judges of the Family Division of the High Court, in addition to the property and financial

---

1 Court of Protection Rules 2001 SI No 824.
2 According to *Halsbury's Laws of England*, prima facie no matter is deemed to be beyond the jurisdiction of a superior court unless it is expressly shown to be so, while nothing is within the jurisdiction of an inferior court (such as a magistrates' court) unless it is expressly shown on the face of the proceedings that the particular matter is within the cognisance of the particular court: *R v Chancellor of St Edmundsbury and Ipswich Diocese ex p White* [1948] 1 KB 195 at 205–206, [1947] 2 All ER 170 at 172, CA, per Wrottesley LJ.
3 MCA 2005 s47(1).

4.8 decision-making jurisdiction which it already had under the Mental Health Acts.

4.8 The court is based at First Avenue House, 42–49 High Holborn, London WC1V 6NP. All applications are filed in London. However, where appropriate and convenient, the case can then be transferred to a 'regional hub' to be dealt with by a nominated Court of Protection judge sitting outside London.

4.9 The court has a President and Vice-President and a resident Senior Judge:

President	Rt Hon Sir James Munby, President of the Family Division of the High Court and Court of Protection
Vice-President	Hon Sir William Charles, Vice-President of the Court of Protection
Senior Judge	Position vacant

4.10 Primarily for purposes of identifying appeal routes, judges are now identified as belonging to one of three tiers, with district judges (and equivalent) being Tier 1, circuit judges (and equivalents) being Tier 2, and High Court judges (and equivalent) being Tier 3. This is discussed further in chapter 18, but in practice this terminology is rarely used to describe the level of judge who will hear a particular case.

4.11 All High Court judges are nominated to sit as Court of Protection judges and some applications must be heard by a judge of at least that seniority.[4]

---

4 Technically, a 'puisne judge of the High Court': in other words a 'full' judge of the High Court, rather than a deputy: MCA 2005 s46(2)(c).

CASES WHICH MUST BE HEARD BY A HIGH COURT JUDGE,[3] etc	
Type of application	Must be heard by:
• Applications in relation to the lawfulness of withholding or withdrawing artificial nutrition and hydration from a person in a permanent vegetative state, or a minimally conscious state.	The President or by another judge nominated by the President: Court of Protection (COP) Rules SI No 1744 r86 and Practice Direction (PD) 12A
• Cases where a declaration of incompatibility is sought pursuant to section 4 of the Human Rights Act (HRA) 1998; • applications in relation to a case involving an ethical dilemma in an untested area; • other cases in relation to serious medical treatment (as to which, see the definitions in PD 9E paras 3 and 4), eg non-therapeutic sterilisation, certain terminations of pregnancy, experimental or innovative treatments, medical treatments or procedures that involve a degree of force or restraint, cases involving organ or marrow donation by an incapacitated person.	A Tier 3 judge: COPR rr83, 86 and PD 11A, PD 12A

Circuit judges and district judges

4.12 The Senior Judge, who has circuit judge rank and is a Tier 2 judge, is supported by 4.8 resident district judges at First Avenue House in London and by circuit judges and district judges across England and Wales who are nominated ('ticketed') to undertake Court of Protection work as required.

Independence of the judiciary

4.13 Because the office of Lord Chancellor is a political appointment and the holder need not have any legal or judicial qualification or experience, it is the Lord Chief Justice who is responsible for judges and their management, performance and discipline. In terms of their Court of Protection work, the judges are led by, and responsible to, the President.

4.14 In order to further ensure judicial independence and the rule of law, section 2(5) of the Courts Act 2003 provides that: 'The Lord

Chancellor may not enter into contracts for the provision of officers and staff to discharge functions which involve making judicial decisions or exercising any judicial discretion'.

HMCTS and court administration

4.15 The Lord Chancellor is under a duty to ensure that there is an efficient and effective system to support the carrying on of the business of the Court of Protection and that appropriate services are provided for it.[5]

4.16 In practice, this duty is discharged day-to-day on the Lord Chancellor's behalf by an agency called Her Majesty's Courts & Tribunals Service (HMCTS).

COURT OF PROTECTION JUDGES	HMCTS
Managed and led by the Lord Chief Justice and the President	A responsibility of the Lord Chancellor
Support system provided by HMCTS	Responsible for ensuring that the judges have the system and support which they require

4.17 The Lord Chancellor may appoint such officers and other staff as appear to him or her appropriate for the purpose of discharging this general duty.[6]

4.18 As at October 2016, the court had an agreed complement of 86 HMCTS staff. In addition, the Office of the Public Guardian funds five staff members to scan court orders.

4.19 HMCTS court staff ('officers') are organised into a number of branches or sections, as described in the table below:

COURT OF PROTECTION — ADMINISTRATION AND CASE WORK	
Branch/Section	Responsibilities
• G1 Branch (Receiving and Issuing Applications)	• Making up case files • Issuing applications • Interim directions • Fast-tracking cases • Applications for permission • Issuing applications

continued

5 Courts Act 2003 s1(1)(aa).
6 Courts Act 2003 s2(1).

Branch/Section	Responsibilities
• G2 Branch (Draft Orders Team)	• Processing applications to appoint a deputy • Processing routine personal welfare applications • Processing applications from existing deputies • Receiving and processing certificates of service and acknowledgments of service (including objections to applications) • Applications within proceedings • Preparing standard drafts of court orders
• G3 Branch (Issuing Orders team)	• Issuing and dispatching final orders • Dispatching security bond forms • Dealing with bond defaulters • Scanning orders to the Public Guardian
• Judicial Support Team (including the regional and appeals team)	• Ushering hearings • Dealing with cases that require listing for an attended or telephone hearing • Case transfers to and from a regional court • Statutory Will, gift and settlement applications • Issuing most orders and directions made by a judge at a hearing • Dealing with applications to vacate or re-list a hearing • Appeals
• Authorised court officers (ACOs)	• ACOs are civil servants who have been authorised to exercise designated court functions of a purely formal or administrative character which previously were exercised by the judges.
• Technical Specialists	• Deprivation of liberty applications • Applications for personal welfare orders • Transfer of welfare cases to regional courts • New trustee applications • EPA and LPA objections and directions • Public Guardian applications • Requests for visitor reports under section 49 • Appointing panel deputies • Orders discharging deputies (recovery/retirement)

Branch/Section	Responsibilities
• Customer Enquiry Service (CES)	• Court's telephone service • General email inquiries • Dispatching court forms to users

Authorised court officers

4.20 A number of civil servants known as authorised court officers ('ACOs') are authorised by the Senior Judge or the President to exercise the jurisdiction of the court in the circumstances set out in Practice Direction PD3A.[7]

4.21 An authorised officer may not conduct a hearing and must refer to a judge any application or question arising in an application which is contentious or which, in the opinion of the officer, is complex, requires a hearing or for any other reason ought to be considered by a judge. The relevant person concerned ('P'), a party and any other person affected by an order can apply to have an authorised officer's order reconsidered by a judge.

APPLICATIONS THAT MAY BE DEALT WITH BY AUTHORISED COURT OFFICERS (COPR r7A; PD 3A para 2.1)

2.1 Subject to paragraphs 2.2, 3 and 4.2 an authorised court officer may deal with any of the following applications:
- (a) applications to appoint a deputy for property and affairs;
- (b) applications to vary the powers of a deputy appointed for property and affairs under an existing order;
- (c) applications to discharge a deputy for property and affairs and appoint a replacement deputy;
- (d) applications to appoint and discharge a trustee;
- (e) applications to sell or purchase real property on behalf of P;
- (f) applications to vary the security in relation to a deputy for property and affairs;
- (g) applications to discharge the security when the appointment of a deputy for property and affairs comes to an end;
- (h) applications for the release of funds for the maintenance of P, or P's property, or to discharge any debts incurred by P;
- (i) applications to sell or otherwise deal with P's investments;
- (j) applications for authority to apply for a grant of probate or representation for the use and benefit of P;
- (k) applications to let and manage property belonging to P;
- (l) applications for a detailed assessment of costs;

---

7 COPR r7A. This rule came into operation on 12 December 2011.

(m) applications to obtain a copy of P's will;
(n) applications to inspect or obtain copy documents from the records of the court; and
(o) applications which relate to one or more of the preceding paragraphs and which a judge has directed should be dealt with by an authorised court officer.

4.22 The case management powers of authorised officers are limited to those matters referred to in PD 3A para 3.

Workload and number of applications

4.23 On average there was a three per cent year-on-year increase in the number of applications to the Court of Protection during the three-year period between 2013/14 and 2015/16.

Year	No of applications
2008/09	19,528
2009/10	21,042
2010/11	23,093
2011/12	24,586
2012/13	24,913
2013/14	25,296
2014/15	26,379
2015/16	27,333

4.24 There were 715 court hearings in London and 1037 outside London in 2014. The 2015 figures were 586 and 1405 respectively as a result of the further development of regional hub courts.

The court's budget

4.25 Published Ministry of Justice (MoJ) data is quite old because of the time it takes to collect data and the need for auditing. Consequently, it is difficult to establish the court's current budget. However, the HMCTS management accounts for 2011/12 indicate an annual expenditure of £4.1 million.[8]

Where to find the law and guidance

4.26 The relevant law and guidance is found in several places:
- Primary legislation: the Mental Capacity Act 2005;
- Secondary legislation: orders, rules and regulations made under the authority of the Act;
- Practice Directions, Practice Guidance and Codes of Practice;
- Case-law decisions of judges;
- European Convention on Human Rights; and
- Textbooks and textbook opinion.

4.27 The precise legal status of these different documents is not always easy to discern. However, the following brief points may help non-lawyers unfamiliar with the various documents and how to refer to them.

4.28 Acts of Parliament ('*primary legislation*') are divided into sections (s), subsections (subs), paragraphs (para) and subparagraphs (subpara). If a document refers to MCA 2005 s22(3)(a)(i), this is a reference to subparagraph (i) of paragraph (a) of subsection (3) of section 22 of the Act.

4.29 Primary legislation takes precedence over '*secondary legislation*', that is over orders, rules and regulations made by the Lord Chancellor or by some other minister with Parliament's permission, ie under the authority of an Act of Parliament.
- The term 'rules' is used for secondary legislation which is concerned with court procedures, eg the COPR. A set of rules is divided into rules (r), paragraphs (paras) and sub-paragraphs (sub-para). Thus, COPR r5(2)(b) refers to sub-paragraph (b) of paragraph (2) of rule 5 of those rules.

---

8 In line with civil courts generally, the Court of Protection fees are expected to fully cover the cost of administering the court although some funding from central government is inevitable because provision is made for fee exemptions, remission and postponement.

- The term 'regulations' is used for secondary legislation that relates to non-court executive procedures, eg the procedures of the Public Guardian. A set of regulations is divided into regulations (reg), paragraphs (para) and sub-paragraphs (sub-para).
- The term 'order' has no single meaning. In relation to the MCA 2005, it is used for secondary legislation that deals with matters directly relating to the Act's implementation, such as transitional arrangements, consequential provisions and prescribed fees. An order is divided into articles (art), paragraphs (para) and sub-paragraphs (sub-para).

4.30 In recent times, primary and secondary legislation has been augmented by a proliferation of *codes of practice, practice directions and practice guidance*:
- *Practice directions*: MCA 2005 s52 provides that the President of the Court of Protection may, with the concurrence of the Lord Chancellor, give directions 'as to the practice and procedure of the court'. Such directions may not be given by anyone else (for example, by the Vice-President or Senior Judge) without the approval of the President of the Court of Protection and the Lord Chancellor.

    The court in *Bovale Ltd v Secretary of State for Communities and Local Government*[9] considered the status of practice directions and the circumstances in which a judge may depart from them. The issue of a practice direction is the exercise of an inherent power of the court even when made under statutory authority. However, this does not mean that a judge dealing with an application can simply vary practice directions or alter rules with general effect; they are binding on her/him. In particular, a judge's wide case-management powers in individual cases cannot be construed 'as giving the power to individual judges or any court simply to vary the rules or practice directions generally' (*Bovale*, para 26). If there is a gap in the rules and practice directions, there is no impediment to a court making the order that is most appropriate to the case before it under its case management powers, or prescribing or suggesting a procedure which should be followed.
- *Practice guidance*: MCA 2005 s52(3) expressly states that providing for practice directions in this way does not prevent the President of the Court of Protection without the concurrence of the Lord Chancellor giving directions which 'contain guidance as to law or making judicial decisions'.

9 [2009] EWCA Civ 171, [2009] 1 WLR 2274.

- *Codes of Practice*: the two codes do not have statutory force, but professionals and some carers must have regard to their provisions, and the courts must take them into account where relevant.

4.31 *Case-law*: judges' decisions that settle or interpret significant points of law – for example, the precise meaning of a section of the Act – may be 'reported', that is published, in one of three historic series of law reports. These are the Official Law Reports; the Weekly Law Reports (WLR); and the All England Reports (All ER). The former should be referred to ('cited') in court if the case is reported in it.

4.32 Transcripts of 'unreported' judgments often appear on the website of the British and Irish Legal Information Institute (Bailii).[10] These transcripts have an uncertain status. They should not usually be cited unless they contain a relevant statement of legal principle not found in reported authority.[11] Many such decisions are simply illustrative of how the law was applied in a novel legal situation or one of obvious public interest. Most often, they are aids to understanding the law and its application rather than legal precedents.

4.33 Many new series of law reports have been established in recent years, the most important of which in this context are Jordan's Court of Protection Law Reports.[12] In practice, they are considered to be wholly reliable, and so are relied upon by the court.

4.34 *Legal textbook opinion* may be quoted if it is likely to assist the court as to the meaning of a disputed or difficult legal provision.

4.35 The *European Convention on Human Rights* (ECHR) is essentially a modern-day Magna Carta. So far as is possible, all primary and secondary legislation must be interpreted so as to be compatible with it.

Mental Capacity Act 2005

4.36 The MCA 2005 consists of 69 sections in three parts. These sections are followed by nine schedules which deal with legal technicalities and formalities that would clog up and make unreadable the main body of the Act if placed there.

---

10 See: www.bailii.org.
11 PD of 24 March 2012: *Citation of authorities* para 10.
12 See also *Community Care Law Reports* published by LAG covering a significant number of Court of Protection cases.

Mental Capacity Act 2005		
Part of Act	Title	What it includes
Part 1	Persons who lack capacity	• Statutory principles • Definitions of incapacity and best interests • Legal protection for professionals and other carers in respect of care and treatment given informally • Payment for necessary goods and services; LPAs • Court declarations and orders • Appointment of deputies by the court • Court's powers in relation to personal welfare matters, property and financial matters, deprivation of liberty, LPAs and advance decisions to refuse treatment • Research • IMCAs (independent mental capacity advocacy service)
Part 2	The Court of Protection and the Public Guardian	• Establishment, jurisdiction and powers of the Court of Protection and the Public Guardian • Court of Protection visitors
Part 3	Miscellaneous and general	• Scope of the Act • International protection of adults • Interpretation • Making of rules, regulations and orders
Schedule 1	Lasting powers of attorney: formalities	Technicalities and formalities relating to LPAs
Schedule 2	Property and affairs: supplementary provisions	Additional provisions relating to matters such as wills and the effect of the court disposing of part of an incapacitated person's property on the distribution of their estate on their death (either by will or under the intestacy rules)

Part of Act	Title	What it includes
Schedule 3	International protection of adults	The schedule gives effect in England and Wales to the Hague Convention (the Convention on the International Protection of Adults, 2000). See also MCA 2005 s63
Schedule 4	Provisions applying to existing enduring powers of attorney	The MCA 2005 repealed the Enduring Powers of Attorney Act 1985. Its provisions are, however, repeated here because, although no new EPAs may be made, EPAs made before the new Act continue to have effect, may be challenged in court on the old terms, etc. See also MCA 2005 s66
Schedule 5	Transitional provisions and savings	
Schedule 6	Minor and consequential amendments	
Schedule 7	Repeals	
Schedule A1	Hospital and care home residents: deprivation of liberty	These schedules set out the 'deprivation of liberty' scheme inserted into the MCA 2005 by the MHA 2007
Schedule 1A	Persons ineligible to be deprived of liberty by this Act	

Rules, practice directions, practice guidance, regulations and orders, and codes

4.37 The MCA 2005 provides for issuing rules, regulations and orders, and the publication of codes of practice. The following are some of the most important for court users.

Rules	
COPR 2007 SI No 1744	These rules govern the procedures of the court. They are somewhat cumbersome: 202 rules in 22 parts, supplemented by 50 practice directions, numerous prescribed forms and where necessary the Civil Procedure Rules 1998 and Family Procedure Rules 2010.
Practice directions[a]	
The practice directions are essentially of two kinds. Some do no more than repeat in plainer English what is said in a part of the rules; others, such as those on the right, are substantive.	• PD 9D – Applications by currently appointed deputies, attorneys and donees in relation to [the person's] property and affairs
	• PD 9E – Applications relating to serious medical treatment
Practice guidance	
Practice guidance	*Lord Chief Justice's Practice Direction: Committal for Contempt of Court – Open Court* issued on 26 March 2015 (this applies to a number of courts, including the Court of Protection)[b]
Regulations and orders	
Lasting Powers of Attorney, Enduring Powers of Attorney and Public Guardian Regulations 2007 SI No 1253	These regulations deal with matters such as the completion and registration of Lasting Powers of Attorney, the registration of enduring powers of attorney, the reports required of deputies and the registers maintained by the Public Guardian.

a See: https://courtofprotectionhandbook.com/legislation-codes-of-practice-forms-and-guidance/.
b See: https://www.judiciary.gov.uk/wp-content/uploads/2015/03/practice-direction-committals-for-contempt.pdf.

Codes of Practice	
There are separate codes on the MCA 2005 as originally passed and the deprivation of liberty provisions added in 2007.	• *Mental Capacity Act 2005: Code of Practice* (Department for Constitutional Affairs, 2007)[c]
	• *Deprivation of liberty safeguards: Code of Practice to supplement the main Mental Capacity Act 2005 Code of Practice* (Ministry of Justice, 2008)[d]

Textbooks

4.38 The main textbook on court practice and procedure is Jordans' *Court of Protection Practice*, a new edition of which appears annually in the spring. The other four standard publications used by practitioners are:

- *Court of Protection Law Reports* (Jordans), which contain decisions made by senior judges on important legal issues;
- *Heywood & Massey: Court of Protection Practice* (looseleaf) (Sweet & Maxwell);
- *Cretney & Lush on Lasting and Enduring Powers of Attorney* (7th ed, Jordans, 2013);
- the monthly *Mental capacity law* newsletter produced by 39 Essex Chambers (A Ruck Keene, V Butler-Cole, N Allen, A Bicarregui, S Edwards, V Butler-Cole, A Lee (eds)) and published at www.39essex.com, and by (free) subscription by contacting marketing@39essex.com.

European Convention on Human Rights

4.39 The HRA 1998 makes it unlawful for a public authority, such as the NHS or a local authority, to act in a way which is incompatible with a convention right unless legislation requires it to act in that way. So far as is possible, all primary and secondary legislation must be interpreted so as to be compatible with the ECHR. If this is impossible, one of the higher courts will make a declaration of incompatibility.

---

c See: https://www.gov.uk/government/uploads/system/uploads/attachment_data/file/497253/Mental-capacity-act-code-of-practice.pdf.
d See: http://webarchive.nationalarchives.gov.uk/20130107105354/http://www.dh.gov.uk/prod_consum_dh/groups/dh_digitalassets/@dh/@en/documents/digitalasset/dh_087309.pdf.

4.40 The articles of the ECHR which are most often 'in play' in Court of Protection proceedings are Articles 5 (right to liberty and security) and 8 (right to respect for private and family life).

4.41 Article 5 is engaged when an incapacitated person is deprived of their liberty. The state is obliged to take effective measures to protect vulnerable persons, including reasonable steps to prevent a deprivation of liberty of which the authorities have or ought to have knowledge. A proper authorisation or court order is required. The person concerned should have access to a court and the opportunity to be heard in person or, where necessary, through some form of representation.

4.42 Article 8 provides a qualified right to respect for one's private and family life, home and correspondence. Any interference with an incapacitated person's family or private life must be authorised by law, proportionate ('necessary in a democratic society') and for a permitted purpose, eg for the protection of their health. The court should consider the nature and strength of the evidence of any alleged risk of harm and there must be a proper, factual basis for such concerns.

Jurisdiction of the Court of Protection

4.43 The court's jurisdiction derives from the MCA 2005 which sets out a number of different types of applications and orders that can be made.

Exempt matters to which the MCA 2005 does not apply

4.44 The MCA 2005 does not apply to some legal situations and cannot be used to authorise certain kinds of interference with a person's life. These exclusions are set out in sections 27–29.

People falling outside the Act

4.45 Depending on the type of decision to be made, the court's jurisdiction may be restricted to adults (eg statutory wills, lasting powers of attorney) or to persons aged 16 or over (eg personal welfare issues).[13]

---

13 MCA 2005 s2(5) and (6).

Family matters falling outside the Act (section 27)

4.46 Nothing in the MCA 2005 permits a decision on any of the following matters to be made on behalf of a person:

- consenting to marriage or a civil partnership;
- consenting to have sexual relations;
- consenting to a decree of divorce being granted on the basis of two years' separation;
- consenting to a dissolution order being made in relation to a civil partnership on the basis of two years' separation;
- consenting to a child's being placed for adoption by an adoption agency;
- consenting to the making of an adoption order;
- discharging parental responsibilities in matters not relating to a child's property;
- giving a consent under the Human Fertilisation and Embryology Act 1990.[14]

Mental Health Act matters (section 28)

4.47 Section 28 excludes certain MHA matters from being dealt with under the MCA 2005. The precise inter-relationship between the two statutes was considered in chapter 3 above.

Voting rights (section 29)

4.48 Nothing in the MCA 2005 permits a decision on voting at an election for any public office, or at a referendum, to be made on behalf of an incapacitated person.[15]

The range of applications and orders that may be made

4.49 The different types of application and orders that may be made are dealt with in greater detail in the appropriate chapters. However, it is useful at the outset to have an understanding of the range of orders that can be made:

- Declarations;
- Court orders and decisions under section 16;

14 MCA 2005 s27(1).
15 MCA 2005 s29(1).

- Appointing deputies under section 16;
- Powers in relation to Lasting Powers of Attorney;
- Powers in relation to Advance Decisions to Refuse Treatment;
- Powers in relation to Enduring Powers of Attorney;
- Other powers; and
- Interim Orders.

Declarations

4.50 Section 15 of the MCA 2005 provides that the Court of Protection may make declarations as to:
- whether a person has or lacks capacity to make a decision specified in the declaration;
- whether a person has or lacks capacity to make decisions on such matters as are described in the declaration;
- the lawfulness or otherwise of any act done, or yet to be done, in relation to that person.

Section 15(2) provides that the term 'act' includes an omission and a course of conduct.

4.51 As its name suggests, a declaration involves the court declaring the law or a person's rights or interests in relation to a particular matter, historically without any reference to enforcement (see further in this regard para 17.1). It registers what exists and declares what it finds. However, it is not an academic process. There has to be a real issue to resolve between the parties so that declaring something to be lawful or otherwise clarifies for the parties what may and may not be done under the Act.

Court orders and decisions under section 16

4.52 MCA 2005 s16 applies if a person lacks capacity in relation to a matter or matters concerning their personal welfare or property and affairs.[16] It enables the court by order to make the necessary decisions on their behalf or to appoint a deputy to make those decisions for the person. The powers of the court are subject to the provisions of the Act and, in particular, to sections 1 (the principles) and 4 (best interests).[17] Any order of the court may be varied or discharged by a

16 MCA 2005 s16(1).
17 MCA 2005 s16(3).

subsequent order.[18] In *Re MN*,[19] Sir James Munby P suggested the court should usually reflect its determination as to an incapacitated person's best interests not by way of making a declaration, but by making an order under MCA 2005 s16: ie by making a decision on their behalf. Where necessary, such an order can be coupled with a declaration under MCA 2005 s15(1)(c) as to the lawfulness of actions to be taken by others (for instance by medical professionals providing treatment to the individual).

Section 16 and personal welfare matters

4.53 The court's section 16 powers as respects an incapacitated person's personal welfare extend in particular to:[20]
- deciding where the person is to live;
- deciding what contact, if any, the person is to have with any specified persons;
- making an order prohibiting a named person from having contact with the person;
- giving or refusing consent to the carrying out or continuation of a treatment by a person providing health care for the person;
- giving a direction that a person responsible for the person's health care allow a different person to take over that responsibility.

Section 16 and property and financial matters

4.54 The court's section 16 powers as respects an incapacitated person's property and affairs extend in particular to:[21]
- the control and management of their property;
- the sale, exchange, charging, gift or other disposition of their property;
- the acquisition of property in their name or on their behalf;
- the carrying on, on their behalf, of any profession, trade or business;
- the taking of a decision which will have the effect of dissolving a partnership of which the person is a member;
- the carrying out of any contract entered into by the person;
- the discharge of the person's debts and any of their obligations, whether legally enforceable or not;

---

18 MCA 2005 s16(7).
19 [2015] EWCA Civ 411, [2016] Fam 87, (2015) 18 CCLR 521.
20 MCA 2005 s17(1), (2).
21 MCA 2005 s18(1).

- the settlement of any of their property, whether for their benefit or for the benefit of others;
- the execution for them of a will (although no will may be made under this power at a time when the person has not reached 18 years of age[22]);
- the exercise of any power (including a power to consent) vested in the person whether beneficially or as trustee or otherwise;
- the conduct of legal proceedings in the person's name or on their behalf.

Appointing deputies under section 16[23]

4.55 MCA 2005 s16 provides that the court may:

- by making an order, make the decision or decisions on the person's behalf in relation to the matter or matters, or
- appoint a person (a 'deputy') to make decisions on the person's behalf in relation to the matter or matters.[24]

4.56 Naturally, if the judge can make the decision, it will generally be inappropriate for him or her to authorise someone else to make it.

4.57 Consequently, the Act provides that a decision by the court is to be preferred to the appointment of a deputy to make a decision; and that the powers conferred on the deputy should be as limited in scope and duration 'as is reasonably practicable in the circumstances': see section 16(4).

4.58 Without prejudice to section 4, the court may make an order or appoint a deputy on such terms as it considers are in the incapacitated person's best interests, and may do so even though no application is before it 'on those terms'.[25]

Who may be a deputy

4.59 A deputy must be an adult (aged 18 or over) or, in the case of property and affairs deputyships, a trust corporation.[26]

4.60 A person may not be appointed as a deputy without their consent.[27]

---

22 MCA 2005 s18(2).
23 See further chapter 7.
24 MCA 2005 s16(2).
25 MCA 2005 s16(6).
26 MCA 2005 s19(1).
27 MCA 2005 s19(3).

4.61　　The court may appoint the holder of a specified office or position as the person's deputy,[28] for example the holder of a particular local authority finance office. This avoids the need for a new order when the current holder of the post moves on and is replaced.

Two or more deputies

4.62　　The court may appoint two or more deputies to act jointly, jointly and separately ('severally'), or jointly in respect of some matters and jointly and separately in respect of others.[29]

Appointment of successors

4.63　　When appointing a deputy or deputies, the court may at the same time appoint one or more other persons to succeed the deputy or deputies in such circumstances, or on the happening of such events, as may be specified, and for such period as may be so specified.[30]

Property and affairs deputyships

4.64　　With regard to property and affairs deputyships, the court may confer on a deputy powers to:
- take possession or control of all or any specified part of the person's property;
- exercise all or any specified powers in respect of it, including such powers of investment as the court may determine.[31]

Restrictions on deputies

4.65　　The MCA 2005 provides that certain powers may not be conferred on or exercised by a deputy. These restrictions are described in chapter 3 above.

Security, reports and the Public Guardian

4.66　　The court may require a deputy:
- to give to the Public Guardian such security as the court thinks fit for the due discharge of his functions; and

---

28　MCA 2005 s19(2).
29　MCA 2005 s19(4).
30　MCA 2005 s19(5).
31　MCA 2005 s19(8).

- to submit to the Public Guardian such reports at such times or at such intervals as the court may direct.[32]

Reimbursement and remuneration

4.67 The deputy is entitled:
- to be reimbursed out of the incapacitated person's property for their reasonable expenses in discharging their functions; and
- if the court so directs when appointing them, to remuneration out of the incapacitated person's property for discharging them.[33]

Revoking a deputy's appointment

4.68 The court may revoke the appointment of a deputy or vary the powers conferred on them if it is satisfied that the deputy:
- has behaved, or is behaving, in a way that contravenes the authority conferred on them by the court or is not in P's best interests; or
- proposes to behave in a way that would contravene that authority or would not be in P's best interests.[34]

Powers in relation to LPAs[35]

4.69 MCA 2005 ss22 and 23 set out the court's powers where a person has:
- executed[36] or purported to execute a document ('an instrument') with a view to creating an LPA; or
- such a document has been registered as an LPA by the Public Guardian.[37]

Determining whether an LPA exists or still exists

4.70 The court may determine any question relating to:

---

32 MCA 2005 s19(9).
33 MCA 2005 s19(7).
34 MCA 2005 s16(8).
35 See further chapter 7.
36 'Executed' simply means to sign a document and to complete any other necessary formalities to give it legal effect, such as having it sealed (which does not apply here). The document or 'instrument' is simply the standard LPA form prescribed under the MCA 2005.
37 MCA 2005 s22(1).

- whether one or more of the requirements for the creation of an LPA have been met;[38]
- whether the power has been revoked or has otherwise come to an end.[39]

Impropriety or failure to act in P's best interests

4.71 MCA 2005 s20(4) applies if the court is satisfied:
- that fraud or undue pressure was used to induce the relevant person to execute an instrument for the purpose of creating a lasting power of attorney, or to create a lasting power of attorney; or
- that the donee (or, if more than one, any of them) of an LPA (i) has behaved, or is behaving, in a way that contravenes his authority or is not in the person's best interests, or (ii) proposes to behave in a way that would contravene his or her authority or would not be in the person's best interests.[40]

4.72 In such a case, the court may:
- direct that an instrument purporting to create the lasting power of attorney is not to be registered; or
- if the person lacks capacity to do so, revoke the instrument or the LPA.[41]

4.73 If there is more than one donee, the court may revoke the instrument or the LPA so far as it relates to any of them.[42]

Powers of court in relation to the operation of lasting powers of attorney

4.74 MCA 2005 s23(1) provides that the court may determine any question as to the meaning or effect of an LPA or an instrument purporting to create one. The court may:
- give directions with respect to decisions which the donee of an LPA has authority to make, and which the person lacks capacity to make;[43]

---

38 An LPA is not created unless section 10 is complied with, the prescribed document is registered, the person creating it is an adult who had capacity to execute it: MCA 2005 s9(2).
39 MCA 2005 s22(2).
40 MCA 2005 s22(3).
41 MCA 2005 s22(4).
42 MCA 2005 s22(5).
43 MCA 2005 s23(2)(a).

- give any consent or authorisation to act which the donee would have to obtain from the person if the person had capacity to give it.[44]

4.75 Where the relevant person lacks capacity to do so, the court may:
- give directions to the donee with respect to the rendering by them of reports or accounts and the production of records kept by them for that purpose;[45]
- require the donee to supply information or to produce documents or things in their possession as donee;[46]
- give directions with respect to the remuneration or expenses of the donee;[47]
- relieve the donee wholly or partly from any liability which they have or may have incurred on account of a breach of their duties as donee.[48]

Gifts

4.76 The court may authorise the making of gifts which are not permitted gifts (such as customary birthday presents and charitable donations) within the meaning of section 12(2).[49]

Powers in relation to advance decisions to refuse treatment

4.77 The court may make a declaration as to whether an advance decision exists; is valid; or is applicable to a treatment.[50]

4.78 Nothing in an apparent advance decision stops a person from providing life-sustaining treatment, or from doing any act they reasonably believe to be necessary to prevent a serious deterioration in the relevant person's condition, while a decision in respect of any relevant issue is sought from the court.[51]

---

44 MCA 2005 s23(2)(b).
45 MCA 2005 s23(3)(a).
46 MCA 2005 s23(3)(b).
47 MCA 2005 s23(3)(c).
48 MCA 2005 s23(3)(d).
49 MCA 2005 s23(4).
50 MCA 2005 s26(4).
51 MCA 2005 s26(5).

Powers in relation to EPAs

4.79 The court's powers in relation to EPAs are set out in Schedule 4 to the MCA 2005 and derive from the Enduring Powers of Attorney Act 1985. The case-law on that Act therefore continues to be relevant. It is undecided whether and to what extent the main body of the MCA 2005 applies to EPAs.

Objections to the registration of an EPA

4.80 If the Public Guardian receives a valid notice of objection to the registration of an EPA from a person entitled to notice then he or she must not register it unless the court directs that it is registered.

4.81 A notice of objection to registration is valid if made on one or more of the following grounds:

1) that the power purported to have been created by the instrument (ie EPA form) was not valid as an EPA;
2) that the power created by the instrument no longer subsists;
3) that the application is premature because the donor is not yet becoming mentally incapable;
4) that fraud or undue pressure was used to induce the donor to create the power;
5) that, having regard to all the circumstances and in particular the attorney's relationship to or connection with the donor, the attorney is unsuitable to be the donor's attorney.

4.82 If any of these grounds is established to the satisfaction of the court, it must direct the Public Guardian not to register the instrument. If the court is not satisfied that any of the grounds are established then it must direct registration.

4.83 If the court directs the Public Guardian not to register an instrument on the fraud, undue pressure or unsuitability ground then it must by order revoke the EPA. This is not necessary under the first two grounds because no EPA exists, and it would be premature under the third ground because it does not rest on a finding of fault and the EPA may require registration in the future.

4.84 In all cases other than the no-fault prematurity ground, the EPA document must be delivered up to the Public Guardian to be cancelled, unless the court otherwise directs. Again, this is logical. In all of the other cases, the EPA document either has no legal effect (in which case one usually one does not want it circulating in someone's possession) or at best the attorney has been found to be unsuitable (in which case one usually does not want them retaining possession of it).

Powers in connection with a registered EPA

4.85 Once an EPA has been registered, the court may be asked to revoke it or to give directions to the attorney as to the management of the donor's property.

Giving directions concerning the operation of the EPA

4.86 Where an instrument has been registered the court may:
   a) determine any question as to the meaning or effect of the instrument;
   b) give directions with respect to:
      i) the management or disposal by the attorney of the property and affairs of the donor;
      ii) the rendering of accounts by the attorney and the production of the records kept by them for the purpose;
      iii) the remuneration or expenses of the attorney whether or not in default of or in accordance with any provision made by the instrument, including directions for the repayment of excessive or the payment of additional remuneration;
   c) require the attorney to supply information or produce documents or things in their possession as attorney;
   d) give any consent or authorisation to act which the attorney would have to obtain from a mentally capable donor;
   e) authorise the attorney to act so as to benefit themselves or others otherwise than in accordance with Schedule 4 para 3(2).

Revocation of a registered EPA

4.87 Once an EPA has been registered, because the donor is becoming mentally incapable, it can only be revoked by the donor if the court confirms the revocation. On such an application, the court must confirm the revocation of the power if it satisfied that the donor:
   a) has done whatever is necessary in law to effect an express revocation of the power; and
   b) was mentally capable of revoking a power of attorney when they did so (whether or not they are still capable of doing so by the time the court considers the application).

Objections to a registered EPA

4.88 The court must direct the Public Guardian to cancel the registration of a registered EPA in any of the following circumstances:

a) on confirming the revocation of the power by the donor (see immediately above);
b) on directing under MCA 2005 Sch 4 para 2(9)(b) that the power is to be revoked (this is where the court makes a deputy order and when doing so directs that a pre-existing EPA shall be revoked);
c) on being satisfied that the donor is and is likely to remain mentally capable;
d) on being satisfied that the power has expired or has been revoked by the mental incapacity of the attorney;
e) on being satisfied that the power was not a valid and subsisting enduring power when registration was effected;
f) on being satisfied that fraud or undue pressure was used to induce the donor to create the power;
g) on being satisfied that, having regard to all the circumstances and in particular the attorney's relationship to or connection with the donor, the attorney is unsuitable to be the donor's attorney.

4.89 If the court directs the Public Guardian to cancel the EPA's registration on one of the fault grounds (fraud, undue pressure or unsuitability) then it must also revoke the EPA itself, ie the EPA document is no longer valid and therefore there can be no future attempts to re-register it.

4.90 In all cases other than the no-fault 'donor is and is likely to remain mentally capable' ground, the EPA document must be delivered up to the Public Guardian to be cancelled, unless the court otherwise directs. Again, this is logical. In all of the other cases, the EPA document either has no legal effect or at best the attorney has been found to be unsuitable.

Other powers

4.91 The court's other main powers relate to COPR r202 and MCA 2005 Sch 3.

Applications under COPR r202

4.92 The court receives applications from persons subject to a deputyship order for the deputy order to be revoked on the ground that the person concerned no longer lacks capacity in relation to the matter or matters in question and therefore no longer falls within the court's jurisdiction.

Applications under MCA 2005 Sch 3

4.93 The court sometimes receives applications in relation to Schedule 3 to the Act which is concerned with the Hague Convention and the international protection of adults with incapacity. For example, a person may apply to the court for a declaration that a protective measure taken in a country other than England and Wales is enforceable in England and Wales. The Convention and Schedule 3 are dealt with in chapter 26.

Interim orders where there is reason to believe person lacks capacity

4.94 The Court of Protection's jurisdiction is directed towards making decisions on behalf of people who lack capacity to make their own decision. By the end of the case there is usually ample evidence on which the judge can determine whether or not the person concerned has that capacity.

4.95 What, though, is the position where it appears that a person lacks capacity to make a decision for themselves, and in consequence is at risk, but that person will not agree to a capacity assessment and the evidence which can be put before the court is incomplete?

4.96 The answer is that the court has power to make interim orders and directions under MCA 2005 s48 if there is reason to believe that the relevant person lacks capacity in relation to the matter and it is in their best interests for the court to do so.

4.97 The specific issue raised in the case of Re F[52] was whether the court has any jurisdiction to hear an application about a person unless and until the presumption of capacity is first rebutted. What if the medical evidence concerning capacity is equivocal?

4.98 It was observed by HHJ Hazel Marshall QC that there are two stages to the court's jurisdiction under section 48. The section enables the court to make 'Interim orders and directions' provided, firstly, that 'there is reason to believe that [the person] lacks capacity in relation to the matter'. This is plainly a lower threshold than 'proof on balance of probability that [the person] lacks capacity'. What is required is simply sufficient evidence to justify a reasonable belief that the person may lack capacity in the relevant regard. There are various phrases which might be used to describe what is required, such as 'good' or 'serious cause for concern' or 'a real possibility' that

---

52 (2009) COPLR Con Vol 390.

the person lacks capacity, but the concept behind each is the same and quite easily recognised.

4.99 It is the second stage which provides the real protection for the citizen against undue interference with their affairs and their right to make their own decisions. The first stage involves considering whether there is evidence giving good cause for concern that the person may lack capacity in some relevant regard. Once that is raised as a serious possibility, the second stage requires the court to consider whether 'it is in the person's best interests to make the order or give the directions, without delay'.

Court of Protection procedures

4.100 The court's procedures are dealt with in the relevant chapters. However, it is helpful to emphasise the following points by way of general introduction.

Case Management Pilot

4.101 It should firstly be noted that a Case Management Pilot came into effect on 1 September 2016, designed to address a perception that (at least some) cases before the court are taking too long to resolve, and too great expense.[53] The Pilot, which will run until 31 August 2017, sets pathways for health and welfare cases, property and affairs cases, and mixed cases. Not all types of cases are on pathways,[54] but for cases which are the Pilot places an obligation on applicants to provide improved analysis of the issues at the start of a case, allowing for more robust case management decisions to be taken at the outset and all issues to be identified at the earliest opportunity in proceedings. It will also seek to encourage early resolution of cases, to reduce the number and length of hearings required in contested cases and to promote judicial continuity.

---

53 See in particular the comments of the President, Sir James Munby, in *Re MN* [2015] EWCA Civ 411, [2016] Fam 87 at paras 100–105.
54 The exceptions are (a) uncontested applications; (b) applications for statutory wills and gifts; (c) applications made by the Public Guardian; (d) applications relating to serious medical treatment; (e) applications in Form COPDOL10 (ie applications challenging deprivation of liberty authorisations under Schedule A1); and (f) applications in Form DLA (ie so-called *Re X* applications for judicial authorisation of deprivation of liberty): see further in relation to these last two chapter 21.

4.102 At the time of writing, it is not clear whether cases that are not on a pathway fall outside the scope of the Pilot altogether. We understand that this was the intention behind the Case Management Pilot, but the wording of the Practice Direction appears to have brought *all* applications issued on or after 1 September 2016 within the scope of the Pilot, and therefore to apply to *all* cases both the new numbering in Pilots Part 1-5 of the Court of Protection Rules (COPR) and the substantively different obligations imposed under some parts of Pilots Part 1-5 and Pilot Part 15 (relating to expert evidence).[55]

4.103 We anticipate that the issue of whether *all* cases now fall within the scope of the Pilot will be the subject of a judgment sooner rather than later; news of any such judgment will be provided at www.courtofprotectionhandbook.com. In the interim, we identify in the chapters below the different effect of the rules depending upon whether the case falls within the scope of the Pilot or not. In any event, and as a rule of thumb, we suggest that wherever a stricter obligation is imposed under the Pilot it is advisable to proceed on the basis that this stricter obligation is to be applied even if, strictly, the case falls outside the scope of the Pilot.

The overriding objective

4.104 COPR r3 sets out the overriding objective of the rules which is to enable the court to deal with a case justly 'having regard to the principles contained in the Act'.

4.105 The principles contained in the MCA 2005 are those set out in section 1. So, for example, a person should not be held to lack capacity to make litigation decisions merely because they make what others regard as an unwise decision or until all practicable steps to help them litigate their own case have been taken without success.

4.106 Where the Case Management Pilot applies, COPR r3 is re-titled COPR Pr1.1, and the overriding objective is modified to make specific reference not just to dealing with the case justly but also to enabling the court to deal with it at proportionate cost. See further chapter 9.

---

55 There is a mismatch between the wording of paras 1.1 and 1.3 of Case Management Pilot PD the former suggesting that the Pilot applies only to cases on a pathway (supported by Para 3.1); the latter suggesting that all cases issued between 1 September 2016 and 31 August 2017 fall within the scope of the Pilot.

Duty of the parties

4.107 COPR r4 (or COPR Pr1.4 where the Case Management Pilot applies) then provides that 'the parties are required to help the court to further the overriding objective'. Thus, for example, so far as practicable they must help to save litigation expense and deal with the case in ways which are proportionate to the nature, importance and complexity of the issues. In an appropriate case, the penalty for not doing so would be not to allow the party all of their costs in a property and financial affairs case or to require them to contribute to another party's costs in a case involving, eg health and welfare. This is discussed further in chapter 9.

Who are the parties to the proceedings

4.108 Unlike proceedings in other courts, the parties do not define themselves – although they will generally be the applicant(s), any objectors and, in significant personal welfare cases, the person said to be incapacitated. The district judge dealing with a case initially must identify the persons who should be parties and ensure that notice is given to other relevant people to enable them to be joined if they wish.

Involvement of the person concerned

4.109 COPR r3A (or COPR Pr1.2 where the Case Management Pilot applies) is concerned with the participation of the relevant person. Having considered the issues raised in the case, whether it is contentious and any response of the person on being notified of the application, the court must always consider making one of a number of directions. These directions are joining the person as a party to the proceedings, appointing an accredited legal representative or non-legal representative for them, arranging for them to have an opportunity to address the judge, giving some other appropriate direction, or (having considered the matter) making no direction at all. In practice, the options available to the judge are often severely limited by the unavailability of legal aid and the financial circumstances of the public authorities and family members involved. A flexible approach is necessary which has regard to the person's wishes and feelings and seeks to facilitate their attendance and participation in decisions affecting them. Depending on the particular circumstances, this may be achieved by their attendance at hearings; telephone hearings;

inviting and considering their letters and written representations; the use of advocates; a visit to the person at their home, hospital or place where they are detained; or by a combination of all of these approaches. See further, in this regard, chapters 10 and 15.

Litigation friends

4.110 Because the COPR are based on the Rules of the Supreme Court, rather than the Mental Health Tribunal Rules, they require (at present) the relevant person to have a litigation friend if they are made a party to the proceedings (or intend to be a party) and lack capacity to conduct the proceedings.[56] This issue is dealt with in chapter 10.

Case management

4.111 By COPR r5, the court is required to further the overriding objective by actively managing cases. Where the Case Management Pilot applies, the relevant rule is COPR Pr1.5, and the requirements upon the court to undertake active case management are significantly strengthened. See further chapter 9.

Hearings

4.112 Most hearings take place in court, but they can take place in a hospital, nursing home or other agreed venue where this is necessary in order to enable the relevant person to participate. As now retired District Judge Gordon Ashton OBE has observed on many occasions, the approach may be adversarial, inquisitorial or conciliatory according to the needs of the case.

4.113 Historically, the general rule in the Court of Protection has always been that hearings are held in private. This was considered to reflect the personal, private, nature of the information which the court is usually considering. However, a transparency pilot scheme has been in operation since 29 January 2016 (see *Court of Protection Practice Direction – Transparency Pilot*). This provides that the court will ordinarily now order that any attended hearing shall be in public, subject to certain restrictions in relation to the publication of information about the proceedings, in particular the identity of the person concerned and family members. See further chapter 13.

56 COPR r141(1).

Legal aid

4.114 For property and affairs cases, public funding is not available. In most kinds of personal welfare cases it is severely restricted, and where available generally means-assessed. This issue is dealt with in chapter 6.

Personal Support Unit (PSU)

4.115 The PSU volunteers at First Avenue House do not give legal advice. However, subject to resources, they may be able to support litigants in person by:
- prompting them to order their thoughts;
- tidying paperwork into a rational order, and indexing it;
- helping them to find out which forms they need to fill in, to complete them if they know what they want to say, and to take the paperwork to the appropriate customer service desk or court office;
- helping people find their way around the court building;
- assisting in discussions with court staff;
- going into court with the person to offer support;
- signposting clients to free legal advice or representation, or to access relevant advice online.

McKenzie friends and lay representation

McKenzie friends

4.116 Litigants who cannot arrange legal representation have the right to have reasonable assistance from a suitable layperson, sometimes called a 'McKenzie friend'.

4.117 A McKenzie friend may:
- provide moral support;
- take notes;
- help with case papers;
- quietly give advice on any aspect of the conduct of the case.

4.118 A McKenzie friend may not act as advocate or to carry out the conduct of litigation. Specifically, they may not:
- act as the litigant's agent in relation to the proceedings;
- manage the litigant's case outside court, for example by signing court documents;
- address the court, make oral submissions or examine witnesses.

See further chapter 6.

Lay representation

4.119 COPR r3A (COPR Pr1.2 where the Case Management Pilot applies) now provides that the court may appoint a non-legal representative for the relevant person. Their function is to provide the court with information about the person's wishes, feelings, beliefs and values, and to discharge any other functions directed by the court.

4.120 That rule aside, lay representation is not generally allowed. The court should only be prepared to grant a right of audience or a right to conduct litigation to a layperson where there is good reason to do so, taking into account all the circumstances of the case, which are likely to vary greatly. Such grants should not be extended to laypersons automatically or without due consideration, and should not be granted for mere convenience.

4.121 Examples of the type of special circumstances which have been held to justify the grant of a right of audience to a layperson, including a McKenzie friend, are that:

- the person is a close relative of the litigant;
- health problems preclude the litigant from addressing the court, or conducting litigation, and the litigant cannot afford to pay for a qualified legal representative;
- the litigant is relatively inarticulate and prompting by that person may unnecessarily prolong the proceedings.[57]

Appeals

4.122 The appellate court will not interfere with the original decision unless the judge erred in principle or reached a conclusion that was wrong. See further chapter 18.

Enforcement of orders and declarations

4.123 The court has all the powers of the High Court within the scope of its jurisdiction, and the COPR incorporate many of the enforcement provisions contained in the Civil Procedure Rules 1998. See further chapter 17.

---

57 In this respect, see the Practice Guidance: *McKenzie friends (Civil and Family Courts)* issued on 12 July 2010 by Lord Neuberger of Abbotsbury (the then Master of the Rolls) and Sir Nicholas Wall (the then President of the Family Division).

CHAPTER 5

Is an application appropriate?

5.1	Introduction
5.3	Maxims and principles
5.4	**Considering the evidence**
5.16	Analysing one's own case and evidence
5.17	Admissibility and weight of the evidence
5.21	The standard of proof
5.23	Evidence meeting
5.24	**Possible alternative remedies**
5.28	Non-contentious property and financial matters
	Steps to take • Lasting power of attorney • Enduring power of attorney Trusts • Banking arrangements • Limitations and disadvantages • Ordinary power of attorney • Appointeeships • Other options
5.76	Contentious property and financial matters
5.78	Non-contentious personal welfare matters
5.83	Contentious personal welfare matters

Introduction

5.1 There are many reasons why people 'go to law'. Not all of them are well thought out, and many people have later regretted doing so in haste. It is sensible, therefore, to consider carefully whether an application to the Court of Protection is necessary as a matter of law, or appropriate as being in the person's best interests.

5.2 The matters to think through before applying include the following:

Jurisdiction → Legal necessity → Appropriateness → Permission

JURISDICTION	
Does the Court of Protection have jurisdiction to consider the proposed application?	• There is little point applying to the court unless it has power to grant the remedy sought. • The court's jurisdiction is defined by the Mental Capacity Act (MCA) 2005. Most obviously, it is a jurisdiction exercisable only over people who lack (or, on an interim basis, appear to lack) capacity. • Remember that a person must be assumed to have capacity unless it is established that they lack capacity. Furthermore, a person is not to be treated as being unable to make their own decision unless all practicable steps to help them to do so have been taken without success, or merely because they make or propose making an unwise decision. • Even if the person is incapacitated, certain family law matters (such as consenting to the making of an adoption order) and Mental Health Act (MHA) matters (treatment without consent under that Act) are excluded from its jurisdiction: see sections 27 and 28. • Depending on the type of decision to be made, the court's jurisdiction may be restricted to incapacitated adults (eg statutory wills, lasting powers of attorney (LPAs)), to persons aged 16 or over (eg treatment or care issues) or available to people of all ages (property and financial affairs matters where the child's incapacity is likely to last into adulthood). • Court of Protection Rules (COPR) 2007 SI No 1744 r87 and Practice Direction (PD) 12B contain provisions for disputing the court's jurisdiction.

	LEGAL NECESSITY
Is an application necessary?	In various situations, an application is a legal necessity. For example, in the personal welfare sphere, a case involving non-therapeutic sterilisation or organ donation; in the financial sphere, situations where there is a need for someone with capacity to manage an incapacitated person's property.
	APPROPRIATENESS
Is an application appropriate?	Even if an application is not necessary, it may still be appropriate to apply because an application is reasonably believed to be in the relevant person's best interests. This is case-specific and depends on many things. For example: • Whether what is required can be done lawfully and in the person's best interests without the court's involvement (ask what is in their best interests having regard to their legal rights and circumstances). • The person's wishes, feelings, beliefs and values and all of the other relevant circumstances. • The likely benefits for the person concerned (ask in what ways the application will benefit them). • The likely cost for the person concerned, not just financially but emotionally if personal or family discord is likely to result (ask in what ways the application may cause them harm). • The affordability of proceedings for the relevant person. Even relatively modest costs may be unaffordable. The Court of Protection has the same status as the High Court and the fees charged for applications, legal assistance and reports tend to reflect this. It is essential to avoid *Jarndyce v Jarndyce* situations where the costs of litigation approach or exceed the value of the estate. Everyone involved is under a duty to deal with the underlying issues in a proportionate and cost-effective manner. • Who is at risk of bearing the litigation costs. It should not be assumed that whatever the merits of the application each party will pay their own litigation costs or that the costs will be recoverable from the incapacitated person's estate. The rules enable the court to have regard to the conduct of the parties, which includes their conduct before as well as during the proceedings, whether it was reasonable for them to raise, pursue or contest a particular issue, etc.

continued

	• The strength of the evidence and the chances of the application succeeding (is there sufficient evidence in support of it and is the court likely to be persuaded to exercise its powers?).
	• The suitability and appropriateness of the applicant (ought it to be obvious that another person such as a spouse or partner is better placed to apply and will reasonably object?).
	• Relevant guidance in the Codes of Practice.
	• The availability of more appropriate alternative procedures or remedies:
	  – Can the matter wait until the person recovers capacity and is able to take the decision for themselves?
	  – Is this the simplest and most appropriate legal way to address this person's needs?
	  – Can the purpose which the applicant has in mind be as effectively achieved in another way which is less restrictive of the person's rights and freedom of action?
	  – Where relevant, does the person still have capacity to complete an LPA or advance decision?
	  – Can what is proposed lawfully and appropriately be done in the person's best interests under MCA 2005 s5?
	  – Does anyone such as an attorney or deputy already have authority to make this decision for the person?
	  – Is it more appropriate to proceed under a different statute, eg guardianship under the MHA 1983, the Children Act 1989 or public health legislation?
	  – If the matter is contentious, are discussions and negotiations really at an end? Is there a possibility of mediation? Would the appointment of an independent mental capacity advocate (IMCA) or a person with a similar independent role help?

PERMISSION	

If permission to make the application is required, is it likely to be granted?	• In order to prevent applications which are frivolous, vexatious, an abuse of process or otherwise an illegitimate interference with the interests and rights of the relevant person, the court's permission is required to make some applications: see MCA 2005 s50 and COPR rr50–52.
	• When deciding whether to grant permission, MCA 2005 s50(3) requires the court to consider:
	  (a) the applicant's connection with the person concerned;
	  (b) the reasons for the asking the court to appoint a deputy to make personal welfare decisions for the person concerned;

> (c) in what ways the person concerned will benefit from having a deputy appointed to make personal welfare decisions for them;
> (d) whether those benefits can be achieved in any other way.
> - Even when permission is required, it is simply a filtering stage. Permission ought to be granted where, having regard to these and any other relevant considerations, on the material available to the court the application deserves fuller investigation by it and, realistically, the order sought may be in the best interests of the relevant person.

Maxims and principles

5.3   Opinion varies otherwise it would not be an opinion. Having acknowledged that, there is a good case for saying that the following common-sense maxims and principles have proved their utility when it comes to reflecting on whether to intervene in someone else's life:

1) First, do no harm – there are many we cannot help, but none we cannot avoid harming. This principle is as important to the practice of law as it is to the practice of medicine.[1]
2) Give due weight to the importance for the person concerned of their liberty and wish to determine their own course in life.
3) In order to avoid disappointment later, be realistic about the proper function of the law and its limits. One can legislate for marriage but not for a happy marriage. The law provides a useful framework for managing conflict, conferring authority, enforcing legal duties and restraining the unlawful exercise of power. It cannot solve family conflict and underlying resentment, that feeling of not being a loved or favoured child, a scarcity of resources, the disease process itself or the fact that the person concerned must soon die.
4) Accept that risk cannot be avoided. All personal welfare decisions involve balancing competing risks of which the risk to the person's physical safety is but one. Where appropriate, in order to avoid practising too defensively consider applying (or applying in the alternative) for a declaration that it *is* lawful and in the person's best interests to take the conventional safeguarding risk rather

---

[1] 'The wicked are wicked, no doubt, and they go astray and they fall, and they come by their deserts; but who can tell the mischief which the very virtuous do?,' Thackeray, *The Newcomes,* Book 1 chapter 20. There is a great deal to be said for 'legal homeopathy': the application of minute, sub-clinical, doses of law. That is tongue-in-cheek, but the lightest touch is often the best.

than to avoid it (by, for example, separating them from their life-partner and removing them to a care home). Let the judge take the strain; that is why they are there.

5) Consider the adequacy of your evidence.

Considering the evidence

5.4 Lawyers spend much time discussing new case-law and the nuances of particular sections. However, for every case lost on a point of law, a thousand are lost for want of evidence; and a few more for procedural reasons such as missing time-limits and non-compliance with directions.

5.5 The lawyers' old maxim 'only a fool bags himself as a brief' acknowledges that everyone finds it difficult to be objective about a case in which they have a strong personal interest.

5.6 Much litigation in the Court of Protection is the result of historic family tensions, in particular disagreements between siblings and step-relations. Strained relationships over many years now colour each child's personal assessment of the evidence as to which of them is best placed to take on day-to-day decision-making for an incapacitated parent.

5.7 Where there are longstanding family issues and an application is likely to be opposed, it is sensible to take legal advice on the evidence and merits of a possible application. Litigation is easy to start, often demanding to pursue and sometimes costly to withdraw or settle.

5.8 Given human nature, it is also often quite easy for a person to satisfy themselves that an application for a proposed gift or will in their favour is one in the incapacitated person's best interests. Again, it is prudent to take neutral advice on the weight of the evidence and what to expect before setting out. At this point the question to ask is not 'What do I make of it?' but 'What is a judge likely to make of it?'

5.9 In the case of local authority safeguarding applications, evidential problems often have a different cause. Local safeguarding investigations rarely involve full disclosure, forensic questioning or independent scrutiny. Consequently, in court the findings reached may not withstand that level of scrutiny. See further chapter 23 in relation to the interaction between safeguarding obligations and going to the Court of Protection.

5.10 To summarise, before embarking on litigation that is likely to be contested it is particularly important to assess objectively the strength of one's case and the adequacy of one's evidence.

Example

5.11 Mrs Smith is a 95-year-old widow who suffers from moderate to severe dementia. She lives with her son and daughter-in-law, Ms Jones. She is taken to a day centre three times a week by a paid carer. Staff at the day centre notice that she has a bruise and Mrs Smith says that her daughter-in-law caused it and that she is frightened of her. Wessex County Council are contacted and place Mrs Smith in a care home under a 'DOLS order' (Deprivation of Liberty Safeguards), ie a standard authorisation. Several months later, an adult safeguarding investigation concludes on the balance of probabilities that the bruising was non-accidental. The family start Court of Protection proceedings seeking a declaration that it is in Mrs Smith's best interests to return home.

What is the local authority's submission?	That it is in Mrs Smith's best interests not to return to the family home and that she should remain in the care home.
What is the local authority trying to prove?	Ill-treatment by her family.
How does it prove this?	By evidence.
What is the evidence?	The evidence consists of: i) the fact that bruising was observed by care home staff; and ii) Mrs Smith's statement as to its cause.
How reliable is the evidence?	Given that the family deny ill-treatment, the key evidential questions are: a) What is the evidence that the bruising is of a kind consistent with non-accidental injury? b) What is the evidence that Mrs Smith is or is not a reliable witness of events, eg that her dementia has not affected her reliability, that she was not led in her account and that she is not motivated by malice?

continued

5.12 As to a), bruising may be related to factors such as age, gender, health status and medication. It is necessary to consider the location, age and pattern of the bruising and any other injuries, the physical indicators of abuse, the behavioural indicators of abuse and the pool of possible perpetrators. Ideally, an applicant requires expert contemporaneous mapping and recording of the injuries by a forensic medical examiner and expert interpretation of the evidence recorded by this examination.

5.13 Although one would never take a child care order application to court without obtaining this evidence, strangely, in the case of alleged elder abuse this is very rarely obtained; and by the time the case comes to court, it is too late to obtain it.

5.14 As to b), there are clear evidential problems given the severity of Mrs Smith's dementia, the passage of time, the fact that the allegations are strongly denied and the number of demonstrably inaccurate allegations made by her in respect of other people.

5.15 By the time of the trial, the situation facing the local authority is that there are a number of possible explanations and a pool of possible perpetrators of any non-accidental injury. The alleged perpetrator has no relevant history and Mrs Smith has been living with her family for some years with no previous concerns of this kind being raised. On the evidence, it is accepted that Mrs Smith has made other allegations which must be the result of confusion. The key evidential omission was not obtaining contemporaneous medical evidence and a forensic opinion on the significance (if any) of the bruising.

Analysing one's own case and evidence

5.16 The approach adopted in the following table is not a substitute for analysing the evidence and taking appropriate advice in each particular case. It is merely an example of how one can devise a simple structure to test the quality and internal consistency of one's own case.

	Example 1	Example 2	Example 3
Type of case	Place of residence dispute	Suitability of a deputy	Contact dispute
Jurisdiction: can the court do what you want? (the application)	The court may determine P's place of residence (MCA 2005 s17)	The court may revoke a deputy's appointment (MCA 2005 s16)	The court may decide contact issues (MCA 2005 s17)

Is an application appropriate? 125

	Example 1	Example 2	Example 3
The local authority's best interests submission (the submission)	It is in P's best interests to reside at care home X, not at her own home	It is in P's best interests to remove his current deputy	It is in P's best interests not to have unsupervised contact with Y
What the local authority is alleging/seeking to prove (the findings sought)	Ill-treatment at home by relatives	The existing deputy has stolen money from P	Sexually inappropriate behaviour by Y
The evidence for the allegation (the facts which prove the allegation)	Bruising P's oral account	Bank statements Failure to account Failure to explain	Staff observations P's oral account
Possible alternative explanations which will need to be ruled out on the balance of probabilities (likely defences)	Innocent alternative cause of the bruising P is an unreliable witness	P gifted the money P has capacity P owed the money Money spent on P	P has capacity/consents P enjoys sexual contact Faulty observation P is an unreliable witness
Evidence re any less restrictive options	Exclude a particular relative or restrict contact with them? Arrange alternative carers?	Retrospective validation of the transaction if no dishonesty, etc	The friendship is in P's best interests
P = the incapacitated person			

Admissibility and weight of the evidence

5.17   Evidence is discussed in detail in chapter 12, but nowadays there are few strict rules concerning the admissibility of evidence, particularly in the Court of Protection.

5.18   Part 14 of the COPR deals with evidence and the court's power to control it. Subject to complying with the rules, the court's discretion and the odd caveat, the general position is simply that to be admissible evidence must be relevant. 'Relevance' means relevant to the issues which the court must decide and evidence is relevant if it makes a matter which requires proof more or less probable.[2]

5.19 If evidence is relevant, one must next consider the weight which a court is likely to give it, that is how credible and persuasive it is. The case may consist of a mixture of agreed first-hand evidence (things actually said to or observed by a witness), disputed first-hand evidence, valid and invalid inferences from agreed or disputed first-hand evidence, hearsay (agreed or disputed 'facts' communicated to a witness), inferences from hearsay, assumptions and suspicions ('It must be, or is likely to be, the case that . . .'), professional presumptions, professional opinions, 'independent expert opinions'.

5.20 If a matter is likely to be contested, some of the questions to consider at this stage are:

- Can all of our 'evidence' be used in court? (This often raises issues of confidentiality; the availability, willingness and compellability of witnesses; and the unrepeatability of some suspicions and corridor conversations.)
- What are the gaps in our evidence?
- Assuming the facts are as stated, are the inferences that have been drawn valid?
- What are the weaknesses in our case?
- How impressive are our witnesses and how expert is our expert evidence?
- What will the other side be saying or putting to our witnesses?
- Does the other side have any good points and is their evidence accurate and reliable?
- Even if our witnesses are right, do we have sufficient evidence that we can provide a better alternative for the incapacitated person to the situation which we are trying to remedy?

The standard of proof

5.21 The standard of proof in Court of Protection proceedings is always 'the balance of probabilities'. However, to leave it there is an oversimplification. The more serious the allegation the less likely it is that the event occurred. Hence, the stronger should be the evidence

---

2 See *Director of Public Prosecutions v Kilbourne* [1973] AC 729, 756. As Lord Bingham once noted, contested trials last long enough as it is without spending time on evidence which is irrelevant and cannot affect the outcome.

before the court concludes that the allegation is established on the balance of probability:[3]

> The balance of probability standard means that a court is satisfied an event occurred if the court considers that, on the evidence, the occurrence of the event was more likely than not. When assessing the probabilities the court will have in mind as a factor, to whatever extent is appropriate in the particular case, that the more serious the allegation the less likely it is that the event occurred and, hence, the stronger should be the evidence before the court concludes that the allegation is established on the balance of probability. Fraud is usually less likely than negligence. Deliberate physical injury is usually less likely than accidental physical injury. A step-father is usually less likely to have repeatedly raped and had non-consensual oral sex with his under age stepdaughter than on some occasion to have lost his temper and slapped her. Built into the preponderance of probability standard is a generous degree of flexibility in respect of the seriousness of the allegation.
>
> Although the result is much the same, this does not mean that where a serious allegation is in issue the standard of proof required is higher. It means only that the inherent probability or improbability of an event is itself a matter to be taken into account when weighing the probabilities and deciding whether, on balance, the event occurred. The more improbable the event, the stronger must be the evidence that it did occur before, on the balance of probability, its occurrence will be established. Ungoed-Thomas J expressed this neatly in *In re Dellow's Will Trusts* [1964] 1 WLR 451, 455:
>
>> 'The more serious the allegation the more cogent is the evidence required to overcome the unlikelihood of what is alleged and thus to prove it.'
>
> This substantially accords with the approach adopted in authorities such as the well known judgment of Morris LJ in *Hornal v Neuberger Products Ltd* [1957] 1 QB 247, 266. This approach also provides a means by which the balance of probability standard can accommodate one's instinctive feeling that even in civil proceedings a court should be more sure before finding serious allegations proved than when deciding less serious or trivial matters.

5.22   It is also necessary to consider the setting within which the 'evidence' was given; as to this, see the observations of McFarlane J (as he then was) in *Re SA*:[4]

> 68. When looking at evidence from a witness who is engaged in providing therapy to an individual who then, during the course of the therapeutic relationship, makes statements which are then produced

---

3   *Re H (minors) (sexual abuse: standard of proof)* [1995] UKHL 16 paras 73–75; [1996] AC 563, D–H.
4   [2010] EWHC 196 (Admin).

as evidence of the truth, the words of Butler-Sloss LJ in *Re D (Child Abuse: Interviews)* [1998] 2 FLR 10 must be borne in mind:

> 'It is essential to distinguish between interviewing the child to ascertain the facts and interviewing to provide the child with help to unburden her worries. The therapeutic interview would seem to me to be generally unsuited to use as part of the court evidence, although there may be rare cases in which it is necessary to use it.'

69. Often the therapist will alert others to matters of concern arising from the therapeutic interview and the child or vulnerable person may then be subject to an interview aimed at the forensic process – as indeed happened here with the ABE interview. In the event the ABE interview did not provide any evidence to support the local authority case and thus reliance is made on the original statements made to AL. I do not regard AJ's reports as being inadmissible or to be automatically of no weight, but I do have regard to the observations of Butler-Sloss LJ and, the reasons behind them, in being cautious as to the amount of weight that can be attached to the material that originates from the drama therapy sessions.'

Evidence meeting

5.23 Time and resources permitting, there is a lot to be said for having an evidence meeting before issuing what is likely to be a contested application.

Possible alternative remedies

5.24 The practice of law is concerned with remedies – people go to a lawyer or a court for the same reason they see a doctor, in order to obtain a remedy.

5.25 Sometimes there will be a more appropriate alternative to making an application to the Court of Protection.

5.26 Most courts deal only with litigious matters. The Court of Protection is unusual in that much of its work, particularly on the property and financial side, is non-litigious. Here there is often a common goal, which is to put in place a protective legal framework for a person who is unable to protect and promote their own personal interests.

5.27 The remainder of this chapter considers or lists possible alternative remedies under the following headings:

- Non-contentious property and financial matters;
- Contentious property and financial matters;

- Non-contentious personal welfare matters; and
- Contentious personal welfare matters.

Non-contentious property and financial matters

Steps to take

5.28 Where a person appears to be incapable of managing their property and affairs or a particular transaction, the first step is to verify this. Capacity often fluctuates, no one is to be found incapable unless all practicable steps to help them make their own decision have been taken unsuccessfully, the correct legal test must be applied and the answer may depend on the significance and complexity of the matter in hand.

5.29 If the person does lack capacity, the second step is to establish if and when they may recover capacity, and whether the decision(s) can be postponed until they are able to act for themselves.

5.30 If a decision is required now, the third step is to check whether arrangements are already in place for managing the situation. For example, did the person execute an enduring power of attorney (EPA) or LPA when they had capacity, or has a deputy already been authorised to make decisions of this kind?

5.31 If not, the fourth step is the check whether the person's affairs are sufficiently complicated to require the appointment of a deputy or whether an alternative procedure will or may suffice.

5.32 The court process for appointing a deputy is not onerous in most cases. It consists of ensuring that there is adequate evidence of incapacity, information about the person's finances, identifying possible conflicts of interest and ensuring that close family members are notified and have an opportunity to object to the proposed arrangement.

5.33 However, the appointed deputy must then usually take out security, file annual reports with the Public Guardian, pay an annual supervision fee and so forth. It is therefore worth considering whether there are any other suitable ways of managing the person's finances in their best interests which avoid supervision of what hitherto has been the individual's private life and all the expense that goes with that.

5.34 Some of the main options are those given in the following table, which is based on one in Ashton's *Elderly people and the law*:[5]

---

5 G Ashton, *Elderly people and the law*, Butterworths, London, 1995, p299.

```
                    ┌─────────────────┐
                    │ Relevant Person │
                    └─────────────────┘
         ┌─────────────────┼─────────────────┐
┌─────────────┐   ┌─────────────┐   ┌─────────────┐
│  Survives   │   │  Does not   │   │  Requires   │
│  incapacity │   │   survive   │   │  incapacity │
│             │   │  incapacity │   │             │
└─────────────┘   └─────────────┘   └─────────────┘
   ┌──┴──┐      ┌────┬────┬────┐      ┌────┬────┬────┐
┌──────┐┌─────┐┌──────┐┌──────┐┌─────┐┌──────┐┌──────┐
│Lasting││Trust││Joint ││Ordinary││Appointee-││Other:││Deputy│
│Power ││     ││banking││Power ││ship ││Necessaries││application│
│of    ││     ││mandates││of   ││     ││Direct ││or court│
│Attorney││   ││      ││Attorney││   ││Payments││order │
└──────┘└─────┘└──────┘└──────┘└─────┘└──────┘└──────┘
```

Lasting power of attorney

5.35 The best way of avoiding the need for a court-appointed deputy is for the relevant person to execute an LPA, provided of course that they still have capacity to do so.

5.36 The important point to bear in mind is that a person may lack capacity to manage their property and affairs in a general sense, so that the court could lawfully appoint a deputy to manage their estate, but still have sufficient capacity to execute an LPA.

5.37 In other words, the person concerned may retain sufficient capacity to be able to make their own arrangements for the future management of their estate. If so, they can appoint (say) their spouse or partner as their attorney, which avoids the need for the latter to apply to be appointed as their deputy.

5.38 The possibility arises because capacity is 'issue-specific' and depends on the transaction or decision in hand.

5.39 Because the relevant individual's capacity is borderline in such cases, it is imperative to ensure that the certificate of capacity is completed by an independent professional such as a general practitioner or solicitor and to establish that close family members and any other key individuals accept the capacity finding.

5.40 Provided there is nothing untoward, the arrangement has clear advantages in terms of maintaining the historic privacy, simplicity and trust of a long-standing relationship. Although there is a fee to be paid for registering an LPA, this is less than the standard court fee payable when filing a deputy application.

Enduring power of attorney

5.41 Once the MCA 2005 came into force on 1 October 2007 it was no longer possible to execute an EPA. However, EPAs made before then were not revoked by the Act and continue to have legal effect, subject to the need for registration if the attorney has reason to believe that the donor is becoming mentally incapable of managing and administering their property and affairs.

Trusts

5.42 It is possible for a person who is concerned that they may be becoming mentally incapacitated to create a trust. This involves transferring money and assets to trustees on terms that require the trustees to manage the trust fund for the benefit of the individual who has created it (and perhaps for the benefit of others also). The relevant test is whether the person has capacity to make the trust at the same time and *Re Beaney*[6] provides some guidance as to this.

5.43 As Ashton noted in 1995, this approach lost some popularity once it became possible for an individual who was beginning to lose capacity to create an EPA. It was then easy for them to enter into a lasting arrangement with a trusted person for the latter to manage the former's property as their agent without the need to create a trust and give up legal ownership of the property to trustees.

There is usually a tension between the settlor's various objectives. He or she will often wish to retain ultimate control over the money and to be able to call for it to be spent on them. However, to obtain tax advantages or to avoid it being taken into account in the assessment of means-tested benefits, it is usually necessary to give up any form of control.

5.44 The tax consequences of placing money in trust need to be carefully considered, as do the extent to which the trustees will be legally obliged to maintain the person who created it. In addition, unless the trust was of a very specific nature, and entered into before there was any reason to believe that the settlor may need residential or nursing care it is extremely unlikely that the trust would be effective at sheltering assets from local authority assessment. Professional advice is essential if a trust is being contemplated. For these reasons the trust is no longer popular as a vehicle for planning for future incapacity.

Banking arrangements

5.45 Joint accounts and other banking arrangements often seem an attractive proposition from a planning point of view compared with other more formal mechanisms. However, as with all mechanisms, they also have limitations and drawbacks.

6 [1978] 2 All ER 595.

Third-party mandates

5.46 An account holder who has mental capacity can authorise someone to access their account, for example because they have physical disabilities. This is called a 'third-party mandate'.[7] A common alternative is for an individual to appoint someone to act as their agent under an ordinary power of attorney. However, neither arrangement survives mental incapacity.

Joint bank accounts

5.47 It is, of course, common for people to operate a joint account with a spouse, partner, child or other trusted person. A joint account involves two different kinds of legal relationship:

Legal relationship between the joint account holders	This is a private matter for the individuals. The individuals agree who pays what amounts in, what may be withdrawn, how the money in the account is split, how any borrowing on the account will be repaid.
Their legal relationship with the bank	This is controlled by a document called a mandate or authority which each joint-account holder must sign. Often this document forms part of the joint-account application form. Depending on the terms of the mandate, either or both account-holders can withdraw money separately or two signatures may be required.
	Either way, the general position is that both are individually as well as jointly responsible for all debts on the account, even if one of them puts all the money in and one of them takes all of it out. For this reason, on becoming aware that one of the joint account-holders lacks capacity, a bank will often cancel the joint authority to withdraw funds and effectively 'freeze' the account.
	The legal justification is that authority to sign on a joint account entails a continuing consent which is broken by mental incapacity. From the bank's viewpoint, there is also a risk management issue if one of the account holders lacks capacity to monitor the account and understand how the funds are spent.

Source: 'You and your joint account' (AE256), British Bankers' Association Enterprises, July 2013.

---

7 *Guidance for people wanting to manage a bank account for someone else*, AE254, March 2013, British Bankers' Association, Pinners Hall, 105–108 Old Broad Street, London EC2N 1EX.

Is an application appropriate? 133

5.48 There is no single procedure which all banks and building societies adopt when a joint account-holder loses capacity. Different banks have different procedures. The degree of flexibility may sometimes depend on their knowledge of the account and their relationship with the account-holders. In some cases the bank may continue to pay pre-existing direct debits and standing orders for utilities, household bills, residential care fees and living expenses until a deputy has been appointed or a power of attorney has been registered.

Joint accounts and attorneys

5.49 If one joint account holder loses the capacity to operate their account and a registered EPA or LPA is in place, the bank will allow the attorney and account holder with capacity to operate the account independently unless the account holder with capacity objects. In such cases the bank will then usually only allow the account to continue to operate on a 'both-to-sign' basis.[8]

Limitations and disadvantages

5.50 The effect of the death of either account holder may be a particularly relevant consideration if one of them is frail. The general (but rebuttable) rule is that on death money in a joint account passes to the surviving account holder. This leaves room for disagreement in some cases if a parent's will provides for dividing their estate equally among all of their children. In practice, in the event of a dispute about the ownership of funds in an account this will come down to evidence as to the sources of the funds in the account.[9]

5.51 A second disadvantage relates to local authority means assessments. There can be a risk that some of the non-incapacitated account

---

8 *Guidance for people wanting to manage a bank account for someone else* (see fn 7 above).
9 The mere fact that the legal title to an account is held in two names does not mean that the beneficial title is held in the same manner – an example of the money in a joint bank account belonging beneficially to one of its signatories can be found in *Day v Harris* [2013] COPLR 254. The beneficial ownership of joint bank accounts is often a difficult question. One difficulty is often proving what was intended, and is often complicated by the competing presumptions of result trust and advancement. *Re Figgis* [1969] 1 Ch 123 is a case where the presumption of advancement was held to apply when a husband in ailing health put an account in his, and his wife's, joint names. In *Re Bishop* [1965] Ch 540 a husband and wife who had contributed unequally to a joint account were each held to be entitled to draw on the proceeds for joint purposes or for their own purpose (the presumption of advancement is to be abolished from a date to be appointed: Equality Act 2010 s199).

holder's funds are means-assessed by the local authority when it comes to assessing the contribution payable towards the incapacitated person's care home costs.

5.52 A third disadvantage materialises where a person added to the account then withdraws funds from it for their own benefit. If both had authority to draw on the account, it can be very difficult to prove that the withdrawals were not authorised and difficult to recover the funds.

Ordinary power of attorney

5.53 An ordinary or general power of attorney can be effective for a specified period of time (for example, to cover a trip abroad) or run indefinitely until the donor brings it to an end by revoking it. The authority granted by the document is automatically revoked if the donor becomes mentally incapacitated.

5.54 Because the donor must be legally competent, an ordinary or general power of attorney does not need to be registered by the Public Guardian.

Appointeeships

5.55 A deputyship may be unnecessary where the person's income consists solely of a state pension or benefits and they have no savings or equity in a house that needs to be sold.

5.56 In such cases, a spouse, partner or other suitable person can apply to the Department for Work and Pensions (DWP) for the pension or benefits to be paid to them as the person's 'appointee'. The appointee is authorised to receive the benefits and manage the benefit income. The appointee has various responsibilities and functions. The appointee:

- must report any change in the person's circumstances that may affect benefit entitlement;
- may sign on behalf of the person if they are a non-tax payer to enable bank and building society interest to be paid without deducting income tax;
- can only deal with the person's income from benefits, except for small amounts of savings which can be used to meet unforeseen emergencies.

5.57 Once the proposed appointee has completed the usual form, a representative from the DWP may visit the relevant person or ask for evidence confirming that they are no longer able to act on their own behalf.

Is an application appropriate? 135

5.58 Current departmental guidance is that the appointee should, wherever possible, be a close relative who lives with the person or visits them frequently. In certain circumstances, the appointee may be a friend, neighbour or professional carer.

5.59 An appointee who does not wish to continue in the role can resign and the DWP can revoke an appointeeship if it has evidence that the appointee is not acting in the person's best interests.

5.60 The regulations provide that a court-appointed deputy automatically becomes the relevant person's appointee in place of any existing appointee, but are silent as to the effect of registering an EPA or LPA.

Limitations and disadvantages

5.61 The limitations of an appointeeship arrangement are fairly obvious: an appointee does not have authority to deal with capital or with other income belonging to the incapacitated person. A court order and/or the appointment of a deputy will be necessary if authority is required to manage other assets which the relevant person lacks capacity to manage, such as real property, personal possessions, cars, shares and so on.

5.62 Unspent pension and benefits may constitute capital. The general view for some time now has been that a deputy application is unnecessary provided that the appointee only holds a 'reasonable sum' of accrued savings. However, some banks set limits on the amount of money that a person can have in an appointeeship account.

Other options

5.63 A number of other provisions are helpful on occasion.

Payment for necessary goods and services

5.64 MCA 2005 s7(1) provides that: 'If necessary goods or services are supplied to a person who lacks capacity to contract for the supply, he must pay a reasonable price for them.' By subsection (2), 'necessary' means suitable to a person's condition in life and to his actual requirements at the time when the goods or services are supplied.

5.65 This provision combined the old common law rule relating to services with the statutory rule in the Sale of Goods Act 1979 relating to goods. Thus, if the milkman carries on delivering milk to the house of someone who has a progressive dementia, they can expect to be paid. If, however, a roofer puts a completely unnecessary new roof on to that person's house, when all that was required was a minor repair, then the rule will not apply.

Expenditure on the person's behalf

5.66 MCA 2005 s8(1) provides that where someone does an act to which section 5 applies which involves expenditure in connection with another person's care or treatment then it is lawful for them to pledge payment from the person's estate and also to apply money in the person's possession to meet the expenditure.

5.67 Furthermore, if expenditure is borne on the person's behalf by the individual acting under section 5, it is lawful for the latter to reimburse themselves from any money in the person's possession or to be otherwise indemnified by them.

5.68 This restates the common law rules which provided that a person acting as an 'agent of necessity' for another person should not be out of pocket as a result. However, nothing in the clause allows a carer to gain access to the relevant person's funds where they are held by a third party such as a bank or building society.

Direct payments

5.69 Direct payments are local authority cash payments for people who have been assessed as being entitled to help from social services and who would like to arrange and pay for their own, independently contracted, care and support services.

5.70 Where a person with eligible needs lacks capacity to consent to the making of direct payments, a suitable person can be appointed to manage the payments on their behalf.[10] This could be an attorney, deputy, DWP appointee or other person such as a carer.

5.71 The suitable person is the only person who can access and manage the direct payment. The account should be in their name but identified as being held on behalf of the person the payments are for (for example, 'Joan Smith on behalf of Edward Smith').[11]

---

10 See (in England) Care Act 2014 s32, and the Care and Support (Direct Payments) Regulations 2014 SI No 2871. In Wales, the relevant provisions are contained in the Social Services and Well-being (Wales) Act 2014 s50 and the Care and Support (Direct Payments) (Wales) Regulations 2015 SI No 1815.
11 *Guidance for people wanting to manage a bank account for someone else* (see fn 7 above).

Personal health budgets

5.72 Since October 2014, people receiving NHS Continuing Healthcare at home have had the right to receive a personal health budget. This can be paid to someone suitable on behalf of an incapacitated person: see regulations 5 and 6 of the National Health Service (Direct Payments) Regulations 2013[12] which are concerned with the appointment of representatives and nominees for incapacitated persons.

Court orders other than deputyship

5.73 Where the authority of the Court of Protection is required, it is not always necessary to appoint a deputy.

5.74 The court is frequently asked to make single orders dealing with matters such as authorising an individual to sign or surrender a tenancy agreement, to litigate on an incapacitated person's behalf, to access their health or social care records, to challenge NHS funding decisions, to ratify a gift and so on. In some cases it ought not to be necessary to obtain a court order, for example in relation to access to records, but the applicant has been frustrated in their attempts to persuade the relevant authority that they are suitable or that the step is in the incapacitated individual's best interests.

5.75 Apart from one judge who occasionally does so, the court no longer makes the kind of old-style 'short order' previously made under the pre-MCA legislation or any contemporary variant of it. However, the legislation does include the principle that a single order is to be preferred to the appointment of a deputy and some estates are small and simple enough that what is required can be achieved in a single order.

Contentious property and financial matters

5.76 Litigation or some formal action may be inevitable if a matter is contentious. The alternative ways forward then need to be explored. Consider the time limits for each possible court action[13] or complaint, the funding options for each and the remedies afforded by each. The aggrieved person needs to be clear about the outcome they wish to achieve – damages, the reversal of a funding decision, better services, disciplinary proceedings, the investigation and deregistration of a care home or service provider, an injunction, a prosecution, an

---

12 SI No 1617.
13 Where the claim is not for damages but what is known as equitable relief, for example an injunction, the equitable defence of laches (unreasonable delay in bringing the claim) may be raised.

apology, publicity – and who has power to provide that kind of remedy. Remember that the Court of Protection is not a regulatory, investigatory or complaints body, nor is it an inspectorate. Ombudsmen and regulators usually require that a complaint has been investigated locally and the service provider been given a fair opportunity to deal with the situation before considering a complaint.

5.77 Where possible, take professional legal advice or advice from Citizens Advice or a similar organisation. Be fair. Avoid multiple complaints to multiple bodies. This demoralises professionals, creates chaos and delay and damages the complainant's case. Be polite – apart from the fact that unpleasant emails and tweets are upsetting for those concerned, and may constitute a criminal offence, they are damaging when later produced in court and may have a bearing on who pays the litigation costs. Most important of all, if any step is being taken on behalf of an incapacitated person, remember that you must act in their best interests. Therefore apply the MCA 2005 s4 considerations and try to maintain a good relationship, or at least a working relationship, with their professional carers, family members, representatives and friends.

PROPERTY AND FINANCIAL AFFAIRS – POSSIBLE ALTERNATIVE REMEDIES	
Remedy	Possible relevance
MCA 2005 matters	
Best interests meetings	If the contentious matter is connected with different opinions as to what is in an incapacitated person's best interests with regard to their property and finances, consider whether there is a professional such as a solicitor or a neutral family member who could convene a best interests meeting. Explore what kinds of formal mediation and alternative dispute resolution (ADR) are available locally.
Complaints about a deputy or donee	• The Public Guardian supervises court-appointed deputies and deals with representations (including complaints) about the way in which a deputy or donee of an LPA is exercising their powers. These functions may be discharged in co-operation with any other person who has relevant safeguarding functions such as a local authority or the police. • On application by the Public Guardian, the Court of Protection can order that any security bond in place is 'called in' to make good the loss.

Is an application appropriate? 139

Remedy	Possible relevance
Complaints about court funds	Contrary to inaccurate press reports, the Court of Protection does not hold or administer funds on behalf of incapacitated people. It is the Court Funds Office (CFO) which provides a banking and administration service for the civil courts throughout England and Wales. See the Court Funds Rules 2011 SI No 1734 or contact the Court Funds Office, Glasgow G58 1AB.
Complaints about an NHS or social services funding decision	
NHS	As to appeals against NHS decisions that a person does not qualify for NHS continuing healthcare, see the section below dealing with personal welfare matters.
Local authority	As to local authority community care means assessments and charges, see the section below dealing with personal welfare matters.
Ombudsmen and regulatory bodies	
Ombudsmen	Depending on the nature of the grievance, a number of ombudsmen and regulatory bodies may exercise a relevant function: • The Financial Ombudsman Service deals with complaints about banking, insurance, loans, credit and other financial services. • The Pensions Ombudsman deals with complaints and disputes about the way that occupational pension schemes and personal pensions are run. The complainant must usually have asked the Pensions Advisory Service for assistance first. • The Solicitors Regulation Authority (SRA) is a regulatory body which deals with failures to comply with professional obligations such as the duty to keep the person's affairs confidential or the duty to act honestly and with integrity. • The Bar Standards Board (BSB) is the equivalent regulatory body for barristers. • The Legal Ombudsman deals with complaints that a poor service has been provided by a barrister, solicitor or legal executive, eg a failure to keep the client properly informed. • The Housing Ombudsman Service deals with complaints from people who receive a direct service from registered social landlords in England and certain other landlords who are members of the scheme, including bodies which take over homes transferred from local authorities. *continued*

Remedy	Possible relevance
Raising the matter with an elected representative or publicising it	
MP	A request to the relevant person's MP concerning the provision of a public service often produces positive action. However, MPs cannot properly become involved in litigation issues being dealt with by a court.
Councillor	Similarly, a request to the person's local councillor about the provision of social services by (or through) the local authority can be effective.
Media/press	This may be an option but it is a legal minefield and one to be exercised with tremendous caution in relation to someone who lacks capacity to decide for themselves whether to waive their usual right to privacy and confidentiality. Consider their capacity to make the decision for themselves, whether *you* have any legal right to waive their right to privacy or confidentiality, whether therefore you may be liable to the incapacitated person, the best interests considerations in MCA 2005 s4, the law relating to defamation (libel, slander) and the legal rights and remedies of the other people involved.
Other kinds of legal proceedings (civil)	
Actions relating to vulnerable or incapacitated persons	• As to the enforceability of contracts entered into by an incapacitated person, a contract is not enforceable against them if a) the relevant person was incapable of understanding the nature of the contract they were entering into and b) the other contracting party knew of their incapacity at the time, or knew of such facts and circumstances that they must be taken to have known of the incapacity. A separate rule applies to the supply of necessary goods and services, which is now set out in MCA 2005 s7. • A gift made by an incapacitated person may be avoided in the circumstances set out in *Re Beaney* ([1978] 2 All ER 595 at 600). In the case of a simple and trivial gift, such as giving a small present to a friend, there is not much to it and very little to grasp in order to make a valid gift. More significant transactions – those where the reasonably foreseeable consequences are more significant for the person concerned – by definition require the capacity to understand and weigh the more significant consequences. • Unless the commission of a tort (civil wrong) requires specific intention, such as malice, avoiding legal liability may be limited to acts done while in a state of automatism, although there is a lack of recent authority.

Is an application appropriate? 141

Remedy	Possible relevance
Standard actions	• The common law duties of an attorney include duties a) of utmost good faith, b) to keep accounts, c) to disclose all relevant facts in certain transactions, d) not to make secret profits, e) to discharge duties with reasonable care. The relevant person has the usual range of available remedies in relation to breach of trust, breach of contract and torts (other civil wrongs which give rise to a right to a remedy, eg conversion, deceit, trespass to land, trespass to goods, nuisance, negligence).
Other kinds of legal proceedings (criminal)	
Offences relating to vulnerable or incapacitated persons	Fraud Act 2006 s4 (abuse of position) makes it a criminal offence where a person intentionally and dishonestly takes advantage of their position.
Standard offences	Incapacitated persons have the protection of the usual criminal laws relating to property, theft, fraud, false accounting, etc. Where justified, a concerned person may ask for an investigation to be undertaken by the police, the local authority adult safeguarding team, the DWP Fraud Investigation Unit or the fraud unit of a bank or other financial institution.

Non-contentious personal welfare matters

5.78 Non-contentious routine care and treatment is usually provided under the protection of MCA 2005 s5 without any application to a court.

5.79 If the relevant person still has capacity to appoint an attorney in relation to their future care and treatment, or some aspect of it, then this mechanism ensures that decisions are always made either with their own consent or that of a trusted person. They may also wish to consider making an advance decision to refuse treatment.

5.80 Direct payments and personal health budgets paid to a suitable person acting for, and hopefully with, the individual also enable care and treatment to be provided in a way which is consistent with the principles of the MCA 2005.

5.81 Guardianship under the MHA 1983 can provide a useful light-touch safety-net for citizens who are vulnerable to self-neglect or abuse but historically it is not favoured by local authorities, for reasons that appear to be almost entirely irrelevant.

5.82 The Children Act 1989 provides an alternative age-dependant framework in some cases.

Contentious personal welfare matters

5.83 Most personal welfare litigation in the Court of Protection involves either:
- a public authority (such as a local authority or NHS trust) in dispute with a person alleged to lack capacity and/or one or more family members; or
- a dispute between family members, in particular siblings, as to what personal welfare arrangements are in an incapacitated person's best interests.

5.84 Before commencing court proceedings, it is important to:
- Remember the duty to act in the relevant person's best interests, not one's own.
- Remember that the normal rule in personal welfare proceedings is that each party bears their own legal costs and that the cost of independent expert reports is usually apportioned between the parties. Unless legally aided, the expense can be significant.
- Remember that the Court of Protection cannot review NHS and local authority funding decisions. Provided they do not act so irrationally that it constitutes acting unlawfully, etc, it is for local and other public authorities, not judges, to decide how to allocate their limited resources. Furthermore, the funds available to public authorities, and levels of taxation and public expenditure, are political decisions, that is matters for all of us, ie for voters not judges.
- Consider the likely emotional cost of being involved in prolonged litigation.

PERSONAL WELFARE MATTERS – POSSIBLE ALTERNATIVE REMEDIES	
Remedy	Possible relevance
MCA 2005 matters	
Best interests meetings, ADR	• Consider, and where practicable explore, non-litigious ways of resolving the outstanding issues. The court expects those involved in an incapacitated person's care to co-operate where possible in seeking to ascertain and promote that person's best interests before asking a court to intervene and rule on the matter.

Is an application appropriate? 143

Remedy	Possible relevance
	• Where relevant, ask the local authority or NHS body to convene a 'best interests meeting' at which the outstanding issues can be discussed and hopefully a way forward agreed. • Alternatively, or in addition, ask the local authority or NHS body for a professional second opinion as to the matter in dispute and the person's best interests. • Explore what kinds of formal mediation and ADR are available locally. • Consider whether a neutral family member or professional such as a solicitor not involved in the dispute may be willing and able to mediate.
Alleged unlawful deprivation of liberty	If an incapacitated person is being deprived of their liberty in a care home or hospital without there existing any legal order or authority which authorises this, consider requesting the relevant local authority to review whether there is an unauthorised deprivation of liberty before applying to the Court of Protection. The non-court procedures relating to unauthorised deprivation of liberty are set out in MCA 2005 Sch A1 paras 67–73.
Deprivation of liberty: requesting a Part 8 review	An application may be made to the Court of Protection challenging a standard authorisation authorising a deprivation of liberty. An alternative procedure in appropriate cases which does not rule out applying to the court if the outcome is adverse is to ask the local authority to undertake a 'Part 8 review'. In general, it must do so if it receives a request from the person concerned or their representative. The procedure is set out in MCA 2005 Sch A1 Part 8.
Complaints about a deputy or donee	The Public Guardian supervises court-appointed deputies and deals with representations (including complaints) about the way in which a donee of an LPA or a court-appointed deputy is exercising their powers. These functions may be discharged in cooperation with any other body with relevant statutory functions such as a local authority or police.

continued

Remedy	Possible relevance
Complaints about an NHS or social services decisions in relation to funding and services	
NHS	• 'NHS continuing healthcare' (CHC) refers to a package of ongoing care arranged and funded solely by the NHS where it has been assessed that the individual's primary need is a health need. It can be provided in any setting. In a person's own home, it means that the NHS funds all of the care required to meet the person's assessed health needs. In care homes, it means that the NHS makes a contract with the care home and pays the fees for the person's accommodation as well as all their care. • The *National framework for NHS continuing healthcare and NHS funded nursing care* sets out the principles and processes for determining eligibility. (Available at: https://www.gov.uk/government/publications/national-framework-for-nhs-continuing-healthcare-and-nhs-funded-nursing-care) • The initial assessment consists of a screening checklist completed by a healthcare professional or social worker. Depending on the outcome, the relevant person will either be found to be ineligible for NHS continuing healthcare or be referred for a full multi-disciplinary assessment. A 'decision support tool' (ie detailed form) must then be completed which records the person's assessed needs – no needs, low, moderate, high, severe, priority – across a number of 'domains' (behaviour, cognition, psychological needs, communication and mobility, etc) in order 'to inform' the final decision as to whether the person does have a primary health need. • There is a three-stage appeals process: Stage one involves an appeal to the relevant clinical commissioning group (CCG). Stage 2 involves a request to NHS England for an independent review. Stage three involves requesting a review by the Parliamentary and Health Service Ombudsman (see below). • NHS continuing healthcare should not be confused with NHS-funded nursing care. A person who lives in a care home who requires care from a registered nurse may be entitled to NHS-funded nursing care (FNC). The standard rate is £112 per week, and the higher rate £154.14 per week.

Remedy	Possible relevance
Local authority	• If the relevant person does not qualify for NHS continuing healthcare, their local authority will be responsible for their care needs and for providing services for which they are eligible. Care services from the local authority are usually means-tested. In other words, if the person is eligible for local authority community care services, their finances are assessed and they may be required to pay some or all of the cost of the services. • Complaints about community care assessments and services are subject to the Local Authority Social Services and National Health Services Complaints (England) Regulations 2009 SI No 309. • The complaint is made initially to the local authority. A further complaint to the Local Government Ombudsman may then be possible if the complainant remains dissatisfied. • The Local Government Ombudsman cannot question the merits of community care funding decisions or professional judgements which have been reached properly. However, the Ombudsman can consider how those decisions were reached and whether they have been implemented properly (maladministration and service failure issues).
Judicial review	In some cases, it may be possible to apply to the Administrative Court (a specialist court within the Queen's Bench Division of the High Court) for judicial review of a funding decision on the basis that the decision was unlawful. This might be because the decision of the NHS body or local authority was irrational, procedurally unfair, outside its legal powers, in breach of the Human Rights Act (HRA) 1998 or in breach of European Union law.
Other complaints about the person's treatment or care	
NHS complaints	• The NHS Constitution explains people's rights when it comes to making a complaint. • In England, every NHS organisation must make arrangements for dealing with complaints in accordance with the Local Authority Social Services and National Health Services Complaints (England) Regulations 2009. Regulation 14 imposes a duty on NHS bodies to provide a written response to complaints.

continued

Remedy	Possible relevance
	• The standard complaints procedure is a two-tier procedure. The complaint must initially be made to the service provider (eg the GP or hospital) or to the commissioner of the service. Since the abolition of primary care trusts (PCTs) in 2013, NHS England commissions most primary care services, such as GP and dental services, while CCGs oversee the commissioning of secondary care such as hospital care and some community services. • A patient advice and liaison service (PALS) is available in all hospitals. It offers confidential advice, support and information to patients, families and carers. • In addition, an NHS Complaints Advocacy Service was established on 1 April 2013. Local authorities now have a statutory duty to commission independent advocacy services to provide support for people making, or thinking of making, a complaint about their NHS care or treatment. • Where a complaint is not resolved at the first-tier, the complainant may take it to the second stage, which is to refer the matter to the Ombudsman. • In England, the Parliamentary and Health Service Ombudsman is the final step for people who want to complain about being treated unfairly or receiving a poor service from the NHS, government departments (including the Ministry of Justice, the Department of Health and the DWP) and other public organisations (such as the Care Quality Commission (CQC)). • Much of the primary legislation governing the Ombudsman's remit is set out in the Parliamentary Commissioner Act 1967; Health Service Commissioners Act 1993; Parliamentary and Health Service Commissioners Act 1987; Health Service Commissioners Act 1993; Health Service Commissioner (Amendment) Act 1996. • In Wales, the bodies which the Public Services Ombudsman for Wales may investigate include the Welsh Assembly Government; a local health board; an NHS trust managing a hospital or other establishment or facility in Wales; an independent health provider; and a family health service provider. • See the Public Services Ombudsman (Wales) Act 2005.

Remedy	Possible relevance
Local authority and other care services	• The Local Authority Social Services and National Health Service Complaints (England) Regulations 2009 apply if a local authority provided or commissioned the care service. • The complainant must normally make the complaint initially to the local authority or to the person or body which provides the commissioned service. If the complaint cannot be resolved at this level, the second stage is to refer it to the Local Government Ombudsman. • Where the care is provided under a private contract with the provider, rather than commissioned by a local authority, the CQC requires all registered care providers to have an effective complaints process. The Local Government Ombudsman may now also investigate the complaint but expects the complaint to be made to the service provider in the first instance. • Provided that (in most cases) the local authority or care provider has had a reasonable opportunity to deal with the matter, the Ombudsman can investigate complaints about issues such as alleged poor-quality care, fees and charges, poor complaint handling, delay, assessments of need, safety and safeguarding. The Ombudsman's remit in some matters extends to personal care at home and supported living services for someone with learning disabilities. • A complaint may be made by a suitable representative if the person is incapable of nominating someone to make it for them. • Much of the relevant primary legislation is set out in the Local Government Act 1974 Parts III and IIIA; Health Act 2009; Regulatory Reform (Collaboration etc between Ombudsmen) Order 2007 SI No 1889. • In Wales, the bodies which the Public Services Ombudsman for Wales may investigate include local authorities (including county/county borough councils and community councils); independent social care providers and social landlords such as housing associations.

continued

Remedy	Possible relevance
Access to health and social care records	
NHS and social services records	• The Data Protection Act (DPA) 1998 applies to the records of living persons. • It provides that an individual who makes a request in writing and pays the relevant fee is generally entitled to given a copy of information held about them in an intelligible and permanent form unless this would involve 'disproportionate effort'. • There is a discretion to disclose information to the carers of an incapacitated adult in order to allow them to exercise their rights as carers where the consent of the person being cared for cannot be obtained. • Special rules apply to health and social work records. Access to health records may be refused on medical advice by the information holder ('data controller') if disclosure would be 'likely to cause serious harm to the physical or mental health or condition of the data subject or another person'. The information holder can only do this after consulting the 'appropriate health professional' (meaning the person most recently responsible for the patient's clinical care in connection with the subject matter of the request). • There is a similar provision in relation to social work records. In this case, however, the decision rests with the social work authority alone, with no obligation to consult the relevant professional. • The Access to Health Records Act 1990 now applies only to records of deceased persons created since 1 November 1991. • The Access to Medical Reports Act 1988 concerns medical reports prepared for employers and insurance companies. • Complaints that information has been disclosed to a third-party without a court order requiring or authorising this usually turn on whether there has been an unlawful breach of confidentiality or privacy or a breach of the DPA 1998 principles in relation to processing personal data fairly and lawfully.

Remedy	Possible relevance
The Information Commissioner	The Information Commissioner enforces and oversees the DPA 1998 and the Freedom of Information Act 2000, for both England and Wales. A person denied access to records may complain using the NHS and local authority complaints procedures and then, if a local resolution is not achieved, to the Information Commissioner's Office.
Other Ombudsmen and Commissioners	
Older People's Commissioner for Wales	The Commissioner may review the way in which the interests of older people are safeguarded and promoted when public bodies discharge, propose to discharge or fail to discharge their functions. It can also investigate whether certain bodies' advocacy, whistle-blowing and complaints arrangements are effective in safeguarding and promoting the interests of relevant older people in Wales. The Commissioner may examine the case of an older person in relation to a matter which affects the interests of a wider group of older people and not just the individual concerned. See the Commissioner for Older People (Wales) Act 2006.
Regulatory bodies	
NHS hospitals, local authority care services, private and voluntary sector	• The CQC is the regulator of health and social care in England. In general terms, it registers and inspects all health and social care provision and seeks to ensure that they meet essential standards of quality and safety. • The Health and Social Care Act 2008 (Regulated Activities) Regulations 2010 SI No 781 set out the essential standards of quality and safety expected from service providers of regulated activities, such as care homes. These are set out in regs 9–24 and are supported by compliance guidance. • The CQC deals with complaints about the standards of care homes, hospitals and other registered services as a whole rather than with the kind of individual complaint of poor service dealt with by ombudsmen.

continued

Remedy	Possible relevance
	• Monitor is responsible for authorising, monitoring and regulating NHS foundation trusts. Whereas the CQC is responsible for service standards and safety, Monitor is concerned with governance issues – the ability of an NHS foundation trust board to do their job and to provide the necessary service. • In Wales, the Care and Social Services Inspectorate Wales (CSSIW) is the body equivalent to the English CQC. It regulates and inspects domiciliary services and care homes for adults including those providing nursing care in order to ensure that they meet national minimum standards.
Individual practitioners	• The General Medical Council (GMC) regulates doctors.
	• The Nursing and Midwifery Council (NMC) regulates nurses and midwives.
	• The Health and Care Professions Council (HCPC) regulates psychologists, social workers in England (in Wales, this is done by the Care Council for Wales) and speech and language therapists.
Other 'avenues' for complaints and grievances	
MPs, local authority councillors, media/press	As to these options, see the section above dealing with property and financial affairs.
Other kinds of legal applications and proceedings (civil)	
The relevance of these options depends on whether a public authority or family member is seeking a safeguarding-type remedy or an incapacitated person (or someone on their behalf) is seeking to enforce their legal rights.	
Possible remedies for public authorities[a]	

[a] See also the guide published by the Social Care Institute for Excellence: *Gaining access to an adult suspected to be at risk of neglect or abuse* (www.scie.org.uk/care-act-2014/safeguarding-adults/adult-suspected-at-risk-of-neglect-abuse/) addressing an issue which often arises in the context of the discharge of safeguarding obligations under the Care Act 2014 (in England) or the Social Services and Well-Being (Wales) Act 2014 (in Wales).

Is an application appropriate? 151

Remedy	Possible relevance
Application under the High Court's inherent jurisdiction	• The exercise of the High Court's inherent jurisdiction may be used to obtain appropriate orders where a person not incapacitated by mental disorder or mental illness is vulnerable and is reasonably believed to be (i) under constraint; or (ii) subject to coercion or undue influence; or (iii) for some other reason deprived of the capacity to make the relevant decision, or disabled from making a free choice, or incapacitated or disabled from giving or expressing a real and genuine consent. See *DL v A local authority* [2012] EWCA Civ 253, (2012) 15 CCLR 267. • The purpose of the jurisdiction is facilitative rather than dictatorial. Its purpose is to facilitate the process of unencumbered decision-making by those with capacity free from external pressure or physical restraint.
MHA 1983 powers	The MHA 1983 includes various provisions relating to compulsory admission to hospital, in particular sections 2, 3 and 4. The community provisions include reception into guardianship and sections 115 (entry to and inspection of private premises); 135 (warrants to search private premises and to remove to a place of safety persons suspected to suffer from mental disorder); and 136 (removal by police to a place of safety of persons in public places who appear to be suffering from mental disorder and to be in immediate need of care or control).
Protecting the person's moveable property under the Care Act 2014	• Care Act 2014 applies when a person is provided with accommodation under the Care Act 2014 or admitted to hospital. • It imposes a statutory duty on the relevant local authority to take reasonable steps to prevent or mitigate loss or damage to the person's movable property if the person is unable to protect or deal with it and no other suitable arrangements are in place. • A power is given to the local authority to enter the person's premises in order to take the steps necessary to protect their moveable property. Any reasonable expenses incurred in protecting the property are recoverable from the person concerned. *continued*

Remedy	Possible relevance
Emergency police powers to save life, limb, etc	Police and Criminal Evidence Act (PACE) 1984 s17(1)(e) authorises a police constable to enter and search any premises for the purpose of saving life or limb or preventing serious damage to property.
Public health remedies	• Public Health Act 1936 s83 allows the local authority to require the cleansing (by disinfecting and decorating) of any premises which are in such a filthy or unwholesome condition as to be prejudicial to health or are verminous. • Sections 84 and 85 contain supplementary provisions concerning the 'cleansing or destruction of filthy or verminous articles' and the 'cleansing of verminous persons and their clothing'. • Environmental Protection Act 1990 Part 3 provides local authorities with abatement powers in relation to 'premises in such a state as to be prejudicial to health or a nuisance'. • Powers of entry, if need be under warrant, are contained in Public Health Act 1936 s287 and Environmental Protection Act 1990 Sch 3. • Local authorities and social landlords may take action under the no-nuisance terms in tenancy agreements. • See *Professional Practice Note: Hoarding and how to approach it – Guidance for Environmental Health Officers and others*, Chartered Institute of Environmental Health, September 2012. (Available at: www.cieh.org/uploadedFiles/Core/Policy/Publications_and_information_services/Policy_publications/Publications/Hoarding_PPN_May09.pdf.)
Possible remedies for the incapacitated person	
Damages claim in the civil courts	Under English law, an individual may be entitled to compensation if they have been injured as a result of the negligence of another person. Other actionable civil wrongs include trespass to the person (assault, battery), nuisance, breach of privacy and breach of confidentiality.

Is an application appropriate? 153

Remedy	Possible relevance
HRA 1998 claim	The HRA 1998 makes it unlawful for a public authority to act incompatibly with the rights conferred by the European Convention on Human Rights. It allows a case to be brought in a UK court or tribunal against the authority if it does so. However, a public authority will not have acted unlawfully under the Act if as the result of another Act of Parliament it could not have acted differently. The Act extended the power to award damages for the breach of a convention right to any court that has the power to order payment of damages or compensation in a civil case.

Equality Act (EqA) 2010	• The EqA 2010 provides that a person is disabled if they have a physical or mental impairment which has a substantial and long-term adverse effect on their ability to carry out normal day-to-day activities. All employers and service providers in England, Wales and Scotland must follow the EqA 2010.
	• A person (A) discriminates against a disabled person (B) if:
	  (a) A treats B unfavourably because of something arising in consequence of B's disability, and
	  (b) A cannot show that the treatment is a proportionate means of achieving a legitimate aim.
	• This prohibition does not apply if A shows that A did not know, and could not reasonably have been expected to know, that B had the disability.
	• EqA 2010 s19 deals with indirect discrimination, section 26 with the harassment of disabled people, section 27 with victimisation and Part 3 of the Act with the provision of services.
	• The EqA 2010 repealed and replaced the Disability Discrimination Act 1995.

Family law remedies	• The Family Law Act 1996 allows non-molestation orders and occupation orders to be made in respect of 'associated persons' such as married persons, civil partners, cohabitants, relatives, parties to family proceedings and persons who have or have had an intimate personal relationship.

continued

Remedy	Possible relevance
	• A power of arrest may not be attached to a non-molestation order. However, breach of such an order without reasonable excuse is a criminal offence and also a contempt of court. • An occupation order is an order by which the court regulates occupation of the home by declaring a person's entitlement to occupy it, prohibiting someone's right to occupy it and so on. Such orders may be made in respect of associated persons who share, have shared or intend to share a dwelling house as their home. • It is often said that the Court of Protection cannot prohibit the rights of occupation of capacitated people and cannot therefore exclude a joint owner or spouse from a dwelling-house. However, there is no case in point. • A power of arrest may be attached to an occupation order and breach of such an order is also a contempt of court.

Anti-harassment injunction	• The High Court and the county court have jurisdiction to grant an injunction under the Protection from Harassment Act (PHA) 1997.
	• Section 1 provides that a person must not pursue a course of conduct:
	    (a) which amounts to harassment of another, and
	    (b) which the person knows or ought to know amounts to harassment of the other.
	• An actual or apprehended breach may be the subject of a claim in civil proceedings. An injunction may be made and the court may also award damages for (among other things) any anxiety caused by the harassment and any financial loss resulting from it. (A person who pursues a course of conduct in breach of section 1 also commits a criminal offence.)

Common law injunctions	It is still possible to obtain a common law injunction in the context of common law proceedings for torts such as assault, battery, trespass to the person and nuisance. However, it is relatively unusual for a situation not to be covered either by the Family Law Act 1996 or by the PHA 1997, eg where the behaviour complained of does not amount to a course of conduct involving associated persons.

Remedy	Possible relevance
Compensation for criminal injuries	Victims of violent crimes can apply to the Criminal Injuries Compensation Authority (CICA) for compensation. It does not matter that a prosecution was not brought or that the perpetrator could not be held responsible because they were suffering from a mental disorder. The claim must be brought within two years from the date of the incident. A responsible person can make a claim on behalf of an incapacitated victim.
	Other kinds of legal proceedings (criminal)
	A remand in custody, bail conditions and/or term of imprisonment may serve to protect an incapacitated person.
Offences relating to vulnerable or incapacitated persons	• MCA 2005 s44 created an (ambiguous) offence of ill-treatment or wilful neglect. It applies to deputies, donees (LPA or EPA) and anyone who has the care of a person who lacks capacity or whom the carer reasonably believes lacks capacity. • Courts and Criminal Justice Act 2015 s20 created an offence for a paid care worker to ill-treat or wilfully to neglect an individual for whom they are caring. A care worker also includes those with managerial responsibility and directors (of equivalents) of organisations providing such care. A separate offence under section 21 exists in relation to care providers in respect of serious management failures giving rise to offences committed by care providers within their employ. • Domestic Violence, Crime and Victims Act 2004 s5 makes it an offence to cause or allow the death of a vulnerable adult. • MHA 1983 s127 makes it an offence for an officer or employee of an NHS hospital, independent hospital or care home to wilfully neglect or ill-treat a person who suffers from or appears to be suffering from a mental disorder. A like offence is committed if someone who has such a person in their custody or care ill-treats or wilfully neglects them. • The Sexual Offences Act 2003 includes various relevant offences such as sexual activity with a person with a mental disorder impeding choice and sexual activity by a care worker with a person with a mental disorder.

continued

Remedy	Possible relevance
Standard offences	Incapacitated persons are also protected by the general criminal law (eg the Offences Against the Person Act 1861 and public order offences) but the likelihood of a successful prosecution may be affected by their inability to give evidence at trial.
Harassment and malicious communications, etc	• PHA 1997 s1 is dealt with above. • Criminal Justice and Police Act 2001 s42A makes it an offence to harass a person in their home. • The Malicious Communications Act 1988 provides that persons who send letters, electronic communications or make telephone calls with intent to cause distress or anxiety are guilty of a criminal offence.
	• Communications Act 2003 s127 makes it an offence to send a message which the perpetrator knows to be indecent, obscene, of a menacing character or grossly offensive for the purpose of causing annoyance, inconvenience or needless anxiety.

CHAPTER 6

Funding and representation

6.5	Being a litigant in person
6.15	Legal representation
6.20	Finding a lawyer
6.24	**Legal aid in the Court of Protection**
6.26	Legal Aid, Sentencing and Punishment of Offenders Act 2012
6.30	Legal aid contracts
6.32	The different levels of legal aid
6.33	Securing legal aid
6.34	Scope of legal aid
6.39	The inherent jurisdiction
6.40	Breaches of ECHR rights by a public authority
6.41	The merits test
	The merits test for Legal Help • The merits test for Help at Court • The merits test for Legal Representation
6.59	The Lord Chancellor's Guidance
6.61	Financial eligibility (means test)
6.71	Evidence of financial eligibility
6.73	Practical issues
6.76	The statutory charge
6.80	Experts' fees
6.88	Very high cost cases

6.1 This chapter looks at sources of advice, funding and representation to parties in the Court of Protection.
6.2 It will provide an overview of the sources of support available in the absence of formal legal representation. It then considers the sources of legal advice and how these can be funded.
6.3 It will then provide an explanation of the legal aid scheme as it applies in the Court of Protection. The aim of this section is to assist both practitioners and their clients in navigating the scheme and in understanding the impact of the relevant legislation and guidance.
6.4 Issues concerning the representation of P and other protected parties are considered in detail in chapter 11.

Being a litigant in person

6.5 There is no compulsion to instruct a lawyer in court proceedings in England and Wales. A person appearing in court proceedings without a legal representative is known as a 'litigant in person' and has the right to address the court directly. The Case Management Pilot rules require the court to 'have regard' to the fact that at least one party is unrepresented in exercising its case management powers.[1] This may include, for example, the judge finding out what questions a litigant in person may wish to put to a witness, and either putting them to the witness directly or causing the questions to be put.[2] If there are, in fact, cases which fall outside the Case Management Pilot (as to which, see further paras 4.101–4.103), it is likely that the same approach will be applied in any such case in which a party is acting in person.

6.6 Litigants in person have the same responsibilities to the court as represented parties to help the court further what is described as 'the overriding objective' (see further paras 10.7–10.11). This means dealing with the case justly, and at proportionate cost, having regard to the principles contained in the Mental Capacity Act (MCA) 2005.[3] This includes complying with orders, keeping to timetables, being full and frank in their disclosure to the court and the parties. The Case Management Pilot imposes a specific duty on litigants in person to engage with the court process, to co-operate with the court and the

1 COPR Pr3.2.
2 COPR Pr3.2.4.
3 COPR Pr1.1.1, COPR r4. The reference to proportionate cost only applies in relation to cases falling within the Case Management Pilot, but the same approach is likely also to be applied if there are cases falling outside the Pilot.

parties, to present their case fairly and to seek early resolution of disputes where practicable.[4] Parties who fail to comply with their duties risk being ordered to pay costs.[5]

6.7 We suggest that it is wise for anyone involved in Court of Protection proceedings at least to consider the possibility of obtaining legal advice. Court of Protection judges will sometimes make a specific recommendation to a litigant in person that he or she should seek legal advice. This should be followed up where possible. Furthermore, legal advice is likely to be more effective if it is provided early on in the case, and obtaining legal advice at the outset may mean that it is possible to narrow the issues in the case so that either the case can be brought to a close more quickly, or a litigant in person may then be in a better position to deal with those remaining issues themselves.

6.8 Sources of support available to litigants in person include the Personal Support Unit (PSU)[6] which is an independent charity, staffed by volunteers. It operates in thirteen courts around England and Wales. Its aim is to help those facing civil proceedings unrepresented manage their cases better. PSU volunteers will not offer legal advice but can sometimes put litigants in touch with relevant agencies. PSU volunteers are able to offer practical support including guidance round the court building, help organising documentation and emotional support. Information about the PSU is prominently displayed in the courts where it operates.

6.9 A 'McKenzie friend' is someone who provides reasonable assistance to a litigant in person. A McKenzie friend does not represent the litigant, but can sit beside them in court and 'quietly assist'.

6.10 In the light of an increase in the number of litigants in person, the Master of the Rolls and the President of the Family Division issued *Practice Guidance on McKenzie friends* on 12 July 2010.[7] This has been held to apply in the Court of Protection (*LBX v TT*[8]). The following points should be noted:

---

4 COPR Pr1.6.
5 COPR r4(3), COPR Pr1.4.3.
6 www.thepsu.org/.
7 *Practice Guidance: McKenzie friends (Civil and Family Courts)* ('Practice Guidance'), 12 July 2010; available at: https://www.judiciary.gov.uk/wp-content/uploads/JCO/Documents/Guidance/mckenzie-friends-practice-guidance-july-2010.pdf.
8 [2014] EWCOP 24, [2014] COPLR 561.

- A McKenzie friend can only act on behalf of a person with litigation capacity.[9]
- Litigants in person can receive reasonable assistance from a McKenzie friend, subject to the discretion of the court. The court may refuse to permit assistance by a McKenzie friend if satisfied that the interests of justice and fairness do not require it.[10]
- A litigant seeking assistance from a McKenzie friend should seek the court's permission as soon as possible and the McKenzie friend should submit a short CV and confirm their independence of the case and their understanding of their duty of confidentiality.[11]
- A McKenzie friend *may*: provide moral support; take notes; help with case papers; quietly give advice on any aspect of the conduct of the case.[12]
- A McKenzie friend may *not*: act as agent; manage the case outside court; address the court; or make submissions.[13]
- The right to a fair trial is engaged by the decision whether to permit a McKenzie friend, and the litigant should be given the chance to argue the point. Unless the proceedings are in private, the proposed McKenzie friend should be allowed in court to help the litigant. If the case is being heard in private, then it is for the litigant to justify the proposed McKenzie friend's presence in court.[14]
- Refusal would not be justified simply because the case is straightforward, or because the proposed McKenzie friend belongs to an organisation that promotes a particular cause, or that the proceedings are confidential. Refusal could be justified if the assistance was for an improper purpose; or the McKenzie friend was using the litigant as a 'puppet', or does not appear to understand the duty of confidentiality.[15]
- Rarely courts may grant rights of audience, or the right to conduct litigation, to McKenzie friends.[16]

---

9 This is not stated in the Practice Guidance, but it is suggested from the scope of the role of such a friend as an assistant to the litigant.
10 Practice Guidance paras 2 and 5.
11 Practice Guidance para 6.
12 Practice Guidance para 3.
13 Practice Guidance para 4.
14 Practice Guidance paras 8 and 9.
15 Practice Guidance paras 12 and 13.
16 Practice Guidance paras 18–26.

- Litigants may agree to pay fees to McKenzie friends for the provision of reasonable assistance, and these costs cannot be recovered from the opponent. If the court has granted the McKenzie friend the right to conduct litigation or a right of audience, then costs incurred in these activities are in principle recoverable from the litigant, and may be recoverable from the opponent as a disbursement.[17]

6.11 The role of the McKenzie friend in Court of Protection proceedings, and the risk of conflicts of interest, was considered in *HBCC v LG*.[18] Eleanor King J had permitted P's daughter to receive assistance from CP, a McKenzie friend who was also a local councillor. The judge described the positive contribution that McKenzie friends can make:

> 141. This court is always keen to welcome McKenzie friends; they give time and support of inestimable value to the litigant they have agreed to assist. McKenzie friend[s] come from all walks of life: often they are personal friends or connections of the litigant; sometimes they are 'professional' McKenzie friends. Sometimes, as here, they are respected members of the community who have been approached by a litigant for support and advice. Each has their place.

6.12 The judge considered that C had exceeded his role as McKenzie friend, not in his conduct during the trial itself, but in his behaviour outside court which she described as inflammatory, including his 'dogged maintenance of his stated position' in correspondence which had gone beyond what was proper. She commented that

> 147. ... I understand that democratically elected representatives be they Members of Parliament or local Councillors will often, appropriately, take up issues on behalf of their constituents. It follows that any elected representative must be cautious that in doing so they do not find themselves in conflict with their role as a McKenzie friend.

6.13 At the time of writing a consultation into the role of McKenzie friends has recently concluded. The consultation sought views on a number of matters, including as to whether the term should be replaced, whether the guidance should be replaced by rules, the possible use of a code of conduct and fee recovery.[19] Whilst the consultation is not specific to the Court of Protection, it is likely that any changes in practice and procedure that are introduced will either apply directly in the court, or be mirrored by equivalent provisions

---

17 Practice Guidance paras 27–30.
18 [2010] EWHC 1527 (Fam).
19 Judicial Executive Board Working Group: *Reforming the courts' approach to McKenzie friends: a consultation* (closed 9 June 2016).

6.14 It may be useful to ask the following questions to anyone offering services as a McKenzie friend:
- How are charges worked out, and what is the likely cost of support for the case in question?
- What is the professional background of the proposed McKenzie friend? They may be able to provide a CV.
- What experience does the McKenzie friend have? Are they able to supply references?
- Does the McKenzie friend hold a particular view about the issues involved in the case – for example, are they involved in relevant campaigns? This does not mean that they cannot act as McKenzie friend; but it may have a bearing on the advice they provide.

Legal representation

6.15 Unless the court (unusually) gives permission for a McKenzie friend to conduct the litigation, legal representation in the Court of Protection will be by a qualified lawyer, who will be a solicitor, a barrister, or in some cases a Fellow of the Institute of Legal Executives.

6.16 As we have seen, cases in the Court of Protection may be heard by district judges, circuit judges or judges of the High Court. Until 29 January 2016 most Court of Protection hearings took place in private, sometimes referred to as 'in chambers'. The exception to this rule were serious medical treatment cases, which have usually been heard in public.

6.17 The Transparency Pilot reversed the default position so that cases are now normally heard in public, with reporting restrictions to protect the identity of P and members of P's family.[20] The Transparency Pilot Practice Direction[21] provides that legal representatives with rights of audience in private proceedings in the Court of Protection can continue to appear in Court of Protection cases when they were heard in public, unless there is 'good reason' not to allow them to do so.[22]

6.18 Solicitors' firms are regulated by the Solicitors Regulation Authority (SRA) and barristers are regulated by the Bar Standards Board (BSB). Traditionally barristers are instructed by solicitors, but those who have been through suitable training can now receive

---

20 The Transparency Pilot is discussed in chapter 13 at para 13.13 onwards.
21 Transparency Pilot PD para 2.6.
22 Transparency Pilot Model Order at para 11.

instructions directly from members of the public (referred to as 'public access').

6.19 Fellows of the Chartered Institute of Legal Executives (CILEx) are regulated by Cilex Regulation and may appear at hearings in chambers before the district court, circuit court and High Court. They may address the court on unopposed applications for adjournment or to enter judgment by consent.

Finding a lawyer

6.20 For members of the public seeking legal advice about Court of Protection cases, the following may be useful sources of information:

- The Law Society maintains a register of qualified solicitors and firms. This can be accessed through the 'Find a Solicitor' page in the Law Society's website.[23]
- The Law Society runs a number of accreditation schemes; and is in the process of designing a scheme for health and welfare work under the MCA 2005. Members of the scheme will have a 'Kitemark' showing that they have demonstrated experience in this area of law.
- The Law Society's Lexcel accreditation scheme is a practice management standard.[24] Firms with Lexcel accreditation have to show that they have met certain standards in client care, risk management and case management.
- The Bar Council maintains a list of all barristers, and a further list of those offering public access, on its website.[25] There is a dedicated telephone number for questions about public access: 020 7611 1472.
- Some publications provide information about solicitors and barristers practising in the Court of Protection, for example *Chambers and Partners* and the *Legal 500*.

6.21 Solicitors and barristers acting on a public access basis are also obliged to provide information about their charges and the likely costs of the case at the outset of a case. Legal aid is available for certain cases in the Court of Protection, as is discussed further in the next section.

---

23 See www.lawsociety.org.uk.
24 See: www.law.society.org.uk/accreditation/lexcel.
25 See: www.barcouncil.org.

6.22 Where legal aid cannot be secured, clients will have to pay privately for legal representation. Providing privately funded representation in contested welfare cases can bring challenges, because of the difficulties in predicting the costs that will be incurred.

6.23 In some cases, practitioners may be able to take on cases under a partial retainer – sometimes referred to as 'unbundling'. The Law Society has issued a practice note about partial retainer cases in family legal services.[26] Practitioners considering this option should consider the advice given in the practice note. The professional obligations of the solicitor on a partial retainer are significant and include a greater responsibility to clients of unbundled services to clearly set out the responsibilities of both solicitor and client. The practice note does not recommend a partial retainer in cases of 'great complexity or where you have concerns that the client does not have the intellectual or emotional capacity to carry out tasks that fall within their responsibility. In such cases you should carefully consider whether and to what extent it is in your client's interests to provide an unbundled service'.[27]

Legal aid in the Court of Protection

6.24 This section is not an exhaustive description of the legal aid scheme and readers are referred to the *LAG Legal aid handbook* for a comprehensive guide.[28] Regular updates appear on www.legalaidhandbook.com, which is an invaluable resource.

6.25 There is no single document which describes the legal aid scheme. Below is a list of the materials referred to, to which practitioners will need to access from time to time:

Primary legislation
- Legal Aid, Sentencing and Punishment of Offenders Act 2012 (LASPO) Schedule 1.

Secondary legislation
- Civil Legal Aid (Merits Criteria) Regulations 2013 SI No 104;
- Civil Legal Aid (Financial Resources and Payment for Services) Regulations 2013 SI No 480;
- Civil Legal Aid (Statutory Charge) Regulations 2013 SI No 503;

---

26 *Unbundling family legal services*, 1 May 2013; available at: www.lawsociety.org.uk/advice/practice-notes/unbundling-family-legal-services/.
27 Para 4.31.
28 V Ling and S Pugh (eds), *Legal aid handbook 2015/6* (LAG).

Funding and representation 165

- Civil Legal Aid (Procedure) Regulations 2012 SI No 3098.

Guidance
- Lord Chancellor's Guidance under section 4 of Legal Aid, Sentencing and Punishment of Offenders Act 2012;
- VHCC: a solicitors' information pack (non-family) (2013).

LAA contracts
- Standard Civil Contract 2014;
- 2013 Individual Case Contract (High Costs Cases) Specification.

Legal Aid, Sentencing and Punishment of Offenders Act 2012

6.26 Publicly funded advice and representation ('legal aid') is governed by the Legal Aid, Sentencing and Punishment of Offenders Act 2012 (LASPO), which came into force on 1 April 2013 and removed a number of areas of law from the scope of legal aid. The Legal Services Commission (LSC), which had previously administered legal aid in England and Wales, was replaced by the Legal Aid Agency (LAA) by the Act. The LAA is headed by the Director of Legal Aid Casework.

6.27 Schedule 1 to LASPO lists those areas of law where advice and/or representation can be provided under legal aid. If an area of law is not in Schedule 1, then no legal aid in any form may be provided to a client seeking help in this area of law unless it is necessary because to deny legal aid would be a breach of the European Convention on Human Rights (ECHR).[29]

6.28 Those areas of law listed in Schedule 1 are then subject to further exclusions and criteria which appear in the regulations. These should be considered in order to ascertain whether a client presenting with a particular case is eligible to receive legal aid for their problem, and what form of legal aid should be provided.

6.29 The purpose of LASPO has been described by the Supreme Court as:

---

29 Under LASPO s10, legal aid (Legal Help and certificates) may be made available on an 'exceptional' basis if it is necessary under the ECHR. The threshold for such exceptional funding is extremely high, requiring the applicant to show that to deny them legal aid would be a breach of the ECHR. Only a handful of the hundreds of applications under section 10 made since 1 April 2013 have been granted. There is no funding for making the application for exceptional funding unless it is actually granted.

... in very summary terms, to channel civil legal aid on the basis of the nature and importance of the issue, an individual's need for financial support, the availability of other funding, and the availability of other forms of dispute resolution.[30]

Legal aid contracts

6.30 All providers of legal aid must hold a contract with the LAA which covers the areas of law which they offer. The provider must at all times comply with the terms of the contract. These include the duty on both the provider and the LAA to act in good faith in relation to the contract.[31] Providers of legal aid who hold contracts in the areas of mental health and community care may also provide legal aid in cases arising under the MCA 2005. Currently the position is governed by the 2014 Standard Civil Contract and the associated category specifications.

6.31 As from April 2016 practitioners are required to make use of the Client and Cost Management System when submitting applications to the Legal Aid Agency.

The different levels of legal aid

6.32 Legal aid is provided at different levels. The usual first level of funding is Legal Help. This will cover an adviser taking instructions at the start of a case, writing letters and advising whether further action is required. Informal assistance at a particular hearing can be provided as 'Help at Court'.[32] Neither cover ongoing representation of a client in court proceedings. If the practitioner wishes to represent the client in the Court of Protection, a legal aid certificate must be obtained, which is linked to the specific proceedings.

Securing legal aid

6.33 In order to qualify for any form of legal aid, the following criteria have to be met. Each of these is addressed in more detail below:
- The case must be within 'scope' of legal aid.
- The client must meet the 'merits test' as to whether legal aid is warranted.

---

30 *R (Public Law Project) v Lord Chancellor* [2016] UKSC 39, [2016] 3 WLR 387 at [37].
31 General Terms, 2014 Standard Contract, 2.1.
32 Civil Legal Aid Procedure Regulations 2012 reg 5.

- The client must meet the 'means test' and be financially eligible for legal aid (unless the case is a section 21A challenge, and the client is either P or the relevant person's representative (RPR)).
- The client must produce the relevant evidence of their means (benefits, bank statements etc) to satisfy the requirements of the LAA.

Scope of legal aid

6.34 The relevant paragraph of Schedule 1 to LASPO for cases where the Court of Protection has jurisdiction is paragraph 5, which provides that civil legal services can be provided 'in relation to matters arising under the Mental Capacity Act 2005'.[33]

6.35 This means that legal aid can – provided all the other criteria are met – be provided in respect of legal issues arising under the MCA 2005.

6.36 This is subject to certain exclusions. No legal advice at all can be provided about:
- The creation of lasting powers of attorney (LPAs) under the MCA 2005; or
- The making of advance decisions under that Act.[34]

6.37 Therefore, practitioners may not provide any advice at all under legal aid to a client who wishes to prepare an LPA (whether financial or welfare) or an advance decision. Such clients will have to pay privately for advice. However, if a client requires advice or representation about a case before the Court of Protection which concerns determinations and declarations about the effect, meaning validity or applicability of a LPA or advance decision, then it may be possible to provide legal aid, in some form, assuming that all other criteria are satisfied.[35]

6.38 Advocacy services can be provided in the Court of Protection[36] if the case concerns at least one of the following issues:
- a person's right to life;
- a person's liberty or physical safety;
- a person's medical treatment (within the meaning of the Mental Health Act (MHA) 1983),

33 LASPO Sch 1 Part 1 para 5(1).
34 LASPO Sch 1 Part 1 para 5(3).
35 LASPO Sch 1 Part 1 para 5(4).
36 LASPO Sch 1 Part 3.

- a person's capacity to marry, to enter into a civil partnership or to enter into sexual relations; or
- a person's right to family life.[37]

The inherent jurisdiction

6.39 Civil legal services can be provided in relation to the 'inherent jurisdiction' of the High Court in relation to children (persons under the age of 18) and vulnerable adults (persons aged 18 and over).[38]

Breaches of ECHR rights by a public authority

6.40 Claims for damages in respect of acts and omissions by public authority remain in scope of legal aid, if these involve a 'significant breach' of convention rights. As explained in para 6.58 below the LAA has accepted that such claims can be litigated in the Court of Protection.

The merits test

6.41 Once it has been established that the case is within the scope of legal aid, the next matter to be considered is whether the case meets the merits criteria. If it does not, legal aid will not be available for advice, or in the case of court proceedings, granted.

6.42 The relevant merits tests are set out in the Civil Legal Aid (Merits Criteria) Regulations 2013 SI No 104. These include definitions of the tests of prospects of success (regs 4–5); public interest (reg 6); reasonable private paying individual (reg 7); and proportionality (reg 8).

6.43 The criteria for the grant of legal help are not the same as the criteria for the grant of full representation, so these are considered separately.

The merits test for Legal Help

6.44 The criteria for qualification for Legal Help are set out at regulation 32 of the Merits Regulations 2013. They are that it must be reasonable to provide Legal Help having regard to other potential sources of funding and that there will be sufficient benefit to justify the cost of

---

37 LASPO Sch 1 Part 3.
38 LASPO Sch 1 Part 1 para 9.

Funding and representation 169

Legal Help. A person's conduct is relevant to whether it is reasonable to provide legal services (including legal help).[39]

6.45 It will be seen from para 6.32 above that advice about any matter arising under the MCA 2005 could be provided under legal help, apart from those areas excluded by LASPO Sch 3 para 5(1)(3). This could include advice to a representative under COPR r3A(2)(c) about how to discharge their role.

The merits test for Help at Court

6.46 The test is the sufficient benefit test as above. In addition, the circumstances and complexity of a case must be such that 'advocacy is appropriate and will be of real benefit to that individual'.[40]

The merits test for Legal Representation

6.47 Legal representation may only be provided if the relevant merits tests are met and it is reasonable in the light of the person's conduct (reg 11(7)).

6.48 There are standard criteria which apply in a number of categories of civil proceedings, and then specific criteria which are relevant in the Court of Protection. The standard criteria are set out in regulation 39 below. If they are not all satisfied, the individual will not get legal aid:

39. An individual may qualify for legal representation only if the Director is satisfied that the following criteria are met –
(a) the individual does not have access to other potential sources of funding (other than a conditional fee agreement) from which it would be reasonable to fund the case;
(b) the case is unsuitable for a conditional fee agreement;
(c) there is no person other than the individual, including a person who might benefit from the proceedings, who can reasonably be expected to bring the proceedings;
(d) the individual has exhausted all reasonable alternatives to bringing proceedings including any complaints system, ombudsman scheme or other form of alternative dispute resolution;
(e) there is a need for representation in all the circumstances of the case including–
   (i) the nature and complexity of the issues;
   (ii) the existence of other proceedings; and
   (iii) the interests of other parties to the proceedings; and
(f) the proceedings are not likely to be allocated to the small claims track.

39 Civil Legal Aid (Merits Criteria) Regulations 2013 reg 11(7).
40 Civil Legal Aid (Merits Criteria) Regulations 2013 reg 33.

6.49 The impact of the test in regulation 39(c) was considered in *R (Moosa) v Legal Services Commission*.[41] This case was brought prior to LASPO, but the same test had formed part of the previous merits criteria. The case concerned a dispute between a family and local authority as to where their son who had significant difficulties would live. The son was being cared for in residential care. The family wanted him to return home. The local authority commenced proceedings in the Court of Protection to determine P's best interests in terms of his residence. His mother was a respondent on the Form COP1 and pursuant to COPR r73 she automatically became a party. She was financially ineligible for legal aid as she had an amount of equity in her home (where she hoped to accommodate P) that took her over the capital limits. Mr Justice Charles agreed to join P's brother as a party. P's brother was a student and was financially eligible for legal aid. It was made clear to the Court of Protection that the reason for joining the brother was to ensure that there was one family member who was eligible for public funding. That member would then become the voice of the family.

6.50 The LSC refused the brother funding on the basis that the mother could reasonably bring the case. The refusal was challenged. It was argued that a refusal to fund the brother simply made it impossible for anyone to argue the family's position with the benefit of legal aid, because the mother could not access the equity in her home, and the home was the place where the family wished to accommodate their son. It was unrealistic to consider for example the sale of that property to allow the mother to realise some of her capital. While the judge expressed some sympathy to the family the application for judicial review was refused.

6.51 The *cost-benefit* criteria and the *prospects of success* test must also be met.[42]

6.52 The cost-benefit criteria require the Director to be satisfied that (assuming the case is not for damages, or of significant wider public interest) the reasonable private paying individual test is met. If the case is of significant wider public interest then the proportionality test must be met (reg 42).

6.53 As from 22 July 2016, the prospects of success test is as follows.[43] The test will be met where the Director is satisfied that the prospects

---

41 [2013] EWHC 2804 (Admin).
42 Civil Legal Aid (Merits Criteria) Regulations 2013 reg 41.
43 https://www.gov.uk/government/news/civil-news-merits-criteria-regulations-amended-from-22-july/.

of success are very good, good or moderate. All other cases must be classified as one of the following:

- 'Marginal' – where there is between 45 and 50 per cent chance of a successful outcome;
- 'Borderline' – where it is not possible to say whether there is a greater than 50 per cent chance of success or whether the prospects of success should be classified as poor or marginal, because of disputed law, fact or expert evidence;
- 'poor' – where there is less than 50 per cent chance of obtaining a successful outcome.

The test will not be met where the prospects of success are poor but may in some cases be met where the prospects are marginal or borderline, for example because the case is of overwhelming importance to the individual or of significant wider public interest.

6.54 If all the criteria above are met, a further test still needs to be carried out if the case is being heard in the Court of Protection. This is set out in regulation 52 and provides that full representation will only be granted if two further tests are met.[44] The *first test* is that the Court of Protection has ordered or is likely to order an oral hearing, *and* that it is necessary for the individual to be provided with full representation in the proceedings.[45] This therefore excludes 'streamlined' applications for authority to deprive P of his or her liberty which are uncontentious? the so-called '*Re X*' applications.[46] Legal help however may be available to parties to such cases, or to a person who has been appointed to represent P under COPR r3A(2)(c).

6.55 The Lord Chancellor's guidance as to when it is 'necessary' to provide representation is considered below at para 6.59.

6.56 The *second test* is that the case relates to:

a) a person's right to life;
b) a person's liberty or physical safety;
c) a person's medical treatment (within the meaning of the Mental Health Act 1983);
d) a person's capacity to marry, to enter into a civil partnership or to enter into sexual relations; or
e) a person's right to family life.

6.57 From the list above it can be seen that cases which concern a person's right to respect for their home or for their private life and which may

44 Note that reg 52 does not apply to cases heard under the 'inherent jurisdiction'.
45 Civil Legal Aid (Merits Criteria) Regulations 2013 reg 52(2).
46 Discussed in more detail in chapter 21.

also engage rights under Article 8 ECHR could fall outside the merits criteria.

6.58 In *R (SL) v Director of Legal Aid Casework and Cambridgeshire County Council*[47] the Legal Aid Agency conceded that legal aid funding is available to P to bring a claim for damages under the Human Rights Act in the Court of Protection. Such claims can be brought in relation both to ongoing and historic violations of P's rights under the ECHR.

The Lord Chancellor's Guidance

6.59 It is important to be aware of this Guidance which sets out the approach that will be taken to questions such as what 'other sources of funding' might be (para 7.14); and when a case is unsuitable for a conditional fee agreement (CFA) (para 7.16). Paragraph 7.23 of the guidance deals with when it will be 'necessary' to represent an applicant for legal aid, and comments:

> It should not be necessary for there to be more parties legally represented than there are positions to be argued. This may be particularly relevant in a welfare case in the Court of Protection where an additional family member seeks representation....

6.60 Section 9 of the Lord Chancellor's Guidance deals with mental health cases, and includes the following relevant provisions:

- Legal representation (ie a legal aid certificate) may be refused if it is premature or if legal help is more appropriate (para 9.5).
- For Court of Protection work, the expectation will be that 'support will be available through legal help' (para 9.8).
- Accommodation cases will only be in scope if they affect P's family life.
- Although legal help is not available to create an advance decision or LPA, it is available to advise on potential or actual proceedings about the validity or applicability.

Financial eligibility (means test)

6.61 The means test is governed by the Civil Legal Aid (Financial Resources and Payment for Services) Regulations 2013 SI No 480.

---

47 Unreported, CO/5916/2015.The sealed order can be viewed at https://courtofprotectionhandbook.com/sealed-final-order-04-04-16/

Funding and representation 173

6.62 There is only one exception to the rule that the client must satisfy the means test before getting legal aid in the Court of Protection. This is where a person is deprived of their liberty under a standard authorisation under MCA 2005 Sch A1 and there is an appeal against the authorisation under MCA 2005 s21A. In this case, the person under the authorisation can obtain legal aid without their means being assessed, and so can their 'relevant person's representative' (RPR).

6.63 The relevant regulation (reg 5(1)(g)) is below and shows when legal aid can be provided without the applicant satisfying the means test:

g) legal representation in relation to a matter described in paragraph 5(1)(c) (mental capacity) of Part 1 of Schedule 1 to the Act to the extent that–
  (i) the legal representation is in proceedings in the Court of Protection under section 21A of the Mental Capacity Act 2005; and
  (ii) the individual to whom legal representation may be provided is–
    (aa) the individual in respect of whom an authorisation is in force under paragraph 2 of Schedule A1 to the Mental Capacity Act 2005; or
    (bb) a representative of that individual appointed as such in accordance with Part 10 of that Schedule;

6.64 From this it will be seen that the exemption from the means test relates to legal representation only. Legal help could only be provided in relation to a section 21A case if the client satisfied the means test.

6.65 Guidance from Charles J in *Re HA*[48] (determined before the regulations came into effect) encouraged judges in section 21A cases to make interim orders depriving P of his or her liberty under MCA 2005 s16. The authorisation would then fall away and P's entitlement to non-means tested legal aid would be lost. In *UF v (1) A Local Authority (2) AS (3) Director of Legal Aid Casework (4) Ministry of Justice*.[49] UF appealed against a standard authorisation. The district judge made orders depriving UF of her liberty under MCA 2005 s16. On the expiry of the standard authorisation, UF was advised by the LAA that her means would now be assessed because she no longer came within regulation 5(1)(g)(ii)(aa) above. UF's means would have made her ineligible for legal aid. She applied to the court to vary the court's order so that the court's authorisation of her deprivation of

48 [2012] EWHC 1068 (COP), [2012] COPLR 534.
49 [2013] EWHC 4289 (COP), [2014] COPLR 93.

liberty would be set aside. Charles J held that in the vast majority of cases the court could exercise its powers under MCA 2005 s21A(3)(a) to vary the standard authorisation; and could extend an extant authorisation pursuant to MCA 2005 s21A(2)(b).

6.66 The Director of Legal Aid Casework and Ministry of Justice assured Charles J that if a court adopted either of the courses in a) or b) or the course adopted in that of *UF*, it would not treat the orders as contrivances and refuse public funding for that reason when applying the merits test for public funding. The effect of these concessions is that it is clear that non-means tested legal aid should remain available on any application under MCA 2005 s21A for so long as P is deprived of his or her liberty, including under orders of the court which are framed as set out in *UF*. An example is set out below:

Example

P brings proceedings a) challenging a standard authorisation and b) seeking declarations that his Article 5 rights have been breached by an act done in relation to the standard authorisation. At the first hearing the authorisation is about to expire but the judge varies the standard authorisation by extending it to the next hearing. P will continue to be eligible for non-means tested legal aid. At the second hearing the judge terminates the standard authorisation and P returns home. The proceedings continue while P seeks declarations about the lawfulness of the authorisation. P will no longer be eligible for non-means tested legal aid.

6.67 In *UF*, Charles J also indicated that, where the court varied the standard authorisation by extending it, the court may need to consider making an order under MCA 2005 s21A(6) exonerating the supervisory body from liability for the extended period as the court would have assumed the responsibility for the deprivation of liberty.

6.68 Non–means tested legal aid is not, however, available if P is deprived of his or her liberty through the order of the court, because he or she lives in a setting where MCA 2005 Sch A1 (DOLS) cannot be used.

6.69 In both *Re NRA*[50] and *Re JM*,[51] Charles J considered the position an uncontentious application is made for orders depriving P of his or

50 [2015] EWCOP 59, [2015] COPLR 690.
51 [2016] EWCOP 15, [2016] COPLR 302.

her liberty (so-called '*Re X*' cases)[52] under MCA 2005 s16. Such cases rarely involve an oral hearing and therefore do not satisfy the merits test (see para 6.46 above); legal help would also only be available if P were financially eligible. He encouraged the Secretary of State to consider whether to amend the legal aid scheme for such cases. Charles J found in *Re JM* that the 'minimum procedural requirements' to satisfy Article 5 necessitated 'some assistance from someone on the ground who considers the care package through P's eyes'.[53] A litigation friend (or an accredited legal representative (ALR): see para 11.4) could fulfil that role, and non-means tested legal aid in such cases would make this a potential solution to the dearth of representatives for P in '*Re X*' cases. However as at the time of writing, there has been no change in policy to reflect these observations.

6.70 In some cases, if the applicant for legal aid is in receipt of certain benefits, then their income will not need to be further assessed.[54] However, in all cases at all levels of legal aid, an applicant for legal aid must have their capital assessed (discussed in the next section).

Evidence of financial eligibility

6.71 All applicants for legal aid need to provide evidence of their capital, even if they are in receipt of 'passporting benefits' where the Department for Work and Pensions (DWP) has already undertaken an assessment of their capital in order to decide that they qualify for benefits.

6.72 When acting for P, or a protected party, it is P's means which must be assessed, and not those of P's litigation friend. The LAA encourages practitioners having difficulty obtaining evidence of means in these cases to email: contactcivil@legalaid.gsi.gov.uk with the heading 'Vulnerable Client Means Assessment'.

Practical issues

6.73 Although it will be P's means which are assessed for the purpose of an application for legal aid, legal aid forms should be signed by the

---

52 See further para 21.56 onwards.
53 *Re JM* at para 140.
54 Civil Legal Aid (Financial Resources and Payments for Services) Regulations 2013 SI No 480 reg 6.

litigation friend (if appointed) or, if there are no proceedings on foot, by the person who intends to act as litigation friend. The Civil Legal Aid (Procedure) Regulations 2012 permit the signature of applications for legal services on behalf of a protected party by a person acting or proposing to act as litigation friend; or by any other person where there is good reason why the litigation friend or proposed litigation friend cannot make the application. This does not include the provider of legal services.[55] The Standard Civil Contract authorises a third party to sign forms on behalf of a protected party where there is sufficient connection between the protected party and the third party to ensure that the third party is likely to act reasonably; and when the third party has sufficient knowledge of the protected party's means to provide instructions[56].

6.74 The appointment of an ALR does not bring funding with it. ALRs will need to be authorised by the court to investigate P's means in cases other than section 21A applications.

6.75 The regulations do not currently cater for ALRs to sign legal aid forms on behalf of P. It is suggested that until such time as the regulations are amended, courts appointing ALRs should specifically authorise the ALR to sign the application form on behalf of P.

The statutory charge

6.76 LASPO s25 provides that the LAA's charge attaches to:
   (a) any property recovered or preserved by the individual in proceedings, or in any compromise or settlement of a dispute, in connection with which the services were provided (whether the property is recovered or preserved for the individual or another person), and
   (b) any costs payable to the individual by another person in connection with such proceedings or such a dispute.

6.77 The definition above is wide and is not limited to property recovered or preserved in the same set of proceedings in which legal aid was made available.

6.78 The Civil Legal Aid (Statutory Charge) Regulations 2013 SI No 503 give the Lord Chancellor discretion to waive all or part of the statutory charge in limited circumstances.[57] Regulation 8 applies when

---

55 Civil Legal Aid (Procedure) Regulations 2012 reg 22.
56 Standard Civil Contract 2014, General Specification, para 3.12.
57 Civil Legal Aid (Statutory Charge) Regulations 2013 regs 8 and 9.

the statutory charge is in favour of a provider of legal aid services (in other words, in cases where legal help or 'help at court' have been provided. The Lord Chancellor can permit the provider to waive all or part of the charge when it would cause grave hardship or distress to a legally aided party to enforce the charge; and when enforcing the charge would be unreasonably difficult because of the nature of the property. Regulation 9 allows the Lord Chancellor to waive all or part of the charge when it is equitable to do so and where at the time of granting legal aid, the Director of Legal Aid Casework had been satisfied that the proceedings has a significant wider public interest and that there were other claimants or potential claimants who might benefit from the proceedings.

6.79 In *R (Faulkner) v Director of Legal Aid Casework*[58] Mostyn J rejected a challenge to the (then) Legal Services Commission not to waive the statutory charge which would have the effect of eliminating the damages awarded to Mr Faulkner for breach of Article 5. He held that damages for Convention breaches do not bring immunity with them and are subject to the same costs regime as any other damages.

Experts' fees

6.80 This section should be read in conjunction with paras 12.64–12.78 which discusses the tests that the court will apply in deciding whether to allow the instruction of an expert and on what terms.

6.81 Experts' fees can be claimed as a disbursement on a party's legal aid certificate. The LAA sets rates which it will agree to pay experts. The current rates were set on 2 December 2013.[59] If a certain type of expert is not listed in the remuneration regulations, they will be remunerated at a rate determined by the LAA, which will have regard to the codified rates in setting such a rate. The LAA published guidance on the remuneration of experts in September 2014.[60] Practitioners will need to be aware of this guidance, which includes indications of typical hours spent in various types of work.

6.82 If an expert charges a rate in excess of the current codified rate, the LAA will only pay this if it considers it is reasonable to do so in exceptional circumstances *and* it has granted prior authority. The LAA considers the following to be exceptional circumstances:

---

58 [2016] EWHC 717 (Admin), [2016] 2 Costs LR 237.
59 Civil Legal Aid (Remuneration) (Amendment) Regulations 2013 Sch 2.
60 www.gov.uk/government/uploads/system/uploads/attachment_data/file/420106/expert-witnesses-fees-guidance.pdf.

- the expert's evidence is key to the client's case, and either
- the complexity of the material is such that a high level of seniority is required, or
- the material is of such a specialised nature that only very few experts are available to provide the necessary evidence.[61]

6.83 Practitioners considering instructing an expert who charges above the codified rates must therefore obtain prior authority before instructing the expert. Practitioners will be expected strictly to demonstrate that the request for prior authority comes within the conditions set out above.

6.84 Where the expert charges the rate set by the LAA prior authority may be sought if the item of costs is unusual in size or nature; or if there are no codified rates set for a particular expert.[62]

6.85 In all cases where an expert is instructed it is helpful to invite the court to approve the instructions of the particular expert when the court gives permission for the expert to be instructed. Precedents can be found on the Court of Protection Handbook website: www.courtofprotectionhandbook.com. Whether or not the case falls within the Case Management Pilot (see further paras 4.101–4.103), it may be persuasive for the order to make it clear that the court is satisfied that the more stringent test in COPR Pr121 is met; namely that the evidence is necessary to assist the court to resolve the issues in the proceedings and cannot otherwise be provided (see further in this regard para 12.68).

6.86 Whilst the Legal Aid Agency's starting point will frequently be to expect costs of experts to be apportioned equally, the case of *JG v The Lord Chancellor and others*[63] is a useful reminder that equal apportionment of experts' fees is not inevitable and will depend on the facts of the case including for whose benefit the report is sought. Black LJ's judgment contains a review of Strasbourg cases where the securing of expert evidence engaged rights under Articles 6 and 8 ECHR. The guidance on remuneration recognises that equal apportionment will not always be the norm in public law children cases, because some parties may have limited involvement in the case (such as an intervenor),[64] or because the case concerns children with different fathers and the issue relates to one child only. There are potential analogies

---

61 Standard Civil Contract 2010 para 6.62, Draft Standard Civil Contract 2014 para 6.61.
62 Guidance on the Remuneration of Expert Witnesses 4.2, 4.14, 4.15.
63 [2014] EWCA Civ 656, [2014] 2 FLR 1218.
64 Guidance on the Remuneration of Expert Witnesses, 4.5.

in Court of Protection cases. A Trust may be providing inpatient care for P and may thus be a party to an application; but may not have an interest in P's care arrangements after discharge.

6.87 In *AB (A Child) (Temporary Leave to Remove from Jurisdiction: Expert Evidence, Re)*,[65] a family case involving the instruction of an expert in Indian law, HHJ Bellamy noted that neither the Civil Legal Aid (Remuneration) Regulations 2013 nor the LAA's contract defined the term 'expert'. He commented:

> That is unsurprising. The determination of whether expert evidence is necessary in order to resolve a case justly and whether a particular witness 'is qualified to give expert evidence' (s3(1) of the Civil Evidence Act 1972) are issues for determination by the court not by the LAA. I am concerned that in this case the LAA should have disregarded a decision by the court that Mr Kumar is an expert. In my judgment it was not open to the LAA to disregard a judicial decision on this issue.

Very high cost cases

6.88 Very high costs cases (VHCCs) are defined in Civil Legal Aid (Procedure) Regulations 2012 SI No 3098 ('the Procedure Regs') reg 54(3). These cases are managed under an individual contract which is agreed between the practitioner and the Special Cases Unit and the LAA. For the purpose of Court of Protection cases, the VHCC provisions will apply when the Director of Legal Aid Casework has reason to believe that the actual or likely cost of the case exceed £25,000.

6.89 Practitioners will keep the overall costs of any certificated case under careful review. If it appears that the likely costs of the case – taking into account counsel's fees and disbursements – are likely to exceed £25,000, then the practitioner must follow the steps set out in the LAA's information pack, *VHCC – A solicitors information pack (non-family)* ('Solicitors Information Pack').[66] It is not difficult for a contested Court of Protection case to become a VHCC, particularly if there are substantial interim hearings or experts are used.

---

65 [2014] EWHC 2758 (Fam), [2015] 1 FCR 164.
66 Available at: www.justice.gov.uk/downloads/legal-aid/vhccs/solicitors-information-pack.pdf.

CHAPTER 7

Making an application: property and affairs cases

7.1	Introduction
7.4	**Preliminary matters**
7.4	Initial considerations
7.6	Application procedure
7.19	Process
7.23	Service and notification
7.28	Dispensing with service
7.29	Service abroad
7.30	Notifying P
7.33	Next steps
7.36	**Deputyship applications**
7.36	When is a deputy needed?
7.40	Choice of deputy
7.51	Security bond
7.53	Supervision
7.54	Restrictions
7.56	Powers and duties of a deputy
7.60	Investment
7.64	Family care payments: 'gratuitous care'
7.70	**Deputyship in personal injury award cases**
7.84	**Statutory wills and gifting**

continued

7.93 Powers of attorney
7.102 Jointly owned property and other trustee matters
7.105 Removal of attorney or deputy
7.117 Redress
7.120 Recovery of capacity
7.123 Death of P
7.124 Mixed applications
7.129 Bulk applications

Introduction

7.1 The vast majority of the applications dealt with by the Court of Protection concern property and affairs. These make up in the region of 95 per cent of the work of the court.[1]

7.2 This chapter looks first at the application process for property and affairs applications, focussing on a deputyship application. It then goes on to look at issues relating to deputyship and other types of applications to the court as well as the court's powers in relation to Lasting and Enduring Powers of Attorney (LPA/EPA). Chapter 8 looks at responding to an application and the procedure when an application is contested.

7.3 A flowchart summarising the procedure is set out at the end of this chapter. The very significant majority of applications concerning P's property and affairs are not contested, and are necessary simply because court authority is needed lawfully to make the necessary decisions.

Preliminary matters

Initial considerations

7.4 Before making an application to the court it is worth considering if other less costly and cumbersome options could offer a solution (see also in this regard chapter 5). Where P's life expectancy is short or funds are very limited then an application may not be appropriate. If the prospective applicant is aware that there is any possibility that the application could be contentious it is wise to try to consult with P's family and wider support network to establish if a consensus can be achieved before taking matters before the court.

7.5 If the appointment of a deputy is necessary there are particular considerations as to the choice of deputy, these can be found below at para 7.40.

Application procedure

7.6 All property and affairs applications begin following the same procedure. Permission is not required to make any application concerning

---

1 By way of example, of the 23,525 applications received by the court in 2015, 20,876 (89 per cent) concerned property and affairs and only 2,469 (11 per cent) concerned health and welfare (statistics provided by former Senior Judge Lush).

P's property and affairs, whether for the appointment of deputy or any other issue.[2]

7.7 The court application documents were revised in 2015 with the aim of simplifying the application process and ensuring that the court had all necessary information at an early stage. The core application documents for property and affairs applications are:

- COP1 Application form;
- COP1A Supporting evidence for property and affairs; and
- COP3 Assessment of capacity.

7.8 COPR Part 9 deals with beginning proceedings. Practice Direction (PD) 9A provides guidance on completing the COP1, which is the main application form for starting proceedings. The COP1 form sets out the order or decision that the court is being asked to make, why the decision needs to be made and how it is in P's best interests to make the decision.

7.9 All applications relating to property and affairs (unless made by an existing deputy or attorney under the procedure set out in PD 9D) require a COP1A form to provide the court with P's financial context. It is important to give as much information as possible to ensure that the order ultimately made by the court suits P's circumstances. Where the application is for the appointment of a deputy this information will be used by the court to set the appropriate guarantee bond and decide how much the deputy may access of P's funds in any given year without further authority or such other restrictions as it deems appropriate. This ensures that the court does not unnecessarily curtail the deputy's authority or leave P exposed by the deputy being under-bonded. In other applications relating to P's property and affairs the question of affordability is often key to any decision to be made so it is essential to robust decision making that all parties have detailed financial information.

7.10 The COP1A form also identifies who is a respondent to the application and who is to be notified. A respondent is 'any person (other than P) whom the applicant reasonably believes to have an interest which means he ought to be heard in relation to the application (as opposed to being notified of it)'.[3] The applicant should attempt to identify at least three people to notify of the application.[4] People to be notified are people who have a reasonable interest in being notified of the application. Those who are notified of an applic-

2 COPR r51(2)(a).
3 COPR r63(c)(iii).
4 COPR r70 and PD 9B para 4.

ation may apply to be joined as parties.[5] There is a presumption (which can be displaced) that close members of P's family will have such an interest and PD 9B para 7 lists those who should ordinarily be notified, in descending order of closeness to P.[6] If someone in that list is not notified, then the application form should explain the reasons for their omission.

7.11 Form COP3 provides the court with an assessment of P's mental capacity in relation to the specific decision to be made by the court. It is usually completed by a medical practitioner, social worker or other suitably qualified professional. The Court of Protection's jurisdiction is only engaged where there is evidence that on the balance of probabilities it is more likely than not that a person is not capable of making certain decisions for themselves because of a lack of capacity (see further paras 3.33–3.39). When completing Part A of the form, advisers should ensure that they have correctly identified the issue or issues in respect of which P's decision-making capabilities need to be assessed. The tests in relation to statutory wills and gifts are touched on below at para 7.84 onwards and are addressed in detail in the BMA/Law Society's *Assessment of Mental Capacity*.[7]

7.12 Occasionally there will be uncertainty as to a person's capacity or lack of capacity. If there is conflicting evidence all relevant evidence as to capacity should be put before the court for consideration.[8] The judge can then consider the evidence available and make a decision or give directions to resolve the issue of P's mental capacity. This may be by way of an oral hearing.

7.13 If the court is not satisfied with the medical evidence available, or if there has been some difficulty in having P's capacity assessed, the court is able to order under MCA 2005 s49 that a Special Visitor meets P to assess their capacity (see further in respect of section 49 reports, paras 12.45–12.53). A Special Visitor is a member of a panel appointed by the Lord Chancellor, with a medical qualification and special knowledge of and experience in cases of impairment of or disturbance in the functioning of the mind or brain;[9] one of their roles is to carry out assessments of capacity in these more difficult or unusual cases.

5 COPR r72(6) and (8); PD 9C para 4.
6 PD 9B para 7.
7 4th edition, 2015.
8 See, by analogy, *Loughlin v Singh and others* [2013] EWHC 1641 (QB), [2013] COPLR 371.
9 MCA 2005 s61(2).

186 Court of Protection Handbook / chapter 7

7.14 Medical evidence must be recent. If the court deems that the evidence is too old it may order that an updated assessment of capacity needs to be carried out which will delay the application. If the COP3 form is dated more than six months before the application then the court is likely to ask for an updated assessment.

7.15 Additional forms are required depending upon the particular application to be made:
- deputy application – COP4 deputy's declaration;
- authorisation of a Statutory will, codicil, gift or other disposition of P's property – COP1C;
- applications to appoint or discharge a trustee – COP1D;
- applications by an existing deputy or attorney – COP1E;
- applications relating to the validity or operation of an EPA/LPA – COP1F.

Applicants are directed to these additional forms when completing the COP1.

7.16 Form COP4 is the prospective deputy's declaration that they are a fit and suitable person to act. Each person who wishes to be appointed as deputy must compete a copy of this form.

7.17 Forms COP1C, COP1D, COP1E and COP1F each use a check-list approach to ensure that the applicant has provided all the information that the court will need to reach a decision for the specified matter.

7.18 In most applications other than a straightforward deputy application a COP24 witness statement will also be required. This allows applicants to explain more fully the matter they wish the court to decide and to set out the evidence available and the reasons for the decision proposed being in P's best interests. The rules relating to evidence are explored in more detail in chapter 12.

Process

7.19 The completed documents must be submitted (the address is in appendix G below) along with the appropriate application fee. In some circumstances a fee remission may be available. Details of fees and remissions are to be found in appendix F below.

7.20 For a straightforward application, such as that for the appointment of a deputy, the application form will usually be sealed and issued without the need for it to be referred for judicial scrutiny. To issue an application the court logs the details of the applicant and P on their system, allocates a case reference and makes up the court's paper file. A copy of the COP1 form, stamped with the date of issue

7.21 and with the court reference number completed, will be returned to the applicant to carry out service.

In some cases the application will need to be referred to a judge before it is issued. This may be where there is conflicting evidence as to P's capacity, if some information is incomplete, interim directions have been requested or the application is for a statutory will or gift for example. Depending upon the circumstances or the nature of the application the court may make enquiries or issue initial directions to obtain further information before issuing the requested application. Where the application is for a statutory will or gift the court will make an order at this stage joining the Official Solicitor to represent P.

7.22 Once the applicant receives back the issued COP1 form and any initial directions, the next step is to deal with service and notification.

Service and notification

7.23 The applicant is responsible for serving anyone named as a respondent[10] or anyone who is to be notified of the proceedings.[11] The applicant must serve the respondents, and those to be notified of the issue of proceedings, within 14 days of the date of the issue of the application.[12] The time limit was reduced by the Court of Protection (Amendment) Rules 2015, in an attempt to speed up the processes of the court. The provisions as to service appear in Part 6 of the COPR, supported by PD 6A, which sets out how service should be effected (for example, by document exchange or electronically). Rule 32 explains the provisions for service on children or protected parties.

7.24 When serving respondents[13] the applicant must send each of them a copy of the following documents:
- a copy of the issued application form;
- a copy of any documents filed with the application form (for example, the COP1B, COP3, COP4 if the application relates to a deputyship, any witness statements);
- a copy of any orders made by the court;
- notice of acting (if this has not been served) – COP30;
- notice of issue of legal aid certificate (if appropriate);
- COP5 acknowledgment of service for the individual to complete.

10 COPR r66
11 COPR r70.
12 COPR r66(1).
13 See para 8.5.

7.25 Those who are notified of an application do not need to be served with a full copy of the application papers. When serving those notified the applicant must send them:
- COP15 notice that an application has been issued, this provides details of the applicant and the order sought;
- COP5 acknowledgement of service for the individual to complete.

7.26 When carrying out service, the applicant or their legal adviser should consider whether to include documents other than those required by the procedure. For instance, it is good practice to include information about the general rule as to costs should the party notified wish to take independent legal advice.

7.27 Once the applicant has served all those who are to be served or notified she must complete form COP20B confirming that dates or service and notification and return this to the court.

Dispensing with service

7.28 There are certain circumstances under which service can be dispensed with, either upon application to the court or of the court's own motion.[14] It has been held that a decision to dispense with service is not an act done or decision made on behalf of P, such that the principles of the MCA 2005 do not strictly apply to the decision: *I v D*.[15] It will only be in exceptional cases that it would be appropriate to dispense with service on an individual (or individuals) who is directly and adversely affected by an application. An applicant who is considering making an application to dispense with service is advised to familiarise themselves with the decision in *I v D* and to note the warning set out in the final paragraph that the Official Solicitor may well on behalf of P seek a costs order against an applicant who, in unexceptional circumstances and for no compelling reason, apply to dispense with service on someone who is materially and adversely affected by an application for the execution of a statutory will.

Service abroad

7.29 Service outside the jurisdiction is dealt with at COPR rr39-39H, introduced by the 2015 amendments. These rules supported by PD 6B. We do not address the issue of such service further here because

14 COPR r38.
15 [2016] EWCOP 35, [2016] COPLR 432, endorsing an earlier decision of District Judge Batten in *A v B* [2013] EWHC B39 (COP).

it is an issue which only arises infrequently, and because PD 6B is comprehensive in its guidance.

Notifying P

7.30 The applicant is responsible for notifying P of the issue of an application, within 14 days of the issue of the application, unless P has already been made a party.[16] Decisions about whether to join P and, if P is joined, how he or she will be represented are governed by COPR r1.2/COPR r3A, which is discussed in detail in chapter 11. If P has been made a party, then the court will decide how service should take place.[17] If P has not been made a party, then P must be provided with the information personally, in a manner that is appropriate to P's circumstances, for example using simple language or visual aids.[18] P must be given a form COP14, which should explain clearly the matter which the court has been asked to decide, and a COP5 (acknowledgement of service).[19] Once this has been done, form COP20A must be filed.

7.31 If at all possible, it is good practice for a prospective deputy – especially one acting in a professional capacity without personal knowledge of P – to meet P and take steps to discuss the proposed application *prior* to making any application.

7.32 COPR r49 allows an applicant or appellant or anyone directed to effect notification on P to apply to the court for an order dispensing with the requirement to comply with the provisions relating to the notification of P or requiring some other person to comply with those provisions. Moreover, the court can in any case, either on its own initiative or on application, direct that he must not be notified of any matter or document, or provided with any document.[20] The court might dispense with the requirement to notify P if P were in a permanent vegetative or minimally conscious state, or if notification by the applicant is likely to cause significant and disproportionate distress to P.[21]

16 COPR r46.
17 COPR r33(1).
18 COPR r46.
19 PD 7 para 6.
20 COPR r40(3).
21 PD 7A para 9.

Next steps

7.33 Unless a specific application has been made on the basis of particular urgency, the court will take no steps during the 14-day period during which those who have been notified must make their response.[22]

7.34 If no objections are received by the court during this period, the file will be referred back to the court for consideration, either by a judge or authorised court officer (depending on the nature of the application). If everything is in order at this stage, then the order will usually be made. If the application concerned the appointment of a deputy the applicant, or their legal adviser, will receive a letter notifying them that the court has made an order appointing them as deputy and advising them that the order will be released to them on the security bond has been put in place.

7.35 If the application is urgent or contested further guidance as to the procedure is provided below in chapter 8.

Deputyship applications

When is a deputy needed?

7.36 If a person loses their capacity to make some decisions about their finances and they have not planned for this eventuality by making an EPA (before 1 October 2007) or an LPA for property and affairs (from 1 October 2007 onwards) then it may be necessary for an application to be made to the court for the appointment of a property and affairs deputy. Without an attorney or deputy, the general rule is that no transactions concerning P's property or finances can be validly undertaken.

7.37 When deciding if an application for the appointment of a deputy is necessary, the nature of P's assets and income should be considered. If the only income of the person concerned is state benefits then the appointment of a deputy may be disproportionate and costly, an application can be made by an individual (such as a family member) or an organisation (eg a council) to the Department for Work and Pensions (DWP) to be made their appointee to manage those benefits. This does not require an application to the court.[23]

---

22 COPR r72 allows 14 days after service for acknowledgment of the application by the person upon whom the application is served.
23 See www.gov.uk/become-appointee-for-someone-claiming-benefits.

7.38 If, however, there are other assets or income that need to be managed, then it is likely that a deputy will need to be appointed. This would include situations such as P owning a property or savings and investments that needed to be sold or accessed, for example to pay for the costs of a care home or to meet P's day-to-day expenses or regular payments.

7.39 It is important to keep in mind that under the Mental Capacity Act (MCA) 2005 capacity is 'decision-specific', there are no absolutes in terms of a person's decision-making capabilities (see paras 3.33–3.64). There is no contradiction between having a deputy and retaining the ability to make some decisions. For example, a deputy may need to make decisions about investing a large sum of money while P retains the capacity to manage their weekly income to buy groceries and personal items.

Choice of deputy

7.40 The MCA 2005 does not set out any order for individuals to be considered for the role of deputy. The choice of who would be a suitable deputy will depend largely upon P's family and circumstances.

7.41 In *Re M; N v O and P*[24] Senior Judge Lush noted that pre-MCA 2005 authorities were still pertinent to the question of who to appoint as a deputy, and set out an 'order of preference' in which P's family was to be preferred by the court over strangers such as professional advisers or statutory bodies. Senior Judge Lush observed that:

> The court prefers to appoint a family member or close friend, if possible, as long as it is in P's best interests to do so. This is because a relative or friend will already be familiar with P's affairs, and wishes and methods of communication. Someone who already has a close personal knowledge of P is also likely to be better able to meet the obligation of a deputy to consult with P, and to permit and encourage him to participate, or to improve his ability to participate, as fully as possible in any act done for him and any decision affecting him. And, because professionals charge for their services, the appointment of a relative or friend is generally preferred for reasons of economy. There are, of course, cases in which the court would not countenance appointing a particular family member as deputy. For example, if there had been physical or financial abuse; if there is a conflict of interests; if the proposed deputy has an unsatisfactory track record in managing his own financial affairs; and if there is ongoing friction

24 [2013] COPLR 91.

between various family members that is likely to interfere with the administration of P's affairs. This list is not exhaustive.[25]

7.42 In this case, in applying the balance-sheet approach, the various factors the court considered in assessing the merits of the two proposed deputies were:
- ability to act;
- willingness to act;
- qualifications;
- place of residence;
- security;
- conduct before and during the proceedings;
- nature of relationship with M;
- M's wishes and feelings;
- views of others;
- effect of hostility;
- conflicts of interest;
- remuneration; and
- the terms of M's will.

7.43 Senior Judge Lush found that the two factors of 'magnetic importance' in deciding who the court should appoint as deputy for P, where there were competing candidates for the role were 'M's past and present wishes and feelings and the unanimous views of others, who are particularly close to him, as to what would be in his best interests'.[26] He went on to comment that there were also cases in which the court would not appoint a family member, such as where P has recovered damages in personal injury litigation specifically to fund a professional deputy appointment.

7.44 Some individuals will be considered as unsuitable to act as deputy. In *Re BM; JB v AG*[27] and again in *Re PAW*[28] Senior Judge Lush set out a list of those the court would not consider appointing, this list includes:

a) A proposed deputy who has physically, emotionally or financially abused P;
b) Where there is a need to investigate dealings with P's assets prior to the matter being brought to the court's attention, and the proposed deputy's conduct is the subject of that investigation;

---

25 Para 39.
26 Para 78.
27 [2014] EWCOP B20.
28 [2015] EWCOP 57, [2015] WTLR 1785.

c) Where there is an actual conflict of interests, rather than simply a potential conflict;[29]
d) The proposed deputy has an unsatisfactory track record in managing his or her own financial affairs;
e) When there is ongoing friction between various family members, which is likely to interfere with the proper administration of P's affairs; and
f) If there is a need to ensure that P is free from undue influence, particularly the influence exerted by the person who is seeking to be appointed as deputy.[30]

Other factors that may influence the decision about who should be appointed as deputy include locality, health, family and work commitments.

7.45 In *DGP Law v DGHP and others*,[31] the traditional position was reversed with regard to appointing a deputy who lives outside the jurisdiction. In this case Senior Judge Lush appointed a deputy who lives in the USA. In his judgment Senior Judge Lush observed that 'in the two decades since Justice Cunningham delivered his judgment there have been further technological advances in communications, such as online banking, digital reporting, mobile phone, email and Skype, and cheaper air travel as a result of a proliferation of budget airlines'.

7.46 The court has also recently considered the situation where a deputy has limited command of English in the case of *Re FH*[32] and concluded that this is not an absolute bar being appointed deputy.

7.47 These may be cases that need to be looked at on their facts as in each case features existed that mitigated the disadvantage suffered by the proposed deputy. In the first case the proposed deputy had access to up to date technology which facilitated administration of P's affairs and in the second a close family member was available to translate for the proposed deputy. Once again we suggest that the court will look at all the circumstances of P and the proposed deputy when coming to a decision.

7.48 It is possible for an application to be made for joint deputies to be appointed. This can help to share the burden but does require good communication to work efficiently. The updated application forms

---

29 For comments on the court's approach to managing conflict see *Re JW* [2015] EWCOP 82, [2016] COPLR 36.
30 *Re PAW* [2015] EWCOP 57, [2015] WLTR 1785 at para 26.
31 [2015] EWCOP 58.
32 [2016] EWCOP 14, [2016] COPLR 287.

make it easier to make a joint application, providing spaces to specify up to four prospective deputies.

7.49 Most deputies appointed are lay deputies, ie private individuals acting as deputy, usually for a family member. There are, however, professionals who specialise in this area of work and whose appointment is appropriate in some circumstances. Many local authorities continue to have a deputyship department but they will often only act as deputies of last resort where a suitable relative cannot be traced to undertake the role. A professional deputy is usually appointed where P has received substantial funds in compensation for a personal injury, or where P has complex or very high value personal finances or if the court concludes that is in P's best interests for a neutral professional to undertake the role, usually where there is discord within a family. The Public Guardian also maintains a panel of deputies to whom cases can be referred to as a deputy of last resort (see also paras 20.44). Panel deputies are often appointed to act where there has been significant friction within the family about who should act as deputy for P. If the court believes that on-going family friction would impact upon the proper management of P's finances a panel deputy will be invited to take on the role. For a discussion of the court's approach to deciding amongst competing professionals see *Re RP Z*.[33]

7.50 Finally, it should be noted that a trust corporation can be appointed to be a property and affairs deputy (but not a health and welfare deputy).[34]

Security bond

7.51 The court has discretion to require a deputy to provide security for the discharge of the functions conferred upon them.[35] Generally, all deputies, whether lay or professional, are required to provide security by way of a bond, with the exception of local authority deputies. The level of the bond and the premium charged for it is determined by the court in reference to P's assets and the amount of money to which the deputy has access.[36] The security bond is to protect P from financial loss caused by the deputy, whether deliberately or by negligence.

33 [2016] EWCOP 1.
34 MCA 2005 s19(1)(b).
35 MCA 2005 s19(9); see also COPR r200.
36 *Re H (a minor and incapacitated person); Baker v H and the Official Solicitor* [2009] COPLR Con Vol 606.

Making an application: property and affairs cases 195

There is a bond arrangement in place which deputies can use or they may wish to try to obtain their own cover. Once the bond is in place, the court will be notified and sealed copies of the order will be sent out to the deputy.

7.52 Deputies and their legal advisers should note that they should apply to the court as circumstances change for the level of the security bond to be reviewed. During P's lifetime the nature and extent of their assets will alter and therefore the appropriate level of bond should be reviewed at regular intervals.

Supervision

7.53 When a new deputy is appointed the Office of the Public Guardian (OPG) will be notified by the court. The OPG will then provide a suitable programme of supervision to the deputy depending upon P's circumstances. The OPG requires that every deputy submit an annual report detailing how P's funds have been spent in the previous year and how any capital is invested. They check that the deputy obtains appropriate financial advice and acts upon it and they will schedule a visit by a court visitor to check that the deputy is coping with the new role. For more information on the role of the OPG, see chapter 20.

Restrictions

7.54 It is not uncommon for a deputy order to contain restrictions to the deputy's authority. When a new order is received, the deputy or their legal adviser should read it carefully and note any limits to their authority. Common restrictions include preventing the sale of a property without a further application to the court, or a limit to the amount of money that a deputy can spend in a year. If any of the restrictions are going to prove problematic, then so long as the application is made within 21 days of the order being served, a request can be made for a reconsideration under the provisions of COPR r89 (see further paras 18.3–18.6). Such a request can be made without incurring a further application fee.

7.55 A deputy order cannot be exhaustive in setting out what a deputy is and is not authorised to do; the new deputy, or their legal adviser, should ensure that they are aware of the limits to the scope of the powers that they may exercise without further authorisation of the court.

Powers and duties of a deputy

7.56 The order made by the court will set out the deputy's powers and their limits; typical orders are to be found on the Court of Protection Handbook website.[37]

7.57 A deputy has what is known as a fiduciary duty towards P. This means that there is a relationship of utmost trust and confidence between the deputy and P. Where a fiduciary relationship exists, money and property must be managed in P's best interests, without regard to any interest of the deputy. This means (among other things) that the deputy cannot profit personally by acting as P's deputy and the funds and assets of P must be kept entirely separate from those of the deputy. In relation to property, the deputy cannot sanction a sale to him or herself, or a family member, particularly for less than full market value, without the additional approval of the court. It is also not appropriate for the deputy to receive any of P's funds into an account in their own name. All of P's assets and funds must remain be clearly in P's name at all times. Most bank accounts and other assets should be named 'A as deputy for Y' so that it is immediately clear who the asset belongs to.

7.58 A discussion of the full range of a deputy's powers and duties falls outside the scope of this chapter, and indeed of this book. However, any person considering putting themselves forward as a deputy would be well advised to familiarise themselves with the Code of Practice to the Mental Capacity Act, the principles of the MCA 2005 and the COPR. There continues to be a steady flow of cases[38] which demonstrate that the court will not be lenient on deputies, or attorneys, who simply do not understand the true nature and scope of the role.

7.59 We suggest the following by way of good practice upon the initial appointment of a deputy:
- The deputy should begin their task by circulating the deputy order to all of the financial institutions with whom P has a relationship. It is good practice to ask for an up-to-date statement or valuation and consider updating the court if it becomes clear once appointed that P had considerably more or fewer assets than were detailed in the COP1A. If P is living independently, the deputy should ensure as far as possible that their actions do not jeopardise P's day-to-day activities. If P relies upon a particular current account to access a

---

37 https://courtofprotectionhandbook.com/precedents/.
38 See *Re GM* [2013] COPLR 290; *Re Buckley* [2013] COPLR 3; *Re AB* [2014] WLTR 1303, [2014] EWCOP 12; *The Public Guardian v AW and DH* [2014] WLTR 1705, [2014] EWCOP 28 and *The Public Guardian v DA, YS and ES* [2015] WLTR 1647, [2015] EWCOP 41.

pension to buy groceries, the deputy should make it clear to the bank and the DWP at the time of notifying them of the deputy order that they do not want any changes to the present arrangement.
- Ensure that P is receiving all the income to which they are entitled (and none that they are not). This means that an early task for any new deputy is to review P's benefits and make sure that claims are up-to-date. Benefits will need to remain under review by the deputy in the event of P's circumstances changing.
- Check that insurance policies are updated and relevant to P's circumstances. If the deputy has been appointed because of an accident sustained by P, it may be, for instance, that P has a critical illness policy which would pay out a sum to P.
- If P lives in their own home, the deputy should visit and check how well-maintained it is. If repairs or adaptations are needed, the deputy should seek quotes and take professional advice about the suitability of any changes. If there is a property that needs to be sold, the deputy should check that the deputy order allows sale without further court approval, and if so, then approach estate agents to get a range of valuations before choosing whom to market a property with. If not, the deputy should seek specific approval from the court.
- Consider P's care arrangements and how they are funded. Explore options to maximise funding for example having an assessment for NHS Continuing Care or applying to the local authority for an assessment of P's needs. If family members are being paid for caring for P from P's funds the new deputy should follow the court's guidance in *Re HC* which is discussed below at para 7.64.

Investment

7.60 A deputy should take care to review P's finances and investments, preferably with the assistance of a suitably qualified Independent Financial Adviser (IFA). This is true not simply of new deputies but equally applies to long-standing appointments. P's needs and circumstances will alter over time and the deputy should be alive to these changes.

7.61 In *Re Buckley*[39] Senior Judge Lush took the opportunity to look at the investment responsibilities of an attorney, noting that:

> 20. There are two common misconceptions when it comes to investments. The first is that attorneys acting under an LPA can do whatever

39 [2013] COPLR 39.

they like with the donors' funds. And the second is that attorneys can do whatever the donors could – or would – have done personally, if they had the capacity to manage their property and financial affairs.

21. Managing your own money is one thing. Managing someone else's money is an entirely different matter.

22. People who have the capacity to manage their own financial affairs are generally not accountable to anyone and don't need to keep accounts or records of their income and expenditure. They can do whatever they like with their money, and this includes doing nothing at all. They can stash their cash under the mattress, if they wish and, of course, they are entitled to make unwise decisions.

23. None of these options are open to an attorney acting for an incapacitated donor, partly because of their fiduciary obligations and partly because an attorney is required to act in the donor's best interests. Section 1(5) of the Mental Capacity Act 2005 (the 2005 Act) states that, 'an act done, or decision made, under this Act for or on behalf of a person who lacks capacity must be done, or made, in his best interests.'

...

25. Attorneys hold a fiduciary position, which imposes a number of duties on them. Like trustees and other fiduciaries, they must exercise such care and skill as is reasonable in the circumstances when investing the donor's assets and this duty of care is even greater where attorneys hold themselves out as having specialist knowledge or experience.

26. Although it does not expressly apply to attorneys, s4 of the Trustee Act 2000 requires trustees to have regard to what are known as the 'standard investment criteria' when exercising any power of investment.' [Senior Judge Lush then set out how these investment criteria apply]

7.62 This guidance was given in the context of a case concerning an LPA, but both the comments should be read as being equally applicable to a property and affairs deputy.

7.63 The investments made by the deputy (or attorney) on behalf of P must be in P's best interests, and in line with any other restrictions set out in the deputy order.

Family care payments: 'gratuitous care'

7.64 In the case of *Re HC*[40] the court considered the issue of family members being paid for care from P's funds. This is usually known

40 [2015] EWCOP 29.

as 'gratuitous care', as it refers to a situation where the person being paid (often one of P's parents) provides care out of love and affection for P but in doing so they save P considerable money on the provision of commercial care arrangements and also make a sacrifice of their own career and earning potential. In these circumstances gratuitous care payments can be made to the carer to recognise their contribution, so long as court authority is obtained.

7.65 A deputy order does not automatically allow a lay deputy to make payments to themselves or a close relative for providing care to P. A lay deputy wishing to make gratuitous care payments should follow the steps set out in *Re HC* for ascertaining the appropriate level of payment:

1) What is the commercial value of the care that the family member provides?
2) The ceiling for payment is the value of commercial care reduced by 20 per cent to reflect the savings of tax and National Insurance;
3) Is the proposed payment affordable for P?

The case also sets out a mechanism for increasing the payment each year on the anniversary of the order.

7.66 The method for deciding the commercial value of the care provided will differ depending upon the circumstances of each particular case. Some applicants may need to commission a report from a care expert to assist with this point. The issue of affordability will also be highly variable from case to case and to be able to make decision about what is in P's best interests the court will require up to date information about all P's capital, income and expenditure as well as the proposed gratuitous care payment and the impact this will have as well as medical information about P's life expectancy.

7.67 The case of *Re HNL*[41] saw the court examine the situation of families where care payments commenced under pre-MCA arrangements and were continued by the lay deputy. In this case the court had sufficient information to give retrospective approval to payments that had been made and to authorise the continuation of payments in future. It is not uncommon for lay deputies to have begun making gratuitous care payments without being aware that court authorisation was required. It is clear now that the court will look to regularise these situations when they come before it.

7.68 A deputy making gratuitous care payments would also be wise to notify HMRC of the arrangement to ensure that the payments will not be subject to income tax. The recipient of the payments should

41 [2015] EWCOP 77.

be made aware that unlike paid employment they will be responsible for their own National Insurance payments and they may wish to take independent financial advice about the likely impact on their state pension entitlement.

7.69 The Office of the Public Guardian has now produced a Practice Note on gratuitous care, taking into account decisions such as those set out above.[42]

Deputyship in personal injury award cases

7.70 Many of the highest value deputyships arise from claims for personal injury where P has sustained a brain injury. As mentioned above, in these cases the court will usually prefer a professional deputy. They raise specific considerations which merit brief highlighting here.

An applicant in this type of case should also be aware of the recent decision in *Watt v ABC*[43] which considered the question of when damages should be managed by a deputy and when the creation of a personal injury trust would be appropriate. Charles J commented that when a decision is made as to the best vehicle for future management of P's funds, those making this decision should not proceed on the basis that there is a strong presumption that the COP would appoint a deputy and would not make an order that a trust be created of the award.

7.71 The deputy will usually become involved at a stage of the litigation where there has been an interim payment, or liability has been settled and an interim payment is anticipated. More rarely, a deputy is needed well before liability is established – for example, where P had an insurance policy that has paid out to a sole name account and their family need to access it to meet day-to-day bills.

7.72 If a referral is made before liability is established or any funds are available, the deputy must act cautiously; there is the possibility that the claim will fail and they should bear in mind how the court and other fees are to be funded. It may be necessary to advise the family of P on other options, eg appointeeship, to claim benefits, local authority funding etc.

7.73 Once liability has been settled and an interim payment is made, the deputy should take steps to ensure that they know the terms of

---

42 www.gov.uk/government/uploads/system/uploads/attachment_data/file/524111/PGnote_2016_05_family_care_payments.pdf.
43 [2016] EWCOP 2532.

the payments made and the professional recommendations for P's care and case management. In cases of this sort, interim payments will be made for a particular purpose and a failure to manage funds in line with these purposes can have an adverse impact on the overall value of P's claim. The deputy needs to ensure that they have regular communication with the litigation team. The deputy should consider asking for certain litigation documents such as a copy of any order relating to interim payments as these are useful to have on the file to refer back to in the future.

7.74 Reports obtained in the course of litigation can also include valuable guidance as to how it is recommended that P's funds be applied, as well as how best to communicate with P to maximise their understanding and participate in decision-making. Professionals engaged to provide services to P such as case mangers, physiotherapists, occupational therapists and neuropsychologists will all provide costs estimates for their intervention. All this information can then be used by the deputy to formulate a proposed budget for the management of P's funds.

7.75 When establishing a budget, the deputy will typically communicate with family members or care-providers depending upon P's circumstances. Sadly it is often the case that a family will be under a huge amount of financial pressure if they have managed for some years without P's financial contribution or they have been frequently travelling to a distant hospital to visit P. The deputy may be able to consider alleviating some of this pressure by reimbursing some of these past losses. The legal team involved in running the personal injury claim will be able to guide on this point, and in some cases the order obtained in the personal injury claim approving the interim payment will make specific allowance for a sum to be paid to the family for these costs.

7.76 Clarity is important at this stage, first because whoever is paying sums out needs to be clear about the authority to make those payments; and second, because litigation can take many years to settle, it is important to make sure that everyone understands and records accurately what each payment is for.

7.77 In many personal injury cases insufficient funds are made available at the interim payment stage to implement all of the recommendations made to the claimant's litigation team. In an appropriate case, the deputy should consider exploring other funding avenues such as local authority funding in the form of direct payments.

7.78 The deputy is responsible for scrutinising the quality of the services they pay for on behalf of P. If a service or treatment provider is falling below an acceptable standard, or not providing what has been recommended for P, then there may be the risk that the cost of the service or treatment is disallowed when the damages are assessed.[44]

7.79 Occasionally the deputy may feel that they are being asked to perform a role outside that of simply managing P's property and affairs. If the deputy is being asked to make a decision that goes beyond the financial and budgetary, this is beyond the scope of the deputy's authority. For example, if P wants to go on holiday, the deputy would be expected to set a suitable budget and make sure that the costings include all the expected items; but it is not the deputy's role to decide if it is in P's best interests to go on that particular holiday at that particular time.

7.80 The case of *Re SRK* has placed the additional responsibility on a professional deputy, in cases where P benefits from a private care regime at home, to make contact with the local authority if they are of the view that P's care regime could amount to an objective deprivation of liberty to which P cannot consent.[45] This case concluded that where there is a court appointed deputy this is sufficient state involvement to engage the state's obligations to secure the person against arbitrary deprivation of their liberty. A professional deputy in this position would be well advised to familiarise herself with the case. This case is subject to an appeal at the time of writing and professional deputies will therefore need to ensure they remain alive to developments in relation to their duties.

7.81 Depending upon the level of funds available and the expected expenditure where there is ongoing litigation, the deputy will usually want to consider putting in place regular budget updates. This allows the deputy to see if funds are being spent in accordance with recommendations and if budgets are being kept to. P's circumstances, and the recommendations for their care, can change rapidly; the deputy should keep pace with these changes.

7.82 Once a claim for compensation is settled the deputy will need to review the financial position P has been left in and begin to make plans for the longer term. Many cases settle for a lump sum plus periodical payments to meet P's care needs. The deputy will typically want to focus on investing the lump sum in such a way that P's needs are met now and in the future.

---

44 *Loughlin v Singh and others* [2013] EWHC 1641 (QB), [2013] COPLR 371.
45 [2016] EWCOP 27, [2016] 3 WLR 867. See further in this regard chapter 21.

7.83 Other matters that the deputy should consider once any litigation has been finalised will include reviewing P's testamentary provision.

Statutory wills and gifting

7.84 The Court of Protection has the power under MCA 2005 s18 to authorise the execution of a will (or a codicil) on behalf of a person who lacks the relevant capacity, and also to authorise gifts on behalf of P that fall outside the very limited scope to gift that is enjoyed by deputies and attorneys alike. These applications raise particular issues which fall outside the scope of this book to discuss fully.[46] What follows is a summary of the key points that arise.

7.85 In each case the applicant should obtain specific medical evidence as to P's capacity in relation to the decision that the court will be invited to make. There are different tests for each decision.

1) In *A, B and C v X and Z*,[47] Hedley J held that the test of testamentary capacity before the Court of Protection is the common law test formulated in *Banks v Goodfellow*,[48] ie that:

> It is essential . . . that a testator shall understand the nature of the act [of making a will] and its effects; shall understand the extent of the property of which he is disposing; shall be able to comprehend and appreciate the claims to which he ought to give effect, and . . . that no disorder of mind shall poison their affections, pervert his sense of right, or prevent the exercise of his natural faculties – that no insane delusion shall influence his will in disposing of his property and bring about a disposal of it which, if his mind had been sound, would not have been made.

> Note that the test in *Banks v Goodfellow* differs in some ways from the approach adopted under MCA 2005 ss2–3 (see further paras 3.33–3.64), in particular because it does not allow the reliance on supported decision making that applies to all other decisions under the MCA 2005.[49] It may well be that in due course there will be a case in which this question is revisited before the Court of Protection.

---

46 For more detail, readers are referred to Ashton et al, *Court of Protection Practice 2016* Jordans, chapter 5, and D Lush and D Rees, consultant editors, *Heywood & Massey: Court of Protection Practice* (looseleaf), Sweet & Maxwell, chapters A20 (wills) and A21 (settlements and gifts).
47 [2012] EWHC 2400 (COP), [2013] COPLR 1.
48 (1870) LR 5 QB 549, [1861–1873] All ER 47.
49 See for further discussion Alex Ruck Keene and Annabel Lee, 'Testamentary capacity' [2013] Eld LJ 272.

2) The test for the capacity to make a gift is – again – derived from the common law, this time from the test in *Re Beaney*.[50] The essence of this test is that it is calibrated to the circumstances of the gift, in particular the size of the gift in question in relation to the donor's assets.

7.86 The application for the court to approve a statutory will or gift is subject to the procedures outlined in PD 9F. In essence, it proceeds in the same fashion as outlined above for the basic application, with the addition of a detailed witness statement on the part of the applicant setting out:

- proposed draft will (for an application to approve a will) or details of the gift(s) proposed;
- details of previous wills (if applicable);
- schedule of capital;
- schedule of income;
- schedule of expenditure;
- family tree;
- schedule showing impact of inheritance tax and distribution of estate with and without proposed will or gift.

7.87 The applicant's witness statement needs to explain the reasoning behind the proposals and why it is in the best interests of P.

7.88 The case of *Re P*[51] sets out in some detail the relevant jurisprudence and the tests that will be applied by the court in deciding if a statutory will should be approved. Further helpful comments can also be found in *Re Peter Jones*.[52]

7.89 Careful consideration needs to be given to ensuring that the correct parties are identified and served as respondents in this type of application. If a person is named as a residuary beneficiary in an existing will of P they will need to be named as a respondent in any application to approve a statutory will. A pecuniary or specific legatee under P's will, whose entitlement would be unchanged by the proposed will, can be named as a person to be notified. If P is intestate (ie they have never made any testamentary provision) then the deputy will need to ascertain their family tree to establish who would inherit from P under the Intestacy Rules set out in the Administration of Estates Act 1925 ss46–47. Anyone who would inherit under P's

---

50 [1978] 1 WLR 770; see also *Re P (capacity to tithe inheritance)* [2014] EWHC B14 (COP).
51 [2010] Ch 33, [2009] EWHC 163 (COP).
52 [2014] EWCOP 59.

intestacy must be notified as a respondent in any application to approve a statutory will.[53]

7.90 Deputies have a very limited ability to make gifts on behalf of P. The standard wording of a deputy order gives the power to make gifts of 'a seasonal and customary nature' (see appendix D below). The case of *Re GM*[54] addressed the scope of a deputy's powers to make gifts from P's assets and Senior Judge Lush took the opportunity to provide some guidance on this topic. Having noted that the deputyship order permitted the deputies to make gifts 'on customary occasions to persons who are related to or connected with them, provided that the value of each such gift is not unreasonable having regard to all the circumstances and, in particular, the size of their estate' and that 'a customary occasion' is defined in MCA 2005 s12(3) as 'an anniversary of a birth, a marriage or a civil partnership, or any other occasion on which presents are customarily given within families or among friends or associates' and also that 'the value of the gift must be 'not unreasonable' (s12(2)). Senior Judge Lush set out very clearly the approach to be followed in determining what is reasonable in a given case:

> First, regard must be had to the totality of P's current and anticipated income and capital, expenditure and debts.
>
> Second, consideration must be given to P's best interests, including the following factors:
> - the extent to which P was in the habit of making gifts or loans of a particular size or nature before the onset of incapacity;
> - P's anticipated life expectancy;
> - the possibility that P may require residential or nursing care and the projected cost of such care;
> - whether P is in receipt of aftercare pursuant to section 117 of the Mental Health Act 1983 or NHS Continuing Healthcare;
> - the extent to which any gifts may interfere with the devolution of P's estate under their or their will or intestacy; and
> - the impact of Inheritance Tax on P's death.
>
> Third, any gift that is not de minimis, must be approved in advance by the Court of Protection. A de minimis gift is to be construed as follows: 'covering the annual IHT exemption of £3,000 and the annual small gifts exemption of £250 per person, up to a maximum of, say, ten people in the following circumstances:
> (a) where P has a life expectancy of less than five years;
> (b) their estate exceeds the nil rate band for Inheritance Tax ('IHT') purposes, currently £325,000;

---

53 *Re D* [2016] EWCOP 35, [2016] COPLR 432.
54 [2013] COPLR 290.

(c) the gifts are affordable having regard to P's care costs and will not adversely affect P's standard of care and quality of life, and
(d) there is no evidence that P would be opposed to gifts of this magnitude being made on their behalf.'

7.91 Bearing this very clear guidance in mind, if a deputy thinks that:

a) a more significant gift should be made on behalf of P;
b) that to do so would be in P's best interests; and
c) the gift is affordable in P's circumstances;

the deputy must apply to the court for approval *before* the gift is made.

7.92 In cases concerning the approval of a will or substantial gifting, P will usually be joined to proceedings as a party, and be represented by the Official Solicitor.

Powers of attorney

7.93 Prior to the implementation of the MCA 2005 on 1 October 2007, an EPA allowed a donor (the person who wishes to make arrangements for someone else to look after their finances if they are unable to do so in future) to appoint an attorney (or attorneys) to deal with their finances both immediately after the signing of the document and in the future, should the donor lose their capacity. An EPA could only be made to cover the donor's financial affairs; no power was conferred by it to allow decision-making with regard to health or welfare matters.[55]

7.94 To be valid, an EPA must be in the prescribed format and have been signed by all parties on or before 30 September 2007.[56] The attorneys named in an EPA are under a duty to register the document with the OPG when the donor has lost, or is losing their capacity.

7.95 LPAs were introduced by the MCA 2005 and come in two varieties:

1) health and welfare; and
2) property and affairs.

The new property and affairs LPA is similar in function to the old EPA, but crucially it cannot be used until it has been registered with the OPG.

---

55 For more detail on EPAs and LPAs, see chapter 3 and D Lush, *Cretney & Lush on Lasting and Enduring Powers of Attorney*, 7th edn, Jordans, 2013.
56 Provisions relating to EPAs can now be found in MCA 2005 Sch 4.

7.96 The special feature enjoyed by both the EPA and LPA is that the authority conferred by them continues even after the donor has lost their capacity. All other types of power of attorney (usually referred to as a 'general power of attorney') are automatically revoked by the donor's incapacity.

7.97 The OPG has a range of documents available to download[57] that can take the prospective donor through the process of making an LPA, and registering it. This is an administrative process, falling outside the scope of this book, with one important exception detailed in the bullet points below:

- The process of registration requires notification to any person named in the LPA for that purpose on a form LPA001.[58] If a person notified wishes to object to the registration of an LPA on a prescribed ground,[59] ie most obviously, that either fraud or undue pressure was used to execute an instrument for the purpose of creating an LPA or to create a LPA,[60] then they must within three weeks from the date on which notice is given make an application to the Court of Protection in a form COP7 (not a COP1), and notify the OPG of their application in a form LPA008. There is no fee payable. The COP7 form will then be issued by the court; it must then be served as soon as practicable and in any event within 14 days; the COP7 form must be accompanied with a COP5 form for the person upon whom it is served to respond, and a certificate of service will be required under COP20. Taking these steps will have the effect of preventing the OPG from registering the LPA until the court has determined the application and directed the OPG to do so.[61]
- If the person who wishes to object to the registration was not a person notified on a LPA001 form, the application is made not on an COP7 form, but on a COP1 form; the OPG must also be notified. There is a fee payable in such case (see appendix F below). This will also apply if the LPA has already been registered, but the person wishes the power to be cancelled.

---

57 See www.justice.gov.uk/forms/opg.
58 MCA 2005 Sch 1 para 6.
59 MCA 2005 Sch 1 para 13(3), referring to MCA 2005 s22(3).
60 MCA 2005 s22(3)(a).
61 MCA 2005 Sch 1 para 13(4).

7.98 The Court of Protection has a range of powers in relation to determining both the validity of LPAs[62] and their operation.[63] The most relevant for present purposes are those related to the jurisdiction that the court exercises over the conduct of attorneys (which also extends to the conduct of attorneys under EPAs[64]); see further paras 7.117–7.119 below.

7.99 The court may determine the validity of an LPA[65] and if it finds that it was not properly created may order that the instrument is not registered. Other powers of the court include severing the appointment of an attorney under an LPA if there is more than one appointed. For example, if only one attorney were found to be in breach of their duties this would in itself not invalidate the appointment of any other attorney validly appointed in the same instrument.

7.100 The court also has powers to require attorneys to provide accounts or other information if the donor lacks the capacity to call for these themselves,[66] as well as giving directions about the remuneration of a donee[67] or alleviating them from liability for any breach of their duty as attorney.[68]

7.101 The court also has jurisdiction to authorise gifts that fall outside of the attorney's existing powers under the LPA, see para 7.84 above. The court's power to revoke an LPA is discussed below at para 7.105.

Jointly owned property and other trustee matters

7.102 In cases where P is a trustee, a deputy may not be given power to exercise P's functions as a trustee.[69] An application will need to be made to the court for the appointment of a new trustee to act in P's place.

7.103 This is most commonly found where P is the co-owner of real property as this is a form of trusteeship. P will usually need to be removed from the title to the land and a new trustee appointed in order for a sale of the land to take place.

---

62 MCA 2005 s22.
63 MCA 2005 s23.
64 Under the – slightly different – provisions in MCA 2005 Sch 3 para 16.
65 MCA 2005 s22(2)(a).
66 MCA 2005 s23(3)(a).
67 MCA 2005 s23(3)(c).
68 MCA 2005 s23(3)(d).
69 MCA 2005 s20(3).

7.104 An application to the court to appoint a trustee can be made by reference to PD 9G. This sets out the information that the court will require in order to consider the application.

Removal of attorney or deputy

7.105 A deputy or attorney may retire from their role and cease to act if circumstances change. They may do this by disclaiming the role. There are, however, occasions when another will apply to the court for the removal of a deputy or attorney. The MCA 2005 gives the court the power to revoke an LPA if P is unable to do so and the attorney:
a) has behaved, or is behaving, in a way that contravenes their authority or is not in P's best interests; or
b) proposes to behave in a way that would contravene their authority or would not be in P's best interests.'[70]

7.106 The Court of Protection can also revoke the appointment of a deputy if it is satisfied that the deputy:
a) has behaved, or is behaving, in a way that contravenes the authority conferred on them by the court or is not in P's best interests; or
b) proposes to behave in a way that would contravene that authority or would not be in P's best interests.[71]

7.107 An application may be made by the OPG (following an investigation – see chapter 20),[72] local authority safeguarding team if there are fears about financial abuse or by someone interested in P's welfare that has well-founded fears about the management of P's finances.

7.108 As more cases continue to be reported, there is more guidance emerging about what the court considers to be behaviour that justifies the removal of either an attorney or a deputy.

7.109 The cases of *Re J*[73] and *Re Harcourt*[74] both comment upon the relevant behaviour to be taken into account when considering applications of this type. In *Re J* HHJ Marshall QC considered the

---

70 MCA 2005 s22(3)(b).
71 MCA 2005 s16(8).
72 See, for instance, *Public Guardian v JM* [2014] EWHC B4 (COP).
73 [2011] COPLR Con Vol 716.
74 [2013] COPLR 69.

question of what conduct of the attorney would be of relevance to the question of revocation, holding that:

> ... on a proper construction of s22(3), the court can consider any past behaviour or apparent prospective behaviour by the attorney, [and], depending on the circumstances and apparent gravity of any offending behaviour found, it can then take whatever steps it regards as appropriate in P's best interests (this only arises if P lacks capacity), to deal with the situation, whether by revoking the power or by taking some other course.[75]

7.110 Senior Judge Lush commented in *Re Harcourt* that: 'Essentially, the Lasting Powers of Attorney scheme is based on trust and envisages minimal intervention by public authorities.'[76] He went on to note that: 'The factor of magnetic importance in determining what is in Mrs Harcourt's best interests is that her property and financial affairs should be managed competently, honestly and for her benefit.'[77]

7.111 In *Re AB*[78] the court sets out the different test that applies in the revocation of an EPA as opposed to that of an LPA. In *The Public Guardian v PM and SH*[79] the court commented upon the different approach that would be taken when asked to revoke an LPA for property and affairs and an LPA for health and welfare.

7.112 The cases of *Re Buckley* and *Re GM* discussed above also resulted in the removal of the deputies involved. Other examples of the type of behaviour that will result in the removal of the attorney or deputy can be found in *Re AB*;[80] *The Public Guardian v AW and DH*[81] and *The Public Guardian v DA, YS and ES*.[82] Finally, while *Re DB*[83] is a decision relating to costs, the case is also of note for the approach taken by the court to the suitability of a proposed deputy.

7.113 The process for making an application for the removal of an attorney or deputy follows that of all other applications relating to P's property and affairs. Firstly, the applicant should obtain an assessment of capacity addressing the questions to be put before the court. Depending upon the situation the questions to be considered may include:

75 Para 13.
76 Para 39.
77 Para 60.
78 [2014] EWCOP 12, [2014] WTLR 1303.
79 [2016] EWCOP 25, [2016] COPLR 488.
80 [2014] EWCOP 12, [2014] WTLR 1303.
81 [2014] EWCOP 28, [2014] WTLR 1705.
82 [2015] EWCOP 41, [2015] WTLR 1647.
83 [2014] EWHC 483 (COP), [2014] COPLR 275.

Making an application: property and affairs cases 211

- whether P lacks the capacity to revoke their LPA;
- whether P can validly enter into a new LPA;
- whether P lacks capacity to request accounts from their attorney;
- whether P lacked the capacity to make a gift (or other relevant detrimental financial decision) at the relevant time.

7.114　The applicant would be wise to consider the outcome for P that would be achieved through making the application, if an LPA is to be revoked and P lacks capacity to enter into a new LPA, who will manage P's finances? It may be appropriate to ask the court, for example, not only to revoke the appointment of an attorney but to order the appointment of a neutral panel deputy.

7.115　The applicant may find that they do not have access to all the information that they need to support their application. P's financial documents are likely to be kept by the attorney or deputy. In these cases it may be preferable to approach the OPG to investigate and use its powers to obtain documents and to make any necessary application. If the applicant has access to sufficient evidence that the deputy or attorney may be acting in such a way that the court should consider their removal, then proceeding straight to apply to the court will be the quickest route to take.

7.116　The applicant may consider asking for immediate directions to protect P's position, but these are rarely granted in cases that solely concern P's property and affairs.

Redress

7.117　As mentioned earlier in this chapter, every deputy (with the exception of a local authority deputy) must purchase a security bond, which is in effect an insurance against them causing financial loss to P. If the court removes a deputy in circumstances in which their actions have caused loss to P, then it is possible to recover those funds for P, up to the value of the relevant security bond if the court orders it.

7.118　It may be possible to make an application for a security bond to be called in within the course of the proceedings to remove the deputy. If there is insufficient information at the time of the removal proceedings about the full scale of P's financial loss, a later application can be brought by the new deputy on behalf of P.

7.119　If P has suffered financial loss through the actions of their attorney or if this loss caused by his deputy exceeds the value of the security bond, the only remedy open is for the new deputy acting on behalf of P is to take civil action against the former attorney or deputy personally. Before considering this step (which would require the endorsement of the Court of Protection) the deputy would need to be sure that the removed attorney or deputy had sufficient resources to meet any liability.

Recovery of capacity

7.120 The Court of Protection's jurisdiction only extends to those who lack capacity to make certain decisions. It follows, therefore, that if P ceases to lack capacity in relation to their property and affairs, an application should be made for the discharge of the deputy.[84]

7.121 If a deputy believes that P has regained their capacity to manage their property and affairs, they should obtain updated medical evidence to this effect and then apply to the court, following the procedure described above, to approve the discharge of the deputyship.

7.122 The court will consider the evidence and if the application is approved will make an order for final accounts to be submitted, the ending of the security bond, the transfer of all assets to P's name and for final costs to be dealt with.[85]

Death of P

7.123 The death of P automatically ends both the valid appointment of a deputy and also that of an attorney. The deputy should liaise with the personal representatives of P's estate to make information available to allow them to administer P's estate. A professional deputy will be entitled to final costs for winding up the deputyship. The deputy should notify the OPG of the death of P, by submitting a copy of the death certificate. Other matters for a deputy to deal with will include submitting a final report to the OPG and discharging the security.

---

84 See PD 23B para 5.
85 See PD 23B, COPR r167, and the Lasting Powers of Attorney, Enduring Powers of Attorney and Public Guardian Regulations 2007 SI No 1253 regs 37 and 40. See also paras 15.69 onwards.

Mixed applications

7.124 During the course of proceedings issues may arise that go beyond those concerning P's property and affairs, to touch on health and welfare issues as well. A common scenario is a dispute arising within a family about who should act as attorney or deputy for an incapacitated relative that also includes an aspect about where the individual should reside or the care they should receive.

7.125 Parties and their advisers need to be clear as to the differences between the two sets of issues. For welfare matters permission will only need to be sought for the part of the application where permission is required.[86] For the procedure for obtaining permission in relation to health and welfare decisions, see chapter 9.

7.126 Advisers should also be aware of the differing costs regimes in property and affairs matters and health and welfare matters. Details on the appropriate treatment of costs in mixed applications can be found in chapter 16.

7.127 Mixed applications will also be subject to case management on the relevant pathways as described in chapters 9 and 10. There are two stages before the court decides which pathway, or mixture of the two, is most appropriate:

1) Pre-issue stage – where potential parties are to identify most appropriate pathway and comply with the requirements and seek to resolve issues.

2) Point of issue of application – where the parties must file a list of issues to allow the court to identify the appropriate pathway or mixture of the two.[87]

7.128 Where an application contains both welfare and property and affairs issues the papers will be placed before a judge for initial case management who will either:

1) order allocation to a pathway and give directions accordingly; or
2) give directions as to which elements of each pathway are to apply and procedure to follow.[88]

---

86 COPR r53(2).
87 PD Case Management Pilot para 6.1(2).
88 PD Case Management Pilot para 6.1(3).

Bulk applications

7.129 Following comments made in the *The Friendly Trust's Bulk Application*,[89] previous guidance about bulk applications has been withdrawn. It had been thought possible to make a bulk application where the same issue affected all or many of the deputyships held by one deputy. Attention is now drawn to the fact that the COPR make no provision for bulk applications.

---

89 [2016] EWCOP 40.

Making an application: property and affairs cases 215

Property and affairs applications

Application papers
- COP1
- COP1A
- COP3

Additional papers for specific applications:
- COP4
- COP1C
- COP1D
- COP1E
- COP1F

↓

Are interim directions required? Or is application for stat will/gift? — Yes → **Judicial attention for initial directions**

↓ No

Court issues application and returns sealed COP1 to applicant with any initial directions order

↓

14 days for applicant to serve P and respondents and notify interested parties

↓

Applicant returns COP20A and COP20B to the court

↓

14 days for those served/notified to respond by returning COP5

↓

Has anyone objected/asked for a different order? — No → **Papers referred back to court for final order**

↓ Yes

First stage of PAA Pathway applicant served with copy of order allocating case to pathway and respondent's COP5

↓

Second stage of PAA pathway. Judicial attention respondent may be ordered to file summary of reasons for opposing application

↓

Matter transferred to appropriate regional court

↓

Dispute Resolution Hearing Listed

↓

Third of PAA Pathway. Dispute Resolution Hearing. Refinement of issues — Agreement → **Court makes final order if in P's best interests**

↓ No agreement

Further case management and direction to take matter to final Hearing

↓

Final hearing, Court hears evidence and decides on P's best interests and makes final order.

→ **Costs - dealt with at final hearing**

CHAPTER 8

Responding to an application and contested applications: property and affairs

8.1	Introduction
8.4	Initial steps
8.9	Consenting to an application
8.13	Becoming a party
8.18	Being removed as a party
8.19	Contesting an application
8.26	Contested applications – the Case Management Pilot
8.29	The stages of the property and affairs pathway
8.30	When the application becomes contested
8.31	Case management on allocation to the pathway
8.32	Dispute resolution hearing
8.41	Final hearing
8.43	Costs
8.45	Urgent applications

Introduction

8.1 Most applications concerning P's property and affairs are not contested and are dealt with 'on the papers,' ie without a hearing. However some will meet with disagreement. This chapter looks at the steps that are necessary when responding to an application, whether the decision is to consent to it or the party served or notified wishes to oppose it or suggest an alternative order.

8.2 Those who are served with application papers, or notified of an application, should consider (where necessary with the benefit of legal advice) as soon as possible how they wish to respond and what part they wish to play in the proceedings. The COPR provide for a number of variations, which will have different consequences for the shape of any proceedings.

8.3 All parties should bear in mind the impact of their behaviour on the costs of the matter, a timely response will be most effective at curbing costs.

Initial steps

8.4 Permission is not required prior to making an application to the court about a matter concerning P's property and affairs.[1] Service or notification that an application form has been issued will therefore usually be the first information that a respondent or a person notified will have of proceedings.

8.5 A respondent will be served (by the applicant) with a copy of the COP1 as issued by the court as well as a copy of the complete application papers and any orders made by the court, a COP5 acknowledgement of service or notification will also be provided. A person notified will be served (by the applicant) with a COP15 notice of proceedings and a COP5.

8.6 Those who are served or notified of proceedings should consider taking appropriate legal advice about their response to the application as soon as possible. The general rule about funding in property and affairs cases[2] is that P's estate pays the costs of all parties. There is no public funding available for property and affairs cases. For more information on the treatment of costs see chapter 16.

---

1 COPR r51(2)(a), although exceptions to this do appear in r52.
2 COPR r156.

8.7 There can be significant variations in the amount of detail provided within an application. The receipt of the application will, however, offer the respondent an opportunity to consider the issues raised by the application and how he or she may be able to counter them. This is all part of the vital exercise of ensuring the actual issues in the case are identified as quickly and precisely as possible. The receipt of the application may be a useful time to consider not only the evidence that the respondent may be able to provide, but whether there are others in P's life who will be able to provide a helpful perspective as well. See further in this regard paras 8.19 onwards below.

8.8 It is vital that the matters are not set in stone at the outset. In other words, those served with the application as much as the person or body bringing the application should remain flexible as to the possible outcome of the application. Parties' views will alter as evidence is gathered and others may have a very markedly different opinion as to P's best interests.

Consenting to an application

8.9 If a person notified, or a respondent, considers that the application is one which is reasonable and which they support, then they can indicate this simply by completing and filing the COP5 form to the effect that they agree with the application proposed. This response should be filed the court within 14 days of service.[3]

8.10 There is no obligation on the part of a person notified or a respondent to make any response to the application, but a failure to do so will not prevent the making of the order that is sought. Respondents or those notified who do not respond will still be bound be the decision of the court as if they had been a party.[4]

8.11 A person who has been notified will not become a party to the proceedings simply by filing a COP5 form consenting to the application. However, if a person notified has taken legal advice before reaching the conclusion that they wish to consent to the application as proposed, it would be appropriate to seek a direction that they be joined as a party to the proceedings only for purposes of seeking to

---

3 COPR r72.
4 COPR r74(2), emphasised in *Mrs P v Rochdale BC* [2016] EWCOP B1 at para 26.

recover their costs.[5] This is likely only to be of relevance in property and affairs case where the costs are in principle recoverable from the estate of P.[6]

8.12 By contrast with proceedings in some other courts, there is no such category as 'interested party' in proceedings before the Court of Protection. A person (or body) is either a party or they are not.[7]

Becoming a party

8.13 A person who has been served as a respondent will automatically become a party to proceedings by filing a COP5 form.[8]

8.14 If a respondent wishes to oppose the application or to propose an alternative order, then the acknowledgement of service should be accompanied by a witness statement which contains any evidence upon which the respondent intends to rely.[9] In practice, however, it is not always appropriate or indeed possible to serve a witness statement along with the COP5 form. The respondent may not have access to documents that would support his or her position. In these circumstances, directions should be sought for the provision of any information that the respondent requires, for example (for instance, in a financial case) bank statements or other financial information.

8.15 If a person who is notified wishes to oppose the application, or to propose an alternative order, he must apply to be joined as a party to proceedings. The person does this by indicating his or her wish to be joined as a party on the COP5 and filing this response with the court within the appropriate timescale. The COP5 must set out the person's reasons for wishing to be a party and should be accompanied by a witness statement setting out his or her interest in the proceedings. The court will decide whether or not to join that person as a party.[10] The relevant test for whether a person should be joined as a party is whether the court considers it desirable for the purpose of deciding the application.[11] If the court approves the application then the person notified will be made a party to proceedings

5 COPR r166.
6 COPR r156; see further chapter 16.
7 See *Re SK* [2012] EWHC 1990 (COP), [2012] COPLR 712 at para 21.
8 COPR r73(1)(b).
9 COPR r52(5).
10 COPR r72(8).
11 COPR r73(2).

8.16 and the applicant will be required to serve him or her with a copy of the full application papers.

8.16 A person who subsequently becomes aware of an application may apply to become a party. To do so, they must demonstrate 'sufficient interest' in the proceedings.[12] That interest must be a sufficient interest in the proceedings themselves – ie 'the ascertainment of the incapacitated person's best interests' – as opposed to any commercial (or other interest) of the applicant's own.[13] This approach was approved by the President in Re G.[14]

8.17 A person who wishes to be joined as a party must file an application notice (COP9) and a statement explaining his or her interest in the proceedings and – if he intends to ask the court to make an order that is different to the order sought by the applicant – the evidence on which he relies.[15] The person seeking to join should send enough copies of the application for all the parties and the court will serve it.[16] Again, the test will be whether it is desirable to join the person to the proceedings for the purpose of dealing with the application.[17]

Being removed as a party

8.18 It is convenient to deal here with the position of a person who wishes to be removed as a party. A person who wishes to be *removed* as a party must apply using form COP9.[18] There is no guidance in either the COPR or the accompanying practice directions as to the test that the court will apply (nor are there any reported decisions on the point), but logic suggests that the application will be granted only if the court considers that the continued participation of the person as a party is no longer desirable for the purpose of dealing with the application. As a half-way house, and in line with the overriding objective in COPR r3, courts will sometimes allow parties to cease to play any active steps for

---

12 COPR r75(1).
13 Re SK [2012] EWHC 1990 (COP), [2012] COPLR 712 at paras 41–43 per Bodey J (refusing application by defendant to personal injury proceedings brought by P to be joined to Court of Protection proceedings concerning P).
14 Re G, London Borough of Redbridge v G (by her litigation friend the Official Solicitor), C and F [2014] EWHC 1361 (COP).
15 COPR r75(3).
16 COPR r75(4).
17 COPR r73(2).
18 COPR r76; see also paras 11.19 onwards.

certain stages in the proceedings where their contribution will not be required at all points (or will provide that the party in question only need file documentation or attend directions hearings 'if so advised').

Contesting an application

8.19 Careful consideration should be given to the available evidence when considering whether to contest an application, or to suggest an alternative order. In property and affairs cases, which commonly concern the management or movement of money within families it is important for each party to remain focused on what is in P's best interests and what is realistically achievable. Any party considering contesting an application should ensure that they are familiar with and adhere to the overriding objective[19] which places emphasis on controlling costs through compliance with procedure in order to resolve issues quickly and fairly. Parties have explicit duties[20] designed to further the overriding objective. For cases falling within the Case Management Pilot, there are additional duties imposed upon legal representatives and unrepresented litigants;[21] and even in cases falling outside the Pilot, it is likely that the court will look to those duties as the 'gold standard' by which to judge their conduct (see further paras 4.101–4.103 as to the scope of the Pilot).

8.20 The grounds on which an application may be contested will depend upon the facts of the case and the evidence available. For details about a range of specific applications and situations see chapter 7.

8.21 In property and affairs cases, if there is a dispute, it is often likely to be between family members, rather than family members and a statutory body. In such cases – and especially given that the general rule as to costs is that the costs (of all parties) will be payable out of P's estate[22] – the temptation must be resisted for respondents to oppose applications on the basis of a point or points that do not relate to the issues in the case and which will serve no purpose but to increase the cost to P. The court will primarily be concerned with P's present circumstances, and the resources of the court do not exist to allow the ventilation of unrelated allegations of the nature that can, sadly, often arise in the case of family disputes. Parties must remain focussed on the issues that are before the court and the relevance of

19 COPR Pr1.1.
20 COPR Pr1.4.
21 COPR Pr1.5 and 1.6; see further chapter 11.
22 COPR r156; see also chapter 16.

the information they wish to put before the court both in the application and in any potential response.

8.22 Parties should maintain a flexible approach, focused on P's best interests and avoid entrenched positions as far as possible. This allows alternative options to be explored by way of mediation and other forms of ADR (see chapter 19), and may help to avoid incurring the expense of attended court hearing(s).

8.23 Advisers should, however, be alert to the danger of attempting to persuade parties to take an approach that fundamentally they do not agree with.

8.24 If the parties are able to reach a negotiated way forward that represents a compromise between the position advocated by the applicant and that desired by the respondent(s), the court should be notified and a consent order submitted, with each party or their legal representative confirming their consent to the order as agreed: see further para 10.48.

8.25 If the parties cannot agree a negotiated way forward within a reasonable timescale, the court will proceed to determine how best to put itself in a position to reach a conclusion. This means that the case will usually proceed on the basis of directions given when the case becomes contested, allowing the parties time to attempt to reach a negotiated agreement before a final hearing is listed.

Contested applications – the Case Management Pilot

8.26 On 1 September 2016 the Case Management Pilot Practice Direction (PD) came into force (see further para 4.101). At the time of writing the pilot is due to run until 31 August 2017. The Case Management Pilot PD sets out the pathways which the court will use to manage applications which are contested. All property and affairs applications will be subject to the property and affairs procedure set out in the Case Management Pilot except for:

- uncontested applications;
- applications by the Public Guardian; and
- applications for the approval of statutory wills and gifts.

8.27 It may appear from these exclusions that requirements set down in the relevant parts of the property and affairs pathway will affect only the minority of applications. However, in practice the courts are likely to use the property and affairs pathway to case manage *all* cases which are contested and where it appears that the parties are not able to refine the issues and work towards a negotiated agreement in a reasonable timescale.

8.28 It is important that all applicants and respondents aware of the procedure, however, as property and affairs applications tend not arise out of an existing disagreement and the applicant will only become aware at a later stage that that the application is opposed, or a different order sought.

The stages of the property and affairs pathway

8.29 The property and affairs pathway[23] set out in the practice direction comprises four stages:
1) when the application becomes contested;
2) case management on allocation to the pathway;
3) the dispute resolution hearing; and
4) the final hearing.

When the application becomes contested

8.30 The property and affairs pathway begins at a later stage than the personal welfare pathway, and has no pre-issue stage. Until it is contested all property and affairs applications will follow the procedure in chapter 7 at para 7.6 onwards. The first stage therefore commences when court is notified by one of the respondents or those notified returning a completed COP5 form indicating that the application is opposed or a different order sought. When this happens the case will be allocated to the pathway. The court will then serve on the applicant a copy of the COP5 form and an order allocating the case to the pathway.

Case management on allocation to the pathway

8.31 At the second stage the papers are placed before a judge who will either:
a) list for a dispute resolution hearing; or
b) transfer case to the most appropriate regional court for listing of the dispute resolution hearing.

---

23 COPR Pr3.9 and Case Management Pilot PD.

Dispute resolution hearing

8.32   The third stage, the dispute resolution hearing (DRH),[24] is a new concept for property and affairs cases. It is modelled upon the financial dispute resolution (FDR) hearing found in the family courts. The purpose of the hearing is to enable the court to determine if the case can be resolved and avoid unnecessary litigation, and by extension costs.

8.33   The DRH will usually take place before a district judge. All parties must attend unless the court directs otherwise, and are to approach the hearing 'openly and without reserve'.[25] The content of the hearing is not to be disclosed and evidence of anything said or admission made at the hearing will not be admissible in evidence at a final hearing. The exception to this being at a trial for an offence committed at the hearing.

8.34   Parties attending a DRH are likely to find that the process will involve negotiations between the representatives of the various parties, and unrepresented parties if there are any, coupled with the making of offers and counter-offers. Positions adopted and concessions made will be treated as being made 'without prejudice' to allow parties to make genuine attempts to reach an agreement.

8.35   The parties will be expected to appear before the court when the judge will wish to be advised on the progress towards refining the issues and reaching agreement, and also the areas where this has not been possible. At the hearing the court will give a view on the likely outcome of the matter if it were to proceed to a final hearing. This allows the parties to consider the strengths and weaknesses of their respective positions and to make further offers in the light of this.

8.36   If the parties are able to reach an agreement at this stage the court will make a final order if it is in P's best interests to do so. If the parties are unable to reach an agreement at the DRH the court will make directions for further case management up to the final hearing.

It should be noted that DRHs are not an attended hearing for purposes of the Transparency Pilot.[26]

---

24 Case Management Pilot PD 5.4.
25 Case Management Pilot PD 5.4(3)(a).
26 PD Transparency Pilot, para 2.2.

8.37 The court may turn to either the Civil Procedure Rules (CPR) or Family Procedure Rules (FPR) in cases where the COPR do not provide express guidance,[27] and given that DRHs are modelled upon FDRs, we consider that it is likely that the courts will draw upon those parts of the FPR which apply to FDRs, Until and unless specific guidance is given, we suggest that parties preparing for a DRH should therefore turn to FPR rr9.14 and 9.17 as a guides. These set out the requirements on parties preparing for the first appointment and FDR appointment in family proceedings. The COPR do not provide for the equivalent of a first appointment but the court would be greatly assisted by the provision of the documents required by those Rules, including:

- a chronology;
- a list of the issues between the parties; and
- details of all offers and proposals, and responses to them.

These must be filed at court at least seven days before the hearing. The court would welcome the provision of these documents as part of a bundle which also includes copies of all the application papers and any torders.

8.38 At the conclusion of the DRH, any documents containing details of the offers and proposals, and any filed documents referring to them, must, at the request of the party who filed them, be returned to that party and not retained on the court file. This is not express from the provisions of the Case Management Pilot, but we suggest must flow from the analogous position prevailing in relation to FDRs.[28]

8.39 If an agreement is not reached at a DRH, a final hearing is not inevitable. It is possible for the parties to go away and reflect upon the indication given by the court and to make other offers before reaching a final hearing. Sometimes parties need more time than is available in the day to reflect upon the developments at the DRH.

8.40 In a case where one party considers that an offer made at the DRH was unreasonably refused, there is considerable merit in that offer being repeated following the DRH in correspondence reflecting the terms of the offer made at the DRH. That offer[29] cannot refer to the contents of the negotiations at the DRH. However, if, at the conclusion of the proceedings, the court reaches a conclusion that is

27 COPR Pr2.5/COPR r9(1).
28 See FPR r9.17(5).
29 Which could be made on a without prejudice or an open basis depending on the circumstances (the former meaning, in essence, that it could not be put before the court until the conclusion of the substantive proceedings).

broadly in line with (or, where relevant) more favourable (in whatever way) than the offer, it would then be entirely proper to refer to the offer when submissions are made as to costs (see further chapter 16).

Final hearing

8.41 The final hearing will be listed before a different judge to that who heard the DRH. This is a necessary consequence of the nature of a DRH, but we anticipate that this may cause practical difficulties in some areas where there are only very few 'ticketed' Court of Protection judges.

8.42 The final hearing will proceed in accordance with the directions given at or following the DRH. The applicant will usually be required to prepare the bundle for the hearing, although the court may make a different order to vary this if the applicant is unrepresented. For more detail on preparing for and conducting the final hearing please see chapter 10 below.

Costs

8.43 At the conclusion of the case, whether by consent or by judicial decision, the court will deal with costs. For a full discussion of costs, see chapter 16.

8.44 Parties who proceed to a final hearing should be clear as to the potential costs implications and prepare accordingly. Parties who proceed to a final hearing must be sure that their opposition is objectively in P's best interests.

Urgent applications

8.45 Urgent applications in property and affairs matters are rare, and the court will only treat a matter as urgent if P's life expectancy is very short and the matter must be resolved before their death, for example to make a statutory will.

8.46 The Case Management Pilot PD sets out[30] how the court will approach a property and affairs application which is urgent from the outset. Parties are reminded of the requirement in the COPR to co-operate.[31] The applicant must include the following with the application papers:

---

30 Case Management Pilot PD para 5.6.
31 COPR Pr 1.4(2)(c).

- an explanation of why the case is urgent and what the consequences will be if the case is not treated as urgent;
- if the application is made without notice, an explanation why it was not possible to make the application on notice, and what the consequences would be if the application were to proceed on notice and the order or an interim order were not made immediately;
- confirmation of any specific deadline;
- information identifying and separating the issues which are urgent from those which are not urgent.

8.47 The court will consider the papers and on issue will, if the matter appears or is confirmed to be contentious, either order:

a) the case will proceed to a DRH but listed urgently; or
b) the case may be listed for an interim hearing to decide the urgent matter or matters in the case, and the court can decide at that hearing whether any further hearing is necessary and if so, whether that further hearing should include a DRH or not.

8.48 Applications which are not contentious but are urgent can be dealt with on the papers if all the relevant consents have been received by the court.

8.49 Sometimes applications are not urgent at the time they are commenced but become so as matters proceed. This is especially likely to be the case in statutory will applications where P's health may decline suddenly making the issue of their will more urgent. Where this occurs it is important to advise the court and other parties of the change in circumstances as soon as possible and to share any available medical evidence. The court will then be able to take steps to consider the matter urgently and decide if a final order can be made or if a hearing should be listed urgently.

CHAPTER 9

Making an application: health and welfare cases

9.1	Introduction
9.2	Before making an application
9.5	Types of application
9.8	The Case Management Pilot
9.12	The personal welfare pathway: the pre-issue stage
9.15	How to make an application
9.21	Completing the forms and supporting information
9.22	Form COP1
9.38	Evidence of capacity
9.43	Supporting evidence
9.44	Human rights issues
9.45	Fees
9.46	Confidential matters
9.48	Urgent applications
9.49	Issue of the proceedings
9.50	Permission
9.51	Disputing the court's jurisdiction
9.53	Service and notification

continued

9.54   Responding to an application
9.56   Consenting to an application
9.58   Becoming a party
9.59   Contesting an application
9.66   Being removed as a party

Making an application: health and welfare cases 231

Introduction

9.1 This chapter considers the process of initiating a case in the Court of Protection which concerns P's health or personal welfare. It examines the 'personal welfare pathway' which was introduced as part of the Case Management Pilot, and goes on to provide guidance on completing the relevant COP forms, obtaining permission and dealing with service. It then discusses how to respond to an application. A flowchart summarising the procedure is set out at the end of this chapter. It should be read with chapter 10 on interim hearings and interim applications, because that chapter takes the life of the application forward.

Before making an application

9.2 In chapter 5 we consider how to decide when an application is appropriate in the context of P's health or personal welfare. In chapter 19 we consider mediation and other forms of alternative dispute resolution (ADR). Readers are advised to refer to those chapters before commencing litigation, and should also bear in mind that the Code of Practice anticipates that attempts will be made to resolve disputes outside the court arena in the first instance.[1]

9.3 There are broadly four types of case where a health or welfare application to court will need to be made:

- First, *serious medical treatment cases* must be brought to court even if there is no dispute. The particular issues arising from medical treatment cases are considered in chapter 22.
- The second type concerns *potentially risky medical or welfare questions*, where even if there is no dispute, the implications of the decision are such that the court should be asked to authorise the proposed course of action so as to put the lawfulness of the actions taken in relation to the person beyond doubt.[2]
- The third is where the court's authority is needed because P's care plan deprives him or her of his or her liberty, in a placement

---

1 Mental Capacity Act 2005 Code of Practice chapter 15: www.justice.gov.uk/downloads/protecting-the-vulnerable/mca/mca-code-of-practice-0509.pdf and *G v E (Deputyship and Litigation Friend)* [2010] EWHC 2512 (COP), (2010) 13 CCLR 610.
2 Why this is so is discussed in more detail in: Alex Ruck Keene, 'Powers, defences and the 'need' for judicial sanction' [2016] ELJ 244.

which is not a hospital or care home. These cases, and those relating to challenges against authorisations under Schedule A1 to the MCA 2005, are considered in chapter 21.
- The fourth is where there is a *genuine dispute*.

9.4 If one of the parties is a public body, then that body will be expected to take the initiative in bringing the matter before the court.[3] Parties should be aware that their conduct before proceedings start can be taken into account if the court is considering departing from the general rule in health and welfare cases that the parties should bear their own costs.[4]

Types of application

9.5 It is important to decide before making an application both whether an application should be made at all, and precisely what declarations and/or orders should be sought: see further chapter 5.

9.6 In general, applications in relation to P's welfare will be for specific declarations and/or decisions, rather than for the appointment of a deputy. As set out in chapter 3, the court has the power to make decisions on P's behalf[5] or appoint a deputy to make them for P.[6] However, it is clear that a decision of the court is preferred to the appointment of a deputy[7] and the powers conveyed upon a deputy should be as limited as possible.[8] These powers are limited by Mental Capacity Act (MCA) 2005 s20. For example, a deputy cannot prohibit contact between P and a named person,[9] or refuse consent to life-sustaining treatment.[10] The Code of Practice indicates that the appointment of a health and welfare deputy would be appropriate where a series of linked decisions will be needed over time, or where someone with final authority to make decisions will be needed, or

3 *Hillingdon LBC v Neary* [2011] EWHC 1377 (COP), [2011] COPLR Con Vol 632; also (by way of example of the approach adopted by district judges): *The Local Authority v Mrs D and another* [2013] EWHC B34 (COP) and *Re RR (Costs)* [2014] EWCOP 34. See also chapter 5.
4 Court of Protection Rules (COPR) 2007 SI No 1744 r159.
5 MCA 2005 s16(1).
6 MCA 2005 s16(2).
7 MCA 2005 s16(4)(a).
8 MCA 2005 s16(4)(b).
9 MCA 2005 s20(2) and *Re TZ (No 2)* [2014] EWHC 973 (COP), [2014] COPLR 159 at para 83.
10 MCA 2005 s20(5).

where there is a history of family disputes.[11] There is a difference of judicial opinion as to whether a health and welfare deputy should only be appointed in the most serious cases, but the statistics show that the courts are reluctant to appoint such deputies.[12] A welfare deputyship should not be sought, therefore, if the underlying decision that the deputy wishes to make is a 'one off' decision, such as a change of residence. A welfare deputyship, however, might be appropriate where there is a need to make decisions over time about the level and frequency of contact in P's best interests with a family member.

9.7 In many cases, the issues that the court needs to address will relate both to P's health and welfare and to P's property and affairs. These 'mixed' applications are addressed in paras 7.124–7.128.

The Case Management Pilot

9.8 The Case Management Pilot ('the Pilot')[13] has significantly modified the requirements on litigants. It represents an attempt to standardise the progress of contested cases in the Court of Protection, and has many features in common with the Public Law Outline in care proceedings. It is outlined in chapter 4. It provides that health and welfare applications are allocated to a dedicated personal welfare pathway with limited exceptions, namely (for these purposes): uncontested applications; applications relating to serious medical treatment[14] applications using form COPDOL10 (so-called *Re X* applications);[15] and applications using form DLA (applications under MCA 2005 s21A).[16] As set out at paras 4.101–4.103, the broader requirement of the Pilot may also apply to such cases even If they fall outside the scope of the personal welfare pathway.

9.9 The personal welfare pathway has four stages: pre-issue, the point of issue; case management on issue; the case management conference; the final management hearing and the final hearing. There are

---

11 Code of Practice para 8.38.
12 In 2015, for instance, 276 health and welfare deputies were appointed. By contrast, 16,528 property and affairs deputies were appointed.
13 See: Case Management Pilot PD. The Pilot was made under the authority of COPR r9A, which permits the modification of the court's practice and procedure for the purpose of pilot schemes.
14 Considered in chapter 22.
15 see paras 21.56 onwards.
16 see paras 21.19 onwards.

requirements at each stage: this chapter concerns the pre-issue and issue stages; case management thereafter is dealt with in chapter 10 and the final hearing in chapter 15.

9.10 The pre-issue stage puts an explicit obligation on the applicant in non-urgent cases to identify and engage with potential respondents and set out proposals for resolving the issue outside the court arena. We will consider the requirements in more detail as we discuss the process of making and responding to an application. Because almost all welfare cases fall within the scope of the Pilot, this chapter uses the Pilot Rules and rule numbering.

9.11 It is important for both potential applicants and potential respondents to be aware that the the court will take into account in deciding whether or not to depart from the general rule as to costs (ie in welfare proceedings, that each party bears their own) the conduct of the parties *before* as well as during the proceedings.[17] This rule has been on the statute books for some time, but it is likely that greater attention will be paid to it given the express introduction of a pre-issue stage in welfare applications, to which we now turn.

The personal welfare pathway: the pre-issue stage

9.12 The Case Management Pilot PD requires the applicant to 'take all necessary steps'[18] to identify all potential respondents and interested parties[19] and inform them and (if possible) P of the applicant's intention to start proceedings unless the matters which the court may be asked to determine can be resolved. The applicant must set out the nature of the proceedings that the applicant intends to commence and the issues concerned. Importantly the applicant must set out proposals for resolving the issues and engage with the potential respondents in order to do so. Thus the focus is on narrowing the issues from an early stage and aiming to resolve as much as possible without litigation.

9.13 Applicants may find it useful to send a pre-issue letter, and a suggested example appears at appendix D. The tone of any such letter should reflect the priority attached to the resolution of issues without litigation. Equally, potential respondents receiving such communication from applicants should ensure that they engage with the pre-issue stage, in keeping with their own duties.

---

17 COPR r159(2)(a).
18 Case Management Pilot PD para 4.2.1.
19 This not a category of person defined in the COPR, so it must be given a common sense interpretation.

9.14 An urgent application should only be made once the applicant has given thought to the consequences if the case is not treated as urgent; the consequences of not carrying out pre-issue steps; whether there is a specific deadline and if so what that deadline is.[20] An applicant who then goes ahead without complying with the pre-issue requirements will have to explain any omissions on issue.[21]

How to make an application

9.15 The majority of applications in health and welfare cases (including for the appointment of a deputy) will require permission from the court.[22] Permission for such cases is not required where an application is made by:

- a person who lacks, or is alleged to lack, capacity;[23]
- a person with parental responsibility for someone under 18 who lacks or is alleged to lack capacity;[24]
- the donor or donee of a lasting power of attorney (LPA) to which the application relates;[25]
- a deputy appointed for P;[26]
- a person named in an existing order, where the application relates to that order;
- an application under MCA 2005 s21A by the relevant person's representative (RPR);[27]
- the Official Solicitor or Public Guardian[28]
- Nor is the court's permission required to apply for an order under MCA 2005 s16(2)(a) the purpose of which is to authorise the deprivation of P's liberty,[29] as to which see further chapter 21.

9.16 The following forms will be needed to commence an application for health and welfare declarations and decisions:

20 Case Management Pilot PD para 4.2.2.
21 Case Management Pilot PD para 4.3.2; also paras 9.22 onwards.
22 MCA 2005 s50.
23 MCA 2005 s50(1)(a).
24 MCA 2005 s50(1)(b).
25 MCA 2005 s50(1)(c).
26 MCA 2005 s50(1)(a).
27 MCA 2005 s50(1)(c).
28 COPR r51(1)(a).
29 COPR r51(d), introduced by the rule changes in 2015.

- COP1 – the application form;
- COP1B – supporting information for health and welfare applications;
- COP3 – capacity assessment.

9.17 The following forms will be needed to commence an application for a health and welfare deputyship:

- COP1 – the application form;
- COP1B – supporting information for health and welfare applications;
- COP3 – capacity assessment;
- COP4 – deputy's declaration.

9.18 All the relevant forms can be found via the Court of Protection Handbook website.[30] In both cases, supporting evidence should be provided either in the body of the COP1 or, more usually, by way of a witness statement in form COP24 (witness statements are addressed in para 12.14 onwards).

9.19 Following the 2015 rule changes, there is now no separate permission form (the old COP2). Where permission is required, it should be addressed in the relevant part of the COP1 form (section 6).

9.20 Once these forms have been completed, they must be sent to the Court of Protection at First Avenue House, together with the appropriate fee (see para 9.34). The full address of the court appears at appendix G below, together with the telephone contact details.

Completing the forms and supporting information

9.21 COPR Part 9 deals with starting proceedings. Practice Direction (PD) 9A provides guidance as to how to complete the application form (COP1). In addition, the Case Management Pilot PD sets out in para 4.3 a comprehensive list of the information that the applicant must include either within the application itself, or must refer to in the application and which must be filed alongside it. The checklist is designed, in particular, to ensure that such matters as the available options for P are identified as soon as possible. It is therefore advisable to use Case Management Pilot PD para 4.3 as a checklist to ensure that everything the court is likely to need has been included.

---

30 https://courtofprotectionhandbook.com/legislation-codes-of-practice-forms-and-guidance/.

Form COP1

9.22 This form is not complex. However, the following issues need to be considered with particular care.

9.23 Section 4 of the form requires the applicant to set out the order that he or she is asking the court to make. Ideally, pre-issue correspondence and engagement will have helped to narrow the issues. In any event it is helpful to focus here on precisely what the court will need to determine. The more precision that can be brought to bear the better. For cases on the personal welfare pathway, Case Management Pilot PD para 4.3.1(a) requires a draft order or an explanation of the order that is sought.

9.24 It is of course essential to draft the form in a balanced manner and not to ask for inappropriately broad orders or powers.[31] The application form and the permission form contain a statement of truth, and proceedings for contempt of court may be brought if a person makes a false statement in a document verified by a statement of truth.[32] All litigants are 'required to help the court to further the overriding objective',[33] as are their lawyers.[34] Solicitors are further subject to the mandatory principles of the Solicitors Regulation Authority (SRA) Code of Conduct to act with integrity and maintain the trust of the public.[35]

9.25 In a complex case, there is no reason why this section cannot be drafted in a separate document to which the COP1 can refer. A useful rule of thumb is to ask whether it will be easier for the judge reading the 'package' of materials in the application to understand what is being asked for, and why, by reference to one standalone document, rather than having to navigate between different forms.

9.26 Section 5.1 provides that respondents to the application should be listed, together with their relationship to P and full postal address. Individuals listed here will automatically become parties[36] unless the court orders otherwise. PD 9A requires that the applicant must list as a respondent 'any person (other than P) whom the applicant reasonably believes to have an interest which means he ought to be heard in relation to the application (as opposed to being notified of it)'.

---

31 *Hillingdon LBC v Neary* [2011] EWHC 1377 (COP), [2011] COPLR Con Vol 632.
32 COPR r14.
33 COPR Pr1.4.
34 COPR Pr1.5.
35 SRA Code of Conduct 2011, Principles 2 and 6.
36 COPR r73(1)(b).

9.27 It may seem anomalous that P does not become a party automatically given that P's future is at stake in the application. Rule 73(4) provides that P should not be named as a respondent to any proceedings without the leave of the court. COPR r3A/COPR Pr1.2 attempts to offer the court a range of options in ensuring the participation of P and the implications are considered at paras 11.6 onwards. To this end, for cases on the personal welfare pathway, Case Management Pilot PD para 4.3.1(o) requires the applicant to address how it is proposed that P will be involved in every case. It should be noted that P is bound as if P were a party by orders of the court in any event.[37]

9.28 Specific issues arise in relation to the ability of P themselves to bring proceedings. The MCA 2005 provides that P can make an application without permission.[38] However, if P lacks capacity to conduct the proceedings, they must have a litigation friend.[39] See chapter 11 for a full discussion of the role of litigation friend; this is also considered in the context of applications under MCA 2005 s21A in chapter 21.

9.29 Practical difficulties can arise if the adviser has represented P directly – perhaps in a forum such as a mental health tribunal where patients are represented without an intermediary – and an issue has arisen which the adviser reasonably believes requires resolution by the Court of Protection. The Official Solicitor will not normally accept an invitation to act unless proceedings have already started. If P has a family member or friend who might be willing to act as litigation friend, or an advocate who is willing to support P, that individual should be approached. In *Re UF*,[40] Charles J recognised that it may be necessary for pragmatic reasons for an interim litigation friend to be named in order to commence proceedings, but for the court at a later stage to invite the Official Solicitor to act.

9.30 In some cases P may lack capacity to conduct the proceedings, but may have capacity to decide to make the application in the first place. This may allow P to make the application in his/her own right. See para 11.12 for further discussion.

9.31 There will be some cases where there really is no individual who is willing to act as litigation friend, even for a limited period. In some cases this may mean that it is not possible to take the matter forward

---

37 COPR r74(2)(a).
38 MCA 2005 s50(1)(a).
39 COPR Pr1.2.4/COPR 3A(2)(4). It would not be possible, we suggest, for P to bring proceedings by an Accredited Legal Representative because such will only ever be appointed 'reactively' by the court.
40 [2013] EWHC 4289 (COP), [2014] COPLR 93.

to the court, unless another party – for example, the relevant local authority – can be persuaded to issue proceedings. There may be some cases where the adviser reasonably considers that P's best interests will be seriously compromised if proceedings cannot be brought. In such cases, which will be rare, we consider the adviser could act as litigation friend, solely in order to bring the case to court. The adviser should prepare a detailed witness statement in which the attempts to locate a suitable litigation friend are described. This is not entirely without precedent, as a solicitor was appointed litigation friend to a protected party whom he knew well.[41] Advisers may find it useful to refer to the Law Society's Practice Note on Meeting the Needs of Vulnerable Clients.[42]

9.32 In addition to listing respondents, section 5.1 of form COP1 requires the applicant to list the people who will be notified of the application, once it has been issued by the court. PD 9B requires the applicant to try to identify at least three people who have an interest in being notified that the application has been issued.[43] Such individuals will have the opportunity of asking to be joined as parties.[44] They will be bound by the court's orders as if they were parties.[45] There is a presumption (which can be displaced) that close members of P's family will have such an interest and the Practice Direction lists those who should ordinarily be notified, in descending order of closeness to P.[46] If someone in that list is not notified, then the reasons must be explained. (For example, P may have several siblings, only one of whom has any contact or involvement with P. There might in that case be good reason not to notify the remaining three.)

9.33 In addition to P's family, the following persons should generally be notified:[47]

- if P is under 18, anyone with parental responsibility for P;
- any person – including a legal entity such as a trust or local authority – likely to be affected by the outcome of the application;
- a deputy or attorney whose powers relate to the issue involved in the application.

---

41 Re RGS [2013] EWHC 1417 (COP).
42 www.lawsociety.org.uk/support-services/advice/practice-notes/meeting-the-needs-of-vulnerable-clients-july-2015/.
43 PD 9B para 4.
44 COPR r72(6), (8); PD 9C para 4.
45 COPR r74(2)(b).
46 PD 9B para 7.
47 PB 9B para 10.

9.34 There now no longer being a separate permission form, section 6 of form COP1 deals with the question of permission. This section asks three questions:
1) What is the matter you want the court to decide?
2) Please state the order you are asking the court to make?
3) How would the order benefit the person to whom the application relates?

9.35 The test for the grant of permission is not set down either in the Mental Capacity Act (MCA) 2005 or in the COPR. The questions at section 6 reflect the guidance in *NK v VW and others*.[48]

9.36 There is no requirement to send proposed respondents copies of the application before it is issued, but it is good practice to do so, especially as the proposed parties should have been in correspondence in any event during the pre-issue stage.

9.37 Form COP1B requires some additional supporting information. This form is largely self-explanatory.

Evidence of capacity

9.38 Form COP3 is the assessment of capacity. It is important to note that this does not need to be completed by a medical practitioner – form COP3 was revised in 2013 to make expressly clear that it can be completed by a registered:

- medical practitioner, for example the GP of the person to whom the application relates;
- psychiatrist;
- approved mental health professional (AMHP);
- social worker;[49]
- psychologist;
- nurse; or
- occupational therapist.

---

48 [2012] COPLR 105.
49 In *A Local Authority v SY* [2013] EWHC 3485 (COP), [2014] COPLR 1, decided before the change in the COP3, the COP3 had been completed by a social worker; Keehan J noted that: 'The assessment in this case demonstrates that an appropriately qualified social worker is eminently suited to undertake such capacity assessments. I commend the practice which I hope will be followed in ropriate future cases' (para 22).

Making an application: health and welfare cases 241

9.39 The form also makes clear that in some circumstances it might also be appropriate for a registered therapist, such as a speech therapist or occupational therapist, to complete the form.

9.40 Some medical practitioners, in particular GPs, will charge to complete a COP3. There is a good argument that it should fall within the scope of the medical services that they provide to P, and advisers should always seek to query the basis upon which any charge is made before simply agreeing to pay.

9.41 Whoever completes the COP3 form, it is important that the practitioner completes the COP3 correctly and provides an appropriate level of detail. In particular, section 7.1 requires the practitioner to set out the areas of decision-making where P lacks capacity. These might, for example, be P's place of residence, P's care arrangements and contact with others. When the practitioner completes the rest of the form he or she must ensure that evidence of lack of capacity is set out in respect of all those three areas of decision-making. The COP3 does not ask about capacity to conduct the proceedings but if the assessor can also provide a view on this question, this will assist when the court considers P's participation in the proceedings at a later stage (see below, para 11.6).

9.42 PD 9A, para 14 explains that if the applicant cannot complete a COP3 ('for example, where P does not reside with the applicant and the applicant is unable to take P to a doctor, or where P refuses to undergo the assessment'), then the applicant should file a witness statement explaining why he or she cannot obtain an assessment of capacity, what attempts have been made to do so and why he or she believes that P lacks capacity to make a decision that is relevant to the application. It is worth bearing in mind that the test for the engagement of the MCA 2005 is whether there is evidence giving good cause for concern that P may lack capacity in some relevant regard: *Re F*.[50]

Supporting evidence

9.43 COPR r64 provides that the evidence which supports the application should be filed at court with the application. PD 9A states that this can be provided in the form COP1, provided it is verified by a statement of truth, or by way of a witness statement in form COP24. It is suggested that in most cases it will be desirable for the applicant to

50 [2009] EWHC B30 (Fam), [2009] COPLR Con Vol 390, (2009) 12 CCLR 530.

provide a witness statement explaining the background to the case in appropriate detail. Questions of evidence are addressed in greater detail in chapter 12.

Human rights issues

9.44 Any claim for remedies under the Human Rights Act 1998 must be clearly pleaded and particularised. This issue is considered in chapter 25.

Fees

9.45 There is a fee for making an application. The current fees at the time of writing are set out in appendix F below.

Confidential matters

9.46 There may be cases where a party does not wish to reveal certain personal details to some or all of the other parties. The position is governed by COPR r15 or, where the Pilot applies, COPR Pr5.7.[51] This provides that if a party does not wish to reveal his or her home or business address or telephone number, or P's address or telephone number, or details of a person with whom P is living, then those details must be provided to the court in any event. These details will, however, not be provided to any other party unless the court directs this. The party must provide an address for service that it within the jurisdiction of the court.

9.47 Anyone who does not wish to reveal the details set out above should explain their reasons in a witness statement. If the party wishes to withhold more details than this, then it will be necessary to follow the procedure discussed at paras 12.102–12.111 (withholding of disclosure).

---

51 COPR r15, COPR Pr5.7.

Urgent applications

9.48 There will be some cases which are so urgent that it is not possible to carry out all the steps set out above or to wait for the court to grant permission. The majority, though not all, will be cases involving serious medical treatment. There is provision for urgent cases to be heard without notice, sometimes out of hours, where this is strictly necessary. PD 10B provides guidance as to how to contact the court to set up an urgent hearing (see para 10.65). For cases falling within the personal welfare pathway, Case Management Pilot PD para 4.3.2 requires the applicant to

- explain why the case is urgent;
- explain why any of the steps in the 'checklist' at Case Management Pilot PD para 4.3.1 have not been taken, and the consequences (presumably in terms of delay) if they had been taken;
- confirm any specific deadline; and, importantly,
- separate the issues that are urgent from those which are not.

Issue of the proceedings

9.49 There is no longer a separate permission stage, and the court will issue the application form as soon as practicable after the application form is filed.[52] The court will seal the application form and stamp it with the date of issue. This is the date on which the proceedings formally commence.[53] The application form will be returned to the applicant for the applicant then to serve the proceedings in accordance with the procedure set out below. Issue is the trigger for the start of the 28-day period within which a case management conference must be held under for cases on the personal welfare pathway within the Case Management Pilot (unless one is required within a shorter period in cases of urgency).[54]

Permission

9.50 Although there is no longer a separate permission stage, the court must, as part of its initial consideration of how to deal with the

---

52 COPR r65.
53 COPR r62.
54 Case Management Pilot PD para 4.4(1)(b).

application – decide whether not permission should be granted in any case where it is required.[55] Although this is not expressly referred to as part of the court's initial case management obligations under the Case Management Pilot PD,[56] it would undoubtedly fall as one of the issues to be considered by the court on the papers at that stage (ie without a hearing). Where permission is required, then the court must considered whether or not it should be granted whether or not permission has been applied for.[57] The court may grant or refuse permission on the papers, or in some – unusual – cases the court will direct a permission hearing.[58] The court will send the applicant the order granting or refusing permission, together with reasons if permission has been refused.[59] This provision is only really of relevance where permission has been refused without a hearing. If permission has been refused following a hearing, the expectation would be that the reasons would be delivered at that hearing or in the judgment provided after the hearing. See further in relation to judgments, paras 15.60–15.62.

Disputing the court's jurisdiction

9.51 Disputes as to whether permission should be granted are rare, and given the removal of a separate permission stage, it would be an unusual case where it was possible to raise an argument as to permission prior to the court's consideration of the issue. An – unusual, but important – example of where it is appropriate to contest permission is where a proposed party wishes to apply under COPR r87 for an order that either (a) the Court of Protection has no jurisdiction to hear an application; or (b) the Court of Protection will not exercise its jurisdiction. Such an application is governed by Practice Direction (PD) 12B: it should be made on a COP5 form and be accompanied by witness evidence.[60] One reported example of an application under both of these grounds being made (and succeeding, in fact, on both of these grounds in relation to different aspects of the proceedings

---

55 COPR r84(1A).
56 Case Management Pilot PD para 4.4(1).
57 COPR r84(1A).
58 COPR r84(1A).
59 COPR r59.
60 PD 12B paras 2 and 8.

that the applicant wished to bring) is that of Re PO,[61] a cross-border case (discussed further in chapter 26) in which the local authority in the 'foreign' (Scottish) jurisdiction to which the person in question had been moved wished to dispute the jurisdiction of the Court of Protection on the basis that the person was no longer habitually resident in England and Wales.

9.52 It is possible to make an application under rule 87 even after the grant of permission if this was done without a hearing; in this case, the party wishing to make the application would need also to seek a reconsideration of the order under rule 89 (see chapter 18). As noted above, given the removal of the permission stage, most applications under rule 87 are likely to take such a form; the court would then consider how and when such application should be determined at the case management hearing. It would be open to a party to seek to make an application under rule 87 later during the course of proceedings, but the court would wish to see clear evidence as to why the issue was not taken at the outset. An example when this might be appropriate is where it is said that P has either gained or regained the capacity to make the decisions in question: see further paras 11.53–11.56.

Service and notification

9.53 The applicant is responsible for serving anyone named as a respondent or anyone who is to be notified of the proceedings,[62] as well as notifying P. This is dealt with in paras 7.23–7.32, the procedure being the same, in principle, for all applications.

Responding to an application

9.54 In proceedings relating to health and welfare, a respondent, or person notified of proceedings, should already be aware of the possibility of proceedings, given the pre-issue obligations imposed upon potential applicants by the Case Management Pilot.

9.55 Otherwise, the same steps as set out at paras 8.5–8.12 apply where responding to a health and welfare application as they do to a property and affairs application.

61 [2013] EWHC 3932 (COP), [2014] COPLR 62.
62 COPR r66.

Consenting to an application

9.56 If a person notified, or a respondent, considers that the application is one which is reasonable and that they support, then they can indicate this simply by completing and filing the COP5 to the effect that they agree with the application proposed. This response must be filed the court within 14 days of service.[63] Consenting is addressed further at paras 8.9–8.12.

9.57 Finally, it should perhaps be noted that, by contrast with proceedings in some other courts, there is no such category as 'interested party' in proceedings before the Court of Protection. A person (or body) is either a party or they are not.[64]

Becoming a party

9.58 A person who has been served as a respondent will automatically become a party to proceedings by filing a COP5 form.[65] The requirements for respondents and the circumstances under which other persons or bodies may become a party are addressed at paras 8.13–8.18.

Contesting an application

9.59 Careful consideration should be given to the available evidence when considering whether to contest an application, or to suggest an alternative order. Given that the initial case management conference will take place within 28 days of the issue of the proceedings, speed is of the essence here.

9.60 The grounds on which an application may be contested will depend upon the facts of the case and the evidence available. In welfare cases, costs will always be a consideration, as the costs of any contested hearings will (most likely) be met out of the resources of the parties themselves.[66] This does not mean that genuinely contested applications should not be fully explored and prepared. Clearly, if after careful investigations and taking material from potential

63 COPR r72.
64 See *Re SK* [2012] EWHC 1990 (COP), [2012] COPLR 712 at para 21.
65 COPR r73(1)(b).
66 COPR r157; see also chapter 16.

witnesses the adviser reaches the view that contesting an application will not succeed, then the adviser must give their client the appropriate advice. However, in welfare cases, families seeking to oppose the removal of P – or to seek P's return – must be given the opportunity fully to put their case to the court or their own rights under Articles 8 (right to respect for private and family life) and indeed 6 (right to a fair trial) of the European Convention on Human Rights (ECHR) may be compromised. In deciding whether the case is one that should be contested, it is in the authors' experience often useful to look outside the areas of dispute between the applicant, often a statutory body, and the respondent(s), often family member(s) caring for P. In such a case, the following questions can usefully be considered at this very early stage:

- What does the party think that P would want to happen?
- What were the care arrangements for P before the dispute arose? Has anything changed (for example, was additional support given by another carer who has died or moved away)?
- Has there been any change in the amount of support provided to P by the relevant statutory bodies?
- Who are the other important individuals in P's life apart from the respondent and members of the relevant statutory body? Can any of them provide evidence about positive aspects of P's care (past or current)? What, if anything, can they say about P's likes and dislikes and what is important to P?
- If the relationship between the respondent and the statutory body is currently poor, has this always been the case? Is the respondent in contact with any professionals with whom he or she has worked well in the past?
- Is evidence needed about any cultural issues or expectations? Who might be able to provide such evidence?
- Are there likely to be significant disputes of fact? If so, what evidence needs to be gathered to corroborate the respondent's case?
- Is it likely that expert evidence may be needed? It may not be possible on receipt of an application to make this judgment. However, once the need for an expert is identified by any party, they would be well advised to make enquiries as soon as possible about the costs and availability of suitable experts. This subject is discussed in detail in chapter 12.

9.61 In all cases, the relevance of the information put before the court both in the application and in any potential response should always be considered.

9.62 The authors further suggest that parties should seek to maintain a flexible approach, focused on P's best interests and avoid entrenched positions as far as possible. This allows alternative options to be explored by way of mediation (see chapter 19), and may help to avoid incurring the expense of attended court hearing(s).

9.63 Advisers should, however, be alert to the danger of attempting to persuade parties to take an approach that fundamentally they do not agree with. In a welfare case, for instance, a family carer recently served with an application seeking a draconian step in relation to P should of course be given the opportunity to consider the benefits of consenting at an early stage. However, advisers will not at that stage have gathered all the available evidence that might point away from the application. It is important that advisers are scrupulous in following their client's instructions and gathering evidence that may support their position. Advisers will need to be astute to making clear to the court at the case management conference why more time may be required, and to giving a clear time-frame within the task is to be carried out.

9.64 If the parties are able to reach a negotiated way forward that represents a compromise between the position advocated by the applicant and that desired by the respondent(s), the court should be notified and a consent order submitted, with each party or their legal representative confirming their consent to the order as agreed: see further in this regard para 10.48.

9.65 If the parties cannot agree a negotiated way forward, the court will proceed to determine how best to put itself in a position to reach a conclusion. This is discussed in chapter 10.

Being removed as a party

9.66 The position of a person (or body) who wishes to be *removed* as a party is addressed further at para 8.18.

Health and welfare applications

Consideration of whether an application is necessary
- No → Use alternative remedy (see chapter 5)
- Yes → **STAGE 1- PW Pathway** Pre-issue steps: (CMPD 4.2) including identifying and seeking to resolve issues outside court.
  - Issues resolved?
    - Yes → No further steps needed
    - No → **STAGE 2: PW pathway:** Point of issue. Comply with CMPD 4.3.1 Application papers: COP1, COP1B, COP3 and COP24. Issue fee; Notify respondents of application

STAGE 3; PW Pathway: Case management on issue. CMPD 4.4. To include: allocation to correct level of judge; CMC in 28 days or earlier if urgent; participation of P; directing advocates meeting if appropriate; preparation of core bundle; Pilot order. Sealed application and order sent to applicant for service

Applicant complies with directions and serves respondents within 14 days. Applicant to file COP 20A (if P has been notified) and COP20B. Applicant diarises time limits for CMC

Respondents to file and serve COP5 within 14 days and comply with any further directions made

Preparation for CMC–parties identified? Litigation friend or ALR/3A representative appointed? If s49 report needed, comply with s49 Pilot. If experts sought, consider new Part 15 COPR.

- Advocates' meeting?
- Communication between parties before hearing

STAGE 4: PW pathway. CMC. See CMPD 4.5. Court makes directions and fixes Final Management Hearing and Final Hearing

Evidence filed. Parties review positions in light of evidence

- RTM or other ADR?
  - Yes → If agreement reached-file consent order
  - No → No agreement reached → **STAGE 5- PW Pathway: pre-hearing meeting**

STAGE 5- Final Management Hearing See CMPD 4.7. Directions to ensure proper preparation. Parties comply with directions

STAGE 6 PW Pathway- Final Hearing. Court makes decision on application. Costs considered at conclusion of case.

CHAPTER 10

Interim hearings and interim applications

10.1	Introduction
10.4	The jurisdiction of the court to make interim orders and give directions
10.7	**Case management**
10.7	The overriding objective
10.12	The powers of the court
10.15	Initial case management
10.19	Case management on the personal welfare pathway
10.21	Applications during proceedings
10.26	Interim hearings: general provisions
10.29	**Pilot Practice Direction 4B**
10.32	Bundles
10.37	Preliminary documents and position statements
10.45	**Making effective use of court time**
10.45	The advocates' meeting
10.49	Before the directions hearing
10.50	The day of the hearing
10.53	The hearing
10.55	After the hearing: the order
10.58	**Interim relief and interim hearings**
10.65	**Urgent applications**

251

Introduction

10.1 In all applications which require consideration by a judge at a hearing (as opposed to a decision made on the papers), there will be at least one and often several, hearings before a final decision is made. At these hearings, the court will both be:
- setting down the steps necessary for the determination of the central issues in the case; and
- making such interim declarations and decisions under the provisions of Mental Capacity Act (MCA) 2005 s48[1] as are necessary to secure P's interests pending the final determination of those central issues.

10.2 This chapter addresses both aspects of such hearings, as well as addressing the (related) issue of making applications during the course of proceedings. It focuses on the procedures applicable to interim hearings in cases allocated to a pathway under the Case Management Pilot, and for ease of reference uses the Pilot Rule numbering (where relevant) throughout. The main categories of case in which interim hearings are likely and which are not on a pathway are those relating to serious medical treatment (covered in chapter 22) and deprivation of liberty (covered in chapter 21). The specific issues that arise in relation to such cases are addressed in the relevant chapter. There is at the time of writing an issue, discussed in para 4.101, as to whether the Pilot Rules apply to such cases. Even if, strictly, they do not, it is suggested that practitioners should always proceed on the basis of the stricter obligations imposed by the Pilot Rules.

10.3 The chapter does not address Dispute Resolution Hearings, which are an important feature of the property and affairs pathway.[2] These are covered at paras 8.32 onwards.

The jurisdiction of the court to make interim orders and give directions

10.4 Where an application has been made, the court has jurisdiction to exercise its powers on an interim basis to make orders and give directions where:

1 See para 10.6 below.
2 Case Management Pilot PD para 5.4.

- there is reason to believe that P lacks capacity in relation to the matter;
- the matter is one to which its powers under the MCA 2005 extend; and
- it is in P's best interests to make the order, or give the directions, without delay.[3]

10.5 The first of these requirements was interpreted in *Re F*[4] as requiring no more than that there be sufficient evidence to justify a reasonable belief that P may lack capacity, or evidence which gives good cause for concern or raises a real possibility that P may lack capacity. This means, therefore, that the court does not need to make a decision as to whether *in fact* lacks capacity in the material regard (which would often be impossible at the outset of the proceedings). The decision in *Re F* also makes it clear that the threshold that must be crossed is lower than that required (for instance) for the making of a final declaration under MCA 2005 s15.

10.6 While MCA 2005 s48 only talks of 'orders' and 'directions', this includes both decisions and declarations. In other words, assuming that the threshold is crossed, the court can – and will very often – make interim decisions and declarations to 'hold the ring' pending the final determination of the application before it. To emphasise the limited basis upon which they are made, interim declarations are very regularly phrased using wording such as: 'Pursuant to the provisions of section 48 of the Mental Capacity Act, in the interim and on the evidence currently before the Court it is declared that: . . .'. (For precedent orders, see www.courtofprotectionhandbook.com/precedents).

Case management

The overriding objective

10.7 Pilot Part 1 of the COPR has significantly strengthened the duties upon the court and the parties (and their legal representatives) to secure the overriding objective of enabling the court to deal with a case justly. It has also introduced a new element to the overriding

---

3 MCA 2005 s48(a)–(c).
4 [2009] EWHC B30 (COP), [2009] COPLR Con Vol 390, at para 36 per HHJ Marshall QC, (2009) 12 CCLR 530.

objective of enabling the court to deal with cases at proportionate cost.

10.8 There are now specific duties to further the overriding objective upon the court, the parties, legal representatives and unrepresented litigants, each of which we examine briefly in turn.

10.9 The **court** has a duty under COPR Pr1.3 actively to manage cases at all times, and in particular at certain key points such as the referral of the case file to a judge, at every hearing, and at all stages of a final hearing.[5] Key aspects of the duty include:

- ensuring that the appropriate judge is allocated to the case and judicial continuity so far as practicable;
- avoiding delay and keeping costs down;
- encouraging the parties to co-operate with each other in the conduct of the proceedings;
- identifying at an early stage the issues and who should be a party to the proceedings;
- deciding promptly which issues need a full investigation and hearing and which do not, and the procedure to be followed in the case;
- deciding the order in which issues are to be resolved;
- encouraging the parties to use an alternative dispute resolution procedure if the court considers that appropriate;
- fixing timetables or otherwise controlling the progress of the case;
- considering whether the likely benefits of taking a particular step justify the cost of taking it;
- dealing with as many aspects of the case as the court can on the same occasion;
- dealing with the case without the parties needing to attend at court;
- making use of technology; and
- giving directions to ensure that the case proceeds quickly and efficiently.

10.10 The **parties** have a duty to help the court further the overriding objective,[6] a particularly important aspect of which is the requirement actively to ask the court to take steps to manage a case if it appears that an order or direction of the court appears not to deal with an issue, or a new circumstance, issue or dispute arises

---

5 COPR Pr1.3(2).
6 COPR Pr1.4.

of which the court is unaware.[7] It is important to note that the court can take into account a failure without reasonable excuse to comply with the duty imposed by COPR Pr1.4 when deciding whether or not to depart from the general rules as to costs (see further chapter 16).

10.11 **Legal representatives** have their own specific duty (newly imposed by the Case Management Pilot) to help the court further the overriding objective.[8] This does not override their duty to their clients, but does emphasise the extent to which they have obligations to the court as to how they conduct the proceedings.[9]

The powers of the court

10.12 To enable it to further the overriding objective, the court is given general powers of case management by COPR Pr3.1 which details a wide-ranging suite of tools that judges can deploy, tools which (unsurprisingly) match closely the obligations imposed by COPR r1.3. Judges are given added flexibility by COPR Pr3.6, which provides that, in addition to its general powers and those listed in COPR Pr3.1, the court may dispense with the requirement of any rule. COPR Pr3.7 then provides the court with specific powers to make directions.

10.13 The powers of a court at a directions hearing are therefore very wide. They extend as far as determining a case summarily upon its own motion, but that jurisdiction 'must be exercised appropriately and with a modicum of restraint': *KD and LD v Havering LBC*,[10] in which an appeal was allowed where the district judge brought proceedings to an end summarily before a best interests report (which the judge had previously directed be prepared) was filed.

10.14 Authorised officers of the court may exercise certain case management powers in (broadly) non-contentious applications relating to property and affairs.[11] Authorised court officers may not conduct a hearing, and must refer to a judge any application or any question arising in any application which is contentious or which, in the opinion of the officer:

---

7 COPR Pr1.4(2)(a).
8 COPR Pr1.5.
9 See also in this regard *Farooqi and others v R* [2013] EWCA Crim 1649 para 108 and also para 15.32.
10 [2009] COPLR Con Vol 770 at para 28 per HHJ Horowitz QC, (2009) 12 CCLR 671.
11 COPR r7A.

256 Court of Protection Handbook / chapter 10

- is complex;
- requires a hearing; or
- for any other reason ought to be considered by a judge.[12]

As this chapter is for the most part concerned with case management hearings, the powers of authorised officers are not addressed further here.

Initial case management

10.15 Judges will make a significant number of initial directions upon consideration of the papers (and, where the grant of permission is required, at the same time as granting permission).[13] For cases on the personal welfare pathway, the Case Management Pilot specifically provides for judges to make a number of important decisions on the papers at the point of issues, including:

- gatekeeping (ie allocating the case to the right level of judge);
- listing for a case management conference within 28 days, unless the matter is urgent, in which case consideration must be given as to whether it is a case which should be allocated to a Tier 3[14] (ie a High Court or equivalent) judge;
- considering whether it is necessary that P be joined as a party (as to which see further chapter 15 below);
- considering whether an advocates meeting is required before the case management hearing and ordering such a meeting if appropriate; and
- ordering the preparation of a core bundle (not usually to exceed 150 pages) for the case management conference.[15]

10.16 For cases on the property and affairs pathway, the judge will list the case for a Dispute Resolution Hearing (see further chapter 18 below), or transfer the case to the most appropriate regional court outside the Central Office and Registry for listing of the Dispute Resolution Hearing and future case management.[16] The judge will also order the respondent(s) to file a summary of the reasons for opposing the application or for seeking a different order if the reasons are not clear from

---

12 PD 3A para 2.2.
13 The express power to do so is contained in COPR Pr3.7(1)(a).
14 See para 18.11 in relation to the tiering of judges in the Court of Protection.
15 Case Management Pilot PD para 4.5(1).
16 Case Management Pilot PD para 5.3(2).

the COP5 form submitted.[17] Where the matter is urgent, the judge may either list for an urgent Dispute Resolution Hearing, or list an interim hearing to decide the urgent matter(s) in the case.[18]

10.17 In mixed cases, the judge will on the papers either allocate it to a specific pathway, and give directions accordingly, or give directions as to which elements of each pathway are to apply and the procedure that the case will follow.[19]

10.18 Anyone affected by an order made without a hearing has an automatic right to seek review of such orders by virtue of COPR r89 (see paras 18.3–18.8), but such review will inevitably add delay and expense. So as to avoid unnecessary delay, it is therefore important when making an application to ensure that it is clear on the face either:

- any of the 'standard' directions are inapplicable; or
- any unusual directions are required at the outset.

Case management on the personal welfare pathway

10.19 An important innovation under the Case Management Pilot is that the court must list a case management hearing within 28 days (unless the matter is urgent, as to which see further para 10.65 below).[20] The Case Management Pilot PD then specifies in some detail what the court is expected to do at that Case Management Pilot.[21] The most important tasks for the judge include:

- to decide – and record – which issues are in dispute, what has been agreed between the parties, and what issues are not to be the subject of adjudication.[22] The President of the Court of Protection, Sir James Munby, has called for a 'culture change' in the Court of Protection[23] and it is likely that judges will be under significant pressure to be much more robust about only allowing the key issues in any case to go forward for determination. Further, judges are going to be astute to the fact that a 'common driver of delay and expense is the search for the ideal solution, leading to decent but imperfect outcomes being rejected ... the requirement in s1(5) of the Mental Capacity Act 2005 that "An act done, or decision

17 Case Management Pilot PD para 5.3(2).
18 Case Management Pilot PD para 5.6(2).
19 Case Management Pilot PD para 6.1(3).
20 Case Management Pilot PD para 4.4(1)(b).
21 Case Management Pilot PD para 4.5.
22 Case Management Pilot PD para 4.5(a)–(e).
23 *Re MN* [2015] EWCA Civ 411, [2016] Fam 87, (2015) 18 CCLR 521.

made, under this Act for or on behalf of a person who lacks capacity must be done, or made, in his best interests" calls for a sensible decision, not the pursuit of perfection.'[24] To take a practical example: if the application is for a decision that an adult with learning disabilities should no longer live at the family home but in a residential placement, the key issues for the court will be the 'macro' issues of (1) the adult's future residence; and (2) (likely) whether they should have contact with their family. The judge will not be expected to wish to list for determination the 'micro' elements of the day to day care arrangements for the adult at the placement;

- to allocate a judge to the case, judicial continuity being recognised as one of the key drivers to ensuring that cases are resolved proportionately;
- decide how P is to participate in the proceedings (see further chapter 11);
- consider the evidence required, and in particular, whether a section 49 report or a COPR Pr1.2 representative (see para 11.7) could achieve a better result than an expert. (As to evidence see chapter 12); and
- fix a date for the final management hearing and set a target date for the final hearing (or a trial window).

10.20 The personal welfare pathway also provides that there should be a final management hearing at which the court can decide whether the case can be resolved, and, if not, to give directions for the proper preparation of the final hearing.[25] Importantly, at least five days before the final management hearing, the Case Management Pilot expects that a meeting will take place between the advocates and (so far as practicable) any unrepresented parties with the purpose of resolving or narrowing the issues to be decided at the final management hearing.[26] Unless otherwise directed, a further advocates' meeting is then to be held no less than five days before the final hearing.[27] Advocates' meetings are discussed in more detail at para 10.45 below.

---

24 A & B (Court of Protection: Delay and Costs) [2014] EWCOP 48, [2015] COPLR 1 at para 14.
25 Case Management Pilot PD para 4.6(1).
26 Case Management Pilot PD para 4.6(2).
27 Case Management Pilot PD para 4.7(1).

Applications during proceedings

10.21　Even within the much tighter structure envisaged by the Case Management Pilot, a party may well need to make an application during the proceedings either for additional directions, or for interim relief, most usually by way of declarations or decisions relating to P (interim relief is considered further at paras 10.58 onwards below). Not all applications will need to be determined at a hearing, many can be made on the papers (often by consent).

10.22　The procedure for making an application within proceedings is set out in COPR Part 10, as well as in PD 10A. Part 10 of the Rules also covers the position in respect of urgent applications (as to which, see further paras 10.65 onwards below). In short, when making an application, it is necessary to file an application notice (on a form COP9)[28] setting out the order or direction the applicant seeks and the grounds on which it is sought.[29] Where an unusually long or complex order is sought, an electronic copy should be provided; PD 10 provides that this should be done on a disk[30] but increasingly the practice is for email to be used. The applicant should also file the evidence upon which they rely unless it is already before the court.[31] The court has the power to dispense with the need to file an application notice (for instance, by treating a letter sent during the currency of proceedings as if it were an application).[32]

10.23　As a general rule, it is necessary for the applicant to serve a copy of the application notice on anyone named as a respondent in the application notice, every party to the proceedings and on any other person directed by the court, as soon as practicable and in any event within 21 days of service.[33] The application notice must be accompanied by a copy of the evidence filed in support,[34] and the applicant must file a COP20 certificate of service within seven days of the date on which documents were served;[35] where a person has already been served with evidence, the applicant does not need to file a further

---

28　COPR r78(1).
29　COPR r79. COPR r79(c) refers to information being required by a practice direction; PD 10A provides that certain basic information (for instance, the case number) is required, but does not materially add to the requirements.
30　PD 10A para 4.
31　COPR r78(2).
32　COPR r78(5).
33　COPR r80(1).
34　COPR r80(2).
35　COPR r80(3).

copy of such evidence but should instead give notice of the evidence upon which they intend to rely.[36] The applicant can dispense with service only where there is exceptional urgency, where the overriding objective is best served by so doing, by consent of all the parties, with the permission of the court, or where a rule or other practice direction permits (the material practice direction here being PD 10B, discussed further at paras 10.60 onwards below).[37] Where the applicant has dispensed with service, the court can nonetheless still direct that service should be effected and specify who should be served with or notified of the application.[38]

10.24 Wherever possible, an application should be made so as that it can be considered at a hearing which is already listed.[39] If a hearing date has already been fixed and a party wishes to make an application at that hearing but does not have sufficient time in which to file an application notice, PD 10A provides that the applicant should inform the court (in writing if possible) and, if possible, the other parties as soon as they can of the nature of the application and the reason for it, and should then make the application orally at the hearing.[40]

10.25 Parties should also be aware of the power under COPR Pr3.7(4)[41] to vary the time specified for a person to 'do any act' either by the rules or the practice directions or the court, by the written agreement of the parties. This cannot be used to vary the date of a final hearing or to vary the period within which a final hearing can take place. This will always require an application to the court.[42] Nor can it be used if the outcome of the variation would require variation of the date of the final hearing or the period in which the final hearing takes place.[43] However if – for example – it becomes clear that the timetable set by the court for the filing of evidence is unlikely to be met, and the parties agreed to vary it, a consent order recording that agreement pursuant to COPR Pr3.7(4)[44] could be filed at court, thus avoiding the need for an application.

36 COPR r80(4).
37 PD 10A para 9.
38 PD 10A para 11.
39 PD 10A para 15.
40 PD 10A para 16.
41 COPR r85(4) outside the Case Management Pilot.
42 COPR Pr3.7(5)/COPR r85(5).
43 COPR Pr3.7(6).
44 COPR r85(6) outside the Case Management Pilot.

Interim hearings: general provisions

10.26 However they have been listed, interim hearings will usually be listed for between 30 minutes and one hour, and it is very common for a direction to be made that parties are to attend one hour before for purposes of discussions. As set out further below, such discussions can be immensely productive, and every effort should be made to attend in good time for such discussions. In the case of final management hearings on the personal welfare pathway, this requirement has been strengthened by the introduction of mandatory advocates' hearings in advance of the hearing.[45]

10.27 Interim hearings can also take place by telephone or video-link.[46] This can save time and expense in terms of travel, but frequently at the cost of additional expense before and after the hearing in terms of seeking to agree an order to put to the judge or to agree the terms of an order reflecting the directions made by the judge at the hearing. In anything other than a straightforward interim hearing, therefore, careful consideration needs to be given (both by the representatives and the court) to whether the cause of effective case management is not better served by personal attendance.

10.28 Interim hearings in serious medical treatment cases will be held in public (see further chapter 22), as will any interim hearing on a case falling within the Transparency Pilot (as to which, see further chapter 13).

Pilot Practice Direction 4B

10.29 Pilot PD 4B[47] applies expressly to final management hearings.[48] It will also apply whenever a hearing is listed for more than an hour before a district or circuit judge, and whenever it is listed before the President of the Family Division, the Chancellor or a High Court. The Practice Direction applies to directions hearings, interim hearings and also final hearings, with the exception of any urgent application if and to the extent that it is impractical to comply with it. Even where the practice direction does not strictly apply (for instance, in relation to a 30-minute directions hearing before a district judge), the

---

45 Case Management Pilot PD para 4.6(2).
46 COPR r25(2)(d). See also PD 10A paras 18–21 in respect of applications made within proceedings.
47 This is otherwise known as PD 13B for non-pilot cases.
48 Case Management Pilot PD para 4.6(3).

principles that it sets down should still be adhered to where possible so as to maximise the effectiveness of the hearing.

10.30 Where Pilot PD 4B does apply, paragraph 12 of the practice direction makes clear the penalty for failure to comply with any part of it may result in the judge removing the case from the list or moving it further back in the list, as well as adverse costs orders.

10.31 For present purposes, the two most important aspects of Pilot PD 4B are those relating to the preparation of the bundle, and the preparation of the so-called preliminary documents to accompany the bundle. Each of these is discussed in turn below.

Bundles

10.32 The general rule is that the party which is the applicant at the hearing (or the first applicant if there is more than one application) has the responsibility for producing the bundle for the use of the court at that hearing.[49] However, if that person is a litigant in person, then subject to any direction by the court, the responsibility falls upon the first listed respondent who is not a litigant in person or P.[50] If the first named respondent is P and he or she is represented by the Official Solicitor, the responsibility for preparing the bundle will fall to the next named respondent who is represented.[51] It is suggested that the same should apply if a litigation friend other than the Official Solicitor has been appointed to act on P's behalf.

10.33 If possible, the contents of the bundle must be agreed by all parties.[52] This can cause difficulties where one or more of the parties is a litigant in person (especially if they do not have access to a computer for purposes of reviewing and commenting upon a draft index). In such cases, while reasonable steps should be taken to try to agree the index with the litigant in person, a decision will need to be taken as to a cut-off point after which the process of agreement should be completed by the represented parties. Pilot PD 4B provides a timetable for the process of preparing and lodging the bundle, thus:

- The party preparing the bundle must (whether or not it has been agreed) provide a paginated index and, where practicable, paginated copies of material additional to that provided with the original application, to all other parties not less than five working days

---

49 Pilot PD 4B para 3.1.
50 Pilot PD 4B para 3.1.
51 Pilot PD 4B para 3.1.
52 Pilot PD 4B para 3.1.

Interim hearings and interim applications 263

before the hearing.[53] It should be noted that this does not mean that a new, complete, bundle be supplied to each party in advance of a hearing, but experience has taught that it is much better for paginated copies of additional material to be supplied rather than relying upon parties to paginate their additional documents themselves. In such cases, it is almost invariably the case that at least one of the parties will end up operating from a differently paginated bundle at the hearing, with consequential delays and judicial frustration.

- Where counsel is to be instructed at any hearing, then if the bundle is not already in counsel's possession, the bundle must be provided to counsel by the person instructing that counsel not less than four working days before the hearing.[54]
- The bundle (with the exception of the preliminary documents if they are not then available) must be lodged with the court not less than three working days prior to the hearing, unless some other time has been specified by the judge.[55] Specific provisions are set out as to the appropriate office for lodging the bundle dependent on where the case is to be heard. It is always strongly advisable to confirm by telephone the day before the hearing with the relevant office whether the bundle has been received,[56] as it is sadly very common for bundles to go astray in the system.

10.34 Bundles should contain copies of all documents relevant to the hearing in chronological order, indexed and divided into separate sections.[57] They should also be paginated, either within the sections or separately – it is much better to paginate within sections because this allows for easier updating of the bundle. The sections required are as follows:

- preliminary documents (discussed at para 10.37 below);
- case management documents required by any other practice direction (in practice, at present, there are no such documents);
- applications and orders including all Court of Protection forms filed with the application;
- any registered, enduring or lasting power of attorney;
- any urgent or standard authorisation given under MCA 2005 Sch A1 (ie authorising a deprivation of P's liberty in a hospital or care home);

---

53 Pilot PD 4B para 6.1.
54 Pilot PD 4B para 6.2.
55 Pilot PD 4B para 6.3.
56 Useful telephone numbers are given in appendix G below.
57 Pilot PD 4B para 4.1.

- statements and affidavits (which must state on the top right-hand corner of the front page the date when it was signed or sworn[58]);
- care plans (where appropriate[59]);
- experts' reports and other reports;[60]
- other documents, divided into further sections as may be appropriate.

10.35 Bundles should be contained in one or more A4-size ring-binders or lever-arch files (each lever-arch file being limited to 350 pages), clearly marked on the front and the spine with the title and the number of the case, the court where the case has been listed, the hearing date and time, (if known) the name of the judge hearing the case, and where there is more than one ring-binder or lever-arch file, a distinguishing letter or number and confirmation of the total number of binders or files (eg '1 of 3' etc).[61] It is *not* advisable to prepare even short bundles using treasury tags, because it makes it very difficult for the parties and the judge to take out or insert documents.

10.36 Perhaps the key principle to bear in mind in relation to the preparation of bundles is that they should contain those documents relevant to the specific hearing in question, but should not contain more than those documents. Especially where a matter has been ongoing for a considerable period of time, the documents generated in the proceedings can start to run to a (significant) number of lever-arch files: it may very well not be necessary for all of the documents in all of the files to be before the court on each occasion, and having too many before the court will slow the process down. In this regard, it is useful to have in mind that for cases on the welfare pathway under the Case Management Pilot, the bundle prepared for the final hearing in the case must ultimately not only comply with these provisions, but also must: (1) not generally exceed 350 pages; and (2) in any event must not contain more than one copy of the same document.[62]

Preliminary documents and position statements

10.37 For directions and interim hearings to which Pilot PD 4B applies, each party (ie not just the applicant) *must* prepare a document (or documents) which sets out – either within the document(s) or by

---

58 See further para 12.14.
59 See further para 12.14 and appendix E.
60 See further para 12.54.
61 Pilot PD 4B paras 5.1–5.2.
62 Case Management Pilot PD para 4.7(2).

Interim hearings and interim applications 265

cross-reference to another document that will be in the bundle before the court:

- a case summary;
- a chronology of relevant events;
- the issues for determination at the hearing;
- an outline of the likely factual and legal issues at the trial of the case;
- the relief sought at the hearing; and
- a list of essential reading.[63]

10.38 In practice, this information is most usually set out in a 'position statement' (a term which does not appear in Pilot PD 4B, but which is common currency before the court and will be used here). Position statements are vital documents, and should be prepared even if Pilot PD 4B does not strictly apply.

10.39 Directions regularly provide that position statements should be limited, often to no more than a page. Especially in the case of a position statement prepared on behalf of the applicant at a hearing, it can, though, frequently be difficult properly to encapsulate the necessary information in so short a space. If the position statement runs to more than two or three pages, a clear introduction should be given which sets out a route map so that the judge can identify clearly where the necessary information will be found in the statement. A sample position statement is to be found at appendix D below.

10.40 Pilot PD 4B goes on to provide that 'where appropriate', the preliminary documents for a directions or interim hearing should include:

- a description of relevant family members and other persons who may be affected by or interested in the relief sought;
- a particularised account of the issues in the case;
- the legal propositions relied on, and in particular whether it is asserted that any issue is not governed by the MCA 2005;
- any directions sought concerning the identification and determination of the facts that are agreed, the facts the court will be invited to find and the factors it will be invited to take into account based on such agreed facts or findings of facts;
- any directions sought concerning the alternatives the court will be invited to consider in determining what is in P's best interests;

---

63 Pilot PD 4B para 4.2. Case Management Pilot PD para 4.6(3) draws the particular attention of those preparing for final management hearings to these provisions.

- any directions sought relating to expert evidence;
- any other directions sought; and
- a skeleton argument.[64]

10.41 These requirements stem from the judgment of Charles J in *LBL v PB and P*,[65] in which the judge made clear that the direction of preparation of position statements and skeleton arguments 'at an appropriate stage' containing this information will be necessary in most welfare cases.[66] The *LBL* case raised complex questions as to the scope of the jurisdiction of the Court of Protection, and the directions that were made in it therefore were arguably more extensive than will be required in many cases. Nonetheless, where Pilot PD 4B applies, it is incumbent upon the person preparing the preliminary document to consider whether it is appropriate to include each of the types of information set out above.

10.42 In almost all cases, and whether or not Pilot PD 4B strictly applies, it is advisable for the position statement to be accompanied by a draft of the directions that the court will be asked to make. This will be important not just so that the court can see precisely what is being asked of it, but also so that the other parties can have sight in advance of the draft of the directions and – potentially – so that agreement can be reached upon the basis of one of the drafts.

10.43 Whenever a directions hearing has been listed, the directions will usually provide a specific point by which the preliminary documents should be filed (whether by reference to a specific date or the period before the hearing). It is always advisable, wherever possible, for the preliminary documents to be served upon the other parties in advance of this deadline so that the process of negotiation can begin quickly.

10.44 For final management hearings, the core bundle complying with the requirements of Pilot PD 4B must be filed no later than three days before the hearing.[67] Otherwise, where Pilot PD 4B applies, the preliminary documents (and any documents referred to in them which are not already in the bundle) must be lodged with the court no later than 11am on the day before the hearing.[68] Pilot PD 4B provides that they should also be sent by email to the judge's clerk where the hearing is before a High Court judge and the judge's name

---

64 Pilot PD 4B para 4.3.
65 [2011] EWHC 502 (COP), [2011] COPLR Con Vol 166.
66 Para 46.
67 Case Management Pilot PD para 4.6(3).
68 Pilot PD 4B para 6.4.

is known;[69] most of the courts in which directions hearings are heard now also have dedicated email addresses for this purpose.[70] It is always better to err on the side of caution as regards lodging preliminary documents and to seek to ensure (for instance) that they have been sent both by fax and by email. Even where Pilot PD 4B does not apply, it is in any event *strongly* advisable that care is taken to make sure that the documents are with the court by 11am the day before.

Making effective use of court time

The advocates' meeting

10.45   The Case Management Pilot has introduced a specific requirement for advocates' meetings for cases on the personal welfare pathway.[71] Such meetings are to be held both with the legal representatives for the parties and, wherever practicable, any unrepresented parties. Their specific purpose is:
- to resolve or narrow the issues to be determined at the final management hearing, to address the case and bundle preparation matters set down in Pilot PD 4B (see above) and to produce a draft order;[72]
- to resolve or narrow the issues to be determined at the final hearing.[73]

10.46   Experience suggests that advocates' meetings are likely to be most effective where:
- the advocates instructed are those with conduct of the case;
- one party's representative (often that instructed by the Official Solicitor if the Official Solicitor is acting on behalf of P) takes the lead in setting the agenda by identifying areas of agreement and disagreement;
- one party's representative takes the lead in taking a note of the order as it evolves;
- areas where agreement will not be reached are parked quickly, with an agreement to raise them before the judge;

---

69   Pilot PD 4B para 6.4.
70   Useful addresses are given in appendix G below.
71   Case Management Pilot PD para 4.6(2).
72   Case Management Pilot PD para 4.6(2).
73   Case Management Pilot PD para 4.7(1). Note that an advocates' meeting must be held at least five days prior to the final hearing unless the court orders to the contrary.

- arrangements have been made in advance to make sure that, where information may be needed from (for instance) a social worker that social worker will be easily contactable so that information can be provided quickly;
- where interim relief is being negotiated (for instance, as to contact restrictions or the interim management of P's property and affairs: see further paras 10.52 onwards below), a clear distinction is drawn between discussions as to the progression of the case and negotiations as to such relief and sufficient time is allocated to both. In many cases, what (say) the family members will be most concerned about will be about the interim relief, whereas what will actually be most important for the speedy resolution of the application as a whole will be negotiations as to case management orders. If all parties are represented by solicitors and counsel, it can sometimes be possible for both sets of negotiations to be taking place simultaneously, but in such circumstances it is important that all those involved in one set of negotiations are clear as to what the other part of the legal team will be doing.

10.47 Careful thought and preparation – and chairing – will be required wherever one or more of the parties attending is unrepresented. It may in such cases be sensible to have a 'pre-meeting' beforehand between the legal representatives.

10.48 If complete agreement is reached, then a consent order should be submitted for endorsement. Such a consent order should be submitted with an accompanying letter (jointly drafted if possible) outlining a short background summary of the case, the written details of each party who consents, and enough information to allow the court to decide whether to take the case out of the list and whether to make the proposed order.[74] Where not all parties consent, an order can still be submitted together with details of the steps taken to obtain that party's consent and, where known, an explanation of why that consent has not been given.[75] The likelihood of the court endorsing an order in such circumstances will depend greatly on whether: a) it has not been possible to contact the person to obtain their consent (for instance, because they are a litigant in person who has not given the proper contact details); or b) the person is actively objecting to all or part of the order.

---

74 Pilot PD 4B para 11. This will apply by analogy given the wording of Case Management Pilot PD para 4.6(2).
75 Pilot PD 4B para 11.

Before the directions hearing

10.49 Even where an advocates' meeting is not strictly required, it nonetheless remains the case that it is sensible to seek to agree as many of the directions as possible or, at a minimum, to outline the key areas of agreement and disagreement. The process at para 10.48 above should be followed as regards providing a consent order to the court recording either partial or complete agreement as to the directions that are to be required, and the court should also be notified by telephone.[76] If the directions hearing is not going to be effective for any other reason Pilot PD 4B (where it applies) mandates the same notification procedure, by telephone and letter. It is suggested that it is sensible to follow as much of Pilot PD 4B as is possible whether or not it strictly applies.

The day of the hearing

10.50 If the hearing is to take place in person, then (as noted above at para 10.26), it will often be the case that the parties are directed to attend one hour beforehand for discussions. It is in any event very sensible to try to agree with the other parties to attend (at least) one hour before. Depending on how busy their list is, judges are usually happy to give parties additional time to discuss matters, especially if this means that it is more likely that a consent order can be submitted for endorsement, but it is much better to start the discussion process sooner rather than later.

10.51 Finding suitable rooms for discussions at court can often be difficult, especially as it will usually be the case that more than one will be needed so that instructions can be taken in private away from the negotiations. This is another good reason to be at court earlier rather than later, as this will maximise the chances of obtaining suitable numbers of conference rooms.

10.52 Much the same approach as that set out above in relation to advocates' meetings also applies in relation to productive discussions outside court. Two further points apply:
- More and more judges are in a position (and happy) to receive drafts of orders by email directly and/or it may be possible to persuade the court office to print off copies of the draft orders generated as a result of discussions. If it is possible for one of the

---

76 Pilot PD 4B para 11.

parties' representatives to bring a laptop with internet access, therefore, it may well be possible for a draft order to be produced during the course of discussions and for it then to be given to the judge in type-written form. If this is not possible, then the choice of representative to chair the discussions is likely to be dictated by the individual with the best handwriting;
- In many cases, especially those brought by public bodies concerning P's health and welfare, it is a productive use of staff resources for the relevant professionals to attend (at least the first) directions hearing, ie the case management hearing for cases on the welfare pathway. This is for two reasons: 1) because it will allow instructions to be received rapidly from the professionals involved; and 2) because of the importance of the interim declarations and decisions that are likely to be made at that hearing 'holding the ring' pending the final determination by the court of the application. Further, where (as is often the case) the underlying issues involve those of trust as between family members and the relevant public authorities, having the opportunity for the professionals to meet with the family members outside court can provide a surprisingly productive forum for discussions: if nothing else, knowing that a judge will be scrutinising whatever agreements are reached or reaching (interim) decisions upon any areas of disagreement serves very usefully to focus the minds of those attending.

The hearing

10.53 Whilst the hearing is likely to be relatively informal, especially before a district judge, the Case Management Pilot PD is prescriptive as regards the matters that will require consideration and resolution at both case management and final management hearings on the personal welfare pathway (see further paras 10.19–10.20) above, and parties should therefore be prepared to address the relevant matters set down in the PD for the particular hearing in question.

10.54 It is unusual for evidence formally to be given in a directions hearing (as to the requirements in this regard, see para 12.13), but it is not uncommon for a judge to want to hear information directly from those with possession of it rather than through a legal representative. This is another reason why it makes sense in cases involving social services that the relevant social worker for the individual in question attends court.

After the hearing: the order

10.55 It is now very common for the judge to ask the representative for one of the parties (usually either the applicant, if legally represented, or the party represented by the Official Solicitor if the Official Solicitor is acting as litigation friend) to submit an order to the court reflecting the directions made during the hearing. Some judges will in essence dictate the order down to the last detail, such that the task of drawing together the order for submission is relatively straightforward. Some judges will identify the broad thrust of their directions and leave it to the parties to agree the details to be put into an order for endorsement.

10.56 It is clear that, if a party is charged with drawing up an order it is the duty of its solicitors and counsel to produce a draft that fairly reflects what they think the judge decided or directed.[77] Experience has shown that the more that details are left to be discussed by the parties after the hearing, the more room there can be for difficulties, in particular if one or more of the parties starts (in essence) re-running matters discussed during the hearing or (even worse) raising entirely new matters. While it is not always practical to do so, especially if the hearing has run late in the day, it is always a good idea to try to agree as many of the points in the order as possible before parties leave the court building because face-to-face discussion is almost invariably more effective in resolving debates than emails sent on the next or subsequent days. It is also likely to be more efficient in the majority of cases where disputes arise *not* to spend the subsequent days/weeks re-arguing the points between the parties, but rather to put two (or if necessary) more versions of the order to the judge by email so that the judge can decide. It is also suggested that unreasonable conduct in the post-hearing period is capable of attracting a costs sanction (ie it represents a basis under COPR r159 for departing from the normal costs rules set out in rules 156–157: see further, chapter 16 below).[78]

10.57 One specific wrinkle arises in respect of cases in which the Official Solicitor is instructed to act as litigation friend for P. The Official Solicitor's caseworker – ie the member of the Official Solicitor's office with delegated responsibility for giving instructions on behalf of the

---

77 See, by analogy, *Webb Resolutions Ltd v JT Ltd* [2013] EWHC 509 (TCC), [2013] TCLR 6 at para 19 per Edwards-Stuart J.
78 See, by analogy, *Webb Resolutions* at para 23.

Official Solicitor – often requires sight of an order for purposes of giving approval. This can sometimes give rise to difficulties where matters have taken an unanticipated turn at the hearing and the Official Solicitor's caseworker (not having been present) takes the view that a different order to that set down by the judge should have been made. In such circumstances, and assuming that the provision in question reflects a direction made by the judge, the proper course of action is for the Official Solicitor to seek leave to appeal the direction, rather than re-open matters in post-hearing correspondence.

Interim relief and interim hearings

10.58 On very many occasions that the court is considering making directions, it will also be considering what interim declarations or decisions are required to 'hold the ring' prior to the determination of the underlying application before it. For instance, in welfare cases, it will usually be necessary for the court to make interim declarations and decisions as to where P should live and with whom they should have contact prior to the final hearing. In property and affairs cases, it will very often be necessary to identify on an interim basis who should administer P's assets so as to secure them prior to a final determination of the application.

10.59 In some situations, especially those urgent ones discussed further at para 10.65 below, the primary focus of the hearing will be to consider the question of interim relief. As discussed at the outset, such hearings should technically be called interim hearings. Even in such hearings, though, the court is very likely to make directions as to the further consideration of the issues that have arisen or matters that flow in consequence of the decisions made.

10.60 Whenever interim relief is sought during the course of proceedings, the process for doing so is the same as set out above at paras 10.21–10.25 in relation to seeking directions.

10.61 The court has the power to enforce its interim decisions. Enforcement is dealt with at chapter 17 below, but in addition to the general powers granted the court under MCA 2005 s48, COPR r82 confirms that the court has the power to grant an interim injunction, an interim declaration or any other interim order it considers appropriate.

10.62 Any order for an interim injunction must set out clearly what the person to be subject to the injunction must or must not do. The courts have repeatedly emphasised the importance of clarity in this regard, together with the importance of ensuring that any injunction must not require the person subject to it to cross-refer to other material so as to understand their obligations: see, in particular, the comments of Munby LJ in *Re X and Y (children)*.[79]

10.63 Judges will usually seek, at least at the outset of proceedings, not to make injunctions (for instance) restricting contact between P and family members, but rather to seek undertakings from the family members in question to abide by contact restrictions. Negotiating the terms of such undertakings will often represent some of the most important, if difficult, work done outside court at the hearing. It may not always be appropriate to proceed in such a way, most obviously if the proposed subject of the restriction is not present at the hearing; indeed, if they are represented but not actually present, some judges will not accept an undertaking because they consider it necessary to accept the undertaking personally from the individual and to explain its significance.

10.64 PD 10B provides that an interim injunction can be varied or discharged by any judge of the Court of Protection.[80] In other words, it is not necessary that the matter be brought back before the same judge, or even the same level of judge. It is important to note, however, that an appeal against a decision to grant an injunction must follow the usual appeal routes[81] – in other words, a district judge could consider an application to vary an injunction granted by a High Court judge, but could not consider the basis upon which it was granted in the first instance.

Urgent applications

10.65 While PD 10B emphasises[82] that applications that become urgent merely because steps were not taken sufficiently promptly at an earlier stage should be avoided, the court has the ability to deal with truly urgent applications 24 hours a day throughout the year. During court hours (ie weekdays between 10:30 and 16:30), it will usually be necessary for the application to be made before the judge at court,

79 [2012] EWCA Civ 1500, [2013] Fam Law 148 at paras 61–63. See also *Re Whiting* [2013] EWHC B27 (Fam), [2014] COPLR 107 at para 12(7).
80 PD 10B para 16.
81 See chapter 18.
82 PD 10B para 4. See also *Sandwell and West Birmingham NHS Trust v CD & Ors* [2014] EWCOP 23, [2014] COPLR 650, (2014) 17 CCLR 395, (medical treatment case not brought to court in sufficiently good time to enable proper participation by family members).

most frequently before the Urgent Applications judge in the Family Division.[83] Out of hours, or in the case of extreme urgency, applications can be made by telephone. Not all urgent applications will require a hearing, but in the majority of cases applications which are properly characterised as urgent will carry with an element of complexity which will necessitate one being arranged in short order.

10.66 If sufficiently urgent, an application can be determined even though an application form has not been issued, or even filed;[84] in all circumstances, the defining characteristic of an urgent application will be that the respondent will not have been formally notified of it. It is always necessary to explain in the application form (or, if none is being filed, in clear terms to the court office or – if out of hours – the security office at the Royal Courts of Justice) precisely how urgent the application is, what level of judge is required to determine it and whether it requires a hearing.[85]

10.67 The guiding principle as regards urgent applications is that, as far as possible, the provisions relating to applications made on notice set out at paras 10.21–10.25 above should be complied with.[86] In other words, the court and the respondent(s) should be provided with as much information as soon as possible (unless, in the respondent's case, to do so would be to defeat the purpose of the application), and that, as a minimum, steps should be taken to inform the respondent of the application by telephone or in writing.[87] The rationale for this is obvious. It means that, even if the respondent cannot properly be said to have been notified of the application, the respondent may still be able to advance their views to the court at the hearing of the application, even only in writing.

10.68 The courts have repeatedly emphasised the stringency of the requirements upon those appearing before them on without notice applications and the care that must be exercised by judges in scrutinising them. In *KY v DD (Without notice applications)*,[88] Theis J gave guidance applicable equally to applications regarding children in the Family Division of the High Court and applications in the Court of Protection. She emphasised the importance of the duty

---

83 Contact details are contained at appendix G below.
84 PD 10B paras 1 and 6–7.
85 PD 10B para 13; although this is in discretionary terms, the reality is that these obligations are mandatory.
86 PD 10B para 7.
87 PD 10B para 5.
88 [2011] EWHC 1277 (Fam), [2012] 2 FLR 200, (2011) 14 CCLR 648.

upon applicants to give full and frank disclosure,[89] including of matters that would suggest that the application should not be granted, and noted further that:

- If information is put before the court to substantiate a without notice order, it should be the subject of the closest scrutiny and, if the applicant is not present in person to verify it, be substantiated by production of a contemporaneous note of the instructions. If that is not available, there may need to be a short adjournment to enable steps to be taken to verify the information relied upon.
- If additional information is put before the court orally, there must be a direction for the filing of sworn evidence to confirm the information within a very short period of time.
- It is incumbent on those advising whether such an application is justified to consider rigorously whether an application is justified and be clear as to the evidential basis for it.

10.69 PD 10B provides that, where an order is made without notice to any party, the order should ordinarily contain:

- an undertaking by the applicant to serve the application notice, evidence in support and any order made upon the affected parties as soon as possible or as ordered by the court; and
- a return date for a further hearing at which the other parties can be present.[90]

10.70 COPR r81 further provides that a copy of the application notice, the order and the evidence in support is to be served by the applicant on anyone named as a respondent in the application notice (if not otherwise a party to the proceedings), every party to the proceedings and any other person directed by the court, such service to take place as soon as practicable or within such date as the court may direct. Where the application has been made in a situation of exceptional urgency and no application form has been issued, an undertaking will be required that the application form in the terms of the oral application be filed on the next working day, or as required by the court.[91]

---

89 Endorsing guidance previously given by Munby J (as he then was) in in *Re W (ex parte orders)* [2000] 2 FLR 927 and *Re S (ex parte orders)* [2001] 1 FLR 308, [2001] 1 WLR 211 and by Charles J in *B Borough Council v S and another* [2006] EWHC 2584 (Fam), [2007] 1 FCR 574, (2006) 9 CCLR 596. See also the comments of McFarlane J (as he then was) in *LLBC v TG, JG, and KR* [2007] EWHC 2640 (Fam), [2009] 1 FLR 414, (2008) 11 CCLR 161.
90 PD 10B para 6.
91 PD 10B para 9.

10.71 While PD 10B is silent on the subject, it is at a minimum good practice, if not even obligatory, for a detailed note to be made of submissions made to the judge when the respondent is not present or represented, and of the reasons given by the judge for making (or not making) the order sought. The court will often order that such a note be filed in advance of the return date; in any event, without such a contemporaneous note it can be very difficult at any later date to identify with clarity precisely how any without notice order came to be made.

10.72 Where a hearing of an urgent application takes place by telephone, PD 10B envisages that, where practicable, that hearing will take place by way of a conference call arranged (and in the first instance, paid for) by the applicant through a service provider (such as BT Connect), and that the service provider will record the call. In such situations, the applicant should order a transcript of the hearing from the service provider.[92] In the authors' experience, however, the majority of urgent telephone hearings in such cases (and especially those out of hours) take place by way of a direct telephone call between the applicant's representative and the judge and there is no possibility of recording the call for transcription. It is further not unheard of for the judge not to have all the papers before them, and for the judge then to be relying almost exclusively upon what they are being told by the applicant's representative. In such situations, the obligation to take a proper note of relevant matters is particularly onerous.

---

92 PD 10B para 12.

CHAPTER 11

P, protected parties and children

11.1	Introduction
11.4	**Participation of P**
11.4	Background
11.6	The menu of options
11.14	**Protected parties**
11.21	**Children**
11.26	**Litigation friends**
11.26	Pre-appointment
11.27	Appointment
	Appointment without a court order • Appointment with a court order
11.40	Who may be appointed as a litigation friend?
	For P
	Acting for a child or a protected party other than P
11.45	Duties of the litigation friend
	General • Deprivation of liberty cases • Litigation friends acting for a child
11.53	Terminating the appointment of a litigation friend
	Litigation friend acting on behalf of P: capacity gained or regained • Litigation friend acting on behalf of an adult protected party: capacity gained or regained • Litigation friend acting on behalf of a child: capacity gained or regained • Litigation friend acting on behalf of a child: child reaching majority • Any litigation friend: other situations
11.65	Costs and the litigation friend
	Costs incurred by the litigation friend
11.69	Costs payable to other parties *continued*

277

11.74	**COPR Pr1.2/COPR r3A representatives**
11.74	Appointment
11.76	Duties
11.81	Directions and variation or termination of appointment
11.83	Funding
11.84	**Accredited Legal Representatives**
11.84	Definition
11.86	When will an ALR be appointed?
11.92	Requirements for appointment as an ALR
11.93	Appointment
11.94	Duties
11.101	Directions and variation or termination of appointment
11.102	Good practice guide

Introduction

11.1 This chapter addresses the participation and representation of P before the Court of Protection. With effect from July 2015, and the amendments introduced by the Court of Protection (Amendment) Rules (COP(A)R) 2015,[1] very much greater attention is now being paid to the issue of participation. Whilst it will remain the case that P will not be joined as a party to the majority of applications, P is now able to participate through a wider range of options than previously addressed in this chapter.

11.2 The chapter will also address the position where a party to the proceedings is a protected party (ie they are an adult who lacks litigation capacity) or they are a child, as in both cases they will require a litigation friend (in the case of a child, unless the court orders otherwise). It should be noted that the 2015 rule changes included a complete replacement for Part 17 of the Court of Protection Rules (COPR), the governing rules in relation to these situations. Whilst, for the most part, the provisions are materially the same, care should be taken to ensure that the current version of Part 17 is consulted (and also the updated accompanying Practice Direction, PD 17A).

11.3 A good practice guide to acting as a litigation friend or an Accredited Legal Representative (ALR) is to be found at the end of this chapter.

Participation of P

Background

11.4 By 2014, the participation of P had become a particular issue for two main reasons:
- A line of cases decided in the European Court of Human Rights[2] had made it increasingly clear that the proper participation of the subject of proceedings for declarations as to their capacity was

---

1 SI No 548.
2 *X and Y v Croatia* (App No 5193/90, decision of 3 November 2011), *Shtukaturov v Russia* (App No 4409/05), [2008] ECHR 223 and *Lashin v Russia* (App No 33117/02, decision of 22 January 2013). See also, subsequently *Ivinovic v Croatia* (App No 13006/13, decision of 18 September 2014) and *AN v Lithuania* (App No 17280/08, decision of 31 May 2016). See also the paper by Lucy Series entitled 'The participation of the relevant person in proceedings before the Court of Protection' available at http://sites.cardiff.ac.uk/wccop/files/2014/09/Briefing-on-Personal-Participation-in-the-CoP-v1-2.pdf.

necessary so as to secure their rights under both Articles 6 and 8 of the European Convention on Human Rights (ECHR);
- More pressingly, the decision of the Supreme Court in *Cheshire West*[3] (see further para 21.3) led to a perception that there would be an enormous increase in the number of applications to the Court of Protection for judicial authorisation of deprivations of liberty outside care homes and hospitals. The question then arose as to whether the person concerned had to be a party to such proceedings in all cases and, if they were not to be a party, how their participation could be sufficiently ensured so as to secure their rights under Article 5 ECHR. How the courts then grappled with that issue is addressed further in chapter 21.

11.5 The ad hoc Rules Committee which met in late 2014/early 2015 with a remit to focus upon the most pressing issues that had been identified as requiring changes in the practice and procedures of the Court of Protection therefore devoted the majority of its energies to addressing the participation of P.[4] The result was therefore what is now COPR Pr1.2/COPR r3A.

The menu of options

11.6 The participation of P is now provided for in COPR Pr1.2/COPR r3A.[5] This rule, which came into force on 1 July 2015, requires in each case the court to consider, either on its own initiative or on the application of any person, whether it should make one or more directions relating to P's participation set down in a 'menu' provided by the rule. Consideration of P's participation is expressly required at the first case management hearing for cases falling under the personal welfare pathway under the Case Management Pilot (see para 10.19).

11.7 The menu of options for P's participation includes:
- P being a party;[6]
- P's participation being secured by the appointment of an ALR to represent P in the proceedings and to discharge such other

---

3 [2014] UKSC 19, [2014] COPLR 313, (2014) 17 CCLR 5.
4 For more detail of the background to the amendments, see Alex Ruck Keene, *The next stage of the journey – the Court of Protection (Amendment) Rules 2015* [2015] 2 Eld LJ 150.
5 The accompanying Practice Direction is PD Pilot 1A/PD 2A.
6 COPR Pr1.2(2)(a) / COPR r3A(2)(a).

functions as the court may direct. The position of such ALRs is considered at paras 11.84–11.114 below;[7]
- P's participation being secured by the appointment of a representative whose primary function is to give P a 'voice' by relaying information as to P's wishes and feelings. The position of such representatives is considered at paras 11.74 below;[8]
- specific provision for P to address (directly or indirectly) the judge determining the application;[9] or
- no direction or an alternative direction (meeting the overriding objective) if P's interests and position can properly be secured.[10]

11.8 Which of the directions set out above is made is a decision for the court having regard to (a) the nature and extent of the information before the court; (b) the issues raised in the case; (c) whether a matter is contentious; and (d) whether P has been notified in accordance with the provisions of Part 7 of the COPR (see further para 7.30) and what, if anything, P has said or done in response to such notification. In practice, a further important consideration is the limited availability of funding for representatives (of whatever kind). This has become a particular issue in relation to applications for authorisation of deprivation of liberty, and is addressed further in chapter 21.

11.9 Practice Direction Pilot 1A/PD 2A, which accompanies these provisions, envisages that in many cases no sort of representative will be needed because these are non-contentious property and affairs cases and 'experience has shown that they can be dealt with on paper and without joining P as a party or appointing anyone to represent P'.[11] The practice direction comments that as a result of COPR Pr1.2/COPR r3A the court 'is both enabled and required to tailor the provision it directs for P's participation and representation to the circumstances of the individual case'.[12]

11.10 Where P is to be a party and does not have capacity to conduct the proceedings, the court must either appoint a litigation friend to act on their behalf,[13] or appoint an ALR to act without a litigation friend being appointed to act for P.[14] The appointment and duties of

7 COPR Pr1.2(2)(b) / COPR r3A(2)(b).
8 COPR Pr1.2(2)(c) / COPR r3A(2)(c).
9 COPR Pr1.2(2)(d) / COPR r3A(2)(d).
10 COPR Pr1.2(2)(e) / COPR r3A(2)(e).
11 Pilot PD1A / PD 2A para 3.
12 Pilot PD1A / PD 2A para 6.
13 COPR Pr1.2(4)(a) / COPR r3A(4)(a).
14 COPR Pr1.2(2)(4)(b) / COPR r3A(4)(b).

litigation friends are considered at paras 11.26–11.48 below; the appointment and duties of ALRs are set out at paras 11.84–11.100 below. An order joining P as a party will only take effect where either a litigation friend or an ALR has been appointed.[15] If the court has directed that P should be joined as a party but it has not taken place because no litigation friend or ALR has been appointed, the court must record in a judgment or order the fact that one has not been appointed, and the reasons given as to why not.[16] This is designed to 'flush out' situations in which funding has not been forthcoming to enable such appointments to take place.

11.11 In deciding whether P has capacity to conduct the proceedings (often called 'litigation capacity'), the court will apply Mental Capacity Act (MCA) 2005 ss2–3. A detailed examination of the issue of litigation capacity lies outside the scope of this work.[17] In summary, however:

- the *test* that the court will apply is that under MCA 2005 ss2–3 (see further paras 3.33 onwards), which means – importantly – that it must have regard to the principles of the presumption of capacity and that all practicable support must have been given to the person without success before they can be found to lack capacity. What this means in practical terms for those representing P is set out in the guide at the end of this chapter.
- In applying that test, the court will have regard to cases decided under the common law as to the key *information* that the person must be able to retain, understand, use and weigh. In particular, in *A, B and C v X and Z*,[18] Hedley J considered that the 'heart of the test' were the observations of Chadwick LJ at para 75 of *Masterman-Lister*[19] that:

[T]he test to be applied, as it seems to me, is whether the party to the legal proceedings is capable of understanding, with the assistance of proper explanation from legal advisers and experts in other

---

15 COPR Pr1.2(4) / COPR r3A(4).
16 COPR Pr1.2(5) / COPR r3A(5).
17 For a more detailed discussion, see chapter 8 of the Law Society/British Medical Association's *Assessment of mental capacity: a practical guide for doctors and lawyers*, 4th edn, 2015.
18 [2012] EWHC 2400 (COP), [2013] COPLR 1.
19 *Masterman-Lister v Brutton & Co, Masterman-Lister v Jewell and another* [2002] EWCA Civ 1889, [2003] 1 WLR 1511, (2004) 7 CCLR 5. The approach adopted in *Masterman-Lister* was endorsed by the Supreme Court in *Dunhill v Burgin (Nos 1 and 2)* [2014] UKSC 18, [2014] WLR 933, (2014) 17 CCLR 203.

disciplines as the case may require, the issues on which his consent or decision is likely to be necessary in the course of those proceedings. If he has capacity to understand that which he needs to understand in order to pursue or defend a claim, I can see no reason why the law – whether substantive or procedural – should require the interposition of a next friend.[20]

11.12 Three points are particularly important when it comes to considering litigation capacity:

- the question of capacity to litigate is not something to be determined in the abstract: it is always necessary to ask whether P has the capacity to litigate in relation to the particular application before the court.[21]
- P may well have capacity to conduct the proceedings even though it is asserted that they do not have capacity to make the decisions in question.[22] The position where P, in fact, has capacity to conduct the litigation although they do not have the capacity to take the decisions in issue is discussed further at para 11.53 onwards. Whilst possible, the converse situation – ie that P *has* litigation capacity but lacks the capacity to make the underlying decisions – is not common in practice.[23]
- P may well have capacity to wish to challenge a decision but lack the capacity to conduct the entirety of the consequent proceedings.[24] This is particularly relevant in the context of applications under MCA 2005 s21A, discussed further in chapter 21.

---

20 *A, B and C v X and Z* [2012] EWHC 2400 (COP), [2013] COPLR 1, para 42.
21 *Sheffield City Council v E and another*, para 38.
22 See, for instance *Re SB* [2013] EWHC 1417 (COP), [2013] COPLR 445 and *KK v STCC* [2012] EWHC 2136 (COP), [2012] COPLR 627, both cases in which the court ultimately held that the person did have the capacity to make their own decisions.
23 For an example of the case where the person was held to have litigation capacity whilst ultimately being found to lack subject-matter capacity, see *Islington LBC v QR* [2014] EWCOP 26, (2014) 17 CCLR 344.
24 See, by analogy, *Hillingdon LBC v WW (Special Educational Needs: Other)* [2016] UKUT 253 (AAC), para 8, distinguishing capacity to appeal from capacity to make other decisions to be made in the course of proceedings.

11.13 Where P is a child,[25] it is suggested that the court should approach that child *as if* they were an adult P for the purposes of deciding their capacity to conduct the proceedings and therefore apply the capacity test set down in MCA 2005 ss2–3. The child may, though, be unable to take the decision (or litigate in respect of that decision) not because they have a material impairment in the functioning of their mind or brain but because they are not 'competent': ie applying the test set down by the House of Lords in the case of *Gillick*,[26] they do not have sufficient maturity and intelligence to understand the nature and implications of the proposed decision.[27] In such a case, if relief is required from a court, then that court is not the Court of Protection, but, depending on the precise nature of the relief sought, then either the Family Court or the Family Division of the High Court. This is not addressed further here.[28]

Protected parties

11.14 An adult other than P who lacks capacity to conduct the proceedings is called a 'protected party'.[29] A protected party requires a litigation friend.[30]

11.15 The same principles as set out in relation to P above apply to the determination of the litigation capacity of an adult party. However, because the focus of the proceedings will not initially be upon the litigation capacity of the adult party, it is often the case that it will only become apparent after proceedings have started that they lack

---

25 MCA 2005 provides for the Court of Protection to make certain types of decision in respect of those between the age of 16 and 18, and indeed, in respect of those below 18, to make any decision relating to P's property and affairs save for the making of a will, if the court considers it likely that P will still lack capacity to make decisions in respect of that matter when he reaches 18: MCA 2005 ss2(5) and 18(3).

26 *Gillick v West Norfolk and Wisbech Area Health Authority* [1985] UKHL 7, [1986] 1 AC 112.

27 [1986] 1 AC 112 at 189 per Lord Scarman. For a more detailed discussion of the position of children potentially subject to the MCA 2005, see Ashton et al, *Court of Protection Practice 2016*, Jordans, paras 2.92–2.94.

28 For more on decision-making and remedies in relation to children, see chapters 7 and 11 respectively Broach et al, *Disabled Children: a legal handbook*, Legal Action Group, 2nd edition, 2016, also available (free) online at www.councilfordisabledchildren.org.uk/11566.

29 COPR r6.

30 COPR rr141(2) and 6.

litigation capacity. This gives rise to practical issues as to what should happen in such a case.

11.16 In some ways the situation is relatively straightforward if the person has legal representation – it is clear that a responsible solicitor who has concerns as to the capacity of his or her client should take steps to obtain a medical opinion;[31] if that opinion suggests that the client lacks litigation capacity, then the solicitor should take steps to ensure that a litigation friend is appointed before proceeding further.[32]

11.17 If the person is acting for themselves, however, then a difficult question can arise. It is ultimately a judicial question whether an individual is or is not a protected party.[33] If the court is in possession of information raising a question as to the capacity of a litigant in person to conduct the litigation, how is it to satisfy itself as to whether the person has the requisite capacity? It may be that the litigant in person is prepared to agree to undergo a medical examination, but what if they refuse? A party to proceedings cannot be ordered to undergo a medical examination[34] and the court is therefore faced with a difficult dilemma. In *Baker Tilly (a firm) v Makar*,[35] Sir Raymond Jack made clear that:

> The absence of medical evidence cannot be a bar to a finding of lack of capacity but where most unusually circumstances arise in which medical evidence cannot be obtained, the court should be most cautious before concluding that the probability is that there is a disturbance of the mind. Section 2(3)(b) of the [Mental Capacity] Act must be kept in mind. A finding of lack of capacity is a serious matter for both parties. It takes away the protected party's right to conduct

---

31 Whether that is from a GP, a psychiatrist or a psychologist will depend upon the circumstances of the case. For more on the duties of solicitors in relation to vulnerable clients, see the Law Society's Practice Note: *Meeting the Needs of Vulnerable Clients*: http://www.lawsociety.org.uk/support-services/advice/practice-notes/meeting-the-needs-of-vulnerable-clients-july-2015/.
32 See *Masterman-Lister v Brutton & Co, Masterman-Lister v Jewell and another* [2002] EWCA Civ 1889, [2003] 1 WLR 1511, (2004) 7 CCLR 5 at para 30.
33 See *Carmathenshire CC v Lewis* [2010] EWCA Civ 1567 at para 8 per Rimer LJ.
34 See also para 4.59 of the Code of Practice accompanying the MCA 2005: 'Nobody can be forced to undergo an assessment of capacity'. Although see *Re SA* [2010] EWCA Civ 1128 where the court sought to require both P and her mother to cooperate in the carrying out of a capacity assessment upon P (for purposes of determining her capacity to make the underlying decisions in the case). On a proper analysis, there was an element of bluff deployed here because there was a strong suggestion that P was being influenced in her refusal by her mother.
35 [2013] EWHC 759 (QB), [2013] COPLR 245.

their litigation. It may constitute, and here would constitute, a serious disadvantage to the other party.

11.18 These comments were made in the context of adversarial civil proceedings, but it is suggested that they are equally applicable before the Court of Protection.

11.19 We suggest, however, that in appropriate cases the court can – and should – make findings as to litigation capacity even where a party refuses to attend a medical examination where there is sufficient evidence. Such evidence may emerge from a variety of sources. In *Re RGS*,[36] for instance, the court had limited medical information about RBS, P's son, who was known to have a history of contact with psychiatric services but who refused to attend a medical examination. The court found RBS to lack litigation capacity. The court found that such information as there was from the professional witnesses and RBS' own account founded the conclusion that RBS had an impairment or disturbance of the mind or brain. RBS' own conduct during the proceedings gave rise to the finding that the impairment/disturbance had compromised his ability to understand, retain and weigh the information relevant to the litigation.

11.20 In extreme cases, where a litigant in person refuses to take part in a medical examination, the court may be able to direct disclosure of the litigant's medical records to an independent medical examiner who could then prepare a report based on the clinical record. A party's medical records are confidential, but in *Bennett v Compass Group*[37] (a case relating to the disclosure of medical records in a personal injury case where the claimant's capacity was not in issue), comments made by both Chadwick LJ[38] and Pill LJ[39] would suggest that a (civil) court could make an order requiring a GP or hospital to disclose records directly to a party to the litigation without the consent of the person in question, although it is clear from the comments made in that case that such an order would be wholly exceptional. There is no reason in principle why such an approach could not be adopted by the Court of Protection, albeit after a very careful balancing exercise between the litigant's rights to maintaining the confidentiality of their medical records under Article 8 (right to respect for private and

---

36 [2012] EWHC 4162 (COP), [2012] EWCOP 4162.
37 [2002] EWCA Civ 642, [2002] CP Rep 58.
38 At paras 67–68.
39 Para 88.

family life) of the ECHR[40] and the potential benefits to them of being represented by a litigation friend.

Children

11.21 A child – ie someone under 18[41] – who is a party to proceedings but is not P, will require a litigation friend unless the court orders otherwise.[42] An application must be made for the court to make such an order; if the application is made by the child, then if a litigation friend has already been appointed to act on their behalf, it must be made on notice to that litigation friend.[43] It may otherwise be made without notice.[44] There is no guidance in the MCA 2005, the COPR or PD 17A as to the circumstances under which a court will permit a child to conduct proceedings without a litigation friend.

11.22 There are two bases upon which a child may lack capacity to conduct proceedings. The first is on the basis that they are not 'Gillick-competent';[45] the second is because they suffer from a material disturbance or impairment of the mind or brain.

11.23 If the concern in respect of the child arises not because of a suggestion that they are in some way suffering from a disability, but rather because of their age, then it is suggested that useful guidance can be found in the approach adopted in the Family Procedure Rules (FPR) 2010,[46] which also contain a provision for the court to dispense with the requirement that a child be represented by a litigation friend (or a children's guardian) in certain circumstances. The FPR provide that an application by the child will be granted 'if [the court] considers that the child has sufficient understanding to conduct the proceedings concerned or proposed without a litigation friend or children's guardian'.[47] The FPR contain differences to the COPR, not least as they provide that the court can nonetheless require the litigation

40 See in this regard Z v Finland (1997) 25 EHRR 371 at para 95.
41 COPR r6.
42 COPR r141(3)–(4).
43 COPR r141(5)(b).
44 COPR r141(5)(c).
45 Ie they do not have sufficient maturity and intelligence to understand the nature and implications of the proposed decision: Gillick v West Norfolk and Wisbech Area Health Authority [1985] UKHL 7, [1986] 1 AC 112. See also para 11.13 above.
46 SI No 2955, as amended.
47 FPR r16.6(6).

friend or guardian to continue to play a part in the proceedings, but it is suggested that the approach set down in the FPR is likely to be adopted before the Court of Protection.

11.24 If the concern in respect of the child's ability to participate in the proceedings arises out of a concern that they are suffering from a disability affecting their capacity to conduct litigation, then while the guidance in the FPR does not cease entirely to be relevant, it is suggested that the primary considerations should be those set out at paras 11.11–11.12 onwards above in relation to adults.

11.25 Even where an order has been made permitting a child to act without a litigation friend, the court retains the power to appoint a litigation friend if it subsequently appears to the court that it would be desirable for such a litigation friend to conduct proceedings on the child's behalf. There is no guidance in the MCA 2005, the COPR or PD 17A as to when such a step would be desirable. At least where the appointment of a litigation friend for a child has taken place on the basis out of a concern that they are not sufficiently mature, then by analogy with the FPR[48] it is suggested that a court should be slow to re-appoint a litigation friend save where it has become clear that the child, in fact, lacks the understanding to conduct the proceedings. To do otherwise – for instance, on the basis that the child's conduct is disruptive – would be to risk depriving the child of a voice in the proceedings; the court has other mechanisms to control such disruptive conduct by way of its case management powers granted it under COPR rr25 and 85 (or COPR Pilot Part 3 where this applies).

Litigation friends

Pre-appointment

11.26 The COPR are silent as to what the court may or may not do as regards the proceedings generally where a party who requires a litigation friend (including P) has not yet had one appointed. It is suggested that the court does have the power to proceed, either under its general case management powers in COPR Pr3.1/COPR r25 and/ or, if required, by importing the provisions of the Civil Procedure Rule (CPR) r21.3(3) through the provisions of COPR Pr2.5(1)/

---

48 FPR r16.6(8).

COPR r9(1),[49] enabling it to give permission to the other parties to proceed to take steps in the proceedings absent the relevant appointment. The court will seek to do the minimum possible to 'hold the ring', pending such an appointment, especially in relation to P, although if needs be the court can proceed simply to make decisions in a suitably urgent case.[50]

Appointment

11.27 There are two ways in which a litigation friend can be appointed: without a court order and with one. A litigation friend can never be appointed for P without a court order.

Appointment without a court order

11.28 A deputy appointed with the specific power to conduct legal proceedings in the name of the protected party is entitled to act as litigation friend without a further order if their power extends to the proceedings in question.[51] The conduct of legal proceedings is considered an aspect of the management of P's property and affairs for purposes of MCA 2005;[52] it would therefore be very unlikely that a deputy appointed to make decisions in relation to a protected party's health and welfare would also be given the power by the court to make decisions in relation to the conduct of legal proceedings where that person is then a protected party. If a deputy is to act as litigation friend, the deputy must file and serve an official copy of the order on the other parties (or, if a party is represented by a litigation friend, upon that party's litigation friend).[53]

11.29 If there is no deputy, a person can become a litigation friend for a protected party or for a child (but not for P) without a court order if

---

49 Which provide that: 'In any case not expressly provided for by these Rules or the practice directions made under them, the Civil Procedure Rules 1998 (including any practice directions made under them) may be applied with any necessary modifications, insofar as is necessary to further the overriding objective'.
50 See, for instance, *Newcastle-upon-Tyne Foundation Trust v LM* [2014] EWHC 454 (COP), [2015] 1 FCR 373, where the medical treatment decision had to be taken in circumstances where it was not possible (in the time available) to appoint the Official Solicitor to act as P's litigation friend.
51 COPR r142(2).
52 MCA 2005 s18(1)(k).
53 COPR r142(4) and PD 17A para 5.

they file a certificate of suitability (with a statement of truth[54]) on a form COP22[55] stating (among other things) that:

- they can fairly and competently conduct proceedings on behalf of the individual in question;[56]
- they have no interests adverse to the individual in question;[57]
- that the litigation friend knows or believes that the child or protected party lacks capacity to conduct the proceedings themselves;[58]
- the grounds of the belief set out above (and, if the belief is based upon medical opinion, or the opinion of another suitably qualified expert, attach any relevant document to the certificate).[59] It is suggested that a court would wish to consider carefully any situation in which a litigation friend had been appointed pursuant to this process absent medical evidence.[60]

11.30 The first two bullet points are discussed further at paras 11.45 onwards below.

11.31 The proposed litigation friend must serve the certificate of suitability on the other parties (or, if a party is represented by a litigation friend, upon that party's litigation friend).[61] Unless the court directs otherwise, the proposed litigation friend does not need to serve any document relating to the medical or other opinion noted at the last bullet point above.

11.32 The proposed litigation friend must then file the certificate of suitability together with a certificate of service on a COP20 form when they first take a step in the proceedings.[62]

11.33 The procedure set out above cannot be used if the court has previously appointed a litigation friend,[63] because in such situations an order will be required to terminate the appointment of the existing litigation friend (see further paras 11.53 onwards below). It also

---

54 PD 17A para 8.
55 Which will serve as the requisite consent for purposes of PD 17A para 7(a).
56 COPR r142(3)(a) read together with COPR r140(1)(a).
57 COPR r142(3)(a) read together with COPR r140(1)(b).
58 PD 17A para 7(b).
59 PD 17A para 7(c).
60 Whether that is from a GP, a psychiatrist or a psychologist will depend upon the circumstances of the case. See *Masterman-Lister v Brutton & Co, Masterman-Lister v Jewell and another* [2002] EWCA Civ 1889, [2003] 1 WLR 1511, (2004) 7 CCLR 5 at para 17.
61 COPR r142(3)(b) and PD 17A para 9.
62 PD 17A para 11.
63 COPR r142(1)(b).

cannot be used by the Official Solicitor[64] (perhaps because the Official Solicitor is to be taken automatically to satisfy the suitability requirement and hence should not be required to file such a certificate).

Appointment with a court order

11.34 An order appointing a person as a litigation friend for a protected party, a child or – importantly – P (if P is joined to the proceedings) can be made either at the court's own initiative or upon application by any person (ie not just by the proposed litigation friend).[65] Any application must be made by filing a COP9[66] and be supported by evidence[67] that will allow the court to be satisfied (as it must also be satisfied if it is contemplating making the order of its own initiative) that:

- the proposed litigation friend can fairly and competently conduct proceedings on behalf of the individual in question;[68]
- the proposed litigation friend has no interests adverse to the individual in question;[69]
- the proposed litigation friend consents to the appointment.[70]

11.35 The last of these criteria is self-evident, although note that a litigation friend can make their consent (and continuing consent) contingent on receiving appropriate funding (see para 11.60 below); the first two are discussed at paras 11.46 onwards below. Because the evidence matches that set out in a COP20 certificate of suitability, there is no requirement to file such a certificate where an application is being made.

11.36 As noted above, a court order is required in order to appoint the Official Solicitor as litigation friend for a protected party, a child or P.[71] Although the COPR are silent on this, it would seem that the Official Solicitor is automatically taken to meet the suitability criteria and the Official Solicitor would never be required to file evidence to address these criteria.

---

64 COPR r142(1)(c).
65 COPR r143(2).
66 PD 17A para 13. See further para 10.21 for applications within proceedings.
67 COPR r143(1).
68 COPR r140(1)(a).
69 COPR r140(1)(b).
70 COPR r143(2).
71 COPR r142(1)(c).

11.37 If the court considers that it requires further evidence before it can grant an application to be appointed as litigation friend, or if it appears to the judge during the course of proceedings that a party (other than P) may require a litigation friend, but that further evidence is required, directions can be made.[72] If P has previously made a successful application to be allowed to instruct representatives directly (see further paras 11.53–11.55 below) but it then appears that the position has changed subsequently, then the same provisions will apply.

11.38 The court has the power, exercisable on its own initiative or at the application of any person (whether or not that person is a party) to prevent someone acting as a litigation friend (for any party).[73]

11.39 Where the application is made on the basis of the proposed litigation friend's conduct, it must be supported by evidence.[74] Where the application is made on the basis that the person (whether that is P, a protected party, or a child) does not require a litigation friend because they, in fact, have the capacity to litigate (or in the case of a child, that one is unnecessary having regard to the factors set out at para 11.23 above), no evidence is required. This is addressed further below at paras 11.53 onwards.

Who may be appointed as a litigation friend?

For P

11.40 The Official Solicitor describes himself as, and because of resource constraints takes very seriously his position as, litigation friend of last resort. This means that he will only consider acting where no suitable and willing person can be identified to act. Further, and save in the case of serious medical treatment cases (as to which, see chapter 22), even assuming that there is no other suitable and willing person, the Official Solicitor will only accept an appointment to act subject to being given suitable security for (a) the costs of any external solicitors he or she retains to act for P; or (b) where he acts as solicitor and conducts the litigation, those costs of so acting. In other words, and while the Official Solicitor does not seek to recover his costs of acting as litigation friend, he must be satisfied that the costs incurred either by external solicitors or by his or her staff in acting as

---

72 COPR r143(5). The position where it appears that an adult party other than P may require a litigation friend is addressed at paras 11.14–11.20 above.
73 COPR r144(1).
74 COPR r144(2).

solicitors will be met, whether that be from P's own assets or by way of legal aid. If the Official Solicitor is not given this security he will not act, and if it emerges during the course of proceedings that his legal costs can no longer be met, he will stop acting – and cannot be compelled to continue to act.[75]

11.41 It is therefore extremely important in any case both to identify whether another person may be suitable to act as a litigation friend and, if it would appear that the Official Solicitor may be the only candidate, to identify the basis upon which the Official Solicitor can be satisfied that his legal costs will be met. A precedent order setting out how the relevant security can be provided can be found online in the precedent section of the *Court of Protection Handbook*.[76]

11.42 The appointment of family members, friends and advocates (such as Independent Mental Capacity Advocates[77]) as P's litigation friend has become increasingly common over the past few years, especially in the context of applications in relation to deprivation of liberty (discussed further in chapter 21). Detailed guidance for such individuals considering acting as a litigation friend was commissioned in 2014 by the Department of Health,[78] but the following points are of particular importance in relation to such appointments:

- The mere fact that a person (for instance, a family member) has strong views as to where P's best interests lie does not automatically disqualify them from acting as P's litigation friend. Indeed, a person with strong and vocal views may very well be the best 'champion' for P;[79]
- However, where there is a family dispute concerning P's best interests, it would be rare for it to be appropriate for a family member to be appointed as P's litigation friend in proceedings relating to that dispute. If they were to be so appointed, they would have 'to demonstrate that he or she can, as P's litigation

---

75 See *Bradbury and others v Paterson and others* [2014] EWHC 3992 (QB), [2015] COPLR 425. This was a decision in civil proceedings, but the same approach would be applied before the Court of Protection.
76 https://courtofprotectionhandbook.com/precedents/.
77 See, for instance, *Re M* [2013] EHWC 3456 (COP), [2014] COPLR 35.
78 www.law.manchester.ac.uk/medialibrary/Main%20site/LAC/Acting-as-a-Litigation-Friend-in-the-Court-of-Protection-October-2014.pdf. This guidance has been superseded to some extent by events, and should be read subject to the discussion below as to the duties of litigation friends, and also the ability of a litigation friend to act without instructing lawyers.
79 See *Re NRA and others* [2015] EWCOP 59, [2015] COPLR 690, (2015) 18 CCLR 392 at paras 163–164.

friend, take a balanced and even-handed approach to the relevant issues';[80]
- In the case of those subject to the deprivation of liberty safeguards (DOLS) regime (see further chapter 21 below), the courts have specifically endorsed the appointment of P's relevant person's representative (RPR) as their litigation friend: see *AB v LCC (A Local Authority) and the Care Manager of BCH*.[81] In *Re UF*, Charles J, endorsing *AB*, suggested that the possibility of whether the RPR could act as a litigation friend should 'often' be investigated;[82]
- Although it would be unusual for a solicitor to be appointed as litigation friend, this has happened in one publicly available case;[83]
- It has now been clarified that a litigation friend can act in person (ie without instructing legal representatives).[84] However, in all cases, a litigation friend should consider very carefully whether they can properly discharge their obligation to conduct the proceedings competently without the assistance of legal representatives. If they consider that they cannot, then there would be nothing improper for the person to decline to act absent receiving appropriate security for cost of instructing legal representatives. The terms of the orders that would then be made would be very similar to those made in cases where the Official Solicitor consents to act;
- To act properly as a litigation friend can be an onerous undertaking. Where a paid RPR or an independent mental capacity advocate (IMCA) employed by an advocacy provider acts, it is important therefore that both they and – more importantly – their organisation are aware of the potentially significant amounts of time that may be required on their part properly to conduct litigation on P's behalf. Specific arrangements will also need to be made to ensure that their costs of acting as P's litigation friend (and, where appropriate, of instructing legal representatives) are met. The question of the basis upon which RPRs and IMCAs are entitled to reimbursement of their costs is addressed below at para 11.67–11.68,

---

80 *Re UF* [2013] EWHC 4289 (COP), [2014] COPLR 93, (2014) 17 CCLR 445 at para 23 per Charles J. See also *Re NRA and others* at para 169.
81 [2011] EWHC 3151 (COP), [2012] COPLR 314.
82 *Re UF* at para 19.
83 *Re RGS* [2012] EWHC 4162 (COP).
84 *Re NRA and others* [2015] EWCOP 59, [2015] COPLR 690, (2015) 18 CCLR 392 at para 135.

but for present purposes it is important to note that there is a difference between an entitlement to reimbursement and a guarantee that they will not be left out of pocket – ie security for their costs. It should also be remembered that when considering an application for legal aid it is P's means, and not those of the litigation friend, which will be assessed (see further, chapter 6).

11.43 The MCA 2005, the COPR and the practice directions are silent as to whether it must be an individual who acts as litigation friend, or whether the responsibility can be taken on by a body. This is of particular relevance in the context of the involvement of RPRs and statutory advocates who may well – understandably – feel more comfortable (and more sure of themselves in demanding proper time to discharge their roles) if the formal responsibility for acting as litigation friend lies with their organisation, rather than resting solely upon their shoulders. The natural reading of the relevant provisions of the COPR would suggest that the draftsman had in mind the appointment of individuals, rather than organisations, but the position is not entirely clear.[85] We would strongly suggest that if any application to be appointed as a 'corporate' litigation friend is advanced, then it is made very clear in that application precisely who will have day-to-day responsibility for the conduct of the case on P's behalf and what arrangements are in place to ensure continuity of consideration in the event that that individual is unavailable.

Acting for a child or a protected party other than P

11.44 Essentially the same considerations as set out above in relation to P also apply in terms of the appointment of a suitable litigation friend to represent children or adult protected parties other than P. In particular, it should be noted that it is not unheard of for the Official Solicitor to act for other parties in addition to P: the authors have experience of one case in which the Official Solicitor was acting for two other family members as well as P. In such cases, where it is quite possible that it is necessary that different individuals have different cases advanced on their behalf, the Official Solicitor will put in place 'Chinese walls' to ensure that such can be carried out ie,

---

85 A trust corporation can be appointed as a deputy to manage P's property and affairs: MCA 2005 s19(1)(b). Management of property and affairs is specifically said to extend to the conduct of legal proceedings on P's behalf (MCA 2005 s18(1)(k)). If appointed as deputy, therefore, and if the relevant order included specific provision relating to legal proceedings, a trust corporation could therefore properly bring proceedings on P's behalf as P's litigation friend.

strict rules to ensure that each caseworker only sees the information relevant to their case.

Duties of the litigation friend

General

11.45 The first edition of this work contained an extensive discussion of the duties of the litigation friend, noting in particular the absence of guidance in case-law or elsewhere. Since then, decided cases have made the position clearer, and this section is therefore considerably shorter than in the previous edition. However, whether the decided cases are correctly decided, and whether litigation friends should not be adopting a rather different role, at least in relation to P, are difficult questions. Lack of space precludes consideration of it here, but interested readers are referred to an article published by Alex Ruck Keene, Peter Bartlett and Neil Allen in which these issues are examined in detail.[86]

11.46 The COPR draws no distinction between the roles of a litigation friend depending upon whether they are acting on behalf of P or on behalf of a protected party (or, indeed, a child, a position addressed further at paras 11.49–11.52 below). In all cases, a litigation friend must (in order to be appointed) be able fairly and competently to conduct the proceedings.[87] Whether rightly or wrongly, the case law (which has not to date included consideration of child parties) also proceeds on the basis that a litigation friend is under the same obligations no matter who they act for.

11.47 The role of the litigation friend has been held to be to form a view as to what is in the person's best interests and then advance that view to the court, although it may not accord with what the person is asserting.[88] Where the litigation friend is acting on behalf of P, the 'solution' that they must advance on P's behalf is the substantive outcome that they consider would best meet P's interests. Moreover, whether acting for P or for another party (or child) the litigation friend is not required to advance a case that would accord with the person's wishes if they consider that to do so would be unarguable, on the (to us the questionable) basis that such would not be in their

---

86 *Litigation Friend or Foe? Representation of P before the Court of Protection* [2016] Medical Law Review (forthcoming).
87 COPR r140(1).
88 *Re NRA and others* [2015] EWCOP 59, [2015] COPLR 690, (2015) 18 CCLR 392 at para 170.

best interests.[89] However, in all cases, the litigation friend must take all necessary steps to relay the individual's wishes and feelings to the court upon the relevant issues in the case.[90]

Deprivation of liberty cases

11.48 It is suggested that litigation friends should proceed with particular caution where P's right to liberty under ECHR Article 5 is engaged, and in particular in cases brought under MCA 2005 s21A in relation to authorisations granted under the DOLS regime (see further chapter 21). There is a considerable body of case-law from the European Court of Human Rights emphasising the importance of ensuring that the right to challenge a deprivation of liberty under Article 5(4) is effective.[91] In light of that case-law, it is suggested that in a case involving a deprivation of liberty:

- a litigation friend for P must *always* consider testing whether it is correct that the assertion implicit in a request that the court uphold an authorisation or otherwise approve a deprivation of liberty that the regime in question is the least restrictive option. In other words, and to use the language of the ECtHR, the litigation friend must consider testing whether other, less severe measures have been considered and found to be insufficient to safeguard the individual or public interest which might require that the person concerned be detained;[92]
- where P wishes to challenge that deprivation, then we would suggest that the litigation friend is, in fact, *obliged* to do so unless satisfied, after the most careful deliberation, that there truly is no properly arguable case that the deprivation of liberty does not represent the least restrictive requirement. If this is the case, then we would further suggest that it would never be appropriate for the litigation friend actively to concede that the deprivation of liberty was in P's best interests. At most, we would suggest, the

---

89 *Re NRA and others* [2015] EWCOP 59, [2015] COPLR 690, (2015) 18 CCLR 392 at para 144, citing *RP v UK* (App No 38245/08, decision of 9 October 2012), [2013] 1 FLR 744, (2013) 16 CCLR 135.
90 See by analogy *RP v UK* (App No 38245/08, decision of 9 October 2012), [2013] 1 FLR 744, (2013) 16 CCLR 135.
91 Summarised in *AJ (Deprivation of Liberty Safeguards)* [2015] EWCOP 5, [2015] Fam 291, (2015) 18 CCLR 158 at para 35. See also, subsequently, the decision of the ECtHR in *AN v Lithuania* (App No 17280/08, decision of 31 May 2016).
92 As, for instance, did the Official Solicitor in *Y County Council v ZZ* [2013] COPLR 463, in which ZZ vigorously disputed the necessity for the restrictions imposed upon him – primarily so as to secure against the risk that he would commit sexual offences against children.

litigation friend could leave it to the judge to decide (having ensured that P's views were relayed to the court). We suggest this is likely in most cases also to require an oral hearing.

Litigation friends acting for a child

11.49 As set out at paras 11.21–11.25 above, whilst a child must have a litigation friend unless the court orders otherwise,[93] there are – logically – two different reasons why this might be so: a) because their age and maturity means that they are not '*Gillick*-competent';[94] or b) because they suffer from a material disturbance or impairment of the mind or brain.

11.50 A litigation friend acting on behalf of a child over the age of 16 who suffers from a material disturbance of the mind or brain giving rise to a lack of litigation capacity is, we suggest, in the same position as a litigation friend acting on behalf of an adult protected party.

11.51 Strictly speaking, then whether or not litigation friends are, in general, bound to act pursuant to MCA 2005 s1(5),[95] the same does not go for:

- a litigation friend acting on behalf of a child under the age of 16 who suffers from a material disturbance or impairment of the mind or brain, as MCA 2005 s1(5) could never apply to the litigation friend's actions given the wording of MCA 2005 s2(5);[96]
- a litigation friend acting on behalf of a child under 18 who requires a litigation friend because of their age and lack of maturity, MCA 2005 s1(5) not being capable of applying to them because there is no relevant impairment or disturbance of the mind or brain.

11.52 In either of these circumstances, it is therefore suggested that a litigation friend acting for a child takes their duties from COPR r140, albeit (by analogy with the situation where a litigation friend is appointed for a child in family proceedings), all steps and decisions

93 COPR r141(3)–(4).
94 *Gillick v West Norfolk and Wisbech Area Health Authority* [1985] UKHL 7, [1986] 1 AC 112.
95 As to which, see the article by Alex Ruck Keene et al cited at footnote 86 above.
96 Which provides that no power may be exercised by a person under the MCA 2005 in relation to a person who lacks capacity under the age of 16; the exception in section 18(3) would not apply.

the litigation friend takes in the proceedings must be taken for the benefit of the child.[97]

Terminating the appointment of a litigation friend

Litigation friend acting on behalf of P: capacity gained or regained

11.53 Any person – including P themselves – can apply to discharge the appointment of P's litigation friend if P has (1) gained, (2) regained or (3) asserts that they have always had capacity to conduct the proceedings.[98] By contrast to the position where an application is brought to terminate the appointment of the litigation friend on the basis of their conduct, there is no need to file evidence with the application.[99] The court will no doubt decide what evidence is required in any given case, bearing in mind the presumption of capacity contained in MCA s1(1). The appointment of the litigation friend will continue in force until the court brings it to an end by an order,[100] in which it will no doubt make appropriate directions consequential upon the termination of the appointment (for instance as to where documents are to be sent to P in circumstances where they are no longer to be sent to the litigation friend).

11.54 Examples of applications made by or on behalf of P to discharge a litigation friend appointed to act on their behalf are rare. Indeed, the authors are aware of only one reported application, made in the medical treatment case of *Re SB*,[101] where the Official Solicitor applied successfully to be discharged on the basis of expert evidence that P had litigation capacity.[102]

11.55 However, save in a case where it is entirely clear that P can never have litigation capacity because of the severity of their underlying disability, the litigation friend acting on P's behalf should be very astute to keep P's capacity to conduct the litigation under review and, if it appears that they may have regained it, take immediate steps to bring matters before the court in short order.

11.56 If P has either gained or regained capacity in relation to the matter or matters to which the application relates, then the court will have no jurisdiction under the MCA 2005 and an application should be

---

97 FPR PD 16A para 2.1.
98 COPR r144(1).
99 The silence in COPR r144(2) in this regard is deliberate.
100 COPR r144(4).
101 [2013] EWHC 1417 (COP), [2013] COPLR 445.
102 See paras 27–30.

made to bring the proceedings to an end[103] (see further chapter 15). Such an application must be supported by evidence.[104]

Litigation friend acting on behalf of an adult protected party: capacity gained or regained

11.57 Where an adult protected party ceases to lack capacity to conduct the litigation, an application can be made for the litigation friend's appointment to be discharged, in the same way as discussed above in respect of P themselves[105] (para 11.53 above). Any person may make such an application, including the protected party themselves.[106] There is no need for evidence to be filed to support such an application.

Litigation friend acting on behalf of a child: capacity gained or regained

11.58 An application can be made during the currency of proceedings that a child no longer requires a litigation friend to conduct the proceedings on their behalf.[107] This would be appropriate if, for instance, the litigation friend considers that a child not suffering from any disability but previously requiring a litigation friend because they were not *Gillick*-competent[108] has now matured sufficiently to understand and conduct their own litigation. Formally, there is no requirement for evidence to support such an application, but it is suggested that the court would be likely to wish (at a minimum) a statement from the litigation friend explaining the basis upon which they consider that the child is now *Gillick*-competent.

Litigation friend acting on behalf of a child: child reaching majority

11.59 When a child party to proceedings turns 18, then, if they are not a protected party (ie an adult without litigation capacity), the appoint-

---

103 Under COPR r87, the application being made on a COP9 form (see further para 10.21for applications within proceedings).
104 COPR r87(2)(b).
105 COPR r144(1).
106 COPR r144(1).
107 ie for an order under COPR r144(1).
108 *Gillick v West Norfolk and Wisbech Area Health Authority* [1985] UKHL 7, [1986] 1 AC 112.

ment of the litigation friend will come to an end automatically.[109] The child must, though, serve notice on every other party stating that they have reached full age, that the appointment of the litigation friend has ended, and providing their address for service.[110]

Any litigation friend: other situations

11.60 Any litigation friend can also be removed by the court:
- on their own application (if, for instance, P is no longer eligible for public funding and the litigation friend cannot continue to discharge their functions without such funding to pay for legal advice and representation);[111]
- on the application of any person (including, logically, both any party or indeed P); or
- of the court's own motion.[112]

11.61 Where the application is brought on the basis of the litigation friend's conduct, the application must be supported by evidence.[113]

11.62 COPR r144 does not place any limit on the power of the court to terminate the appointment of a litigation friend. In *Re A (conjoined twins: medical treatment) (No 2)*,[114] Ward LJ commented on the:

> ... particular situation in which the court is asked to replace a guardian ad litem because the guardian has in the conduct of litigation taken a course of action (in which we include an omission), or is about to take a course of action, which is manifestly contrary to the best interests of the child whose interests it is the guardian's duty to safeguard. If the guardian (or litigation friend) does act manifestly contrary to the child's best interests, the court will remove him even though neither his good faith nor his diligence is in issue.

11.63 It is suggested that a similar approach would be adopted in the Court of Protection (subject to the discussion at paras 11.45–11.48 above as to the precise scope of the litigation friend's duties).

11.64 In any case where a litigation friend's appointment is terminated, the court will strive, if at all possible, to appoint a suitable person to

---

109 COPR r145A.
110 COPR r145A.
111 See by analogy *Bradbury and others v Paterson and others* [2014] EWHC 3992 (QB), [2015] COPLR 425.
112 COPR r144(1).
113 COPR r144(2).
114 [2000] EWCA Civ 254, [2001] 1 FLR 267.

act as replacement litigation friend[115] so that the proceedings can continue in an uninterrupted fashion.

Costs and the litigation friend

Costs incurred by the litigation friend

The Official Solicitor

11.65 The Official Solicitor is placed in a special position by virtue of COPR r163, which provides that his or her costs (if they are not met by payments made out of P's estate, by P's deputy, donee or attorney) shall be paid by such person or out of such funds as the court may direct. As noted above, the Official Solicitor will not accept an invitation to act as litigation friend if he or she is not satisfied that there is provision for the (in-house or external) litigation costs to be met.

11.66 Largely for historical reasons, the Official Solicitor receives sufficient central government funding to conduct (in-house) proceedings relating to serious medical treatment cases (as to which, see further chapter 21), and is also conventionally awarded half the costs of so doing against the relevant NHS body: see *An NHS Trust v D*.[116] The Official Solicitor will in general decline to act in such cases until an undertaking to meet half of his or her costs has been received from the NHS body in question.

Other litigation friends

11.67 There are no equivalent statutory provisions to those relating to the Official Solicitor to guarantee reimbursement for others who act as litigation friend (whether for P or another individual requiring such representation). In *B v B*,[117] a case concerned with the ability of the Official Solicitor to recover his costs of acting as the litigation friend of an adult in matrimonial proceedings, Bennett J held that a litigation friend acts as the agent of the protected party and is entitled to be reimbursed by the protected party for the properly incurred costs of so acting.[118]

11.68 It is suggested that this principle holds true in Court of Protection proceedings for all litigation friends. There is, though, a difference

---

115 COPR r144(1)(c), the substitute litigation friend being required to fulfil the conditions set by COPR r140(1): COPR r144(3).
116 [2012] EWHC 886 (COP), [2012] COPLR 499.
117 [2010] EWHC 543 (Fam), [2012] COPLR 480.
118 Paras 15, 30 and 41.

between an entitlement to reimbursement and security for costs – ie a guarantee that the costs incurred (if properly incurred) will be repaid. As set out at para 11.40 above, it is suggested that – as with the Official Solicitor – it is entirely proper for a litigation friend such as an IMCA or family member to decline an invitation to act without sufficient security for their costs of so doing.

Costs payable to other parties

11.69   A curious feature of the COPR is that (unlike the CPR[119]) they do not provide any circumstance under which the litigation friend is required personally, as a condition of acting, to undertake to pay the costs incurred by other parties in proceedings before the Court of Protection. That most likely reflects the general rules on costs in such proceedings which are to the effect that either a) P is to pay the costs of proceedings relating to their property and affairs;[120] or b) there should be no order as to costs in proceedings relating to P's health and welfare[121] (see further chapter 16 below).

11.70   It is clear, however, that the party on whose behalf the litigation friend acts can be made the subject of a costs order – and, indeed, at present, the general rule in property and affairs proceedings is that P will be required to pay the costs of those proceedings (including those costs incurred by others).[122] There is no reason in principle why a child or an adult protected party could not also be made the subject of a costs order. It would be the responsibility of the litigation friend to take appropriate steps to ensure that these costs are met (it is suggested as part of their duties to the court in the conduct of the litigation). It is not clear, however, that this would, formally give rise to a personal liability on the part of the litigation friend to meet the costs.[123] Even if it did, however, it is suggested that the litigation friend can look to the individual to reimburse them, at least if the proceedings have been properly conducted on the part of the litigation friend.[124]

---

119 CPR 21.4(c).
120 COPR r156.
121 COPR r157.
122 COPR r156.
123 It may be that the obligation arises at common law, see *ex p Brocklebank* (1877) 6 Ch D 358 at 360.
124 See, by analogy, *Re E (Mental Health Patient)* [1984] 1 WLR 320 at 324H per Sir Robert Megarry V-C, and also *B v B* [2010] EWHC 453 (Fam), [2012] COPLR 450.

11.71 Any litigation friend (theoretically including the Official Solicitor) is, however, potentially at risk of being ordered to pay costs *themselves*. Even though they are not, themselves, a party to proceedings, the COPR has provision for costs orders to be made against non-parties.[125]

11.72 In the absence of further guidance to clarify the scant provisions of the COPR as they relate to litigation friends other than the Official Solicitor, it has become an increasing practice for RPRs and IMCAs in welfare proceedings to make their agreement to act as litigation friend conditional on the giving of an undertaking on the part of the relevant public authority that they will not seek their costs against the RPR/IMCA. It is suggested that this is a useful mechanism by which RPRs/IMCAs can be given reassurance in the discharge of what is an important public function, although it cannot (and would not be seen by the court as) acting as a carte blanche to the RPR/IMCA acting as litigation friend to depart from the proper and proportionate conduct of litigation.

11.73 There are no reported cases in which a litigation friend has themselves been made the subject of a costs order in the Court of Protection, and it is suggested that such an order would only be made in the event of serious misconduct on the part of the litigation friend, especially if such misconduct had the consequence of increasing the costs of the proceedings. In the event of such misconduct, it is further suggested that a local authority that had given an undertaking of the nature described in the paragraph immediately above would readily be relieved of its obligation by a judge and given permission to seek their costs as against the litigation friend personally.

COPR Pr1.2/COPR r3A representatives

Appointment

11.74 As set out at para 11.7 above, one of the options that the court can adopt to ensure the participation of P is to appoint a representative for them 'to provide the court with information as to the matters set out in section 4(6) of the Act [ie P's wishes, feelings, beliefs and values] and to discharge such other functions as the court may direct'.[126] It would, in principle, be possible to appoint such a repres-

---

125 COPR r166.
126 COPR Pr1.2(2)(c) / COPR r3A(2)(c).

entative even where P is joined as a party to proceedings, but in practice it is likely that a representative will only be appointed where the court has decided that P's participation can be secured other than by joining them. These representatives are commonly known as 'Rule 3A representatives', the term used in this section, although they are in fact Rule 1.2 representatives for purposes of the Case Management Pilot.

11.75 The court may appoint a COPR Pr1.2/ COPR r3A representative of its own motion or on the application of any person, but only with the consent of the representative.[127] Such an application must be made using form COP9[128] and must be served on all parties, as well as on any current representative or ALR and the proposed representative.[129] The representative must be able to discharge his or her functions[130] 'fairly and competently.'[131]

Duties

11.76 Pilot PD 1A/PD 2A envisages a COPR Pr1.2/COPR r3A representative as being someone with knowledge of P, such as a family member or friend, or an IMCA or Care Act advocate.[132] Whilst, in theory, a legally qualified person could be appointed, it is suggested that they would not, if appointed as such a representative, be discharging any functions as a lawyer. If the court wished to appoint the person to act as a lawyer, then it would be required to do so under the provisions relating to ALRs, addressed further below.

11.77 In *Re NRA and others*,[133] Charles J approved the appointment of family members or friends of P, who have 'fought P's corner' over the years, in uncontentious cases where a statutory body applies to the court under MCA 2005 ss15 and 16 for authority to deprive P of his or her liberty (known as '*Re X* cases') (see further chapter 21). As he indicated, such appointments provide a means of:

(i) eliciting P's wishes and feelings and making them and the matters mentioned in s 4(6) of the MCA known to the court, without causing P any or any unnecessary distress, and

---

127 COPR r148(2); PD 2A para 8.
128 PD 17B (3).
129 COPR r148C.
130 See COPR Pr1.2(2)(c) / COPR r3A(2)(c) and the paragraph above.
131 COPR r147.
132 Pilot PD1A/PD 2A para 12.
133 [2015] EWCOP 59, [2015] COPLR 690, para 234

(ii) critically examining from the perspective of P's best interests, and with a detailed knowledge of P, the pros and cons of a care package, and whether it is the least restrictive available option.[134]

11.78 In the context of *Re X* cases, Charles J drew an express analogy between the role of a COPR Pr1.2/COPR r3A representative and the role of the Relevant Person's Representative under Schedule A1.[135] In other words the role requires a continuing commitment to the representation of P's wishes and feelings and the scrutiny of P's circumstances. In *Re VE*,[136] Charles J set out an extensive list of functions that would be expected of the representative including:

- checking the court documentation for accuracy;
- discussing points of difference with the statutory body making the application;
- discussing the package of care and support and the application to the Court with P in so far as P is able to understand them; and ascertaining P's views if this can be done without unnecessary distress including asking P what he thinks about the package of care and support
- deciding whether to support the application;
- considering how P should participate in the application; and
- preparing a statement to set out all of the above matters.

11.79 However, and especially outside the context of cases involving the authorisation of deprivation of liberty, the appointment of a representative will not always require the long term involvement envisaged in *Re NRA* and *Re JM*.[137] Such an appointment could be limited to a single report to the judge in, for example, a property and affairs case where the judge does not wish to join P to save P the legal costs but wants to ensure that they have heard a neutral voice relaying P's views to the court.

11.80 The COPR do not prohibit a COPR Pr1.2/COPR r3A representative seeking to instruct a lawyer to assist them in the discharge of their duties. As discussed in chapter 6, public funding in the form of Legal Help is in principle available to assist a COPR Pr1.2/COPR r3A representative who is, themselves, financially eligible for such assistance, and a family member wishing to understand their duties may well wish to enlist legal advice by way of Legal Help. It would

---

134 *Re NRA*, para 164.
135 *Re NRA*, para 111.
136 [2016] EWCOP 16.
137 [2016] EWCOP 15, [2016] 4 WLR 64.

also be possible – by analogy with the position in relation to litigation friends (see para 11.68) for a person to decline to consent to be a COPR Pr1.2/COPR r3A representative without being given the necessary funds to instruct a lawyer. However, we suggest that a COPR Pr1.2/COPR r3A representative who finds that are needing recourse to more than outline advice as to the nature of the duties (and, for instance, how to draft a witness statement) should consider very carefully whether it is in fact appropriate for them to continue in their role, or whether they should not take the matter back to court for further directions under the provisions discussed in the following paragraph.

Directions and variation or termination of appointment

11.81 COPR r148A allows any representative appointed under COPR Pr1.2/COPR r3A to apply to the court for directions at any time, and does not require notice to be given to the parties. The directions sought may concern the 'performance, terms of appointment, or continuation of the appointment.' An application by the representative must be made on form COP9.[138] PD Pilot 1A/PD 2A recognises the possibility that representatives may find themselves in either a personal or professional position where they cannot properly represent P, or provide the court with information about P or carry out functions directed by the court.[139]

11.82 Other persons may also apply for the appointment of a representative to be brought to an end or varied; and may also apply for orders that a person does not act as a COPR Pr1.2/COPR r3A representative, or for an order that the representative is replaced.[140] If any such application is based on the conduct of the representative then this must be supported by evidence.[141] The court can also make any such order on its own initiative.[142] The court must bring the appointment of a representative to an end if P has capacity to

---

138 PD 17B para 2.
139 Para 13.
140 COPR r148B(1).
141 COPR r148B(2).
142 COPR r148B (2).

appoint a representative and does not wish the appointment to continue.[143]

Funding

11.83 Many COPR Pr1.2/COPR r3A representatives will be family members who would be expected to act as a representative without recompense. However, as noted above, it is also entirely possible for an IMCA or another statutory advocate to act as such a representative. Charles J confirmed in *Re JM and others*[144] (in the context of *Re X* applications) that local authorities are under no statutory duty, and cannot be compelled, to fund advocates to act as COPR Pr1.2/COPR r3A representatives. By analogy with a litigation friend (see paras 11.40–11.43 above), we suggest that a statutory advocate can decline to consent to act as a COPR Pr1.2/COPR r3A representative absent confirmation that they will be recompensed for their time, or withdraw their consent if it suitable funding is no longer available.

Accredited Legal Representatives

Definition

11.84 An ALR is defined in COPR r6[145] as 'a legal representative authorised pursuant to a scheme approved by the President to represent persons meeting the definition of P in this rule in proceedings before the Court'. A legal representative is also defined in COPR r6/ COPR r2.1 as one of a number of categories of legally qualified individuals who has been instructed to act for a party in relation to any application.[146]

11.85 At the time of writing no scheme has yet been approved, and no ALRs can therefore be appointed. However, the Law Society have taken steps to establish an accreditation process which will – if

---

143 COPR 148B (5). In *YA v CNWL* [2015] UKUT 37 (AAC), Charles J held (at para 8) that to have capacity to appoint a representative for the purpose of an application to the Mental Health Tribunal required an appreciation of the patient's inability to conduct the proceedings unaided. It is suggested that this test should be applied for the purpose of COPR 148B(5).
144 [2016] EWCOP 15, [2016] 4 WLR 64.
145 COPR Pr2.1 where the Case Management Pilot applies.
146 The reference to 'being instructed to act' is not strictly accurate in the context of ALRs, and it is likely that this will be amended in due course to 'being appointed for' or 'being appointed on behalf of.'

When will an ALR be appointed?

11.86 Pilot PD 1A/PD 2A gives the judge 'pointers' when considering which of the options in COPR Pr1.2/COPR r3A to select. In light of the novelty of the role, paragraphs 9–12 are set out below.

> 9. An accredited legal representative is defined in Rule 6. When such representatives exist one can be appointed whether or not P is joined as a party and this may be of assistance if urgent orders are needed, particularly if they are likely to have an impact on the final orders (eg an urgent order relating to residence).
>
> 10. When P lacks capacity to conduct the proceedings and is made a party an accredited legal representative is not intended as a substitute for a litigation friend, but as an alternative in a suitable case (or in the early stages of the case).
>
> 11. When P lacks capacity to conduct the proceedings and an order that he is to be a party is made factors relevant to the choice between appointing a litigation friend and an accredited legal representative to represent him as a party will include –
>
> - whether there will be a need for expert or other evidence to be obtained and filed, or other material gathered, on P's behalf;
> - the nature and complexity of the case;
> - the likely range of issues.
>
> 12. In other cases their nature and complexity, the issues raised or likely to be raised in them and the stage they have reached could mean that the assistance of an accredited legal representative is not required or is inappropriate and that P's participation is best secured and the court will be properly informed by the appointment of a representative under Rule 3A(2)(c) (who could be a friend, an IMCA, an advocate appointed under the Care Act 2014, a family member or anyone with relevant knowledge) or by directions being made under [COPR Pr1.2(2)(d) or (e)/COPR r3A(2)(d) or (e)].

11.87 Whilst COPR Pr1.2(2)(b)/COPR r3A.2(b) envisages that an ALR can be appointed to represent P in the proceedings without P being joined as a party, we anticipate that this form of appointment will be relatively rare; rather, we anticipate that ALRs will be more usually appointed where the court considers that P's participation requires them to have party status but P does not have the capacity to conduct the proceedings. At that point, and as set out at para 11.10 above, the court must either appoint an ALR or a litigation friend.[147]

---

147 COPR Pr1.2(4)/COPR r3A(4).

11.88 It is also clear that the court does not envisage that ALRs will lead to litigation friends becoming redundant. Paragraph 11 explains the factors which the court would consider when deciding between an ALR and a litigation friend:
- whether there will be a need for expert evidence or other evidence to be obtained or filed, or other material gathered, on behalf;
- the nature and complexity of the case and
- the likely range of issues.

11.89 This suggests that the court is more likely to appoint an ALR in a case where the issues are relatively defined. Paragraph 10 suggests that there may be cases where an ALR is appointed in the early stages of the case but that subsequently a litigation friend is needed because – for example – the case is more complex than first appeared. See further paras 11.97–11.100 below.

11.90 Given the novelty of the role, there is at the time of writing limited case-law to assist in terms of their potential duties and role, but as the scheme for ALRs is rolled out it is likely that their role will be subject of judicial comment and/or guidance. In *Re PD* Baker J held that in an application for recognition and enforcement of a foreign order (see further chapter 26), P does not always need to be a party but could participate through an ALR who could 'facilitate a quick but focussed analysis of the particular requirements of Schedule 3. It is therefore to be hoped that the scheme for accreditation is swiftly established.'[148] In *Re JM*[149] Charles J described ALRs as a possible solution for the representation of P in uncontentious welfare cases where there is an application to deprive P of his or her liberty in a setting where DOLS cannot be used.

11.91 It is hoped that the availability of ALRs may reduce the pressure on the Official Solicitor's office, especially in urgent cases. It is not always possible to identify other paid litigation friends (eg IMCAs, RPRs) because of capacity and funding issues. There was vivid evidence of the pressure on advocacy services from some of the statutory bodies in *Re JM*.[150] It is suggested that ALRs may be of particular benefit is in section 21A appeals, where P will be entitled to non-means-tested legal aid (see chapters 6 and 21).

---

148 [2015] EWCOP 48, [2015] COPLR 544
149 [2016] EWCOP 15, [2016] 4 WLR 64, at para 73.
150 At para 96.

Requirements for appointment as an ALR

11.92 COPR r147 provides that a COPR Pr1.2/COPR r3A representative (including an ALR) must be able to discharge his or her functions in relation to P 'fairly and competently.' COPR r148 requires the consent of the COPR Pr1.2/COPR r3A representative before he or she is appointed.

Appointment

11.93 COPR r148 provides that the court may appoint an ALR at any time, either on its own initiative or on the application of any person,[151] provided it is satisfied that the person to be appointed satisfies the requirements of COPR r147 (see para 11.34 above). The same requirements apply as regards the appointment of ALRs as they do COPR Pr1.2/COPR r3A representatives (see paragraph 11.74 above).

Duties

11.94 An ALR has the following responsibilities:
- A duty to the court to comply with COPR Pr1.2/COPR r3A and r147, and to help the court to further the overriding objective;[152]
- Professional responsibilities to the client and others in line with the relevant regulatory framework applicable to the relevant category of legal representative;[153] and
- (In legal aid cases) a duty to the LAA to comply with the contracting arrangements (see further chapter 6).

11.95 The ALR's role has some elements in common with that of so-called Rule 11(7)[154] representative in English Mental Health Tribunals (MHTs) where again the representative acts for a client without capacity to appoint them (and who is also likely to lack capacity to conduct their appeal before the Tribunal) without a litigation friend or other individual appointed to give instructions to the representatives.

---

151 COPR r148(2).
152 COPR r4/COPR Pr1.4.
153 For instance the SRA Code of Conduct for solicitors or the BSB Code of Conduct for barristers.
154 Ie representatives appointed (in England) under rule 11(7)(b) of the Tribunal Procedure (First-tier Tribunal) (Health, Education and Social Care Chamber) Rules SI 2008 SI No 2699. The equivalent rule for the Mental Health Review Tribunal for Wales is rule 13(5)(b) of the Mental Health Review Tribunal for Wales Rules SI 2008 No 2705.

11.96 There will be some cases where the guidance issued to Rule 11(7) representatives will be useful to ALRs,[155] but care should be taken not to equate the two roles. MHTs tend to be recurring events which will almost always involve an oral hearing and which essentially consider a snapshot in which the MHT applies the statutory criteria set out in MHA 1983 ss72, 73, 74 and 75.[156] Cases in the Court of Protection will cover a more extensive range of issues in which it may make one-off decisions with life-changing consequences. If a patient detained in hospital loses his or her application to the MHT, he or she can apply again. If P is moved away from his or her home by the COP, which also authorises the sale of the home, this decision cannot be easily revisited.

11.97 ALRs are likely to face the dilemmas regularly faced by those acting for litigation friends and considered at paras 11.45 onwards. The following are familiar scenarios:
- P desperately wants to leave the care home but there is strong evidence this will put him or her at life-threatening risk;
- P wants to continue a relationship with a person who is abusive and manipulative, and takes advantage of the client's vulnerability;
- P wants to refuse treatment but this could result in death.

11.98 In the absence of guidance from the courts we note that Pilot PD 1A/PD 2A recommends a cautious approach to the use of ALRs and concludes with the following paragraph:

A Rule 3A representative must be able to discharge his or her functions fairly and competently It is possible that a Rule 3A representative may be in, or find himself or herself in, a personal or professional position in which he or she cannot properly represent P, provide the court with information about P or carry out other functions directed by the court. In such a case, Section 2 of Part 17 allows for the court to vary the terms of the appointment with a view to resolving the difficulty, or to discharge the appointment altogether (in which case the court will consider afresh whether it should make one or more of the directions in paragraph (2) of [COPR Pr1.2/COPR r3A].

11.99 This suggests in turn that ALRs (or COPR Pr1.2/COPR r3A representatives) should not attempt to 'soldier on' if they find themselves in difficulty discharging the various duties they owe. We suggest that

---

155 See in particular the Law Society's Practice Note: Representation before Mental Health Tribunals, available at www.lawsociety.org.uk/support-services/advice/practice-notes/representation-before-mental-health-tribunals/.
156 For more detail, see Johnston, Miles and Royston, *Mental Health Tribunals Handbook* (Legal Action Group, 2015).

the circumstances in which the ALR should consider approaching the court will include cases where there is a divergence between the ALR's view of P's best interests and P's wishes, and where the ALR is satisfied that P lacks capacity to make the decision.

11.100 ALRs may therefore wish to apply a relatively low threshold for approaching the court under Part 17. The court will then have a range of Rule 3A options open to it, including the appointment of a litigation friend who could then instruct the former ALR in the usual way. In their forthcoming article referred to at footnote 86 above, Alex Ruck Keene and others suggest the appointment of an 'amicus curiae' in such cases, allowing the ALR to argue P's wishes without reservation.

Directions and variation or termination of appointment

11.101 The relevant provisions apply in relation to ALRs in this regard as they do in relation to COPR Pr1.2/COPR r3A representatives: see para 11.82 above.

Good practice guide

11.102 Although primarily directed to legal representatives acting for P after appointment as ALR, the following suggestions may also be of assistance by analogy for legal representatives acting for P in the following cases:
- when instructed by the Official Solicitor;
- when instructed by another litigation friend;
- (In rare cases) instructed by P directly where P has litigation capacity.

11.103 The appointment as an ALR is an appointment of the individual representative and not the representative's organisation. In our view this entails the individual who is appointed carrying out attendances on P personally other than in circumstances where this is simply impracticable. We would suggest that this is good practice in any event.

11.104 Key to the task of representing P is effective communication with P. In some cases the representative may know P already from other proceedings (most commonly from tribunal proceedings). In the majority of cases the representative will receive a set of papers about an individual and his or her family whom the representative knows nothing about. In the case of an appeal under MCA 2005 s21A these should include the current authorisation and assessments for the purpose of the Deprivation of Liberty Safeguards ('DOLS') authorisation. These will provide the representative with the factual background; and with some information about P's diagnosis and presentation. DOLS assessments may provide valuable information about P's communication and may provide pointers as to how this can be maximised.

11.105 In addition to diarising key dates, case management tools such as chronologies can be vital time-savers allowing the representative to keep track of what is likely to be fast-moving litigation. As we have seen, the courts are likely to turn to ALRs in urgent cases, perhaps where an interim decision on residence needs to be made quickly which will have a significant bearing on the remainder of the case.

11.106 It is hoped that orders appointing ALRs will also contain provision for disclosure of records to the ALR from social service, relevant health bodies and placements, and that such orders will make it explicit that other professionals involved – including advocates or paid RPRs – have permission to speak to the ALR, so as to minimise delay in the ALR familiarising himself or herself with the case and with P.

11.107 Family members will in many cases have a wealth of information about P. Such family members may or may not be parties to the case. If they are represented then communication will take place through their solicitors but at the start of all cases the representative should ensure that family members are aware of the identity and the role of the ALR or litigation friend and that they have relevant contact details. It is important to be aware of the inevitable sensitivity that some family members may feel when a stranger is appointed to represent their parent, child or spouse.

11.108 When preparing to meet P it is helpful to have some information about P's condition and how this affects P's communication. The Advocate's Gateway is an invaluable free resource which provides toolkits giving insight into conditions such as autism or learning disability and offer practical guidance about tailoring questions to enhance effective communication by P.[157] Charities or NGOs campaigning on behalf of those with specific conditions may also have useful factsheets on their websites. See appendix G for contact details of relevant organisations. The Law Society has provided guidance on providing legal services to vulnerable clients ('the Vulnerable Clients Practice Note') which may be useful.[158] See also paras 15.34–15.44 in relation to how P may be enabled to give evidence or information to the court.

11.109 If P is in a hospital or care setting it may be useful to find out something about it before visiting P. The placement's most recent Care Quality Commission report will be a good starting point.[159]

11.110 If at all possible visits to P should be planned with P's schedule in mind; although in urgent cases this may not be achievable. If P has an advocate, IMCA or RPR, consider whether the visit should take place with them. It is essential to take a careful note of visits to P. These should include as far as possible the representative's observations of the setting where P resides: for example the physical structure, the accessibility for P; availability of open air space; evidence of activities. It is helpful to note down observations of P: where is P at the time of the visit; is it possible to see how P has spent the time just before the visit; how does P appear; what interaction between P and staff or residents can be observed? P may prefer someone to be with him or her during the visit and this should be respected.

11.111 When meeting P for the first time, even in cases where interim declarations as to P's capacity have been made, the representative should retain an open mind as to P's capacity to make the relevant decisions and to conduct the proceedings. See paras 11.11–11.12 above, as well as the Vulnerable Clients Practice Note.

11.112 It is good practice to document the conversation with P fully and directly rather than using reported speech. This is time consuming but plays an important part in ensuring P's voice really is heard, in P's own words. Attendance notes of the visit

---

157 www.theadvocatesgateway.org/toolkits.
158 www.lawsociety.org.uk/support-services/advice/practice-notes/meeting-the-needs-of-vulnerable-clients-july-2015/.
159 www.cqc.org/.

should be timed and dated and exhibited to a COP24. Members of staff at placements may also provide helpful information but must always be told in advance of any conversation that they are not speaking to the representative and that what they say will be made available to the court and the parties.

11.113 An ALR may have been given a specific remit on appointment by the court but in all cases the representative will wish to explore P's wishes as to the issues under consideration by the court and how P wishes to participate in the proceedings. P may wish to attend court or may wish the judge to visit. Consideration can then be given to how this can be facilitated. Judicial visits will need to be arranged with the court and will usually require P's representative to take a note to be filed and served. In some cases the use of an intermediary may be warranted: see para 15.73 for further details.

11.114 In most cases it will be important to keep P informed of the progress of the case. Where possible there should be continuity in who visits P. This is likely to be preferable to P and facilitates an accurate picture of P's views, wishes and in some cases progress being relayed to the court.

CHAPTER 12

Evidence and disclosure

12.1	Introduction
12.4	**Evidence**
12.4	The powers of the court
12.6	What evidence is required?
12.12	Admissions
12.13	Factual evidence
	Overview • Witness statements: formalities and contents • Witness statements – timing • Hearsay evidence • Affidavits • Documentary evidence • Notarial acts and instruments • Witness summons • Depositions • Witnesses outside the jurisdiction
12.44	Documents held by the police
12.45	Section 49 reports
12.54	Expert evidence
	Overview • Permission • Instructing the expert • The duties upon an expert • The expert's report – content • Once the report has been provided
12.91	**Disclosure**
12.91	Overview
12.94	Disclosure issues in practice
	Withholding disclosure on confidentiality/welfare grounds • Privilege

317

Introduction

12.1 This chapter deals with the process by which sufficient evidence is obtained and put before a judge to enable him or her to decide upon the application before them. It deals, in particular, with the different categories of evidence that may be necessary, whether that be factual evidence or expert evidence. It addresses questions relating to hearsay evidence. It then turns, finally, to disclosure, in particular the questions of when and how disclosure is or should be withheld.

12.2 The matters covered in this chapter are very wide-ranging, and space precludes detailed discussion of the intricacies of such matters as the law relating to hearsay evidence. The reader is directed to such works as *Phipson on Evidence*;[1] there is also valuable commentary to be found about the application of the principles to public law proceedings relating to children (which bear certain analogies to proceedings relating to incapacitated adults) in works such as *Hershman and McFarlane: Children Law and Practice.*[2]

12.3 The Case Management Pilot (discussed in chapter 4) has introduced with effect from 1 September 2016 changes to the rules in relation to expert evidence in relation to cases falling within the Pilot. As noted at para 4.102, there is an issue as to whether all new cases fall within the Pilot, or only those allocated to a pathway. For completeness, the 'old' rules are noted where relevant in this chapter but it is suggested that practitioners should proceed by reference to any tighter obligation contained in a Pilot rule even in relation to a case falling outside a pathway. A Pilot running from 1 September 2016 has also introduced changes to reports produced at the direction of the court under Mental Capacity Act (MCA) 2005 s49.

Evidence

The powers of the court

12.4 The provisions of Part 14 of the COPR amplified by Practice Direction (PD) 14, set out a detailed framework by which the court can ensure that (ideally) it has before it that evidence, but only that evidence, which it needs to make the decision(s) it is asked to make.

---

1 Sweet & Maxwell, 18th edn, 2015.
2 Bloomsbury, looseleaf, Section 7.

The heart of Part 14 is rule 95, which, as amended in July 2015,[3] provides that:

95(1) The court may–
  (a) control the evidence by giving directions as to:
    (i) the issues on which it requires evidence;
    (ii) the nature of the evidence which it requires to give those issues; and
    (iii) the way in which the evidence is to be placed before the court;
  (b) use its power under this rule to exclude evidence that would otherwise be admissible;
  (c) allow or limit cross-examination; and
  (d) admit such evidence, whether written or oral, as it thinks fit; and
  (e) admit, accept and act upon such information, whether oral or written, from P, any protected party or any person who lacks competence to give evidence, as the court considers sufficient, although not given on oath and whether or not it would be admissible in a court of law apart from this rule.

12.5 The powers granted to judges under this rule are in addition to the general case management powers granted them by COPR rr3.1 and 3.7/COPR rr25 and 85. They are very broad, and reflect the fact that a very wide range of cases come before the Court of Protection, requiring a carefully calibrated approach so as to ensure that (in line with the overriding objective set down in rule 4) evidence is obtained – and limited – in a proportional fashion.

What evidence is required?

12.6 The MCA 2005 and COPR are silent as to the evidential requirements that must be satisfied before the court can decide the application(s) before it. There are, though, two obligations of particular importance that are imposed upon the court:

- to act in the best interests of the adult without capacity if the decision before it is one falling within the scope of MCA 2005 s1(5), which requires that an act done or decision made under the MCA 2005 for or on behalf of a person who lacks capacity 'must be done, or made, in his best interests';
- to act compatibly with the rights under the European Convention on Human Rights (ECHR) of the adult without capacity (and, to the extent relevant, the rights of the other parties to the

3 By the Court of Protection (Amendment) Rules 2015 2007 SI No 548.

application or potentially affected by its decision) (see further chapter 25).[4]

12.7 Determining the nature and scope of the evidence required by the court is a matter that is complicated by the fact that:

> The processes of the Court of Protection are essentially inquisitorial rather than adversarial. In other words, the ambit of the litigation is determined, not by the parties, but by the court, because the function of the court is not to determine in a disinterested way a dispute brought to it by the parties, but rather, to engage in a process of assessing whether an adult is lacking in capacity, and if so, making decisions about his welfare that are in his best interests.[5]

12.8 That having been said:
- In all cases, the burden lies upon the party asserting that P lacks capacity to take the material decisions in question to establish that they lack such capacity, on the balance of probabilities.[6]
- Further, it may be necessary that a party prove a particular fact or facts in a way akin to conventional civil litigation:
  - In *LBB v JM, BK and CM*[7] Hedley J held that, where the intervention of the court would engage a potential breach of rights under the ECHR, as is particularly likely in welfare cases, it is incumbent upon the applicant to establish a factual basis upon which the court can be satisfied both that the jurisdiction should be exercised and that any interference is lawful.
  - Another (not uncommon) scenario is where it is said that a deputy or attorney has behaved in a way which justifies the intervention of the court; in such instance, it will fall to the party asserting such misconduct to establish it upon the basis of appropriate evidence.

12.9 Questions of the resolution of disputed facts are addressed further in chapter 14 below. The resolution of disputes as to capacity is addressed further in the context of the final determination of proceedings at chapter 15 below.

12.10 Further, even if a judge is presented with a consent order for approval by parties to an application, the judge is required to consider

---

4 Human Rights Act (HRA) 1998 s6(1), read together with s6(3).
5 *Cheshire West and Cheshire Council v P and M* [2011] EWHC 1330 (Fam), [2011] COPLR Con Vol 273 at para 52 per Baker J, endorsed by Sir James Munby P in *Re G (An Adult)* [2014] EWCOP 1361, [2014] COPLR 416 at para 26.
6 MCA 2005 ss1(2) and 2(4). See also *PH v A Local Authority and others* [2011] EWHC 1704 (Fam), [2012] COPLR 128 at para 16, per Baker J.
7 [2010] COPLR Con Vol 779.

for themselves as an independent matter whether they can properly endorse that order, and must do so by reference to the evidence before them. In a contested application, one of the first questions for the court will be to determine as precisely as possible what evidence it will require before it can make any final decision(s) (in this regard see also chapter 10, on interim hearings).

12.11 A failure to bring proceedings upon the basis of proper evidence can lead to substantial costs consequences. A good example of this is *A Local Authority v HS and others*,[8] in which the local authority maintained allegations that P's brother had sexually abused her but then withdrew them shortly before a hearing was to take place to determine them, on the basis that it accepted that it would not be able to establish them. The local authority applicant was ordered to pay all of the costs claimed by the Official Solicitor on behalf of P and of P's brother in respect of the steps taken towards the determination of the allegation up to and including the point that the local authority withdrew the allegation. As the court noted: 'Cogent evidence never existed. It should have been obvious long before these proceedings were commenced ... that there was never any cogent evidence'.[9] Those costs amounted (together) to some £88,000. See also in this regard chapter 22 on safeguarding and the Court of Protection.

Admissions

12.12 The COPR provide for the making of admissions by a party of the truth of the whole or another part of another party's case by giving notice in writing.[10] This provision is, in the authors' experience, rarely invoked, but it serves as a formal mechanism by which factual matters can be agreed between the parties and advanced to the court as an agreed basis upon which it can then be invited to take a decision. There is no necessary formality to the notice that is required (nor is it necessary that the notice be filed at court), but it is prudent to ensure that, where an admission is being made, express reference is made to the provisions of COPR r94(1) and care is taken to ensure that the precise scope of what is being admitted is defined.

---

8 [2013] EWHC 2410 (COP).
9 Para 185, per District Judge Eldergill.
10 COPR r94(1). The court may allow a party to amend or withdraw an admission: COPR r94(2).

Factual evidence

Overview

12.13 Very broadly, most evidence before the court will fall into one of two categories: factual evidence and expert evidence. The latter is discussed at paras 12.54 onwards below. The former constitutes a range of different types of material, the most obvious being evidence from witnesses as to facts relevant to the decision(s) that the court is being asked to take. The different categories of such evidence are discussed below.

Witness statements: formalities and contents

12.14 The general rule is that any fact that needs to be proved by the evidence of a witness must be proved by the oral evidence of that witness if there is a final hearing, and by their evidence in writing at any other hearing (or if there is no hearing).[11] It would appear that a permission form, an application form or an application notice can stand as evidence at a hearing other than a final hearing if verified by a statement of truth.[12]

12.15 Almost without exception, and in line with the position that prevails in civil litigation and proceedings involving children, a witness will be required to provide a witness statement in advance of the final hearing, which will stand (if they are to give oral evidence) as their evidence in chief.[13] In other words, the court will accept their statement (if it complies with the formal requirements discussed below) at a final hearing *as if* they had given its contents orally in response to questions from the representative of the party on whose behalf the witness has been called. The corollary of this is that a witness will only be allowed to amplify their statement and/or to give evidence relating to new matters if there is good reason to do so.[14] The latitude granted by judges to witnesses to go beyond the contents of their witness statement in oral evidence will depend greatly upon the circumstances of the case, but as a general rule it is prudent to proceed on the cautious basis that the main opportunity that the witness will get to give oral evidence will be in response to questions

---

11 COPR r96(1).
12 COPR r11(3)(a).
13 COPR r96(2).
14 COPR r96(3)–(4).

asked in cross-examination by other parties or to questions asked by the judge.

12.16 While permission is not required to serve written evidence with an application (including an interim application) or in response to an application (and indeed, it is in some circumstances mandatory to file such evidence[15]), as a general rule it is only possible to rely upon written evidence filed subsequently if permission has been given by the court.[16] As noted above (and discussed further in chapter 9), one of the primary questions for the court as part of its case management functions will be to decide whether to grant such permission; indeed, it is required by the COPR to give directions as to the service of witness statements in advance of the final hearing.[17] Judges will be astute in deciding whether to grant permission to ensure – insofar as possible – that the written evidence filed only goes to the issues in question.

12.17 Witness statements to be used at a final hearing are the subject of particular requirements. They must contain a statement of truth and comply with the requirements of paras 33–50 of PD 14A.[18] While, strictly, witness evidence prepared for other purposes (for instance, at an interim hearing), does not need to comply with these requirements, it is advisable that, wherever practicable, witness evidence is put before the court in a form that can stand, if necessary, at the final hearing.

12.18 A sample witness statement is to be found in appendix D below. The most important points to emphasise in relation to the preparation of witness statements are as follows:

- Witness statements should be clearly headed so that it is immediately obvious who is giving the statement, on whose behalf they are giving it, whether it is the first statement that they are making (and, if not, which number it is), and the date upon which it was made.
- While witness statements must be attached to a COP24 form, it is not necessary that they are included in the form itself. The form

15 For instance, a party served with an application who opposes it or seeks a different order must file a witness statement with their acknowledgment of service containing any evidence upon which they intend to rely: COPR r72(5); an interim application must also be accompanied by evidence if it the evidence not already before the court: COPR r78(2).
16 COPR r97(c).
17 COPR r99(2).
18 COPR r100 read together with PD 14A. PD 14B makes detailed provisions relating to statements of truth.

is unwieldy; unless the statement is very short, it is often much better to prepare the statement as a stand-alone document and attach it to a COP24. If this is done, then it is advisable to include a statement of truth at the end of the stand-alone document as well as in the box contained in the COP24.
- Only evidence that is relevant to the issue(s) before the court should be included. Indeed evidence that is not relevant is strictly not admissible.[19] For cases on the welfare pathway under the Case Management Pilot (see further para 4.101), specific tasks for the judge at the case management conference include recording the issues in dispute, what has been agreed between the parties, and which issues are not to be the subject of adjudication in the case.[20] Care should be exercised not to include in the witness statement evidence that goes to issues that have been specifically recorded as not being the subject of adjudication, otherwise (at a minimum) judicial criticism will be likely.
- It is important clearly to distinguish in the statement between facts that are directly within the knowledge of the person making the statement and those which are matters of information or belief (and, where the latter, the source for those matters). While it may be quite proper for a witness statement to contain hearsay evidence (ie evidence relating to matters that they have not witnessed directly, discussed further below at para 12.23 below), it is necessary that this is clearly identified.
- Any exhibits should be clearly referenced in the statement by the witness; where the witness gives more than one statement, the numbering of the exhibits should run consecutively throughout, rather than starting again with each statement. The mechanics of exhibiting documents (and other items) to a witness statement are set out at PD 14A paras 20–31.[21]

12.19 A common error in statements prepared by public bodies in welfare proceedings is that they do not set out in sufficient detail what is proposed for P, why the proposed option is considered to be in P's best interests and how, if there is to be a change in the arrangements for P (for instance a move) how any transition is to be managed. It is

---

19 *Hollington v Hewthorn and Co Ltd* [1943] KB 587 at 594. For a detailed discussion of questions of relevance and admissibility, see *Phipson on Evidence* chapter 7.
20 Case Management Pilot PD para 4.5(a)–(c).
21 Which apply not to just to affidavits, as suggested by their placement in the practice direction, but also to witness statements: see PD 14A para 39.

(often) the case that further investigation in fact reveals that the necessary issues have been considered, but that the analysis underpinning the conclusions set out in the statement is not set out in sufficient detail. A checklist for the preparation of such statements is to be found at appendix E.

12.20 By the same token, if any other party wishes to advance an alternative suggestion as to what is in P's best interests in welfare proceedings (or, indeed, suggestions are being advanced as to P's best interests in proceedings relating to property and affairs), it is suggested that the maxim of 'show your workings' in terms of outlining the reasons why the course of action advanced is in P's best interests will always serve well.

Witness statements – timing

12.21 The court will usually consider, when giving directions as to service of witness statements, the order in which they are to be served.[22] Where P is a party to the proceedings, and the Official Solicitor acts as their litigation friend, it is usual for the Official Solicitor to serve his evidence last. That evidence (save in the most straightforward of cases) takes a standard form and is not, formally, a witness statement, but simply a statement, as the Official Solicitor does not have direct knowledge of the facts and matters in question. It is prepared by the solicitors instructed on the Official Solicitor's behalf (or by a lawyer or case-worker in the Official Solicitor's office if the matter is being handled in-house), but will be signed by the Official Solicitor or one of his or her deputies. It will set out the Official Solicitor's summary of the relevant background to and the procedural developments in the proceedings, and setting out the Official Solicitor's views as to P's best interests in the light of the evidence as it stands as at the time of the statement. Such views are almost invariably expressed as being subject to the caveat that they will be the subject of further consideration at the conclusion of the hearing, to cater for unanticipated developments at the hearing. It is suggested that a broadly similar approach should also be followed where another litigation friend is appointed to act on P's behalf.

12.22 In some circumstances, it is not possible for witness statements to be prepared and served in the way outlined above. There are two potential scenarios:

22 COPR r99(3).

- The party wishing to rely upon the evidence of the witness may not be able to take the formal steps required to enable the witness to give their statement (for instance, because the witness is unwell at the time). In such circumstances, the party can apply without notice to be permitted to file a witness summary, which is a summary of a) the evidence, if known, which would otherwise be included in a witness statement; or b) if the evidence is not known, the matters about which the party proposes to question the witness.[23] Unless the court directs otherwise, the summary must include the name and address of the intended witness, and the summary must be filed within the period in which the statement would have had to be filed.[24] The court will then apply, as far as practicable, the provisions relating to the amplification of witness statements discussed at para 12.15 above and also the provisions relating to the service of witness statements (for instance, as to the order in which the summary is to be served).[25]
- It may become clear shortly before a hearing that a witness is able to give evidence necessary to the resolution of the matters before the court, but permission has not previously been granted to the relevant party to rely upon the evidence of the witness. In such circumstances, it is strongly advisable to notify the other parties and the court as soon as possible of the existence of the witness and the nature of the evidence that they will be able to give if permission is granted to rely upon their evidence at the hearing. Depending upon the timing, it may be possible for the question of permission to be determined in advance of the hearing; it may well, however, be necessary for the question to be decided at the outset of the hearing. If it will not be possible for the question of permission to be decided before the hearing, it is advisable that as full a statement as possible is obtained from the witness and served upon the other parties so as to reduce any element of surprise. The statement should also be filed with the court, but it is particularly important to flag up in any list of pre-reading prepared for the judge that permission has not been granted to rely upon the statement; if any party has indicated that they will object to the late service of the statement and/or the giving of evidence by the witness, the judge should not be invited to read the statement prior to the hearing.

23 COPR r101(1)–(2).
24 COPR r101(3)–(4).
25 COPR r101(5).

Hearsay evidence

12.23 Space precludes a detailed discussion of the law relating to hearsay evidence, ie statements made otherwise than by a person while giving oral evidence in the proceedings which are tendered as evidence of the matters stated.[26] In contrast to the statutory schemes for both civil and family proceedings, the MCA 2005 and COPR make no express reference to hearsay. However, in *Enfield LBC v SA and others*,[27] McFarlane J held that Court of Protection proceedings under the MCA 2005 fall within the very wide definition of 'civil proceedings' under the Civil Evidence Act (CEA) 1995. The CEA 1995 therefore applies to such proceedings, and hearsay evidence is admissible in accordance with the provisions of the CEA 1995.[28]

12.24 In the light of the decision in *SA*, the formal position is that:

- If a party wishes to rely upon hearsay evidence, they must give to the other party or parties such formal notice of and (on request) such particulars of or relating to the evidence, as is required to enable them to deal with any matters arising from its being hearsay.[29] It would appear that there is no requirement to give notice to rely upon a hearsay statement contained in a document within the agreed bundle (see paras 12.29–12.32 below).[30] In any event, in light of the flexibility granted by COPR r95(d), it is unlikely that a judge would decline to consider hearsay evidence in respect of which formal advance notice had not been given. The judge would, however, no doubt consider the extent to which the other party or parties had been disadvantaged by the fact that the maker of the original statement had not been produced for cross-examination.
- In estimating the weight (if any) to be given to the hearsay evidence the court shall have regard to any circumstances from which any inference can reasonably be drawn as to the reliability or otherwise of the evidence, and, in particular, may have regard to:
  – whether it would have been reasonable and practicable for the party by whom the evidence was adduced to have produced the maker of the original statement as a witness;
  – whether the original statement was made contemporaneously with the occurrence or existence of the matters stated;

---

26 The statutory definition contained in Civil Evidence Act (CEA) 1995 s1(2)(a). A detailed discussion can be found in chapter 29 of *Phipson on Evidence*.
27 [2010] EWHC 196 (Admin), [2010] COPLR Con Vol 362.
28 *SA* at paras 29–30.
29 CEA 1995 s2(1).
30 By analogy with *Charnock v Rowan* [2012] EWCA Civ 2, [2012] CP Rep 18.

- whether the evidence involves multiple hearsay;
- whether any person involved had any motive to conceal or misrepresent matters;
- whether the original statement was an edited account, or was made in collaboration with another or for a particular purpose;
- whether the circumstances in which the evidence is adduced as hearsay are such as to suggest an attempt to prevent proper evaluation of its weight.[31]

12.25 If a witness is not competent to give evidence it can be received as hearsay. As a result of the 2015 rule changes and the introduction of COPR r95(e), it is now clear that the court can accept hearsay evidence (in the form of 'information') from P, any protected party or any person who lacks competence to give evidence.[32] Competence to give evidence should not be confused with capacity to conduct proceedings: the test for competence is whether the witness is capable of understanding the nature of an oath and of giving rational testimony.[33] A person may not be able to conduct proceedings and require a litigation friend, but be entirely competent to give evidence.[34]

12.26 However, even if the evidence from a witness who is not competent to give evidence is admissible, as McFarlane J noted in *SA*:

> Admissibility is one thing, and the weight to be attached to any particular piece of hearsay evidence will be a matter for specific evaluation in each individual case. Within that evaluation, the fact that the individual from whom the evidence originates is not a competent witness will no doubt be an important factor, just as it is, in a different context, when the family court has to evaluate what has been said by a very young child.[35]

12.27 The position in respect of hearing from P is addressed at paras 15.34–15.44.

---

31 CEA 1995 s4.
32 See also *A County Council v AB and others (Participation of P in Proceedings)* [2016] EWCOP 41.
33 *Phipson on Evidence*, Sweet & Maxwell, 12th edn, 2012, para 9–08.
34 See by analogy *Milroy v British Telecommunications Plc* [2015] EWHC 532 (QB), in which the claimant in personal injury proceedings did not have capacity to litigate those proceedings, but was competent to give evidence as the training he had received and the circumstances under which he had suffered the material injury.
35 *SA* at para 36.

Affidavits

12.28 The COPR and PD 14A both make reference to the giving of evidence by witnesses within the jurisdiction by way of affidavit instead of or in addition to a witness statement.[36] Save for the making of an application for an order for committal to prison for contempt of court,[37] there are no rules or practice directions (or other enactments) which require that evidence be given in such a form. A judge may require such to be given, but such is in practice unusual, especially given that proceedings for contempt of court can be brought against a person who makes or causes to be made a false statement in a witness statement verified by a statement of truth without an honest belief in its truth.[38]

Documentary evidence

12.29 PD 14 provides both that a court may give directions requiring the parties to use their best endeavours to agree a bundle or bundles of documents for use at any hearing,[39] and that all documents contained in such bundle(s) shall be admissible at that hearing as evidence of their contents unless a) the court orders otherwise; or b) a party gives written notice of objection to the admissibility of particular documents.

12.30 In practice, it is routine in welfare cases for a direction to be made at an early stage in the proceedings that social services and/or medical records relating to P be provided by the relevant public authorities to the litigation friend appointed to act on behalf of P, most usually the Official Solicitor. It is then not uncommon for parts of those records to be included (whether by the public authority or those acting on behalf of P) in the bundles before the court, and then to form a significant part of the evidence upon which the court will make its decision. It is therefore important that if a family member (say) wishes to object to the admissibility of any or all or those documents that this is made very clear in the preparation of the agreed bundles before the final hearing. Questions of the wider disclosure

---

36 COPR rr102–103; PD 14A paras 1–19. The position of witnesses outside England and Wales is considered separately at para 12.42 below.
37 COPR r186(1) and PD 21A.
38 COPR r14.
39 For welfare cases on the personal welfare pathway under the Case Management Pilot, specific provision is made in relation to the preparation of bundles for the case management hearing, final management hearing and the final hearing (see Case Management Pilot PD paras 4.4(1)(h), 4.6(3) and 4.7(2) respectively and chapter 10).

of such records during the currency of proceedings and (in particular) the circumstances under which such disclosure can be withheld raise difficult issues that are discussed further below at para 12.102.

12.31 Another mechanism by which factual information can be put before the court is by the power granted under COPR r107 to the court to direct that a party with access to information which is not reasonably available to another party to direct the former to prepare and file a document recording the information and to serve it on the other party (or parties). Any document prepared pursuant to this rule must include sufficient details of all the facts, tests, experiments and assumptions which underlie any part of the information to enable the party on whom it is served to make, or to obtain, a proper interpretation of the information and an assessment of its significance.[40] This provision is rarely, if ever, invoked, but can serve a purpose if one party has information which is not reduced to documentary form which can and should properly be provided to the other parties to the court in a document which can be the subject of proper scrutiny. Rule 107 does not, itself, provide that a document produced under the provision is evidence of its contents, but if it is included within the agreed bundle for a hearing, the rule discussed at para 12.29 above will apply.

Notarial acts and instruments

12.32 A notarial act or instrument may, without further proof, be received in evidence as duly authenticated in accordance with the requirements of law unless the contrary is proved.[41] Such acts or instruments will, in most cases, originate from a foreign country in which notaries play an important role in authenticating documents.

Witness summons

12.33 A party can apply for the issue of a witness summons requiring a named individual to attend court and give oral evidence or to produce a document.[42] Permission to issue such a summons must be sought upon application using a COP9 form (see further paras 10.21 onwards), and the application notice must include particulars of the applicant, the proposed witness, any document which the proposed

---

40 PD 14A para 54.
41 COPR r105.
42 COPR r106(1).

witness is required to produce, and the grounds upon which the application is made.[43] A witness summons can also be issued by the court of its own motion, and in Re NRA, Charles J noted the use of such summons as one of the tools that the court should consider using as part of its 'investigatory jurisdiction'.[44]

A summons to produce documents to the court must either identify the individual document(s) or by reference to a specific category or event, but 'with sufficient certainty to leave no real doubt in the mind of the person to whom the summons is addressed about what they are required to do'.[45]

12.34 If the application is granted, the witness summons will then be prepared by the court[46] (PD 14D provides for the correction of errors in the name or address of the person to be summoned prior to service). The usual rule is that the party that made it must serve the summons; at the time of service, the party must be offered or paid a) a sum reasonably sufficient to cover his travelling expenses to and from court; and b) compensation for his loss of time.[47] Both of these sums are fixed by reference to those payable in criminal cases;[48] compensation for ordinary witnesses (ie those who are neither experts nor professionals) is capped at £33.50 for a period of absence not exceeding four hours and £67.00 for a longer period.[49] The court can also order that a witness be paid such general costs as it considers appropriate.[50] Although the COPR and the accompanying practice direction (PD 14D) are silent as to who should pay, the silence suggests that payment should be made by the party who sought the application.

12.35 In general, a witness summons is only binding if a) it is served more than seven days prior to the date on which the witness is required to attend court; and b) the requirements as to offering or

43 COPR r106(2); PD 14D para 3.
44 Re NRA and Others [2015] EWCOP 59, [2015] COPLR 690 at 261, (2015) 18 CCLR 392.
45 Tajik Aluminium Plant v Hydo Aluminium AS [2005] EWCA Civ 1218, [2006] 1 WLR 767 at para 28 per Moore-Bick LJ.
46 PD 14D para 4.
47 COPR r106(6)(a) and (b).
48 PD 14D para 10 and the Costs in Criminal Cases (General) Regulations 1986 SI No 1335 (made under the Prosecution of Offenders Act 1985 (as amended)).
49 Annex A to the Guide to Allowances under Part V of the Costs in Criminal Cases (General) Regulations 1986, 2007; available at: www.justice.gov.uk/downloads/information-access-rights/foi-disclosure-log/courts-tribunals/foi-76520-annex-a.pdf.
50 COPR r106(7).

paying compensation have been met.[51] It is possible, though, for the court to shorten the time period in an appropriate case (although not to dispense with the compensation requirements).[52]

12.36 Where the summons is issued solely so as to obtain documents and prove their authenticity, it is suggested that the same practice as is used in civil proceedings would be followed, ie that the summons specify a date for the production of the documents that is in advance of the substantive hearing.[53] This power is of little application in terms of documents held by the parties, because of the operation of COPR r107 (see above, para 12.31).

12.37 It should be noted, finally, that witness summons are not issued solely to comply reluctant witnesses to attend court, but also as a mechanism by which (for instance) an employer can be forced to allow an employee to attend to give evidence.

12.38 The COPR are silent as to the sanctions that follow a failure to comply with a witness summons. It is suggested, however, that, by analogy with the position that prevails in the High Court, such a failure can be punished as a contempt of court: see further chapter 18 below.

Depositions

12.39 It is possible for an order to be obtained for a person to be examined on oath before the relevant hearing takes place. Such an order must be sought upon application using a COP9 form (see further paras 10.21 onwards), although it is not necessary that it be made on notice to the other parties.[54] The deponent can be examined before a circuit judge or a district judge (whether or not nominated as a judge of the Court of Protection), an examiner of the court or such other person as the court appoints,[55] and the order can require the production of any document which the court considers is necessary for the purposes of the examination.[56] The court can also order that the party who

---

51 COPR r106(3).
52 COPR r106(4).
53 See *Khanna v Lovell White Durrant* [1995] 1 WLR 121 and the *White Book 2014*, Sweet & Maxwell, at para 34.0.3.
54 COPR r108(1); PD 14B para 9.
55 COPR r108(3); 'examiners of the court' are appointed by the Lord Chancellor: see COPR r111.
56 COPR r108(4).

Evidence and disclosure 333

obtained the order to file a witness statement or witness summary in relation to the evidence to be given by the person be examined.[57]

12.40 A deposition that has been ordered under COPR r108 may be put in evidence at a hearing unless the court orders otherwise.[58] If a party intends to put such a deposition in evidence, they must file notice of their intention to do so with the court and serve it on every other party; absent order to the contrary, they must file such notice at least 14 days before the hearing date.[59] The court can require the deponent to attend the hearing and give evidence orally.[60]

12.41 Detailed provisions relating to the conduct of depositions to be taken in England and Wales are set out in PD 14B,[61] aimed primarily at ensuring the creation of an accurate record of the questions put and the answers given, and also at setting out the consequences of a failure of a deponent to attend the examination or a refusal to be sworn, answer any lawful question or produce any document. They are not addressed further here because the process is so rarely invoked before the Court of Protection.

Witnesses outside the jurisdiction

12.42 The COPR and PD 14A contain detailed provisions relating to the obtaining of evidence from witnesses outside England and Wales; they also (along with PD 14B) contain provisions relating to the taking of depositions outside England and Wales. In summary:

- a person may make an affidavit outside England and Wales in the same (limited) circumstances as provided for within England and Wales, or as in accordance with the law in the place where they make the affidavit;[62]
- the procedure for taking evidence outside the jurisdiction will vary depending upon whether or not the person in question is in an EU member state;[63]
- the same procedural requirements apply in relation to the putting before the court of evidence obtained outside the jurisdiction as

57 COPR r108(7).
58 COPR r113(1).
59 COPR r113(2)–(3).
60 COPR r113(4).
61 PD 14B paras 1–15.
62 COPR r104.
63 COPR rr115–116; PD 14B paras 16–33. If the person is within an EU member state, the Taking of Evidence Regulation (Council Regulation (EC) 1206/2001) applies.

do in relation to depositions taken from witnesses in England and Wales.[64]

12.43 Where a witness is outside the jurisdiction, it is more likely that steps will be taken to enable them to give any oral evidence required by way of video link, as provided for at COPR r98, and discussed further at paras 15.53–15.57.

Documents held by the police

12.44 Where the police force of a particular area is not a party to the proceedings, but where the court agrees that documents are required from the police, the police normally require that any order be made in terms that a) are directed to the chief constable of the force in question; b) invite, rather than require, the production of documents; and c) include the full name and date of birth of the person to whom they relate. Many police forces have in place local protocols with local authorities for the disclosure of documents in proceedings relating to children; it is usually easiest if such protocols (modified as necessary) are adopted in proceedings relating to incapacitated adults. A model order can be found at www.courtofprotectionhandbook.com/precedents.

Section 49 reports

12.45 The court has the power under MCA 2005 s49 to call for a report in respect of such matters relating to P as it may direct from:
- the Public Guardian;
- a Court of Protection Visitor, appointed by the Lord Chancellor to one of two panels, Special Visitors and General Visitors, the former requiring a medical qualification and special knowledge of and experience in cases of impairment of or disturbance in the functioning of the mind or brain;[65]
- a local authority or NHS body (such report to be produced by one of its officers or employees or such other person other than that the Public Guardian or a Court of Protection Visitor as the authority/NHS body considers appropriate).

12.46 There are specific provisions in MCA 2005 s49 and COPR r117 relating to the powers of those charged with producing such reports

64 COPR r113.
65 MCA 2005 s61(2).

(which are normally, but not necessarily, provided in writing[66]). In summary:

- The Public Guardian or a Court of Protection Visitor is entitled, at all reasonable times, to examine and take copies of any health record, any record of or held by a local authority and compiled in connection with a social services function, and any record held by a person registered under Care Standards Act 2000 Part 2 or Health and Social Care Act 2008 Part 1 Chapter 2 (broadly, records held by those managing private residential and nursing homes) relating to P.[67]
- Any person compiling a report can inspect and take copies of any document in the court records, unless the court orders to the contrary (or orders that they may only have access to the information on an edited basis).[68]
- A Public Guardian or Court of Protection Visitor can interview P in private for purposes of producing a report.[69]
- A Special Visitor can, if the court directs, carry out a private medical, psychiatric or psychological examination of P's capacity and condition.[70]
- An officer or an employee of a local authority or NHS body (or person reporting on their behalf) is expected to contact or seek to interview such persons as he thinks appropriate or the court directs, but is not granted any specific power to interview or examine P for purposes of producing a report.[71]

12.47 Section 49 reports, especially those produced by Court of Protection Visitors, bear a strong resemblance to expert reports, in that they will include both discussion of factual matters and also opinions reflecting the expertise of the maker of the reports. Both those providing reports under MCA 2005 s49 and experts reporting to the court owe a duty to the court (rather than to the parties) to assist on the matters within their expertise.[72] However, even though many section

---

66 MCA 2005 s49(6). The model order attached to Pilot PD14E (see further below) provides alternative wording for oral and written reports: see para 4.
67 MCA 2005 s49(7).
68 COPR r117(5) and (7).
69 MCA 2005 s49(8).
70 MCA 2005 s49(9).
71 COPR r117(3)(a).
72 COPR r117(2) (reports under MCA 2005 s49); COPR r122 (experts). The maker of a section 49 report must also give a statement of truth that relates both to the facts contained within their report and the expression of their professional opinions: Pilot PD 14E para 23(e).

49 reports are in substance identical to expert reports, they are treated distinctly to such reports for purposes of the COPR,[73] and therefore conceptually occupy a somewhat curious position in the conventional categorisation of evidence.

12.48 In many circumstances, the power exercisable under MCA 2005 s49 serves as an effective route by which the court can obtain independent evidence as to matters relevant to the application, and thus as an alternative to the grant of permission to the parties to instruct (jointly or separately) an expert to give evidence. For welfare cases falling within the Case Management Pilot the court must actively consider whether such a report[74] could achieve a better result than an expert.[75]

12.49 There is one substantial advantage to the parties in the obtaining of such a report, namely that the MCA 2005 and the COPR make no express provision for the payment of any fees. This is in contrast to the position in relation to experts where the default position is that the instructing parties are jointly and severally liable for the payment of the expert's fees and expenses[76] (see further para 12.79 below). In practice, this means that the costs fall upon the body required to produce the report (in the case of Special and General Visitors, they are remunerated for their work by Lord Chancellor, including for the provision of section 49 reports[77]).

12.50 In part because of concerns expressed by NHS bodies at the burdens being placed upon them by orders to provide section 49 reports (especially in relation to individuals with whom they had had no previous contact),[78] and in part also because of practical difficulties that were being encountered on a regular basis in obtaining timely and appropriately detailed section 49 reports from public bodies, a Pilot was introduced on 1 September 2016 in relation to such reports. The Pilot, which runs until 31 August 2017, applies

---

73 By COPR r119(b), an expert does not include any person instructed to make a report under MCA 2005 s49.
74 Or from a COPR Pr1.2 representative (see further chapter 11).
75 Case Management Pilot PD para 4.5(m).
76 COPR r131(5).
77 MCA 2005 s61(4).
78 See *RS v LCC & Ors* [2015] EWCOP 56, in which District Judge Bellamy emphasised that there is no provision is made within MCA 2005 s49 for fees or expenses incurred by the relevant public bodies, but that '[w]hat the court will do is to carefully consider resources and listen to any argument from the [public body] particularly in relation to the time for compliance and the scope of the work to be undertaken. That would appear to be both a reasonable and proportionate approach.'

to all cases where a section 49 report is ordered, whether on application, or on the court's own initiative.[79]

12.51 The section 49 Pilot contains, in Pilot PD14E, detailed guidance both as to when a section 49 report is likely to be ordered, and also as to the contents of the report. It also contains details as to the steps that should be taken by a party before applying for an order for a section 49 report directed against a public body, in particular as to the identification of a suitable person ('the senior officer') at the local authority or NHS body in question who will be in a position to receive the order and take action upon it. There is also a detailed model order attached to the Pilot PD, which includes specific provisions for such matters as the contents of the report, persons to whom it is likely to be disclosed and access to records.

12.52 For purposes of the Pilot (and, indeed, as we previously recommended in the first edition of the book as good practice) the rule of thumb will therefore be to prepare *as if* an expert is being instructed (see further below paras 12.79 onwards). In other words:

- If the report is to be provided by a public body and requires any specific expertise (for instance the preparation of a report addressing P's capacity), an individual should, if possible, be identified at the relevant body with that expertise; alternatively, a particular category of individual (for instance a psychologist, or psychiatrist). Whilst MCA 2005 s49 provides for a report to be provided by the public body, rather than by a specific person within the public body,[80] if an appropriate person can be identified and agreed with the 'senior officer' then this will speed matters up considerably as regards the preparation of the report;
- A realistic time-frame should be identified within which the report can be prepared;
- A draft letter of instruction should be prepared for consideration by the court,[81] which contains a summary of the relevant background matters (including, in many cases, relevant documentation); and a summary of the relevant legal tests to apply (including not just the provisions of the MCA 2005 but any relevant cases). It should also ask detailed and specific questions. This does not apply just to situations where the report is being sought of a public body, but also of a Court of Protection Visitor: experience

---

79 Section 49 Reports Pilot PD para 1.3.
80 And Pilot PD14E provides for how the public body is to nominate the person to prepare the report: paras 11–12.
81 This is a specific requirement: Pilot PD14E para 8.

has taught that both General and Special Visitors can on occasion be asked to report in extremely vague terms, producing in consequence extremely vague – and unhelpful – reports;

12.53 A report made in response to an order under MCA 2005 s49 is made to the court, rather than to the parties. It will then be sent by the court to the parties; it can also be sent to such other persons as the court may direct.[82] A party (but not another person to whom the report has been sent) can apply for permission to put written questions to the maker of the report.[83] Such questions must be directed via the court, which will make such amendments as it sees fit; the court will then send the replies received to the parties and such other person as it may direct.[84]

Expert evidence

Overview

12.54 More than in many other types of proceedings, judges sitting in the Court of Protection will often require assistance from suitably qualified individuals as to such matters as:

- whether P has or lacks capacity to take the decision(s) in question; and
- what course of action is in P's physical and/or psychological best interests, especially if there are specific clinical or social work concerns.

12.55 That evidence will go beyond evidence of fact and, indeed, it will be of value to the court predominantly insofar as it constitutes evidence of opinion based upon the expertise of the individual in question. As such evidence would not otherwise be admissible, the MCA 2005 and COPR Part 15 contain provisions enabling such evidence can be put before the court in a proportionate fashion.[85] COPR Part 15 is accompanied by a practice direction (PD 15A); this is very much less detailed than the suite of practice directions that are now in force accompanying the Family Procedure Rules (FPR) 2010 SI No 2955

---

82 COPR r117(4). Paragraph 12 of the model order attached to Pilot PD14E directs the minds both of the parties and the court to identifying whom the report is to be disclosed to other than the parties.
83 COPR r118(1).
84 COPR r118(2)–(3).
85 Space precludes a detailed discussion of the law relating to expert evidence; the reader is referred to *Phipson on Evidence* at para 33-09 onwards.

Part 25, the equivalent provisions in proceedings relating to children. At present, there is no immediate prospect of PD15A being amended to introduce a similar degree of detail. The Case Management Pilot has substituted a new Pilot Part 15 governing expert evidence which for the most part is identical to the 'old' Part 15 but contains a number of areas in which obligations are tightened highlighted below.

12.56 Slightly oddly, neither the MCA 2005 nor the COPR provide any definition of an 'expert',[86] but it is suggested that for these purposes an 'expert' is a person qualified to express an expert opinion upon a relevant matter by virtue of their qualifications or experience upon such matters. By analogy, Civil Evidence Act (CEA) 1972 s3 provides that where a person is called as a witness in any civil proceedings, the person's opinion on any relevant matter on which he or she is qualified to give expert evidence shall be admissible in evidence, and that 'a relevant matter' includes an issue in the proceedings in question. It is suggested that proceedings before the Court of Protection are 'civil proceedings' for these purposes (by analogy with *Enfield LBC v SA and others*[87]).

12.57 It is further suggested that an expert is a person who must have a degree of independence from P,[88] such that a family member could not properly qualify as an expert for these purposes. In the ordinary run of events, it would be unusual for a treating clinician (or a social worker involved with P's case) to be asked to provide expert evidence falling within the scope of COPR Part 15. However, in *O-M and Others v The Local Authority and Others*,[89] the Court of Appeal held that there is no blanket rule which prevents, in an appropriate case, a treating doctor becoming a jointly instructed expert in public law proceedings relating to children. It is suggested that there is no reason in principle why the same approach could not apply in proceedings in relation to adults.

12.58 In any event, 'specialist' professional witnesses employed or acting on behalf of a public body party to proceedings often give evidence that contains both evidence of fact and what would in layperson's terms be considered to be expert opinion evidence. For instance,

---

86 Although, as noted above, it cannot be a person who gives a report under the provisions of MCA 2005 s49.
87 [2010] EWHC 196 (Admin), [2010] COPLR Con Vol 362, discussing the CEA 1995, which contains the same definition of 'civil proceedings'. See CEA 1972 s3; compare CEA 1995 s11.
88 See PD 15A paras 3–4, discussed further below.
89 [2009] EWCA Civ 1405, [2010] 2 FLR 58. See also *Hershman and McFarlane: children law and practice*, at para 3060-1.

a social worker will very often both relate events that they have witnessed directly (or have knowledge of from their reading of social services records) and then also express their professional opinion as to where P's best interests may lie on the basis of their perception of those events. That opinion may well be due (and be given) significant weight by the court. As noted extra-judicially by Sir James Munby P (in comments relating to care proceedings but of equal relevance to proceedings under the MCA 2005):

> Social workers may not be experts for the purposes of FPR Part 25 [the equivalent of COPR Part 15], but that does not mean that they are not experts in every other sense of the word. They are, and we must recognise them and treat them as such.[90]

12.59 As discussed below, therefore, where there is evidence before the court from a witness such as a social worker on behalf of a public authority, this will factor into the question of whether expert evidence falling within the scope of COPR Part 15 is in fact required.

12.60 It is also vital as a preliminary point to remember in respect of all expert evidence (both that falling within the scope of Part 15 and that of the quasi-expert nature discussed immediately above) that:

- where the opinion of an expert is based upon the report of facts, those facts, unless within the expert's own knowledge, must be proved independently;
- an expert may (in an appropriate case) give evidence upon 'ultimate questions' going to factual matters, for instance as to the accuracy or truthfulness of a witness, but the final decision remains that for the judge;[91]
- likewise, the 'ultimate' questions of whether P has capacity and as to what is in their best interests are matters for the court.[92]

---

90 Sir James Munby P, 'View from the President's Chambers (3) The process of reform: expert evidence' [2013] Fam Law 816.
91 See, by analogy, *Re M and R* [1996] 2 FLR 195 at 205–213 per Butler-Sloss LJ and *Re M (sexual abuse allegations: interviewing techniques)* [1999] 2 FLR 92 per Sir Stephen Brown P. See also the discussion in *Hershman and McFarlane: children law and practice*, at para 3056.
92 *CC v KK and STCC* [2012] EWHC 2136 (COP), [2012] COPLR 627 at para 24 per Baker J.

12.61 In other words, and as Charles J observed in *A County Council v K, D and L*,[93] after a detailed review of the authorities:

> ... it is important to remember (i) that the roles of the court and the expert are distinct; and (ii) it is the court that is in the position to weigh the expert evidence against its findings on the other evidence ... the judge must always remember that he or she is the person who makes the final decision.

12.62 Allied to this is the fact that the judge is not limited in their determination even of questions upon which expert evidence might be thought to be of particular weight solely to consideration of that evidence. In particular, it is clear that capacity is a question ultimately to be determined by the court, and it must do so on the basis of:

> all the relevant evidence. Clearly, the opinion of an independently-instructed expert will be likely to be of very considerable importance, but in many cases the evidence of other clinicians and professionals who have experience of treating and working with P will be just as important and in some cases more important.[94]

12.63 A corollary of the matters set out above is that the judge is entitled to depart from the expert evidence put before them, as happened in the *CC* case referred to above, where Baker J held in the face of all the professional and expert evidence before him that P had the capacity to decide where she wished to reside, largely (it appears) on the basis of his own assessment of P when she appeared before him. By analogy with the position that prevails in relation to children, it is suggested that a departure where it concerns the potential level of risk to the welfare of P must be accompanied by appropriately detailed reasons.[95]

Permission

12.64 Although it is not necessary to obtain permission to file expert evidence as to capacity and/or best interests with the initial application to the court,[96] the court's permission must be obtained before filing any

---

93 [2005] EWHC 144 (Fam), [2005] 1 FLR 851, at paras 39 and 44. This case related to an application for a care order under the Children Act 1989, but its principles were held to be equally applicable to proceedings under the MCA 2005 by Baker J in *CC v KK and STCC* [2012] EWHC 2136 (COP), [2012] COPLR 627 at para 24.
94 *PH v A Local Authority and others* [2011] EWHC 1704 (Fam), [2012] COPLR 128 at para 16(xiii) per Baker J.
95 See *Re B (care: expert witnesses)* [1996] 1 FLR 667 and *Hershman and McFarlane: children law and practice* at para 3056.
96 COPR Pr120(1)(a)–(b)/COPR r120(1)(a)–(b).

subsequent expert evidence[97] (and evidence filed with the application can only be relied upon to the extent and for the purposes that the court allows).[98]

12.65 The requirement to obtain permission is an important tool in the court's case management armoury. In addition to its general obligation to have regard to the general requirement to deal with cases in a proportionate fashion,[99] the court is also under a specific duty to limit expert evidence to that which is reasonably required to resolve the proceedings.[100] This duty extends not just to requiring careful consideration of whether expert evidence is required at all,[101] but also, where possible, requiring expert evidence upon a particular issue to be dealt with by a single expert.[102] In guidance sanctioned by the President of the Court of Protection, the provisions of the COPR and PD 15A were amplified to make clear that: 'Unnecessary expert assessments must be avoided. It will be rare indeed for the court to sanction the instruction of more than one expert to advise in relation to the same issue'.[103]

12.66 It is perhaps worth noting that there are advantages to the instruction of single joint experts other than those of proportionality and cost-saving. As Ryder J (as he then was) noted after a review of the authorities in *JG (a child) v Legal Services Commission and others*[104] (in the context of a discussion of the principle of the equal apportionment of the costs of joint expert evidence (see further para 12.77 below)):

> 47. There are sound reasons, recognised in the decided cases, why there should be apportionment of costs in cases where there is joint expert evidence. Such evidence will:

---

97 COPR Pr123(1)/COPR r123(1).
98 COPR Pr120(2)/COPR r120(2).
99 COPR Pr1.1(c)/COPR r3(3)(c).
100 COPR Pr121/COPR r121.
101 See *City of Westminster v FS* (unreported, 9 September 2009) at paras 12–16, per HHJ Horowitz QC (consideration of whether first instance judge erred in refusing permission to the Official Solicitor to instruct an independent social work expert).
102 COPR Pr130(1)/COPR r130(1) and PD 15A para 1.
103 *Guidance in cases involving protected parties in which the Official Solicitor is being invited to act as guardian ad litem or litigation friend*, 2010, available at: www.familylaw.co.uk/system/uploads/attachments/0001/4515/Guidance_in_cases_involving_the_Official_Solicitor_-_December_2010.pdf.
104 [2013] EWHC 804 (Admin), [2013] 2 FLR 1174. This decision was reversed on appeal: [2014] EWCA Civ 656 but these dicta remain valid.

(a) be something which each party has an interest in making available to the court . . .;
(b) be something from which each party has the potential to benefit (whether or not they ultimately do so) . . .; and
(c) inform the positions of the parties . . .

48. These points do not apply to evidence obtained, and paid for, on a single party's behalf. In *Lambeth*,[105] the court approved (at para [59](viii)) the comment of Bodey J in *Calderdale*[106] (at para [37](e)) in relation to the cost of a joint report prepared for care proceedings brought by a local authority that:

'. . . there is much force in the Local Authority's point that parents need to know that reports which may prove to have a "preponderant influence" (per Munby J at paragraph 113(ii) of *Re L*) are not being prepared at the sole expense of the Local Authority – in which event they may feel that the Local Authority calls the tune.'

12.67 These comments were made in the context of a discussion of expert evidence in private law proceedings concerning a child, but it is suggested that they are equally applicable in proceedings under the MCA 2005.

12.68 For cases on the Case Management Pilot, the provisions in relation to experts have been modified so as to make the test for permission more stringent.[107] The court's duty is to restrict expert evidence to that which is necessary to assist the court to resolve the issues in the proceedings, and the court may only give permission to file or adduce expert evidence if it is satisfied that it is both necessary and cannot otherwise be provided.[108] In deciding whether to give permission to file or adduce expert evidence, the court must have specific regard to (a) the issues to which the expert evidence would relate; (b) the questions which the expert would answer; (c) the impact which giving permission would be likely to have on the timetable, duration and conduct of the proceedings; (d) any failure to comply with any direction of the court about expert evidence; and (e) the cost of the expert evidence.[109] Additionally, the Case Management Pilot Practice Direction (PD) provides that for cases on the welfare pathway, the

105 *Lambeth LBC v S, C, V and J (by his guardian); Legal Services Commission (intervening)* [2005] EWHC 776 (Fam), [2005] 2 FLR 1171.
106 *Calderdale MBC v S and the Legal Services Commission* [2004] EWHC 2529 (Fam), [2005] 1 FLR 751.
107 Note that PD15A, the practice direction accompanying Part 15, has not been amended, so para 1 is incorrect in respect of the test applicable under the Case Management Pilot.
108 COPR Pr121.
109 COPR Pr123(2A).

court must at the case management hearing (see further para 10.19) actively consider whether a section 49 report[110] could achieve a better result than the use of an expert.[111]

12.69 The more stringent test to be applied under the Case Management Pilot echoes that to be found in the Family Procedure Rules.[112] 'Necessity' was interpreted in the context of those rules in *Re H-L (A Child) (Expert Evidence: Test for Permission)*[113] as having 'the connotation of the imperative, what is demanded rather than what is merely optional or reasonable or desirable'.[114]

12.70 As set out at paras 4.101–4.103 above, it is at the time of writing not clear whether cases falling outside one of the pathways also fall outside the scope of the Case Management Pilot. However, the authors strongly suggest that practitioners should proceed on the basis that it will be necessary to satisfy the stricter test in all cases so as to avoid the potential for unhelpful and potentially costly arguments as to which test to apply.

12.71 A further hurdle to the obtaining of expert evidence in cases in which one or more parties are in receipt of public funding is the increasing reluctance of the Legal Aid Agency (LAA) to fund expert evidence (whether at the particular rate sought by the expert, or indeed at all). That the LAA has the power to refuse all or part of the instruction, even if permission has been granted by the court was confirmed by Collins J in *R (T) v Legal Aid Agency*.[115]

12.72 It is strongly advisable that (in line with the approach that applies in family proceedings[116]):

- Where the court takes the view that the expert's report is required (under whatever test is applicable) for the resolution of the case, it should say so and should give reasons (and should do so even if the order is a consent order being endorsed by the court, as it is still a judicial decision).

---

110 Or from a COPR Pr1.2 representative (see further chapter 11).
111 Case Management Pilot PD para 4.5(m).
112 FPR r25.1 as amended by the Family Procedure (Amendment) (No 5) Rules 2012 SI No 3061.
113 [2013] EWCA Civ 655, [2014] 1 WLR 1160, at para 3 per Sir James Munby P; see also Sir James Munby P, 'View from the President's Chambers (3) The process of reform: expert evidence' [2013] Fam Law 816.
114 [2013] EWCA Civ 5, [2013] 1 FLR 1250, at para 30 per Sir James Munby P
115 [2013] EWHC 960 (Admin), [2013] Fam Law 805.
116 *A Local Authority v S and others* [2012] EWHC 1442 (Fam), [2012] 1 WLR 3098 at para 45 per Sir Nicholas Wall P.

- While the reasons need not be lengthy or elaborate, they must, however, explain to anyone reading them why the decision-maker has reached the conclusion he or she has, particularly if the expert's rates exceed the maximum rates ordinarily allowable. This can be done by way of preamble to the order, or by a short judgment, delivered at dictation speed or inserted by the parties with the judge's approval. It is suggested that the preamble or judgment should include (and hence the material put to the court must indicate clearly):
  - what relevant papers it has read;
  - the reasons why it considers that the expert evidence is required to resolve proceedings, which should include the reasons why the evidence would not otherwise be available to it as part of the proceedings (for instance, from a social worker or a treating clinician who has given evidence on behalf of a public body);
  - the reasons why the volume of work is required, if it is a particularly complex report;
  - (if one or more parties is publicly funded) the reasons for why there is any need to exceed the maximum rates usually allowable by the LAA; and
  - the reasons why there is any departure from: i) the principle that the costs of a single joint expert will be shared equally between the instructing parties, particularly if this has the effect of placing a disproportionately high cost burden on a party or parties in receipt of public funding (this should include a robust scrutiny of the means of any party claiming to be unable to afford the cost of the instruction); or ii) the principle that the instructing parties are to be jointly and severally liable for the costs of single joint expert.

12.73 The last point above requires some amplification because a question that arises relatively often is whether all the parties to proceedings *need* to join in the instruction of an expert and, if they do not, what, if any a) right do they have to have input into the instruction; and b) obligation do they have to pay the costs of the expert report?

12.74 The starting point in respect of both is simple: only a party who wishes to submit expert evidence is an 'instructing party';[117] only such a party has the right (but not the duty) to give instructions to the

---

117 COPR Pr130(2)/COPR r130(2).

expert;[118] and the status of instructing party carries with it the obligation to meet jointly and severally the expert's fees and expenses.[119] The Court of Protection cannot force a party to join in the instructions; if a party refuses to do so, it is suggested that this should be recorded on the face of the directions giving permission to other party or parties to instruct the expert in question.

12.75 Conversely, especially where one party is a litigant in person and/or is of limited means, the argument is often run that the letter of instruction should be circulated to the relevant party for their input and comment, but that they should not then be required to meet any part of the costs of the report. There is undoubtedly a pragmatic attraction to this, not least as written questions can be put to an expert by any party, not just an instructing party, and the presumption is that the costs of producing the replies will in the first instance be met by the instructing party or parties.[120] It may therefore be thought easier to ensure that the expert is asked to consider all matters compendiously, rather than having to respond to subsequent questions by a party who has not taken part in the instruction. Care needs to be exercised, however, both by the parties and the court, if this course is adopted. This is in part because it offends against the principle of the joint apportionment of costs which is enshrined in COPR r125(7). It is also, pragmatically, a course which is likely to lead to substantial problems if the LAA consider that there has been any degree of 'loading' of the costs of an expert report upon a public funding certificate for any party.

12.76 However, the position may now be somewhat more flexible at least where one (or more) parties is of limited means and one party is publicly funded following the decision in *JG v Lord Chancellor and others*.[121] This case was decided in the context of a private law dispute involving a child, but the central principles are equally applicable before the Court of Protection (see also the discussion of this case at paras 6.86 onwards). In this case, the Court of Appeal made a number of general observations, including that:

- no party could be compelled to join in instructing an expert (under the FPR – this also applies to the COPR);
- the involvement of other parties will not necessarily convert an expert instructed on behalf of one party into a single joint expert;

---

118 COPR Pr131(1)/COPR r131(1).
119 COPR Pr131(5)/COPR r131(5).
120 COPR r125(1) and (7). See further para 12.90 below.
121 [2014] EWCA Civ 656, [2014] 2 FLR 1218.

- there are good practical reasons to be cautious about treating an expert as a joint expert, as it would be undesirable for non-instructing parties to be deterred from contributing to an expert's instruction, and thus from providing useful information to an expert, for fear they will be treated as a joint expert;
- if, on proper analysis, the expert is a joint expert, the possible grounds for departing from the principle of equal apportionment could be a) impecuniosity, b) the need to avoid a breach of the ECHR[122] and c) a 'very exceptional case'. If it is established that a lack of an expert report would breach an individual's rights under the ECHR, there was no need to consider exceptionality as an additional requirement.

12.77 It is important to remember that the pressure of work means that a judge at a case management hearing may not have time to master the details of the documents in the case. This means that it is particularly important to flag up all relevant matters clearly (and succinctly) for the judge, ideally in the position statement filed in advance of the hearing (discussed further at paras 10.37 onwards).

12.78 Wherever possible, the court being invited to grant permission to instruct an expert should be asked to give permission to instruct a specific expert, rather than a category of expert. In other words, the identity of the expert together with the professional qualifications should be made clear to the judge at the time that permission is sought, rather than permission being sought to rely upon (say) a consultant psychiatrist to report upon P's capacity in one or more domains. This has two advantages:

- The court can make clear in its reasons for the grant of permission that it has considered the value that the specific expert proposed can add (assuming that such expert is endorsed by the court; if the expert is not, then appropriate steps can then be directed to put forward a suitable alternative for judicial endorsement).
- Where more than one party is to be involved in the instruction of the expert, the order appointing that expert will name them. In the authors' experience, while there is a mechanism in the COPR for the resolution by the court of disputes as to the identity of the

---

122 A failure by the court to allow expert evidence can be a violation of Article 8 ECHR (see *Elsholz v Germany* (2002) 34 EHRR 58).

expert between joint instructing parties,[123] leaving matters open in the order can give rise to unhelpful and time-consuming debates subsequently that can be avoided by ensuring that any such discussions take place prior to the making of the order.

Instructing the expert

12.79 An expert must be instructed before they can report. In other words, they must be provided with:
- a summary of the background to the case;
- a summary of the relevant legal provisions (and of any relevant case-law); and
- relevant documentation.

12.80 The questions upon which their opinion is sought must also be set out with clarity. A sample letter of instruction is included at appendix D below, but particular points to emphasise are that:
- As noted above, the presumption is that expert evidence will be provided by way of an expert jointly instructed by all those parties who wish to submit expert evidence upon a particular issue or issues. In such circumstances, and while the COPR provide for separate instructions to be given by the instructing parties to the expert,[124] courts are in practice astute to seek to ensure that only one letter of instruction is sent, and will use their general case management powers to bring about (if all possible) one letter, agreed, if possible between the instructing parties. This means, in practice, that the solicitors for one of the parties should take the lead in drafting the letter and then circulate it to the other instructing parties for comment. Wherever the Official Solicitor is instructed as P's litigation friend and is participating in the instruction, it is conventional that the solicitors instructed by the Official Solicitor take on the task of producing the first draft. If agreement cannot be reached as to the terms of the letter, it is almost invariably quicker if rival drafts (with the differences clearly marked) are provided in writing along with submissions to the merits of the different drafts to the judge who made the original order granting permission for the judge to make the final decision as to the terms of the letter, rather that engaging in protracted rounds

---

123 COPR Pr130(3)/COPR r130(3) providing that the court can either select the expert from a list prepared or identified by the instructing parties or direct the manner by which the expert is to be selected.
124 COPR r131(2)/COPR r131(2).

Evidence and disclosure 349

of correspondence. Under the Case Management Pilot COPR Pr131(1A) provides, expressly, that, where instructions are to be contained in a jointly agreed letter, in default of agreement the instructions may be determined by the court on the written request of any instructing party copied to the other instructing parties.

- Where an expert is jointly instructed, the expert must be reminded that any communications that they have with one instructing party should be copied to the others; there is a real risk, otherwise, that the independence of the expert will (even if only apparently) be compromised.[125]
- Thought must be given as to the documentation that it is necessary that the expert reviews in order to give their report, and the mechanics by which the expert can review that documentation. In this regard two considerations arise, in particular:
  - The expert may well not need to see the entirety of files held upon P by relevant public bodies, but must be entitled to inspect and/or be provided with copies of sufficient documents in order to be able to reach their conclusions.
  - It is quite possible that the expert will need to see documents relating to P (for instance, their social services files) to which the other parties in the proceedings (most obviously family members) may well not have had sight of and which there are legitimate reasons to suggest the other parties should not see. In *Re L (care assessment: fair trial)*, Munby J (as he then was) held in relation to care proceedings that there might be a breach of Article 6 ECHR (right to a fair trial) where a jointly instructed or other sole expert's report was 'likely to have a preponderant influence on the assessment of the facts' by the court, if a litigant were denied the opportunity, before the expert produced his report, a) to examine and comment on the documents being considered by the expert and b) to cross-examine witnesses interviewed by the expert and on whose evidence the report was based, and hence to participate effectively in the process by which the report was produced.[126] It is suggested that the same principle applies in relation to proceedings under the MCA 2005; this does not necessarily mean that an expert cannot have

125 See in this regard *SMBC v WMP* [2011] EWHC B13 (COP), (2011) 14 CCLR 413, [2011] COPLR Con Vol 1177 at para 57(vii) per HHJ Cardinal (discussions between the Official Solicitor's solicitor and the expert).
126 [2002] EWHC 1379 (Fam), at paras 113–118, applying *Mantovanelli v France* (App No 21497/93) (1997) 24 EHRR 370.

sight of documents withheld from other parties – rather, it means that consideration must be given to the basis upon which those documents are withheld both by the party wishing to withhold those documents and the court. These difficult issues are examined further at paras 12.102 onwards below.
- Arrangements must be made for the expert to be able to visit P (which will, in the majority of cases, be necessary for them to be able to form any proper conclusion as to their capacity and/or best interests[127]), and interview any individuals such as carers or family members whom the expert considers necessary in order to be able to produce a sufficiently rounded picture. If an expert is unable to obtain access to see P because of the actions of a family member, this is something that should be raised with the court at the earliest possible opportunity so that – if appropriate – steps can be taken to consider the making of injunctions (and, ultimately, initiating proceedings for contempt of court).
- While the court is likely to have indicated in the order granting permission the matters to be covered in the report,[128] it is unlikely that the order will set down the questions in detail (nor, in the ordinary run of events, is it likely that the judge making the order will have had sight of the letter of instruction before it is sent out). It is therefore important that care is taken to formulate the questions so as to direct the expert's attention to answering the issues that actually fall for consideration in the case. In the authors' experience, unclear reports are very frequently the result of unclear questions having been asked in the first place (and it is also difficult to 'salvage' such an unclear report by way of questions asked upon receipt of the report, discussed further at para 12.86 below).
- The expert should be reminded that they should exercise extreme care before expressing any provisional views to P: in *SC v BS and A Local Authority*,[129] the expert was criticised for having given an indication to P that he thought she had capacity in the material domains without having read the very extensive records. As Baker J noted: 'Although his comments to her were hedged

---

127 As an independent consultant neuro-psychiatric expert noted in *Wandsworth CCG v IA and TA* [2014] EWHC 990 (COP): 'assessment of capacity based on case notes is of necessity a relatively inadequate substitution for the complex assessments that occurs in a clinical interview' (*IA* at para 43).
128 COPR Pr126(1)/COPR r126(1) provides that the court may give directions as to the matters to be covered in such a report.
129 [2012] COPLR 567.

with qualifications, it was highly probable that [P]'s hopes were raised that she would shortly be allowed to leave her current accommodation.'[130] No expert should give a patient a 'provisional' view of the patient's capacity without reading the patient's history.
- The expert should be reminded that they have the right to ask the court for directions to assist them in carrying out their functions as an expert.[131] While in the first instance, an expert would usually be expected to look to the representatives of the instructing parties to assist them to overcome any logistical difficulties, experts must, themselves, take responsibility for ensuring that they are satisfied that they have obtained the information necessary to report to the court. In *SMBC v WMP*, HHJ Cardinal indicated that, as a matter of good practice: 'An expert ... ought ... to seek clarifications and raise questions under r129 Court of Protection Rules 2007 before completing a report referring to lacunae in the information before him.'[132]
- Instructions to an expert are not privileged against disclosure:[133] in other words, nothing should be put to an expert in a letter of instruction which cannot properly be seen by all the other parties to the proceedings.

The duties upon an expert

12.81 The expert must assist the court on the matters within his or her expertise.[134] This encompasses two equally important aspects:
- No matter who the expert is instructed by or who pays them, the expert does not owe their duty to any party or parties, but to the court (and, to that end, their report is to be addressed to the court, rather than to any party from whom they have received their instructions[135]). An expert whose report lacks objectivity may themselves be at risk not just of having all or part of their fees

---

130 Para 39.
131 COPR Pr129(1)/COPR r129(1). Any such application must (in the absence of direction to the contrary) be provided in advance to the instructing party and to the other parties to the proceedings.
132 *SMBC v WMP* [2011] EWHC B13 (COP), [2011] COPLR Con Vol 1177, (2011) 14 CCLR 413, at para 57(i).
133 COPR r126(5).
134 COPR Pr122/COPR r122.
135 PD 15A para 8.

disallowed, but may, themselves, be at risk of having to pay costs incurred by other parties in consequence of their report.[136]
- The expert must only advise upon the matters within their expertise, and make clear if a matter upon which their opinion is sought lies outside their expertise.[137] While this is in large part, a matter for the expert, it also reflects the need to ensure that the right person is chosen by the instructing parties. In *SC v BS and A Local Authority*,[138] the court (in granting permission for another expert to be instructed to report upon capacity, where the first expert, although a nationally recognised expert on autism, had not demonstrated the requisite degree of knowledge of the MCA 2005 but offered to undergo training) noted that: 'It cannot be satisfactory to seek the expert opinion from someone who perceives the need to undergo training before he can give that opinion.'[139]

The expert's report – content

12.82 PD 15A, amplifying COPR Pr126(2)–(4)/COPR r126(2)–(4),[140] sets out in some detail the requirements that apply both as to the form and the content of an expert's report, and they are not rehearsed here, save to emphasise that an expert report which does not comply with the requirements of paragraph 15 of PD 15A is unlikely to be accepted by the court, not just because of the formal defects, but more importantly because paragraph 15 sets out the 'route map' by which an expert can produce a report that establishes the proper building blocks by which reliable conclusions can be reached. As Henderson J put it in *Re S*: 'The rules are there for a good reason, and if they are not complied with a report, even from the most eminent of experts, is likely to lack the transparency and objectivity which the court rightly insists upon in expert evidence.'[141]

136 See, by analogy, *Phillips v Symes* [2004] EWHC 2330 (Ch), [2005] 1 WLR 2043. COPLR r166 provides for costs orders to be made against non-parties.
137 PD 15A para 6(a). See also in this regard *A Local Authority v M & Ors* [2014] EWCOP 33, [2015] COPLR 6 at 88 per Baker J: 'in assessing the expert evidence ... the court must be careful to ensure that each expert keeps within the bounds of their own expertise and defers where appropriate to the expertise of others – see the observations of Eleanor King J in *Re S* [2009] EWHC 2115 Fam.'
138 [2012] COPLR 567.
139 *SC* at para 37 per Baker J.
140 PD15A has not been amended under the Case Management Pilot.
141 [2010] EWHC 2405 (COP), [2010] COPLR Con Vol 1112, at para 146.

12.83 Further, and as set out above (para 12.60), an expert must be very careful in their report not to seek to determine factual issues that are outside their direct experience. If – as is regularly the case in reports relating to best interests – the view of the expert as to where P's best interests will lie will vary depending upon which interpretation of the facts is preferred, the proper course of action is for the expert to set out both alternative chains of reasoning from factual scenario to opinion as to best interests. In other words, the expert should give their opinion as to where P's best interests will lie depending on whether the court accepts that the particular factual issue(s) is/are made out. The most obvious example is where the allegation is made that a named individual has abused or otherwise caused harm to come to P; in such a case, the expert should give their view as to (say) contact between P and that individual based upon either a) the allegation being established; or b) the allegation not being established (see chapter 14 below for further discussion of the resolution of factual disputes).

12.84 There are two particular risks that the courts have identified that experts must guard against in the assessment of capacity:

- The first, which applies equally (if not with greater force) to those involved in the ongoing care and treatment of P, is succumbing to the 'protection imperative', namely feeling 'drawn towards an outcome that is more protective of the adult and thus . . . fail[ing] to carry out an assessment of capacity that is detached and objective';[142]
- The second is not paying sufficient weight to the fact that (as necessarily occurs in most cases) the expert only has the benefit of a limited exposure to P by comparison with the more 'longitudinal' picture enjoyed by other professionals with longer-term contact with P. While on the one hand, this may make it easier to produce a detached report, the risk is that the resulting report will represent a snapshot alone.[143] There is, in reality, unlikely to be any way in which this risk can be entirely avoided; the best that can be done is to ensure that the expert is alive to its existence.

---

142 *PH v A Local Authority and others* [2011] EWHC 1704 (Fam), [2012] COPLR 128 at para 16(xiii) per Baker J. See also *CC v KK and STCC* [2012] EWHC 2136 (COP), [2012] COPLR 627 and also *X and Y v Croatia* (App No 5193/90, decision of 3 January 2011) (criticism by the ECtHR of the fact that the psychiatrist charged with determining X's capacity saw her for only 20 minutes, at a time when she was 'tired and under the influence of medication' (para 87)).
143 *PH* at para 56.

354 Court of Protection Handbook / chapter 12

Once the report has been provided

12.85   An expert report disclosed by a party can be used by any party as evidence at any hearing in the proceedings. The report cannot be used by a party to whom it has been disclosed for any other purpose, unless:
- the document has been read to or by the court or referred to at a public hearing; or
- the court otherwise permits.[144]

12.86   As noted above, any party (not just an instructing party) can put written questions to an expert.[145] That entitlement is limited in that (subject to a different order of the court or the agreement of all the relevant parties[146]):
- the questions can only be put once;
- must be put within 28 days beginning with the date upon which the report was served; and
- can only be for purpose of clarification of the report.[147]

This last restriction is particularly important – courts take a very dim view of attempts to cross-examine experts in writing. Both to try to stop such questions being put and also so as to ensure that the expert is not bombarded with a sequence of questions from different parties, judges sometimes direct that any questions are to be put via the solicitors for one of the parties, most obviously those instructed on behalf of the Official Solicitor where P is a party and represented by the Official Solicitor.

12.87   The Case Management Pilot PD imposes a further obligation in relation to putting written questions to an expert, namely that the question must be copied and sent to the other parties at the same time as they are sent to the expert.[148]

If an expert fails to respond to a question put to them under the procedure put to them, then the court may order:
- that the instructing party or parties may not rely on the evidence of the expert; and/or

---

144 COPR Pr5.10/COPR r18.
145 COPR Pr125(1)/COPR r125(1)
146 COPR Pr125(3)/COPR r125(3) also provides for a practice direction to make alternative provision; none at present does so.
147 COPR Pr125(2)–(3)/COPR r125(2)–(3).
148 COPR Pr125(2)(d).

- that the party may not recover all or part of the fees and expenses of the expert or part from any other party.[149]

12.88 Any answers given by the expert to questions put under the procedure set out above are treated as part of their report,[150] and subject to any different order of the court or final costs order, the instructing party or parties are responsible for meeting the costs both of the original report and of the answers.[151]

12.89 If permission has been granted to two (or more) experts to report upon an issue, then specific powers are granted to the court in addition to its general case management powers contained in COPR r25 and 85 (COPR Pr3.1 and Pr3.7). The court may at any stage direct that the experts meet for purposes of identifying and discussing the expert issues in the proceedings and, where possible, reaching an agreed opinion on those issues.[152] The court can specify the issues the experts must discuss, and can direct that the experts prepare a joint statement for the court setting out issues upon which they agree and issues upon which they disagree (together with a summary of their reasons for disagreeing).[153] Whether contained in a statement or otherwise, the contents of the discussions may, absent order to the contrary, be referred to at any hearing or at any stage in the proceedings (including, although the COPR do not say so expressly, for purposes of considering the conduct of any party for purposes of determining the final allocation of costs).[154]

12.90 The MCA 2005 and COPR are silent as to what should happen in the event that a party who has taken part in a joint instruction is dissatisfied with the expert report. By analogy with the position that prevails under the CPR, it is suggested that: 'If having obtained a joint expert's report, a party, for reasons which are not fanciful, wishes to obtain further information before making a decision as to whether or not there is a particular part (or indeed the whole) of the expert's report which he or she may wish to challenge, then they should, subject to the discretion of the court, be permitted to obtain that evidence.'[155] In the light of the statutory provisions and authorities discussed above, it is clear that the court will be astute to ensure that every other avenue is explored first before such permission is granted.

149 COPR Pr125(5)–(6)/COPR r125(5)–(6).
150 COPR Pr125(4)/COPR r125(4).
151 COPR Pr125(7)/COPR r125(7).
152 COPR Pr128(1)/COPR r128(1).
153 COPR Pr128(2)–(3)/COPR r128(2)–(3).
154 COPR Pr128(4)/COPR r128(4).
155 *Daniels v Walker (practice note)* [2000] 1 WLR 1382 at 1387 per Lord Woolf MR.

Disclosure

Overview

12.91 COPR Part 16 contains provisions relating to disclosure which are based upon those in CPR Part 31. In both, a party discloses a document by stating that it exists or has existed;[156] the CPR defines a 'document' broadly as 'anything in which information of any description is recorded.'[157] While no equivalent description is given in the COPR it is suggested that the same definition should apply.

12.92 Because proceedings before the Court of Protection are, at heart, inquisitorial rather than adversarial,[158] it has become increasingly apparent that the provisions of COPR Part 16 are not altogether well-suited to the requirements of applications under the MCA 2005. In *Enfield LBC v SA and others*,[159] McFarlane J (as he then was) commented adversely on the fact that the rules contained in COPR Part 16 were based upon:

> ... ordinary civil litigation with the expectation that disclosure will be based on whether documents 'adversely affect [a party's] own case' or 'support another party's case' (COPR r133(2)(b)) whereas the approach of the family court is that there is a duty to give *the court* all relevant material.[160]

He continued that there could be:

> ... no justification for there being a difference of this degree on the issue of disclosure between the family court and the Court of Protection in fact finding cases of this type where really the process and the issues are essentially identical whether the vulnerable complainant is a young child or an incapacitated adult. For the future in such cases in the Court of Protection it would seem to be justified for the court to make an order for 'specific disclosure' under COPR 2007 r133(3) requiring all parties to give 'full and frank disclosure' of all relevant material.[161]

See further in this regard, para 12.101 below.

12.93 Because they essentially do not 'fit' the approach of the Court of Protection, the majority of the provisions relating to disclosure in

---

156 CPR 31.1; COPR r132.
157 CPR 31.4.
158 *Re G* [2014] EWCOP 1361, [2014] COPLR 416 at para 26 per Sir James Munby P, endorsing *Cheshire West and Cheshire Council v P and M* [2011] EWHC 1330 (Fam), (2012) 15 CCLR 48, [2011] COPLR Con Vol 273 at para 52 per Baker J.
159 [2010] EWHC 196 (Admin), [2010] COPLR Con Vol 362.
160 *SA* [2010] EWHC 196 (Admin) at para 57 (emphasis in original).
161 *SA* at para 58.

Evidence and disclosure 357

COPR Part 16 will not be invoked in most applications. It may be that this will change in future, as the Case Management Pilot directs that the court must in relation to cases on the welfare pathway give specific consideration to disclosure at the case management hearing (see further para 10.21).[162] For the present, however, these provisions are not discussed in detail in this chapter, the focus rather being upon the disclosure issues that arise most commonly in practice.

Disclosure issues in practice

12.94 It is important to note that disclosure issues can arise at the very outset of proceedings in (at least) two ways.

12.95 First, if an application is brought on an ex parte basis (ie in the absence of the respondent) then, as discussed at para 10.68 above, there is a duty upon the advocate making that application to give full and frank disclosure of all relevant matters, including those tending to suggest that the application should not be brought.

12.96 Second, the decision in *Loughlin v Singh and others*[163] stands as a clear endorsement of the propositions:

- that the rules that apply in civil proceedings as regards the privileged status of expert reports do not apply before the Court of Protection (see further para 12.116 below); and
- (in consequence) that there is a duty to bring relevant material contained in expert evidence within the possession of the applicant to the attention of the court at the outset of proceedings.

12.97 In that case, an application had been made to the Court of Protection for a professional deputy to be appointed to manage the property and affairs of an adult who had suffered a number of serious injuries in a road traffic accident. The solicitors making the application were in possession of expert evidence which suggested that he *had* the requisite capacity, but did not bring this to the attention of the court. A district judge appointed the deputy without a hearing. In subsequent personal injury proceedings, the issue of the man's capacity to manage his property and affairs was hotly contested by the defendant. Kenneth Parker J found – on a fine balance[164] – that the claimant lacked capacity, such that there was ultimately no inconsistency between his decision and that which underpinned the appointment of the deputy.

162 Case Management Pilot PD para 4.5(l).
163 [2013] EWHC 1641 (QB), [2013] COPLR 371.
164 Para 45.

The judge was, however, highly critical of the actions of the solicitors, noting in an appendix to his judgment that:

> 14. In my view, this was a case where *all* available medical evidence relevant to the issue of capacity should have been disclosed to the court [of Protection] . . . It is then almost certain that the court, faced with this welter of conflicting medical opinion and aware [of other unsatisfactory aspects of an expert's report] would have refused to determine the application on paper, but would have insisted on an oral hearing at which the issue could have been fully and properly considered. I am unwilling to speculate as to what the outcome might have been if a proper procedure had been followed at that time, but the possibility cannot be ruled out that the court might at that time have found that the claimant had capacity. In the light of my own conclusion such a finding, although not unreasonable, would have been incorrect.
>
> 15. All I need add is that the lamentable failures that occurred here, and the invidious position in which the judge in the Court of Protection was unwittingly placed, must never be repeated. The issue of capacity is of very great importance, and all involved must ensure that the Court of Protection has all the material which, on proper reflection, is necessary for a just and accurate decision.

12.98 While the decision in *Loughlin v Singh* is not, strictly, binding on practitioners appearing before the Court of Protection, as it was a decision taken in the Queen's Bench Division, nor do these passages appear to reflect argument advanced to the court based upon analysis either of the MCA 2005 or of the COPR, it is suggested that the passages set out above are entirely correct in their approach and should be followed.

12.99 Once proceedings are under way, it would appear that the injunction given by McFarlane J in *SA* discussed at para 12.92 above is routinely ignored, orders for full and frank disclosure in welfare proceedings being made very rarely (if at all). It is to be hoped that this will change in light of the specific focus upon disclosure in the Case Management Pilot.

12.100 It is also at present unusual for the Court of Protection routinely to make an order for general disclosure, ie for each party to disclose those documents on which he relies, and documents which adversely affect his own case; adversely affect another party's case; or support another party's case. Indeed, in some cases, no disclosure orders will be made at all.

Evidence and disclosure 359

12.101 In welfare cases, however, orders are commonly made for the provision of specific categories of documents (for instance of medical or social services records), not to all the parties to the proceedings, but rather only to those with a specific need to have sight of them. This happens most obviously where P is a party to the proceedings and orders are made requiring (for instance) either all or part of the records held by the local authority's social services department relating to P to be provided to their litigation friend. The authors' experience is that these orders are made without judicial examination of the basis of the power under which they are made. It may, on a proper analysis, actually be that they are not specific disclosure orders[165] at all, but rather orders made under the provisions of COPR r107 (discussed at para 12.31 above) for the provision of information that one party has unique access to.

Withholding disclosure on confidentiality/welfare grounds

12.102 No matter the power under which such orders are made, one question arises with some regularity, namely the extent to which it is permissible for orders to be made allowing for documents to be seen by one party but not by others. Orders are regularly made providing (for instance) that social services records relating to P are to be provided to P's litigation friend (and can, in turn, be provided to any independent expert instructed to report to the court), but either making no provision for those records to be provided to other parties to the proceedings, or giving P's litigation friend a 'vetting' role so as to allow their litigation friend to determine which documents should be provided to other parties. The COPR do not contain any test or threshold for denying disclosure (whether to one or to more than one party), rule 138 merely providing in material part that:

(1) A party who wishes to claim that he has a right or duty to withhold inspection of a document, or part of a document, must state in writing –
 (a) that he has such a right or duty; and
 (b) the grounds on which he claims that right of duty.

12.103 Moreover, as COPR r138 can only be invoked at the time that a disclosure list is provided,[166] and as such disclosure lists are rarely, if ever, in fact used in the Court of Protection, it would appear that rule 138 does not, in fact, serve as the basis upon which disclosure of such

165 Made under COPR r133(3).
166 COPR r138(2).

materials as social work records is limited. The precise basis upon which such orders are made is therefore not entirely clear.

12.104 Following the decision of Sir James Munby P in *RC v CC and X Local Authority*,[167] it is, however, clear that the court does have the power to withhold disclosure of reports or records. *RC* did not spell out the basis upon which the power arose,[168] but it is suggested that it is perhaps most obviously under the court's general powers under COPR r25 (COPR Pr3.1 for cases falling under the Case Management Pilot).

12.105 The decision in *RC* also set out the test for the circumstances under which such orders can be made where a party wishes to withhold documents on the basis of their confidentiality and/or their adverse impact upon P (the position where disclosure is withheld on the basis of privilege is discussed at paras 12.112 onwards below).

12.106 Before addressing the decision in *RC*, it is worth noting the competing principles in play, in particular:

- P's right to the maintenance of confidentiality in relation to what will often be highly sensitive personal data (a right which is recognised at common law and by Article 8 ECHR right to respect for private and family life), and is enshrined in statutory provisions such as the Data Protection Act 1998). In the case of children, there has also been a historical acceptance that the particular circumstances in which social services records are created give rise to a presumption that they should be immune from disclosure on a public interest basis.[169]
- The rights of other parties to have sight of, and the ability to respond to, information contained in those documents if any reliance is to be placed by the court upon that information, whether that reliance is to be direct – ie the judge himself reading the documents – or indirect – ie an expert reporting to the court based upon the documents. The proper exercise of those rights is integral to enabling the fairness of the proceedings, a principle enshrined both at common law and in Article 6 ECHR.

12.107 In *RC*, Sir James Munby P drew direct analogies between the position that prevailed in proceedings in relation to children and those that

---

167 [2014] EWHC 131 (COP), (2014) 17 CCLR 127.
168 See para 20.
169 *Re M (a minor) (disclosure of material)* [1990] 2 FLR 36. This case must now be treated with caution: *Dunn v Durham CC* [2012] EWCA Civ 1654, [2013] 1 WLR 2305 at para 45 per Munby LJ.

should apply in the Court of Protection. He placed particular reliance upon three decisions,[170] and his conclusions can be summarised thus:

- It is a fundamental principle of fairness that a party is entitled to the disclosure of all materials which may be taken into account by the court when reaching a decision adverse to that party.
- When deciding whether to direct that a party referred to documentation should not be able to inspect the part which refers to them, the court should first consider whether disclosure of the material would involve a real possibility of significant harm to P.
- If it would, the court should next consider whether the overall interests of P would benefit from non-disclosure, weighing on the one hand the interest of P in having the material properly tested, and on the other both the magnitude of the risk that harm will occur and the gravity of the harm if it does occur.
- If the court is satisfied that the interests of P point towards non-disclosure, the next and final step is for the court to weigh that consideration, and its strength in the circumstances of the case, against the interest of the parent or other party in having an opportunity to see and respond to the material. In the latter regard the court should take into account the importance of the material to the issues in the case.
- In all cases, the test for non-disclosure is whether it is strictly necessary to meet the risk identified by the court.[171]

12.108 Sir James Munby P also noted in RC that consideration should always be given to the fact that disclosure is never a binary exercise, and a proper evaluation and weighing of the various interests may lead to the conclusion that i) there should be disclosure but ii) the disclosure needs to be subject to safeguards such as limits to the use that may be made of the documents, in particular so as to limit the release into the public domain of intensely personal information about third parties. Further, he emphasised, the position initially arrived at is never set in stone; it may be appropriate to proceed one step at a time.[172]

12.109 A further factor that did not arise in RC but may well do in a future case is where P themselves has views as to whether or not

---

170 In re D (minors) (adoption reports: confidentiality) [1996] AC 593; Re B (disclosure to other parties) [2001] 2 FLR 1017; and Dunn v Durham CC [2012] EWCA Civ 1654, [2013] 1 WLR 2305.
171 See paras 15–17.
172 See paras 18–19.

information should be disclosed to a particular party or parties. Whilst those views will not be determinative, it is likely that considerable weight will be placed upon them by analogy with the position adopted in *Local Authority X v HI*,[173] concerning whether sensitive information revealed by a boy subject to care proceedings which he did not wish disclosed to his parents or stepmother.

12.110 *RC* is of also significance because Sir James Munby P confirmed that the first instance judge had had the power to direct that some documents could be disclosed solely to the advocate for a party, with a direction that the representative could not disclose or discuss it with the client.[174] He made it clear that such limited disclosure can only be ordered if there is clear and express consent on the party of the affected party's legal representative, who should only give such consent if they are satisfied that they can do so without harming their client's case.[175]

12.111 Notwithstanding the endorsement by Sir James Munby P of 'confidentiality rings', it is suggested that any legal adviser should be very cautious before advancing or agreeing to one. The 'very serious problems' it creates between lawyer and client have led to doubts being placed upon the decision in *Mohammed* upon which Sir James Munby P relied.[176] The decision in *RC* may therefore not necessarily be the end of the story in this regard.

Privilege

12.112 Disclosure of documents can also be resisted on the basis that they are subject to legal professional privilege: ie that they represent 'protected' communications between lawyer and client (and, in certain circumstances, with third parties).

12.113 This is a very large topic. Space precludes a detailed discussion of it here,[177] but the position is set out in summary form in the paragraphs that follow. These paragraphs must be read subject to the caveat that, with the limited exception of the case of *Loughlin v Singh* discussed above (para 12.96), there has been no reported judicial

---

173 [2016] EWHC 1123 (Fam).
174 See paras 21–23. The appeal was allowed in this regard because of a doubt as to the basis upon which the power had been exercised.
175 *RC* at para 38, endorsing dicta of Moses LJ in *R (Mohammed) v Secretary of State for Defence* [2012] EWHC 3454 (Admin), [2014] 1 WLR 1071.
176 *AHK, AM, AS, FM v Secretary of State for the Home Department* [2013] EWHC 1426 (Admin) at paras 20–28 per Ouseley J.
177 The reader is directed, in particular, to C Passmore *Privilege*, Sweet & Maxwell, 3rd edn, 2013.

consideration of the application of the law of privilege to proceedings before the Court of Protection. The paragraphs below therefore represent the authors' view that the closest analogy to such proceedings are those involving children, and that the principles derived in those proceedings can and should be applied before the Court of Protection.

12.114 There are two forms of legal professional privilege: legal advice privilege and litigation privilege.

- **Legal advice privilege** protects confidential communications between a client and their professional legal adviser that is made for the purpose of seeking or giving any legal advice or related legal assistance. It is not necessary for it to apply that there is litigation in prospect.[178]
- **Litigation privilege** protects confidential communications between either the client or their legal adviser or their legal adviser and a third party (such as a factual or an expert witness), where such communications come into existence for the dominant purpose of being used in connection with actual, pending or contemplated litigation.[179]

12.115 Where a litigation friend has been appointed to act on behalf of a party (whether that be P or a protected party: see chapter 11), and whilst there is no reported case from the Court of Protection on the point, it is suggested that for these purposes the litigation friend stands in the shoes of the client. By analogy, we note that the Court of Appeal accepted in *RP v Nottingham City Council* (it appears without argument) that the file maintained by a solicitor retained by the Official Solicitor where he was acting as litigation friend for a protected party in care proceedings contained privileged material.[180]

12.116 Litigation privilege is 'essentially a creature of adversarial proceedings'; it does not therefore extend to protect expert reports obtained in the context of care proceedings involving children.[181] It is suggested that this applies equally in the context of proceedings under the MCA 2005. Indeed, this would appear to be (albeit implicitly rather than expressly) the basis upon which Kenneth Parker J held in *Loughlin v Singh* (para 12.96 above) that all relevant

178 Passmore, *Privilege*, para 1-002.
179 Passmore, *Privilege*, para 1-002.
180 [2008] EWCA Civ 462, (2008) 11 CCLR 316 at paras 34–35, per Wall LJ.
181 *Re L (a minor) (police investigation: privilege)* [1997] AC 16 at 27 per Lord Jauncey.

expert reports in the possession of the claimant's solicitors should have been disclosed to the Court of Protection when making an application for the appointment of a deputy to manage his property and affairs. It should also be noted that it is clear from the COPR that *instructions* to an expert are not privileged against disclosure.[182]

12.117 It would, further, appear that it may well be the case that litigation privilege cannot be claimed in the context of other classes of documents or correspondence created in the context of proceedings before the Court of Protection.[183] Moreover, even if litigation privilege can be claimed, a number of family law cases have suggested this may be overridden by a duty to disclose documents where the court must determine what is in the best interests of the child.[184] It is suggested that such an approach would be likely also to be taken by the Court of Protection.

12.118 The position as regards legal advice privilege, however, is very different. Save for rare exceptions involving fraud or misconduct, the privilege has been held to be an absolute one even in respect of proceedings involving the determination of the best interests of children.[185] It is suggested that the same applies in proceedings under the MCA 2005 so as to protect lawyer-client communications, communications between a litigation friend appointed to act on behalf of P (or a protected party other than P, or a child) and the lawyers that that litigation friend has retained.

12.119 It should be emphasised that the mere fact that a person lacks capacity to conduct the proceedings does not mean that they should not be afforded the same protections as would be afforded to others. This means that, for instance, a litigation friend and lawyers instructed on behalf of P (or a protected party other than P or a child) must be very careful before putting before the court, whether by way of attendance notes of visits or otherwise, material that might incriminate their client if factual allegations are made against the individual in question.[186]

---

182 COPR Pr126(5)/COPR r126(5).
183 Following the approach adopted by the House of Lords in *Three Rivers (No 6)* [2004] UKHL 48, [2005] 1 AC 610.
184 See, in particular, *Oxfordshire CC v M* [1994] 2 WLR 393.
185 *AB (care proceedings: disclosure of medical evidence to police)* [2002] EWHC 2198 (Fam), [2003] 1 FLR 579.
186 See, by analogy, *Re E (A Child)* [2016] EWCA Civ 473.

CHAPTER 13

Publicity, privacy and confidentiality

13.1	Introduction
13.6	The Administration of Justice Act 1960
13.7	The Court of Protection Rules
13.13	The Transparency Pilot
13.25	The Pilot Order
13.43	Assessment
13.44	Cases outside the Transparency Pilot
	Serious medical treatment cases
	Contempt of court
13.61	**The approach of the court to reporting restrictions**
13.71	Restrictions after P's death
13.82	Restrictions on disclosure of documents

Introduction

13.1 The Court of Protection's approach to public and media access has changed dramatically in the two years since the first edition of this book. On 16 January 2014 Sir James Munby P had issued guidance entitled *Transparency in the Court of Protection: publication of judgments*.[1] The President considered that too few judgments in the Court of Protection were made available to the public and that greater transparency was needed to build both understanding of and confidence in the court system. He made it clear that this was part of an incremental approach and that the guidance would be followed by further guidance, then practice directions and changes to the Rules, with a view to harmonising practice in the Court of Protection with that in the Family Court.[2]

13.2 Limited changes were made in July 2015 through amendments to the COPR r91 and to Practice Direction 13A. More fundamental change was implemented with the (initially) six-month Transparency Pilot in January 2016. As explained below at para 13.14 this reversed the default position that the majority of hearings should be in private and instead applies a presumption that hearings will take place in public, with reporting restrictions to protect the identity of P and P's family, unless there is 'good reason' to order otherwise. The Transparency Pilot was extended in July 2016 to last until 31 August 2017.

13.4 In addition to the Transparency Pilot, the provisions governing hearings and publicity have been re-numbered in cases falling within the Case Management Pilot. In cases to which the Pilot applies, the relevant rules are no longer to be found in Part 13 (COPR rr90–93), but rather in Pilot Part 4, COPR Pr4. Practice Direction 13A is now PD Pilot 4A in cases to which the Pilot applies. For the most part, this chapter refers to the numbering that relates to the Case Management Pilot, but will also refer to the numbering where it is considered that this may help the reader. This applies in particular to cases concerning serious medical treatment, which fall outside both the Transparency Pilot and may (as noted in para 4.101 above) fall outside the Case Management Pilot as well.

---

1 Available at: www.judiciary.gov.uk/Resources/JCO/Documents/Guidance/transparency-in-the-cop.pdf.
2 *Transparency in the Court of Protection* [2014] EWCOP B2 paras 5, 6.

13.5 In this chapter, we:
- set out the relevant provisions of in the Administration of Justice Act 1960;
- set out the rules and explain the modifications as a result of the rule changes in 2015;
- explain the implications of the Transparency Pilot;
- consider the position in cases which fall outside the pilot (ie serious medical treatment cases and committal proceedings); and
- consider the issues that may arise in relation to anonymisation.

The Administration of Justice Act 1960

13.6 It is important to be aware of section 12 of the Administration of Justice Act (AJA) 1960, as amended by MCA 2005 Sch 6 para 10. The relevant part of section 12 reads:

Publication of information relating to proceedings in private

12 (1) The publication of information relating to proceedings before any court sitting in private shall not of itself be contempt of court except in the following cases, that is to say–
(a) where the proceedings–
   (i) relate to the exercise of the inherent jurisdiction of wthe High Court with respect to minors;
   (ii) are brought under the Children Act 1989; or
   (iii) otherwise relate wholly or mainly to the maintenance or upbringing of a minor;
(b) where the proceedings are brought under the Mental Capacity Act 2005 or under any provision of the Mental Health Act 1983 authorising an application or reference to be made to a Mental Health Review Tribunal or to a county court . . .

Therefore it is a contempt of court to publish information relating to Court of Protection proceedings when the court is sitting in private. This applies whether or not the court has made any order restricting publication of information about a specific case.

The Court of Protection Rules

13.7 COPR Pilot Part 4/COPR Part 13 deals with hearings. It is supported by two Practice Directions: Practice Direction Pilot 4A (PD Pilot 4A/PD 13A) and the Practice Direction: Transparency Pilot ('the Transparency PD').

13.8 As it will be seen, the rules provide the 'general rule' that hearings are heard in private. The rules contain a degree of flexibility with judges having discretion to allow the publication of information or the attendance of members of the public or the media. Departure from the general rule requires 'good reason'.[3]

13.9 These rules are still in force, but as we will see have been modified in their application by the Transparency Pilot. Before considering this however we note that in July 2015 PD Pilot 4A/PD 13A was amended by adding a new Part 3. These sensible amendments allow for the communication of information without the need for formal authorisation by the court, for example by a party to their GP, to enable them to receive confidential support, or their MP to pursue a complaint. Paragraph 31 of PD 13A/Pilot PD4A makes clear that communication for these purposes will not constitute contempt of court. The court can make a specific direction limiting communication of information if it considers that such is required in a particular case.[4]

13.10 Paragraph 33 of PD Pilot 4A/PD 13A sets out the circumstances in which information about proceedings can be released, for example to a party, a party's legal representative or accredited legal representative (or ALR, see chapter 10), an expert or author of a report directed under MCA 2005 s49 (see para 12.45) as well as the Director of Legal Aid casework.

13.11 Paragraph 34 of PD Pilot 4A/PD 13A reads:

(1) A party or the legal representative of a party, on behalf of and upon the instructions of that party, may communicate information relating to the proceedings to any person where necessary to enable that party–
 (a) by confidential discussion, to obtain support, advice or assistance in the conduct of the proceedings;
 (b) to engage in mediation or other forms of non-court dispute resolution; (c) to make and pursue a complaint against a person or body concerned in the proceedings; or
 (d) to make and pursue a complaint regarding the law, policy or procedure relating to proceedings in the Court of Protection.

13.12 There are restrictions on onward disclosure. It should be noted that if information is communicated under paragraph 34(1)(a) of PD Pilot 4A/PD 13A – perhaps to a party's GP or counsellor – the person who receives the information must not pass it on to anyone else. Further communication is permitted where the initial disclosure is made under paragraph 34(1) (b), (c) or (d), either to take part in some form of ADR or to make a relevant complaint. In these cases success-

---

3 COPR Pr4.4(1).
4 PD1 3A/Pilot PD 4A para 31.

ive communication is permitted but only with the agreement of the party who communicated the information in the first place and for the original purpose. The provisions for onward disclosure appear at paragraph 35 of PD Pilot 4A/PD 13A.

The Transparency Pilot

13.13 The Transparency Pilot ('the Pilot') was announced in November 2015. It was not preceded by consultation. The key documents can be found at www.courtofprotectionhandbook.com. These are:
a) The Practice Direction (as subsequently amended in July 2016 to extend the Pilot to August 2017 and to provide that the order to be made is no longer that contained in the annex to the PD but rather that approved by the President of the Court of Protection and published on the judicial website at www.judiciary.gov.uk/publication-court/court-of-protection;
b) The Pilot Order, which, as noted immediately above, may be varied from time to time (the most recent version will always be found on the Court of Protection Handbook website); and
c) The Vice-President's note explaining the Pilot.

13.14 The Transparency PD provides that, where the Transparency Pilot applies, the court will ordinarily make an order that the hearing shall be in public and at the same time impose reporting restrictions.[5] Thus, it reverses the presumption that hearings will be in private. Now the default position is that they will be in public with standard orders to 'ensure the anonymity of P and, where appropriate, other persons'.[6]

13.15 The practice direction applies to hearings in all proceedings except those cases where there are already established arrangements for them to be heard in public (serious medical treatment cases, which continue to be governed by PD 9E and committal hearings – see below at paras 13.42 onwards).

13.16 The Pilot applies to hearings which were listed on or after 29 January 2016. Thus, cases which commenced before the pilot started were not exempt, although the fact that there had been earlier private hearings in a case is a relevant factor in the court's decision-making if it is considering departing from the (new) general rule that the case will be heard in public.

---

5 Transparency PD para 2.1.
6 Transparency PD para 1.1.

13.17 Paragraph 2.1 of the Transparency PD explains that where the pilot scheme applies the court will ordinarily direct that any attended hearing shall be in public and will make a standard order in relation to the publication of proceedings. So, once the Pilot order has been made it is in place for the remainder of the case and all attended hearings will be in public. There is therefore no need for the court to make more than one Pilot order. A 'dispute resolution hearing' for a case on the property and affairs pathway is not considered to be an attended hearing for the purpose of the Transparency PD.[7]

13.18 Paragraph 2.4 of the Transparency PD allows the court not to make an order under para 2.1, but only if it considers there is 'good reason' for not making the order.

13.19 Paragraph 2.5 of the Transparency PD sets out some of the factors that the court will consider when deciding if there is 'good reason' not to make an order that the hearing should be in public. These are:

...the need to protect P or another person involved in the proceedings;
(b) the nature of the evidence in the proceedings;
(c) whether earlier hearings in the proceedings have taken place in private;
(d) whether the court location where the hearing will be held has facilities appropriate to allowing general public access to the hearing, and whether it would be practicable or proportionate to move to another location or hearing room;
(e) whether there is any risk of disruption to the hearing if there is general public access to it;
(f) whether, if there is good reason for not allowing general public access, there also exists good reason to deny access to duly accredited representatives of news gathering and reporting organisations.
(2) In sub-paragraph (1)(f), 'duly accredited' refers to accreditation in accordance with any administrative scheme for the time being approved for the purposes of this pilot by the Lord Chancellor.

13.20 It should be noted however that the court is not expected to take a binary approach and either make a standard Pilot Order or no such order at all. Instead, para 2.4 provides that the court should always consider as an alternative making an order under that only part of the hearing will be in public or that some persons or classes of persons should be excluded.

---

7 Transparency PD para 2.2, see further para 8.36.

13.21   In *V v Associated Newspapers Ltd and others*[8] Charles J gave the example of a hypothetical case which involved a celebrity but was otherwise not out of the ordinary. In such a hearing the court would be exercising a well-known decision-making process and the impossibility of providing effective anonymisation might lead to a decision to order a private hearing.

13.22   In his accompanying Note on the Pilot,[9] Charles J commented that it is important that reasons are given for any decisions not to make a pilot order. He encouraged judges who make such decisions to give a judgment, which will be a public document explaining his or her reasons for their decision and setting out who took part in the application or consideration. Judges were encouraged to provide details and/or a copy to the Vice-President. It will be seen that the expectation is that a Pilot Order will be the norm.

13.23   Paragraph 2.6 of the Transparency PD provides that:

> Where the court makes an order pursuant to paragraph 2.1 or 2.4 that an attended hearing or part of it is to be in public, the court will grant, to any person who would have been entitled under the Legal Services Act 2007 to exercise rights of audience at that hearing if such an order had not been made and the hearing was held in private (and who is not otherwise entitled to exercise such rights), the equivalent rights of audience at that attended hearing and any further attended hearing, unless the court is satisfied that there is good reason not to do so.

13.24   This was a late addition to the scheme, after it was pointed out by several solicitors who had seen the documentation in its draft form that the effect of holding public hearings would be to deprive them of their rights of audience in the Court of Protection. The new provision does however give rise to the question of when there might be good reason not to allow a solicitor to appear in a public hearing in the Court of Protection. We are not aware of any reported cases in which this has been considered.

The Pilot Order

13.25   As noted above, the extension of the Transparency Pilot in July 2016 saw some modifications to the Pilot. In particular, the model Pilot Order has been simplified to reduce the requirements in relation to anonymisation of documentation, reflecting the fact that very few

---

8   *V v Associated Newspapers Ltd and others* [2016] EWCOP 21.
9   Available at www.judiciary.gov.uk/wp-content/uploads/2016/01/CoP-Transparency-Pilot-Note-from-the-VP-11Dec15final.pdf.

members of the public or media representatives have attended hearings since the Pilot was launched and the concern that motivated such anonymisation (ie that such documentation would be disseminated more widely) has to some extent been alleviated. Further, there is now the ability for the Pilot Order to be amended on an essentially rolling basis, subject to the approval of the President, and it may well be that further amendments are made before 31 August 2017 and the end of the Pilot. The most recent version of the order will always be available on the Court of Protection Handbook website. The discussion below refers to the order as it stands at October 2016.

13.26 The wording of the Pilot Order is complex, reflecting primarily the fact that, absent amendments to the COPR (and potentially primary legislation) careful navigation is required by the court to ensure that it does not, by listing a hearing as a public hearing, thereby lose the ability to ensure that private information relating to P is kept private. The Vice-President, Charles J, explained the basis for the order – and also its differences to those made in serious medical treatment cases (see further para 13.42 below) in a schedule to the judgment he gave in *V v Associated Newspapers Ltd and others*.[10]

13.27 The Court of Protection Handbook website includes an unofficial 'easy read' version of the Pilot Order with annotations by Tor Butler-Cole to explain its implications for litigants in person.[11] Whilst this version refers to the earlier iteration of the Order, it remains useful for explaining to non-lawyers (and indeed to lawyers) the effect of the sometimes complex of the wording. At the time of writing, it is understood that an official, updated, version of this may be forthcoming to explain the current iteration of the Pilot Order.

13.28 The Pilot Order is a public document and therefore P's full name should no longer appear in full in it. Likewise the names of the parties should be 'appropriately anonymised'; although as with judgments[12] public bodies should be named in full.

13.29 The standard order will provide for the next hearing and any further hearing to be in public. Paragraph 2 makes it clear however that admission to hearings under the Pilot will be dependent on the attendees signing a document before they go into court which will give their details and will confirm that they have been given a copy of the order and are aware of its terms.

10 [2016] EWCOP 21.
11 https://courtofprotectionhandbook.files.wordpress.com/2016/02/transparency-order-in-plain-english.pdf.
12 See Transparency and the Court of Protection: publication of judgments, para 20.

Publicity, privacy and confidentiality 373

13.30 The standard order contains some basic details of the issues that the case concerns, from a list of standard descriptions. These are also included in a daily cause list. These are:
a) where P should live;
b) contact with specified persons;
c) prohibiting contact with P;
d) healthcare;
e) capacity to marry or to consent to sexual relations;
f) appointment of deputy for personal welfare;
g) varying or terminating an urgent or standard authorisation under the Deprivation of Liberty Safeguards;
h) authorising a deprivation of liberty (in relation to ... eg care and residence arrangements);
i) appointment of deputy for property and affairs;
j) discharge or conduct of deputy;
k) will, codicil, gift or settlement of property;
l) registration of enduring or lasting power of attorney;
m) discharge or conduct of deputy or attorney (application by Public Guardian/delete as necessary);
n) recognition and enforcement of a protective measure under the law of [name country]; and
o) publication of information about proceedings.

13.31 This should have the effect of making research into the types of cases which come before the courts much easier.

13.32 Paragraph 5 is the injunctive provision and reads as follows:

(A) The following persons (the Persons Bound by this Injunctive Order) are bound by this injunctive order:
(i) the parties and their representatives,
(ii) the witnesses,
(iii) all persons who attend all or any part of an attended hearing,
(iv) all persons who by any means obtain or are given an account or record of all or any part of an attended hearing or of any order or judgment made or given as a result of an attended hearing,
(v) all persons who are provided with or by any means obtain documents and information arising from this application, and
(vi) any body, authority or organisation (and their officers, employees, servants and agents) for whom any such person works or is giving evidence.

(B) The material and information (the Information) covered by this injunctive order is:
(i) any material or information that identifies or is likely to identify that
(a) [*INITIALS TO IDENTIFY P NOT NAME*] and members of [*SAME INITIALS TO IDENTIFY P*]'s family are respectively the subject (and so a P as defined in the Court of Protection Rules 2007) or members of the family of a subject of these proceedings, or that
(b) [*ANONYMISED PERSON*] [*... ANONYMISED REFERENCE TO ANY OTHER PARTY ...*] is a party to these proceedings, or that
(c) [*ANONYMISED PERSON*] [*... ANONYMISED PERSON WHOSE IDENTITY SHOULD NOT BE PUBLISHED ...*] (who the Court has so identified to the parties in private) [*... has taken a part in / or been referred to in ...*] these proceedings; and
(ii) any material or information that identifies or is likely to identify where any person listed above lives, or is being cared for, or their contact details.
(C) Subject to further order of the Court and save as provided by sub-paragraph (D) the Persons Bound by this Injunctive Order shall not by any means directly or indirectly:
(i) publish the Information or any part or parts of it, or
(ii) cause, enable, assist in or encourage the publication of the Information or any part or parts of it.
(D) Subject to further order of the Court this injunctive order does not prevent the Persons Bound by this Injunctive Order from communicating information relating to these proceedings on the basis that Part 3 of Practice Direction 13A to the Court of Protection Rules 2007 (which relates to proceedings held in private) applies to these proceedings.

13.33 It will be noted that members of the media are not specifically listed. The media must be given notice of an order restricting the media from reporting what happens in a given case.[13] Charles J explained in the note accompanying the launch of the Pilot that to give the media formal notice on each occasion that a Pilot Order was made would be impracticable and would cause delays. His view is that this was not necessary anyway as if a member of the media attends a hearing they

---

13 PD 13A/Pilot PD 4A para 10.

will be bound by the terms of the order. The possibility that someone who attends the hearing subsequently breaches the Pilot Order and provides information to a third party is catered for by sub-para 5A(iv) which binds the third party.

13.34 Paragraph 5(B) sets out the information which is covered by the injunction. This broadly protects the identity of

- P and members of P's family;
- Other parties;
- Other persons involved or referred to.

13.35 The injunction does not prevent disclosure of information under Part 3 of Practice Direction Pilot 4A (see para 13.9 above) (see para 5D).

13.36 Paragraph 6 requires any transcripts of judgments as well as orders to be anonymised, but is subject to the position in relation to third party orders addressed below.

13.37 The position in relation to anonymisation of documents has now been simplified by comparison to the position that prevailed when the Transparency Pilot started. There is no longer any requirement to anonymise such documents as position statements. Rather, Paragraph 7 provides that the court may at any time give such directions as it thinks fit (including directions relating to anonymisation, payment, use, copying, return and the means by which a copy of a document or information may be provided) concerning the provision of information or copies of documents put before the Court and the terms on which they are to be provided to any person who attends an attended hearing (and is not a person to whom the document can be provided under Part 3 of Pilot PD4A/Practice Direction 13A).

13.38 Paragraph 8 provides for a record of that information which the court has determined should not be released to be kept and referred to as 'the Record'. This information may be made available 'on such terms as the court thinks fit' to anyone who attends the hearing (para 8) or makes an application supported by evidence (para 9). It is the Record which will contain the full names of the parties.

13.39 Paragraph 10 gives the parties and anyone affected by the order liberty to apply to vary or discharge it. The Vice-President's Note[14] makes it clear that such applications must be supported by evidence, although this is not in the Practice Direction or the draft order.

---

14 https://www.judiciary.gov.uk/wp-content/uploads/2016/01/CoP-Transparency-Pilot-Note-from-the-VP-11Dec15final.pdf.

13.40   Paragraph 11 deals with the question of rights of audience, discussed at paras 6.15–6.19.

13.41   Care should be taken in preparing third party orders under the Pilot (ie orders directed to a person or body who is not a party to proceedings and was not present at the hearing at which they were made – an example being an order for disclosure of records held by a public body). Orders are public and should be endorsed with the following notice:

> This order is covered by the terms of the transparency pilot order served herewith which imposes restrictions upon the identification of the parties. If any person disobeys that order in paragraph (5) they may be found guilty of contempt of court and may be sent to prison, fined or have their assets seized. They have the right to ask the court to vary or discharge the order.

13.42   Because the third party order will be anonymised, Paragraph 6 makes clear that a confidential schedule will also need to be prepared, providing the necessary identification. The schedule should also contain the notice in the paragraph above.[15]

Assessment

13.43   At the time of writing, there has been no formal report as to the success (or otherwise) of the pilot, but readers may find the comments of the Transparency Project, whose authors have been following the Pilot, to be of interest.[16] Anecdotal evidence suggests that there has been very limited take-up of the opportunity to attend hearings both by members of the public and by media representatives. In part, this has been because of considerable inconsistency as to the information provided in and the timing of the listing of cases. A further issue that has been identified is the fact that there is inconsistency in practice as regards explanation of the Pilot and its effects to those who do attend the hearing. It is understood that guidance is to be prepared for judges to ensure that they give a standard explanation concerning attendance and the reporting restrictions at the beginning of the hearing. It is also likely that prior to the end of the Pilot in August 2017 and – if it is to be made permanent – any consequential changes required to the COPR, further work will be done to align the position in relation to cases currently falling under the Transparency Pilot and serious medical treatment cases, discussed further below.

---

15   Model Order.
16   www.transparencyproject.org.uk/category/cop/.

Cases outside the Transparency Pilot

Serious medical treatment cases

13.44 The position is different if the case concerns serious medical treatment, as defined in PD 9E.[17] Paragraph 16 of PD 9E provides that in serious medical treatment cases the court will ordinarily make an order under COPR r92[18] that the hearing will be held in public with restrictions on reporting. For the wider issues arising in medical treatment cases, see chapter 22.[19]

13.45 COPR r91 empowers the judge to authorise publication of information relating to private proceedings, or of all or part of a judgment given in private proceedings. Such an order will again be made when there is good reason to make it.[20] COPR r91(3) provides that such an order can be made in such terms as the court sees fit and gives examples of the types of restrictions the court may consider imposing (for an example, given in proceedings where it is necessary for information contained in an order relating to P to be shared with others for purposes of delivering care to them, see precedents on www.courtofprotectionhandbook.com). Release of information which complies with a direction under COPR r91will not be contempt of court.[21]

13.46 As we have seen, COPR r92 allows the court to direct that all or part of a hearing be held in public. However this remains subject to the court's powers to exclude persons or classes of persons from the hearing or part of it and imposing restrictions on publication. Again the test is that there is good reason for making such an order.

13.47 The relevant practice direction accompanying these rules (PD 13A) is in three parts. The first applies in all cases where an application is being made for orders under COPR rr4.1, 4.2 or 4.3 and provides that such applications must be made by filing an application using form COP9.[22] The court should then consider whether to deal with the application as a discrete issue.[23]

13.48 If the court decides to authorise publication and at the same time sets out restrictions as to what can or cannot be published (for

---

17 PD 9E paras 5–7.
18 Serious medical treatment cases do not fall within the Case Management Pilot, so the governing rules are to be found in COPR Part 13.
19 Where the Court of Protection directs a public hearing control over publicity is governed by the Contempt of Court Act 1981 ss1–4, 11, 19.
20 COPR r93(1)(a).
21 COPR r91(1).
22 Pilot PD 4A/PD 13A Part 1 para 4.
23 Pilot PD 4A/PD 13A Part 1 para 6.

example, when a judge directs that a judgment should be published, but at the same time directs that the parties' names should be anonymised), there is no need to give notice to the news media.[24]

13.49 Different considerations apply where the court has already made an order authorising publication, or has agreed to sit in public, and subsequently either an application is then made to restrict what can be published, or the court is considering exercising its powers to restrict the information.[25] In such cases, P's rights under the European Convention on Human Rights (ECHR) are engaged; but so are the Article 10 ECHR rights to freedom of expression of the person seeking to publish the information.[26] Therefore, the practice direction draws attention to the requirement for notice to be given to the person whose Article 10 rights would be affected (probably one of the media organisations) unless there are compelling reasons why that person should not be notified.[27] In *V v Associated Newspapers Ltd and others*,[28] Charles J noted that this prior notification procedure adds little, if anything, to the service of the order particularly if that order and the listing information contains a description of the subject matter of the proceedings. Urgency, particularly if substantive relief is sought on the first or an early directions hearing may require notice of that hearing but equally may provide the 'compelling reason' why notice was not given. Further, as he noted, '[e]ven in urgent cases, and many serious medical treatment cases are urgent, it is the substantive issues and the content of the evidence that informs the balance that that has to be carried out between Articles 8 and 10. This means that it is unlikely that this balancing exercise can be properly argued and considered at a directions hearing and so disputes on the grant / extent of reporting restrictions are likely to be best dealt with at later stages of the proceedings.'[29] He expressed the view that 'proper notification to the media of the existence of the proceedings and of the date of the public hearing of a case relating to serious medical treatment and the terms of any reporting restrictions order made when a public hearing is directed is what really matters.'[30]

---

24 Pilot PD 4A/PD 13A Part 2 para 8.
25 Pilot PD 4A/PD 13A Part 2 para 12.
26 Pilot PD 4A/PD 13A Part 2 paras 10, 11.
27 Pilot PD 4A/PD 13A Part 2 para 10.
28 [2016] EWCOP 21.
29 Para 211.
30 Para 212.

13.50   It is likely that, in due course, further consideration will be given to aligning the approach under serious medical treatment cases and that under the Transparency Pilot (where prior notification is not required). In the interim however, the procedure that must be followed is set out in paras 13–19 of PD 13A, and it is important that this is followed. National newspapers and broadcasters subscribe to the Press Association's CopyDirect service. A list of the subscribing organisations is available online.[31] CopyDirect is responsible for notifying individual media organisations of an intended application, and notice of an application for an order that would affect the world at large can be given to CopyDirect.[32] However, the CopyDirect service does not extend to regional or local media or magazines who would need to be served directly with notice of the application.[33]

13.51   The CopyDirect website makes it clear that CopyDirect will only notify organisations of applications and does not deal with service of orders once they are made

13.52   Paragraphs 15–18 require the applicant to contact CopyDirect and sets out the information that is required. The court will also give advance notice if considering an order of its own initiative and will then provide much of the information listed in para 15 as it sees fit.[34] The court may also dispense with any of the requirements in paras 15–19.[35] An organisation which wishes to take part in any hearing must file an acknowledgement of service in form COP5 within 21 days of receipt of the notice from CopyDirect.[36] It is essential that the nature of the orders sought are clearly indicated and that anyone seeking restrictions on identifying or contacting individuals or classes of individuals should make this clear.[37] It is necessary to provide the information identifying P (and any other party/person in respect of whom reporting restrictions are sought) when notifying CopyDirect.[38]

---

31 See: www.medialawyer.press.net/courtapplications.
32 PD 13A Part 2 para 14.
33 PD 13A Part 2 para 18.
34 PD 13A Part 2 para 20.
35 PD 13A Part 2 para 19.
36 PD 13A Part 2 paras 21, 22.
37 See also *W v M (reporting restriction order)* [2011] EWHC 1197 (COP), [2011] COPLR Con Vol 1226
38 *A Healthcare Trust v P* [2015] EWCOP 15, [2015] COPLR 147, in which Hayden J made clear that the media could not lawfully then reveal the parties' names on receipt of an application for reporting restrictions.

13.53 The practice direction gives guidance as to the approach to be taken when balancing P's ECHR rights under Article 8 against the right under Article 10 to freedom of expression. There is no precedence between the two and both are qualified.[39] The practice direction[40] draws attention to the need to have particular regard to:

- the importance of freedom expression;
- the extent to which material has or is about to become public (orders will not usually be made prohibiting publication of material which is already in the public domain, apart from in exceptional cases);[41]
- the extent of the public interest in such material being published;
- the terms of any relevant privacy code.

13.54 The practice direction also notes that the aim of any restrictions should be to protect P rather than confer anonymity on others; but restrictions on identifying others could be justified if the absence of such restrictions might lead to the identification of P or restrict the ability of others to care for P. The identity of experts however is not usually subject to restrictions.[42] Paragraph 13.62 below considers the issue of jigsaw identification.

13.55 Orders should last no longer than they are needed to achieve their purpose but may need to last until P's death, or indeed beyond.[43] Post-mortem orders are considered further in paras 13.71 onwards below.

Contempt of court

13.56 Special considerations arise in cases involving contempt of court. A Practice Direction[44] issued on 26 March 2015 applies in all proceedings. It draws attention to the fundamental principle of the administration of justice in England and Wales that applications for committal

---

39 Pilot PD 4A/PD 13A Part 2 para 24.
40 Pilot PD 4A/PD 13A Part 2 para 25.
41 Pilot PD 4A/PD 13A Part 2 para 28.
42 Pilot PD 4A/PD 13A Part 2 para 27.
43 Pilot PD 4A/PD 13A para 28. See also *W v M and S (reporting restriction order)* [2011] EWHC 1197 (COP), [2011] COPLR Con Vol 1205 (injunctions were made in support of reporting restrictions that prevented contact being made with the laypeople at the heart of a high-profile medical treatment case were expressed so as to last for the lifetime of P).
44 Practice Direction of 26 March 2015 Committal for Contempt of Court – Open Court.

for contempt should be heard and decided in public, that is, in open court. Any derogation must be strictly justified.[45] The practice direction specifies how the case should be listed.[46]

13.57 Importantly the Practice Direction makes it clear that 'the fact that the hearing may involve disclosure of material which ought not to be published does not of itself justify hearing the application in private if such publication can be restrained by an appropriate order'.[47] Thus, P's details could be anonymised in any order or judgment, and the hearing could proceed in public.

13.58 If the court is considering holding a committal hearing in private the media should be notified.[48] A reasoned public judgment must explain any decision to hear a committal hearing in private.[49] If, in an exceptional case, a committal application is heard in private and the court finds that a person has committed a contempt of court it must state in public

a) the name of that person;
b) in general terms the nature of the contempt of court in respect of which the committal order [committal order for this purpose includes a suspended committal order] is being made; and
c) the punishment being imposed.

13.59 In addition, it is mandatory for the above information to be notified to the national media. There are no exceptions. The Practice Direction states that:

There are never any circumstances in which any one may be committed to custody without these matters being publicly stated.[50]

13.60 Applications for committal for contempt are discussed in full at paras 17.12 onwards.

The approach of the court to reporting restrictions

13.61 As we have seen, with the advent of the Transparency Pilot the default position is that there will be open access to hearings, but with restrictions aimed at protecting the identity of P and of P's family. This is

---

45 Practice Direction para 4.
46 Practice Direction para 5.
47 Practice Direction para 9.
48 Practice Direction para 8, also see Practice Guidance June 2015 para 2.
49 Practice Direction para 10.
50 Practice Direction para 13.

the thrust of the injunctive provisions in the Pilot order,[51] and is consistent with the President's guidance as to the publication of judgments[52] as well as Pilot PD 4A/PD 13A.[53] In *R (C) v Secretary of State for Justice*[54] (a case concerning proceedings before the Mental Health Tribunal) Lady Hale described the starting point in the jurisdictions dealing with detention, care and treatment of those with mental disorders and disabilities as 'usually privacy and always anonymity, although either or both may be relaxed'.

13.62 The expectation is that statutory bodies or professionals will be identified. In some cases where this has risked 'jigsaw identification' the courts have extended anonymisation. In *NHS Trust and Others v FG*,[55] Keehan J held that it was not in FG's interests for the hospital, the responsible Trust or the county in which she resided to be identified. This was because he accepted there was 'a real risk that if the latter were to be made public it is highly likely FG and /or her baby would be identified given the most unusual circumstances of this case'.[56]

13.63 If an application to extend anonymisation is made in a case where an order has already been has been made under the Transparency Pilot, then it will be necessary to notify the media as a result of paragraph 10 of Pilot PD 4A.

13.64 The tension between protecting P's ECHR rights and the freedom of the press has been considered in several judgments since the Court of Protection acquired its welfare jurisdiction. A detailed examination of these judgments is beyond the scope of this book and what follows is only a summary of the key cases. In *Independent News and Media Ltd v A*,[57] the Court of Appeal approved the approach that Hedley J had taken at first instance. He had taken a two-stage approach to the application for an order under COPR r91. The first stage was to ascertain whether there was good reason to permit the application. If this is established, the court should proceed to weigh up the competing factors. The Court of Appeal noted the paradox whereby matters in respect of which adults with capacity would take their privacy for granted come before the Court of Protection: the incapacitated adult faces a risk to their privacy (because the relevant

---

51 Considered in para 13.32 above.
52 Transparency in the Court of Protection [2014] 1 WLR 235, paras 9 and 10
53 Pilot PD 4A/PD 13A, para 27.
54 [2016] UKSC 2, [2016] 1 WLR 444.
55 [2014] EWCOP 30, [2015] 1 WLR 1984.
56 Para 67.
57 [2010] EWCA Civ 343, [2010] 1 WLR 2262.

decisions are being taken by the court) that an adult with capacity would never face. As the Court of Appeal noted, adults with capacity make decisions about their personal lives all the time, and take their privacy in doing so for granted, but that a person who needs the court to make these decisions, because he or she cannot, faces the potential loss of that privacy as a result.

13.65 In *Hillingdon LBC v Neary*,[58] Peter Jackson J again noted the salutary impact that publication of information could have, commenting that:

> There is a genuine public interest in the work of this court being understood. Not only is this healthy in itself – the presence of the media in appropriate cases has a bracing effect on all public servants, whether in the field of social services or the law – but it may also help to dispel misunderstandings. It is not in the interests of individual litigants, or of society at large, for a court that is by definition devoted to the protection of the welfare of disadvantaged people to be characterised (including in a report about this case, published as I write this judgment) as 'secretive'. It is part of our natural curiosity to want to know other people's secrets, and using pejorative descriptions of this kind may stimulate interest. The opportunity, in appropriate cases, to follow a process that has welfare, not secrecy, at its heart can only help the media to produce balanced reporting, and not fall back on clichés.[59]

13.66 Steven Neary's name and circumstances had been in the public eye before proceedings had started but there was no evidence that the publicity had or was likely to harm him. Stories about named individuals may hold more interest than those about unidentified people.[60] Individuals should not be named at the outset of a case if there is a real possibility that at the end of the case the court would not allow publication; but it would be stultifying to withhold information when it was already in the public domain, as in this case.

13.67 This approach is consistent with paragraph 28 of Pilot PD 4A/PD 13A, which, as we have seen, provides that orders will not normally restrict the publication of information that is already in the public domain, apart from in exceptional cases. These could include circumstances where there would be a 'qualitative difference' between the level of intrusion that would result from unrestrained publication and the current level.[61]

---

58 [2011] EWHC 413 (COP), [2011] COPLR Con Vol 677.
59 Para 15 (emphasis in original).
60 As emphasised in *Re Guardian News and Media Limited* [2010] UKSC 1, [2010] 2 AC 697.
61 For example as in *PJS v NGN Ltd* [2016] UKSC 26.

13.68 *W v M (reporting restriction order)*[62] concerned the proposed withdrawal of artificial nutrition and hydration from a M, a minimally conscious patient. In accordance with PD 9E, Baker J directed that hearings should take place in open court. Orders were granted restricting publication which could identify M, her family and care staff, but also restraining the media –who were not represented – from contacting anyone on a list of 65 persons involved in caring for M. Baker J agreed to reconsider the order on receipt of a letter from Times Newspapers Ltd expressing concern that the media had not been notified of the full nature of the orders to be sought and had therefore been unable to make representations.

13.69 Baker J held that:

- While PD 13A[63] does not require the applicant to serve a draft order, it is essential for the applicant to give an outline of the orders sought and the applicant must indicate the categories of people whose identities it is proposed will be kept confidential.
- If the applicant seeks restrictions on contact by the media with individuals or categories of persons, the application must make this clear.
- There is no automatic precedence between the Article 8 rights of P or P's family and the Article 10 rights of the media organisations.
- There must be a proper evidential basis for concerns about the risk of harm from an interference with the Article 8 rights of P or P's family.
- The public interest in freedom of expression in medical cases will usually lie in information being available about the general issues rather than the identity of individuals.
- There is a public interest in the practices of the Court of Protection being better understood and the urge to take an over-protective stance should be resisted.
- Celebrity cases and super-injunctions involve balancing the same convention rights, but the circumstances of the individuals concerned are so different that decisions in the two types of cases are unlikely to be relevant to each other.

13.70 In *Westminster City Council v Sykes*[64] (which pre-dated the Transparency Pilot) DJ Eldergill decided to allow the publication of the names

---

62 [2011] EWHC 1197 (COP), [2011] COPLR Con Vol 1205.
63 Now Pilot PD4A in cases on the Case Management Pilot.
64 [2014] EWHC B9 (COP), (2014) 17 CCLR 139.

of Manuela Sykes and the local authority where she had once been a councillor and which was at the time depriving her of her liberty. Ms Sykes had been a political campaigner all her life and had always wanted to he heard. On learning of her diagnosis of dementia she had shared her experiences on the internet, campaigning for the rights of those with the condition. Her personality and wishes were a magnetic factor in the balancing exercise.

Restrictions after P's death

13.71 As we have seen Pilot PD 4A/PD13A specifies that reporting restriction orders should last only as long as necessary to achieve their purpose. Some orders may need to last until P's death; and in some cases longer.[65] Three recent cases have considered the question of anonymity after P's death.

13.72 In *V v Associated Newspapers Limited*[66] Charles J considered an application following the death of C whose case had come before the Court of Protection for determination as to her capacity to consent to renal dialysis.[67]

13.73 A reporting restrictions order was made at the outset of the proceedings (in standard terms for a serious medical treatment case) restricting reporting of information leading to the identification of C and her adult daughters. The order was expressed to have effect during C's lifetime. After a hearing at which it was determined that C had the capacity, such that the Court of Protection had no jurisdiction, C died.

13.74 The case was the subject of considerable media interest, and both the tactics adopted by some reporters and the style of some reporting caused distress to C's family. The adult daughters applied for a continuation of the reporting restriction order; by the time that the matter came finally to be determined by Charles J, the relevant media organisations did not contest that the order should be continued to the 18th birthday of C's teenage daughter, although raised an issue as to whether the order could be made by Charles J as a Court of Protection judge (as opposed to a High Court judge). Subsequent to the hearing, a further application was made that the order be extended to cover C's inquest, which the media organisations did not resist, and which Charles J found to be justified on the particular

---

65 Pilot PD 4A/PD 13A para 29 where it applies.
66 *V v Associated Newspapers Limited and others* [2016] EWCOP 21, [2016] COPLR 236.
67 *Kings College NHS Foundation Trust v C and V* [2015] EWCOP 80, [2016] COPLR 50.

facts of the case, especially given the prurient nature of the reporting that had taken place.

13.75 Much of the judgment, therefore, consisted of determination of general principles for future guidance, rather than the resolution of a contest as to how they should apply upon the facts of the instant case. The following conclusions he reached are key.

13.76 First: the Court of Protection has jurisdiction to make a postmortem reporting restrictions order (although in the instant case, and on a 'belt and braces approach,' Charles J also made the order as a High Court judge to avoid any future jurisdictional arguments). Further, reporting restrictions orders in serious medical treatment cases can extend beyond the death of the subject of those proceedings and there is no presumption or default position that such orders should end on P's death.

13.77 Second: the Court of Protection should generally address the following questions:

- Are there good reasons for the hearing to be in public?
- If there are, should that public hearing be ordered with or without reporting restrictions? As part of that determination, how effective are any such reporting restrictions likely to be in protecting and promoting the relevant Article 8 rights and how restrictive are they likely to be of the relevant Article 10 rights having regard to the factors, propositions and public interests that underlie and promote those competing rights?
- In light of the conclusions as to these questions, and applying the ultimate balancing test required by *Re S (A Child) (Identification: Restrictions on Publication)*,[68] should the hearing be in private or in public? If in private, which documents (with or without redactions and anonymisation) should be made public (and when and how should this be done)? If in public, what reporting restrictions order / anonymity order should be made?

13.78 Third, the answer to the first question is almost always going to be 'yes' because of the benefits of open justice and so almost always the *Re S* exercise will be engaged by addressing the second and third questions.

13.79 Fourth: a distinction can be made between (a) cases where pursuant to the default or general position under the relevant Rules or Practice Directions the court is allowing access (or unrestricted access) to the media and the public, and (b) cases in which it is

68 [2005] 1 AC 593.

imposing restrictions and so where the court is turning the tap on rather than off. However, Charles J emphasised that this distinction only reflects the strength of the reasoning underlying those Rules and Practice Direction that in many, perhaps most, cases the important safeguards secured by a public hearing can be secured without the press publishing or the public knowing the identities of the people involved. The distinction therefore provides weight to the general arguments for anonymity to promote the administration of justice by the court generally and in the given case. The distinction therefore does not undermine the general proposition that naming people has a valuable function of rendering news stories personal and therefore effective as journalism.[69]

13.80 Fifth, the weight to be given to the 'naming proposition' and the conclusion as to what generally best promotes the administration of justice will vary from case to case, and may require specific consideration (and reasons) in specific cases. Charles J gave some useful examples of how these considerations might apply in different cases:

- If the case involves a celebrity but otherwise is not out of the ordinary, the court will be exercising a well-known decision making process, and the difficulty or impossibility of providing effective anonymisation may found a decision not to order a public hearing. The question for the trial judge will therefore be what (if any) document or judgment should be made public;
- If the case involves a celebrity but raises new or unusual points and so is out of the ordinary this may found a decision for a public hearing with no (or unusual) reporting restrictions;
- Where findings of serious mistreatment or malpractice are sought or when a member of a family wants (or has initiated) publicity that identifies P and family members issues will arise whether: (1) there should be a public hearing with no reporting restrictions (so the rival arguments and assertions are made public and linked to identified individuals); or (2) whether there should be a private hearing (with disclosure to relevant bodies or persons).

13.81 In *University College London Hospitals NHS Foundation Trust v G*,[70] Peter Jackson J refused an application by the treating Trust and supported by G's family, to extend a reporting restriction order in relation to G, which was to end a month after her death. Noting that

---

69 See *Re Guardian News and Media Limited* [2010] UKSC 1, [2010] 2 AC 697.
70 *University College London Hospitals NHS Foundation Trust v G (by her litigation friend the Official Solicitor)* [2016] EWCOP 28.

the names of those who are born and those die are a matter of public record the judge found that although the circumstances of G's death were understandably distressing, there was no evidence that her identification would harm family members or significantly infringe their privacy. Hayden J reached a similar view in *M v Press Association*,[71] addressing himself to the questions which Charles J had formulated in *V v Associated Newspapers*. He did not consider that M or her family were at risk of intrusive commentary and noted that intrusion by the media on the family's grief would breach the IPSO Code of Conduct. He took the unusual step in his judgment of providing details of IPSO's website.[72]

Restrictions on disclosure of documents

13.82 A final, related, series of points should be noted as regards witness statements and/or other documents filed on behalf of a party. First, where a document has been filed or disclosed, a party to whom it was provided may only use it for the purpose of the proceedings in which it was filed or disclosed, except where:

a) the document has been read to or by the court or referred to at a public hearing (NB, which is now the majority of hearings in proceedings under the MCA 2005); or
b) the court otherwise permits.[73]

13.83 Second, a party to proceedings may (subject to any order to the contrary) inspect or obtain from the records of the court a copy of any document filed by a party to the proceedings.[74]

13.84 Third, where the application has been for the appointment of a deputy or the variation of the order under which the deputy was appointed, the Public Guardian is entitled to be supplied with copies (among other things) of documents filed in the proceedings relevant to the decision to appoint the deputy, any powers conferred upon him, any duties imposed on him if the Public Guardian reasonably considers it necessary for him to have regard to them for purposes of the discharge of his statutory functions in relation to the supervision of deputies. The court can limit disclosure of particular documents

---

71 *M v Press Association* [2016] EWCOP 34.
72 www.ipso.co.uk/IPSO/harassment.html
73 COPR Pr5.10/COPR r18.
74 COPR Pr5.8/COPR r16.

or categories of documents or direct that the documents are provided on an edited basis.[75]

13.85 Finally, upon application, the court may authorise a person who is not a party to proceedings to inspect documents in the court records or to obtain a copy of any such documents or extracts from such documents.[76] The court must consider whether to provide any document on an edited basis.[77]

75 COPR Pr5.12(1)–(6)/COPR rr20(1)–(6).
76 COPR Pr5.9(2)/COPR r17(2).
77 COPR Pr5.9(4)/COPR r17(4).

CHAPTER 14

Fact-finding

14.1	Introduction
14.3	When is fact-finding necessary?
14.11	Preparing for a fact-finding hearing
14.20	The determination of contested facts
14.25	Fact-finding and future risk
14.27	Fact-finding: consequences

Introduction

14.1 Proceedings before the Court of Protection are primarily inquisitorial, not adversarial.[1] However, there will be circumstances in which it is necessary for the court to reach determinations upon contested facts before it is possible for it then to go on to consider where P's best interests lie (or to make other decisions/declarations open to it). It is open to a judge, in the exercise of their case management powers under COPR Part 5 (Pilot Part 3 where the Case Management Pilot applies (see further chapter 4), to decide that it is necessary that such a determination of fact take place.

14.2 This chapter discusses the question of when and how disputes of fact are resolved in the Court of Protection. It addresses, in particular, the circumstances under which a separate fact-finding hearing will be listed (a so-called 'split trial), and the particular steps required to prepare for such hearings. The issues that it raises are likely to be of most relevance in applications concerning P's welfare, and, in particular, in cases brought by local authorities in the discharge of their safeguarding obligations owed to adults at risk (as to which, see further, chapter 23 below).

When is fact-finding necessary?

14.3 Unlike in applications for care or supervision orders under Children Act (CA) 1989, the local authority (or other applicant) does not need to establish that the adult in question is suffering or is likely to suffer significant harm[2] before the court can move on to the second stage of considering whether making the order sought will promote the welfare of the adult. 'The Mental Capacity Act does not contain provisions equivalent to the threshold provisions under CA 1989 s31(2). Nor should any such provisions be imported in it as clearly Parliament intended that they should not be.'[3]

14.4 However, that does not mean that the court can necessarily gloss over disputes of fact as to the conduct of those suspected of acting in a way adverse to the adult in favour of a broader-brush analysis of

---

1 *Re G* [2014] EWCOP 1361, [2014] COPLR 416 at para 52 per Sir James Munby P, endorsing *Cheshire West and Cheshire Council v P and M* [2011] EWHC 1330 (Fam), [2011] COPLR Con Vol 273 at para 52 per Baker J.
2 CA 1989 s31(2). The threshold criteria go further than this, but this requirement is at their core.
3 *LBB v JM, BK and CM* [2010] COPLR Con Vol 779 at para 8 per Hedley J.

where their best interests may lie. This is for several reasons, the most important of which are that:

- In order for any best interests decision to be made, the court needs to be satisfied as to 'all [of] the relevant circumstances' for purposes of the application of the checklist set down in Mental Capacity Act (MCA) 2005 s4. If those circumstances are disputed, it may well be necessary for the dispute to be resolved as a preliminary step to the determination of where the adult's best interests lie. For instance, if the allegation has been made that a family member has mistreated the adult, it is likely to be necessary for the court to determine whether that allegation is made out in order before it can make any best interests decision about contact with that family member; and
- As Hedley J made clear in *LBB v JM, BK and CM*:[4] 'an intervention with parties' rights under Article 8 [ECHR] is a serious intervention by the State which requires to be justified under Article 8(2). If there is a contested factual basis it may often be right ... that that should be investigated and determined by the court'.[5]

14.5 In *Re AG*,[6] Sir James Munby set down when it is necessary to have fact finding proceedings in the Court of Protection, by expressly endorsing the approach adopted by Wall J (as he then was) in the pre-MCA 2005 case of *Re S (adult's lack of capacity: carer and residence)*.[7] In this case, concerning a 33-year-old woman, S, the relevant local authority sought declarations as to S's capacity and best interests as regards her residence, care arrangements and contact with her father. The catalyst for the local authority's application was an alleged incident of assault by S's father upon her; it was also alleged that her father had on a number of occasions been drinking and had been unfit through drink to care for her. The father strongly denied both allegations. In a detailed discussion of the relevant legal principles, Wall J directed himself that:

---

4 [2010] COPLR Con Vol 779.
5 It is suggested that this approach holds good notwithstanding the subsequent decision of the Court of Appeal in *K v LBX and others* [2012] EWCA Civ 79, [2012] COPLR 411, (2012) 15 CCLR 112, that the consideration of Article 8 rights follows on from the application of the MCA 2005 s4 checklist; the Court of Appeal was considering a different question: see para 2 of the judgment.
6 [2015] EWCOP 78, [2016] COPLR 13 at para 30.
7 [2003] EWHC 1909 (Fam), [2003] 2 FLR 1235. That approach was also set down as being the correct test in the first edition of this work (at paras 15.7 onwards).

... unlike care proceedings under the Children Act 1989, the exercise of the jurisdiction over mentally incapable adults is not dependent upon any threshold criteria apart from the fact of incapacity and the existence of what Dame Elizabeth Butler-Sloss P described in *Re F (No 2)*[8] at 47 and 521 respectively as 'a serious justiciable issue' which requires the court's adjudication.[9]

14.6 Applying *Re A (male sterilisation)*,[10] Wall J further directed himself that the central question for the court was as to what outcome was in the best interests of the adult.[11] He continued that both of the factors outlined immediately above, but in particular the absence of any threshold criteria, raise 'the question as to the extent to which (if at all) it is necessary, for the purposes of exercising the jurisdiction and deciding which course of action is in the best interests of S, to make findings of fact relating in particular to disputed historical issues'.[12]

14.7 Importantly, Wall J rejected the submission made on behalf of the father to the effect that absent findings of fact which warranted her removal from her father's care, the local authority would not have made out a case for such removal, and that she should therefore be returned, stating that:

> I do not accept that argument. I agree that there must be good reason for local authority intervention in a case such as the present. Equally, if there are disputed issues of fact which go to the question of Mr S's capacity and suitability to care for S, the court may need to resolve them if their resolution is necessary to the decision as to what is in S's best interests. Findings of fact against Mr S on the two issues identified [above] would plainly reflect upon his capacity properly to care for S. But it does not follow, in my judgment, that the proceedings must be dismissed simply because the factual basis upon which the local authority instituted them turns out to be mistaken, or because it cannot be established on the balance of probabilities. What matters (assuming always that mental incapacity is made out) is which outcome will be in S's best interests. There will plainly be cases which are very fact specific. There will be others in which the principal concern is the future, and the relative suitability of the plans which each party can put forward for both the short and long-term care of the mentally incapable adult. The instant case, in my judgment, is one of the cases in the latter category.[13]

---

8 *Re F (Adult: Court's Jurisdiction)* [2001] Fam 38.
9 Para 13.
10 [2000] 1 FLR 549.
11 Para 14.
12 [2001] Fam 38 para 15.
13 Para 18.

14.8 Wall J continued:

Whilst I acknowledge that in a relatively untried jurisdiction there are dangers in too relaxed an approach to historical issues, I am unable to accept the proposition that the approach to best interests is fettered in any way beyond that which applies to any judicial decision, namely that it has to be evidence based; that it excludes irrelevant material; and that it includes a consideration of all relevant material. In a field as complex as care for the mentally disabled, a high degree of pragmatism seems to me inevitable. But in each case it seems to me that the four essential building blocks are the same. First, is mental incapacity established? Secondly, is there a serious, justiciable issue relating to welfare? Thirdly, what is it? Fourthly, with the welfare of the incapable adult as the court's paramount consideration, what are the balance sheet factors which must be drawn up to decide which course of action is in his or her best interests?[14]

14.9 In this regard, it is, further, important to emphasise that the sole focus of proceedings under the MCA 2005 is (or should be) upon the interests of the adult lacking capacity. They do not exist as a forum to canvass allegations of misconduct save and to the extent it is necessary that such allegations are determined in order to allow the judge properly to determine the application before them. As has been said in the context of private law proceedings under the CA 1989: 'the finite resources of the court do not exist simply to provide a freestanding medium for one party to obtain, for no reason other than vindication, findings of matrimonial misconduct against the other'.[15] The same holds equally true of allegations of misconduct towards the adult without capacity.

14.10 In order to assist the court to determine whether a fact-finding exercise: a) will be necessary; and b) (if it is) should be listed as the first part of a split trial process, it is incumbent upon the parties to identify at an early stage precisely what the issues are and precisely what factual findings will be required from the court in order to ground the relief that is sought. This point is discussed further in chapter 10 above. With the drive towards speedier determination of welfare cases before the Court of Protection it is likely that courts will now require some persuasion that a split trial is necessary given the inevitable delay that this will build in to the final resolution of the application.

---

14 Para 21.
15 *AA v NA (Appeal: Fact-Finding)* [2010] EWHC 1282 (Fam), [2010] 2 FLR 1173 at para 18 per Mostyn J.

Preparing for a fact-finding hearing

14.11 Fact-finding hearings are most commonly directed by the court (either separately or as part of the final hearing) in what might be termed safeguarding cases brought by local authorities (see further chapter 23). In such cases, it is usually the case that the local authority will be seeking adverse findings against an individual or individuals to support its contention that (for instance) their contact with P should be limited, or that P should live other than in the family home.

14.12 In such cases, the practice has developed of requiring the local authority applicant to draw up a so-called 'Scott schedule'[16] of allegations, in other words a table setting out:

- the specific allegation made (for instance that 'X failed to provide adequate care to P');
- the particulars of the allegation (for instance that 'On 9 September 2016 X failed to change P's incontinence pad for a period of 12 hours'); and
- a cross-reference (or cross-references) to the evidence relied upon in support of the particulars of the allegation (for instance 'paragraph 9 of the witness statement of Ms Y, social worker, dated 20 October 2016').

14.13 It is conventional then for the subject of the allegation to be required to set out in the same table their response to the allegation and, if it is denied, cross-references to the evidence upon which they rely in support of their denial. The local authority is then usually permitted to reply to the response, again in the same format. A column can then be provided in which the court can in due course record its finding against each allegation. The end result is a table which (ideally) makes it easier for preparations to be made for the fact-finding hearing by bringing into sharp focus the allegations, whether the allegations are disputed (and, if so, whether in whole or in part) and the scope of the evidence that will be called by the parties.

14.14 Experience shows that the process of preparing and responding to Scott schedules serves significantly to focus the minds of both applicants and respondents as to the issues in the case and the strength of the evidence. Experience has also shown that it is very

---

16 So-called because the original schedule was devised by George Alexander Scott, who held the post of Official Referee (ie judge in what is now the Technology and Construction Court) in the 1920s.

Fact-finding 397

common for applicants to produce *Scott* schedules that run to many pages of allegations when, in reality, the court need only determine a limited number in order to be able to have a secure foundation upon which to determine where P's best interests lie. An important function of the final case management hearing prior to the fact-finding hearing will therefore be to ensure that only those allegations that it is truly necessary for the court to determine are set down for resolution at that latter hearing.

14.15   Pilot PD 4B/PD 13B,[17] in turn, makes clear that at the start of any bundle prepared for the fact-finding hearing, there must be inserted a document or documents prepared by each party which should set out (either within the document(s) themselves or by cross-referring to another document that is, or will be, within the bundle):

- the findings or fact that the court is being asked to make; and
- cross-references to the evidence relied upon to found those findings

(in other words, a *Scott* schedule).[18]

14.16   Where appropriate, the preliminary documents for a fact-finding should also include:

- a chronology;
- a skeleton argument; and
- a description of relevant family members and other persons who may be affected by or interested in the relief sought.[19]

14.17   Where (as is often the case) the documents in the case run to several lever arch files, it is also strongly advisable for the applicant to prepare (on an agreed basis if possible) a core bundle which contains:

- any relevant directions made by the court;
- the completed *Scott* schedule;
- a chronology of relevant dates;
- the witness statements of the relevant witnesses; and
- any documents to which those witnesses are likely to have to be taken for purposes of giving evidence.

14.18   For welfare cases under the Case Management Pilot, the expectation is that the bundle for the final hearing (and it is suggested, by analogy,

---

17   Discussed in greater detail at paras 10.29 onwards.
18   Pilot PD 4B/PD 13B para 4.4.
19   Pilot PD 4B/PD 13B para 4.5.

for any 'split' fact-finding hearing) should run to no more than 350 pages into total.[20]

14.19 One final point needs to be made in this regard. As discussed at paras 12.9 onwards, the provisions relating to disclosure in the COPR are not regularly applied. However, in *Enfield LBC v SA and others*,[21] McFarlane J (as he then was) considered a situation that had arisen where, during the course of a fact-finding hearing held to determine allegations of abusive parenting against a learning disabled woman, it emerged that the police had already conducted an 'achieving best evidence' (ABE) interview with the woman, in which the woman had denied that she had been abused, and had repeatedly asked to go home or to see her parents, and that the authority had a copy of this interview. The local authority had informed the Official Solicitor afterwards that the interview had taken place, but, having signed a police disclaimer, had not disclosed the interview, on the basis that it decided not to rely upon the content of the interview. McFarlane J was highly critical of the local authority, and his reasoning is sufficiently important to merit reproduction in this chapter almost in full:

55. . . . . [I]t would seem that in this case they have provided the disclosure that was required of them [under the directions made], yet the result, from the perspective of a judge who is embedded in the procedure and culture of child protection proceedings under the Children Act 1989, is totally unacceptable. In a fact-finding process, where the case is largely based upon what a vulnerable adult (P) has said and the aim of the court in due course is to make orders to meet P's best interests, how can it be appropriate, fair to the interests of all parties (but particularly P) or in any way acceptable for the applicant local authority to take part in arranging a formal ABE interview of P and subsequently take possession of a DVD recording of the interview yet be under no duty to inform the other parties or the court that that is the case?

56. The position in family proceedings is that 'it is a duty owed to the court both by the parties and by their legal representatives to give full and frank disclosure in ancillary relief applications and also in all matters in respect of children' [*Practice Direction (Family Proceedings: Case Management)* [1995] 1 WLR 332, [1995] 1 All ER 586, sub nom Practice Direction: Case Management (31 January 1995) [1995] 1 FLR 456]. If these were proceedings relating to children, then there is absolutely no doubt that the local authority, under the duty to give 'full and frank disclosure', would have been required to inform the parties and the court of the occurrence of the interview and to disclose the

---

20 Case Management Pilot PD para 4(2)(b).
21 [2010] EWHC 196 (Admin), [2010] COPLR Con Vol 362.

DVD record (subject to the court's power to limit or control disclosure on a case specific basis). Given that the aim of protection is common between child protection proceedings under the CA 1989, Part 4 and proceedings such as the present which aim to investigate allegations of harm to P and, if necessary, protect her, how can it be a requirement in one process for the applicant to disclose the existence of an ABE interview, yet not a requirement, absent of an express order from the court in the other process?

57. The apparent difference in the approach to disclosure as between the family courts and the Court of Protection may well arise from the fact that the rules for the latter are based upon ordinary civil litigation with the expectation that disclosure will be based on whether documents 'adversely affect [a party's] own case' or 'support another party's case' (COPR, r133(2)(b)) whereas the approach of the family court is that there is a duty to give *the court* all relevant material.

58. There can, in my view, be no justification for there being a difference of this degree on the issue of disclosure between the family court and the Court of Protection in fact-finding cases of this type where really the process and the issues are essentially identical whether the vulnerable complainant is a young child or an incapacitated adult. For the future in such cases in the Court of Protection it would seem to be justified for the court to make an order for 'specific disclosure' under COPR 2007, r133(3) requiring all parties to give 'full and frank disclosure' of all relevant material. If such a direction had been made in the present case, the local authority would have been under a duty to disclose the DVD of the ABE interview, and any other records relating to it, once they came into their possession.

The determination of contested facts

14.20 As noted at the outset to this chapter, the processes of the Court of Protection are essentially inquisitorial, which means that questions of the burden of proof are not relevant to some of its tasks. Questions of the burden of proof are, for instance, not relevant to the question of what is in P's best interests, which is 'primarily an inquiry by the courts, weighing into the balance various factors. No party is under a burden of proof; rather the court, after investigating best interests, decides that issue on a balance of probability'.[22]

22 *Cheshire West and Cheshire Council v P and M* [2011] EWHC 1330 (Fam), [2011] COPLR Con Vol 273 at paras 51–52 per Baker J, endorsing the submissions made by the mother of P, supported by the Official Solicitor. This approach was endorsed by Sir James Munby P in *Re G* [2014] EWCOP 1361, [2014] COPLR 416 at para 52

14.21 However, the court nonetheless proceeds on the basis of conventional civil principles when it comes to the determination of a fact or facts that one party must prove in order to obtain the relief that it seeks (properly called 'facts in issue'). These principles have been summarised thus:[23]

> 83. First, the burden of proof lies with the local authority. It is the local authority that brings these proceedings and identifies the findings that they invite the court to make. Therefore, the burden of proving the allegations rests with them.
> 84. Secondly, the standard of proof is the balance of probabilities: *Re B (Children)* [2008] UKHR 35. If the local authority proves a fact on the balance of probabilities, this court will treat that fact as established and all future decisions concerning M's future will be based on that finding. Equally, if the local authority fails to prove any allegation, the court will disregard that allegation completely. In her written submissions on behalf of the local authority, Miss Bretherton contended that the court should apply the principle that
>
>> 'the more serious the allegation the more cogent is the evidence required to overcome the unlikelihood of what is alleged and thus to prove it.'
>
> This principle, originally stated by Ungoed-Thomas J in *Re Dellows Will Trust* [1964] 1 WLR 451, was at one time applied by the courts considering allegations of child abuse in family proceedings under the Children Act 1989. In *Re B*, however, the House of Lords emphatically rejected that approach. Baroness Hale of Richmond, with whose judgment the other four Law Lords agreed, having analysed the case law, stated at paragraphs 70 to 72:
>
>> '70 I would announce loud and clear that the standard of proof in finding the facts necessary to establish the threshold under s31(2) or the welfare considerations of the 1989 Act is the simple balance of probabilities – neither more nor less. Neither the seriousness of the allegation nor the seriousness of the consequences should make any difference to the standard of proof to be applied in determining the facts. The inherent probabilities are simply something to be taken into account, where relevant in deciding where the truth lies.
>>
>> 71. As to the seriousness of the consequences, they are serious either way. A child may find her relationship with her family seriously disrupted or she may find herself still at risk of suffering serious harm. A parent may find his relationship with his child

---

23 *A Local Authority v M and Another* [2014] EWCOP 33, [2015] COPLR 6 per Baker J.

seriously disrupted or he may find himself still at liberty to maltreat this or other children in the future.

72. As to the seriousness of the allegation, there is no logical or necessary connection between seriousness and probability.'

In my judgment, the same approach must surely apply in the Court of Protection where the court is carrying out a similar exercise in determining the facts upon which to base decisions as to the best interests of an incapacitated adult.

85. Thirdly, findings of fact in these cases must be based on evidence. As Munby J (as he then was) observed in *Re A (A Child: Fact-finding hearing: speculation)* [2011] EWCA Civ 12:

> 'It is an elementary proposition that findings of fact must be based on evidence, including inferences that can properly be drawn from the evidence, and not on suspicion or speculation.'

86. Fourth, the court must take into account all the evidence and, furthermore, consider each piece of evidence in the context of all the other evidence. As Dame Elizabeth Butler-Sloss, President, observed in *Re T* [2004] EWCA Civ 458, [2005] 2 FLR 838, at paragraph 33:

> 'Evidence cannot be evaluated and assessed in separate compartments. A judge in these difficult cases must have regard to the relevance of each piece of evidence to the other evidence and to exercise an overview of the totality of the evidence in order to come to the conclusion whether the case put forward by the local authority has been made out to the appropriate standard of proof.'

87. Fifth, whilst appropriate attention must be paid to the opinion of medical experts, those opinions need to be considered in the context of all the other evidence. The roles of the court and the experts are distinct. It is the court that is in the position to weigh up expert evidence against the other evidence: *A County Council v K, D and L* [2005] EWHC 144 Fam, [2005] 1 FLR 851 per Charles J.

88. Sixth, in assessing the expert evidence, which involves a multi-disciplinary analysis of the medical information conducted by a group of specialists, each bringing their own expertise to bear on the problem, one important consideration – and of particular relevance in this case – is that the court must be careful to ensure that each expert keeps within the bounds of their own expertise and defers where appropriate to the expertise of others – see the observations of Eleanor King J in *Re S* [2009] EWHC 2115 Fam.

[...]

90. Eighth, it is not uncommon for witnesses in these cases to tell lies, both before and during the hearing. The court must be careful to bear in mind that a witness may lie for many reasons – such as shame, misplaced loyalty, panic, fear and distress – and the fact that a witness has lied about some matters does not mean that he or she has lied

about everything – see *R v Lucas* [1981] QB 720. The assessment of the truthfulness is an important part of my function in this case.15.24

14.22 The following observations of Mostyn J24 are also important:

ii) The law operates a binary system in which the only values are 0 and 1. The fact either happened or it did not. If the court is left in doubt, the doubt is resolved by a rule that one party or the other carries the burden of proof. If the party who bears the burden of proof fails to discharge it, a value of 0 is returned and the fact is treated as not having happened. If he does discharge it, a value of 1 is returned and the fact is treated as having happened: *Re B (Care Proceedings: Standard of Proof)*, at para [2] per Lord Hoffmann.

[...]

iv) Sometimes the burden of proof will come to the judge's rescue: the party with the burden of showing that something took place will not have satisfied him that it did. But generally speaking a judge ought to be able to make up his mind where the truth lies without needing to rely upon the burden of proof: *Re B (Care Proceedings: Standard of Proof)* at paras [2] and [32]; *Rhesa Shipping Co SA v Edmond and Another: The Popi M* [1985] 1 WLR 948.

v) It is impermissible for a judge to conclude in the case of a series of improbable causes that the least improbable or least unlikely is nonetheless the cause of the event: *Rhesa Shipping Co SA v Edmond and Another: The Popi M; Ide v ATB Sales Ltd; Lexus Financial Services t/a Toyota Financial Services (UK) plc v Russell* [2008] EWCA Civ 424 at para [4].

vi) There is no pseudo-burden or obligation cast on the respondents to come up with alternative explanations: *Lancashire County Council v D and E* [2010] 2 FLR 196 at paras [36] and [37]; *Re C and D (Photographs of Injuries)* [2011] 1 FLR 990, at para [203].

vii) The assessment of credibility generally involves wider problems than mere 'demeanour' which is mostly concerned with whether the witness appears to be telling the truth as he now believes it to be. With every day that passes the memory becomes fainter and the imagination becomes more active. The human capacity for honestly believing something which bears no relation to what actually happened is unlimited. Therefore, contemporary documents are always of the utmost importance: *Onassis and Calogeropoulos v Vergottis* [1968] 2 Lloyd's Rep 403, per Lord Pearce; *A County Council v M and F* [2011] EWHC 1804 (Fam) [2012] 2 FLR 939 at paras [29] and [30].

14.23 It is worth amplifying point ii): if a party decides not to advance an allegation (or withdraws it) because it does not consider that it can properly make out the relevant facts supporting that allegation, for

---

24 *Re D (a child)* [2014] EWHC 121 (Fam), [2014] Fam Law 421 at para 31 per Mostyn J. This was a care case, but the principles are of general application.

purposes of the court's determination of the issues to which the allegation goes, it must proceed on the basis that the facts did not happen.

14.24 Further, where the court is asked to determine allegations of harm it is suggested that, by analogy with the position that prevails in care proceedings relating to children, a conclusion that an adult has suffered from harm at the hands of another must be based upon facts, not just suspicion.[25] It is further suggested that a real possibility alone would not be sufficient.[26]

Fact-finding and future risk

14.25 'Safeguarding' cases are sometimes brought, not on the basis that an adult *has* suffered harm at the hands of another, but rather on the basis that they are *likely* to do so absent preventative action on the part of the court. In care proceedings, the approach that the court must take has been set down by the Supreme Court thus:

> 8. ... [I]f the case is based on the likelihood of future harm, the court must be satisfied on the balance of probabilities that the facts upon which that prediction was based did actually happen. It is not enough that they may have done so or that there was a real possibility that they did. ... [H]owever, if the case is based on the likelihood of future harm, the court does not have to be satisfied that such harm is more likely than not to happen. It is enough that there is 'a real possibility, a possibility that cannot sensibly be ignored having regard to the nature and gravity of the feared harm in the particular case', [*In re H (Minors) (Sexual Abuse: Standard of Proof)* [1996] AC 563] per Lord Nicholls of Birkenhead, at p 585f.
>
> 9. Thus the law has drawn a clear distinction between probability as it applies to past facts and probability as it applies to future predictions. Past facts must be proved to have happened on the balance of probabilities, that is, that it is more likely than not that they did happen. Predictions about future facts need only be based upon a degree of likelihood that they will happen which is sufficient to justify preventive action. This will depend upon the nature and gravity of the harm: a lesser degree of likelihood that the child will be killed will justify immediate preventive action than the degree of likelihood that the child will not be sent to school.[27]

---

25 *In re H (minors) (sexual abuse: standard of proof)* [1996] AC 563 at 591E per Lord Nicholls.
26 *In Re B* at para 70 per Baroness Hale.
27 *Re S-B (children)* [2009] UKSC 17, [2010] 1 AC 678 at para 8 per Baroness Hale.

14.26 This approach was also adopted prior to the coming into force of the MCA 2005 in the exercise of the inherent jurisdiction of the High Court to protect vulnerable adults,[28] and it is suggested that it remains equally applicable for judges of the Court of Protection.

Fact-finding: consequences

14.27 Although, as noted above, fact-finding can (and often will) take place at essentially the same time as the determination of the substantive best interests questions relating to P, where the fact-finding takes place separately it would be usual for the court to give a separate judgment in relation to the fact-finding hearing in order for the parties to take stock prior to the second stage. Part of this taking stock might well be to consider – in an appropriate case – the instruction of the relevant expert to report upon P's best interests. Experience has taught that it is frequently helpful to delay the instruction until this stage so that the expert can proceed upon the basis of clearly established facts, rather than having to give alternative conclusions upon the basis of what may be found in due course to have occurred (it being clear that an expert cannot seek to determine contested facts for themselves: see para 12.61).

14.28 Importantly, as there is no difference in principle between the approach to be adopted to split hearings in the Court of Protection (at least in welfare cases) and public law child protection proceedings, the decision of the House of Lords in *Re B*[29] applies so as to require that once findings of fact have been made the case is part heard and the trial should not resume before a different judge.[30]

14.29 Finally, it should be noted that it is clear that a judge may subsequently revisit the conclusions reached at a fact-finding hearing if subsequent evidence warrants it.[31]

---

28 *Re MM; local authority X v MM (by the Official Solicitor) and KM* [2007] EWHC 2003 (Fam), [2009] 1 FLR 443 at para 119 per Munby J (as he then was).
29 *In re B (children) (care proceedings: standard of proof) (CAFCASS intervening)* [2008] UKHL 35, [2009] 1 AC 11 at para 2 per Lord Hoffmann.
30 *Enfield LBC v SA and others* [2010] EWHC 196 (Admin), [2010] COPLR Con Vol 362 at para 113 per McFarlane J (as he then was).
31 *In re L and another (children) (preliminary finding: power to reverse)* [2013] 1 WLR 634 at para 34; see also *In re S-B (children) (care proceedings: standard of proof)* [2010] 1 AC 678 at para 46.

CHAPTER 15

The final determination of the application

15.1	Introduction
15.3	Determining an application without a final hearing
15.9	Finalising the issues and the evidence; timetabling
15.22	Skeleton arguments
15.23	**The hearing**
15.23	The day of the hearing
15.25	Public or private?
15.26	Opening speeches
15.27	Witness evidence
15.34	Witnesses: special cases (1) hearing from P
15.45	Witnesses: special cases (2) vulnerable witnesses
15.48	Witnesses: special cases (3) interpreters
15.53	Witnesses: special cases (4) 'remote' evidence giving
15.58	Closing arguments
15.59	Negotiations during the hearing
15.60	**Judgment**
15.63	**Final orders**
15.69	P regains capacity or dies
15.73	Case study: facilitating participation of 'P' in Court of Protection proceedings

Introduction

15.1 This chapter deals with how applications are finally disposed of by the court. After touching on the disposal of applications without a final hearing, the focus is on the steps required effectively to prepare and to conduct final hearings, as well as dealing with the subsequent steps of receiving the judgment and drawing up the final order. Because the issues of principle are the same, the chapter covers both proceedings relating to P's property and affairs, and P's health and welfare; many of the examples will, though, be drawn from applications relating to health and welfare because they form the bulk of the reported cases.

15.2 This chapter must be read alongside the preceding chapters, and in particular those relating to directions hearings (chapter 10), evidence and disclosure (chapter 12) and (in an appropriate case) fact-finding (chapter 14). It is clear from the reported cases,[1] that matters will very rapidly go awry in a contested case unless a proper focus is maintained by all parties – and the court – upon the final destination of the proceedings and of the steps required along the route.

Determining an application without a final hearing

15.3 The vast majority of applications to the Court of Protection are disposed of without any hearing at all. By way of example, of the 23,525 applications received by the court in 2015, 20,876 (89 per cent) concerned property and affairs and only 2,469 (11 per cent) concerned health and welfare.[2] Of the applications relating to property and affairs, the vast majority were non-contentious and were dealt without a hearing. There were, in total, 1,991 hearings in 2015 in London and in the regional courts in which Court of Protection judges sit, a very significant proportion of which would have been directions/interim hearings rather than final hearings.

15.4 Moreover, many applications which start out hotly contested end up being resolved by consent without the need for a final hearing. This can be, for instance, because an independent expert has provided a report making entirely clear where P's interests lie which is accepted by all parties and encapsulated in a proposal put to the court to be

---

1 See, for instance, *Re A and B (Court of Protection: Delay and Costs)* [2014] EWCOP 48, [2015] COPLR 1.
2 These statistics are provided by former Senior Judge Lush.

endorsed as a consent order. In other cases, mediation or some other form of alternative dispute resolution (discussed further in chapter 19) can achieve a resolution to the issues dividing the parties that they consider that they can properly put to the court as being in P's best interests.

15.5 As discussed above (para 10.48), where parties have reached agreement, they are required to notify the court as soon as possible. Where a consent order has been submitted for approval which finally disposes of all the issues in the case, the starting position will be that the court will only convene a hearing a) if insufficient notice has been given; or b) there is some specific feature which the court considers it must deal with at an attended hearing. One (extreme) example of the latter would be in an application for withdrawal of clinically assisted nutrition and hydration from a person in a permanent vegetative state; it is often the case that such applications are ultimately agreed by all the parties, but judges will always convene a hearing and deliver a judgment recording their determination (see further in relation to serious medical treatment cases, chapter 22).[3] Another less extreme, but probably – and sadly – more common example, is where the information provided with the consent order is not sufficient to satisfy the judge that they can endorse it without further clarification that the decisions/declarations set out are properly in P's best interests.

15.6 It should be remembered that wherever the court makes an order without a hearing, COPR r89 applies so as to allow P, any party to the proceedings, or any person affected by the order to apply for reconsideration. Reconsideration is addressed further in chapter 18, but is unlikely to be relevant where the court is endorsing a consent order submitted by the parties for approval.

15.7 In some cases, the applicant may decide that they wish to withdraw proceedings. For instance, the safeguarding concern that underpinned a local authority's application to the court for draconian welfare orders (eg removing the person from their own home and restricting contact with a family member) has now been sufficiently alleviated that the relevant local authority no longer considers that they are justified. Or it may become clear that it will not be possible to establish a sufficient factual basis upon which to seek such orders (as to which see further chapter 14). With the introduction of COPR r87A in July 2015, permission is now required to withdraw

---

3 See, for instance, *Re D* [2012] EWHC 885 (COP), [2012] COPLR 493.

proceedings. An application must be made on a COP9 form,[4] following the normal procedure for applications made within proceedings (see para 10.22). It is suggested that a decision upon an application to withdraw proceedings is not a decision falling within MCA 2005 s1(5): ie it is a case management decision on the part of the court, rather than a decision taken for or on behalf of P (and therefore not a 'best interests' decision), albeit that the court will have P's welfare interests squarely in mind.[5]

15.8 As discussed further in para 23.18, whilst the court is likely to endorse an order to withdraw proceedings where it is clear that the underlying basis for the concern motivating the application is no longer present, it is likely that the court will take a dim view of attempts to withdraw proceedings on the basis that the public authority which has brought proceedings now takes a different view of where the person's interests lie than it is likely that the court will do. Indeed, the public body may well find itself directed to file evidence (including care plans), even though the plan's contents may not or do not reflect its formal position.[6] Where the public body decides, in the discharge of its public law obligations relating to funding of care and treatment, that a particular option is no longer on the table, the position is different, and is discussed in chapter 24.

Finalising the issues and the evidence; timetabling

15.9 As discussed in detail in chapter 10 above, and has been given renewed emphasis by the Case Management Pilot, one of the key case management tasks of the court is to ensure that the issues in the case are identified at an early stage, in large part so that directions can be made to ensure that the evidence (but only the evidence) necessary to resolve those issues will be before the court. It is worth emphasising, however, that the issues can – and frequently do – evolve during the currency of proceedings. For instance, if P is elderly, their health may deteriorate and different priorities may assert themselves when it comes to their best interests. A case brought before the court on an urgent basis arising out of a safeguarding concern may evolve dramatically if further investigation reveals that the concern is in part not

4 COPR r87A(2).
5 See, by analogy, *Re W (Care Proceedings: Functions of Court and Local Authority)* [2013] EWCA Civ 1227, [2014] 2 FLR 431 at para 40.
6 *Re W*, see also *Re MN (Adult)* [2015] EWCA Civ 411, (2015) 18 CCLR 521, [2016] Fam 87 at para 37.

The final determination of the application 409

borne out. If a separate fact-finding hearing has been listed (see chapter 14 above), the court may in giving its judgment upon the matters considered at that hearing make findings which require one or other party to take stock of how it wishes to present its case at the subsequent hearing to determine the substantive best interests questions. Alternatively, expert evidence may be directed following such a fact-finding hearing which puts a different complexion upon the best interests exercise. It can also be the case that trial periods of contact (for instance) directed at an interim hearing have proceeded sufficiently successfully that a local authority applicant decides that it can adopt a more 'relaxed' position at the final hearing.

15.10 By the same token, it can also frequently be necessary for provision to be made for the filing of updating evidence relating to P's circumstances: the court will be determining what is in P's best interests *as at* the time of the final hearing, so it is necessary that it is provided with the most up-to-date evidence possible. While witnesses can amplify their written evidence in the witness box (see further para 15.28 below), it is desirable to ensure that that written evidence is as current as possible.

15.11 So as to ensure that final hearings are successful in terms of leading to a determination of the issues on the basis of the necessary evidence, the Case Management Pilot has introduced a final management hearing for cases on the welfare pathway (see further paras 10.19). Even though there is no formal requirement for a final management hearing for cases on the property and affairs pathway, it is likely that an equivalent hearing would be listed in the event that the case was of any complexity.

15.12 A final management hearing will follow the pattern of directions hearings discussed in chapter 10, but with a particular focus on ensuring that both the issues and the evidence have been finalised insofar as possible in advance of the final hearing. To that end, the Case Management Pilot Practice Direction (PD) provides that a meeting should take place five days before the final management hearing between advocates, and, insofar as practicable, any unrepresented parties, with the purpose of resolving and narrowing the issues to be determined at the hearing, addressing each of the matters required by Pilot PD 4B/PD 13B (see further paras 10.20 onwards) and, critically, preparing a draft order.[7] The applicant or (if the applicant is not represented but the respondent is) must also file a core

7 Case Management Pilot PD para 4.6(2).

bundle complying with the provisions of Pilot PD 4B/PD 13B including, in particular, those provisions set out at paras 10.37).[8]

15.13 The judge at the final management hearing will want to see, in particular:

- an agreed time estimate for the final hearing made on the basis of separate provision being made for 1) judicial pre-reading; 2) hearing all the evidence and submissions; and 3) preparation and delivery of judgment.[9] Experience suggests that estimates given by legal representatives often underestimate the time for 2) and almost invariably do not give sufficient time for either 1) or 3);
- a draft witness template identifying precisely who will be giving evidence when and specific arrangements that may be required in relation to any particular witness (see further paras 15.45 onwards for particular considerations that may apply in relation to vulnerable witnesses or where a person is giving evidence by video-link). It is important to be realistic as to how quickly it is possible to hear from each witness, and also to schedule witnesses appropriately, especially where (for instance) clinicians will need to re-arrange clinics in order to attend; and
- specific consideration as to any practical issues that may arise in relation to hearing from P. See further below, paras 15.34 onwards.

15.14 The preparation of bundles for directions hearings is discussed in detail at paras 10.32ff above. The same practical requirements set out in Pilot PD 4B/PD 13B will apply to almost all final hearings as they do to interim hearings (including as to the timing for lodging them), and they are not repeated here. There are, though, specific requirements that apply to the preliminary documents that must appear in the bundle, addressed in the paragraphs which follow.

15.15 At the start of the bundle there must be inserted a document or documents prepared by each party ('the preliminary documents for a final hearing') which should set out (either within the preliminary documents themselves, or by cross-reference to what is set out in another document that is in, or is to be put in the bundle):

- the relief sought;
- a skeleton argument.[10]

---

8 Case Management Pilot PD para 4.6(2) and Pilot PD 4B/PD 13B paras 4.2 and 4.3.
9 Pilot PD 4B/PD 13B para 10.1.
10 Pilot PD 4B/PD 13B para 4.6.

15.16 Where appropriate, the preliminary documents for a final hearing should include

- a chronology;
- the findings of fact that the court is being invited to make and the factors based on such findings or agreed facts that the court is being invited to take into account;
- an appropriately particularised description of the alternatives the court is being invited to consider; and
- a description of relevant family members and other persons who may be affected by or interested in the relief sought.[11]

15.17 Each of the preliminary documents must state on the front page immediately below the heading the date when it was prepared and the date of the hearing for which it was prepared.[12] All case summaries, chronologies and skeleton arguments contained in the preliminary documents must be cross-referenced to the relevant pages of the bundle.[13]

15.18 Where the nature of the hearing is such that a complete bundle of all documents is unnecessary – for instance, because the relief now being sought by the applicant has been refined significantly – the bundle (which need not be repaginated) may comprise only those documents necessary for the hearing, but i) the preliminary documents must state that the bundle is limited or incomplete; and ii) the bundle must if reasonably practicable be in a form agreed by all parties.[14]

15.19 One injunction which is regularly honoured more in the breach, but which is actually of some importance, is that, where a bundle has been taken away after a directions hearing and is then re-lodged, the bundle must be updated and superseded documents must be *removed*.[15] Judges – understandably – become very impatient with bundles that contain numerous iterations of documents: it is very rarely necessary for any but (for instance) the most recent version of the care plan for P to be contained in the bundle.

15.20 For the final hearing (as opposed to the final management hearing), a further requirement is imposed in relation to the court bundle for welfare cases falling within the Case Management Pilot:

11 Pilot PD 4B/PD 13B para 4.7.
12 Pilot PD 4B/PD 13B para 4.8.
13 Pilot PD 4B/PD 13B para 4.9.
14 Pilot PD 4B/PD 13B para 4.10.
15 Pilot PD 4B/PD 13B para 4.11.

the bundle should not normally be more than 350 pages, and should in any event not contain more than one copy of any document.[16]

15.21 Where witnesses are to give evidence at the final hearing, it is important that a separate bundle is provided which can be put into the witness box for them to use during the course of the hearing. It is equally important (but sadly not always the case) that this bundle matches the pagination of the bundles being used by the parties and the judge to avoid unnecessary delays during the hearing.

Skeleton arguments

15.22 As noted above (para 15.15), Pilot PD 4B/PD 13B envisages that the parties will each provide skeleton arguments in advance of the final hearing. The courts have repeatedly emphasised that skeleton arguments should be just that – ie skeletal. In the course of a judgment given in the Court of Appeal, but of equal relevance to proceedings before the Court of Protection, Mummery LJ emphasised that:

> ... skeleton arguments should not be prepared as verbatim scripts to be read out in public or as footnoted theses to be read in private. Good skeleton arguments are tools with practical uses: an agenda for the hearing, a summary of the main points, propositions and arguments to be developed orally, a useful way of noting citations and references, a convenient place for making cross references, a time-saving means of avoiding unnecessary dictation to the court and laborious and pointless note-taking by the court.[17]

The hearing

The day of the hearing

15.23 Even more than is the case with directions hearing, it is important to get to court early on the day of the final hearing. This will allow for any last-minute discussions to take place and for steps to be taken in the event of any logistical problems (a common one being that the bundle provided for the witnesses has not found its way into the witness box). If witnesses are to give evidence, it will also allow time

---

16 Case Management Pilot PD para 4.7(2)(b).
17 See *Raja v Van Hoogstraten (No 9)* [2009] 1 WLR 1143 at para 126 per Mummery LJ.

to take their details and give them to court staff -- who need to know, in particular, whether the witness will swear on the Bible or other Holy Book, or affirm.

15.24 Both in relation to witnesses of fact and expert witnesses, making sure that they are familiar with the layout of the court room is important: wherever possible they should be taken in and shown where they are to sit, where the witness box is and where the judge will sit. It is important to understand that for most witnesses, even social or health care professionals, a court room is an alien and often forbidding environment; much can be done by way of simple familiarisation with that environment. It is also important – and is not (impermissible 'coaching') – to explain to a witness the process of being questioned: one particularly useful tip being to address the answers to any question being asked in cross-examination to the judge so as to avoid the natural tendency to feel that cross-examination represents a personal attack upon the witness by the person conducing the questioning.

Public or private?

15.25 As discussed in greater detail in chapter 13, final hearings will take place in the majority of cases in public.

Opening speeches

15.26 Especially where full skeleton arguments have been provided, it is unlikely that the judge will want to hear lengthy opening speeches from any of the legal representatives; the usual practice is to proceed very rapidly (often within a matter of minutes) to the calling of the first witness for the applicant.

Witness evidence

15.27 Proceedings before the Court of Protection are formal proceedings, such that witnesses will be required to swear on the Bible or other Holy Book, or affirm as to the truth of their evidence.

15.28 As discussed at para 12.15 above, a witness statement will stand as the evidence-in-chief of a witness, such that they will only be permitted to give supplementary evidence in answer to questions from the party on whose behalf they appear with the permission of the court. How readily this will be granted will depend upon the nature of the case; it can, though, be the case that a witness will have done no more than confirm their name and address and that the contents of their statement are true before they are answering questions put by the other parties. This can be disconcerting for the witness, and, where it can properly be done, it is usually advisable for the legal representative for the party calling the witness to ask at least one 'settling in' question. What this question will be will depend upon the context, but most usually it will consist of inviting the witness to update the court as to any developments since the witness statement was prepared.

15.29 A witness called on behalf of a party will then be cross-examined by the other parties, and can then be re-examined by the party on whose behalf they have given evidence. They can also be asked questions by the judge: especially given the inquisitorial nature of the Court of Protection's processes, it is quite frequently the case that many of the questions that are put to the witness in the court are, in fact, asked by the judge. The judge should then give the chance to the parties to ask any further questions of the witness arising out of their questions.

15.30 The usual practice is for all the witnesses of fact to give their evidence, first those called on behalf of the applicant, then those called on behalf of the first respondent, and so forth, before any expert witness gives their evidence. Ideally, an expert witness such as an independent social worker will have had the chance to hear the evidence of the witnesses of fact so that they are able to consider this evidence when giving their opinion to the court; if the hearing is lengthy, however, it may well be too expensive and/or logistically impracticable for the expert to attend all the days of the hearing. In such a case, then the party calling the expert (which will, if the Official Solicitor has been instructed on behalf of P, almost invariably be the Official Solicitor) should make sure that they give a summary to the expert of any relevant evidence given in their absence.

15.31 Space precludes a detailed discussion of the principles of witness handling, the principles of which are the same before the Court of Protection as they are before any other court or tribunal.[18] In very brief summary, *preparation* and *politeness* are the two watchwords that will perhaps most usefully serve. What the judge wants is to have brought out before them the evidence upon which they can:

a) determine any facts in issue; and
b) determine whether

---

18 And are pithily summarised by Parker J in *NCC v PB and TB* [2014] EWCOP 14, [2015] COPLR 118 at paras 140–146.

- P has or lacks the requisite decision-making capacity; and
- (if P lacks capacity), where P's best interests lie.

It is only by being clear as to what submissions will be made in closing arguments as to the evidence going to a) and b) that proper lines of questioning can be developed. Further, while it can frequently be necessary to be robust in cross-examination, and it is important that particular points of contention are put to the witnesses so that they can properly respond, judges respond very negatively to discourtesy in questioning. This is particularly so when it comes to the cross-examination of independent experts, whose duty it is to assist the court rather than one of the parties (see paras 12.81 onwards). Moreover, experience teaches that it is generally extremely unlikely that 'badgering' an expert under cross-examination will lead them to recant their opinions. It is generally far more productive for an advocate to treat the expert as a fellow professional and, in essence, to engage with them upon their own terms so as to tease out the nuances in their views. What is often effective is to examine with the experts the factual premises upon which they have based their opinions, because a good expert will always reassess their opinion if they are given new or different factual information upon which to base that information. As discussed at para 12.60 above, an expert should not be determining the factual matters in issue in the case, so where there are still factual matters that are not determined, it is entirely appropriate to invite an expert to give their opinion on the basis that 'if the court were to find that [xx] took place, how would your opinion differ?'.

15.32   One point cannot be emphasised enough. As obvious as it seems, it is vital to recall that the focus of the hearing will be upon P's capacity and best interests, a matter in respect of which there are no winners or losers. The court will therefore be very impatient with questions that are directed to the canvassing of allegations of misconduct or poor practice save and to the extent necessary for the court to be able to determine where the interests of P lie (see also para 14.9). This can place advocates in particular difficulties where they are being pressured by their lay clients to put questions to others because they want grievances aired. Those grievances – for instance as to how another family member or a local authority social worker has conducted themselves – may well be very deeply felt, but unless they relate to the issues actually before the court they should not be advanced by way of questioning. In this regard, it is useful to recall the strong guidance given by the Court of Appeal that:

Something of a myth about the meaning of the client's 'instructions' has developed. . . . the client does not conduct the case. The advocate is not the client's mouthpiece, obliged to conduct the case in accordance with whatever the client, or when the advocate is a barrister, the solicitor 'instructs' him. In short, the advocate is bound to advance [his client's] case on the basis that what his client tells him is the truth, but save for well-established principles [relating specifically to criminal cases] the advocate, and the advocate alone remains responsible for the forensic decisions and strategy. That is the foundation for the right to appear as an advocate, with the privileges and responsibilities of advocates and as an advocate, burdened with twin responsibilities, both to the client and to the court.[19]

This guidance was given in the context of criminal proceedings, but it is equally applicable to proceedings before the Court of Protection.[20]

15.33 Finally, it should be noted that it is very important to keep a proper note of the evidence given by witnesses; while proceedings before the Court of Protection are recorded, such recordings a) can sometimes contain gaps at the vital moments; b) can take some time to transcribe; and c) will usually only be transcribed upon payment of a fee by the party requesting the transcription.

Witnesses: special cases (1) hearing from P

15.34 As discussed in chapter 4, there is an increasing trend for judges to hear from P, and judges are now required specifically to consider whether they should do so as part of determining how P is to participate in the proceedings (see para 11.4).

15.35 In light of what is now a considerable body of case-law from the European Court of Human Rights (ECtHR) outlining what some have called the 'rule of personal presence,'[21] there is in the authors' view, a strong argument that the presumption should be that the judge determining any case in which either P's capacity or best interests is in issue should take steps to ensure that they have had personal contact with P.[22]

---

19 *Farooqi and others v R* [2013] EWCA Crim 1649 at para 108.
20 *Re PB* [2014] EWCOP 14, [2015] COPLR 118 at paras 140–146.
21 Summarised most recently in *AN v Lithuania* [2016] ECHR 462. See also Lucy Series, 'The participation of the relevant person in proceedings in the Court of Protection: A briefing paper on international human rights requirements,' available at http://sites.cardiff.ac.uk/wccop; a further, more detailed discussion paper, drawing on work funded by the Nuffield Foundation, is anticipated as at the date of writing.
22 This argument is reinforced by considerations arising out of the Convention on the Rights of Persons with Disabilities: see chapter 25.

15.36 'Personal contact,' however, can take various forms, not all of which will necessarily involve P participating as a witness, ie giving information to the court in a formal fashion in the presence of the parties and being questioned by the parties. The use of the word 'information' here is deliberate: P may well not be competent to give evidence (see further para 12.25), but following the introduction in July 2015 of COPR r95(e), the court 'can admit, accept and act upon such information, whether oral or written, from P [. . .] as the court considers sufficient, although not given on oath and whether or not it would be admissible in a court of law apart from this rule'.[23]

15.37 Even if P does give information in open court, it would be an unusual case in which P was cross-examined in a conventional fashion by the representative of a party (and, we suggest, an extremely unusual case in which the court would allow such questioning by an unrepresented party). The main circumstances where we suggest that such might be permissible – and possibly even in some circumstances required – is where P is giving information as to factual matters which have to be determined before the court can make determinations as to best interests, most obviously where the court has to resolve factual allegations against one or more parties. In some (rare) cases, most obviously where the allegation is one that essentially relates to P's word against that of another, P may well have to be cross-examined. In such a case, however, we suggest that the court will proceed with extreme care and will follow the guidance we discuss in relation to vulnerable witnesses below in controlling the questioning process.

15.38 The courts have not yet authoritatively determined exactly what is happening where P is giving information to a court which is determining their capacity. However, in *CC v KK and STCC*, Baker J proceeded on the basis that KK was able to give evidence as to her own capacity which he both and should weigh up alongside all the other evidence (including that from the experts instructed). This was in some ways an unusual case because KK had been found to have capacity to conduct the proceedings, and it is also clear that KK was cross-examined as to her evidence as to (or possibly, strictly, her assertion of) her own capacity.[24]

15.39 Nor have the courts authoritatively determined whether P can give evidence (or information) going to their best interests. The

---

23 See also *A County Council v AB and others (Participation of P in Proceedings)* [2016] EWCOP 41.
24 See para 49.

determination of P's best interests is not the determination of a fact, but an evaluative exercise.[25] As the identification of and giving suitable respect to P's wishes and feelings assumes greater importance in decision-making under the MCA 2005 (see further chapter 3), it is clear that the courts are becoming increasingly alive to the need to hear those wishes and feelings, wherever possible, directly from P. Strictly, the court is in doing so probably not taking information or evidence in any conventional sense, but rather discharging its obligation under MCA 2005 s4(4) to 'permit and encourage [P] to participate . . . as fully as possible in any act done for him or any decision affecting him.'[26]

15.40 However it is characterised, the judge seeing P will in the right circumstances give a very valuable picture which may be very different to that presented at second hand on the papers by others.[27] It cannot be emphasised enough that this must be in the right circumstances: it may well be entirely inappropriate, if not actively counter-productive and damaging, to bring P from their home or care placement to court.[28] Rather, it may well be necessary for the judge to visit P – including, for instance, at P's bedside – and in the presence of only a limited number of representatives so as to minimise any pressure upon P.

15.41 Wherever a judge is seeing P other than in the presence of the parties, a proper record should be kept of any discussion, usually by the representative of the Official Solicitor if instructed on P's behalf. It is also important that P is assisted insofar as possible to understand both nothing that P says to the judge can be kept confidential as between P and the judge, and also that the judge will have to reach their decision on the relevant issues on the basis of everything that they have heard, not just the information that P has given them.

15.42 A further reason for the judge to see P has nothing, strictly, to do with the gathering of evidence, but is simply to allow P to feel 'connected' to the proceedings.[29] There is also a risk that this can come across as both patronising and demeaning, but it can be extremely important to allow P to understand who it is who is taking often very significant

---

25 See *Aintree University Hospitals NHS Foundation Trust v James* [2013] UKSC 33, [2013] 1 WLR 1911, (2013) 16 CCLR 554 at para 42.
26 See *Wye Valley NHS Trust v B Court of Protection* [2015] EWCOP 60, [2015] COPLR 843, (2015) 18 CCLR 733 at para 18.
27 See in this regard *A Hospital NHS Trust v CD and Another* [2015] EWCOP 74, [2016] COPLR 1 at para 31.
28 See the comments in *Re M* [2013] EWHC 3456 (COP) at para 42.
29 *Re M* [2013] EWHC 3456 (COP) at para 42.

The final determination of the application 419

decisions in their life. Many, even with relatively severe levels of cognitive impairment, have a concept of a 'judge,' and to see the judge who will be deciding the case can be extremely important for them.

15.43 Wherever it is suggested that the judge should see P, consideration will always need to be given to the practicalities. For instance, it may well not be appropriate for P to be brought into the well of a large and intimidating court room, but the judge might well be able to see P in a smaller conference room. It may well also be a good idea, if such is practicable, for P to be brought to the court before the day of hearing so that they are familiar with the journey and reassurance can be given as to the practical arrangements: a small but important example being whether tea is available: the calming power of a cup of tea can never be overestimated. If the judge is to visit P in their care home, then suitable arrangements will need to be made for somewhere private to be made available for the relevant meeting to take place. Guidance is expected at the time of writing amplifying these points, and will be found at www.courtofprotectionhandbook.com.

15.44 See further the end of this chapter for practical examples of steps taken in a case to maximise P's participation in the proceedings.[30]

Witnesses: special cases (2) vulnerable witnesses

15.45 Although it is likely to be rare that the court will need to hear from a witness who themselves is vulnerable (by reason of age, disability or otherwise), the possibility cannot be ruled out. There are no specific provisions in the COPR to cater for the putting in place of special measures to cater for vulnerable witnesses; however, there are a suite of such measures that are regularly deployed in family proceedings that can be pressed into service by the court.[31] Some of these steps include:[32]

- Using a live video-link so that the witness can give evidence remotely, most usually so that they can give evidence other than in the presence of a person who may be subjecting them to intimidation;

---

30 See also the guidance issued by Charles J in 'Facilitating participation of 'P' and vulnerable persons in Court of Protection proceedings' available at courtofprotectionhandbook.com/legislation-codes-of-practice-forms-and-guidance.
31 Using, in particular, COPR rr3 and 95(a)(iii).
32 For more detail, see Alex Ruck Keene, Penny Cooper and Claire Hogg, 'Special measures in the Court of Protection' [2016] Eld LJ 62.

- Pre-recording evidence, whether evidence in chief, or (in special cases) cross-examination;[33] and
- Using an intermediary, whose function is to communicate (a) to the witness, questions put to the witness, and (b) to any person asking such questions, the answers given by the witness in reply to them, and to explain such questions or answers so far as necessary to enable them to be understood by the witness or person in question.[34] Although originally a development in the criminal sphere, intermediaries are seeing increasing use in the family as well as criminal courts, where they have received praise for their effectiveness in facilitating communication. In *Newcastle City Council v WM and Others*,[35] Mr Justice Cobb described the two intermediaries as 'excellent', and as having performed their role 'with great skill and discretion'. He found himself to be 'indebted' to the intermediary service for enabling the mother, who suffered from learning disabilities and spoke English as a second language, 'to participate in the process as fully and effectively as could possibly be achieved'.[36]

15.46 Perhaps the most crucial step is recognising that both the court and the advocates must adjust their approach to questioning so as to ensure that the witness is enabled to give their best, most accurate and most coherent account. This can be facilitated by:
- The use of Ground Rules Hearings, which are established practice in the criminal sphere, and at which specific, advance, consideration can be given to the approach to take to questioning so as to ensure both fair treatment and proper participation.[37] In a welfare case falling under the Case Management Pilot (see further chapter 4), we would suggest that the final management hearing should also, where appropriate, include the relevant ground rules determination (although we also suggest that adapting to the particular needs of relevant witnesses and – especially – P is something that starts much earlier in the process, from the first case management hearing);
- Prior vetting of the planned examination or cross examination. Where examination is necessary, advocates may submit their proposed questions in advance to an individual (often an interme-

---

33 See in the criminal context, Youth Justice and Criminal Evidence Act 1999 s27.
34 Youth Justice and Criminal Evidence Act 1999 s29(2).
35 [2015] EWFC 42.
36 At paras 5–6.
37 *R v Lubemba (Cokesix)* [2014] EWCA Crim 2064, [2015] 1 WLR 1579.

diary) who is well placed to advise on vocabulary, order of questioning and general approach in light of the needs and limitations of the vulnerable witness.
- A collaborative rather than adversarial approach to questioning.

15.47 A particularly useful recourse in this regard is the Advocate's Gateway, a free resource designed to assist in the questioning of vulnerable witnesses, including specific resources to assist in (for instance) the questioning of those with learning disability.[38]

Witnesses: special cases (3) interpreters

15.48 Her Majesty's Courts and Tribunals Service (HMCTS) will meet the reasonable costs of interpreters for deaf and hearing-impaired litigants for hearings in civil proceedings, including those before the Court of Protection.[39] If an interpreter is needed, the court will make arrangements for an interpreter to attend. Many people have a friend or relative who usually interpret for them. Permission will be required from the judge before such a friend or relative can translate, and the judge must be satisfied that the friend or relative can interpret exactly what is being said to the court and what the court is saying to the individual in question.

15.49 Unless the relative or friend has a recognised qualification in relaying information between deaf and hearing people, it may be better to use a qualified interpreter. The friend or relative may still be able to attend and provide support, but permission should be sought from the judge first.

15.50 Language interpreters will be arranged at public expense in certain limited circumstances:
- proceedings for committal for contempt of court (see further chapter 17), where the subject of the application cannot understand or speak the language used in court;
- where it is the only way in which a litigant can take part in proceedings, ie where the person:
  - cannot speak or understand the language of the court well enough to take part in the hearing;
  - cannot get public funding;
  - cannot afford to fund an interpreter privately; and

---

38 See: www.theadvocatesgateway.org/.
39 See: www.justice.gov.uk/newsite/courts/interpreter-guidance.

- has no family member, or friend, who can attend to interpret for them and who is acceptable to the court.
- Where a party is exercising the right given by the Welsh Language Act 1993 to any party to speak Welsh in legal proceedings in Wales.

15.51 It is vital to give as much notice as possible wherever an interpreter will have to be arranged by the Courts Service, especially where the services are required for interpretation to and from an unusual language.

15.52 It will also be necessary to factor in extra time for the giving of evidence whenever the services of an interpreter is required – a rough rule of thumb is that it is sensible to double the time-estimate for any given witness because of the inevitable impact upon the speed at which questions can be put and answered.

Witnesses: special cases (4) 'remote' evidence giving

15.53 COPR r98 provides that the court can allow a witness to give evidence through a video-link or other communication technology.

15.54 Increasing numbers of court centres are now equipped to receive evidence from witnesses by video, and it is now a relatively routine procedure. A video-link can be an important special measure taken to secure the giving of evidence by a vulnerable witness. However, in general:

> It is, however, inevitably not as ideal as having the witness physically present in court. Its convenience should not therefore be allowed to dictate its use. Consideration should be given in each case as to whether its use is likely to be beneficial to the efficient, fair and economic disposal of the proceedings.[40]

15.55 It is necessary to make an application for a video-link to be used in good time, not least as most court centres will only have a limited number of court rooms in which it is possible to use the necessary equipment. The application must be made on a COP9[41] form by the party wishing to call the relevant witness by video. Detailed guidance as to the process that should be followed is set out in annex 2 to PD 14A. This annex also sets out in some detail the practical considerations that arise when taking evidence by video, in particular given the 'lag' that can arise between receipt of the picture and accompanying

---

40 PD 14A annex 2 para 2. In *Re Jones* [2014] EWCOP 59, the daughter of P gave evidence by video from Canada as she was unable to travel to London for the hearing.
41 See further paras 10.20 onwards.

15.56 In urgent medical treatment cases (see further chapter 22), it is not uncommon for evidence to be given by the treating clinicians by telephone; the courts discourage the use of telephone evidence in final hearings in other cases, and it would be very unusual indeed for it to be acceptable for a witness giving evidence as to contested facts to give telephone evidence because of the difficulties to which this gives rise in terms of assessing their credibility absent the ability to see their face and body language. If it is proposed that evidence should be taken from a witness by telephone in anything other than the most urgent hearing, a detailed application for permission should be submitted on a COP9 form in good time. Wherever telephone evidence is taken, particular care must be taken to ensure that the loudspeaker on the telephone in the court room is set to a sufficiently loud volume to be able to be picked up by the tape transcription of the proceedings.

15.57 Finally, it should be noted that the courts have been prepared, in cases involving children, to accept evidence by Skype, but only with a considerable degree of caution:

> The technology can be very effective for informal use, but does not lend itself to the court environment. There are problems in everyone seeing and hearing the picture and in the evidence being recorded. There are also issues about security. I would not be willing to use this method if there was any alternative.[42]

It is possible, however, for a specialist service to be employed to provide a bridge between the witness using Skype and the ISDN system in place at court. This technology mediates between the systems and provides some protection against hacking. The Skype user is provided with a download allowing them to connect to the court's system. In addition to the program, the witness requires a PC, an internet connection, a webcam, a microphone and a mobile or landline number with which to contact the company for instructions. Again, if there is a suggestion that Skype should be used, this is something that should be raised as early as possible and by way of a detailed COP9 application. It is something in respect of directions will undoubtedly be need to be sought at the final management hearing under the Case Management Pilot (see further para 10.20).

---

42 *Re ML (Use of Skype Technology)* [2013] EWHC 2091 (Fam), per Peter Jackson J at para 13.

Closing arguments

15.58 The normal practice is that the applicant will make their closing submissions first, followed by the respondent(s), and then the applicant will have the last word by way of a reply. Where P is a party, the court will usually wish to hear from the Official Solicitor (if he is acting as P's litigation friend) after all of the other respondents. As noted at para 12.21 above, the Official Solicitor will usually have filed a statement in advance of the final hearing setting out a summary of the relevant background to and the procedural developments in the proceedings, and setting out the Official Solicitor's views as to P's best interests in the light of the evidence as it stands as at the time of the statement. Such views are usually expressed as being subject to the caveat that they will be the subject of further consideration at the conclusion of the hearing, to cater for unanticipated developments at the hearing. The court will therefore be particularly astute to glean from the Official Solicitor what his final position is as to P's best interests in light of all the evidence heard. It is suggested, again, that broadly the same procedure should be followed if a litigation friend other than the Official Solicitor has been appointed to act on P's behalf.

Negotiations during the hearing

15.59 It is very common for the positions of parties to shift during the course of a final hearing, especially if it lasts any length of time. This is particularly so if the evidence given by a witness (or witnesses) is either particularly compelling or is demonstrated to be particularly weak by way of cross-examination. It is important always to keep in mind that there is no reason why agreement in such circumstances cannot be reached upon part (or even the whole) of the application. While judges are reluctant to risk letting a case overrun by granting too many adjournments, it is usually the case that a judge will be happy to retire to allow discussions to take place during the time set aside for the final hearing if they can be satisfied that constructive progress is being made.

Judgment

15.60 In some cases, the judge will be in a position to give an oral judgment immediately following the close of oral arguments or after a

The final determination of the application 425

short period of reflection. Judgments given orally (known as ex tempore judgments) are recorded; again, though, it is important for as full as possible a note to be taken. If permission to appeal the judgment is to be sought from a higher court (as to which, see chapter 18 below), the time limits are sufficiently short that it can frequently be necessary to seek permission from that higher court before a transcription can be prepared. This makes it particularly important that a proper note be taken of the judgment so that, if necessary, it can be filed with the application for permission to appeal.[43]

15.61 In cases of any complexity, it is likely that the judgment will be 'reserved:' in other words, the judge will take a longer period of time to deliberate and will then, most often, prepare their judgment in written form. Where judgments are given in writing, the practice increasingly is for a draft to be circulated to the legal representatives in advance. The purpose of so doing 'is to introduce an orderly procedure for the delivery of reserved judgments, whereby the parties' lawyers can have time to consider and agree the terms of any consequential orders they may invite the court to make and the process of delivering judgment can be abbreviated by avoiding the need for the judge to read the judgment orally in court'.[44] Such draft judgments must be kept strictly confidential to the parties' lawyers. While judges will normally invite the submission of corrections of typographical errors, the circulation of a draft judgment is not intended to afford an opportunity to the parties to re-argue their case.[45] Where a party or parties are not legally represented, the practice commonly adopted is not to circulate a draft judgment for correction, but rather to hand down a draft judgment 'subject to editorial corrections', allowing for any revisions to be incorporated before a final approved version is handed down.[46]

15.62 One matter that will usually have to be resolved after judgment has been given is as to costs. This is addressed further at chapter 16 below.

---

43 Note also that there can be a duty upon an advocate for the respondent to any application to appeal to provide their note promptly and free of charge to an unrepresented appellant: see para 18.29 below.
44 *Prudential Assurance Company v McBains Cooper and others* [2000] 1 WLR 2000 at 2008E–F per Brooke LJ. See also Civil Procedure Rules (CPR) PD 40E (Reserved judgments).
45 See *Egan v Motor Services (Bath) Ltd* [2007] EWCA Civ 1002, [2008] 1 All ER 1156 and *G v A* [2009] EWHC 11 (Fam).
46 See, by analogy, *R (S) v General Teaching Council for England* [2013] EWHC 2779 (Admin) at para 5.

Final orders

15.63 The precise nature of the relief that the court can grant is discussed at paras 4.49 onwards. The actual decision of the court, whatever it may be, must be recorded in an order.

15.64 If the judgment has been circulated in draft ahead of it being handed down, the judge will expect that the parties will have tried to agree the terms of that order. If the judgment has been given orally, and if the order records anything more than a simple decision/declaration, then it may well prove difficult for all the details of the order made to be finalised at the end of what is likely to have been a long court day. For similar reasons as discussed at para 10.55 above in relation to directions hearings, however, every effort should be made to ensure that the broad outlines of the order have been agreed and (if possible) endorsed by the judge before the parties leave for the day to avoid lengthy – and expensive – debates in the ensuing days via correspondence as to the terms of the order.

15.65 One oddity of proceedings under the MCA 2005 is that it is far from unusual that an order made at what all parties and the court treat as final hearing will not, in fact, be a final order. A good example of this is where the court has, itself, authorised the deprivation of P's liberty (for instance, because P is deprived of their liberty in supported accommodation, so cannot be made the subject of the DOLS regime discussed in chapter 21 below). In such a case, it is necessary in order to secure P's rights under Article 5 ECHR (right to liberty) that the court undertakes regular reviews of that deprivation.[47] In such cases, particular care needs to be paid to the way in which the order made at the hearing provides for the payment of the costs of any publicly funded party so as to ensure that such funding is readily available for purposes of any further review by the court.

15.66 A final point should be made here. In many cases, the court will be asked to take a one-off decision on P's behalf. In other cases, the court will be asked to make a declaration under MCA 2005 s15 as to P's capacity in respect of a particular decision, or to decide on P's behalf (for instance) where to live. It is quite possible that circumstances will change after the hearing, however, such that P's best interests may dictate a different course of action. The question that

---

47 *Cheshire West and Chester Council v P* [2011] EWCA Civ 1257, [2012] COPLR 37, (2012) 15 CCLR 48 at para 4 per Munby LJ. This aspect of the judgment of the Court of Appeal was not contested before the Supreme Court on the Official Solicitor's (successful) appeal against the decision.

arises immediately in this regard is whether it is necessary to return the matter to court, or whether the parties to the proceedings are bound by the declaration(s) contained in the final order.

15.67 Although the question has not yet come before the courts to be determined (at least in any recorded cases), it is suggested that, by analogy with the position that prevails in respect of decisions taken by mental health tribunals, the parties must consider themselves bound by the decision unless they reasonably and in good faith consider that they have information unknown to the court 'which put a significantly differently complexion on the case as compared with that before the [court]'.[48] If there has not been such a material change of circumstances, but the circumstances are such that they nonetheless require revisiting by the court then, depending upon the length of time since the original proceedings were concluded (and especially if all questions relating to costs have been resolved), it may be necessary for a fresh application to be made. If a fresh application has to be made, then it would be prudent for the applicant to make clear that the proceedings were previously before the court and to seek an order at the first directions hearing that (if the court bundle from the previous proceedings is still in readily accessible form and remains relevant) that the documents contained in the bundle stand as evidence in the new proceedings, so as to ensure that all relevant materials are before the court in the new proceedings.

15.68 The position where P regains capacity after the proceedings have come to an end is covered by PD 23B (primarily concerned with property and affairs). Where P ceases to lack capacity after proceedings have concluded, an application may be made to the court to discharge any orders made (including an order appointing a deputy or an order in relation to a security bond) by filing a COP9 application notice, together with any evidence in support of the application. The application notice should set out details of the order or orders the applicant seeks to have discharged, and should in particular be supported by evidence that P no longer lacks capacity to make decisions in relation to the matter or matters to which the proceedings relate.[49] Note that if the Court Funds Office is holding funds or assets on behalf of P, it will require an order of the court to the effect that P no longer lacks capacity to make decisions with regard to the

---

48 *R (von Brandenburg) v East London and City NHS Trust* [2004] 2 AC 280, (2004) 7 CCLR 121 at para 10 per Lord Bingham.
49 PD 23B para 5.

use and disposition of those funds or assets before any funds or assets can be transferred to him.[50]

P regains capacity or dies

15.69 There are two other events that will bring about a final determination of the proceedings in a way other than provided for in the balance of this chapter, namely P regaining the relevant capacity to take the decision(s) in question or P dying. What should happen in these circumstances is, in part, set out in PD 23B, and in part in PD 12B.

15.70 If P regains capacity (or, to use the terminology of PD 23B, 'ceases to lack capacity'), then steps should be taken forthwith to end the proceedings and discharge any orders made in respect of P. Whilst PD 23B refers to an order being sought under COPR r202 (disposal of property where P ceases to lack capacity), PD 12B makes clear that an order should also be sought under COPR r87(1)(b) for the court to declare that it no longer has jurisdiction over P.[51] Such an application can be made by P, their litigation friend or any other person who is party to the proceedings, and should be made on a COP9 form together with, in particular, evidence that P no longer lacks capacity to make decisions in relation to the matter or matters to which the proceedings relate.[52]

15.71 If P dies during the currency of proceedings (which is, sadly, not an altogether unusual experience), then this should be brought to the attention of the court as soon as practicable. At that point, proceedings will come to an effective halt,[53] although the court retains a residual jurisdiction in respect of matters such as:

- costs;[54]
- the remuneration of a deputy, donee or attorney;[55]
- fees;
- the discharge of security;[56]

---

50 PD 23B para 6.
51 PD 12B para 5.
52 PD 23B paras 3–4, PD 12B paras 5–7.
53 See *Re RC (deceased)* [2010] COPLR Con Vol 1022 at paras 50–54 per Senior Judge Lush.
54 COPR r165 and PD 23B para 10.
55 COPR r167.
56 Lasting Powers of Attorney, Enduring Powers of Attorney and Public Guardian Regulations 2007 SI No 1253 reg 37.

- (if a deputy has been appointed), the deputy's final report on the termination of his appointment;[57] and
- the transfer and delivery of funds.[58]

15.72 The court will also have a jurisdiction to take necessary steps as regards the protection of P's identity: see further chapter 13.

Case study: facilitating participation of 'P' in Court of Protection proceedings

15.73 In the body of this chapter, we set out some of the ways in which practice needs to change within the Court of Protection to ensure that the court and representation process is looked at through P's eyes, rather than just adding P as an afterthought. Whilst the COPR and accompanying Practice Directions may well need to be amended in due course to secure this goal, creative steps are already possible within the framework of the COPR as they stand. As a case study, we set out here those which were implemented to facilitate P's participation in a fact-finding hearing listed to determine allegations of abuse at the hands of his parents.[59]

P had expressed a wish to attend Court to come to the fact finding hearing to listen to what his parents and other witnesses were saying, as well as to 'tell his story' to the court. This was opposed by both his parents and the local authority, but the court ruled that he should attend. The court also ruled that, whilst P was:

almost certainly not competent to give evidence [this is] is no reason not to seek with appropriate help to elicit 'information' from him via a skilled intermediary . . . . using Rule 95 (e) the Court may admit the information but there is no guarantee that

---

57 Lasting Powers of Attorney, Enduring Powers of Attorney and Public Guardian Regulations 2007 reg 40.
58 PD 23B para 11.
59 *A County Council v AB and others (Participation of P in Proceedings)* [2016] EWCOP 41. This case study is written by Nicola Mackintosh QC (Hon), who acted as P's solicitor, instructed by the Official Solicitor as his litigation friend.

it would accept or act upon it ..... the Court's ability to have information provided by P is wide and flexible . . .
In the light of the judgment the practical arrangements which had already been made were implemented. These steps show clearly how vital it is when securing and enhancing P's participation that each and every detail of the arrangements is planned from P's perspective and not simply limited to a meeting with the judge (important as that is). This involved the following:

1) P's lawyers meeting with P and securing appropriate Speech and Language Therapy support to prepare for the hearing by exploring concepts such as the following:
   a) 'what is happening in court, what is a case, why is your case in court, what is the case about'?
   b) 'what is a judge, what will the judge be deciding, why is it important to you'?
   c) 'what will happen at the hearing, who will speak when, how long will it take etc.'?
   d) 'how can I tell my story'?
2) Considering which court location would best meet the needs of the case, taking into account all physical facilities, travel time for P and others etc.
3) As the court's video facilities did not allow for P to be in an adjacent room viewing the proceedings from a distance so as to minimise distress, an alternative facility was found nearby which could provide a video link to the court. Arrangements were made for this between the IT specialists of the court and the other facility, and for the video link to be tested in advance to ensure it was working. In the event this facility was not used as P remained in court throughout the proceedings.
4) (With consent) taking photographs of the judge, the courtroom and all the lawyers involved in the proceedings to explain to P the physical location and the identity of all involved in advance of the hearing.
5) Before the hearing arranging a visit by P to the courtroom when the court was not sitting to see the layout, and also to meet the court clerk who was to be allocated to the hearing days.
6) Deciding where it was best for P to sit in his wheelchair in the courtroom to listen to the proceedings, taking into

account the position of other parties and 'lines of sight' with others.
7) Arranging for P to be supported by staff regarding personal care, and ensuring mobile hoists were provided for P in both locations for care.
8) Ensuring that there was enough physical space in the court complex so that P had a separate room just next to the courtroom, with a fan (P being a wheelchair user had reduced temperature control).

The first day of the hearing was listed as a Ground Rules Hearing, as provided for in the Advocates' Gateway (see paragraph 15.46). On the first day, as planned, the judge met with P in a side room next to the courtroom. P's solicitor was present, and P's SALT also assisted by explaining to the judge that P was able to respond 'yes, no, happy and sad' through different Makaton signs. P showed the judge how he communicated each of these expressions, enabling the judge better to understand how to interpret P's wishes and reactions.

Although the fact finding hearing was listed for nine days, after the initial part of the first day of the hearing (P being present in court with his carers and intermediary) the parties set out their updated positions which then resulted in negotiations to see if a settlement could be reached without the need for the fact finding process. This lasted the first day and the terms of an order were agreed on the second day of the hearing. P was present during all discussions between lawyers and the court, and communicated his wish to continue to be involved and to listen to the proceedings. Between updates to the court he was permitted by the judge to remain in the courtroom with his support workers, watching a DVD. This reduced the need for him to be taken in and out of the courtroom, waiting for long periods in a small stuffy side room, and was invaluable. This could not have been arranged without the court's co-operation and flexibility of the court staff.

Once agreement had been reached in principle between the parties as to the core issues in the case, it was considered vital for P's wish to 'tell his story' to be facilitated. A very careful consideration of the issues raised, and the broad themes set out in the fact finding schedule was undertaken. Questions of P were drafted by P's legal representatives with the assistance of

P's SALT and intermediary. As P's communication was limited to responses such as 'yes, no' etc, it was necessary for leading questions to be posed however these were broken down into questions so that the leading element was minimised. Examples of questions included 'Do you want to talk about when you were living at home?', 'How did you feel when you were living at home?', When you were living at home did anyone do X to you?', and if the answer was affirmative, 'How did it make you feel?' These questions were devised to ensure that P's broad wishes were communicated to the court notwithstanding the agreement between the parties, so that P felt that he had been listened to by the parties and the judge, but avoiding detailed questioning on the fact finding schedule which eventually proved to be unnecessary.

The question and answer sessions were broken down into more than one session to allow P to rest and refocus. With agreement they were filmed on a mobile phone and then played to the judge in his chambers. They were then also played to the other parties. This flexibility avoided all the delays and organisational problems associated with using the court video facilities.

By the end of the second day, agreement had been reached in the form of a detailed order. The judge held a further short hearing and again explained the outcome to P, coming into the courtroom and sitting by P to confirm what was going to happen. P was repositioned in his wheelchair to be solely in the line of sight of the judge and not the other parties.

In conclusion, P's wishes and story had been communicated to the judge, and P had been present throughout the proceedings in accordance with his wishes. P communicated that he felt he had 'told his story', and he did not need to say anything more. He was clearly excited by the eventual outcome (that he could return to his own home, without his parents, but having regular contact), and felt that he and his wishes had been central to the process.

CHAPTER 16

Costs

16.1   Introduction
16.2   **The statutory provisions**
16.2   Mental Capacity 2005
16.4   Court of Protection Rules
16.5   Application of other statutes and the Civil Procedure Rules
16.7   The general rule
16.11 Serious medical treatment cases
16.12 Departing from the general rule
16.17 Alternative dispute resolution/mediation – costs consequences
16.18 Wasted costs orders
16.19 Appeals
16.20 Summary

Introduction

16.1 This chapter sets out how costs are dealt with in the Court of Protection. The costs rules that apply are unique to the court, balancing as they do a number of interests that are not necessarily in play in other forms of litigation. They also make different provisions for applications involving property and affairs on the one hand, and health and welfare on the other. This chapter addresses both categories of application, together with the (common) scenario where the two are mixed.

The statutory provisions

Mental Capacity 2005

16.2 Mental Capacity (MCA) 2005 s55 provides that:
(1) Subject to Court of Protection Rules, the costs of and incidental to all proceedings in the court are in its discretion.
(2) The rules may in particular make provision for regulating matters relating to the costs of those proceedings, including prescribing scales of costs to be paid to legal or other representatives.
(3) The court has full power to determine by whom and to what extent the costs are to be paid.
(4) The court may, in any proceedings–
 (a) disallow, or
 (b) order the legal or other representatives concerned to meet, the whole of any wasted costs or such part of them as may be determined in accordance with the rules.
(5) 'Legal or other representative', in relation to a party to proceedings, means any person exercising a right of audience or right to conduct litigation on his behalf.
(6) 'Wasted costs' means any costs incurred by a party–
 (a) as a result of any improper, unreasonable or negligent act or omission on the part of any legal or other representative or any employee of such a representative, or
 (b) which, in the light of any such act or omission occurring after they were incurred, the court considers it is unreasonable to expect that party to pay.

16.3 Practitioners should be aware of the powers in MCA 2005 s55(3)–(6) to use costs sanctions against legal representatives when the court considers this to be justified. These powers replicate the powers in Senior Courts Act 1981 s51(6), and will be deployed according to the same criteria.[1]

Court of Protection Rules

16.4 COPR Part 19, as amended most recently by the Court of Protection (Amendment) Rules 2015,[2] sets out the general provisions dealing with costs. We set out the key provisions below.

Application of other statutes and the Civil Procedure Rules

16.5 Some of the provisions in the Civil Procedure Rules (CPR) 1998 apply to Court of Protection cases, with modifications.[3] The relevant provisions in the COPR importing specific rules from the CPR were drafted prior to the re-writing of the CPR in 2013. Confusingly for practitioners, the COPR were not immediately updated to take account of changes in the CPR. Therefore, the numbering set out in COPR r160 no longer corresponded with the CPR as they then stood. However, the Court of Protection (Amendment) Rules 2015 removed this anomaly by substituting a new COPR r160 and we set out in the table in appendix C the provisions of the CPR (as at 1 April 2015[4]) that apply in the Court of Protection by virtue of the current iteration of COPR r160.

16.6 By virtue of provisions contained in the Legal Aid, Sentencing and Punishment of Offenders Act 2012 (LASPO), a costs order can be made against a party who holds a legal aid certificate, but these cannot exceed the amount which it is reasonable for that party to pay, having regard to the circumstances including the conduct and financial resources of all the parties. If a legally aided party is ordered to pay an amount of costs which is less than the costs incurred by the receiving party, then the receiving party may apply for an order that the shortfall is met by the Lord Chancellor. There is no reason why,

1 *Sharma and Judkins v Hunters* [2011] EWHC 2546 (COP), [2012] COPLR 166.
2 SI No 548
3 COPR r160, PD 19A.
4 COPR r9(2) and PD 3C (COPR Pr2.5(2) and Pilot PD 2C where the Case Management Pilot applies). This can be updated by updating PD 3C (COPR r9(2)).

in principle, such an order could not be made in favour of a public body.[5]

The general rule

16.7 The COPR currently sets out two very different general rules (although at the time of writing a consultation is understood to be likely as to whether to amend that relating to P's property and affairs[6]):
- The general rule in cases concerning P's welfare is that there will be no order as to the costs of the proceedings, or of that part of the proceedings that concerns P's welfare.[7] This means that in 'pure' welfare cases, the parties should expect to bear their own costs. Clients who are not legally aided therefore need to be advised that they cannot expect to recover costs they incur in those proceedings.
- In respect of cases concerning P's property and affairs, the general rule is that the costs will be met from P's estate.[8]

16.8 Special provisions apply in relation to the appointment of deputies:
- An order appointing a property and affairs deputy will deal with both with any legal costs incurred by the deputy in making the application and the expenses incurred by the deputy in the discharge of their functions. Where a lay deputy is appointed, the costs will be limited to reasonable out-of-pocket expenses.[9] Where a professional is appointed, either as a sole appointment or jointly with a lay deputy, a clause will be included to permit fixed costs to be taken,[10] or for the costs to be assessed by the Supreme Court Costs Office. The rates that can be charged by a professional deputy are subject to the Guideline Hourly Rates.[11] Where an hourly rate is authorised, PD 19B provides that solicitors will ordinarily be entitled to a higher rate than local authorit-

---

5 See LASPO s26; Civil Legal Aid (Costs) Regulations 2013; and the detailed Guidance Notes on the application of LASPO s26(1), issued by the Senior Costs Judge.
6 For updates, see www.courtofprotectionhandbook.com/posts/.
7 COPR r157.
8 COPR r156.
9 MCA 2005 s19(7).
10 COPR r164, PD 19B.
11 See www.judiciary.gov.uk/guideline-hourly-rates-2011.

ies. The Practice Direction explicitly leaves to the court's discretion in each case the issue of whether and how to apply its provisions to a not-for-profit organisation deputy or to a deputy from another discipline, such as an accountant. For a detailed exposition of the law and practice on this point, see *The Friendly Trust's Bulk Application*.[12]

- Health and welfare deputies will not usually be allowed to recover either the legal costs of making the application or of the expenses incurred in discharging their functions. Professional deputies are – rarely – appointed to act as health and welfare deputies, and it is suggested that the same approach would be adopted as if they were a property and affairs deputy.
- Good practice guidance on professional costs incurred by deputies in the discharge of their duties was issued by the Office of the Public Guardian and the Supreme Court Costs Office in July 2016.[13] See further chapter 20.

16.9 Many cases involve a mixture of welfare and property and affairs issues. It is important to differentiate between the different elements of the case to ensure that there is clarity as to who is responsible for what. The court will, insofar as possible, apportion the costs between the issues.[14]

16.10 In *Re E*,[15] Senior Judge Lush considered the origin of the 'general rules' in COPR 156–7 and commented:

34. The origin of the general rule in property and affairs cases goes back to the decision of the Lords Justices in Lunacy in *Re Windham* (1862) 4 De G. F. & J. 53, following which the Lunacy Amendment Act 1862 conferred upon the court a wide discretion as to costs.

35. As both Mr Holland and Miss Hughes observed, the current rule 156 is largely a replication of the principles laid down by the Court of Appeal in *Re Cathcart* [1892] 1 Ch 549, with a few exceptions, such as a requirement in *Re Cathcart*, which does not appear in the Court of Protection Rules 2007, to have regard to the respective means of the parties.

36. By contrast, the general rule in personal welfare cases is of recent origin, dating from 1989, and reflects the fact that most personal welfare cases are of a public law nature.

---

12 [2016] EWCOP 40.
13 www.gov.uk/government/uploads/system/uploads/attachment_data/file/538901/19_07_16_Professional_deputy_costs__FINAL.pdf.
14 COPR r158.
15 [2014] EWCOP 27.

Serious medical treatment cases

16.11 While the general rule in health and welfare cases is as set out above, it is important to note that the courts have recognised what amounts to a further general rule in cases relating to serious medical treatment (see further in respect of such cases, chapter 22). Reflecting the position that prevailed before the MCA 2005 came into force, the invariable practice is for the NHS Trust that made the application to pay half of the costs of the Official Solicitor (who will, in all cases where P is made a party – ie almost all[16] – act as P's litigation friend).[17]

Departing from the general rule

16.12 As COPR r159 makes clear, the court can depart from rules set out above (rules 156–157) if the circumstances so justify. Rule 159 provides that:

(1) The court may depart from rules 156 to 158 if the circumstances so justify, and in deciding whether departure is justified the court will have regard to all the circumstances, including–
  (a) the conduct of the parties;
  (b) whether a party has succeeded on part of his case, even if he has not been wholly successful; and
  (c) the role of any public body involved in the proceedings.
(2) The conduct of the parties includes–
  (a) conduct before, as well as during, the proceedings;
  (b) whether it was reasonable for a party to raise, pursue or contest a particular issue;
  (c) the manner in which a party has made or responded to an application or a particular issue; and
  (d) whether a party who has succeeded in his application or response to an application, in whole or in part, exaggerated any matter contained in his application or response.
(3) Without prejudice to rules 156 to 158 and the foregoing provisions of this rule, the court may permit a party to recover their fixed costs in accordance with the relevant practice direction.

16.13 It will be seen that the court retains a broad discretion to award costs and to take into account the parties' behaviour before and during the

---

16 Essentially the only exception being where urgency makes this impossible: for an example, see *Newcastle-upon-Tyne Foundation Trust v LM* [2014] EWHC 454 (COP).
17 *Re D (Costs)* [2012] EWHC 886 (COP), [2012] COPLR 499.

proceedings. Given the pre-issue obligations imposed upon potential parties to welfare proceedings under the Case Management Pilot (see further chapter 10), it is likely that greater focus is going to be placed in due course upon the conduct of parties before litigation concerning P's welfare is started.

16.14 COPR r4 (COPR Pr1.4 where the Case Management Pilot applies) imposes a duty on the parties to help the court to further the overriding objective, and sets out a non-exhaustive list of expectations, considered at paras 10.7 onwards. These include, amongst others, full and frank disclosure[18] and co-operation in all aspects of the proceedings, including the preparation of bundles.[19] The expectations upon parties in cases under the Case Management Pilot are more stringent, but it is prudent even in cases outside the Pilot to proceed on the basis that the court will hold parties to the higher standards of the Pilot. The Case Management Pilot also introduces duties upon legal representatives[20] and also upon unrepresented parties,[21] both discussed in chapter 10.

16.15 The following warning was added in 2015 to COPR r4[22] and is clearly intended to focus the minds of parties and their advisers on the importance of compliance:

> If the court determines that any party has failed without reasonable excuse to satisfy the requirements of this rule, it may, under rule 159 depart from the general rule about costs in so far as they apply to that party.

16.16 It is also the experience of the authors that with more hearings taking place in the regions local judges are more willing to exercise their powers to undertake a summary assessment of costs. Advisers need to be alert to these issues which should be drawn to clients' attention in the appropriate client care letter and/or terms and conditions.

---

18 COPR r4(2)(d)/Pr1.4(2)(f).
19 COPR r4(2)(e)/Pr1.4(2)(g).
20 COPR Pr1.5.
21 COPR Pr1.6.
22 COPR r4(3)/COPR Pr1.4(3) where the Pilot applies.

Alternative dispute resolution/mediation – costs consequences

16.17 There is an increasing emphasis upon forms of alternative dispute resolution (ADR) including mediation as a way both to prevent disputes reaching the Court of Protection and to bring about a speedier resolution to proceedings if they do. This is discussed in more detail in chapter 19. As noted in that chapter, the court has no power to require parties to engage in a form of ADR. We suggest, however, that, by analogy with the approach adopted in family proceedings,[23] an unreasonable failure to engage in ADR might give a basis for departure from the general rule.

Wasted costs orders

16.18 It is important that legal advisers are clear that case management directions must be complied with- even when it is another party who has been directed to take the steps in question. By way of analogy, in *Re L (Case Management: Wasted Costs)*[24] HHJ Bellamy made wasted costs orders against all the legal representatives in a care case, finding that they were all negligent for the purpose of section 51 of the Senior Courts Act 1981, so as to give rise to the power to make a wasted costs order. The local authority had failed to disclose relevant material and bore the brunt of the responsibility: but the other parties should have noticed this and were negligent in 'failing to take pro-active steps in drawing the omission to the attention of the local authority and court.' Given the express duty on all parties to ask the court to make directions if an issue arises 'of which the court is unaware,[25] and the duty on legal representatives to comply with the rules,[26] it is entirely possible to imagine a similar approach being taken in the Court of Protection.

Appeals

16.19 Appeals are dealt with in chapter 18. It should be noted, however, that the Court of Appeal has made clear that the bar for appealing a

---

23 Eg *Mann v Mann* [2014] EWHC 537 (Fam).
24 [2016] EWFC B8.
25 COPR Pr1.4(2)(a).
26 COPR Pr1.5(2)(a).

costs order is set high. In *Re G (An Adult) (By Her Litigation Friend the Official Solicitor) (Costs)*,[27] Lord Justice Ryder noted that 'an appeal against the exercise of by a judge of his discretion [in making a decision as to costs] faces a high hurdle', and that the Court of Appeal will only interfere if the judge exceeds the generous ambit of his discretion. The same approach will also prevail in respect of appeals within the Court of Protection (ie from a lower 'tier' of judges to a higher 'tier': see further para 18.11).

Summary

16.20 The following practice points derived from the reported cases should be borne in mind:

- It is essential for anyone embarking on litigation, however it is to be funded, to be properly advised about the likely costs risks at the start of the case and throughout it.
- Any decision to depart from the general rule will turn on the facts of the individual case.
- A costs order can, in a suitable case, be made against a legally aided party and ultimately against the Lord Chancellor.
- The fact that a party seeking costs is legally aided is not relevant.[28]
- Costs do not necessarily follow the outcome of the case, although they may do.[29]
- Bad faith is not necessary to establish a reason to depart from the general rule.[30]
- Refusal to co-operate prior to the issue of proceedings may be relevant to costs at the conclusion of the case.[31]

---

27 [2015] EWCA Civ 446, [2015] COPLR 438 at para 22.
28 *WBC v CP* [2012] EWHC 1944 (COP).
29 *G v E (by his litigation friend the Official Solicitor) and F* [2010] EWHC 3385 (Fam), (2011) 14 CCLR 140, [2010] COPLR Con Vol 454; *Hillingdon LBC v Neary* [2011] EWHC 3522 (COP), [2011] COPLR Con Vol 632; *AH v (1) Hertfordshire Partnership NHS Trust, (2) Ealing Primary Care Trust* [2011] EWHC 3524 (COP, [2012] COPLR 327.
30 *G v E* [2010] EWHC 3385 (Fam), (2011) 14 CCLR 140, [2010] COPLR Con Vol 454; *AH and others* [2013] EWHC 2410 (COP).
31 *AH and others* [2013] EWHC 2410 (COP).

- A failure to comply with the provisions of the MCA 2005 or other statutes or guidance may be relevant to the question of costs.[32]
- Failure to comply with the rules or the court's case management directions may justify the court in departing from the general rule.[33]
- A party that refuses to modify its position in the face of the evidence may be vulnerable to a costs order.[34]
- Public bodies can be expected to know the risks of litigation and warnings are not pre-conditions for costs orders against public bodies, though warnings may be appropriate before costs are awarded against private individuals, especially those acting in person.[35]
- There are particular obligations on public bodies bringing applications in the context of safeguarding concerns, and failure to take appropriate steps to consider the evidential basis for such applications can give rise to an award of costs against them: see further chapter 23.
- The risk of a costs order should not deter applicants from bringing disputes to the court for resolution.[36]
- Failure to bring a dispute to court in a timely fashion may be a relevant factor leading to a costs order.[37]
- An unreasonable refusal to engage in ADR may leave a party vulnerable to a costs order.[38]
- Legal representatives should be alert to the need to advise the court and seek directions when another party has failed to take necessary steps which might put a hearing at risk.[39]

---

32 *AH and others* [2013] EWHC 2410 (COP); *WBC v CP* [2012] EWHC 1944 (COP).
33 COPR Pr1.4(3).
34 *AH and others* [2013] EWHC 2410 (COP); *A Local Authority v HS* [2013] EWHC 2410 (COP).
35 *AH and others* [2013] EWHC 2410 (COP); *SC v LBH* [2010] EWHC B29 (COP), *sub nom Re RC (deceased)* [2010] COPLR Con Vol 1022.
36 *G v E* [2010] EWHC 3385 (Fam), (2011) 14 CCLR 140, [2010] COPLR Con Vol 454; *AH and others* [2013] EWHC 2410 (COP); *Re HS* [2013] EWHC 2410 (COP).
37 *Hillingdon v Neary* [2011] EWHC 3522 (COP), [2011] COPLR Con Vol 632; *AH and others* [2013] EWHC 2410 (COP).
38 *Mann v Mann* [2014] EWHC 537 (Fam).
39 *Re L* [2016] EWFC B8.

CHAPTER 17

Enforcement

17.1	Introduction
17.5	**The powers of the Court of Protection**
17.5	Powers drawn from those of the High Court
17.7	Specific powers contained in the COPR
17.12	**Committal proceedings**
17.12	Bringing proceedings
17.17	The hearing
17.20	**Continuing contempt**
17.21	Powers to protect court's own processes

Introduction

17.1 Previous chapters in this book have set out the steps by which a judge can be placed in a position to determine applications relating to P (and to grant interim relief pending such final determination). Sometimes, all the court will be required to do is to grant a declaration, either as to P's (lack of) capacity or that a course of action is lawful,[1] and no substantive decisions will be taken by the court that will require enforcement. In such situations, there would be no need for the judgment and the accompanying order of the court to be enforced. Indeed, it would appear that a declaration alone is not capable of being enforced by way (for instance) of committal proceedings.[2]

17.2 However, on occasions, one (or more) of the parties to the proceedings may be required either to take or to refrain from taking specific actions. This requirement can arise in three main ways:

- by way of case management directions made so as to secure the effective resolution of the application;
- as a necessary consequence of a decision (for instance, that P is to be moved from their home into a care home), which can only be given effect by one or more of the parties;
- by the court making an injunction specifically requiring one of the parties to do something or not to do something (for instance, not to have contact with P save under specified circumstances).

17.3 Court of Protection judges are well aware (especially in welfare cases) that:

> ... the mere fact that a litigant, perhaps in the heat of a frenzied battle, may breathe defiance is not to be taken by the court as necessarily an accurate reflection of what will happen in the future. The court assumes, is entitled to assume, has to assume, because otherwise the road leads to anarchy, that its orders will be complied with.[3]

---

1 Under Mental Capacity Act (MCA) 2005 s15(1)(a) or (c) respectively.
2 See *MASM v MMAM and others* [2015] EWCOP 3, [2015] COPLR 239 and *Re MN (Adult)* [2015] EWCA Civ 411, [2015] COPLR 505 at paras 87–91.
3 *Re SA* [2010] EWCA Civ 1128 at 52 per Munby LJ, a case in which the court made orders directing that both P and her mother comply with a capacity assessment of P in circumstances where P, apparently under the influence of her mother, was indicating her refusal to do so.

17.4 Absent the ability to enforce decisions falling into the categories set out above, however, the Court of Protection would be toothless. This chapter discusses the mechanisms by which the court can enforce its judgments and its orders as well as its own processes.

The powers of the Court of Protection

Powers drawn from those of the High Court

17.5 Before turning to the detail of the enforcement mechanisms set out in COPR Part 21, it is necessary first to discuss the more general powers of the Court of Protection. The Court of Protection is a superior court of record,[4] which has 'in connection with its jurisdiction the same powers, rights, privileges and authority as the High Court'.[5] This has the following consequences:

- A judge sitting in the Court of Protection can grant an injunction so as to give effect to their decision and to secure the best interests of the adult. Senior Courts Act 1981 s37 provides that 'the High Court may by order (whether interlocutory or final) grant an injunction . . . in all cases in which it appears to the court to be just and convenient to do so'. The Court of Protection is, by MCA 2005 s47(1), given these same powers.[6] Such an injunction will either require a person to do a specified act or (more usually) not to do a specified act or acts. Its terms must be clear and unambiguous in order for it to be effective,[7] and the person to whom it is addressed must have proper notice of its terms.[8]
- That the High Court would use its powers to grant an injunction so as to secure the interests of an adult without capacity (at least pending the final resolution of the application) had been

---

4 MCA 2005 s45(1).
5 MCA 2005 s47(1). See also *MASM v MMAM and others* [2015] EWCOP 3, [2015] COPLR, (2015) 18 CCLR 80 239 at para 13.
6 *W v M and S (reporting restriction order)* [2011] EWHC 1197 (COP), [2011] COPLR Con Vol 1205 at para 21.
7 *Iberian Trust Ltd v Founders Trust and Investment Co Ltd* [1932] 2 KB 87; *R v City of London Magistrates' Court, ex p Green* [1997] 3 All ER 551. See also the commentary in *Halsbury's Laws* Volume 22 (5th edn, 2012), at para 75, and *Re Whiting* [2013] EWHC B27 (Fam), [2014] COPLR 107 at para 12.
8 *R v City of London Magistrates' Court ex p Green* [1997] 3 All ER 551. See also the commentary in *Halsbury's Laws*, Volume 22, 5th edn, LexisNexis, 2012, at para 75.

established prior to the coming into force of the MCA 2005.[9] The power to grant an interim injunction has now been codified in the Court of Protection Rules 2007,[10] and is regularly exercised so as to 'hold the ring' pending the determination of an application.
- It is also possible to grant an injunction that will continue in force after the end of proceedings. In *W v M*, a high-profile case regarding the withdrawal of treatment from M, a person in a minimally conscious state, injunctions were made in support of reporting restrictions that prevented contact being made with the lay people at the heart of the case; those injunctions were expressed so as to last for M's lifetime.[11] An analogy can also be drawn with the circumstances of *Re SA (vulnerable adult with capacity: marriage)*,[12] a case decided under the inherent jurisdiction of the High Court. In this case,[13] Munby J (as he then was) made final orders prohibiting the family members of a vulnerable adult from either themselves or by others removing her from the jurisdiction and/or arranging for her marriage save in very clearly defined circumstances. A time-limited power of arrest was attached to one provision (relating to the use of violence), but the remainder of the injunctions were expressed to run on an indefinite basis.[14]
- An order made by a Court of Protection judge (of no matter what level) has the same status as that made by a High Court judge.
- A breach of an order made by a Court of Protection judge, whether for purposes of case management or for purposes of giving effect to a judgment, can amount to a contempt of court and the court has the power to punish such contempt.[15] There are detailed provisions in COPR Part 21 relating to the procedural steps for applications for committal to prison for contempt of court,

9 See, for example, *Re S (hospital patient: court's jurisdiction)* [1996] Fam 1, [1995] 1 FLR 1075 and the commentary in Ashton et al *Court of Protection Practice 2016*, Jordans, at para 1.40.
10 COPR r82(1)(a). See further paras 10.58 onwards above.
11 *W v M* at para 70. It may be possible for reporting restrictions to continue after P's death: *Newcastle upon Tyne Hospitals Foundation Trust v LM* [2014] EWCOP 454 and *V v Associated Newspapers Ltd and others* [2016] EWCOP 21.
12 [2005] EWHC 2942 (Fam), [2006] 1 FLR 867.
13 Which pre-dated the MCA 2005 and concerned an adult with capacity, but who was vulnerable to coercion.
14 Paras 136–137.
15 See, for a discussion of the relevant powers of the High Court, *Halsbury's Laws*, Volume 22 (5th edn, 2012), at paras 66ff, and the commentary in the *White Book 2016* at section 3C.

addressed further at paras 17.12 onwards below. It is suggested that the underlying power to commit a person to prison (or to fine them) does not derive from the COPR, but rather, from MCA 2005 s47(1) and, in turn, the inherent, common law power of the High Court both to control its own processes[16] and to enforce compliance with its decisions.[17]

17.6 The range of orders that the court can make under its general powers so as to compel compliance with its decisions is extensive. By way of example, in *Re HM*,[18] a case involving the abduction of an adult with impaired capacity, PM, from the jurisdiction to Israel, orders were made including:

- injunctive orders directed to PM, HM's father, including a collection order;
- orders inviting the assistance of both domestic and foreign public (including judicial) authorities;
- orders seeking information from various individuals, friends or associates of HM (including summonses to court to give evidence), from various banks, insurers and travel agents, from an airline, various telephone and email service providers and the DVLA, and from others thought to be holding monies for PM;
- freezing orders, some directed to specific individuals in relation to specific assets held by them, the other a general freezing order in respect of all of HM's assets which had been renewed from time to time;
- orders permitting frozen funds to be used to fund living expenses and to fund not merely PM's legal costs in this country and in Israel but also the living costs of HM and her mother (KH), costs both in England and Israel and the costs of HM's guardian in Israel, together with directing a third party to transfer monies from an account in his name to an account in the name of the Official Solicitor's solicitors, directing the relevant bank to honour those instructions whatever contrary instructions they might

---

16 See *Days Healthcare UK Ltd (formerly known as Days Medical AIDS Ltd) v Pihsiang Machinery Manufacturing Co Ltd* [2006] EWHC 1444, [2007] CP Rep 1 at paras 20–23 per Langley J.
17 See *Griffin v Griffin* [2000] 2 FLR 44, CA at para 21 per Hale LJ.
18 *Re HM (Vulnerable Adult: Abduction)* [2010] EWHC 870 (Fam), [2010] 2 FLR 1057. Although HM lacked the material decision-making capacity, this case was decided under the inherent jurisdiction of the High Court essentially as an accident of history. It is clear that similar relief can be granted by the Court of Protection, and the authors are aware of unreported cases in which such has been done.

have from PM, and subsequently directing the solicitors as to the utilisation of funds in that account; and
- orders designed to prevent PM knowing what was going on, though at the same time permitting appropriate disclosure to others.

Specific powers contained in the COPR

17.7 The COPR[19] contains specific provisions relating to the enforcement powers of the Court of Protection. In particular:
- The court is given a specific power to direct that a penal notice be attached to any order. Such a notice makes clear that any person upon whom a copy of the order is served that disobedience would be a contempt of court punishable by imprisonment or a fine.[20] It should be made in the following terms: 'You must obey this order. If you do not, you may be sent to prison for contempt of court.'[21] In practice, such penal notices – which are not infrequently used in welfare cases – usually also specify the precise paragraphs of the order which contain the particular act(s) that the person in question must do or not do.
- If the court does not make a penal notice direction, then a penal notice may not be attached to the order.[22] It should be noted, however, that this does not mean that – in a suitable case – the court cannot consider whether disobedience of the order represents a contempt of court: this flows both from the provisions of the COPR themselves[23] and also from the wide powers granted to the court by MCA 2005 s47.

17.8 Further, COPR r184 imports into the COPR the material provisions of the Civil Procedure Rules (CPR). These provide a suite of tools which are, in practice, relatively infrequently used by the Court of Protection. They enable the party entitled to enforce a judgment or order ('the judgment creditor') to enforce such a judgment or order against another party ('the judgment debtor'). As the use of the terms 'creditor' and 'debtor' suggest, these tools are primarily directed to the enforcement of judgments or orders in relation to property and

---

19 See also MCA 2005 s51(2)(j), providing specific authority for rules to be made for the enforcement of orders made and directions given in proceedings.
20 COPR r192(1).
21 COPR r192(3).
22 COPR r192(2).
23 In particular COPR r194.

affairs. They are applicable also to enforce undertakings given to the court.

17.9 In summary, these tools (all of which are only applicable at the instigation of the judgment creditor, and in some cases only with the permission of the court) are as follows:

- The Court of Protection can transfer enforcement proceedings to the county court.[24]
- The court may make an order requiring the judgment debtor to provide specific information to court about such matters as their means.[25]
- The court may make an order requiring a third party to pay a judgment creditor a specified sum.[26]
- The court may make a charging order (which is the equivalent of a mortgage) in favour of the judgment creditor over land or other property owned by the judgment debtor.[27]
- The court may prevent certain steps being taken (by way of a stop order and stop notice) in relation to securities and funds held by the judgment debtor.[28]
- The court may issue a writ or warrant of control to enable the taking control and sale of the debtor's goods.[29]
- The court may make other provision for enforcement by way of taking control of the debtor's goods.[30]

17.10 CPR Part 89 (attachment of earnings), which was introduced with effect from 6 April 2016,[31] was not incorporated into the COPR as the amendment to the CPR post-dated the 2015 rule changes. However, this makes little difference as the county court has sole jurisdiction to make an order under the Attachment of Earnings Act 1971, so a transfer to the county court would have been all but inevitable under CPR 70.3, incorporated by COPR r184(a).

17.11 Space precludes a discussion of the procedural steps required to invoke enforcement proceedings, but the central steps are set out clearly in CPR Practice Direction (PD) 70 (Enforcement of

---

24 COPR r184(a); CPR Part 70; CPR 70.3.
25 COPR r184(a); CPR Part 71.
26 COPR r184(a); CPR Part 72.
27 COPR r184(a); CPR Part 73.
28 COPR r184(a); CPR Part 73.
29 COPR r184(a); CPR Part 83.
30 COPR r184(a); CPR Part 84.
31 By the Civil Procedure (Amendment) Rules 2016 SI No 234.

judgments and orders). They are, in the authors' experience, rarely invoked.

Committal proceedings

Bringing proceedings

17.12 The COPR contains detailed provisions[32] (accompanied by a practice direction[33]) relating to the procedure that applies when an application is made to a Court of Protection judge to commit a person for contempt of court. Such an application can be made in a range of circumstances, including where the person has: a) refused or neglected to do an act required by a judgment or an order within the specified time; b) disobeyed a judgment or order requiring them to abstain from doing a specific act; or c) breached the terms of an undertaking given to the court.[34] With one exception, no permission is required to bring such an application. That exception is where the application is brought on the basis that made or caused to be made a false statement in a document verified by a statement of truth (such as a witness statement). Such an application can only be brought by the Attorney-General and with the permission of the court.[35]

17.13 The provisions of the COPR do not govern the *power* to commit a contemnor to prison which, as discussed at para 17.5 above, is derived (via MCA 2005 s47(1)) from the High Court's common law powers in this regard. Rather, they govern the *procedure* for such applications.

17.14 The provisions of the COPR rr185–191 are largely self-explanatory, requiring as they do the filing of an application notice on a COP9, accompanied (unusually) by an affidavit containing specific details set out in PD 21A, most importantly of the alleged act(s) of contempt.[36]

17.15 In *Re Whiting*,[37] an application for committal for alleged breaches of orders made by the Court of Protection, Hayden J emphasised some crucial features of the committal process:

(1) the procedure has an essentially criminal law complexion. That is to say, contempt of court must be proved to the criminal stand-

32 COPR rr185–191.
33 PD 21A.
34 PD 21A para 6.
35 COPR r14(2)(a).
36 COPR r186(1).
37 [2013] EWHC B27 (Fam), [2014] COPLR 107.

ard, i.e. so that the judge is sure. The burden of proof rests throughout on the applicant (see: *Mubarak v Mubarak* [2001] 1 FLR 698);

(2) contempt of court involves a deliberate contumelious disobedience to the court (see: *Re A (A Child)* [2008] EWCA Civ 1138);

(3) it is not enough to suspect recalcitrance; it must be proved (see: *London Borough of Southwark v B* [1993] 2 FLR 559);

(4) committal is not the automatic consequence of a contempt, though the options before the court are limited – for example: (a) do nothing; (b) adjourn where appropriate; (c) levy a fine; (d) sequester assets; (e) where relevant, make orders under the Mental Health Act (see: *Jamie Malcolm Hale v Rachel Tanner* [2000] 2 FLR 879);

(5) the objectives of the application are usually dual, ie to punish for the breach and to ensure future compliance;

(6) bearing in mind the dual purpose of many committal proceedings, they should be brought expeditiously, whilst primary evidence is available and the incidents are fresh in the mind of the relevant witness. This is particularly important in the Court of Protection where there may be reliance on a vulnerable witness and where capacity might have to be assessed.

(7) It follows, therefore, that where injunctive orders are made, they should be clear, un-ambivalent and drafted with care. In my judgment, simplicity should be the guide.[38] Similarly, where breaches are alleged, they should be particularised with care, both so that the alleged contemnor knows exactly what, where, when and how it is contended that he is in breach, so as to be able to marshal his defence, but also to help the applicant focus on what evidence is likely to be required to establish the breach to the requisite standard of proof.[39]

17.16 In the same case, and criticising the vagueness of the evidence advanced by the local authority which brought the application for committal for contempt, Hayden J, further, emphasised that:

What is required ... is an intellectually rigorous relationship between the lawyers and the social workers in every aspect of the Court of Protection, of course, but particularly on an application of this kind. The lawyers preparing the case must realise that establishing breaches to the criminal standard of proof requires forensic precision and the careful identification of evidence to support each of the particulars of the breach ... The process requires the lawyer and the social worker to work closely together to look at the order, to identify the breach and to marshal the material as if proving the constituent parts on a count

---

38 See also the comments of Munby LJ (as he then was) in *Re X and Y (children)* [2012] EWCA Civ 1500, [2013] Fam Law 148 at paras 61–63.
39 Para 12.

on an indictment. Nothing less will do where the liberty of the individual is at stake.[40]

The hearing

17.17 COPR r188(2) makes clear that, even if the underlying proceedings are (or were) taking place in private, applications for committal are to be heard in public unless the court directs otherwise. The position is also confirmed by the Lord Chief Justice's Practice Direction: Committal for Contempt of Court – Open Court issued on 26 March 2015, which should be read also with subsequent clarificatory guidance issued.[41] That Practice Direction and Guidance gives details as to the steps that must be taken to ensure that the hearing is properly publicised, the (exceptional) circumstances under which a committal hearing can take place in private, and also as the need for publication of judgments. To emphasise the seriousness of the hearing, they will almost invariably take place with Counsel robed.

17.18 If a person wishes at the hearing of the committal application to give oral evidence, they must be allowed to do so,[42] as well as to obtain legal advice if they are not represented.[43]

17.19 The court, when determining an application for contempt, may, in an appropriate case, commit the person to prison. COPR r193, however, also makes clear that the powers granted to the court under MCA 2005 s47 in respect of the punishment of contempt are not limited solely to committal to prison, but that the court can also require a person guilty of contempt of court to pay a fine or give security for his good behaviour: see also the passages from *Re Whiting* set out at para 17.15.

Continuing contempt

17.20 In *A Local Authority v B, F and G*,[44] HHJ Cardinal confirmed that the Court of Protection has the power to make a *Hadkinson* order[45] – ie

---

40 Para 15.
41 Available at www.judiciary.gov.uk/publications/practice-guidance-committal-for-contempt-of-court-open-court/
42 COPR r187.
43 See, by analogy, *Hammerton v Hammerton* [2007] EWCA Civ 248 at para 52 per Wall LJ.
44 [2014] EWCOP B18.
45 Named after *Hadkinson v Hadkinson* [1952] P 285.

an order refusing to hear further representations in the proceedings from a person who has been found to be in contempt of court in those proceedings until such point as they have 'purged' their contempt and acceded to the court's powers. Such an order can be made in respect of any party to the proceedings who has been held in contempt. The question for the court upon such an application is:

> ... whether, taking into account all the circumstances of the case, it is in the interests of justice not to hear the contemnor. Refusing to hear a contemnor is a step that the court will only take where the contempt itself impedes the course of justice. What is meant by impeding the course of justice in this context comes from the judgment of Lord Justice Denning in *Hadkinson v Hadkinson* [1952] P 285 and means making it more difficult for the court to ascertain the truth or to enforce the orders which it may make.[46]

Powers to protect court's own processes

17.21 In *Re A (A Patient)*[47] Sir James Munby P confirmed that the Court of Protection has the power to make civil restraint orders. Specific provisions are likely to be added to the COPR relating to such orders in due course.

---

46 *JSC BTA Bank v Mukhtar Ablyazov* [2013] EWHC 1979 (Comm) at para 13 per Popplewell J.
47 [2016] EWCOP 38.

CHAPTER 18

Reconsideration and appeals

18.1	Introduction
18.3	Reconsideration
18.9	What can be appealed?
18.10	Who can appeal?
18.11	Appellate structure
18.13	Permission
18.26	The appellant's notice and skeleton argument
18.34	The respondent's notice and skeleton argument
18.43	The position between the grant of permission and the determination of the appeal
18.44	Determination of appeals
18.52	Second appeals
18.55	Appeals to the Court of Appeal and Supreme Court

Introduction

18.1 This chapter sets out how and when decisions can be reconsidered; how they can be appealed; and the basis upon which appeals will be considered by the higher courts.

18.2 The framework for such appeals is set down in COPR Part 20, amplified by Practice Direction (PD) 20A and PD 20B. These provisions were substantially altered (and made very much simpler) by the 2015 rule changes, which introduced an entirely new Part 20 and new Practice Directions. The new framework is based around three 'tiers' of judges, outlined in new Practice Direction (PD) 3B.[1] In broad terms, tier 1 judges are district judges or their equivalent; tier 2 judges are circuit judges or their equivalent (including the Senior Judge if one is appointed to replace Senior Judge Lush), and tier 3 judges are puisne (ie full) judges of the High Court or their equivalent nominated to sit in the Court of Protection. These terms will be used in this chapter, because they make explanation of the appellate structure much easier, but they will rarely be encountered in day to day practice.

Reconsideration

18.3 P, or any party or person affected by an order made without a hearing or without notice to them, has an automatic right to seek a reconsideration of that order.[2] An application should be made within 21 days of the date of the order being served (or such other period as the court may direct).[3]

18.4 Reconsideration may be undertaken on the papers or at an oral hearing,[4] and COPR r89 spells out who can undertake reconsideration:

- a decision taken by an authorised court officer can only be reconsidered by a judge, but can be reconsidered by any judge;[5]
- an order made by a Tier 1 judge can be reconsidered by any judge;[6]

---

1 And given their statutory definition in COPR r6.
2 COPR r89(2).
3 COPR r89(3)(a).
4 COPR r89(4). An oral hearing can be requested: COPR r89(10).
5 COPR r89(6)(a) read together with COPR r 7(2)(a).
6 COPR r89(6A).

- an order made by a tier 2 judge can be reconsidered by any tier 2 judge or tier 3 judge;[7]
- an order made by a tier 3 judge can be reconsidered by any tier 3 judge.[8]

18.5 It is possible for a judge to reconsider their own decision.[9]

18.6 The COPR are silent as to whether it is possible to appeal a decision made upon without a hearing (or without notice to the party in question) if reconsideration has not been sought.[10] However, given that reconsideration is not an appeal but is, instead, an opportunity for the court to look at matters again afresh, it will therefore usually be better to seek reconsideration where possible. The proposition that reconsideration is preferable to appeal is reinforced by COPR r174 (introduced in July 2015), which provides that an application for permission to appeal may be treated, where a practice direction provides (which it does not at present) or the court directs, as an application for reconsideration under Rule 89, where the applicant would have been entitled to seek such reconsideration.

18.7 If there are proper grounds to do so, there is nothing inappropriate in asking in the application notice that the reconsideration should be undertaken by a different judge to the one who made the first order.

18.8 The purpose of COPR r89 and the way in which it operates were described by Her Honour Judge Hazel Marshall QC in *Re S and S*[11] in the following terms:

> [61] ... Such a reconsideration is not an appeal. The processes in the Court of Protection are intended to give the court wide flexibility to reach a decision quickly, conveniently and cost effectively where it can, whilst preserving a proper opportunity for those affected by its orders to have their views taken into account in full argument if necessary. To that end, on receiving an application, the court can make a decision on the papers, or direct a full hearing, or make any order as to how the application can best be dealt with. This will often lead to a speedy decision made solely on paper which everyone is content to accept, but any party still has the right to ask for a reconsideration.

---

7 COPR r89(6B).
8 COPR r89(6C).
9 This flows from the use of the word 'any' in the relevant provisions of COP r.89(6A)–(6C).
10 They do, though make clear that a decision made after reconsideration has to be appealed – it cannot be further reconsidered: COPR r89(7).
11 [2008] COPLR Con Vol 1074.

[62] If this occurs, the court should approach the matter as if making the decision afresh, not on the basis that the question is whether there is a justifiable attack on the first order. The party making the application has not had a proper opportunity to be heard, and should be allowed one without feeling that s/he suffers from the disadvantage of having been placed in the position of an appellant by an order made without full consideration of his points or his views.

What can be appealed?

18.9 Any decision of the court can be appealed.[12] This means any judicial decision can be appealed, including case management decisions, the grant or refusal of an interim application or a final decision. A decision of an authorised court officer, however, cannot be appealed, and reconsideration must be sought from a judge.[13]

Who can appeal?

18.10 Any person bound by the order of the court by virtue of operation of COPR r74 is, in principle, entitled to seek to appeal that order.[14] This has two consequences:

- P is entitled to seek to appeal, even where they were not joined to the proceedings;
- a person who has been served with or notified of an application form but who has not been joined as a party will also be entitled to seek to appeal.

Appellate structure

18.11 Three useful tables are set out in PD 20B setting out the routes of appeal from tier 1, tier 2 and tier 3 judges respectively. In brief terms, however, usually:

---

12 COPR r169.
13 COPR r171A(3).
14 COPR r172(2).

- A decision of a tier 1 judge is appealed to a tier 2 judge.[15] Any second appeal from the decision of that tier 2 judge will be to the Court of Appeal.[16]
- A decision of a tier 2 judge is appealed to a tier 3 judge.[17] Any second appeal from the decision of that tier 2 judge will be to the Court of Appeal.[18]
- A decision of a tier 3 judge is appealed to the Court of Appeal.[19]
- A decision of the Court of Appeal is appealed to the Supreme Court.

18.12 Where either the judge whose decision is being granted or a judge one or more tiers above them certifies that the appeal would raise an important point of principle or practice or there is some other compelling reason for a tier 3 judge to hear the appeal, an internal 'leapfrog' can take place from tier 1 to tier 3.[20] There is no appeal against a refusal to make such a leapfrog direction.[21]

Permission

18.13 With the exception of an appeal against an order for committal to prison, an appeal against a decision of the Court of Protection requires permission.[22]

18.14 Unless the decision under challenge is, itself, one made on appeal (in which case, see paras 18.52–18.54 below), an application for permission to appeal can be made to the judge who made the decision in question ('the first instance judge'), or to a judge in a higher tier.[23] A table can be found in PD 20B setting out who can grant permission.

---

15 COPR r171A(2)(a).
16 COPR r171A(1)(b).
17 COPR r171A(2)(b).
18 COPR r171A(1)(b).
19 COPR r171A(1)(a).
20 PD 20B paras 3.1–3.3.
21 PD 20B para 3.4
22 MCA 2005 s53(4) read together with COPR rr171B, 172(1) and r172A.
23 COPR rr172(2)(b) read together with COPR r12(4) and (5). This means that permission to appeal a decision of a tier 1 judge can be made to a tier 3 judge, even though the appeal itself would be heard by a tier 2 judge (unless it was 'leapfrogged' to a tier 3 judge).

18.15 There is no requirement that the application is made to the first instance judge first. There are five reasons, though, why it is prudent to apply to the first instance at the time of judgment:
1) the judge is fully seized of the matter and so the application will take less time;
2) an application at this stage involves neither party in additional costs;
3) no harm is done if the application fails – the party enjoys two bites at the cherry;
4) if the application succeeds and the party subsequently decides to appeal, they avoid the permission stage in the appeal court;
5) no harm is done if the application succeeds but the litigant subsequently decides not to appeal.[24]

18.16 The default position is that the application will be considered by the first instance judge. If the appellant wishes to seek permission directly from the judge of the court to whom an appeal is made ('the appeal judge'), the appellant must spell this out in their appellant's notice (see further para 18.26 below).[25]

18.17 In some circumstances, it may be possible (and appropriate) to seek permission from the first instance judge at the hearing at which the decision is given. This could either be at the end of an interim hearing or at a hearing at which a reserved judgment (see paras 15.60–15.61) is handed down. In such a case, then it is suggested that there is no need to file an appellant's notice in advance: it will, though, be necessary to file an appellant's notice subsequently within the requisite time frame: ie within 21 days of the decision being appealed subject to any different order being made by the first instance judge.[26]

18.18 Note that, if a ground of appeal is that the judge has failed to deal with a particular point, the judge should be given an opportunity to deal with that point at the hearing before the application for permission is made.[27]

18.19 If no application for permission is made to the first instance judge at the relevant hearing, then it will be necessary to file an appellant's

---

24 See T (A Child) [2002] EWCA Civ 1736 at paras 12–13, see also the commentary in the White Book 2016 at para 52.3.4.
25 COPR r175(1).
26 COPR r175(2)(b).
27 English v Emery Reimbold and Strick Ltd [2002] EWCA Civ 605, [2002] 1 WLR 2409 at para 25 and In the matter of S (children) [2007] EWCA Civ 694 at paras 23–25.

notice, a COP35 form.[28] Again, subject to any different order being made by the first instance judge, this notice must be filed within 21 days of the decision being appealed. If the first instance judge announces their decision and reserves their reasons for their judgment, then the date for filing the appellant's notice should be varied so as to take this into account.[29]

18.20 If the appellant wishes to seek permission to appeal from the first instance judge and the time for doing so has not yet extended, it is possible to make an application (on a COP9 form) to that judge for an extension of the time.[30] If the time for seeking to appeal has expired, the appellant's notice should include in it a formal application for an extension of time stating the reason(s) for the delay and the steps taken prior to the application being made.[31]

18.21 Respondents are not generally expected to file any submissions at the permission stage unless the court otherwise directs.[32] Permission applications are usually determined by the first instance (or where appropriate) appeal judge without a hearing. If there is an attended hearing, then it is likely to be given only a short time-listing. There is no expectation that a respondent attend a permission hearing; by analogy with the position that prevails under the Civil Procedure Rules (CPR) (which may not be exact because of the specific rules as to costs that prevail at all stages prior to the Court of Appeal[33]), it is likely that a respondent would be in difficulty seeking their costs of doing so unless their attendance has specifically been requested.[34]

18.22 Permission to appeal will be granted only where:

- the court considers that the appeal would have a real prospect of success (ie a realistic, as opposed to a fanciful, prospect of success[35]); or

---

28 COPR r175(2).
29 PD 20A para 5, read together with COPR r175(2)(a).
30 ie for the judge to exercise their power under COPR r175(2)(a) to set a period for the filing of the appellant's notice.
31 PD 20A paras 8–9. A respondent has the right to be heard on an application for an extension of time where permission to appeal has been given or is not required: PD 20A para 10.
32 PD20A para 31.
33 See chapter 16 as to costs generally.
34 See *Jolly v Jay* [2002] EWCA Civ 277 and PD 52C.
35 By analogy with the equivalent provision in the CPR: see *Tanfern Ltd v Cameron-MacDonald (Practice Note)* [2000] 1 WLR 1311 at para 21 per Brooke LJ, citing *Swain v Hillman* [2001] 1 All ER 91.

- there is some other compelling reason why the appeal should be heard.[36]

18.23 If the first instance judge refuses permission, a further application for permission can be made:
- Where permission was refused by tier 1 judge, to a tier 2 or tier 3 judge.[37]
- Where permission was refused by a tier 2 judge, to a tier 3 judge.[38]

18.24 Where that second judge refuses permission without a hearing, a request can be made to reconsider that decision at a hearing.[39] However, the Senior Judge (if one is appointed to replace Senior Judge Lush) or tier 3 judge can, however, certify an application for permission to appeal that they have determined on the papers to be totally without merit, at which point the application cannot be renewed at an oral hearing.[40] It is also not possible to appeal a refusal by an appeal judge of permission to appeal from the first instance judge (see further paras 18.52–18.54 below).[41]

The provisions of CPR r172 provide for permission to be granted by a judge who is two tiers above the first instance judge in the appellate structure. However, in such a case, the substantive appeal will be heard by the judge of the usual level to hear the appeal. In other words, even if a tier 3 judge has granted permission to appeal a decision of a tier 1 judge, the substantive appeal will still fall to be heard by a tier 2 judge (unless it is to be 'leapfrogged' to the tier 3 judge: see para 18.12).

18.25 An order giving permission may limit the issues to be heard, and be made subject to conditions. If a first instance judge makes an order limiting permission, then it would be open to the appellant to seek permission from an appeal judge in respect of those matters where permission was refused. If the order limiting permission was made by the appeal judge without a hearing, then it is suggested that it would be open to the appellant to seek a reconsideration of this decision at an oral hearing under the provisions of COPR r89.

---

36 COPR r173(1)(a) and (b).
37 COPR rr172(3) and (4).
38 COPR rr172(3) and (5).
39 COPR r172(6).
40 COPR r172(7).
41 *TA v AA and another* [2013] EWCA Civ 1661 (concerning refusal of permission to appeal by judge of the High Court sitting as a judge of the Court of Protection; the same would also apply by analogy, it is suggested, with a refusal of permission to appeal by a circuit judge).

However, if the appeal judge refuses permission to appeal on the remaining issues at or after an oral hearing, it is suggested that the appellant cannot then renew their application for permission in respect of those issues at the hearing of the appeal.[42]

The appellant's notice and skeleton argument

18.26 In all cases where an appellant's notice is required, PD 20A sets out in some detail what must be included.[43] The documents that are required[44] are:

- one additional copy of the appellant's notice for the court;
- one copy of a skeleton argument using, or attached to, a COP37 form, either be filed with the appellant's notice or within 21 days of filing the notice;[45]
- a sealed copy of the order being appealed;
- a copy of any order giving or refusing permission to appeal, together with a copy of the judge's reasons for allowing or refusing permission to appeal;
- any witness statements or affidavits in support of any application included in the appellant's notice;
- the application form and any application notice or response (where relevant to the subject of the appeal);
- any other documents which the appellant reasonably considers necessary to enable the court to reach its decision on the hearing of the application or appeal. PD 20A suggests – correctly – that in almost all cases this will include a chronology;[46]
- a suitable record of the judgment of the first instance judge; and
- such other documents as the court may direct.

18.27 A 'suitable record' of the judgment of the first instance judge will be:

- where the judgment has been officially recorded by the court, an approved transcript (not a photocopy);[47]

---

42 See, by analogy, *Fieldman v Markovic* [2001] CP Rep 119 and *James v Baily Gibson & Co* [2002] EWCA Civ 1690.
43 Which must either accompany the notice or be filed and served on all respondents within 21 days of filing the appellant's notice.
44 PD 20A para 11.
45 PD 20A paras 16–17.
46 PD 20A para 14.
47 PD 20A para 22.

- where the judgment has been given in writing, a copy of that judgment endorsed with the judge's signature;[48]
- where the judgment was not officially recorded or given in writing, a note prepared by the advocate for the appellant. For purposes of an application for permission to appeal, a note would suffice; where permission to appeal has been granted, the note should be agreed (if possible) with the advocate for the respondent and approved by the first instance judge (or, in the absence of agreement), the judge should be invited in writing to approve one of the two rival versions.[49]

18.28 Where an appellant is unrepresented before the first instance judge, it is the duty of any advocate for the respondent to make their note of the judgment promptly available – free of charge – where there is no officially recorded judgment or the court directs; similarly, if the appellant was but is no longer represented, it is the duty of their former advocate to make their note available. The appellant should, in turn, submit the note to the appeal judge.[50]

18.29 In some circumstances, the evidence given during the hearing may be of relevance to the appeal. If so, then an official transcript must be obtained or, if the evidence was not officially recorded, a typed version of the judge's notes of evidence.[51] Where the appellant is unrepresented, or represented on a pro bono basis, an application can be made (wherever possible to the first instance judge at the time of seeking permission to appeal) for a transcript of the evidence or the proceedings to be obtained at public expense.[52] Such a transcript will only be ordered if the court is satisfied that the cost of such a transcript would be an excessive burden on the appellant and there are reasonable grounds for appeal.[53] PD 20A suggests that transcripts or notes of evidence are generally not needed for purposes of seeking permission to appeal,[54] although in a case where the evidence will be of relevance if permission is granted, steps should be put in place as quickly as possible to obtain a transcript of the evidence because it can take some time to obtain.

---

48 PD 20A para 23.
49 PD 20A para 24.
50 PD 20A para 25.
51 PD 20A para 26.
52 PD 20A paras 28–29.
53 PD 20A paras 28–29.
54 PD 20A para 26.

18.30 Where it is not possible to provide a document or documents required by PD 20A with the appellant's notice, the appellant should indicate what documents have not yet been filed, why they have not been filed and when they estimate that they can be filed (and then file and serve them as soon as reasonably practicable thereafter).[55]

18.31 In completing the appellant's notice and the accompanying skeleton argument it is necessary to be clear as to the distinction between:

- the grounds of appeal: ie what it said that the judge did wrong, which can – and should – be summarised shortly (ie 'the judge was wrong to find that P was not deprived of his liberty'), which should be set out in box 5 of the COP35 form; and
- the arguments advanced in support of those grounds of appeal: these will be set out in the skeleton argument and will be longer in form, although (as discussed at para 15.22) they should still be concise and to the point.[56]

18.32 The court will issue the appellant's notice upon it being filed; unless the court orders otherwise, the appellant must serve the appellant's notice upon each respondent and upon such other persons as the court may direct as soon as practicable and in any event within 21 days of the date on which it was issued.[57] The appellant must file a certificate of service within seven days of the date on which the notice was served.[58]

18.33 It should be noted, finally, that it is possible to apply in an appellant's notice either for a remedy incidental to the appeal or for an interim remedy, either by including the application in the notice itself or by attaching a COP9 application form to the appellant's notice (see further chapter 10 in relation to interim remedies).

The respondent's notice and skeleton argument

18.34 Unless the court directs otherwise, or unless they, too, wish to appeal, a respondent need not take any action when served with an appellant's notice until they are notified that permission to appeal has been

---

55 PD 20A para 12.
56 See also PD 20A paras 18–21 in relation to the contents of skeleton arguments accompanying appellants' notices.
57 COPR r175(3).
58 COPR r175(4).

granted (see para 18.21 above in relation to the role of respondents pre-permission).[59]

18.35 Where the respondent has been notified that the permission has been granted (or that the application for permission to appeal has been listed to be heard together with the appeal itself), what they should then do will depend upon what they wish to request of the appeal judge:

- if the respondent wishes to request that the decision of the first instance judge be upheld for the reasons given by that judge, they do not need to file a respondent's notice;
- if the respondent wishes to request that the decision of the first instance judge be upheld for reasons different to or additional to those given by the first instance judge, they need to file a respondent's notice (on a COP36 form), otherwise they will not be able to rely upon such reasons except with the permission of the court.[60]

18.36 If a respondent also wishes to seek permission to appeal, the respondent should file a respondent's notice.[61] Logically, because permission to appeal has already been granted to the appellant, either by the first instance judge or the appeal judge, and the case is therefore destined to be heard on appeal, permission to the respondent to cross-appeal must be sought from an appeal judge, rather than from the first instance judge.[62]

18.37 Where a respondent's notice is necessary, then (unless the first instance judge makes an order to different effect) it must be filed within 21 days of whichever is the soonest of:

- the date on which the respondent was served with the appellant's notice (ie where permission to appeal was given by the first instance judge or permission was not required);
- the date on which the respondent was served with notification that an appeal judge has given the appellant permission to appeal; or
- the date on which the respondent was served with notification that the application for permission to appeal and the appeal itself are to be heard together.[63]

---

59 PD 20A para 32.
60 COPR rr176(1)(b) and 179(5) and PD 20A paras 33–34.
61 COPR r176(1)(a); PD 20A para 31. Permission, where necessary, must be sought in the respondent's notice: COPR r176(2).
62 COPR r176(1)(a) only speaks of seeking permission to appeal from a judge other than the first instance judge.
63 COPR r176(4).

18.38 There is no express equivalent to the provisions set out in in PD 20B providing for applying for extensions of time in relation to the filing of the respondent's notice. However, it is suggested that the same procedure as set out at para 18.20 above would be likely to apply. Especially where an application is made after the expiry of the period for filing of the notice, it is suggested that it would be prudent to ensure that the respondent's notice details the reason(s) for the delay and the steps taken prior to the application being made.

18.39 The same requirements as to service of the respondent's notice and the filing of a certificate of service apply to respondent's notices as to appellant's notices.[64]

18.40 Unsurprisingly, what a respondent must provide in and with a respondent's notice[65] is very similar to what an appellant must provide in and with an appellant's notice, save that the respondent is not under the same obligation as the appellant to provide such documents as a suitable record of the judgment.

18.41 In any case where the respondent wishes to address arguments to the court (ie whether or not they have filed a respondent's notice), they must file and serve a skeleton argument.[66] If the respondent files a respondent's notice, then the skeleton argument must either accompany that notice or be filed and served within 21 days of filing that notice.[67] If the respondent does not file a respondent's notice, then any skeleton argument must be filed and served at least seven days before the appeal hearing.[68]

18.42 The same requirements apply to the contents of the respondent's skeleton argument as to those of an appellant, with the added – unsurprising – requirement that it should, where appropriate, answer the arguments set out in the appellant's skeleton argument.[69]

---

64 COPR r176(5)–(6).
65 Set out in PD 20A para 40. A respondent can also apply for incidental relief: PD 20A para 41.
66 PD 20A para 44.
67 PD 20A paras 45–46. A certificate of service is required: PD 20A para 49.
68 PD 20A para 47.
69 PD 20A para 48.

The position between the grant of permission and the determination of the appeal

18.43 It is not unknown for the appellant's case to change after the grant of permission. In such a case, the appellant's representatives should write to the appeal court and to the other party, indicating the proposed nature of the changed case. The court should be asked to indicate whether it will deal with the matter at the beginning of the hearing of the appeal or whether it will give directions on an earlier date. After being informed of the respondent's attitude, the court can decide whether to shut out the new grounds or allow them to be argued.[70] Similarly, if there has been a material change in circumstances after the grant of permission, which would affect the question of whether permission should have been given, the applicant should inform the court in writing.[71] A failure to take either step will waste money and court time, and may have adverse cost consequences.[72]

Determination of appeals

18.44 It is, in principle, open to the appeal judge to deal with all or part of an appeal without a hearing.[73] However, as reconsideration can be sought of an order made without a hearing (see above paras 18.3–18.8), appeal judges will often err on the side of ordering a hearing, especially where they have gleaned from the prior history that the appellant will be likely to seek reconsideration.

18.45 An appeal judge has all the powers of the first instance judge whose decision is under appeal.[74] The appeal judge can in particular, if they allow the appeal, decide the issue in question themselves, rather than sending it back to the first instance judge (or ordering a new hearing before a first instance judge). Appeal judges will, however, be cautious about deciding cases themselves unless there is plainly only one answer: wherever it is a question of evaluation, it is

---

70 See by analogy, *Shire v Secretary of State for Work and Pensions* [2003] EWCA Civ 1465 at paras 6–7 and the commentary in the *White Book 2016* at paras 52.3.20 and 52.8.
71 See, by analogy, *Walbrook Trustee (Jersey) Ltd v Fattal* [2008] EWCA Civ 427 at para 49.
72 See, by analogy, *R (a child)* [2010] EWCA Civ 303 at paras 14–16.
73 COPR r171(2), having regard to the factors set out in COPR r84(3).
74 COPR r178(1).

more usual for the matter to be remitted to a first instance judge (whether that be the one who initially heard the case or another judge) to consider it in the light of the judgment of the appeal court.

18.46 The starting point in relation to appeals is that they are reviews, rather than re-hearings.[75] It would only be in very unusual circumstances that the appeal court will undertake a re-hearing; the appeal court will therefore not usually receive either oral evidence or evidence that was not before the first instance judge, although the appeal court has the power to do all three.[76] While the MCA 2005 and COPR are silent as to the circumstances under which fresh evidence will be admitted, it is suggested that the appropriate test to apply is that which applies in civil proceedings, namely consideration of whether:

- the evidence could have been obtained with reasonable diligence for use at the trial;
- the evidence is such that, if given, it would probably have an important influence on the result of the case, though it need not be decisive; and
- the evidence is such as is presumably to be believed; ie whether it is apparently credible, though it need not be incontrovertible.[77]

18.47 By way of an example of a circumstance in which it was appropriate to receive fresh evidence, we note the case of *Aintree University Hospitals NHS Foundation Trust v James*,[78] concerned with whether life-sustaining treatment should be withheld from a critically ill patient in a minimally conscious state. Here, the Court of Appeal received fresh evidence as to the deterioration in the patient's condition between the time of the hearing before the first instance judge and the date of the hearing before the Court of Appeal. The Supreme Court ultimately found that the Court of Appeal had been right to determine that – at that point the case was before the Court of Appeal, and on the basis of that fresh evidence – it was in the man's best interests not to receive life-sustaining treatment.[79]

18.48 The COPR provides that an appeal will be allowed where the decision of the first instance judge is (a) wrong; or (b) unjust, because

---

75 COPR r179(1).
76 COPR r179(1)(b) and (2)(a) and (b) respectively.
77 See *Ladd v Marshall* [1954] 1 WLR 1489, *Terluk v Berezovsky* [2011] EWCA Civ 1534 and the commentary in the *White Book 2016* at para 52.11.2.
78 *Aintree University Hospitals NHS Foundation Trust v DJ* [2013] EWCA Civ 65, [2013] 4 All ER 67, (2013) 16 CCLR 554.
79 *Aintree University Hospitals NHS Foundation Trust v James* [2013] UKSC 67, [2014] AC 591.

of a serious procedural or other irregularity in the proceedings before the first instance judge.[80] In the Supreme Court decision in *Aintree University Hospitals NHS Foundation Trust v James*, Lady Hale, relying upon *Re B (a child) (care proceedings: appeal)*,[81] held that, where a judge of the Court of Protection had correctly directed themselves as to the law, an appellate court could only interfere with their decision as to the evaluation of best interests if satisfied that it was wrong.[82] Strictly, this decision only relates to the power of the Supreme Court upon an appeal, but it is – at the very least – powerful guidance as to how lower courts should interpret the provisions of the COPR.

18.49 The decision in *Aintree* and the application of *Re B* gives rise to two important, related, points:

- The majority of the Supreme Court in *Re B* (albeit not Lady Hale herself) had held in the context of proceedings relating to children that it is not for an appellate court itself to conduct a 'de novo' assessment of the proportionality of any interference with rights enjoyed by parties under the European Convention on Human Rights (ECHR). In other words, unless – exceptionally – it considers that it is necessary to conduct a re-hearing, the appellate court is confined to reviewing the decision of the first instance judge as to the proportionality of the interference. Given that almost every best interests decision taken by the Court of Protection will engage one or more rights under the ECHR, this suggests strongly that the same approach will apply in the context of almost all appeals against best interests decisions.
- While the majority of the Supreme Court in *Re B* rejected the addition of any gloss to the word 'wrong' (such as 'plainly'), Lady Hale made clear in *Aintree* that in sensitive and difficult cases (which will, by definition, be those most likely to attract appeals), appellate courts should be very slow to find that a first instance judge's evaluation of best interests is wrong. The threshold for intervention by the appellate courts is therefore a high one.

18.50 Where the appeal lies not against an evaluative decision but against the exercise of a discretion (most obviously in the context of case management decisions), then the test is subtly different: the

---

80 COPR r179(3).
81 [2013] UKSC 33, [2013] 1 WLR 1911.
82 At para 42.

appellate court should only interfere if 'satisfied that the judge erred in principle, took into account irrelevant matters, failed to take into account relevant matters, or came to a decision so plainly wrong that it must be regarded as outside the generous ambit of the discretion entrusted to the judge': *Re TG (children) (care proceedings: case management: expert evidence)*.[83]

18.51 It should be noted that where an appeal is to a tier 2 judge (against a decision of tier 1 judge) or to a tier 3 judge (against the decision of either a tier 2 or (in a 'leapfrog' case a tier 1 judge)), then the normal costs rules contained in the COPR apply (see chapter 16).

Second appeals

18.52 A decision which was, itself, made on appeal, can only be appealed to the Court of Appeal.[84] Permission must be sought from the Court of Appeal for such an appeal, and the test (contained in the Civil Procedure Rules (CPR) 1998, not the COPR is stricter; the Court of Appeal will only grant permission where:

- the appeal would raise an important point of principle or practice; or
- there is some other compelling reason for the Court of Appeal to hear it.[85]

18.53 This rule does *not* apply if the appeal is against a decision of a tier 3 judge sitting in the Court of Protection as a first instance judge; in that case, permission can be sought either from that tier 3 judge or from the Court of Appeal.[86]

18.54 It is important to note that a decision from an appeal court refusing permission to appeal to that court from a lower court is not a

---

83 [2013] EWCA Civ 5, [2013] 1 FLR 1250 per Munby LJ (as he then was) at para 35.
84 COPR r17A(1)(b) and COPR r171B(3).
85 CPR r52.13(2). On a strict reading of the CPR, this provision does not apply to second appeals from the Court of Protection, as this court is not mentioned there, but it is suggested that it is overwhelmingly likely that the Court of Appeal would apply this test in the exercise of its inherent case management jurisdiction.
86 COPR r171B(2).

'decision' for these purposes: it is not possible to appeal such a refusal.[87]

Appeals to the Court of Appeal and Supreme Court

18.55 As noted at the outset of this chapter, appeals to the Court of Appeal and Supreme Court fall outside the scope of the COPR. If, therefore, an appeal is being considered against a decision of a tier 3 judge sitting in the Court of Protection as a first instance judge, then the relevant rules to apply are not the COPR but rather those set out in Part 52 of the Civil Procedure Rules (CPR) 1998, as amplified by PDs 52A and 52C. CPR Part 52 and PDs 52A and 52C can be found in the supporting materials section. They are, in most respects, very similar to the rules set out in the COPR and discussed above, and are not rehearsed here.

18.56 If an appeal lies from a decision of the Court of Appeal to the Supreme Court in relation to a matter that was originally determined by a judge of the Court of Protection, the relevant procedural rules are set out in the Supreme Court Rules 2009[88] and the associated practice directions. These can be found on the Supreme Court website;[89] they are not addressed here because they are beyond the scope of this work. The only point that should be noted is that it does not appear that there is a possibility for a 'leapfrog' appeal to be made directly to the Supreme Court from a decision of a High Court judge sitting in the Court of Protection. The relevant provisions of the Administration of Justice Act (AJA) 1969 allow such a 'leapfrog' appeal in respect of 'civil proceedings in the High Court'.[90] It is, however, suggested that a judge of the High Court sitting as a Court of Protection judge is not hearing civil proceedings in the High Court.[91]

---

87 *TA v AA and another* [2013] EWCA Civ 1661 (concerning refusal of permission to appeal by a judge of the High Court sitting as a judge of the Court of Protection; the same would also apply by analogy, it is suggested, with a refusal of permission to appeal by a circuit judge (now tier 2 judge)).
88 SI No 1603.
89 See: www.supremecourt.uk/procedures/rules-of-the-court.html.
90 AJA 1969 s12(2).
91 See, by analogy, *TA v AA and another* [2013] EWCA Civ 1661 and the discussion at para 55 of that case of the earlier decision in *Re B (a patient) (Court of Protection – appeal)* [2006] 1 WLR 278.

18.57 In any appeal to the Court of Appeal the costs rules set out in the COPR do not apply. Unless an application is made under CPR 52.9A (as to which, see below), the normal costs rules set out in the CPR will apply, and the unsuccessful party will be ordered to pay the costs.[92] In *Cheshire West and Chester Council v P (No 2)*,[93] Munby LJ rejected an argument made on behalf of the unsuccessful party, P, that there should be no order as to costs because proceedings in the Court of Protection were analogous to public law family proceedings (and appeals therefrom) which are exempt from the material provisions of the CPR.[94] Munby LJ held:[95]

> I cannot accept Mr Gordon's argument of principle. It comes perilously close to an impermissible invitation to us to re-write [CPR 44.2], whether by incorporating within it the principle in r157 of the Court of Protection Rules or by adjusting CPR r[44.2(3)] to include a reference to the Court of Protection. Our task is to apply CPR r[44.2]. I accept, of course, that we can properly have regard to the fact that the appeal concerns a vulnerable adult in the context of the court's protective functions and not, for example, a valuable cargo in the context of a commercial dispute, but this is not because of some supposed analogy with either [CPR r44.2] or r157 of the Court of Protection Rules. It is simply because it is one of the 'circumstances' – and, it may be, one of the more important of the circumstances – to which CPR r44.3(4) bids us have regard.

18.58 It is suggested that the Court of Protection is (for these purposes) either a 'no costs' or a 'low costs' jurisdiction, by virtue of the specific costs provisions in COPR Part 19, which differ from those applying in conventional litigation. It is therefore suggested that it is therefore possible for an application to be made by either party for an order under CPR 52.9A limiting the recoverable costs of an appeal to the extent that the court specifies. In making such an order, the Court of Appeal will have regard to:

- the means of both parties;
- the circumstances of the case; and
- the need to facilitate access to justice.

---

92 This is now contained in CPR 44.2(a); prior to 1 April 2013, this was contained in CPR 44.3(a).
93 [2011] EWCA Civ 1333, [2012] COPLR 76.
94 These are now contained in CPR 44.2(3)(a); prior to 1 April 2013 they were contained in CPR 44.3(3)(a).
95 Para 6. The references to the CPR have been amended to reflect the position that prevails post 1 April 2013.

18.59 As the Court of Appeal explained in *JE (Jamaica) v Secretary of State for the Home Department*:[96] 'The rule deals with appeals coming up from a "no costs" or a "low costs" jurisdiction. It enables the appeal court to put in place a similar regime to that which applied in the court or tribunal below'.[97] The Court of Appeal in the same case noted the importance of any application being made at any early stage, so that both parties know the costs regime under which they are proceeding; if the appellant is seeking the order, it may be 'convenient and economic' to include such an application in the appellant's notice, but that is not required by the rule. The application will then be determined in writing unless the court orders otherwise.[98]

18.60 The costs rules that apply in relation to appeals to the Supreme Court are contained in Part 7 of the Supreme Court Rules; they are beyond the scope of this work.

---

96 [2014] EWCA Civ 14, [2014] 1 Costs LR 163.
97 Para 8, per Jackson LJ.
98 CPR 52.9A(4).

CHAPTER 19
Alternative dispute resolution

19.1	Introduction	
19.4	Code of Practice	
19.9	Court of Protection Rules	
19.12	Case-law	
19.15	The Select Committee	
19.17	Mediation and ADR in practice – types of ADR and how to decide between them	
19.17	Round table meetings	
	What they are and how they work • Advantages and disadvantages	
19.26	Mediation	
	What mediation is • Practicalities • Finding a mediator • Preparation for the mediation • The mediation process	

Introduction

19.1 In common with the expectations in other forms of civil and family litigation, advisers are expected to discuss the possibility of mediation or other forms of alternative dispute resolution (ADR) before litigating and to keep this decision under review.

19.2 A wide range of methods of ADR may be used in the life of a Court of Protection case, ranging from informal discussions outside court, to formal mediation processes that are independently facilitated and may run into several days.

19.3 The Case Management Pilot introduces 'Dispute Resolution Hearings' for property and affairs cases[1]. These are a form of judge-led mediation and are discussed in more detail at paras 8.32–8.40 above. More broadly, the Pilot also requires the parties to make efforts to resolve disputes outside the court arena in respect of cases falling within the welfare pathway set out in the Pilot. This chapter will:

- examine the guidance about ADR in the Court of Protection;
- consider the obligations on litigants to use ADR; and
- consider the options and how they may work in the context of the Court of Protection.

Code of Practice

19.4 The Code of Practice[2] to the Mental Capacity Act (MCA) 2005 provides guidance to decision-makers about managing 'conflicting concerns' when establishing the best interests of a person who lacks capacity. Paragraph 5.64 reads:

> The decision-maker will need to find a way of balancing these concerns or deciding between them. The first approach should be to review all elements of the best interests checklist with everyone involved. They should include the person who lacks capacity (as much as they are able to take part) . . . It may be possible to reach agreement at a meeting to air everyone's concerns. But an agreement in itself might not be in the person's best interests. Ultimate responsibility for working out best interests lies with the decision-maker.

---

1 Case Management Pilot PD para 5.4.
2 Available at: www.legislation.gov.uk/ukpga/2005/9/pdfs/ukpgacop_20050009_en.pdf.

19.5 Chapter 15 of the Code concerns settling disagreements. The Code stresses again the importance of the person without capacity having support and representation,[3] including during mediation.[4]

19.6 The Code advocates mediation as a means of solving a problem at an early stage. The Code makes a number of claims for mediation, which it describes as offering a wider range of solutions than court proceedings as well as having the potential to be 'less stressful, more cost-effective and quicker. People who come to an agreement through mediation are more likely to keep to it, because they have taken part in mediation'.[5]

19.7 The Code refers to the availability of legal aid funding for mediation but states this is available mainly for family mediation.[6] This is not entirely correct: see para 19.29 below.

19.8 The emphasis in the Code on co-operation does not detract from the need to refer matters to the court where it is not possible to reach agreement: see *G v E (deputyship and litigation friend)*[7] and *Hillingdon LBC v Neary*.[8]

Court of Protection Rules

19.9 The Court of Protection Rules (COPR) require parties to help the court in furthering the overriding objective of dealing with cases justly.[9] Judges are required to further the overriding objective by 'active case management', described in COPR Pr.13/COPR r5 as including:

(a) encouraging the parties to co-operate with each other . . .

(e) encouraging the parties to use an alternative dispute resolution procedure if the court considers that appropriate . . .

19.10 As discussed in more detail in chapter 10, this is often reflected in practice. For example, judges may routinely include in standard directions a requirement that the parties should take steps to seek to narrow the disputes between them. This may be expressed simply as a requirement to attend court an hour before the hearing takes place,

3 Code of Practice para 15.3.
4 Code of Practice para 15.6.
5 Code of Practice para 15.7.
6 Code of Practice para 15.13.
7 [2010] EWHC 2512 (COP), [2010] COPLR Con Vol 470.
8 [2011] EWHC 1377 (COP), [2011] COPLR Con Vol 632.
9 COPR rr3, 4.

in order to have discussions. Sometimes the Court of Protection may make a direction requiring the parties to make contact with each other before the day of the hearing.

19.11 As set out in chapter 9, the Case Management Pilot requires an applicant before issuing a welfare application to engage with potential respondents and explore how the dispute can be resolved without proceedings.[10] Whilst the Case Management Pilot Practice Direction does not expressly refer to ADR in the issues to be considered by the judge at the case management hearing, it is implicit in paragraph 4.5 of the Practice Direction that the court will consider this as part of its duty of active case management. As noted above, and discussed further in chapter 8, judicial ADR in the form of a Dispute Resolution Hearing is expected to be the norm in contested property and affairs applications.

Case-law

19.12 There are no reported cases that give specific guidance as to mediation or ADR in this jurisdiction. In *A Local Authority v PB and P*,[11] Charles J was invited to comment on the issue of mediation or ADR but declined on the basis that this had not arisen in the facts of the case that he was considering.

19.13 The use of ADR is far more established in the family courts. Some assistance can be found by analogy in the case of *AI v MT (alternative dispute resolution)*[12] Baker J approved a consent order which had been reached after a lengthy arbitration process by a separating couple overseen by the New York Beth Din. The principles he identified in the context of the family courts are of relevance in the Court of Protection:

- the court's jurisdiction cannot be ousted by agreement between the parties;
- unless statute provides otherwise, the child's welfare is the paramount consideration;
- respect for the practice and beliefs of all faiths and cultures does not oblige the court to depart from the welfare principle because this principle is 'sufficiently broad and flexible to accommodate many cultural and religious practices';

---

10 Case Management Pilot PD para 4.2.1.
11 [2011] EWHC 502 (COP), [2011] COPLR Con Vol 166.
12 [2013] EWHC 100 (Fam), [2013] 2 FLR 371.

- it is always in the interests of the parties to try to resolve disputes by agreement if possible and the courts will encourage this but will be cautious not to endorse a process which might oust the jurisdiction of the court.

19.14 In *S v S*[13] Sir James Munby P considered the approach of the courts when there has been an arbitration award, in that case, under the Institute of Family Law Arbitrators Scheme (a not for profit organisation, conducting arbitrations in accordance with the Arbitration Act 1996). He observed that the fact that the parties had bound themselves to accept an arbitral award generated a 'single magnetic factor of determinative importance'; and that in the absence of very compelling evidence to the contrary this should be determinative of the order made. In these circumstances the judge's role was not to be 'a rubber stamp. He is entitled but is not obliged to play the detective. He is a watchdog, but he is not a bloodhound or a ferret.'[14] If an attempt is made to resile from an arbitral award, the court may be robust in case managing the dispute, and may in some cases simply make the order in any event. The President noted the increasing range of forms of ADR and the need for the courts to keep up with developments and the needs of litigants and advisers.

The Select Committee

19.15 The Select Committee of the House of Lords conducting post-legislative scrutiny of the MCA 2005[15] considered the role of mediation. It noted a limited pilot scheme proposed by the Office of the Public Guardian (OPG), though was disappointed by the limited terms of the pilot and the fact that mediation would be conducted by telephone, in an area where building relationship and trust is crucial. It concluded that:

- mediation in the Court of Protection must comply with the decision-making framework of the MCA 2005 and provision must be made to ensure representation of P's views and interests;
- mediation would be beneficial in many cases prior to issue and consideration should be given to making it a pre-requisite for

13 [2014] EWHC 7 (Fam); [2014] 1 WLR 2299.
14 *S v S* at para 20, citing his own judgment in *L v L* [2008] 1 FLR 26.
15 *Mental Capacity Act 2005:post-legislative scrutiny*, HL Paper 139, March 2013, paras 224–232; available at: www.publications.parliament.uk/pa/ld201314/ldselect/ldmentalcap/139/139.pdf.

launching proceedings, especially financial proceedings where the costs will fall to P's estate.

In its response ('*Valuing every voice, respecting every right*'[16]) the government agreed mediation would be suitable in some property and affairs cases, but less so in health and welfare cases. The government did not consider mediation should be a prerequisite to issuing as this would detract from its voluntary nature.

19.16 There is therefore no formal structure to the use of ADR in the Court of Protection, although the parties are strongly encouraged to use it. In practice the two most commonly used forms are round table meetings and formal mediation.

Mediation and ADR in practice – types of ADR and how to decide between them

Round table meetings

What they are and how they work

19.17 Round table meetings (RTMs) are often suggested by parties, or sometimes by judges of their own motion. An RTM is a meeting which would usually take place away from a court setting. RTMs are sometimes hosted by legal advisers or barristers' chambers. They may take place in local authority offices.

19.18 Standard directions will often include a provision encouraging the parties to take part in a RTM and will sometimes specify when it should take place and who is responsible for convening the meeting, arranging minutes and preparing an agreed note. If an expert is to attend the RTM it is prudent to include provision for the expert's fees in the order. The Court of Protection Handbook website includes (as part of a wider precedent directions order for welfare cases) a precedent set of directions for a RTM: see www.courtofprotection handbook.com.

19.19 The difference between an RTM and a mediation is that an RTM is not facilitated by an external mediator. In welfare cases, an RTM is often chaired by the solicitor or barrister acting for P. The rationale

---

16 'Valuing every voice, respecting every right: Making the case for the Mental Capacity Act – The Government's response to the House of Lords Select Committee Report on the Mental Capacity Act 2005 (June 2014)': www.gov.uk/ government/uploads/system/uploads/attachment_data/file/318730/cm8884-valuing-every-voice.pdf.

Alternative dispute resolution 481

behind this is that they are more likely to be seen as neutral than the other parties and to ensure that P's interests are central.

19.20 An RTM will usually involve the parties and their legal advisers. In some cases independent experts attend as well. In most cases solicitors rather than barristers will attend the meeting with their clients, and everyone attending will be present during the meeting. It is often prudent to ascertain if, in addition to the room where the meeting is taking place, any other rooms are available so that confidential discussions between lawyers and their clients can take place and to provide some space if any participant needs a break from the meeting. These rooms are sometimes described as 'breakout rooms'.

19.21 There are no rules governing the conduct of RTMs, so it is essential before such a meeting starts for the participants to address their minds to the following questions:

- Will the discussions be confidential, or can they be referred to in the litigation? If the latter, how will the contents of the meeting be recorded?
- What is the status of any agreement reached at the RTM?
- Who is going to attend the meeting?
- Who is going to chair the meeting?
- What will be on the agenda?
- At what point will the RTM be abandoned?
- Will the venue be suitable? Will there be enough space and is there a 'breakout room' for confidential discussions?

Advantages and disadvantages

19.22 RTMs can be arranged more quickly than formal mediation. They are cheaper as there are no mediation fees. It can often be productive to suggest an RTM at the every early stages of a dispute, perhaps in pre-action correspondence. A dispute between a family member and social work staff may have become entrenched. Sometimes the involvement of lawyers, both for the family member and the statutory body, can help the clients narrow the issues and an RTM at this stage may obviate the need for litigation at all.

19.23 As with all forms of ADR, one advantage of an RTM is it can allow the parties to reach an outcome which could not be achieved through litigation alone – for example, an apology.

19.24 The potential disadvantage at this early stage may be that it is unlikely that P will be represented, and thus it will be difficult to ensure P's effective participation. As we have seen above, the Code suggests that P might be supported by an advocate during mediation, and the same solution might then be used. This may, however, result in two parties to a dispute – for example, the local authority and statutory services – being legally represented at an RTM, while P remains without legal advice.

19.25 RTMs will be challenging if there is a particularly difficult relationship between two or more parties, as they tend to involve the participation of all the parties. Not all lawyers feel comfortable chairing RTMs, and the lawyer may be seen as less objective than an external mediator because the lawyer may already have had to express a view on important issues on an interim basis which may have been unpopular with one or more of the parties.

Mediation

19.26 This section provides a very basic summary of what mediation is, and then looks at the issues arising when mediating Court of Protection cases. Readers interested in learning more about mediation are recommended to read *Making mediation work for you*,[17] on which this section draws.

What mediation is

19.27 Mediation can take various different forms, but all mediations share the following characteristics:
- An independent mediator is used to facilitate the process.
- Mediation is confidential (though there are some exceptions) – the aim is that this encourages parties to be open and flexible. What one party says to the mediator will not be disclosed to the other without permission.
- Mediation is 'without prejudice' – the discussions which take place cannot be referred to in litigation.
- Mediation is a voluntary process – parties cannot be forced to mediate.
- Mediation is non-binding in that the parties are not obliged to reach agreement.
- If the mediation results in agreement, this can be recorded in the form of a legally binding agreement.

19.28 The involvement of an independent trained mediator can bring benefits to a case where the parties may find it difficult to see solutions.

17 Kate Aubrey-Johnson with Helen Curtis, *Making mediation work for you*, LAG, 2012.

Alternative dispute resolution 483

A skilled mediator will try to identify the parties' real interests in the case, which can be masked by the parties' stated positions. The mediator will try to draw out areas of common interest between the parties, which can generate solutions.

Practicalities

19.29 Although mediation may obviate the need for a contested hearing if it is successful and may therefore save money, it is not a cheap option, and it is important to anticipate the likely cost and make arrangements about how this is to be met. A mediator will require the parties and/or their representatives to sign and agreement to mediate, and this will include details as to how the mediator's costs will be met.

19.30 The mediator's fees are usually shared by the parties who are mediating. If any of the parties are legally aided, then the mediator's fees will be a disbursement on the certificate or Legal Help form. Prior authority should be sought from the Legal Aid Authority (LAA) (see chapter 6). Advisers should ensure that they have identified all the potential costs of the mediation. These may, for example, include room hire; whether the length of the mediation has been underestimated; or it may have been suggested that any experts who have reported should also attend the mediation.

Finding a mediator

19.31 Finding a mediator who will be able to conduct an effective mediation in a Court of Protection case can be daunting. There are different types of mediator, reflecting the different specialist areas of mediation – civil, family, workplace and community mediators. There is no single body which regulates mediators. Family mediators are accredited by organisations which belong to the Family Mediation Council. The Civil Mediation Council (CMC) accredits mediation providers, who must have a panel of at least six mediation providers who can show that they meet the CMC's accreditation standards. Thus, individual mediators will not themselves be accredited by the CMC. The Ministry of Justice maintains a directory of mediators accredited by the CMC which can be searched by geographical area. Individual mediators will be accredited if they have been trained by a body recognised by the CMC.[18] The Law Society has an accreditation scheme for civil and commercial mediators.[19]

18 http://civilmediation.justice.gov.uk.
19 See: www.lawsociety.org.uk.

19.32 In addition to checking the mediator's accreditation, it is advisable to ask to see their CV and ask about the cases they have taken on.

Preparation for the mediation

19.33 For those who have proposed mediation or responded to a suggestion by the court or another party, it is essential to consider what to expect from the mediation. Advisers will need to have a clear grasp of the strengths and weaknesses of the client's case. Perhaps for this reason, many Court of Protection mediations take place after the receipt of experts' reports, if these are being used. This is an ideal time to take stock of the evidence as it now stands, in as objective a way as possible. This may be difficult because of the highly charged atmosphere that can develop in Court of Protection disputes, especially in cases involving a relationship between family carers and statutory bodies, which may have been deteriorating over a number of years before matters come to a head and proceedings are issued. Advisers may find it helpful to underline to their clients the potential benefit of the involvement of a neutral mediator who will not take sides. A neutral mediator should manage the mediation process in such a way that parties can adopt a fresh perspective on the strengths and weaknesses of their case without losing face. Perceptions can shift in the course of mediation which can help parties move from their initial stated position to something more flexible.

19.34 In anticipation of the mediation the following issues should be considered:

- Assuming that new evidence (especially in the form of expert reports) has been received, what if any impact have this evidence had on the views and positions of the parties?
- Advisers should explore with their clients as neutrally as possible whether there are any concessions which the client feels they could offer which might promote an agreement. These might be matters that could not be achieved through litigation alone. This could include eg an apology; an agreement to make a gift in kind; or an agreement to work with the other parties in a different manner in the future. Possible concessions that might be sought from the other parties should also be considered.
- It is important to evaluate in the light of the evidence what the client can realistically achieve in the litigation. If mediation fails to deliver an agreement, what is the likely outcome of a contested hearing? If an adviser's client is legally aided, is there any risk that

the client's legal aid will be not be extended to cover a contested hearing if mediation fails?
- Is there any reason (on an objective evaluation) to believe that any of the other parties have not agreed to mediate in good faith?
- The potential benefits to mediation should be weighed, even if it is unlikely to deliver a full resolution: might it narrow the issues or at least improve the parties' ability to communicate?
- With this point in mind, advisers are encouraged to manage their clients' expectations.
- Practicalities – will the parties agree to sit in the same room for all or any of the process?
- In the civil sphere, an unreasonable refusal to mediate can give rise to costs sanctions: see *Halsey v Milton Keynes NHS Trust*.[20] The costs implication of a refusal to mediate in the Court of Protection sphere is considered at para 16.17.

19.35 It is not always necessary for the mediator to be provided with all the papers filed in a given case. However the mediator may need to see at least some of the documents from the Court of Protection proceedings. Before mediating the parties will need to agree the contents of a bundle of core documents for the mediator. The court will need to give permission to disclose this information to the mediator. This could be the subject of an application on COP9, usually by consent.

19.36 The mediator may wish to speak to the parties or their legal advisers in advance of the mediation. This can be a useful opportunity to agree the procedure to be followed and can make attending the mediation itself less daunting. Some mediators invite the parties to prepare a short position statement or make a short opening statement at the beginning of the process. Where parties feel unable to be in the same room, this can be delivered between the legal representatives and then shared with their respective clients in private rooms.

19.37 It is highly likely that the mediator will ask the parties to sign an agreement to mediate in advance of the mediation. The contents of this will vary but the agreement will probably contain the following provisions:
- who is responsible for the mediator's fees and when these will be paid;
- confirmation that the parties have agreed to mediate voluntarily;
- confidentiality, perhaps with a provision that nothing said during the mediation will be referred to in the litigation;

---

20 [2004] EWCA Civ 576, [2004] 1 WLR 3002.

- any ground rules the mediator considers necessary, including the discretion to end the mediation;
- a requirement that whoever attends on behalf of the parties has authority to settle.

The mediation process

19.38 Mediation is a flexible process which can be designed to fit the needs of the parties involved. Many mediations will commence with a plenary meeting, where all the parties gather in one room and where the mediator will introduce him or herself and explain the procedure to be followed. Opening statements may be made during this session. Typically, after this the parties will then retreat to separate rooms, while the mediator speaks to them in turn. This can take time, and mediation can often seem to involve a considerable amount of waiting to hear how the other party has responded or what the other party may propose.

19.39 The mediator will seek to establish the parties' core interests to explore potential common ground which may provide an opening for agreement. The mediator may want to explore how one party would react in the event that a particular concession is made by one of the parties.

19.40 Court of Protection cases can pose particular challenges. P's interests need to remain central to the process. If P is a party, he or she will have a litigation friend who is likely to be present (or be represented) at the mediation. The litigation friend should make every attempt to ascertain P's wishes and feelings on the issues which are being mediated. By definition, P is unlikely to be able to take part in the process of compromise and give-and-take that may be involved in mediation. It is the mediator's role to ensure that P remains the focus of the mediation and to reduce the time spent disproportionately on satellite issues which may be considered important by the other parties.

19.41 The second difficulty is that Court of Protection cases will frequently involve an imbalance of power between the parties, as they may typically involve a dispute between a statutory body and one or more individuals. It is suggested that this requires the mediator to satisfy him or herself that even though one party may be in a much stronger position, that party remains willing genuinely to consider an element of compromise.

19.42 An experienced mediator should be alert to both these issues.

19.43 If agreement is reached, the agreement should be put in writing. In the authors' experience, this is usually done by the legal advisers. This needs to be done with care. Once proceedings have started, the court will need to approve any agreement before it is fully binding. However, it is undesirable to be in the position of resiling from a signed mediation agreement. It is absolutely essential that there is sufficient time, even at the end of what may have been a long day, for advisers to satisfy themselves that their client fully understands, and is willing to comply with, the mediation agreement. If a party needs, for example, to consider their position overnight, see if this can be agreed.

19.44 If the mediation is successful, then the mediation agreement should be approved by the judge, who will need to be satisfied that the outcome is one that can properly be said to be in the best interests of P.

CHAPTER 20
Office of the Public Guardian

20.1	Introduction
20.4	Responsibilities
20.5	Register of lasting powers of attorney and deputies
20.16	Searching the registers
20.23	Supervision
20.27	Annual reports
20.30	Court Visitors
20.38	Investigations
20.44	Panel deputies

Introduction

20.1 The role of Public Guardian, and the Office of the Public Guardian (OPG) were established by sections 57–61 of the Mental Capacity Act (MCA) 2005. Before the MCA a similar role and office had existed but with a narrower focus. Today the Public Guardian is Alan Eccles, who has been in post since 2012. Full contact details for the OPG can be found in appendix G below.

20.2 The OPG is an executive agency of the Ministry of Justice through which the Public Guardian caries out his statutory functions.

20.3 The OPG has continued to see significant year on year increases in its work load. In 2015/16 the number of LPAs registered rose by 34 per cent and the number of deputy orders under supervision rose by eight per cent.[1]

Responsibilities

20.4 Under MCA 2005 s58(1), the Public Guardian is responsible for:
a) establishing and maintaining a register of lasting powers of attorney,
b) establishing and maintaining a register of orders appointing deputies,
c) supervising deputies appointed by the court,
d) directing a Court of Protection Visitor to visit–
   i) a donee of a lasting power of attorney,
   ii) a deputy appointed by the court, or
   iii) the person granting the power of attorney or for whom the deputy is appointed ('P'),
   and to make a report to the Public Guardian on such matters as he may direct,
(e) receiving security which the court requires a person to give for the discharge of his functions,
(f) receiving reports from donees of lasting powers of attorney and deputies appointed by the court,
(g) reporting to the court on such matters relating to proceedings under this Act as the court requires,
(h) dealing with representations (including complaints) about the way in which a donee of a lasting power of attorney or a deputy appointed by the court is exercising his powers,

1 Office of the Public Guardian Annual Report and Accounts 2015 to 2016.

(i) publishing, in any manner the Public Guardian thinks appropriate, any information he thinks appropriate about the discharge of his functions.

Register of lasting powers of attorney and deputies

20.5 The MCA 2005 updated the law with regard to the provisions that can be made by an individual to appoint a decision maker (attorney) to make certain decisions on their behalf should they lose the capacity in the future.[2]

20.6 Prior to 1 October 2007 an enduring power of attorney (EPA) allowed a donor (the person who wishes to make arrangements for someone else to look after their finances if they are unable to do so in future) to appoint an attorney (or attorneys) to deal with their finances both immediately after the signing of the document and in the future, should the donor lose their capacity. The scope of an EPA was limited to financial affairs. To be valid, the EPA must be in the prescribed format and have been signed by all parties on or before 30 September 2007.

20.7 An EPA does not need to be registered to be used, although the attorneys named in the document are under a duty to register the document with the OPG when they believe that the donor has lost, or is losing their capacity.[3]

20.8 Properly created EPAs are still valid, although the authors are aware of considerable anecdotal evidence that banks and other financial institutions refuse to acknowledge these documents unless they are now registered.

20.9 From 1 October 2007 the MCA 2005 replaced EPAs with lasting powers of attorney (LPAs), of which there are two varieties:

- property and affairs – which covers the donor's financial matters; and
- health and welfare – which allows a donor to nominate attorney(s) to take decisions about their future medical treatment, care and other related matters if they lost the capacity to do so themselves.

20.10 A property and affairs LPA is similar in function to the old EPA but crucially it cannot be used until it has been registered with the OPG. The special feature enjoyed by both EPA and LPA is that the

---

2 See also chapter 7.
3 Enduring Powers of Attorney Act 1985 s4(2).

authority conferred by them continues after the donor has lost their capacity. All other types of power of attorney will be automatically revoked by the donor's incapacity.

20.11 The process for validly entering into an LPA lies outside the scope of this work, but is the subject of detailed guidance and commentary[4] (see also chapter 7). The OPG has a range of documents available to download that take the prospective donor through the process of making an LPA, registering it and acting as an attorney.[5]

20.12 The range of options for entering into an LPA now includes an online tool[6] for generating a document to be printed, signed and submitted for registration. It is hoped that innovations like this will help donors to ensure that the document they create is valid and complete and thereby reduce the number of applications for registration that are returned by the OPG each year for the rectification of minor errors or omissions.

20.13 LPAs are more detailed than the EPAs they replaced, and allow more scope for a donor to give specific advice to their chosen attorneys about how they want decisions made on their behalf. It is possible to place restrictions on the powers of the attorneys both in relation to finance and welfare and the donor may set out guidance for her attorneys to follow when discharging their duties. The nature of this guidance will depend upon the wishes and circumstances of the donor, but may include religious or ethical considerations, or stipulations as to specific decisions that attorneys may not take without further authority of the court (for example, to sell a property or valuable artefact). There are also specific requirements to be follow if a donor of an LPA wishes to grant the power to their attorneys to refuse life-sustaining treatment. Those who are advising a donor entering into an LPA should ensure that they make the donor aware of these options and requirements.

20.14 Advisers to both donors entering into LPAs and attorneys acting under an LPA should ensure that their clients are aware of the limits to the scope of their powers under LPAs. In the authors' experience the extent of an attorney's authority is frequently misunderstood. There would seem to be common misunderstandings and assumptions in relation to powers to gift and invest money, as well as their options when deciding on care arrangements under a health and

---

4 See in particular Denzil Lush, *Cretney & Lush on Lasting and Enduring Powers of Attorney*, 7th edn, Jordans, 2013.
5 See: www.gov.uk/government/publications/make-a-lasting-power-of-attorney.
6 See www.lastingpowerofattorney.service.gov.uk.

welfare LPA. Ensuring that all parties have clarity at the time that arrangements are made will help to avoid problems, including possibly interventions by the court, in future. Details about the court's powers in relation to EPAs and LPAs can be found in chapter 7 (it should be noted that the OPG has the power to – and regularly does – apply to the Court of Protection to sever ineffective provisions in LPAs under provisions of MCA 2005 Sch 2 para 11[7]).

20.15 It is also worth noting that the OPG only maintains a register of instruments for England and Wales. Arrangements for decision-making for those who lack capacity will vary significantly in jurisdictions outside England and Wales (including Northern Ireland and Scotland). See further chapter 26.

Searching the registers

20.16 Anyone may apply to search the registers of EPAs, LPAs and deputyships maintained by the OPG.[8] A standard 'first-tier' search is made by completing an OPG100 form[9] and sending it to the OPG. There is no charge for making an application.

20.17 Although more recent statistics are not available, there were 8,778 first-tier searches made between May 2012 and April 2013.[10]

20.18 Information that may be revealed by this search includes:

- the allocated case number;
- known other names of the donor/person the order is about;
- date of birth of the donor/person the order is about;
- name(s) of any deputy/deputies;
- name(s) of any attorney(s);
- whether the LPA, EPA or deputyship order relates to 'property and affairs' or 'personal welfare';
- the date the LPA, EPA or deputyship order was made;

---

7 For examples of orders made in this regard, see: www.justice.gov.uk/protecting-the-vulnerable/mental-capacity-act/orders-made-by-the-court-of-protection/lasting-powers-of-attorney.
8 Under the Lasting Powers of Attorney, Enduring Powers of Attorney and Public Guardian Regulations 2007 SI No 1253 reg 31. See also the *Office of the Public Guardian Registers guidance*, LPA 109, available at: https://www.gov.uk/government/publications/search-public-guardian-registers.
9 Available at the website in the footnote above.
10 *Enabling digital by default – impact assessment*, available at: https://consult.justice.gov.uk/digital-communications/opg-enabling-digital-default/supporting_documents/iaopgdigitaldefault.pdf.

- the date the LPA, EPA or deputyship order was registered;
- the date the LPA or EPA was revoked (if applicable);
- the date the deputyship order expires (if applicable);
- the date the deputyship order was cancelled (if applicable);
- name(s) of any replacement deputy/deputies/attorney(s);
- whether any replacement deputy/deputies/attorney(s) are active;
- whether the deputies/attorneys are appointed jointly;
- whether deputies/attorneys are appointed jointly and severally; and
- whether there are conditions or restrictions on the LPA, EPA or deputyship order (but not details about the conditions or restrictions).

20.19 Information will only be provided if there is an exact match between the details provided on the application form and those held on the registers. If there is a close but not exact match the OPG may contact the applicant for more information.

20.20 A first-tier search will not reveal any details about EPAs/LPAs that have not yet been registered, or any applications for the appointment of a deputy that are pending with the court. It also does not include details of any other types of order made by the court, for example those authorising a statutory will. If this information is sought, then an application must be made to the court and the usual rules of disclosure under the COPR will apply (for more on disclosure, see chapter 12).

20.21 Additional information about the donor/P may be sought by requesting a 'second-tier' search.[11] This is done by making an application in writing to the OPG setting out the name of the donor/P, the applicant's relationship to them, why the applicant needs the information requested and why the applicant has been unable to obtain it by any other route. The OPG considers such applications on their merit and any information provided is at the discretion of the OPG, if he considers that there is 'good reason' to provide the information.[12]

20.22 As part of an ongoing government-wide project to improve transparency and access to information, the OPG has proposed digital

---

11 Under Lasting Powers of Attorney, Enduring Powers of Attorney and Public Guardian Regulations reg 32.
12 Lasting Powers of Attorney, Enduring Powers of Attorney and Public Guardian Regulations reg 32(2).

searches for tier-one requests,[13] although progress has been slower than had been anticipated.

Supervision

20.23   When a new deputyship order is made, the court will notify the OPG so that they can begin to supervise the new deputy to ensure that he understands his duties and is acting correctly.

20.24   In 2015 the OPG overhauled the supervision regime. There had previously been four levels of supervision, each attracting a different annual fee, and a deputy could expect to move between these levels as experience, circumstances and asset levels altered over time.

20.25   There are now two levels of supervision:

1) General Supervision – this is allocated to all cases in their first year; and
2) Minimal supervision – deputies managing total assets of £19,000 or less on behalf of P will normally be moved down to this level after the first year of the deputyship.

20.26   The new supervision regime supports a more targeted approach to supervising deputies with specialised teams focussing on particular groups of deputies such as local authority deputies, lay deputies or professional deputies.

Annual reports

20.27   Deputies are required by the OPG to produce a report each year detailing how they have managed P's funds and with whom they have consulted with when making decisions.[14] These reports may be audited and the OPG may require that invoices, receipts or other evidence of expenditure is submitted.

20.28   From 1 March 2016 the report forms were amended to widen the scope of the report. In particular, the new reports ask for information about how recently P's capacity was assessed. Professional deputies should note that an estimate of future costs is also required. The OPG has recently issued guidance on professional costs, which is

---

13   See: https://www.gov.uk/government/consultations/transforming-the-services-of-the-office-of-the-public-guardian-enabling-digital-by-default.
14   MCA 2005 s19(9)(b).

mandatory reading for those acting in a professional capacity when completing the annual report.[15]

20.29 The annual reports are straightforward for most deputies, but lay deputies may wish to instruct an accountant or solicitor to prepare them if P's finances are more complicated. The costs of professional advice can be met from P's funds.

Court Visitors

20.30 One of the most important ways in which the OPG keeps in touch with deputies and provides ongoing supervision and support is through the network of Court of Protection Visitors.

20.31 The OPG maintains two panels of experts, or Visitors, on behalf of the Lord Chancellor. MCA 2005 s61 provides that:

61(1) A Court of Protection Visitor is a person who is appointed by the Lord Chancellor to–
(a) a panel of Special Visitors, or
(b) a panel of General Visitors.
(2) A person is not qualified to be a Special Visitor unless he–
(a) is a registered medical practitioner or appears to the Lord Chancellor to have other suitable qualifications or training, and
(b) appears to the Lord Chancellor to have special knowledge of and experience in cases of impairment of or disturbance in the functioning of the mind or brain.
(3) A General Visitor need not have a medical qualification.
(4) A Court of Protection Visitor–
(a) may be appointed for such term and subject to such conditions, and
(b) may be paid such remuneration and allowances,
as the Lord Chancellor may determine.

(5) For the purpose of carrying out his functions under this Act in relation to a person who lacks capacity ('P'), a Court of Protection Visitor may, at all reasonable times, examine and take copies of–
(a) any health record,
(b) any record of, or held by, a local authority and compiled in connection with a social services function, and

---

15 https://www.gov.uk/government/uploads/system/uploads/attachment_data/file/538901/19_07_16_Professional_deputy_costs__FINAL.pdf

(c) any record held by a person registered under Part 2 of the Care Standards Act 2000 so far as the record relates to P.
(6) A Court of Protection Visitor may also for that purpose interview P in private.

20.32 Generally a lay deputy can expect to have a visit from a General Visitor within the first 12 months of their appointment. This will usually take the format of a meeting with the deputy, and P, face-to-face to discuss how the deputy is managing in their role.

20.33 As well as routine visits as part of the ongoing supervision regime, the OPG can request a general visit for many reasons, for example:

- when a deputy is new to the role;
- to answer questions and make sure the deputy understands and can meet their responsibilities;
- if the OPG need reassurance that the deputy is acting in accordance with the terms of order and in P's best interests;
- for access to paperwork, for example bank statements, receipts etc; and
- when the OPG is carrying out an investigation.

20.34 The Visitor will contact the deputy in advance to arrange a suitable time for the meeting and to provide details of what information and paperwork they need access to.[16] They will usually wish to meet with the deputy and P separately; they may also wish to meet with third parties such as a care manger, social worker etc. Court Visitors carry identification and will show this when they visit.

20.35 After a visit, a report will be prepared for the OPG, making recommendations – for example, about issues that need to be monitored or the appropriate time before a follow-up visit needs to be scheduled.

20.36 Deputies may request a visit if they feel that the OPG can provide support with a particular issue.

20.37 The court has wide-ranging powers to call for reports.[17] Where a medical report is required, a Special Visitor can be commissioned to undertake this role. This can be useful, for example when P does not wish to co-operate with an assessment of capacity, or if there is a dispute as to P's capacity. See further for the role of Visitors in this regard paras 12.46 onwards.

---

16 Lasting Powers of Attorney, Enduring Powers of Attorney and Public Guardian Regulations 2007 reg 44.
17 MCA 2005 s49.

Investigations

20.38 The Public Guardian has the power to conduct investigations into the conduct of attorneys and deputies. The Court of Protection can order that a report be made to the Public Guardian by a deputy.[18]

20.39 Anyone who has concerns about the conduct of an attorney or deputy may raise these concerns with the OPG. Investigations will usually centre on the attorney or deputy's management of P's finances, and allegations of suspected financial abuse, but may encompass other aspects of the attorney or deputy's behaviour in relation to P.

20.40 Following an investigation, the OPG will produce a report which will make recommendations. In the event that the OPG concludes that it is in P's best interests to do so an application can be made to the Court of Protection. The OPG does not require permission to make such an application.[19]

20.41 In the financial year 2015/16 the Public Guardian received a total of 2,681 safeguarding referrals. Of these, 876 were investigated with 151 resulting in an application to the Court of Protection.[20] It is the experience of the authors that the OPG has grown more robust in recent years and more willing to litigate when necessary.

20.42 The case of *The Public Guardian v JM*[21] looked at the interface between a police investigation into the conduct of an attorney and an investigation by the OPG. In his judgment, Senior Judge Lush noted that:

> 44. There are significant differences between a police investigation and an investigation conducted by the OPG. When the police investigate an alleged crime, they need to consider whether there is sufficient evidence to present to the Crown Prosecution Service ('CPS') to guarantee a realistic prospect of conviction . . .
>
> 45. By contrast, an investigation by the OPG is concerned primarily with establishing whether an attorney or deputy has contravened his authority under the Mental Capacity Act 2005, or has acted in breach of his fiduciary duties under the common law of agency, or has behaved in a way that is not in the best interests of the person who lacks capacity. The standard of proof, 'on the balance of probabilities', is lower than the criminal standard.

---

18 MCA 2005 s19(9)(b).
19 COPR r51(1)(b).
20 *Office of the Public Guardian Annual Report and Accounts 2015–2016*, available at: https://www.gov.uk/government/uploads/system/uploads/attachment_data/file/535456/OPG_Annual_Report_-_2015-16__web_.pdf
21 [2014] EWCOP B4.

20.43 This case is a reminder to attorneys, as well as deputies, and their advisers that the Court of Protection will still act to remove an individual who it believes has not acted in P's best interests, despite that individual not facing prosecution for their actions.

Panel deputies

20.44 The OPG maintains a panel of professional deputies who can be appointed as property and affairs deputy for P where there is no other suitable person to take on the role. Panel deputies are 'deputies of last resort' as in most cases the deputy will be a member of P's family or a legal professional who is already familiar with P.

20.45 The court will often order the appointment of a panel deputy in cases where there has been a dispute within the family as to who should be a property and affairs deputy or where there has been abuse. For further details about disputed applications for the appointment of a property and affairs deputy; the revocation of EPAs, LPAs and deputyships; and the choice of deputy see chapter 7 above.

CHAPTER 21

Deprivation of Liberty applications in the Court of Protection

21.1	Introduction
21.9	**Challenging deprivations of liberty in care homes and hospitals**
21.9	Where no authorisation has been granted
21.13	Where an authorisation has been granted
	Reviews • Application or review?
21.19	**Applications under MCA 2005 s21A**
21.22	Who should make an application?
21.25	What if the RPR does not bring the challenge?
21.30	Making the application
21.33	Preparing the application
21.40	After the application is received
21.44	Preparing for the first hearing
21.51	The approach of the court to section 21A applications
21.56	**'*Re X*' applications**
21.63	Making an application
	The order
	Evidence required
	That the court can in principle make an order • Why the court can consent to the arrangements on P's behalf as being in P's best interests • Ancillary matters about the arrangements • Procedural matters relating to the application

Introduction

21.1 This chapter considers applications to the Court of Protection which concern deprivation of P's liberty, and therefore engage P's rights under Article 5 of the European Convention on Human Rights (ECHR).[1] In very brief terms, Article 5 will be engaged where three elements are present:[2]

- The 'objective element': confinement in a particular restricted space for a not negligible length of time; and
- The 'subjective element': there is no valid consent. Lack of objections from a patient without capacity is not consent; and
- The deprivation must be imputable to the state.

21.2 The chapter falls into two parts. Each part deals with a specific area of the court's jurisdiction: applications under MCA 2005 s21A and 'Re X' applications under MCA 2005 s16. Both types of application fall outside the scope of the pathways set down under the Case Management Pilot[3] and have their own procedures, set out in Practice Direction 10AA. They do not fall outside the Transparency Pilot (discussed in chapter 13), and, as discussed in para 4.101, they may not fall outside the scope of the Case Management Pilot altogether.

21.3 The volume of both types of application has expanded dramatically since the publication of the first edition of this work, in particular following the judgment of the Supreme Court in *P v Cheshire West and Chester Council*[4] ('*Cheshire West*'). The Supreme Court formulated what has become known as the 'acid test' for the objective element of deprivation of liberty – that P is not free to leave and is subject to continuous supervision and control. The concept of deprivation of liberty generally is discussed at paras 3.166 onwards; for more detail as to the decision of the Supreme Court and its implications for different settings, reference should be made to the guidance commissioned by the Department of Health and prepared by the Law Society,[5] but caution is required because the case-law in this area is fast-moving. See appendix G for useful and free resources.

---

1 See Human Rights Act 1998 Sch 1 in appendix A.
2 *Storck v Germany* (App No 61603/00), (2006) 43 EHRR 6.
3 PD Case Management Pilot para 3.1.
4 *P (by his litigation friend the Official Solicitor) v Cheshire West and Chester Council* [2014] UKSC 19, [2014] AC 896.
5 Law Society, *Deprivation of liberty: a practical guide* (April 2015); at www.lawsociety. org.uk/support-services/advice/articles/deprivation-of-liberty/.

21.4 The first part of the chapter considers challenges to standard and urgent applications granted under the so-called Deprivation of Liberty Safeguards (DOLS), where P is detained in a hospital or care home. This important function of the Court of Protection was given to it after the Mental Capacity Act (MCA) 2005 came into force. By amendments to the MCA 2005 made by the Mental Health Act (MHA) 2007, the Court of Protection was given the task of considering applications under MCA 2005 s21A in respect of authorisations granted under the deprivation of liberty safeguards regime introduced by the MHA 2007 in the form of Schedule A1 to the MCA 2005. These safeguards were introduced to seek to fill the legislative lacuna (known as the 'Bournewood gap') which was exposed in the important case of *HL v UK*.[6] The jurisdiction of the Court of Protection under MCA 2005 s21A overlaps with its jurisdiction to make declarations and decisions regarding P's health and welfare under MCA 2005 ss15–16, but it is essentially a standalone jurisdiction. It can only be understood by reference to the – complex – provisions of Schedule A1. These are explained in detail in paras 3.166–3.231.

21.5 An important judgment by Baker J in 2015 (*AJ (by her litigation friend the Official Solicitor) v A Local Authority*[7], discussed in para 21.22 below) raised awareness of the importance of bringing cases before the Court where P wishes to challenge a DOLS authorisation. As a result of both this judgment as well as *Cheshire West*, practitioners will have seen an increase in such challenges.

21.6 The second part of the chapter examines applications made under MCA 2005 s16, on form COPDOL10. This process is for non-contentious applications to deprive P of his or her liberty in settings other than care homes or hospitals. Such applications are often referred to as *Re X* applications, after the series of *Re X* cases.[8] The process of establishing the safeguards to which P is entitled has been a controversial one. For now, the process is as laid down in two judgments of Charles J, *Re NRA*,[9] and *Re JM*.[10] These cases will usually be dealt with on the papers, with P not joined as a party but supported by a

6 *HL v UK* (App No 45508/99), [2004] ECHR 471, (2004) 7 CCLR 498.
7 *AJ (by her litigation friend the Official Solicitor) v A Local Authority* [2015] EWCOP 5, (2015) 18 CCLR 158.
8 *Re X* [2014] EWCOP 25, [2015] 1 WLR 2454; *Re X* [2014] EWCOP 37, [2015] 1 WLR 2454 and *Re X (Court of Protection Practice)* [2015] EWCA Civ 599, [2016] 1 WLR 227.
9 *Re NRA and others* [2015] EWCOP 59, [2015] COPLR 690, (2015) 18 CCLR 392.
10 *Re JM and others* [2016] EWCOP 15, [2016] 4 WLR 64.

representative appointed under COPR Pr1.2(c)/ COPR r3A(2)(c).[11] This section will summarise the procedural requirements for such applications and draw together guidance for those involved.

21.7 With the increase in both types of applications the challenges for all involved is to ensure that the Article 5 safeguards are practical and effective and add value for P in a climate of financial austerity.

21.8 Readers will be aware that the Law Commission has recommended legislative change which would replace both the DOLS and the *Re X* regime. A draft Bill will be published in March 2017, but at the time of writing the precise nature and extent both of the draft Bill and the likely timescale for the implementation of the recommendations are unclear.[12] This chapter is therefore limited to describing the current regime.

Challenging deprivations of liberty in care homes and hospitals

Where no authorisation has been granted

21.9 Schedule A1 provides a useful mechanism which allows a third party who is an 'eligible person' to require that the supervisory body decides whether there is an unauthorised deprivation of liberty.[13] An eligible person is defined as 'any person other than the managing authority of the relevant hospital or care home'.[14] An eligible person could therefore include:

- the individual who is being detained;
- a member of that individual's family;
- a professional working with the individual.

21.10 An unauthorised deprivation of liberty arises where a person is a 'detained resident' in a hospital or care home, and where this has not been authorised under MCA 2005 s4A.[15] A 'detained resident' is defined at MCA 2005 Sch A1 para 6 as:

> ... a person detained in a hospital or care home – for the purpose of being given care or treatment- in circumstances which amount to deprivation of the person's liberty.

---

11 See chapter 11 for a discussion of this role.
12 www.lawcom.gov.uk/project/mental-capacity-and-deprivation-of-liberty/.
13 MCA 2005 Sch A1 paras 67–73.
14 MCA 2005 Sch A1 para 68(5).
15 MCA 2005 Sch A1 para 67.

21.11 This will require consideration of whether the person satisfies the 'acid test' in *Cheshire West*, as a part of deciding whether or not they are deprived of their liberty At this stage, however, no consideration is required as to whether the person fulfils any of the other qualifying requirements for an authorisation.[16]

21.12 To exercise the right to involve the supervisory body, the eligible person must first notify the managing authority that it appears to them that there is an unauthorised deprivation of liberty,[17] and must ask the managing authority to request a standard authorisation in relation to the detention. If the managing authority does not request the authorisation within a 'reasonable period'[18] then the eligible person may request that the supervisory body decides whether or not there is an unauthorised deprivation of liberty. Unless the supervisory body considers the request to be frivolous or vexatious, or unless the question has already been decided and there has been no change in circumstances,[19] then the supervisory body must select and appoint a person to assess whether the relevant person is, in fact, detained.[20] If that assessment concludes that the relevant person is detained, this triggers an obligation for the supervisory body to assess the qualifying requirements for an authorisation, as if the supervisory body had requested it in the usual way.[21]

Where an authorisation has been granted

Reviews

21.13 The supervisory body may carry out a review of a standard authorisation at any time. The supervisory body must carry out a review of a standard authorisation if requested by an eligible person.[22] For the purpose of reviews, an 'eligible person' means P, the RPR or the managing authority.[23] There is no equivalent procedure for urgent authorisations. The process is set out in detail in MCA 2005 Part 8, Sch A1.

---

16 Described at paras 3.176–3.188.
17 MCA 2005 Sch A1 para 68(2).
18 MCA 2005 Sch A1 para 68(4).
19 MCA 2005 Sch A1 para 69 (4)–(5).
20 MCA 2005 Sch A1 para 69(2).
21 MCA 2005 Sch A1 para 71(2).
22 MCA 2005 Sch A1 para 102.
23 MCA 2005 Sch A1 para 102.

21.14 If, following the review process, the supervisory body concludes that one of the qualifying requirements is not met, it should terminate the authorisation with immediate effect.[24]

Application or review?

21.15 There is no requirement to request a review before making an application to the court under MCA 2005 s21A. The Part 8 review process is internal and does not provide P with independent scrutiny of whether the criteria for the authorisation are met. Nor does the review process include the considerations of liability available under MCA 2005 s21A(6) and (7). The review process does not and is not intended to meet the requirements of ECHR Article 5(4), namely the entitlement of a detained person 'to take proceedings by which the lawfulness of his detention shall be decided speedily by a court and his release ordered if the detention is not lawful'.

21.16 Practitioners should seek to resolve issues without litigation if at all possible. This stems from the overriding objective and the parties' duty to assist the court in furthering the overriding objective.[25] It may be appropriate to advise the supervisory body of the issues taken with the authorisation before making an application under section 21A. However, as set out in paragraph 21.2 above, section 21A applications are not on the personal welfare pathway for the purposes of the Case Management Pilot and the obligations in the 'pre-issue' stage do not apply. Equally, applicants are not required to seek a review before commencing proceedings under section 21A and in our view a decision to proceed directly to an application under section 21A, without requesting a review first, should not attract criticism.

21.17 In particular in *any* case where P is known to be objecting to all or part of his or her care and treatment, or to residence in the relevant hospital or care home, one of the lessons of *AJ* is that practitioners should be proactive in bringing applications to the court. This advice applies to those advising P, P's RPR, members of P's family, as well as those advising the supervisory body.

21.18 There may, however, be some cases where practitioners may wish to advise requesting a review before proceeding to court. In the authors' view, the factors below may point to the use of the review process first:

---

24 MCA 2005 Sch A1 para 117.
25 COPR rr3 and 4/COPR Prr1.3 and 1.4.

- There is reason to believe, from correspondence or initial discussion with the supervisory body or their advisers, that there is a realistic possibility that agreement to terminate or vary the authorisation will be reached.
- The practitioner is advising a third party who is not P's RPR and is unlikely to be appointed as P's litigation friend, and that third party is not financially eligible for legal aid.
- In both cases, there is no risk that P will suffer distress and/or harm if the status quo continues pending the review.

Applications under MCA 2005 s21A

21.19 Unlike patients detained under the Mental Health Act 1983 (MHA 1983), those detained under DOLS do not have their case referred automatically to the court. Instead an application under section 21A must be made and MCA 2005 s21A gives the court powers to terminate or vary an authorisation if an application is made. It is important to be aware of the extent of the jurisdiction of s21A. The section is set out in full below and a flow chart setting out the process for applications under section 21A is set out overleaf.

21A(1) This section applies if either of the following has been given under Schedule A1–
  (a) a standard authorisation;
  (b) an urgent authorisation.
(2) Where a standard authorisation has been given, the court may determine any question relating to any of the following matters–
  (a) whether the relevant person meets one or more of the qualifying requirements;
  (b) the period during which the standard authorisation is to be in force;
  (c) the purpose for which the standard authorisation is given;
  (d) the conditions subject to which the standard authorisation is given.
(3) If the court determines any question under subsection (2), the court may make an order–
  (a) varying or terminating the standard authorisation, or
  (b) directing the supervisory body to vary or terminate the standard authorisation.
(4) Where an urgent authorisation has been given, the court may determine any question relating to any of the following matters–
  (a) whether the urgent authorisation should have been given;

Process for applications under section 21A

Decision to issue application. Consider whether any steps in case management Pilot (pre-issue) should be taken.

↓

Application papers: DLA; DLB if urgent Draft order and supporting Evidence; Fee

↓

Judicial directions (usually within 24 hours: may include
- Transfer to regional court
- Service and parties
- Participation of P
- Disclosure
- Attended hearing

↓

Applicant complies with directions Papers served with form DLE; Applicant files form DLD at court

↓

Preparation for first hearing:
- All parties identified?
- Directions needed?
- Section 49 report needed? If so, comply with S49 Pilot;
- Expert needed? If so consider new Part 15 COPRs
- Litigation friend identified?

↓

Communication between parties

↓

Directions agreed?

- **Yes** → Consent order lodged → Court makes agreed order → Parties follow directions
- **No** → Directions hearing: Court makes directions and sets timetable → Parties follow directions

↓

Evidence filed

↓

Preparation for final hearing

↓

Final hearing Court hears evidence and submissions

↓

Parties consider positions in light of evidence

→ RTM or ADR;

Agreement reached
- **Yes** → Consent order filed at court
- **No** → Court makes final order; costs dealt with.

(b) the period during which the urgent authorisation is to be in force;
(c) the purpose for which the urgent authorisation is given.
(5) Where the court determines any question under subsection (4), the court may make an order–
(a) varying or terminating the urgent authorisation, or
(b) directing the managing authority of the relevant hospital or care home to vary or terminate the urgent authorisation.
(6) Where the court makes an order under subsection (3) or (5), the court may make an order about a person's liability for any act done in connection with the standard or urgent authorisation before its variation or termination.
(7) An order under subsection (6) may, in particular, exclude a person from liability.

21.20 From this it will be seen that section 21A fulfils the role required by Article 5(4) ECHR in providing review of the lawfulness of P's detention by a court. As such, the court is able to bring an authorisation to an end.[26] However, it goes further by allowing the court to:

- vary an urgent or standard authorisation or direct that such authorisations are varied;
- direct that the relevant authority terminate a standard or urgent authorisation;[27]
- make an order about a person's liability 'for any act done in connection with the standard or urgent authorisation' which can include excluding a person from liability.[28] This power only arises when the court either varies, or terminates an authorisation, or directs that it is varied or terminated.[29]

21.21 In an application under MCA 2005 s21A, the court's powers are not limited to the matters set out in section 21A, as Baker J made clear in *KK v CC and STCC*:[30]

When a standard authorisation has been made by a supervisory body, s21A(2) empowers the Court of Protection to determine any questions relating to, inter alia, whether P meets one or more of the qualifying requirements. In particular, once the court determines the question, it may make an order varying or terminating the standard authorisation: s21A(3)(a). But once an application is made to the Court under s21A, the Court's powers are not confined simply to

26 MCA 2005 s21A(3)(a), (5)(a) (standard and urgent authorisations respectively).
27 MCA 2005 s21A(3)(b), (5)(b) (standard and urgent authorisations respectively).
28 MCA 2005 ss21A (6), (7).
29 MCA 2005 s21A(6).
30 [2012] EWHC 2136 (COP).

determining that question. Once its jurisdiction is invoked, the court has a discretionary power under s15 to make declarations as to (a) whether a person has or lacks capacity to make a decision specified in the declaration; (b) whether a person has or lacks capacity to make decisions on such matters as are described in the declaration; and (c) the lawfulness or otherwise of any act done, or yet to be done, in relation to that person. Where P lacks capacity, the court has wide powers under s16 to make decisions on P's behalf in relation to matters concerning his personal welfare or property or affairs.

Who should make an application?

21.22 In consequence of the rule changes introduced in July 2015, there is no permission filter in relation to section 21A applications.[31] As has always been the case, P has a right to apply to the court under section 21A in his or her own right, irrespective of whether the RPR supports P's application. Following the strong guidance in *AJ v A Local Authority*,[32] in which Baker J held that the 'fundamental principle' was that 'there is an obligation on the State to ensure that a person deprived of liberty is not only entitled but enabled to have the lawfulness of his detention reviewed speedily by a court',[33] it is clear that RPRs should not allow their views about the merits of an application to hold them back either from making the application themselves or supporting P in doing so. *AJ* spelt out clearly the responsibility on RPRs, and of independent mental capacity advocates (IMCAs) appointed under MCA 2005 s39D, as well as the responsibilities of local authorities to ensure that a person lacking capacity is able to challenge their deprivation of liberty if they wish to do so.

21.23 It should be noted that Charles J touched on this case in *Re NRA*[34] and observed (obiter) that an RPR is not obliged to test every case: instead, as he noted '[o]bjections expressed by P are a relevant but not a determinative factor for a RPR in deciding whether to issue such proceedings.' These remarks do not obviate the risk of a violation of P's rights under Article 5(4) if P objects to his or her placement, especially where the objection is strongly held and consistent, but he or she is not supported to bring the case to court. At the time of writing, a further judgment from Baker J is expected in which it is anticipated that he

---

31 COPR r51(c).
32 [2015] EWCOP 5, (2015) 18 CCLR 158.
33 Paragraph 36, citing the judgment of Peter Jackson J in Peter Jackson J in *Neary v LB of Hillingdon* [2011] EWHC 1377 (COP), [2011] 4 All ER 584.
34 *Re NRA* [2015] EWCOP 59, (2015) 18 CCLR 392, para 171

will give further guidance as to how to identify words or actions on P's part that can be characterised as an objection necessitating an application being brought so as to secure their rights under Article 5(4).

> AJ was 88 and lived in an annexe to the home of her niece and husband, Mr and Mrs C. AJ had vascular dementia and became more dependent on care from Mr and Mrs C who eventually felt unable to provide this. AJ was placed in a unit in X House ostensibly for a respite placement but 'with a view to... staying... on a permanent basis'. AJ was made the subject of an urgent and then a standard authorization under DOLS. Mr C was made RPR and Mr R was appointed as section 39D IMCA. All parties were aware that AJ was extremely unhappy at X House, but no application was made to the court until she had been there six months. The Official Solicitor was appointed as AJ's litigation friend and sought declarations that AJ's convention rights had been breached because the local authority should have ensured an authorisation or an order of the court was in place before she moved to X House; that Mr C should not have been RPR; that the local authority should have ensured the IMCA was able to exercise his responsibilities by acting as litigation friend under a section 21A application or the local authority should have issued proceedings itself.

21.24   Baker J found that AJ's rights under Article 5(4) had been violated. He summarised the wider lessons arising from the case:

133. First, I emphasise that the scheme of the DOLS is that, in the vast majority of cases, it should be possible to plan in advance so that a standard authorisation can be obtained before the deprivation of liberty begins. It is only in exceptional cases, where the need for the deprivation of liberty is so urgent that it is in the best interests of the person for it to begin while the application is being considered, that a standard authorisation need not be sought before the deprivation begins.

134. Secondly, professionals need to be on their guard to look out for cases where vulnerable people are admitted to residential care ostensibly for respite when the underlying plan is for a permanent placement without proper consideration as to their Article 5 rights.

135. Thirdly, a RPR should only be selected or confirmed by a BIA where he or she satisfies not only the criteria in regulation 3 of the Mental Capacity (Deprivation of Liberty: Appointment of Relevant Person's Representative) Regulations 2008 but also the requirements of paragraph 140 of Schedule A1 to the MCA 2005. This requires that

the BIA not only checks that the facts set out in regulation 3 are satisfied but also carries out an analysis and reaches a judgment as to whether the prospective representative would, if appointed, (a) maintain contact with the relevant person; (b) represent the relevant person in matters relating to or connected with the Schedule; and (c) support the relevant person in matters relating to or connected with the Schedule.

136. Fourthly, the local authority is under an obligation to satisfy itself that a person selected for appointment as RPR meets the criteria in regulation 3 and in paragraph 140 of Schedule A1. If the local authority concludes that the person selected for appointment does not meet the criteria, it should refer the matter back to the BIA.

137. Fifthly, it is likely to be difficult for a close relative or friend who believes that it is in P's best interests to move into residential care, and has been actively involved in arranging such a move, into a placement that involves a deprivation of liberty, to fulfil the functions of RPR, which involve making a challenge to any authorisation of that deprivation. BIAs and local authorities should therefore scrutinise very carefully the selection and appointment of RPRs in circumstances which are likely to give rise to this potential conflict of interest.

138. Sixthly, an IMCA appointed under section 39D must act with diligence and urgency to ensure that any challenge to an authorisation under schedule A1 is brought before the court expeditiously. Failure to do so will lead to the evaporation of P's Article 5 rights.

139. Seventhly, the appointment of a RPR and IMCA does not absolve the local authority from responsibility for ensuring that P's Article 5 rights are respected. The local authority must monitor whether the RPR is representing and supporting P in accordance with the duty under paragraph 140 and, if not, consider terminating his appointment on the grounds that he is no longer eligible. The local authority must make sufficient resources available to assist an IMCA and keep in touch with the IMCA to ensure that all reasonable steps are being taken to pursue P's Article 5 rights.

140. Finally, in circumstances where a RPR and an IMCA have failed to take sufficient steps to challenge the authorisation, the local authority should consider bringing the matter before the court itself. This is likely, however, to be a last resort since in most cases P's Article 5 rights should be protected by the combined efforts of a properly selected and appointed RPR and an IMCA carrying out their duties with appropriate expedition.

What if the RPR does not bring the challenge?

21.25 In cases where the RPR – for whatever reason – does not bring a challenge, there are a number of potential routes whereby an application under MCA 2005 s21A may be made. A member of P's family may make the application in their own right (subject to the permission of the court[35]); or as P's litigation friend. *Re UF*[36] concerned a woman who had been deprived of her liberty at a care home under a standard authorisation. UF's RPR supported the deprivation of liberty, as did all her family save AF, one of UF's daughters, who considered her mother to be very unhappy at the care home, to the point that AF felt her mother's life was endangered. Although AF could have made the application herself (which would (at the time) have required permission), Charles J noted there was 'force in seeing whether an application should be made by or on behalf of P'.[37] It was clear that the RPR was unlikely to agree to commence proceedings. The advice given to AF by her 'experienced solicitor' was for AF to apply under MCA 2005 s21A as UF's litigation friend. This was a pragmatic solution which ensured that the case was brought before the court, although Charles J ultimately concluded that AF's understandable emotional involvement in the case made it inappropriate for her to continue as litigation friend.

21.26 Practitioners advising family members or carers concerned about a standard authorisation should check that an RPR has been appointed (as this is sometimes overlooked) and whether the RPR is willing to challenge the authorisation. If they are not, but the family member or carer can provide evidence suggesting that P objects to their placement, then the best solution may be for the family member or carer to facilitate an application by acting as P's litigation friend. If this happens, the proposed litigation friend can apply for non-means tested legal aid on P's behalf. If this course of action is adopted, it must be borne in mind that the court may well consider at a later date that an alternative litigation friend should be appointed.

21.27 As emphasised at para 21.22 above, P has a right to make an application under MCA 2005 s21A in his or her own right. P may well have capacity to make the decision to challenge the deprivation of his or her liberty, even if he or she lacks capacity to conduct the proceedings once they are under way. By way of analogy, we note the decision in *London Borough of Hillingdon v WW (Special Educational Needs: Other)*[38] in which Upper Tribunal Judge Jacobs drew an important distinction between the decision to appeal against a Special Educational Needs Tribunal and the conduct of such an appeal:

---

35 MCA 2005 s50.
36 *Re UF* [2013] EWHC 4289 (COP), [2014] COPLR 93.
37 *Re UF* [2013] EWHC 4289 (COP), [2014] COPLR 93 para 13.
38 [2016] UKUT 253 (AAC).

...capacity depends on the matter in respect of which a decision has to be made: section 2(1). So a person may have capacity at one time but not at another, and may have capacity in respect of one matter but not another. The matter I am concerned with is the bringing of an appeal; that is what I mean when I refer to (lack of) capacity. The young person may have capacity in respect of that, but not in respect of other decisions that have to be made in the course of the proceedings. Equally, a person may lack capacity to bring an appeal, but have capacity to make other decisions in the course of the proceedings.

21.28 Applying the logic of this decision, it is suggested that it would be entirely possible that a person would have the capacity to bring an application under MCA 2005 s21A but not to have the capacity then to instruct his or her legal representatives in respect of all the decisions that may need to be brought during the course of that application. This is consistent with the reasoning of Charles J in *YA v Central and North West London NHS Trust and others*[39] in the context of mental health tribunals, where he drew a distinction between capacity to apply to the tribunal and capacity to appoint a representative for the tribunal:

> So to have capacity to appoint a representative a patient needs to have more than only an understanding that they can make an application to a mental health review tribunal or have someone else make it for them, and thus the limited capacity referred to in *R(H) v SSH* [2006] 1 AC 441.

21.29 Legal aid is available for section 21A cases, in some circumstances without reference to the means test. The provisions are discussed in chapter 6.

Making the application

21.30 The procedure for making an application is not complex. Guidance is provided in Practice Direction (PD) 10AA. It is essential for practitioners to be familiar with this practice direction and to follow the procedure it sets out to ensure that the application is treated with the appropriate urgency.

21.31 Practitioners will see from the practice direction that they are asked to contact the Deprivation of Liberty (DOL) Team as soon as they know that an application is likely to be issued.[40] It is important for practitioners to note that they can and should alert the DOL team

---

39 [2015] UKUT 37 (AAC), [2015] MHLR 144, para 7.
40 PD 10AA paras 2–3.

Deprivation of Liberty applications in the Court of Protection   515

in the event of other very urgent matters that are not applications under section 21A but which may relate to deprivation of liberty and require urgent attention.[41]

21.32   Whilst section 21A applications are not personal welfare cases for purposes of the Case Management Pilot, it is prudent to proceed on the basis that the court will seek, insofar as possible, to apply the same approach to case management.

Preparing the application

21.33   Applications made under section 21A should be made on the forms that have been specially designed for this purpose, and the benefit of these is that they are easily distinguished from other applications and can be dealt with by the right team urgently. If at all possible, it is very helpful to have electronic copies as part of a case management system allowing details to be inputted electronically.

21.34   Form DLA, the deprivation of liberty application form, contains 'prompts' to ensure all relevant issues are addressed:

- Section 2 allows information to be added about interested parties. This term is not used in the rules. Inclusion in this section does not result automatically in the person or body named as interested party being joined as a party, as they have not been named as a respondent. If served with the application, however, the proposed interested party will be bound by orders of the court as if they were a party.[42]
- Section 3 requires consideration of whether an interim application is being made and asks whether other applications are to be made.
- Section 4 asks for a detailed statement of grounds and in most cases it will be advisable to prepare this – or instruct counsel or a Higher Rights Advocate – as a separate document. This is an opportunity to address from the outset the issues that are likely to feature. For example, are there obvious defects in any of the assessments or the authorisation itself?
- It should be noted that that section 8 requires a statement of facts relied on. It is suggested that sections 8 and 5 could conveniently be combined in the same document.
- Section 5 asks the applicant to identify other 'issues that will arise for determination in respect of the relevant person' and any other

41   PD 10AA para 2.
42   COPR rr73(1), 74.

applications that have been made or that the applicant intends to make. These might include broader welfare questions such as an application for a declaration as to P's best interests in terms of residence or contact; or whether an HRA 1998 claim may be made.
- Section 6 seeks information about other pending applications, so that the court can consider whether these should be linked. In addition to outstanding welfare applications, practitioners should check whether they are aware of any outstanding property and affairs applications.
- Section 7 invites the applicant to identify any special assistance or facilities that will be needed to enable the applicant to attend court.
- Section 10 provides a helpful checklist.

21.35 Form DLB is a declaration of exceptional urgency to be used to explain if it is necessary for the court's usual timetable to be abridged.

21.36 Form DLC is no longer required, as there is now no permission filter for section 21A applications.

21.37 It should be noted that the practice direction anticipates that the above forms will be served at the same time that they are lodged with the court.[43] In addition to the forms a fee of £410 is payable (see appendix F below). This can be claimed as a disbursement on the applicant's legal aid certificate, whether the applicant is P or the RPR.

21.38 In addition to the forms, which must be completed, form DLA lists a number of supporting documents which might be filed at court with the forms. These include copies of the authorisation and assessments, a witness statement on form COP24, a copy of the legal aid certificate if any, copies of relevant statutory material, and a draft order which if possible should also be provided electronically on disk.[44] It is our advice to provide as much information as possible, given that the first order will be made on the basis of the information in the papers alone.[45]

21.39 In particular, and where time allows, any witness statements should be carefully prepared. Although significant information can be provided by means of the statement of facts and grounds, this is no substitute for witness evidence in which the applicant is able to set out in full their perspective as well as state the relevant facts. Considerable time will be saved if the documents are paginated and

43 PD 10AA para 10.
44 PD 10AA para 15.
45 PD 10AA para 20.

Deprivation of Liberty applications in the Court of Protection

indexed. A paginated indexed bundle is required for the first hearing in any event.[46]

After the application is received

21.40 Once the documents are received by the court, the practice direction provides that steps will immediately be taken to ensure the papers are considered by a judge who will make a first order. This is likely to deal with the following matters:

- Identifying a litigation friend, if possible; if not this will usually be deferred to the first attended hearing. This may include an invitation to the Official Solicitor to act, if there is no other litigation friend.
- Identifying the parties, or those who may wish to join as parties,
- Initial disclosure from the supervisory body
- A timetable leading up to the first hearing for filing and serving evidence; preparation of the bundle and position statements.
- The order will usually encourage the parties to communicate and narrow the issues before the hearing takes place.

21.41 For a discussion on litigation friends and accredited legal representatives in section 21A cases, see chapter 11.

21.42 The applicant is responsible for following up any directions made and is also responsible for service of the order and any other relevant papers that have not already been served, together with form DLE (acknowledgement of service). The applicant must file form DLD (certificate of service).

21.43 The first attended hearing should be listed within five working days of the judge's first order (ie the date of issue of the application).[47] If the applicant considers this will be too late, this should be made clear on form DLB (see para 21.35 above). The first hearing is likely to take place at the closest regional court to P. It will usually be fixed without reference to the parties' availability.

Preparing for the first hearing

21.44 If the Official Solicitor is invited to act when initial directions are made then any solicitors instructed by him are likely to have very limited time to prepare for the first hearing. The same is likely to be

---

46 PD 10AA para 26.
47 PD 10AA para 24.

true for an ALR in the event that one is appointed by the court. In chapter 11 we propose at paras 11.108ff some practical steps when planning to visit P for the first time. A solicitor instructed by an RPR (whether in their own right or as litigation friend to P) will have the advantage of the background knowledge of the RPR and may well have met with P before making the application.

21.45 Consideration should be given to the directions which will be sought at that hearing. For example, are there any outstanding issues about the appointment of a litigation friend?[48] Is expert evidence required? Given the pressure of time in section 21A appeals, an application for permission to instruct an expert is more likely to be granted if an expert has already been identified and his or her timetable ascertained in advance of the hearing.

21.46 If it has not yet been possible to identify all those parties who should be joined to the application then this should be put in hand now. In particular it is important to ascertain the role which relevant statutory bodies should play in the application. This is important to enable the court to identify what alternatives to P's current placement may be available. The supervisory body will be a respondent; however if P is detained in a hospital consideration should be given to joining the Trust providing care to P. If P is in receipt of NHS continuing healthcare, then the CCG commissioning P's care may have to be joined. There may be family members who should be given an opportunity to join as parties. If at all possible contact should be made with potential respondents before the hearing.

21.47 Practitioners will wish to decide now whether to instruct counsel for the directions hearing or whether to undertake the advocacy themselves. Solicitors are entitled to appear in the Court of Protection (see chapter 6) and directions hearings may be relatively informal. Whether instructing counsel or appearing himself or herself, the ALR should attend court personally as should, ideally, the solicitor instructed by the litigation friend.

21.48 The court will usually require a position statement and a draft order to be submitted by each party. There are precedent orders on the Court of Protection Handbook website.[49] Position statements for the first directions hearing need not be long, especially if relatively detailed grounds have been prepared. The aim should be to:

- either provide a summary of the background to the judge or signpost him or her to such a summary (for example in the grounds);

---

48 See chapter 11.
49 https://courtofprotectionhandbook.com/precedents/.

- explain what steps have been taken so far;
- provide an account of P's wishes if possible;
- identify the issues in the application; and
- explain the orders that will be sought and why. If expert evidence is sought, then it is prudent to proceed on the basis that the more stringent test applicable under the Case Management Pilot will be applied. This is considered further at para 12.69.

21.49 There will be some – relatively rare – cases where it is possible to determine the challenge to the authorisation at the first hearing. However, in the majority of cases further evidence will be needed and therefore the court will consider how to regulate the intervening period, if P is to continue to be deprived of their liberty while the case continues. Paragraph 6.62 provides details as to how this can best be achieved without compromising non-means testing legal aid for P or the RPR.

21.50 If the directions are not contentious it may be possible to vacate the hearing by consent.

The approach of the court to section 21A applications

21.51 The range of issues which can arise in section 21A applications is huge. While some section 21A cases may focus on the level of restrictions to which P is subject,[50] many involve a dispute about P's best interests as regards residence or care. In *Re HA*[51] Charles J provided guidance as to how the key issue of contested residence which underpinned the section 21A appeal he was hearing should be resolved speedily. He considered that the key to this was an investigation of the 'pragmatically available options' which would be achieved in that case through the local authority identifying the potential alternatives (for example, maintaining the status quo, a move to another provider or a home placement) and informing the court and parties how these could be provided and funded. This is consistent with the subsequent decision of the Court of Appeal in *Re MN*.[52]

---

50 Including, for example, the use of covert medication- see *AG (by her litigation friend the Official Solicitor) v BMBC and SNH* [2016] EWCOP 37.
51 [2012] EWHC 1068 (COP), [2012] COPLR 534.
52 *Re MN* [2015] EWCA Civ 411, [2016] Fam 87. This decision is under appeal to the Supreme Court at the time of writing, with a hearing listed for December 2016.

21.52　　North Yorkshire County Council v MAG, GC and ACCG[53] concerned applications under MCA 2005 s16, rather that MCA 2005 s21A. It provides, however, an example of the application of the principles in *Re MN* to cases concerning deprivation of liberty. At first instance District Judge Glentworth refused to endorse a care plan for MAG who lived in a ground floor flat and received one to one support at home, and two to one support in the community. MAG's accommodation was unsuitable – he could not stand independently or use his wheelchair indoors as there was not enough room. It was generally accepted that it would be in MAG's best interests to move to a less restrictive property but no such property was available and the judge was asked – following *MN* – to approve the deprivation of MAG's liberty on the basis of his current care plan. In her decision the judge stated that she accepted the Official Solicitor's argument that the inability of the Court to compel a public authority to agree to a care plan does not apply when the issue is the right to liberty under Article 5.

21.53　　The appeal of the local authority and the CCG was upheld by Cobb J in *North Yorkshire County Council (1) A CCG (2) v MAG (by his litigation friend the Official Solicitor.*[54] Cobb J accepted that *if* MAG's living conditions in fact violated Article 5, the Court would have to refuse to authorise it. However for MAG's conditions to comply with Article 5, he held that they had only to be 'appropriate', not the most appropriate; a 'high threshold' would need to be crossed and conditions would need to be 'seriously inappropriate' to establish a violation. Indeed, 'deprivation of liberty of a person who lacks capacity in his own home, under a care plan delivered by qualified care providers, is most unlikely to breach his Article 5 rights'.[55] Cobb J further held that the judge had exceeded the powers of the court by taking a decision on behalf of MAG that he could not take for himself; that she had made factual findings which were unfair; and exerted impermissible pressure on the local authority.

21.54　　This does not however mean that the need for what the President described in *Re MN* as 'rigorous probing, searching questions and persuasion' is obviated if at the early stages of an application a statutory body indicates an unwillingness to fund a particular option. It will almost always be appropriate to ask for a direction that the relevant body files a statement setting out the available alternatives;

53　[2015] EWCOP 64.
54　[2016] EWCOP 5, [2016] COPLR 346.
55　At para 26.

explaining what they are willing to fund and expressing a view as to P's best interests. In the authors' experience this process can often generate new ideas and options which had not been obvious at the start of the case.

21.55 Some first instance judgments in section 21A applications demonstrate a willingness by the court to accede to strongly held wishes by P to live at home, even where the available care package was not optimal and involved some risk to P. *Re M (Best Interests: Deprivation of Liberty)*[56] concerned a woman with unstable diabetes who was deeply unhappy in a care home, to the extent the placement there was considered to be unstable. The choice was between 24-hour care in the placement and a return home with a 'standard care package', because 24-hour care at home would be prohibitively expensive. Lifting the authorisation, Peter Jackson J observed at para 38:

> In the end, if M remains confined in a home she is entitled to ask 'What for?' The only answer that could be provided at the moment is 'To keep you alive as long as possible.' In my view that is not a sufficient answer. The right to life and the state's obligation to protect it is not absolute and the court must surely have regard to the person's own assessment of her quality of life. In M's case there is little to be said for a solution that attempts, without any guarantee of success, to preserve for her a daily life without meaning or happiness and which she, with some justification, regards as insupportable.

'*Re X*' applications

21.56 Certain applications to the Court of Protection are referred to as '*Re X* applications', after the series of cases under that name.[57] These are uncontentious applications for welfare orders under MCA 2005 s16, authorising the deprivation of P's liberty in settings where the DOLS regime cannot be used. They follow a 'streamlined' procedure, which is excluded from the Case Management Pilot.[58] Such a process was considered to be necessary in the aftermath of the *Cheshire West*

---

56 [2013] EWHC 3456 (COP), [2014] COPLR 35.
57 *Re X* [2014] EWCOP 25, [2015] 1 WLR 2454, (2014) 17 CCLR 297; *Re X* [2014] EWCOP 37, [2015] 1 WLR 2454, (2014) 17 CCLR 464 and *Re X (Court of Protection Practice)* [2015] EWCA Civ 599, [2016] 1 WLR 227.
58 Case Management Pilot PD para 3.1(e).

judgment which, as we have seen, increased the cohort of those whose circumstances engaged Article 5.[59]

21.57 There has been significant litigation as to how P's interests are properly protected during the course of the application. In addition to the three *Re X* cases, *Re NRA*[60] and *Re JM*[61] consider in depth the essential requirements for a procedure which complies with Article 5. For a more detailed analysis of these cases readers are referred to articles in *Legal Action* in January 2016[62] and June 2016.[63]

21.58 Cases where a *Re X* application may need to be made could include cases where P is living in one of the following settings:

- supported living placements;
- extra care housing;
- adult foster placements; or
- care packages delivered to P in his or her own home (including those that are fully funded by P).

21.59 If P is 16 years old or over, lacks capacity to consent to his or her care arrangements, and his or her care package amounts to a deprivation of liberty for the purpose of Article 5, then authorisation will need to be sought from the Court of Protection. Without such authorisation, P is at risk of arbitrary detention, in violation of his or her Article 5 rights, which may lead to liability for damages. It is well-established that, except in emergencies, the authority to detain must be sought before the deprivation of liberty starts.[64] Failure to do so will result, at least, in a procedural breach of Article 5(1).

21.60 A full examination of all the circumstances in which Article 5 is engaged – and when applications to court should be made – is beyond the scope of this chapter. Nor does this chapter consider the position of those under 16, because the Court of Protection will not have jurisdiction over those aged 15 and below. However it is important to stress that the responsibility to seek authorisations is not limited to cases where P's care is arranged or commissioned by a public body. P's deprivation of liberty can be attributable to the State in any case where the State knows or ought to know of 'the situation

---

59 Although the numbers have not been as great as had been predicted: see *Re JM and others* [2016] EWCOP 15, [2016] 4 WLR 64 para10.
60 *Re NRA and others* [2015] EWCOP 59, [2015] COPLR 690, (2015) 18 CCLR 392.
61 *Re JM and others* [2016] EWCOP 15, [2016] 4 WLR 64.
62 Sophy Miles, 'Court of Protection update' Dec 2015/ Jan 16 *Legal Action* 28.
63 Sophy Miles, 'Court of Protection update' June 2016 *Legal Action* 29.
64 See by analogy *Re AJ* at para 133.

on the ground'.[65] If a local authority or other statutory body is in any doubt as to whether an application should be made in a particular case, specialist legal advice should be sought as a matter of urgency.

21.61 The next important point is that '*Re X*' applications are only appropriate where there is no dispute as to whether P's care arrangements are in P's best interests and the least restrictive alternative, either from P or from any other person.[66] If such a dispute exists then an application should be made for a welfare order, using COP1, and following the requirements of the Case Management Pilot. The procedure for such cases is addressed in chapter 9.

21.62 The *Re X* process has the following characteristics:

- it is paper-based and unlikely to involve an oral hearing;
- P will usually not be a party but will instead require a representative appointed under COPR Pr1.2/ COPR r3A.[67] There is no reason in principle, why P cannot be joined and a litigation friend be appointed for purposes of an application under the *Re X* process, but the case-law subsequent to *Re X* itself has made clear that the court will strive to avoid this outcome;
- any order made by the court will be time-limited and will be subject to further review.

Making an application

21.63 To make an application the applicant will have to consider:

- Practice Direction 10AA Part 2;
- Form COPDOL10 (which can be found in an unofficial Word version on the Court of Protection Handbook website), its annexes and guidance;
- The judgment of Charles J in *Re VE*[68], a case linked with *Re JM*. Here Charles J provides a helpful precedent of a letter that should be sent to the Rule 3 A representative, explaining what is expected;

---

65 *Staffordshire County Council v SRK (by his litigation friend SK) and others* [2016] EWCOP 27, under appeal at the time of writing.
66 See *Re NRA*, para 37.
67 For a full account of the role of such representatives, see paras 11.74 onwards.
68 *Re VE* [2016] EWCOP 16, [2016] 4 WLR 64.

- The *Re X* 'Model Order', which must be completed. A Word version of the order can be found on the Court of Protection Handbook website.[69]

21.64 At the time of writing, a new COPDOL10 form is in preparation. The updated version will be found at www.courtofprotectionhandbook.com when it is published.

21.65 The Practice Direction is comprehensive and explains exactly what is required in the application. The form COPDOL10 prompts the applicant to address the evidence which the court will need. In *Re NRA*, Charles J approved the form but suggested a number of improvements, in particular by way of additional information. This means that it is now no longer possibly easily to fit the information into the COPDOL10 form as it stands at the time of writing. Pending revision of that form, and as it no longer addresses all the issues that need to be covered, we suggest that it will make the judge's life considerably easier if: the (1) COP DOL10 form is simply used as a procedural vehicle (ie it is only completed so as to give the necessary names and other procedural matters); (2) that in all places where 'real' questions are asked (eg as to the care arrangements), the box is completed 'please see attached grounds'; and (3) that all substantive matters that need addressing are set out in a separate document entitled 'grounds.' The maker of the main witness statement in support of the application should then attest to the factual accuracy of the grounds.

21.66 It is important to appreciate that the applicant is asking the Court of Protection, by making an order under MCA 2005 s16(2)a), both to consent on P's behalf to living at the placement identified to receive care, and to authorise confinement there. The judge must therefore be satisfied that the arrangements are in P's best interests before they can consent to them.

21.67 Taking the judgment in *Re X* together with the COPDOL10 form and the additional requirements set down by Charles J in *Re NRA* means that the application needs to answer a substantial number of matters, either in the body of the form or in attached documents. We set them out below, re-ordered so as to place them in a logical order, and also amplified where necessary by reference to other relevant case-law.[70]

---

69 https://courtofprotectionhandbook.com/precedents/.
70 This draws upon the guidance note prepared by Alex Ruck Keene, Tor Butler-Cole, Neil Allen and Michelle Pratley of 39 Essex Chambers.

The order

A draft of the precise order sought should be provided, including in particular the duration of the authorisation sought and appropriate directions for automatic review and liberty to apply and/or seek a redetermination in accordance with COPR r89. When completing the order, careful thought should be given to the length of the authorisation sought. The maximum length is twelve months but – as in the case of standard authorisations – this should not be requested unless necessary.[71]

Evidence required

The applicant will be required to satisfy the court as to the following matters:

That the court can in principle make an order

This will require:

- Proof that P is 16 years old or more and is not ineligible to be deprived of liberty under MCA 2005 (the same eligibility requirements applying in respect of DOLS authorisations). We suggest that this evidence will be of the same nature as that required to allow the supervisory body to be satisfied that the (higher) age requirement under Schedule A1 is met. We would anticipate that stating P's date of birth would ordinarily suffice. If in doubt, of course check their birth certificate. If there is doubt and no papers – for example in the case of a paperless asylum seeker – a *Merton*-compliant age assessment may be required (see *B v London Borough of Merton*[72]).
- The basis upon which it is said that P is of unsound mind (together with the relevant medical evidence). Professional medical opinion is necessary to establish unsoundness of mind but where the facts are clear this need not involve expert psychiatric opinion (there will be cases where a general practitioner's evidence will suffice). We note that there therefore may well be a difference between (1) 'standard' applications to the Court of Protection where a COP3 should be filed setting out the basis upon which it is said

71 *P v Surrey CC and Surrey Downs CCG* [2015] EWCOP 54.
72 [2003] EWHC 1689 (Admin), [2003] 4 All ER 280.

that the person lacks capacity to take the relevant decision(s) can be completed by (inter alia) a social worker, and (2) a deprivation of liberty application, where the social worker can complete the evidence as to the lack of capacity to consent, but cannot complete the evidence of P's unsoundness of mind. We note also that the requirement is of evidence of unsoundness of mind, rather than (as under DOLS) evidence of a mental disorder for purposes of the Mental Health Act 1983, but where a person has a specific diagnosis of a mental disorder, such should be given.

- The nature of P's care arrangements (together with a copy of P's care and treatment plan) and why it is said that they do or may amount to a deprivation of liberty. The key restrictive provisions of the care package should be detailed including:

  – the level of supervision (1:1, 2:1 etc);
  – the periods of the day when supervision is provided;
  – the use or possible use of sedation or restraint;
  – the use of assistive technology;
  – what would happen if P tried to leave; and
  – restrictions on contact with others.

  Where any sedation or restraint is being used or may be used, give the details (eg drug name, dose, method of administration especially if covert) and an explanation should be given as to why these are the least restrictive measures to deal with the relevant issues.

  In *Re NRA*, Charles J held that the actual care notes can be very informative and their production may obviate the need for a summary or a lengthy summary. The importance of the care plan accurately recording the use of restraint, especially physical restraint, was emphasised by Baker J in *Re AJ*. Linked to this, because the judge's main concern is as to what is actually happening on the ground, the care plan that will usually need to be supplied with the application will be the care provider's care plan, because that will (or should) be detailing what is taking place on a day to day basis. This is to be contrasted with the care and support plan drawn up by the local authority (or NHS body) whose main function is to set out how the person's assessed needs will be met, and it will often not include the necessary level of detail.

The public body making the application will therefore have to make sure that it has obtained (and where necessary worked with the care provider to improve) the care provider's care plan before making the application so as to ensure that it addresses the matters set out above. Given that a more restrictive care regime will need to be sanctioned by the court, applicants may want to consider incorporating contingency arrangements into the care plan so as to minimise the need for judicial micro-management.

- Whether there has been any recent change or planned change in the care package and the reasons for it.
- The basis upon which it is said that the arrangements are or may be imputable to the state.
- The basis upon which it is said that P lacks the capacity to consent to the care arrangements (together with the relevant medical evidence).

Why the court can consent to the arrangements on P's behalf as being in P's best interests

This will require information as to:

- The basis upon which it is said that the care arrangements are necessary in P's best interests and why the care package advanced is the appropriate one. This will include explanation of why there is no less restrictive option (including details of any investigation into less restrictive options and confirmation that a best interests assessment, which should be attached, has been carried out). It will almost invariably be helpful to include a balance sheet to identify how the best interests decision has been reached. Charles J emphasised in *Re NRA* that the supporting material here is particularly important because it highlights the core of the decision making process and so the reasons why the court can be satisfied that it can properly consent to the arrangements on P's behalf in their best interests.
- Any evidence of conflicting interests within the same placement. This is particularly important in supported living placements because, as Charles J noted in *Re NRA*, in any one supported living placement there can be a number of

service users and the demands of the care package for one service user can impact on the others.
- If the proposed placement is planned and has not yet taken place, an explanation of whether or not a transition plan has been produced, a copy of the transition plan and an explanation as to how the placement will be reviewed, particularly in the context of responding to P's reaction to his or her new placement.
- If P is already living at the placement, information about the date P moved there, where he or she lived before, why the move took place, and how the move is working.
- The steps that have been taken to notify P and all other relevant people in P's life (who should be identified) of the application and to canvass their wishes, feelings and views.
- Any relevant wishes and feelings expressed by P and any views expressed by any relevant person.
- Details of any relevant advance decision by P and any relevant decisions under a lasting power of attorney or by P's deputy (who should be identified).

Ancillary matters about the arrangements

- If there is a tenancy agreement, the applicant should provide clarification of who has the authority or needs to apply for the authority to sign it on P's behalf.

Procedural matters relating to the application

The application will also need to address:

- P's eligibility for public funding. This means providing any details that are available as to P's savings and income, and details of any person (for instance a property and affairs deputy) who may be able to assist providing details of P's means.
- Whether or not it is thought the case is controversial and can be dealt with without an oral hearing and, if so, the reasons why.
- Information about the participation of family and friends over the years including (1) the nature of the care and support they have provided, (2) their approach to issues relating to the provision of care and support in the past and

(3) whether and why it is thought that family or friends have provided and will provide balanced support for P in his or her best interests.
- Whether P's family and friends support P's care package and the reasons why or why not.
- Whether a family member or friend is willing to be a litigation friend or a COPR Pr1.2/COPR r3A representative and whether they are able to keep the care package under review.
- Whether a family member or friend is suitable to be a litigation friend or a COPR Pr1.2/COPR r3A representative, with particular reference to the history of P's care. It should be not assumed that the person needs to be someone who supports the deprivation of liberty. Indeed, sometimes the most vocal are the best advocates for P.
- If no family member or friend is able to act as P's litigation friend or COPR Pr1.2/COPR r3A representative, whether or not there is any other person (for instance a statutory advocate such as an IMCA) who would be able to do so.
- Where possible, a statement from one or more of the actual carers should be provided as to P's wishes and feelings and any deficiencies or possible changes to the care package.
- Any reasons for particular urgency in determining the application.
- Any factors that ought to be brought specifically to the court's attention (the applicant being under a specific duty to make full and frank disclosure to the court of all facts and matters that might impact upon the court's decision), being factors:
  – needing particular judicial scrutiny; or
  – suggesting that the arrangements may not in fact be in P's best interests or be the least restrictive option; or
  – otherwise indicating that the order sought should not be made.

21.68 There is a helpful checklist in form COPDOL10, as well as a list of triggers which may suggest that the case may not be suitable for a *Re X* application.

21.69 Once the forms and all the ancillary documentation (including the draft order) have been completed they should be lodged at court with the application fee (see appendix F). As long as the court is satisfied that consultation with P and others has taken place it will dispense with the requirement that the application is served or that P is notified.[73] Where there is agreement from everyone, including the potential COPR Pr1.2/COPR r3A representative where one can be identified (or a litigation friend for P where one has been identified and confirmed their willingness to act and to consent to the order), the requisite order can be made on the papers. As at the time of preparing writing, orders are usually being returned within 4–6 weeks of issue.

21.70 If no Rule 3A representative has been identified the current guidance in *Re JM*[74] is that the case should be stayed and the Department of Health and Ministry of Justice joined to the proceedings with a view to identifying a potential representative. This is because in *Re JM* Charles J found that without such a representative P's fundamental rights would not be protected. See paras 11.74 onwards for details of the role of the Rule 3A representative; and chapter 6 for details of the legal aid entitlement.

21.71 If the judge considers that the case is not suitable for the *Re X* process he or she make case management directions[75] and may list it for an attended hearing.

21.72 Once the order is received it must be served on all those consulted, including P.[76] The order will contain details as to the review process, ie the process to extend the authorisation at the end of the authorisation period set down in the order. The review can, where appropriate, be done on the papers. Note that there is, as yet, no specific application for purposes of seeking a review, and that the model order provides that it should otherwise be made on a COP DOL10. The order will further contain a requirement to make an application to the court in the event that the care plan becomes more restrictive.

21.73 The draft letter set out in *Re VE*[77] should be used as a template when writing to the Rule 3A representative. From this it will be seen that the role is an ongoing one, and is in some ways an equivalent to the RPR in DOLS cases.

---

73 PD 10AA para 41.
74 At para 25.
75 PD10AA para 47.
76 PD10AA para 48.
77 At para 6.

CHAPTER 22

Medical treatment cases

22.1   Introduction

22.3   The scope of the court's jurisdiction

22.4   Serious medical treatment cases: definition

22.11 Other medical treatment cases

22.12 Pre-action steps

22.13 Urgent applications

22.16 Allocation

22.18 Case management

22.19 Declarations

22.22 Is there really a best interests decision to be taken?

Introduction

22.1 Cases involving medical treatment form a distinct sub-set of the cases that are decided by the Court of Protection, and cases involving serious medical treatment have their own dedicated practice direction. They do not fall within the pathways set down under the Case Management Pilot,[1] although as discussed in paras 4.101, they may not fall outside the scope of the Case Management Pilot altogether. This chapter highlights some of the key features of such cases, but it is likely that in such cases specialist advice and representation will be required going beyond the scope of this work.[2]

22.2 It is important to note that Practice Direction (PD) 9E is under review at the time of writing (October 2016). Reference should be made to www.courtofprotectionhandbook.com for updates to this chapter consequent upon the completion of that review.

The scope of the court's jurisdiction

22.3 As set out in chapter 4, the Court of Protection has jurisdiction regarding (among other matters) medical treatment in relation to those aged 16 and above who lack the material decision-capacity. Conventionally, medical treatment cases involving those below the age of 18 have been brought before the High Court for relief under its inherent jurisdiction; however, where a 16- or 17-year-old is considered to lack decision-making capacity, it would be equally possible to bring the case to the Court of Protection. If the concern on the part of the treating clinicians is not that the individual (aged 16 or over) lacks capacity but that they are vulnerable and under the influence of another, then the appropriate route would be, again, to seek relief from the High Court under the inherent jurisdiction.

Serious medical treatment cases: definition

22.4 Practice Direction (PD) 9E makes specific provision for cases involving 'serious medical treatment', defined for this purpose as

---

1 Case Management Pilot PD para 3.1(d).
2 More detail about the Mental Capacity Act (MCA) 2005 and the role of the Court of Protection in medical treatment cases can be found in Christopher Johnston et al, *Medical treatment*, 3rd edn, Bloomsbury, 2016.

treatment which involves providing, withdrawing or withholding treatment in circumstances where:

- (if a single treatment is proposed) there is a fine balance between its benefits and burdens and risks;
- (if there is a choice) a decision as to which treatment is finely balanced; or the treatment, procedure or investigation would be likely to involve serious consequences for the patient.[3]

22.5 Serious consequences are, in turn, defined, as those which could have a serious impact on P, either from the effects of the treatment, procedure or investigation itself or its wider implications. This may include treatments, procedures or investigations which:

- cause, or may cause, serious and prolonged pain, distress or side-effects;
- have potentially major consequences for P; or
- have a serious impact on P's future life choices.

22.6 PD 9E sets[4] out certain decisions which should be regarded as serious medical treatment decisions and should be brought to the court. These are:

- decisions about the proposed withholding or withdrawal of artificial nutrition and hydration from a person in a permanent vegetative state or a minimally conscious state;[5]
- cases involving organ or bone marrow donation by a person who lacks capacity to consent; and
- cases involving non-therapeutic sterilisation of a person who lacks capacity to consent.[6]

22.7 The word 'should' in PD 9E is ambiguous. Although there is case-law which suggest that cases falling into this category *must* be brought to court,[7] the true position is that there is no requirement of law that such cases be brought, rather that it is required as a matter of good

---

3 PD 9E para 3.
4 PD 9E para 5.
5 NB, in all such cases, reference must now be made to the guidelines issued by the Royal College of Physicians in December 2013 on *Prolonged disorders of consciousness*, available at: www.rcplondon.ac.uk/prolonged-disorders-consciousness-national-clinical-guidelines.
6 See also in this regard *A Local Authority v K and others* [2013] EWHC 242 (COP), [2013] COPLR 194.
7 *W v M and others* [2011] EWHC 2443 (Fam), [2012] COPLR 222 at para 257 per Baker J (in relation to the proposed withdrawing of artificial nutrition and hydration from a person in a minimally conscious state).

practice to ensure that there is no doubt that the relevant clinicians are acting lawfully.[8]

22.8 PD 9E also gives a non-exhaustive list of examples of other decisions which should be considered serious medical treatment.[9] It does not state expressly that such decisions should be brought to court. However, case-law makes clear that at least two categories of case should come to court (again, it is suggested, as an aspect of good practice):[10]

- In respect of a proposed termination of a pregnancy in relation to a person who lacks capacity to consent to such a procedure, an application must be made where:
  - there is dispute over capacity;
  - the patient may regain capacity during her pregnancy;
  - there is any lack of unanimity;
  - the procedures under Abortion Act 1967 s1 have not been followed;
  - the patient or members of her immediate family have opposed a termination; or
  - there are other exceptional circumstances, including that this may be the patient's last chance to bear a child.[11]
- (It appears) the carrying out of Caesarean section operations on incapacitated patients where any degree of force of restraint is contemplated. This follows the media outcry in the case of an Italian national, Ms Pacchieri, who was detained under the Mental Health Act (MHA) 1983 while temporarily present in England and in respect of whom such an operation was authorised.[12]

22.9 That a case falls within the category of serious medical treatment does not itself mean that it *has* to be brought to court, unless it is one of those falling with the categories set out in the paragraphs above. In many cases, the treatment could be provided in reliance upon the defence in MCA 2005 s5 on the basis that it is reasonably considered

---

8 See *R (Burke) v General Medical Council* [2005] EWCA Civ 1003, [2006] QB 273, (2004) 7 CCLR 609 at paras 71–72. It suggested that nothing in the post-MCA case of *Aintree University Hospitals NHS Foundation Trust v James* [2013] UKSC 67, [2014] 1 AC 591, (2013) 16 CCLR 554 casts doubt upon this proposition.
9 PD 9E para 6.
10 Although, as noted above, as an aspect of good practice, rather than by way of a substantive obligation of law.
11 *D v An NHS Trust (medical treatment: consent)* [2004] 1 FLR 1110; see also *Re P (abortion)* [2013] EWHC 50 (COP), [2013] COPLR 405.
12 *Re AA* [2012] EWHC 4378 (COP). See also *NHS Trust 1 and Another v G (Practice Note)* [2014] EWCOP 30, [2015] 1 WLR 1984.

to be in the best interests of the patient.[13] However, the treating NHS trust must, at the very least, consider whether an application to court is necessary if the treatment in question falls within the scope of 'serious medical treatment' as defined in PD 9E, and – we suggest – *must* as a matter of good practice bring the matter to court in the event of dispute either between the treating clinicians as to either P's capacity or best interests or between the treating clinicians and P's family members.

22.10   The expectation in serious medical treatment cases is that the application will be brought by the organisation providing the treatment to P. If they are not the applicant (which would be unusual), then they should be a respondent.[14] If the question is whether P should be admitted to hospital for purposes of being provided with medical treatment, then one would expect to see the relevant clinical commissioning group (CCG) (as the funding body) making the application, and that the treating hospital would either be a joint applicant or joined as a respondent.

Other medical treatment cases

22.11   Merely because a case involving medical treatment does not fall within the categories of serious medical treatment as defined in PD 9E does not mean that it should not be brought to court if – for instance – there is a serious dispute between those properly concerned with P's wellbeing as to whether the medical treatment should be administered or withheld. An example would be a dispute about the withholding of antibiotics. Such an application would, though, fall to be considered for purposes of case management (and the Case Management Pilot) as akin to a 'standard' welfare application. They are not therefore discussed separately in the majority of the balance of this chapter.

Pre-action steps

22.12   A particular feature of serious medical treatment cases is that P will almost invariably be joined as a party, and the Official Solicitor will almost invariably be invited to and will accept the invitation to act as P's litigation friend (see further para 22.18 below). The Official

---

13   See *Aintree v James* at paras 19–22, per Lady Hale.
14   PD 9E para 9.

Solicitor will also almost invariably act both as litigation friend and solicitor for P – in other words, external solicitors will not be instructed and the Official Solicitor's own lawyers will handle the case from start to finish, instructing counsel if needs be. This means that, wherever possible, it is sensible to ensure that contact is made with the Official Solicitor's office before an application is issued (the contact details are in appendix G below), both to discuss the case in outline and to ensure that the Official Solicitor is in a position to respond quickly when the application is issued. The pressure of work upon the Official Solicitor, however, is such that the authors' experience is that the Official Solicitor is increasingly reluctant to become formally involved before an application is lodged unless there is clear provision for his legal costs (see further para 22.18 below).

Urgent applications

22.13 The courts are well used to dealing with urgent medical treatment applications, including those that arise out of normal court hours. The procedures in relation to urgent applications are discussed at paras 10.65ff, and they will apply equally in medical treatment cases. It is particularly important in such cases that the treating clinicians are available by telephone so that the judge is able to hear from them directly if needs be – which may well entail setting up a conference call if the matter is being heard out of normal court hours.

22.14 It should be noted the Official Solicitor does not operate an out of hours service, so on any application brought out of normal court hours the court will normally strive to make the most limited order possible until such point as the matter can be brought back with the Official Solicitor present. The same will also generally apply if the urgency of the application has meant that the Official Solicitor has been unable to attend,[15] although in the case of a decision that simply cannot wait, the court will make the decision on the spot.[16]

22.15 The general rule in medical treatment cases is that it is better to bring the application sooner rather than later so that all the necessary inquiries can be made and information obtained to allow the court to reach a proper conclusion as to where P's best interests lie. It should

---

15 For a good example of the court's approach, see *Nottinghamshire Healthcare NHS Trust v RC* [2014] EWHC 1136 (COP) at para 19.
16 See *Newcastle-upon-Tyne Hospitals Foundation Trust v LM* [2014] EWHC 454 (COP), [2015] 1 FCR 373.

be noted, however, that a somewhat unfortunate consequence of the decision in *Aintree University Hospitals NHS Trust v James*[17] is a lack of clarity as to exactly when applications should be brought in respect of the withholding of life-sustaining treatment. Lady Hale, giving the judgment of the Supreme Court noted that, if an application is brought too early, then there is a risk that that the court may be unable to say that when the treatments are needed that they will not be in the best interests of the patient.[18] The logical corollary of this is that some decisions may be delayed – and that a sudden clinical deterioration may then require an urgent application to be brought.[19]

Allocation

22.16 Where the application relates to the lawfulness of withholding or withdrawing artificial nutrition and hydration from a person in a permanent vegetative state or a minimally conscious state, or it is a case involving an ethical dilemma in an untested area, then the whole proceedings (including the permission stage and the giving of any directions) must be conducted by the President or a judge nominated by the President.[20]

22.17 All other serious medical treatment cases or cases in which a declaration of incompatibility is sought pursuant to Human Rights Act (HRA) 1998 s4 must be conducted by the President, the Chancellor or a High Court judge nominated to sit as a Court of Protection judge.[21]

Case management

22.18 Serious medical treatment cases will be managed according to the same principles as other cases before the Court of Protection, but the following distinctive features should be noted:

---

17 [2013] UKSC 67, [2014] 1 AC 591, (2013) 16 CCLR 554.
18 Para 47.
19 See further in this regard the article by Vikram Sachdeva, Alex Ruck Keene and Victoria Butler-Cole entitled 'The MCA in the Supreme Court – Reflections on *Aintree v James*' [2014] Eld LJ 54.
20 PD 9E para 11.
21 PD 9E para 12.

- As noted above, P will almost invariably be joined as a party and the Official Solicitor be appointed to act as P's litigation friend. The Official Solicitor receives sufficient central government funding to conduct (in-house) such proceedings, and is also conventionally awarded half the costs of doing so against the relevant NHS body.[22] The Official Solicitor will often decline to act until an undertaking is given by the relevant NHS body to meet half of his costs.
- The presumption is that the application will be heard in public with suitable reporting restrictions imposed.[23] This means that it is very likely that the applicant NHS trust will need to apply for a reporting restrictions order under the provisions of COPR r92(2): see in this regard paras 13.61 onwards. The courts are increasingly reluctant to grant anonymity to NHS trusts and the treating clinicians, save where this is necessary to protect the identity of P and their place of treatment (it is therefore likely that an NHS trust responsible for more than one hospital will be named as the chances of P being identified would be materially reduced in such a case).
- Unless the urgency of the case makes it impossible, the Official Solicitor will usually wish to obtain independent expert evidence (and will usually seek to do so on a joint basis). Questions of expert evidence are addressed further in chapter 12. The courts will place considerable weight upon the evidence of any expert(s) instructed, but – as in all other cases – will exercise independent judgment upon the questions both of P's capacity and best interests. A good example of the latter is *An NHS Trust v (1) K (2) Another Foundation Trust*[24] in which Holman J declined to follow the 'unduly pessimistic' evidence of the independent expert as to the risks to the patient surrounding the operation in question.
- Any decision in a serious medical treatment case (whether or not held in public) will prima facie fall to be published (subject to suitable anonymisation) in line with the President's guidance on *Transparency in the Court of Protection: publication of judgments*.[25]

---

22 *An NHS Trust v D* [2012] EWHC 886 (COP), [2012] COPLR 499.
23 PD 9E para 16; see also *W v M and others (reporting restrictions order)* [2011] EWHC 1197 (COP), [2011] COPLR Con Vol 1206.
24 [2012] EWHC 2292 (COP), [2012] COPLR 694.
25 [2014] EWHC B2 (COP), [2014] COPLR 78. See also paras 14.32 onwards.

Declarations

22.19 Serious medical treatment cases are unusual in that the applicant (usually the treating NHS Trust) does not generally seek decisions from the court,[26] but rather declarations as to whether a proposed course of action is lawful.[27] PD 9E gives examples of the wording that should be adopted in respect of particular categories of cases.[28] It is questionable whether this is, in fact, correct, or whether the real relief that should be sought is not a decision (under MCA 2005 s16(2)(a)) consenting (or refusing consent) on behalf of P,[29] coupled (where the treating Trust is particularly concerned to have legal 'cover') with a declaration under MCA 2005, s15(1)(c). It may well be that PD 9E is amended in due course to make this clear.

22.20 In any event, it is important to be precise. In *Aintree*, for instance, the NHS trust in question made an application for a declaration that it would be lawful to withhold three types of life-sustaining treatment from Mr James 'in the event of a clinical deterioration'. As Lady Hale noted, this actually meant 'should his condition deteriorate that they [ie the treatments] become necessary', and that it would have been helpful to say so.

22.21 The courts have also shown themselves to be careful to maintain a distinct line between matters in respect of which they can properly make declarations or decisions under the MCA 2005 and those matters which fall within the scope of the ethical and clinical obligations owed by the treating doctors. In *A NHS Trust v (1) K (2) Another Foundation Trust*,[30] for instance, Holman J authorised the sedation of a woman who needed a hysterectomy before she was to be informed that it was proposed to carry out the proposed surgery so as to reduce the risk that she would be non-compliant.[31] Holman J noted, however, that 'an ethical issue may arise as to the degree of sedation and whether the surgeon can ethically proceed to operate unless he has given to the patient an adequate account of what he

---

26 ie under MCA 2005 s16.
27 Under MCA 2005 s15.
28 PD 9E paras 17 and 18.
29 See *Re MN* [2015] EWCA Civ 411, [2016] Fam 87, (2015) 18 CCLR 521.
30 [2012] EWHC 2292 (COP), [2012] COPLR 694.
31 Relying on *DH NHS Foundation Trust v PS* [2010] EWHC 1217 (Fam), [2010] COPLR Con Vol 346, (2010) 13 CCLR 606. Holman J did not authorise restraint to be used on the patient because of the risk to her given her other medical difficulties.

proposes to do while she retains sufficient awareness to hear it and take it in. But that is an ethical matter for him'.[32]

Is there really a best interests decision to be taken?

22.22 We conclude this chapter by raising a question that is starkly posed by the decision of the Supreme Court in *Aintree v James*, but which has yet fully to be grappled with by the courts. The Supreme Court emphasised – in our view correctly – that the MCA 2005 is concerned with 'enabling the court to do for the patient what he could do for himself if of full capacity, but it goes no further. On an application under this Act, therefore, the court has no greater powers than the patient would have if he were of full capacity'.[33] The Court of Protection cannot therefore order a doctor to provide a particular treatment to a patient; rather, its task is to 'decide whether a particular treatment is in the best interests of a patient who is incapable of making the decision for himself'.[34]

22.23 In some cases, therefore, the treating clinicians will have concluded that they will not offer specific treatment(s) to the patient (or would wish to withdraw such treatment) because they consider that either offering or continue to offer it would be clinically inappropriate, futile or (potentially) on the basis that its costs so far outweigh its benefits to the person that the treatment will not be funded by the relevant funding NHS body. In such a case, it would be irrelevant that the patient lacks the capacity to consent to the treatment because it would not be offered to them even if they had capacity and were requesting it. In this situation then, assuming (as it is not unknown) that no other treating clinician would offer (or continue to offer) such treatment, then there is a good argument that there is, in fact, no best interests decision for the court to take.

22.24 This situation arose in the pre-*Aintree* case of *An NHS Trust v L, FL and TL*[35] in which Moylan J was of the view that there were no treatment options available. He was, however, constrained (with evident unhappiness) to make a best interests decision because none of the parties before him were prepared to submit that such was the case. In a future case, it is quite possible, we suggest, to imagine a

---

32 Para 44.
33 *Aintree* at para 18 per Lady Hale.
34 *Aintree* at para 18 per Lady Hale.
35 [2013] EWHC 4313 (Fam), [2013] COPLR 558.

22.25 This issue may be revisited by analogy when the Court of Appeal decision in *Re MN*[36] is heard before the Supreme Court in December 2016 (see further chapter 22), when the Supreme Court will examine what the Court of Protection should do where a social care option is not put on the table. In the interim, however, we would suggest that, if – on a proper analysis – there is no best interests decision for the Court of Protection to take, then if the NHS trust wishes to have legal 'cover' for its actions (most obviously where there is a dispute between the clinicians and the patient's family) then it should make clear in its application that it is not seeking any form of determination as to the person's best interests, but rather a declaration under MCA 2005 s15(1)(c) that (for instance) not providing a specific form of treatment is lawful because it is futile. Another alternative would be to bring an application in the Queen's Bench Division under Part 8 of the Civil Procedure Rules (CPR) for a declaration that the trust's actions (or potentially proposed omissions) are lawful.[37]

situation in which a judge would decline to make a best interests determination.

---

36 [2015] EWCA Civ 411, [2016] Fam 87, (2015) 18 CCLR 521.
37 See further Vikram Sachdeva, Alex Ruck Keene and Victoria Butler-Cole, 'The MCA in the Supreme Court – Reflections on *Aintree v James*' [2014] Eld LJ 54.

CHAPTER 23

Safeguarding and the Court of Protection

23.1 Introduction

23.4 What is safeguarding?

23.13 The overlap between safeguarding and the Court of Protection

23.19 Safeguarding during the currency of Court of Protection proceedings

23.22 Police involvement

Introduction[1]

23.1 A significant proportion of the welfare applications made to the Court of Protection are made by local authorities on the basis of concerns that an adult lacking decision-making capacity in one or more domains, either has been subjected to or is at risk of harm. Such applications frequently arise, therefore, in the context of the discharge by the local authority of the obligations that are imposed upon it by various routes to safeguard adults at risk within their area. The overlap between actions taken on the basis of safeguarding obligations and applications before the Court of Protection is one that justifies a specific chapter of its own because of the difficulties that can arise where local authorities are not sufficiently clear as to the specific requirements that arise when matters move from investigation to proceedings before the court.

23.2 This chapter therefore outlines briefly what is meant by safeguarding, by specific reference to the changes to the law in England and Wales introduced by the Care Act 2014 and the Social Services and Well-being (Wales) Act 2014 respectively. It then highlights how Court of Protection proceedings form an aspect of safeguarding, before making clear the specific steps required when an adult's circumstances move from being the subject of a safeguarding investigation to an application before the Court of Protection. It, finally, notes what should happen while Court of Protection proceedings are ongoing and further safeguarding concerns arise.

23.3 It is not only local authorities who have safeguarding obligations: other bodies, most obviously NHS bodies, will have responsibilities toward adults at risk, and may find that those responsibilities give rise to a need to bring proceedings before the Court of Protection. While the changes set out in the Care Act 2014 and the Social Services and Well-being (Wales) Act 2014 do not directly apply to such bodies, the principles set out in the subsequent parts of the chapter apply with equal force to them.

---

1 Parts of this chapter originally appeared, in different form, in an article by Alex Ruck Keene entitled 'Safeguarding and the Court of Protection,' in the November 2013 *Encyclopedia of Local Government Law Bulletin*, Sweet & Maxwell. See also Alex Ruck Keene, Kelly Stricklin-Coutinho and Henry Gilfillan, 'The role of the Court of Protection in safeguarding' [2015] Journal of Adult Protection 380.

What is safeguarding?

23.4 Safeguarding has both a broad and a narrow definition.[2] The broader definition encompasses the prevention of abuse, and can encompass consideration of all aspects of a person's general welfare. As such, it forms part of the general approach to be taken to the assessment and delivery of services to adults by local social services authorities. The narrow definition – perhaps more accurately called 'adult protection' – refers to investigation and intervention where it is suspected that abuse may have occurred. In neither case was there traditionally a single legal framework setting out either the responsibilities of local authorities. Their duties arose from a mixture of statutory obligations (in particular, the duty to undertake community care assessments); statutory guidance in the form of the *No Secrets* guidance issued by the Department of Health and Home Office in 2000;[3] and public law requirements, in particular those imposed under Articles 2, 3, 5 and 8 of the European Convention on Human Rights (ECHR).

23.5 In England, the Care Act 2014 changed the law in this area by imposing two duties upon local authorities.

- First, implementing one of the main recommendations of the Law Commission in its review of adult social care, the Care Act 2014 introduced an overarching principle in section 1 to the effect that the general duty of a local authority in the discharge of its functions relating to care and support of specific individual is to promote the well-being of that individual. 'Well-being,' in turn, is defined as including protection from an abuse and neglect.[4]
- Second, and again implementing one of the main recommendations of the Law Commission, the Care Act 2014 introduced[5] a statutory duty of enquiry upon a local authority wherever it has reasonable cause to suspect that an adult in its area (whether or not ordinarily resident there):

---

2 See the Law Commission's report *Adult social care*, Law Com No 326, May 2011, para 9.2; available at: http://lawcommission.justice.gov.uk/docs/lc326_adult_social_care.pdf.
3 *No Secrets: guidance on developing and implementing multi-agency policies and procedures to protect vulnerable adults from abuse*, Department of Health/Home Office, 2000; available at: https://www.gov.uk/government/publications/no-secrets-guidance-on-protecting-vulnerable-adults-in-care.
4 Care Act 2014 s1(2)(c).
5 Care Act 2014 s42.

- has needs for care and support (whether or not the authority is meeting any of those needs) (ie whether or not the adult is eligible for community care services provided by the local authority);
- is experiencing, or is at risk of, abuse or neglect; and
- as a result of those needs is unable to protect himself or herself against the abuse or neglect or the risk of it.

23.6 While 'abuse' is not given a specific definition, the Care Act 2014 makes clear[6] that it includes financial abuse, financial abuse being defined, in turn, as including:

- having money or other property stolen;
- being defrauded;
- being put under pressure in relation to money or other property; and
- having money or other property misused.

23.7 The statutory guidance accompanying the Care Act 2014 provides that it also encompasses physical abuse, domestic violence, sexual abuse, psychological abuse, modern slavery, discriminatory abuse and organisational abuse.[7] 'Neglect' is not defined in the Care Act 2014, but in the statutory guidance is defined as including neglects by acts of omission such as ignoring medical, emotional or physical care needs, failure to provide access to appropriate health, care and support or educational services and the withholding of the necessities of life, such as medication, adequate nutrition and heating. It can also include self-neglect.[8]

23.8 The equivalent duties were introduced in Wales in the Social Services and Well-being (Wales) Act 2014 ss5 (well-being) and 126 (the duty of inquiry). There is a more detailed definition of both abuse and neglect given in the legislation itself,[9] with a non-exhaustive list of examples given in the accompanying statutory guidance.[10] Neither the Act nor the accompanying statutory guidance provide for self-neglect, and it is doubtful that this is capable of triggering the duty of inquiry.

23.9 Where the duty of enquiry arises, the local authority must make or cause to be made whatever enquiries it thinks necessary to enable

---

6 Care Act 2014 s42(3).
7 Department of Health, *Care and Support Statutory Guidance*, chapter 14.
8 Ibid.
9 Social Services and Well-being (Wales) Act 2014 s197.
10 Welsh Government, *Statutory Guidance: Working Together to Safeguard People Volume 1 – Introduction and Overview, Part 7: Safeguarding*, para 26.

it to decide whether any action should be taken in the adult's care and, if so, what and by whom.[11]

23.10 The Care Act 2014 does not, however, introduce any additional *powers* for local authorities in respect of either the prevention or the investigation of abuse or neglect. In particular, the government declined on several occasions during the passage of the Bill through parliament to amend it to introduce a power of entry by which a local authority would be able to seek a judicial warrant to enter a property and speak to an adult at risk. The Social Services and Well-being (Wales) Act 2014 does include such a power for an authorised officer to apply for an adult protection and support order,[12] and practice in England and Wales may well diverge considerably over the coming years in consequence of the differing powers available to local authorities in the two jurisdictions.

23.11 In order to discharge their duty of inquiry, local authorities will need to draw upon a range of pre-existing powers (including the specific statutory power of entry in Wales) and/or draw upon co-operation from other authorities with relevant responsibilities and powers (most obviously, police forces). Space prevents a detailed discussion of these powers, but for purposes of this book, the most relevant is the ability of a local authority – where the adult lacks (or may lack[13]) decision-making capacity in the relevant domains – to bring proceedings before the Court of Protection for declarations and decisions as to such matters as to where they should live and with whom they should have contact.

23.12 The President of the Court of Protection, Sir James Munby, has held on a number of occasions that local authorities or other public bodies must obtain the authority of the court if they consider it necessary to remove a person lacking capacity to consent from their home.[14] It is suggested that, to the extent that he has purported to lay down a

---

11 Care Act 2014 s42(2) (England); Social Services and Well-being (Wales) Act 2014 s126 (Wales).
12 Social Services and Well-being (Wales) Act 2014 s127 (Wales). An equivalent power (and other, broader, powers including a power of removal) can be found in the Adult Support and Protection (Scotland) Act 2007.
13 Sometimes, the issue is in fact whether the adult lacks that capacity or whether they are a vulnerable adult under coercion: see para 5.2, *London Borough of Redbridge v G* [2014] EWCOP 17 and chapter 11 of Ashton et al, *Mental Capacity Law and Practice*, 3rd edition, Jordans, 2015.
14 Most recently in *Re AG* [2015] EWCOP 78, [2016] COPLR 13, but see also *Re A and C (Equality and Human Rights Commission intervening)* [2010] EWHC 978 (Fam), [2010] COPLR Con Vol 10.

substantive rule to this end, such cannot be correct.[15] However, it is clear that any decision by a public body to remove a person from their own home, especially in the face of their objections, and/or to restrict their contact with others,[16] will undoubtedly engage the person's rights to private and family life under Article 8 ECHR (and quite possibly those of others), and that proceeding without the sanction of the court may well give rise to a breach of the implied procedural safeguards that accompany Article 8.[17] Put simply: public bodies are on thin legal ice when they are interfering substantially in the autonomy of those without capacity, and they will always need to be clear as to the precise basis upon which they are acting and alert to the possibility that they may need the court to confirm they are acting lawfully. The mere fact that they are acting pursuant to safeguarding obligations imposed under either the English or Welsh legislation does not, itself, give them the power to take such draconian steps as removal from a person's home or restriction of their contact with others.

The overlap between safeguarding and the Court of Protection

23.13 It can be seen from the very brief review above that what might be entitled adult protection proceedings before the Court of Protection sit within the broader safeguarding context. It is, however, vitally important to recognise that a decision to instigate proceedings before the Court of Protection is a decision that gives rise to a specific set of obligations upon the applicant – be that a local authority or NHS body – arising from the demands of the court process. These obligations are discussed in greater detail in the main part of this work; of particular relevance is chapter 14, because fact-finding will – often – form an important part of adult protection proceedings.

---

15 See, by analogy, *R (Burke) v General Medical Council* [2005] EWCA Civ 1003, [2006] QB 273, (2004) 7 CCLR 609 at paras 71–72, and also Alex Ruck Keene, 'Section 5 MCA and the "need" for judicial sanction' [2016] Eld LJ 244.
16 *Hillingdon LBC v Neary* [2011] EWHC 1377 (COP), [2011] COPLR Con Vol 632, (2011) 14 CCLR 239.
17 See the article by Alex Ruck Keene referred to above and, eg, the decision of the European Court of Human Rights in *Shtukaturov v Russia* [2008] ECHR 223, in which the court reiterated (at para 89) that, whilst Article 8 of the Convention contains no explicit procedural requirements, 'the decision-making process involved in measures of interference must be fair and such as to ensure due respect of the interests safeguarded by Article 8'.

23.14 Perhaps the most important point to emphasise here is that it is inappropriate for Court of Protection proceedings to be used as a 'voyage of discovery',[18] such that it is important that the applicant is satisfied at the outset that it has a satisfactory evidential basis for any allegations that it advances against those whom it contends have harmed the adult or from whom the adult is at risk. That evidential basis may, in a very urgent case, be limited, but as a general rule, it is clear that a local authority should not embark upon Court of Protection proceedings except on the basis that it is satisfied that it has the evidence that it will need at the final hearing to support factual allegations made against any individuals.

23.15 This means that a decision to bring proceedings has to be taken after as rigorous a process as possible in the time allowed (involving senior members of the social work management team and the legal department) so as to ensure that:

- a considered decision is taken as to whether evidence being put before the Court is sufficiently cogent. While the standard of proof before the Court of Protection is the civil standard (see further para 14.20), it is axiomatic that a serious allegation should not be advanced absent proper evidence;[19]
- the sources of information forming the foundation of the decisions being made are checked so as to allow an assessment to be made about its reliability. 'The fact that a piece of information has been repeated many times does not enhance its reliability';[20]
- where orders are being sought that interfere with rights under Article 8 ECHR, the picture being put to the court is a balanced one, rather than one presenting solely the negative information or the facts cast only in a negative light;[21] and
- proper consideration has been given to whether it is necessary to put the allegations to the alleged abuser before taking steps upon the basis of those allegations. The obligation upon public bodies

---

18 *A Local Authority v PB and P* [2011] EWHC 502 (COP), [2011] COPLR Con Vol 166 at para 38, per Charles J.
19 *A Local Authority v HS and others* [2013] EWHC 2410 (COP) at paras 184–186, per District Judge Eldergill. This decision does not have precedent value but is cited here as it contains a very detailed discussion of the consequences of a failure to analyse the evidential basis upon which an adult protection application is brought.
20 *Surrey CC v M and others* [2013] EWHC 2400 (Fam), (2013) 157(32) SJLB 31 at para 77 per Theis J (the comments relate to care proceedings, but are of wider application).
21 *Surrey CC v M and others* at para 78.

to treat parties affected by their actions in a just manner is capable of being overridden by the obligation to protect an adult at risk, but a failure to recognise that obligation can, itself, give rise to flawed decision-making.[22]

23.16 The courts are alive to the fact that, on occasion, local authorities are on the horns of a dilemma, and that it may be necessary urgently to invoke the jurisdiction of the Court of Protection before it has been possible properly to investigate an allegation of abuse.[23] However, in such a case, it is all the more important that stock is taken as soon as possible thereafter of matters. A failure to do so leads to (at least) two adverse consequences:

- leaving allegations '[hanging] like a cloud' over family members or other individuals can act as a substantial distraction to the real welfare issues, by placing those individuals in an unnecessarily adversarial position vis-à-vis the local authority;[24]
- in the worst case scenario, it can lead to very substantial damages and/or costs being incurred unnecessarily by other parties which fall to be paid by the local authority. By way of example, a local authority was ordered to pay the full costs of the Official Solicitor and of P's brother (agreed in the total sum of £88,000) after it withdrew allegations of sexual abuse against the brother almost two years after the proceedings were brought in the Court of Protection. District Judge Eldergill held that:

> There was a prolonged failure on the local authority's part to recognise the weakness of its case. The allegations were vague and insufficiently particularized. The 'evidence' in support was manifestly inadequate. It was internally inconsistent and unreliable. The truth of what was alleged was assumed without any proper, critical, analysis.[25]

---

22 *R (Davis and Davis) v West Sussex CC* [2012] EWHC 2152 (Admin), [2013] PTSR 494.
23 *HS* at para 187.
24 *A London Borough v (1) BB (by her litigation friend the Official Solicitor) (2) AM (3) SB (4) EL Trust* [2011] EWHC 2853 (Fam), [2012] COPLR 16 at para 18 per Ryder J (as he then was).
25 Para 188. For other cases in which local authorities have been heavily criticised and had to pay substantial damages and/or costs, see *Somerset County Council v MK* [2014] EWCOP B25 (damages not quantified) and [2015] EWCOP B1 (indemnity costs); *Milton Keynes Council v RR* [2014] EWCOP B19 and [2014] EWCOP 34 (costs); *Essex County Council v RF* [2015] EWCOP 1: (£60,000 damages, care home fees waived at a cost to the local authority of £23–£25,000, costs).

23.17 The propositions set out above do not affect the general duty to place before the court disputes where the best outcome may not be immediately clear. Court of Protection proceedings need not be adversarial and may be the best forum for resolving finely-balanced questions as to what may constitute the best and least restrictive alternative for P. In all cases, however, it is essential to show that available evidence has been properly evaluated and that it is openly shared with the court and the parties.

23.18 Importantly, if a public body brings a matter to the Court of Protection for determination as to where an individual's best interests lie, then, for forensically similar reasons to those which apply in relation to child care proceedings they must work in partnership with the court. This means that it lies in the court's power to direct the public body to file evidence (including a care plan), even though the plan's contents may not or do not reflect its formal position, 'for it is not for the local authority (or indeed any other party) to decide whether it is going to restrict or limit the evidence that it presents'.[26] Further, as noted at para 15.7, the court's powers in this regard have been strengthened by the introduction of COPR r87A, which means that the permission of the court is required before proceedings may be withdrawn. Where the public body decides, in the discharge of its public law obligations relating to funding of care and treatment, that a particular option is no longer on the table, the position is different, and is discussed in chapter 24.

Safeguarding during the currency of Court of Protection proceedings

23.19 In the authors' experience, there can sometimes be confusion on the part of public authorities as to what it is that they are required to do during the currency of Court of Protection proceedings if a further safeguarding concern arises in relation to P. They can, in particular, sometimes be unclear as to whether they can take any steps without the authorisation of the court.

23.20 The short answer is that the fact that Court of Protection proceedings are on foot does not alleviate the obligations upon the local authority (or NHS body) where they have reason to believe that P has

---

26 *Re MN (Adult)* EWCA Civ 411, [2016] Fam 87, (2015) 18 CCLR 521 at para 37, citing *Re W (Care Proceedings: Functions of Court and Local Authority)* [2013] EWCA Civ 1227, [2014] 2 FLR 431.

suffered harm or is at risk of harm. However, while they should take such steps as are immediately necessary to meet the situation, it is likely always to be necessary to bring the matter back to court if they will involve a substantial change in P's circumstances (for instance, where they are living).

23.21 One specific requirement in such case was identified by McFarlane J (as he then was) in *Enfield LBC v SA and others*.[27] Where there are extant Court of Protection proceedings, then in the absence of an absolutely pressing emergency (using that phrase in an extreme sense), McFarlane J held that any question of whether or not P was to be the subject of an 'achieving best evidence' interview[28] must be raised with the court and be subject to a direction from the judge. He noted that where the substance of the interview might relate to allegations that another party to the proceedings (or someone closely connected to a party) had harmed P then there would be good grounds for the matter being raised, at least initially, without notice to that party. However, in every case, he held, notice should be given to the Official Solicitor or any other person who acted as P's litigation friend.[29]

Police involvement

23.22 One particular feature of adult protection proceedings before the Court of Protection is that they may well require the involvement of the police to implement the decisions and declarations of the court. This is especially so if the judge determines that it is necessary that P be removed from a place that they have been residing with family members or carers whom it is thought will seek to frustrate the process. In such a case, the courts have set down guidance as to the steps should be followed:

> In the event that it is expected that the assistance of the Police may be required to effect or assist with the removal of a vulnerable/

---

27 [2010] EWHC 196 (Admin), [2010] COPLR Con Vol 362.
28 ie an interview carried out by police officers with a possible view to criminal proceedings, complying with the guidance set down in *Achieving best evidence in criminal proceedings: guidance on interviewing victims and witnesses, and guidance on using special measures*, Ministry of Justice, (now) 3rd revision, 2011; available at: www.justice.gov.uk/downloads/victims-and-witnesses/vulnerable-witnesses/achieving-best-evidence-criminal-proceedings.pdf.
29 *Enfield LBC v SA* at para 46.

incapacitated adult ('P') which the Court is being asked to authorise, the following steps should generally be taken:

(1) the Local Authority/NHS body/other organisation/person (the Applicant) applying to the Court for an authorisation to remove P should, in advance of the hearing of the Application, discuss and, where possible, agree with the Police the way in which it is intended that the removal will be effected, to include, where applicable, the extent to which it is expected that restraint and/or force may be used and the nature of any restraint (for example, handcuffs) that may be used;

(2) the Applicant should ensure that information about the way in which it is intended that removal will be effected is provided to the Court and to the litigation friend (in cases where a person has been invited and/or appointed to act as P's litigation friend) before the Court authorises removal. In particular, the Court and the litigation friend should be informed whether there is agreement between the Applicant and the Police and, if there is not, about the nature and extent of any disagreement;

(3) where the Applicant and the Police do not agree about how removal should be effected, the Court should give consideration to inviting/ directing the Police to attend the hearing of the Application so that the Court can, where appropriate, determine how it considers removal should be effected and/or ensure that any authorisation for removal is given on a fully informed basis.[30]

---

30 *LBH v GP and MP* (unreported, 8 April 2009), at para 31 per Coleridge J.

CHAPTER 24

The Court of Protection and the Administrative Court

24.1 Introduction
24.3 The limits of the Court of Protection's jurisdiction
24.6 Parallel proceedings
24.9 The approach of the Administrative Court

Introduction

24.1 For some years after the coming into force of the Mental Capacity Act (MCA) 2005, it was not entirely clear how far the Court of Protection could go in deciding where P's best interests lay. In particular, where P's care was provided by a public body (whether a local authority or a health body), it was not entirely clear whether the Court of Protection was entitled to decide – in the abstract – where (for instance) it was in P's best interests for them to live, or whether the Court of Protection was limited to choosing between the options put on the table by the public body. The position is now significantly clearer, although at the time of writing the Supreme Court is expected to make the authoritative determination of the position when the case of *Re MN*[1] discussed in this chapter is heard before it in December 2016. Readers should therefore make sure that they have regard to the online updates to this book to be found at www.courtofprotectionhandbook.com to keep themselves abreast of developments in this area.

24.2 This chapter outlines briefly the dividing lines between the jurisdiction of the Court of Protection and that of the Administrative Court, before addressing the practical questions that arise where parallel proceedings are likely to be necessary and, finally, the approach that the Administrative Court is likely to take in any challenge arising out of a case before the Court of Protection.

The limits of the Court of Protection's jurisdiction

24.3 For the most part, a public body responsible for the wellbeing of the person concerned (whether in a medical context or in the context of their welfare more generally) will either bring proceedings to seek a decision from the court (especially in the safeguarding context: see further chapter 23) or is a party to the proceedings and is willing to abide by the result. However, there may be cases in which the public body has already taken a decision in discharge of its statutory functions, and the question then arises how that decision can appropriately be challenged. Alternatively, the public body may decide in the currency of Court of Protection proceedings that it does not wish to put before the Court a particular option for consideration. For instance, a local authority may contend that a placement to which P has been moved in discharge of its community care functions

---

1 *Re MN (Adult)* EWCA Civ 411, [2016] Fam 87, (2015) 18 CCLR 521.

sufficiently meets their needs that they are not prepared to incur the substantially greater expenditure that may be required to allow them to move home. The question that then arises is as to the extent the Court of Protection is able to compel a public authority to discharge its statutory functions in a certain way or to make a specific funding decision. Put another way, how and when will parallel public law proceedings be required in such situations?

24.4　Cases decided prior to the enactment of the MCA 2005 suggested that, in the event of an impasse of the nature described above, it would be necessary to proceed by way of judicial review in order to challenge the decision of the public authority.[2] In May 2015, the Court of Appeal confirmed in *Re MN*[3] that this remains the position. Sir James Munby P, giving the sole reasoned judgment of the court, held that:

> 80. The function of the Court of Protection is to take, on behalf of adults who lack capacity, the decisions which, if they had capacity, they would take themselves. The Court of Protection has no more power, just because it is acting on behalf of an adult who lacks capacity, to obtain resources or facilities from a third party, whether a private individual or a public authority, than the adult if he had capacity would be able to obtain himself. [. . .] The Court of Protection is thus confined to choosing between available options, including those which there is good reason to believe will be forthcoming in the foreseeable future.
>
> 81. The Court of Protection, like the family court and the Family Division, can explore the care plan being put forward by a public authority and, where appropriate, require the authority to go away and think again. Rigorous probing, searching questions and persuasion are permissible; pressure is not. And in the final analysis the Court of Protection cannot compel a public authority to agree to a care plan which the authority is unwilling to implement. I agree with the point Eleanor King J made in her judgment (para 57):
>
>> 'In my judgment, such discussions and judicial encouragement for flexibility and negotiation in respect of a care package are actively to be encouraged. Such negotiations are however a far cry from the court embarking on a 'best interests' trial with a view to determining whether or not an option which has been said by care provider (in the exercise of their statutory duties) not to be available, is nevertheless in the patient's best interest.'

2　See, in particular, *A v A Health Authority* [2002] Fam 213 and *Re S (Vulnerable Adult)* [2007] 2 FLR 1095.

3　*Re MN (Adult)* EWCA Civ 411, [2016] Fam 87, (2015) 18 CCLR 521.

24.5 As discussed further at paras 25.5 onwards, there is one important caveat to this proposition that arises in cases where a proper claim can be framed based upon the Human Rights Act (HRA) 1998 that a public authority in declining to fund a particular form of care package is acting in a way incompatible with rights under the European Convention on Human Rights (ECHR).

Parallel proceedings

24.6 Parallel proceedings will be unusual,[4] not least because it is not easy to mount a judicial review challenge (in particular given the ever more limited scope of public funding available). The Administrative Court also applies a permission filter significantly more stringently than does the Court of Protection (the filter not even applying in all cases before the latter: see chapter 9). Administrative Court judges will, further, be astute to ensure that cases that should properly be determined within the four walls of the Court of Protection remain there. In *R (DO) v LBH*,[5] for instance, permission was refused to the sister of P in concurrent Court of Protection proceedings to bring judicial review applications against decisions of the local authority which had the effect of removing her from caring for her brother and making decisions as to his care arrangements. HHJ Jarman QC (sitting as a Deputy High Court Judge) noted that such questions were ones which the Court of Protection with its expertise was particularly suited to deal with and that judicial review was a remedy of last resort which should only be deployed where (for instance) an application or appeal within Court of Protection proceedings was not available.

24.7 However, where a party or parties wish to challenge a failure by a public body to put a particular option on the table, by way of judicial review proceedings, then any delay or increased expense of litigation can be ameliorated to a considerable extent by an early identification of the issues and, if needs be, the matter being listed before a High Court judge who sits both in the Court of Protection and the Administrative Court.[6] If the application was being heard by a district

---

4 An example of a combined judicial review and Court of Protection application (albeit not arising out of a refusal to put an option on the table) is *R (C) v A Local Authority and others* [2011] EWHC 1539 (Admin), [2011] COPLR Con Vol 972.
5 [2012] EWHC 4044 (Admin).
6 All High Court judges who sit in the Family Division are entitled to sit in the Court of Protection. Some also hold a 'ticket' to sit in the Administrative Court.

or a circuit judge, therefore, it will be necessary to apply to have the matter transferred to be heard before a High Court judge with the relevant 'tickets'. Detailed directions will also be required to ensure that matters are considered in the right sequence – ie broadly, all the stages of the judicial review first so as to ensure that there is clarity as to exactly what options are before the Court of Protection when it comes to consider where P's best interests will lie.

24.8 Finally, we should emphasise (as did Eleanor King J at first instance in *ACCG*) that it is vital that there is clarity in respect of the available options as early as can reasonably be achieved (see also paras 10.19 and 10.41). A failure to identify which options are actually on the table and which are not can lead to a party told at the last minute that an option is not available feeling – quite understandably – that the 'ground has been cut from under their feet by ... the public authorities' "knock out blow" '.[7] It may well be the case that the public authority, for good reason, may well not wish to commit itself to a stark statement that 'option A is not available' so as to allow room for discussion and the maintenance of a working relationship. However, if the reality is that it is not, it is likely to be better for this to be established sooner rather than later, if for no other reason than a failure to do so will inevitably lead to a prolonging of proceedings – and of consequent expense – which are, on a proper analysis, futile. It is to be hoped that the introduction of the Case Management Pilot (discussed in chapter 4 and chapter 10) will assist significantly in this regard.

The approach of the Administrative Court

24.9 It is of considerable importance to remember that the fact that a person lacks the capacity to decide (for instance) where they should live:

> ... does not import the test of 'what is in her best interests?' as the yardstick by which all care decisions are to be made ... Section 1(5) of the Act applies to 'an act done, or decision made ... for or on behalf of a person who lacks capacity'. Its decision-making criteria and procedures are designed to be a substitute for the lack of independent capacity of the person to act or take decisions for him or herself. They

---

7 [2013] EWHC 3859 (COP), [2014] COPLR 11 at para 46. See also para 102 of the judgment of Sir James Munby P in the Court of Appeal.

come into play in circumstances where a person with capacity would take, or participate in the taking of, a decision.[8]

24.10 In other words, very many decisions relating to the provision of care by public bodies to adults lacking capacity to take material decisions are not, on a proper analysis, best interests decisions falling within the scope of the MCA 2005. Rather, they are decisions taken as to (1) what the adult's needs are; and (2) how those needs are to be met. They are decisions taken by reference to substantial bodies of legislation and of case-law that apply to all adults, not just those who lack capacity in one or more regards;[9] they are therefore precisely the sort of decisions that have conventionally fallen – and continue to fall – to be decided in the Administrative Court by reference to the well-developed tests that apply when that court is considering whether the public bodies in question have erred in their decision-making.

24.11 Space precludes a detailed discussion here of the tests that apply in judicial review proceedings,[10] but it is important to note that the crucial distinction between the approach of the Administrative Court and the approach of the Court of Protection is that the former is (broadly) focused upon the process by which the public body has taken the decision in question; the latter is, itself, the decision-maker and will therefore engage in a detailed examination of the merits of the various options before it. This hard-edged distinction can appear to be blurred in certain categories of cases, in particular those requiring the assessment by the Administrative Court of the proportionality of any interference with rights under the ECHR, but even in such cases the Administrative Court will not, formally, be conducting a review of the merits of the decision and will not therefore be standing in the shoes of the decision-maker.[11]

---

8 R (Chatting) v (1) Viridian Housing (2) Wandsworth LBC [2012] EWHC 3595 (Admin), [2013] COPLR 108 at paras 99–100 per Nicholas Paines QC sitting as a Deputy High Court Judge. This passage was endorsed by the Court of Appeal in Re MN (at para 24).
9 See eg (for England) Stephen Knafler QC, *Adult Social Care Law*, LAG 2016 and Tim Spencer-Lane, *Care Act Manual*, Sweet & Maxwell, 2nd edition, 2015.
10 See, in this regard, in particular, Jonathan Manning, Sarah Salmon and Robert Brown, *Judicial review proceedings: a practitioner's guide*, LAG, 3rd edn, 2013.
11 See R (A) v Chief Constable of Kent [2013] EWCA Civ 1706; (2014) 135 BMLR 22.

CHAPTER 25

Human rights and the Court of Protection

25.1	Introduction
25.2	Relying upon the ECHR in the course of proceedings
25.6	Human Rights Act 1998 declarations and damages
25.15	The Convention on the Rights of Persons with Disabilities

Introduction

25.1 The Court of Protection is, almost by definition, a court whose every substantive decision will be taken after balancing different rights arising under the European Convention on Human Rights (ECHR), both those of P and – frequently – those of third parties (most often family members) upon whom the court's decisions in relation to P will impact. In this chapter, we outline briefly some of the key points that advisers need to consider in relation to the ECHR, in particularly when it comes to seeking redress for breaches of the ECHR. We also touch upon the impact of the Convention on the Rights of Persons with Disabilities (CRPD).

Relying upon the ECHR in the course of proceedings

25.2 The ECHR permeates all aspects of the decision-making of the Court of Protection, both as to case management and as regards the decisions and declarations that it makes at the end of proceedings. We have touched upon specific procedural considerations at relevant points in the balance of this book. For instance, questions of disclosure (and withholding of disclosure) engage difficult balancing exercises between the different ECHR rights of the parties involved (see paras 12.102 onwards). The particular procedural issues arising in relation to cases involving deprivation of liberty as covered in chapter 21. A brief overview of the provisions of the ECHR that are likely to be most relevant to the court in deciding what substantive declarations and decisions to grant can be found at paras 4.39–4.42.[1]

25.3 The Court of Appeal in *Re MN*[2] confirmed that the Court of Protection has jurisdiction to hear a claim under the Human Rights Act (HRA) 1998 s7 that a public body has acted (or proposed to act) incompatibly with the ECHR. We address the issue of where the breach has already happened in the next section, but for present purposes focus on the issue of what a party should do when the actions of the public body are still 'live' – in other words, where they have the potential, if reversed or changed, to impact upon the decisions that the Court of Protection might make in relation to P. In

---

1 A good introduction to the ECHR and to the Human Rights Act 1998 is Wadham et al, *Blackstone's Guide to the Human Rights Act 1998*, Oxford University Press, 7th edition, 2015.
2 *Re MN (Adult)* [2015] EWCA Civ 411, [2016] Fam 87, (2015) 18 CCLR 521.

MN, the decision in question was a decision not to fund a particular care package. The Court of Appeal confirmed that the court might, exceptionally, have to consider whether the actions of the public body breached the relevant party's human rights (and, for those purposes, consider what decision it might make in P's best interests if the care package or other relevant service was hypothetically 'on the table.').

25.4 The decision of the Court of Appeal is under appeal at the time of writing, listed before the Supreme Court in December 2016. Until and unless reversed, it is clear that it will only be an exceptional case in the court which will engage in a hypothetical assessment of where P's best interests may lie for purposes of determining a claim based upon HRA 1998 s7(1)(b). Otherwise, and as discussed in chapter 24, claims as to whether a public body has acted lawfully (including by reference to their obligations under the HRA) should be brought in the Administrative Court.

25.5 If a party wishes the court to carry out the 'exceptional' assessment of a hypothetical option on the basis set out in the paragraphs immediately above, then the following will apply:

- the claim must be formulated and pleaded properly by reference to HRA 1998 s7(1)(b); and
- the claim will then be dealt with by the Court of Protection as part of the main proceedings: it will not be treated as a discrete issue separated from the rest of the case.[3]

Human Rights Act 1998 declarations and damages

25.6 The Court of Protection has a jurisdiction to grant:

- a declaration that the ECHR rights of P have been breached;[4]
- a declaration that the ECHR rights of another person who can claim to be a victim have been breached;[5]
- damages under HRA 1998 s8 where such are required to afford just satisfaction for either category of breach;[6]

---

3 *Re MN (Adult)* [2015] EWCA Civ 411, [2016] Fam 87 at para 85, applying *Re V* [2004] 1 FLR 944.
4 *YA(F) v A local authority and others* [2010] EWHC 2770, [2010] COPLR Con Vol 1226.
5 *YA(F)*. See also *City of Sunderland v MM and others* [2009] COPLR Con Vol 881.
6 *YA(F)*.

- a declaration under HRA 1998 s4 that a provision of the Mental Capacity Act (MCA) 2005 is incompatible with the ECHR.[7] To date, no declarations have been granted (or, indeed, sought, at least in any reported case).

25.7 There is now an increasing body of first instance decisions from the Court of Protection providing (most commonly by endorsing consent orders) for declarations and/or damages in respect of breaches of Articles 5 and 8 ECHR committed by public bodies. That body of decisions represents the tip of an iceberg of unreported cases in which claims have been settled.

25.8 The case-law was usefully summarised in *Essex County Council v RF*,[8] in which the District Judge also gave an indication of a 'tariff' of damages for an unlawful deprivation of liberty of between £3,000 and £4,000 per month where the individual would not have been detained had the public body in question acted lawfully. The decision is not binding authority, but the authors are aware that this 'tariff' is regularly used by both practitioners and the courts in assessing offers and settlements in relation to compensation in the field of deprivation of liberty.

25.9 It is, however, important to understand that where the responsible body can show that deprivation of liberty would have happened in any event and caused no loss to the individual (ie that the breach of Article 5 was 'technical' or 'procedural'), then the person is likely to recover only nominal damages (ie £1) and/or the court will simply make a declaration that their rights under Article 5 have been breached as the necessary 'just satisfaction'.[9] It is unlikely that public funding will be available to bring a claim where it is likely simply to result in such a declaration (see further chapter 6).

25.10 If a declaration or damages for a breach of rights under the ECHR is sought, it is necessary that the precise basis for this claim be set out. Practice Direction (PD) 11A, dealing with HRA claims, outlines the relevant procedure at paras 1–3 for making a claim, but in summary the most important requirement is that it is set out as soon as practicable so that the other parties and the court are aware that a specific claim in this regard is being made.

25.11 A specific procedure must be followed if a declaration of incompatibility is sought, including notice to and the joining of the Crown.[10]

7 COPR r83(1) and HRA 1998 s4(5)(f).
8 [2015] EWCOP 1.
9 HRA 1998 s8(3).
10 PD 11A paras 4–8.

The entirety of a case from the permission stage onwards in which a declaration of incompatibility is sought must be heard before the President of the Family Division, the Chancellor or by a High Court judge nominated to sit in the Court of Protection.[11]

25.12 Claims for declarations/damages under the HRA 1998 that follow on the substantive determination by the Court of Protection of questions of P's best interests have sometimes been brought either in the county court (or, if it is a high value claim) in the Queen's Bench Division of the High Court. There is no reason in principle why this aspect of the claim cannot be heard before the Court of Protection and, as suggested above, this has the advantage that the judge in question will be familiar with all of the surrounding issues. It also has the advantage that the Court of Protection judge can approve any settlement (ie negotiated compromise) without the need for further judicial intervention. A precedent for a settlement order can be found online at www.courtofprotectionhandbook.com/precedents.

25.13 Some Court of Protection judges are reluctant to address 'historic' breaches of rights under the ECHR, preferring to focus upon P's best interests now and for the future. Whilst understandable, we suggest that this should be resisted, because of the inevitable need for duplication of effort and delay in recovering damages for P in a separate claim in the county court or the Queen's Bench Division of the High Court. At a minimum, we suggest, it is strongly advisable to seek declarations from the Court of Protection judge as to the breaches of P's rights upon which a claim in the county court or Queen's Bench Division can be brought.

25.14 The only sound reason for 'hiving off' HRA 1998 aspects is that the standard costs rules in civil proceedings will apply, by contrast to the specific rules that apply in the Court of Protection (as to which, see chapter 16). If it appears that the defendant public authority is likely to contest the HRA 1998 claim, then it may be prudent to proceed before the civil courts so that a full award of costs can be sought against the public authority. If P is publicly funded then if this civil claim is, in turn, compromised, care will need to be taken to ensure that the costs consequences are considered both by reference to the costs in the civil proceedings and before the Court of Protection so as to ensure that, insofar as possible, any damages awarded to P are not then swallowed up by the statutory charge imposed by the Legal Aid Agency (LAA). This is addressed at paras 6.76–6.79.

---

11 PD 11A para 9.

Practice points

- Identify the HRA issue as early as possible. It should be mentioned in documents such as position statements so that the court is aware of the potential claim, even if the respondent is already aware of it.
- If it is decided to pursue a claim for declarations or damages under the HRA 1998 in the Court of Protection, the court should be invited to make directions to resolve the issue when making case management decisions. Initially these could simply provide a timetable for a letter before claim and response, before a decision is taken as to whether to proceed.
- It is prudent to ensure that it is possible to identify all time that is spent on the HRA points, as opposed to welfare issues. This will make it much easier to produce a schedule of costs.
- PD 11A specifies that in the event that HRA claims are made they are either identified in the COP1 or made on a COP9 form. Either way the claim should be fully pleaded.
- The court will then need to case manage the claim, and it is our advice that these directions should be kept distinct from directions to resolve welfare issues. This will make it easier to keep track of work being carried out for this purpose as opposed to work on the welfare aspect of the case. The first step will be for the respondent to the HRA claim to file and serve a defence. The judge will then be able to assess what further evidence is required to resolve the claim.
- In the event that the claim is compromised the court will need to approve the award. The COPR do not provide for this; and we would advise applying the provisions of CPR Part 21 in drafting an advice or position statement for the court, which explains the rationale for recommending acceptance.

The Convention on the Rights of Persons with Disabilities

25.15 The United Nations Convention on the Rights of Persons with Disabilities (CRPD) was concluded in 2006 and ratified by the United Kingdom in 2009. The convention seeks to bring about a radical change in the approach adopted in the social, political and legal arenas to those suffering from disabilities (and, indeed, to the very concept of disability). Among other provisions, it seeks to bring about a fundamental shift away from the taking of decisions on behalf of individuals on the basis of an asserted lack of capacity. A good guide to the CRPD and its implications for English law can be found in Lucy Series, 'Comparing old and new paradigms of legal capacity'.[12]

25.16 At least as interpreted by the Committee on the Rights of Persons with Disabilities, compliance with Article 12 CPRD (which provides for equal recognition before the law) means that states party to the CPRD should replace legislation providing for substitute decision-making for incapacitated adults based 'on what is believed to be in the objective "best interests" of the person concerned, as opposed to being based on the person's own will and preferences'.[13]

25.17 There is a considerable debate as to the precise meaning of Article 12 and its implications for national legislatures, in particular those of the countries which are also bound by obligations under the ECHR.[14] However, on its face, the MCA 2005 is not compatible with Article 12, not least because reliance on a 'diagnostic threshold' as a component of the test for mental incapacity (see further chapter 3) does not comply with the anti-discrimination requirements of Article CRPD. Further, there is a good argument that the current configuration of its best interests standard fails to incorporate the safeguards required by Article 12(4), by failing to ensure that sufficient weight is placed upon the person's wishes and feelings (or in the language of the Convention) their 'will and preferences'.[15] There are other Articles of the CRPD with which the compatibility of the MCA 2005 is doubtful,[16] but

12 [2014] Eld LJ 62. See also the report by the Essex Autonomy Project Three Jurisdictions Project entitled *Towards Compliance with CRPD Art. 12 in Capacity/Incapacity Legislation across the UK* (2016), available at http://autonomy.essex.ac.uk/eap-three-jurisdictions-report.

13 Committee on the Rights of Persons with Disabilities, 'General Comment on Article 12: Equal Recognition before the law', para 23; available at: www.ohchr.org/EN/HRBodies/CRPD/Pages/GC.aspx.

14 See, for instance, Philip Fennell and Urfan Khaliq, 'Conflicting or complementary obligations? The UN Disability Rights Convention, the European Convention on Human Rights and English law', *European Human Rights Law Review*, No 6 (2011): pp662–674.

15 See further the report by the Essex Autonomy Project Three Jurisdictions Project entitled *Towards Compliance with CRPD Art. 12 in Capacity/Incapacity Legislation across the UK* (2016). Available at http://autonomy.essex.ac.uk/eap-three-jurisdictions-report.

16 Most obviously Article 14, which on its face cannot be squared with ECHR Article 5 (right to liberty).

Article 12 poses the most direct challenge to the MCA 2005 as currently drafted.

25.18 While the CRPD has not been incorporated into domestic law, the Court of Appeal has endorsed it as having persuasive authority as an aid to interpretation.[17] It was referred to by the Supreme Court in the seminal decision upon deprivation of liberty under the MCA 2005, *P v Cheshire West*[18] (discussed in more detail in chapter 21), has been referred to, essentially in passing, in a number of cases before the Court of Protection[19] and it is now regularly referred to by the European Court of Human Rights. It has, though, yet to be the subject of any detailed consideration by the Court of Protection. This may, in part, be because the obligations that it imposes are at the state level, rather than (for instance) at the level of the discharge by either public authorities or courts of their respective functions under domestic legislation. It is also likely, however, that this is as much a function of the fact that the CRPD is – as yet – remarkably little known by practitioners.

25.19 That having been said, the CRPD is already beginning to make its impact in law reform terms. The Law Commission of England and Wales has provisionally proposed that the MCA 2005 should be amended to establish that decision-makers should begin with the assumption that the person's past and present wishes and feelings should be determinative of the best interests' decision.[20] The final report of the Law Commission and draft legislation is anticipated by the end of 2016.

25.20 The Committee on the Rights of Persons with Disabilities is due to consider the UK's compliance with the CRPD (both in respect of England and Wales and the regimes in Northern Ireland and Scotland) in the course of 2017; what will happen in this regard (and what the government will do in response either to the Committee's report or the Law Commission's recommendation) is not clear at the time of writing.

---

17 *Burnip v Birmingham City Council and another* [2012] EWCA Civ 629, [2013] PTSR 117 (obiter, in the context of interpretation of Article 14 ECHR).
18 *P (by his litigation friend the Official Solicitor) v Cheshire West and Chester Council and another, and P and Q (by their litigation friend the Official Solicitor) v Surrey CC* [2014] UKSC 19, [2014] 2 WLR 642, (2014) 17 CCLR 5.
19 The first being *An NHS Trust v DE* [2013] EWHC 2562 (Fam), [2013] COPLR 531.
20 Law Commission, 2015: Mental Capacity and Deprivation of Liberty: A Consultation Paper (Consultation Paper No 222).

25.21 In the interim, however, it is suggested that it is entirely in order for practitioners to rely upon the provisions of the CRPD to support arguments that:

- In deciding whether all practicable steps have been taken without success before concluding that P lacks capacity (MCA 2005 s1(3)), the Court of Protection must be astute to examine precisely what support mechanisms have been put in place to enable P to participate in the decision in respect of which their capacity is questioned and – where necessary – to direct that such support mechanisms be provided. An example of such support – directed during the currency of proceedings – would be that given to DE[21] by way of education, which allowed him to attain capacity to consent to sexual relations.
- P must be supported to participate as fully as possible in the proceedings before the Court of Protection (consistent with the emphasis also placed by the European Court of Human Rights of the importance of such participation by reference to the provisions of the ECHR: see paras 15.34ff);
- Particular weight must be placed upon P's wishes and feelings in the determination of where their best interests may lie. Indeed, it can be suggested that, where it is possible to identify which of the available options P would have chosen then that gives the answer as to where their best interests will lie for purposes of MCA 2005 s4, regardless of whether this is an option that the professionals (or indeed the court) consider to be 'wise'.

---

21 *An NHS Trust v DE* [2013] EWHC 2562 (Fam), [2013] COPLR 531.

CHAPTER 26

Cross-border matters

26.1	Introduction
26.5	What counts as a foreign jurisdiction?
26.6	The basis of jurisdiction of the Court of Protection
26.9	Recognition and enforcement of foreign protective measures
26.12	Foreign lasting powers of attorney

Introduction

26.1 The majority of cases before the Court of Protection concern the property or personal welfare of people who are habitually resident in England and Wales. However, the Mental Capacity Act (MCA) 2005 also includes detailed provisions relating to the powers of the court over people who are habitually resident other than in England but in respect of whom, for whatever reason, declarations or decisions are sought. This might be, for instance, because an incapacitated adult has been kidnapped from their home country and brought to England and Wales. In such a case, an order may well be sought in their home country seeking their return; Schedule 3 to the MCA 2005 contains provisions detailing when and how such an order would be given effect by the Court of Protection. Alternatively, a question might arise as to the proper disposal of property in England belonging to someone habitually resident abroad upon whose behalf decisions are now being taken by a guardian appointed under the laws of that country.

26.2 The private international law rules governing decision-making for incapacitated adults with a foreign connection is a complex topic, a full discussion of which lies outside the scope of this book.[1] The complications are only increased by the fact that MCA 2005 Sch 3 implements – as the law of Wales – many of the provisions of the Hague Convention on the International Protection of Adults 2000 ('Hague 35'), but the UK has not, to date, ratified the convention as regards England and Wales.[2]

26.3 This chapter limits itself to highlighting those jurisdictional questions that are most likely to arise in the court setting before noting the position in relation to foreign lasting powers of attorney (LPAs) (ie powers made under other legal systems which have a similar effect to LPAs).

26.4 Practitioners should be aware that it is likely that procedural rules for applications engaging MCA 2005 Sch 3 will be enacted in due course; updates can be found at www.courtofprotectionhandbook.com.

---

1 Readers are directed to Frimston et al, *International Protection of Adults*, Oxford University Press, 2015.
2 It has done so in respect of Scotland.

What counts as a foreign jurisdiction?

26.5 It is important to realise that, for purposes of proceedings before the Court of Protection, both Scotland and Northern Ireland count as foreign jurisdictions.[3] This means, therefore, that a move of an incapacitated adult from England to Scotland would give rise to a cross-border jurisdictional question; as would questions concerning the exercise of a Scottish power of attorney in England.

The basis of jurisdiction of the Court of Protection

26.6 The Court of Protection has jurisdiction to make declarations and decisions under MCA 2005 ss15–16 in relation to:
- an adult habitually resident in England and Wales;
- an adult's property in England and Wales;
- an adult present in England and Wales or who has property there, if the matter is urgent; or
- an adult present in England and Wales, if a protective measure which is temporary and limited in its effect to England and Wales is proposed in relation to him.[4]

26.7 'Habitual residence' is not defined in the MCA 2005, but the phrase has been the subject of judicial consideration. Above all, it is 'a question of fact to be determined in the individual circumstances of the case'.[5] In the case of an adult who lacks the capacity to decide where to live, habitual residence can in principle be lost and another habitual residence acquired without the need for any court order or other formal process, such as the appointment of an attorney or deputy.[6] If an adult has been moved across borders, then a central question in deciding whether their habitual residence has changed will be whether there has been any element of wrongfulness in the

---

3 MCA 2005 Sch 3 para 1.
4 MCA 2005 Sch 3 para 7(1).
5 *Re MN (recognition and enforcement of foreign protective measures)* [2010] EWHC 1926 (Fam), [2010] COPLR Con Vol 893 at para 22. See also *An English Local Authority v SW* [2014] EWCOP 43, [2015] COPLR 29 and *Re DB*; *Re EC* [2016] EWCOP 30, [2016] COPLR 450.
6 *Re PO* [2013] EWHC 3932 (COP), [2014] Fam 197, para 18.

move.[7] Habitual residence can in principle be lost and another habitual residence acquired on the same day.[8]

26.8 An adult is deemed to be habitually resident in England and Wales if:

- their habitual residence cannot be determined;
- they are a refugee; or
- they have been displaced as a result of disturbance in the country of their habitual residence.[9]

Recognition and enforcement of foreign protective measures

26.9 Perhaps the most important function of the provisions of MCA 2005 Sch 3 is to put in place a mechanism for declarations to be obtained that foreign 'protective measures' be recognised and enforced in England and Wales. Such 'protective measures' will include any measure directed to the protection of the person or property of an adult, who for these purposes is any person over 16[10] who, as a result of an impairment or insufficiency of his personal faculties, cannot protect their interests.[11] The MCA 2005 gives examples of such protective measures;[12] examples that have come before the Court of Protection include:

- an order made by a Californian court requiring the return of an adult to California after her removal from the jurisdiction to England in questionable circumstances;[13] and

---

7 *Re MN* (move in apparent breach of instruction in Californian Advance Healthcare Directive); or *Re HM (vulnerable adult: abduction)* [2010] EWHC 870 (Fam), [2010] 2 FLR 1057 (move in breach of a court order).
8 *Re PO* [2013] EWHC 3932 (COP), [2014] Fam 197 at para 17.
9 MCA 2005 Sch 3 para 7(2).
10 Except if they are aged 16 or 17 and subject to the provisions either of the 1996 Convention on the Jurisdiction, Applicable Law, Recognition, Enforcement and Co-operation in respect of Parental Responsibility and Measures for the Protection of Children or Council Regulation (2201/2003) concerning jurisdiction and the recognition and enforcement of judgments in matrimonial matters and the matters of parental responsibility.
11 MCA 2005 Sch 3 para 4.
12 MCA 2005 Sch 3 para 5.
13 *Re MN*.

- the placement of Irish nationals in an English psychiatric institution by way of an order made in the High Court in the Republic of Ireland.[14]

It is important to note that, for these purposes, a protective measure includes not just single court orders but also the appointment of a guardian or equivalent by the relevant authorities in the foreign jurisdiction.

26.10 Where a measure has been taken on the ground that an adult is habitually resident in any foreign jurisdiction (including, for these purposes, Scotland and Northern Ireland[15]), any interested person can apply to the Court of Protection for a declaration that it is to be recognised in England and Wales.[16] Such an application will almost invariably be accompanied by an application that the measure be declared enforceable here as well.[17] Although neither the MCA 2005 nor (at present) the Court of Protection Rules (COPR) set down any formal procedure by which applications for recognition and enforcement are to be made, they should be made by way of a standard COP1 application,[18] and do not require permission.[19] They should be accompanied by full details and – where relevant – a certified translation of the relevant order(s) and any underlying judgment. As noted at the outset of this chapter, it is likely that specific provision will be made within the COPR for such applications, accompanied by a Practice Direction outlining the relevant evidential requirements.

26.11 A judge of the Court of Protection asked to recognise and/or declare enforceable a foreign protective measure operates within strict limits. Their role is confined, in essence, to scrutinising whether core procedural and substantive rights have been complied with.[20] They cannot, in particular, conduct their own analysis of where the adult's best interests may lie, although they can – and must – consider the adult's best interests in deciding how the measure is to be implemented.[21]

---

14 *Re M* [2010] EWHC 1926 (Fam) [2012] COPLR 430; *Re PA & Ors* [2015] EWCOP 38, [2016] Fam 47.
15 By virtue of the definition of 'country' given in MCA 2005 Sch 3 para 1.
16 MCA 2005 Sch 3 para 20(1).
17 MCA 2005 Sch 3 para 22(1).
18 As happened in *Re MN*.
19 MCA 2005 Sch 3 para 20(2).
20 See *Re PA & Ors* [2015] EWCOP 38, [2016] Fam 47.
21 *Re MN* at paras 29 and 31; and MCA 2005 Sch 3 para 12.

Foreign lasting powers of attorney

26.12 An adult who is habitually resident other than in England and Wales at the point of making a lasting power of attorney (LPA)[22] can specify that they want English law to apply to questions of existence, extent, modification or extinction, if:
- they do so in writing; and
- they are:
  - a UK national;
  - they have previously been habitually resident in England and Wales; or
  - they have property here (subject to the limitation that they are only entitled to specify that English law applies in relation to the property here).[23]

If they do not make any such specification, then the law of the country in which they were habitually resident at the point of making the power will apply.

26.13 A foreign LPA – ie made by someone habitually resident other than in England and Wales at the point of making it – is automatically effective in England and Wales if it satisfies the requirements of the law that applies under the test set out in the paragraph immediately above.[24] If, though, the foreign power is not exercised in a manner sufficient to guarantee the protection of the person or property of the donor, the Court of Protection can – if it has jurisdiction over the person or their property (applying the tests set out in para 26.6 above) disapply or modify the power.[25]

26.14 It should be noted that – as matters stand – the Office of the Public Guardian does not register foreign LPAs alongside those of English powers. If a bank or other institution is not willing to accept that a foreign LPA is effective, then, assuming that the jurisdictional test set out in para 26.6 above is met, it may be necessary to bring an application to the Court of Protection for a declaration that – for instance – the attorney is acting lawfully in exercising the foreign power in England and Wales. Such an application is not an applica-

---

22 Which will include a power of like effect to an English LPA: MCA 2005 Sch 6 para 6(c).
23 MCA 2005 Sch 3 para 12(2)(b).
24 This flows from MCA 2005 Sch 3 para 13(1)–(2).
25 MCA 2005 Sch 3 para 14(1).

tion for recognition and enforcement;[26] it is likely, however, that a specific procedure will be established in due course within the COPR for such applications to be made.

26.15 The situation described immediately above is not satisfactory; in due course, if ratification of Hague 35 is extended to England and Wales, then the situation will improve – at least between contracting states to Hague 35. Under Article 38 of Hague 35, authorities of a contracting state to the Convention where a measure of protection has been taken or a power of representation confirmed can issue to the person entrusted with the protection of the adult's person or property a certificate indicating the capacity in which the person is entitled to act and the powers conferred. Under a provision of the MCA 2005 which will come into force upon ratification with effect to England and Wales,[27] such a certificate would stand – unless the contrary is shown – as proof of the capacity in which the representative acts and the powers conferred upon them by the power of representation.

---

26 See Frimston et al, *International protection of adults*, chapter 9. This is by contrast with an application by a guardian appointed by a foreign court for recognition and enforcement of their appointment, which would be such an application.

27 They are not currently in force: *Re PO* at para 9.

CHAPTER 27

Instructing experts in Court of Protection cases[1]

27.1	Introduction
27.2	**Psychiatrists**
27.2	Persuading psychiatrists to get involved in a case
27.4	Instructions
	Expertise • Evidence of mental disorder • Assessment of capacity • Practicalities
27.13	Supporting the expert in court
27.14	**Nurses**
27.14	How a nursing report can assist the court
27.17	Types of registered nurse
27.19	Instructing the nurse

---

1 The section of this chapter on psychiatrists is written by Dr Ian Hall, Consultant Psychiatrist for People with Learning Disability, East London NHS Foundation Trust; Associate Dean, Royal College of Psychiatrists; the section on nurses by Lynne Phair, Independent Consultant Nurse and Expert Witness.

Introduction

27.1 This chapter is concerned with instructing two different types of experts before the Court of Protection, psychiatrists and nurses. Both sections of the chapter are written by experts in their disciplines who regularly give evidence before the court, and outline the specific considerations relevant to instructing psychiatrist and nurses respectively. In broad terms, however, the points that they make as to how to instruct and support an expert are equally applicable to an expert of any kind. The chapter should also be read with chapter 12 on expert evidence.

Psychiatrists

Persuading psychiatrists to get involved in a case

27.2 Psychiatrists are medically qualified doctors that specialise in helping people with mental disorders. The vast majority of consultant psychiatrists in the UK do most or all of their clinical work in the NHS, and therefore lead busy professional lives. Why would anyone with such commitments be interested in taking on the additional role of being an expert witness for the Court of Protection?

27.3 The simple answer might be because of the fee, or because it is a fairly local case and therefore easy to arrange. But there are other motivators instructing lawyers can appeal to. Psychiatrists working in psychiatric specialties where mental capacity is often an issue – such as psychiatry of learning disability or psychiatry of old age – may have developed a particular interest in Court of Protection work. For any psychiatrist, doing such work gives the opportunity to do a very thorough and detailed assessment of a case, and particularly in cases where an opinion about best interests is sought, it can be very appealing to be essentially speaking up for the person with a mental disorder. Those that are highly experienced in court work may relish particularly interesting cases where new case-law may be made. Others may welcome the whole court experience as something they can use to train junior doctors or other team members.

Instructions

Expertise

27.4 The letter of instruction is obviously crucial to getting a report that addresses the issues you want. It is helpful to be explicit about the role of the expert in the case, and particularly which parties are instructing the expert. Questions need to be as clear as possible, and within the expertise of the psychiatrist. If you are not sure about what might be within their expertise, then it can be helpful to discuss this with the psychiatrist before the letter of instruction is finalised. Having said that, the diagnosis and treatment of mental disorder, and the assessment of capacity are core skills. Commenting on best interests can be within their expertise, particularly when it concerns directly, or has some bearing on medical or psychiatric assessment and treatment. Because of this concern about appropriate expertise, it is important to instruct a psychiatrist from the right subspeciality. As well as General Adult Psychiatrists, there are specialist psychiatrists for Older Adults; for Children and Adolescents; and for People with Learning (Intellectual) Disability. There are also Forensic Psychiatrists for people with mental disorder who are involved in criminal proceedings.

27.5 Some psychiatrists focus almost exclusively on medico-legal work, and have developed great expertise in the technical aspects of report writing and giving evidence. However, if they have not been in clinical practice for some time, then their knowledge and skills about current psychiatric practice may be more limited, and their expertise brought into question.

Evidence of mental disorder

27.6 When outlining the circumstances of the case, the medical and psychiatric history is highly relevant and any psychiatrist would be grateful for as much detail as possible in this area, and permission to access medical records is usually very helpful.

27.7 An essential element to assessing capacity is determining whether there is a mental disorder present, and assessing the nature and severity of that disorder. Therefore any evidence of mental disorder is really helpful. Obviously this may include previous psychiatric assessments, but psychology assessments, especially psychometric assessments (eg IQ assessments), occupational therapy assessments (eg standardised assessments of skills) and speech and language therapy assessments (eg of communication skills) can all be very valuable. It is also helpful to have detailed descriptions of any recent events or behaviour that have led to concerns about the person being mentally unwell. Previous assessments of capacity are also essential material to include, as are details of any particular attempts that have been made to support decision making in the past.

Assessment of capacity

27.8 Assessment of capacity requires a determination of the information needed to make the decision. It is therefore important to have all the background information relevant to the decision, such as social work reports or statements for welfare decisions, and medical reports for medical decisions. It is of course very helpful if the court has made a determination of the information needed to make the decision in the particular case or if there is any relevant case law about the type of decision in question (eg capacity to consent to sex, capacity to decide residence).

27.9 In cases where there are disputes about capacity or best interests, there are often others involved who have a powerful influence on the person. Because this can substantially affect the ability to weigh information up in the process of making a decision (especially where capacity is borderline) it is important to know as much as possible about this. Sometimes where there are disputes about best interests, there can be significant mental health issues in the family (whether diagnosed or not) and it is very helpful to have full details of such concerns.

Practicalities

27.10 It is important to give contact details for people the psychiatrist need to get history from, or will need to discuss best interests with, or who can assist in setting up the assessment. In order to maximise decision-making ability, it is often helpful to see the person in an environment with which they are familiar, and multiple visits may be required, depending on the complexity of the questions, and how the person is able to engage in the assessment.

27.11 Having described above the sort of information that is very helpful to the assessment, this does not mean that the psychiatrist needs to see the whole court bundle, and judicious limiting of the reading is helpful, especially if opinions about best interests decisions are not required.

27.12 Because the psychiatrist is likely to have many other commitments, it is important to set a realistic timetable for the assessment of at least a few weeks unless the clinical or social situation is very urgent.

Supporting the expert in court

27.13 Many psychiatrists can be anxious about giving oral evidence in court, so it is very helpful if a clear idea of issues to be discussed can be given in advance so that they can prepare properly. Often psychiatrists will be asked questions in court that stray outside their area of expertise, and it is of course for the expert witness to point this out. However, it also helps not to be asked the question in the first place. Psychiatrists are usually happy to participate in meetings of experts, as this is more akin to clinical practice than the more adversarial court process. Finally, on a practical note, it is of course very helpful to fix dates and times as far in advance as possible, bearing in mind that if a case is listed for several days, psychiatrists in clinical practice are unlikely to be able to keep the whole period free, so guidance should be given about when their evidence is likely to be required.

Nurses

How a nursing report can assist the court

27.14 Many people who lack capacity will have care and support needs and although the use of an independent social worker is relatively common, it has recently become more common to instruct a registered nurse to assist the court.

27.15 A registered nurse can assist the court in understanding several different matters of importance:

- **P's care needs.** Often the care of P can appear simple, basic or routine, yet is often complex, unpredictable and intense. A nurse expert can give a perspective on current and future care needs, as well as how any medical condition from which P suffers impacts upon those needs, including by way of identifying issues regarding prescribing, administration, effectiveness and use of medication (including as required or 'PRN' medication). Although a nurse cannot give a prognosis an experienced nurse can also assist in advising on advanced care planning and possible end-of-life care needs. Whilst funding of care is not a matter that directly falls for consideration by the Court of Protection, a nurse expert will be able to identify whether the person should be assessed for NHS Continuing Healthcare (if not already in place) which could influence access to an increased level of services. Finally, the need for 24-hour registered nursing involvement at home if P is currently living in a nursing home is often given as a reason for not permitting P to go home. An expert nurse is able to advise as to whether such involvement is, in fact, required, or whether any particular procedure(s) can be undertaken by others with appropriate training or by the oversight of community nurse.

- **P's understanding of their needs.** From visiting and talking to P (often more than once), a nurse expert will be able to establish from P their understanding of their own care needs. A nurse will be able to decipher non-technical terms and P's own perspective as to their condition and assess the level and depth of their understanding of their needs and risks of alternative care provision. Whilst other professionals can also undertake this assessment, a nurse will be able to bring an expert perspective to bear upon whether P is likely to be able to gain further knowledge and understanding of their care needs;
- **How P's current or proposed setting affects their care needs.** Care packages and approaches to supporting a person to live independently are constantly changing. The nurse will be able to give an opinion on the care delivered, its suitability and/or alternative approaches if required. The nurse will also be able to address how P's wellbeing and quality of life is affected by the location of care, type of care and the quality of care. The location of care should be considered not simply by reference to the location, funding and the registration category of the care provider but also whether it meets the social, cultural and emotional needs of P. This not only refers to ethnicity and religion but also refers to social status and to P's personal values. The nurse will also be able to advise the court as to concerns raised in regulatory inspection reports, whether any concerns have been rectified since publication and how any concerns may affect the care of P;
- **The family's perspective.** Family relationships may be straightforward with all members of the family in agreement with their opinions of what is best for P. In other situations there may be complicated family dynamics with fractions, disagreement and diverse opinions. On other occasions the family members may be viewed by health or social care professionals as obstructive, subversive and sometimes responsible for abuse of P. Conversely the family may not trust any professionals and believe they have ulterior motives for their decisions. The reasons for any mistrust are varied and may be due to misunderstanding, poor communication, lack of understanding on either side and unwillingness to listen (to the professionals) or unwillingness on the part of the professional to appreciate the learned skills and knowledge of the family for caregiver. A nurse expert may well be able to assist in identifying the causes of (and potential solutions for) this mistrust

for the benefit of the court. Moreover, and given that families and professionals will have to continue to work together after the court process is finished, a nurse expert may well be able to assist in bringing about the mutual understanding required to enable this continuing relationship;
- **Potential safeguarding concerns.** The nurse may be able to assist the court by making observations about safeguarding matters that are contentious, for example bruising or pressure ulcers. The nurse will not be able to investigate these concerns but may be able to comment on the enquiry that should have taken place at the time of the alleged incident and offer an opinion as to the future risks of any concerns.

27.16 It is also important to note that a good nursing expert, by taking part in a professionals' meeting with those involved in the case, can assist in the resolution of the case for two reasons:
- Firstly by reassuring the professionals that the expert witness is not 'any better than them', merely looking at the same situation from a different perspective.
- Secondly, because health and social care professionals often become anxious when anything 'becomes legal' and lawyers get involved, which only adds to any tension already present between parties. The nurse expert can assist in reducing these anxieties.

Types of registered nurse

27.17 Nursing is a diverse profession and there are numerous specialities within it. The main qualifications relevant to the court of protection are Registered General Nurse (RGN), Registered Mental Nurse (RMN) and Registered Learning Disability Nurse (RLDN).[2] Within these branches of the profession the nurses will specialise according to patient's needs, age or location of care. There will be nurses who have vast experience in one location of care and predominantly treated one care group but have no experience at all in other locations of care which may be considered by the court. A person's diagnosis may appear to be the information most essential in identifying the most appropriate nurse but the diagnosis may be secondary to the care needs now presenting.

27.18 The lawyer should consider whether the nurse has experience and expertise in the identified care needs of the person, rather than

---

2 In each case, 'Registered' means registered with the Nursing and Midwifery Council, which can be checked with the person's name or PIN number.

simply the diagnosis and in the various care settings being suggested. The nurse should have experience that is relevant and up-to-date. Nurses who work independently may be well placed to provide a court report if they have experience in a variety of settings or models of care delivery and they may be more accommodating with court directions and timescales; they may also still be in current practice across a wide range of services. Whilst there are no specific role titles which will indicate whether they have the requisite skill to give an expert report, it is likely that a nurse who has master's degree, is an Independent Prescriber and has fulfilled the role of consultant nurse, nurse specialist or a community matron will have the requisite skills. They will also need to have undertaken training as an expert witness.

Instructing the nurse

27.19 To obtain a satisfactory report, the lawyer needs to consider providing the following to the nurse expert:
- clear instructions setting out all the options required to be examined;
- details of the locations to be visited;
- contact details of the family and professionals involved;
- clear identification of the family groups and any conflicts;
- provide historical and current care records relevant to the issues to be explored (historical records being of importance where the report requires an opinion as to whether P can return to a specific location where a care package has previously failed; and
- details of any advocates or communication aids, or translators that may be required to support P in talking to the nurse.

APPENDICES

A **Primary legislation** 589
   Mental Capacity Act 2005   590
   Human Rights Act 1998 ss3, 6–8 and Sch 1   697

B **Secondary legislation** 705
   Court of Protection Rules 2007   706
   Court of Protection Case Management Pilot Rules 2016   772
   Mental Capacity Act 2005 (Transfer of Proceedings) Order 2007   792
   Court of Protection Fees Order 2007 (as amended)   794

C **Civil Procedure Rules costs provisions as applied in the Court of Protection** 805

D **Statements and letters** 815
   1 Pre-issue letter   816
   2 Position statement   819
   3 Witness statement   822
   4 Letter of instruction to expert   825
   5 Letter of instruction for testamentary capacity assessment from GP   839

E **Checklists for best interests assessment, care planning and transition planning** 841

F **Court of Protection fees** 847

G **Useful addresses and resources** 849

APPENDIX A

Primary legislation[1]

Mental Capacity Act 2005   590
Human Rights Act 1998 ss3, 6–8 and Sch 1   697

---

1 © Crown copyright. Legislation is reproduced up to date to 1 November 2016.

MENTAL CAPACITY ACT 2005

Part 1: Persons who lack capacity

The principles

The principles

1 (1) The following principles apply for the purposes of this Act.
(2) A person must be assumed to have capacity unless it is established that he lacks capacity.
(3) A person is not to be treated as unable to make a decision unless all practicable steps to help him to do so have been taken without success.
(4) A person is not to be treated as unable to make a decision merely because he makes an unwise decision.
(5) An act done, or decision made, under this Act for or on behalf of a person who lacks capacity must be done, or made, in his best interests.
(6) Before the act is done, or the decision is made, regard must be had to whether the purpose for which it is needed can be as effectively achieved in a way that is less restrictive of the person's rights and freedom of action.

Preliminary

People who lack capacity

2 (1) For the purposes of this Act, a person lacks capacity in relation to a matter if at the material time he is unable to make a decision for himself in relation to the matter because of an impairment of, or a disturbance in the functioning of, the mind or brain.
(2) It does not matter whether the impairment or disturbance is permanent or temporary.
(3) A lack of capacity cannot be established merely by reference to–
 (a) a person's age or appearance, or
 (b) a condition of his, or an aspect of his behaviour, which might lead others to make unjustified assumptions about his capacity.
(4) In proceedings under this Act or any other enactment, any question whether a person lacks capacity within the meaning of this Act must be decided on the balance of probabilities.
(5) No power which a person ('D') may exercise under this Act–
 (a) in relation to a person who lacks capacity, or
 (b) where D reasonably thinks that a person lacks capacity,
 is exercisable in relation to a person under 16.
(6) Subsection (5) is subject to section 18(3).

Inability to make decisions

3 (1) For the purposes of section 2, a person is unable to make a decision for himself if he is unable–
 (a) to understand the information relevant to the decision,
 (b) to retain that information,
 (c) to use or weigh that information as part of the process of making the decision, or
 (d) to communicate his decision (whether by talking, using sign language or any other means).

(2) A person is not to be regarded as unable to understand the information relevant to a decision if he is able to understand an explanation of it given to him in a way that is appropriate to his circumstances (using simple language, visual aids or any other means).
(3) The fact that a person is able to retain the information relevant to a decision for a short period only does not prevent him from being regarded as able to make the decision.
(4) The information relevant to a decision includes information about the reasonably foreseeable consequences of–
   (a) deciding one way or another, or
   (b) failing to make the decision.

Best interests

4 (1) In determining for the purposes of this Act what is in a person's best interests, the person making the determination must not make it merely on the basis of–
   (a) the person's age or appearance, or
   (b) a condition of his, or an aspect of his behaviour, which might lead others to make unjustified assumptions about what might be in his best interests.
(2) The person making the determination must consider all the relevant circumstances and, in particular, take the following steps.
(3) He must consider–
   (a) whether it is likely that the person will at some time have capacity in relation to the matter in question, and
   (b) if it appears likely that he will, when that is likely to be.
(4) He must, so far as reasonably practicable, permit and encourage the person to participate, or to improve his ability to participate, as fully as possible in any act done for him and any decision affecting him.
(5) Where the determination relates to life-sustaining treatment he must not, in considering whether the treatment is in the best interests of the person concerned, be motivated by a desire to bring about his death.
(6) He must consider, so far as is reasonably ascertainable–
   (a) the person's past and present wishes and feelings (and, in particular, any relevant written statement made by him when he had capacity),
   (b) the beliefs and values that would be likely to influence his decision if he had capacity, and
   (c) the other factors that he would be likely to consider if he were able to do so.
(7) He must take into account, if it is practicable and appropriate to consult them, the views of–
   (a) anyone named by the person as someone to be consulted on the matter in question or on matters of that kind,
   (b) anyone engaged in caring for the person or interested in his welfare,
   (c) any donee of a lasting power of attorney granted by the person, and
   (d) any deputy appointed for the person by the court,
   as to what would be in the person's best interests and, in particular, as to the matters mentioned in subsection (6).
(8) The duties imposed by subsections (1) to (7) also apply in relation to the exercise of any powers which–
   (a) are exercisable under a lasting power of attorney, or
   (b) are exercisable by a person under this Act where he reasonably believes that another person lacks capacity.

(9) In the case of an act done, or a decision made, by a person other than the court, there is sufficient compliance with this section if (having complied with the requirements of subsections (1) to (7)) he reasonably believes that what he does or decides is in the best interests of the person concerned.
(10) 'Life-sustaining treatment' means treatment which in the view of a person providing health care for the person concerned is necessary to sustain life.
(11) 'Relevant circumstances' are those–
(a) of which the person making the determination is aware, and
(b) which it would be reasonable to regard as relevant.

Restriction on deprivation of liberty
4A(1) This Act does not authorise any person ('D') to deprive any other person ('P') of his liberty.
(2) But that is subject to–
(a) the following provisions of this section, and
(b) section 4B.
(3) D may deprive P of his liberty if, by doing so, D is giving effect to a relevant decision of the court.
(4) A relevant decision of the court is a decision made by an order under section 16(2)(a) in relation to a matter concerning P's personal welfare.
(5) D may deprive P of his liberty if the deprivation is authorised by Schedule A1 (hospital and care home residents: deprivation of liberty).

Deprivation of liberty necessary for life-sustaining treatment etc
4B(1) If the following conditions are met, D is authorised to deprive P of his liberty while a decision as respects any relevant issue is sought from the court.
(2) The first condition is that there is a question about whether D is authorised to deprive P of his liberty under section 4A.
(3) The second condition is that the deprivation of liberty–
(a) is wholly or partly for the purpose of–
(i) giving P life-sustaining treatment, or
(ii) doing any vital act, or
(b) consists wholly or partly of–
(i) giving P life-sustaining treatment, or
(ii) doing any vital act.
(4) The third condition is that the deprivation of liberty is necessary in order to–
(a) give the life-sustaining treatment, or
(b) do the vital act.
(5) A vital act is any act which the person doing it reasonably believes to be necessary to prevent a serious deterioration in P's condition.

Acts in connection with care or treatment
5(1) If a person ('D') does an act in connection with the care or treatment of another person ('P'), the act is one to which this section applies if–
(a) before doing the act, D takes reasonable steps to establish whether P lacks capacity in relation to the matter in question, and
(b) when doing the act, D reasonably believes–
(i) that P lacks capacity in relation to the matter, and
(ii) that it will be in P's best interests for the act to be done.

(2) D does not incur any liability in relation to the act that he would not have incurred if P–
  (a) had had capacity to consent in relation to the matter, and
  (b) had consented to D's doing the act.
(3) Nothing in this section excludes a person's civil liability for loss or damage, or his criminal liability, resulting from his negligence in doing the act.
(4) Nothing in this section affects the operation of sections 24 to 26 (advance decisions to refuse treatment).

Section 5 acts: limitations

6 (1) If D does an act that is intended to restrain P, it is not an act to which section 5 applies unless two further conditions are satisfied.
  (2) The first condition is that D reasonably believes that it is necessary to do the act in order to prevent harm to P.
  (3) The second is that the act is a proportionate response to–
    (a) the likelihood of P's suffering harm, and
    (b) the seriousness of that harm.
  (4) For the purposes of this section D restrains P if he–
    (a) uses, or threatens to use, force to secure the doing of an act which P resists, or
    (b) restricts P's liberty of movement, whether or not P resists.
  (5) [Repealed.]
  (6) Section 5 does not authorise a person to do an act which conflicts with a decision made, within the scope of his authority and in accordance with this Part, by–
    (a) a donee of a lasting power of attorney granted by P, or
    (b) a deputy appointed for P by the court.
  (7) But nothing in subsection (6) stops a person–
    (a) providing life-sustaining treatment, or
    (b) doing any act which he reasonably believes to be necessary to prevent a serious deterioration in P's condition,
  while a decision as respects any relevant issue is sought from the court.

Payment for necessary goods and services

7 (1) If necessary goods or services are supplied to a person who lacks capacity to contract for the supply, he must pay a reasonable price for them.
  (2) 'Necessary' means suitable to a person's condition in life and to his actual requirements at the time when the goods or services are supplied.

Expenditure

8 (1) If an act to which section 5 applies involves expenditure, it is lawful for D–
    (a) to pledge P's credit for the purpose of the expenditure, and
    (b) to apply money in P's possession for meeting the expenditure.
  (2) If the expenditure is borne for P by D, it is lawful for D–
    (a) to reimburse himself out of money in P's possession, or
    (b) to be otherwise indemnified by P.
  (3) Subsections (1) and (2) do not affect any power under which (apart from those subsections) a person–
    (a) has lawful control of P's money or other property, and
    (b) has power to spend money for P's benefit.

Lasting powers of attorney

Lasting powers of attorney

9 (1) A lasting power of attorney is a power of attorney under which the donor ('P') confers on the donee (or donees) authority to make decisions about all or any of the following–
  (a) P's personal welfare or specified matters concerning P's personal welfare, and
  (b) P's property and affairs or specified matters concerning P's property and affairs,
  and which includes authority to make such decisions in circumstances where P no longer has capacity.
(2) A lasting power of attorney is not created unless–
  (a) section 10 is complied with,
  (b) an instrument conferring authority of the kind mentioned in subsection (1) is made and registered in accordance with Schedule 1, and
  (c) at the time when P executes the instrument, P has reached 18 and has capacity to execute it.
(3) An instrument which–
  (a) purports to create a lasting power of attorney, but
  (b) does not comply with this section, section 10 or Schedule 1,
  confers no authority.
(4) The authority conferred by a lasting power of attorney is subject to–
  (a) the provisions of this Act and, in particular, sections 1 (the principles) and 4 (best interests), and
  (b) any conditions or restrictions specified in the instrument.

Appointment of donees

10 (1) A donee of a lasting power of attorney must be–
  (a) an individual who has reached 18, or
  (b) if the power relates only to P's property and affairs, either such an individual or a trust corporation.
(2) An individual who is bankrupt or is a person in relation to whom a debt relief order is made may not be appointed as donee of a lasting power of attorney in relation to P's property and affairs.
(3) Subsections (4) to (7) apply in relation to an instrument under which two or more persons are to act as donees of a lasting power of attorney.
(4) The instrument may appoint them to act–
  (a) jointly,
  (b) jointly and severally, or
  (c) jointly in respect of some matters and jointly and severally in respect of others.
(5) To the extent to which it does not specify whether they are to act jointly or jointly and severally, the instrument is to be assumed to appoint them to act jointly.
(6) If they are to act jointly, a failure, as respects one of them, to comply with the requirements of subsection (1) or (2) or Part 1 or 2 of Schedule 1 prevents a lasting power of attorney from being created.
(7) If they are to act jointly and severally, a failure, as respects one of them, to comply with the requirements of subsection (1) or (2) or Part 1 or 2 of Schedule 1–
  (a) prevents the appointment taking effect in his case, but

(b) does not prevent a lasting power of attorney from being created in the case of the other or others.

(8) An instrument used to create a lasting power of attorney–
(a) cannot give the donee (or, if more than one, any of them) power to appoint a substitute or successor, but
(b) may itself appoint a person to replace the donee (or, if more than one, any of them) on the occurrence of an event mentioned in section 13(6)(a) to (d) which has the effect of terminating the donee's appointment.

Lasting powers of attorney: restrictions

11 (1) A lasting power of attorney does not authorise the donee (or, if more than one, any of them) to do an act that is intended to restrain P, unless three conditions are satisfied.
(2) The first condition is that P lacks, or the donee reasonably believes that P lacks, capacity in relation to the matter in question.
(3) The second is that the donee reasonably believes that it is necessary to do the act in order to prevent harm to P.
(4) The third is that the act is a proportionate response to–
(a) the likelihood of P's suffering harm, and
(b) the seriousness of that harm.
(5) For the purposes of this section, the donee restrains P if he–
(a) uses, or threatens to use, force to secure the doing of an act which P resists, or
(b) restricts P's liberty of movement, whether or not P resists,
or if he authorises another person to do any of those things.
(6) [Repealed.]
(7) Where a lasting power of attorney authorises the donee (or, if more than one, any of them) to make decisions about P's personal welfare, the authority–
(a) does not extend to making such decisions in circumstances other than those where P lacks, or the donee reasonably believes that P lacks, capacity,
(b) is subject to sections 24 to 26 (advance decisions to refuse treatment), and
(c) extends to giving or refusing consent to the carrying out or continuation of a treatment by a person providing health care for P.
(8) But subsection (7)(c)–
(a) does not authorise the giving or refusing of consent to the carrying out or continuation of life-sustaining treatment, unless the instrument contains express provision to that effect, and
(b) is subject to any conditions or restrictions in the instrument.

Scope of lasting powers of attorney: gifts

12 (1) Where a lasting power of attorney confers authority to make decisions about P's property and affairs, it does not authorise a donee (or, if more than one, any of them) to dispose of the donor's property by making gifts except to the extent permitted by subsection (2).
(2) The donee may make gifts–
(a) on customary occasions to persons (including himself) who are related to or connected with the donor, or
(b) to any charity to whom the donor made or might have been expected to make gifts,

if the value of each such gift is not unreasonable having regard to all the circumstances and, in particular, the size of the donor's estate.
(3) 'Customary occasion' means–
   (a) the occasion or anniversary of a birth, a marriage or the formation of a civil partnership, or
   (b) any other occasion on which presents are customarily given within families or among friends or associates.
(4) Subsection (2) is subject to any conditions or restrictions in the instrument.

Revocation of lasting powers of attorney etc
13 (1) This section applies if–
   (a) P has executed an instrument with a view to creating a lasting power of attorney, or
   (b) a lasting power of attorney is registered as having been conferred by P, and in this section references to revoking the power include revoking the instrument.
(2) P may, at any time when he has capacity to do so, revoke the power.
(3) P's bankruptcy, or the making of a debt relief order (under Part 7A of the Insolvency Act 1986) in respect of P, revokes the power so far as it relates to P's property and affairs.
(4) But where P is bankrupt merely because an interim bankruptcy restrictions order has effect in respect of him or where P is subject to an interim debt relief restrictions order (under Schedule 4ZB of the Insolvency Act 1986), the power is suspended, so far as it relates to P's property and affairs, for so long as the order has effect.
(5) The occurrence in relation to a donee of an event mentioned in subsection (6)–
   (a) terminates his appointment, and
   (b) except in the cases given in subsection (7), revokes the power.
(6) The events are–
   (a) the disclaimer of the appointment by the donee in accordance with such requirements as may be prescribed for the purposes of this section in regulations made by the Lord Chancellor,
   (b) subject to subsections (8) and (9), the death or bankruptcy of the donee or the making of a debt relief order (under Part 7A of the Insolvency Act 1986) in respect of the donee or, if the donee is a trust corporation, its winding-up or dissolution,
   (c) subject to subsection (11), the dissolution or annulment of a marriage or civil partnership between the donor and the donee,
   (d) the lack of capacity of the donee.
(7) The cases are–
   (a) the donee is replaced under the terms of the instrument,
   (b) he is one of two or more persons appointed to act as donees jointly and severally in respect of any matter and, after the event, there is at least one remaining donee.
(8) The bankruptcy of a donee or the making of a debt relief order (under Part 7A of the Insolvency Act 1986) in respect of a donee does not terminate his appointment, or revoke the power, in so far as his authority relates to P's personal welfare.

(9) Where the donee is bankrupt merely because an interim bankruptcy restrictions order has effect in respect of him, or where the donee is subject to an interim debt relief restrictions order (under Schedule 4ZB of the Insolvency Act 1986), his appointment and the power are suspended, so far as they relate to P's property and affairs, for so long as the order has effect.

(10) Where the donee is one of two or more appointed to act jointly and severally under the power in respect of any matter, the reference in subsection (9) to the suspension of the power is to its suspension in so far as it relates to that donee.

(11) The dissolution or annulment of a marriage or civil partnership does not terminate the appointment of a donee, or revoke the power, if the instrument provided that it was not to do so.

Protection of donee and others if no power created or power revoked

14 (1) Subsections (2) and (3) apply if–
   (a) an instrument has been registered under Schedule 1 as a lasting power of attorney, but
   (b) a lasting power of attorney was not created,
   whether or not the registration has been cancelled at the time of the act or transaction in question.

(2) A donee who acts in purported exercise of the power does not incur any liability (to P or any other person) because of the non-existence of the power unless at the time of acting he–
   (a) knows that a lasting power of attorney was not created, or
   (b) is aware of circumstances which, if a lasting power of attorney had been created, would have terminated his authority to act as a donee.

(3) Any transaction between the donee and another person is, in favour of that person, as valid as if the power had been in existence, unless at the time of the transaction that person has knowledge of a matter referred to in subsection (2).

(4) If the interest of a purchaser depends on whether a transaction between the donee and the other person was valid by virtue of subsection (3), it is conclusively presumed in favour of the purchaser that the transaction was valid if–
   (a) the transaction was completed within 12 months of the date on which the instrument was registered, or
   (b) the other person makes a statutory declaration, before or within 3 months after the completion of the purchase, that he had no reason at the time of the transaction to doubt that the donee had authority to dispose of the property which was the subject of the transaction.

(5) In its application to a lasting power of attorney which relates to matters in addition to P's property and affairs, section 5 of the Powers of Attorney Act 1971 (c 27) (protection where power is revoked) has effect as if references to revocation included the cessation of the power in relation to P's property and affairs.

(6) Where two or more donees are appointed under a lasting power of attorney, this section applies as if references to the donee were to all or any of them.

General powers of the court and appointment of deputies

Power to make declarations

15 (1) The court may make declarations as to—
  (a) whether a person has or lacks capacity to make a decision specified in the declaration;
  (b) whether a person has or lacks capacity to make decisions on such matters as are described in the declaration;
  (c) the lawfulness or otherwise of any act done, or yet to be done, in relation to that person.
 (2) 'Act' includes an omission and a course of conduct.

Powers to make decisions and appoint deputies: general

16 (1) This section applies if a person ('P') lacks capacity in relation to a matter or matters concerning–
  (a) P's personal welfare, or
  (b) P's property and affairs.
 (2) The court may–
  (a) by making an order, make the decision or decisions on P's behalf in relation to the matter or matters, or
  (b) appoint a person (a 'deputy') to make decisions on P's behalf in relation to the matter or matters.
 (3) The powers of the court under this section are subject to the provisions of this Act and, in particular, to sections 1 (the principles) and 4 (best interests).
 (4) When deciding whether it is in P's best interests to appoint a deputy, the court must have regard (in addition to the matters mentioned in section 4) to the principles that–
  (a) a decision by the court is to be preferred to the appointment of a deputy to make a decision, and
  (b) the powers conferred on a deputy should be as limited in scope and duration as is reasonably practicable in the circumstances.
 (5) The court may make such further orders or give such directions, and confer on a deputy such powers or impose on him such duties, as it thinks necessary or expedient for giving effect to, or otherwise in connection with, an order or appointment made by it under subsection (2).
 (6) Without prejudice to section 4, the court may make the order, give the directions or make the appointment on such terms as it considers are in P's best interests, even though no application is before the court for an order, directions or an appointment on those terms.
 (7) An order of the court may be varied or discharged by a subsequent order.
 (8) The court may, in particular, revoke the appointment of a deputy or vary the powers conferred on him if it is satisfied that the deputy–
  (a) has behaved, or is behaving, in a way that contravenes the authority conferred on him by the court or is not in P's best interests, or
  (b) proposes to behave in a way that would contravene that authority or would not be in P's best interests.

Section 16 powers: Mental Health Act patients etc

16A(1) If a person is ineligible to be deprived of liberty by this Act, the court may not include in a welfare order provision which authorises the person to be deprived of his liberty.

(2) If–
  (a) a welfare order includes provision which authorises a person to be deprived of his liberty, and
  (b) that person becomes ineligible to be deprived of liberty by this Act,
  the provision ceases to have effect for as long as the person remains ineligible.
(3) Nothing in subsection (2) affects the power of the court under section 16(7) to vary or discharge the welfare order.
(4) For the purposes of this section–
  (a) Schedule 1A applies for determining whether or not P is ineligible to be deprived of liberty by this Act;
  (b) 'welfare order' means an order under section 16(2)(a).

Section 16 powers: personal welfare

17 (1) The powers under section 16 as respects P's personal welfare extend in particular to–
  (a) deciding where P is to live;
  (b) deciding what contact, if any, P is to have with any specified persons;
  (c) making an order prohibiting a named person from having contact with P;
  (d) giving or refusing consent to the carrying out or continuation of a treatment by a person providing health care for P;
  (e) giving a direction that a person responsible for P's health care allow a different person to take over that responsibility.
(2) Subsection (1) is subject to section 20 (restrictions on deputies).

Section 16 powers: property and affairs

18 (1) The powers under section 16 as respects P's property and affairs extend in particular to–
  (a) the control and management of P's property;
  (b) the sale, exchange, charging, gift or other disposition of P's property;
  (c) the acquisition of property in P's name or on P's behalf;
  (d) the carrying on, on P's behalf, of any profession, trade or business;
  (e) the taking of a decision which will have the effect of dissolving a partnership of which P is a member;
  (f) the carrying out of any contract entered into by P;
  (g) the discharge of P's debts and of any of P's obligations, whether legally enforceable or not;
  (h) the settlement of any of P's property, whether for P's benefit or for the benefit of others;
  (i) the execution for P of a will;
  (j) the exercise of any power (including a power to consent) vested in P whether beneficially or as trustee or otherwise;
  (k) the conduct of legal proceedings in P's name or on P's behalf.
(2) No will may be made under subsection (1)(i) at a time when P has not reached 18.
(3) The powers under section 16 as respects any other matter relating to P's property and affairs may be exercised even though P has not reached 16, if the court considers it likely that P will still lack capacity to make decisions in respect of that matter when he reaches 18.
(4) Schedule 2 supplements the provisions of this section.

(5) Section 16(7) (variation and discharge of court orders) is subject to paragraph 6 of Schedule 2.
(6) Subsection (1) is subject to section 20 (restrictions on deputies).

Appointment of deputies
19 (1) A deputy appointed by the court must be–
  (a) an individual who has reached 18, or
  (b) as respects powers in relation to property and affairs, an individual who has reached 18 or a trust corporation.
(2) The court may appoint an individual by appointing the holder for the time being of a specified office or position.
(3) A person may not be appointed as a deputy without his consent.
(4) The court may appoint two or more deputies to act–
  (a) jointly,
  (b) jointly and severally, or
  (c) jointly in respect of some matters and jointly and severally in respect of others.
(5) When appointing a deputy or deputies, the court may at the same time appoint one or more other persons to succeed the existing deputy or those deputies–
  (a) in such circumstances, or on the happening of such events, as may be specified by the court;
  (b) for such period as may be so specified.
(6) A deputy is to be treated as P's agent in relation to anything done or decided by him within the scope of his appointment and in accordance with this Part.
(7) The deputy is entitled–
  (a) to be reimbursed out of P's property for his reasonable expenses in discharging his functions, and
  (b) if the court so directs when appointing him, to remuneration out of P's property for discharging them.
(8) The court may confer on a deputy powers to–
  (a) take possession or control of all or any specified part of P's property;
  (b) exercise all or any specified powers in respect of it, including such powers of investment as the court may determine.
(9) The court may require a deputy–
  (a) to give to the Public Guardian such security as the court thinks fit for the due discharge of his functions, and
  (b) to submit to the Public Guardian such reports at such times or at such intervals as the court may direct.

Restrictions on deputies
20 (1) A deputy does not have power to make a decision on behalf of P in relation to a matter if he knows or has reasonable grounds for believing that P has capacity in relation to the matter.
(2) Nothing in section 16(5) or 17 permits a deputy to be given power–
  (a) to prohibit a named person from having contact with P;
  (b) to direct a person responsible for P's health care to allow a different person to take over that responsibility.
(3) A deputy may not be given powers with respect to–
  (a) the settlement of any of P's property, whether for P's benefit or for the benefit of others,

(b) the execution for P of a will, or
(c) the exercise of any power (including a power to consent) vested in P whether beneficially or as trustee or otherwise.

(4) A deputy may not be given power to make a decision on behalf of P which is inconsistent with a decision made, within the scope of his authority and in accordance with this Act, by the donee of a lasting power of attorney granted by P (or, if there is more than one donee, by any of them).

(5) A deputy may not refuse consent to the carrying out or continuation of life-sustaining treatment in relation to P.

(6) The authority conferred on a deputy is subject to the provisions of this Act and, in particular, sections 1 (the principles) and 4 (best interests).

(7) A deputy may not do an act that is intended to restrain P unless four conditions are satisfied.

(8) The first condition is that, in doing the act, the deputy is acting within the scope of an authority expressly conferred on him by the court.

(9) The second is that P lacks, or the deputy reasonably believes that P lacks, capacity in relation to the matter in question.

(10) The third is that the deputy reasonably believes that it is necessary to do the act in order to prevent harm to P.

(11) The fourth is that the act is a proportionate response to–
(a) the likelihood of P's suffering harm, and
(b) the seriousness of that harm.

(12) For the purposes of this section, a deputy restrains P if he–
(a) uses, or threatens to use, force to secure the doing of an act which P resists, or
(b) restricts P's liberty of movement, whether or not P resists,
or if he authorises another person to do any of those things.

(13) [Repealed.]

Transfer of proceedings relating to people under 18

21 (1) The Lord Chief Justice, with the concurrence of the Lord Chancellor, may by order make provision as to the transfer of proceedings relating to a person under 18, in such circumstances as are specified in the order–
(a) from the Court of Protection to a court having jurisdiction under the Children Act 1989, or
(b) from a court having jurisdiction under that Act to the Court of Protection.

(2) The Lord Chief Justice may nominate any of the following to exercise his functions under this section–
(a) the President of the Court of Protection;
(b) a judicial office holder (as defined in section 109(4) of the Constitutional Reform Act 2005).

Powers of the court in relation to Schedule A1

Powers of court in relation to Schedule A1

21A(1) This section applies if either of the following has been given under Schedule A1–
(a) a standard authorisation;
(b) an urgent authorisation.

(2) Where a standard authorisation has been given, the court may determine any question relating to any of the following matters–
   (a) whether the relevant person meets one or more of the qualifying requirements;
   (b) the period during which the standard authorisation is to be in force;
   (c) the purpose for which the standard authorisation is given;
   (d) the conditions subject to which the standard authorisation is given.
(3) If the court determines any question under subsection (2), the court may make an order–
   (a) varying or terminating the standard authorisation, or
   (b) directing the supervisory body to vary or terminate the standard authorisation.
(4) Where an urgent authorisation has been given, the court may determine any question relating to any of the following matters–
   (a) whether the urgent authorisation should have been given;
   (b) the period during which the urgent authorisation is to be in force;
   (c) the purpose for which the urgent authorisation is given.
(5) Where the court determines any question under subsection (4), the court may make an order–
   (a) varying or terminating the urgent authorisation, or
   (b) directing the managing authority of the relevant hospital or care home to vary or terminate the urgent authorisation.
(6) Where the court makes an order under subsection (3) or (5), the court may make an order about a person's liability for any act done in connection with the standard or urgent authorisation before its variation or termination.
(7) An order under subsection (6) may, in particular, exclude a person from liability.

Powers of the court in relation to lasting powers of attorney

Powers of court in relation to validity of lasting powers of attorney

22 (1) This section and section 23 apply if–
   (a) a person ('P') has executed or purported to execute an instrument with a view to creating a lasting power of attorney, or
   (b) an instrument has been registered as a lasting power of attorney conferred by P.
(2) The court may determine any question relating to–
   (a) whether one or more of the requirements for the creation of a lasting power of attorney have been met;
   (b) whether the power has been revoked or has otherwise come to an end.
(3) Subsection (4) applies if the court is satisfied–
   (a) that fraud or undue pressure was used to induce P–
      (i) to execute an instrument for the purpose of creating a lasting power of attorney, or
      (ii) to create a lasting power of attorney, or
   (b) that the donee (or, if more than one, any of them) of a lasting power of attorney–
      (i) has behaved, or is behaving, in a way that contravenes his authority or is not in P's best interests, or
      (ii) proposes to behave in a way that would contravene his authority or would not be in P's best interests.

(4) The court may–
  (a) direct that an instrument purporting to create the lasting power of attorney is not to be registered, or
  (b) if P lacks capacity to do so, revoke the instrument or the lasting power of attorney.
(5) If there is more than one donee, the court may under subsection (4)(b) revoke the instrument or the lasting power of attorney so far as it relates to any of them.
(6) 'Donee' includes an intended donee.

Powers of court in relation to operation of lasting powers of attorney
23 (1) The court may determine any question as to the meaning or effect of a lasting power of attorney or an instrument purporting to create one.
(2) The court may–
  (a) give directions with respect to decisions–
    (i) which the donee of a lasting power of attorney has authority to make, and
    (ii) which P lacks capacity to make;
  (b) give any consent or authorisation to act which the donee would have to obtain from P if P had capacity to give it.
(3) The court may, if P lacks capacity to do so–
  (a) give directions to the donee with respect to the rendering by him of reports or accounts and the production of records kept by him for that purpose;
  (b) require the donee to supply information or produce documents or things in his possession as donee;
  (c) give directions with respect to the remuneration or expenses of the donee;
  (d) relieve the donee wholly or partly from any liability which he has or may have incurred on account of a breach of his duties as donee.
(4) The court may authorise the making of gifts which are not within section 12(2) (permitted gifts).
(5) Where two or more donees are appointed under a lasting power of attorney, this section applies as if references to the donee were to all or any of them.

Advance decisions to refuse treatment

Advance decisions to refuse treatment: general
24 (1) 'Advance decision' means a decision made by a person ('P'), after he has reached 18 and when he has capacity to do so, that if–
  (a) at a later time and in such circumstances as he may specify, a specified treatment is proposed to be carried out or continued by a person providing health care for him, and
  (b) at that time he lacks capacity to consent to the carrying out or continuation of the treatment,
  the specified treatment is not to be carried out or continued.
(2) For the purposes of subsection (1)(a), a decision may be regarded as specifying a treatment or circumstances even though expressed in layman's terms.
(3) P may withdraw or alter an advance decision at any time when he has capacity to do so.
(4) A withdrawal (including a partial withdrawal) need not be in writing.

(5) An alteration of an advance decision need not be in writing (unless section 25(5) applies in relation to the decision resulting from the alteration).

Validity and applicability of advance decisions

25 (1) An advance decision does not affect the liability which a person may incur for carrying out or continuing a treatment in relation to P unless the decision is at the material time–
   (a) valid, and
   (b) applicable to the treatment.
(2) An advance decision is not valid if P–
   (a) has withdrawn the decision at a time when he had capacity to do so,
   (b) has, under a lasting power of attorney created after the advance decision was made, conferred authority on the donee (or, if more than one, any of them) to give or refuse consent to the treatment to which the advance decision relates, or
   (c) has done anything else clearly inconsistent with the advance decision remaining his fixed decision.
(3) An advance decision is not applicable to the treatment in question if at the material time P has capacity to give or refuse consent to it.
(4) An advance decision is not applicable to the treatment in question if–
   (a) that treatment is not the treatment specified in the advance decision,
   (b) any circumstances specified in the advance decision are absent, or
   (c) there are reasonable grounds for believing that circumstances exist which P did not anticipate at the time of the advance decision and which would have affected his decision had he anticipated them.
(5) An advance decision is not applicable to life-sustaining treatment unless–
   (a) the decision is verified by a statement by P to the effect that it is to apply to that treatment even if life is at risk, and
   (b) the decision and statement comply with subsection (6).
(6) A decision or statement complies with this subsection only if–
   (a) it is in writing,
   (b) it is signed by P or by another person in P's presence and by P's direction,
   (c) the signature is made or acknowledged by P in the presence of a witness, and
   (d) the witness signs it, or acknowledges his signature, in P's presence.
(7) The existence of any lasting power of attorney other than one of a description mentioned in subsection (2)(b) does not prevent the advance decision from being regarded as valid and applicable.

Effect of advance decisions

26 (1) If P has made an advance decision which is–
   (a) valid, and
   (b) applicable to a treatment,
   the decision has effect as if he had made it, and had had capacity to make it, at the time when the question arises whether the treatment should be carried out or continued.
(2) A person does not incur liability for carrying out or continuing the treatment unless, at the time, he is satisfied that an advance decision exists which is valid and applicable to the treatment.

(3) A person does not incur liability for the consequences of withholding or withdrawing a treatment from P if, at the time, he reasonably believes that an advance decision exists which is valid and applicable to the treatment.
(4) The court may make a declaration as to whether an advance decision–
   (a) exists;
   (b) is valid;
   (c) is applicable to a treatment.
(5) Nothing in an apparent advance decision stops a person–
   (a) providing life-sustaining treatment, or
   (b) doing any act he reasonably believes to be necessary to prevent a serious deterioration in P's condition,
   while a decision as respects any relevant issue is sought from the court.

Excluded decisions

Family relationships etc
27 (1) Nothing in this Act permits a decision on any of the following matters to be made on behalf of a person–
   (a) consenting to marriage or a civil partnership,
   (b) consenting to have sexual relations,
   (c) consenting to a decree of divorce being granted on the basis of two years' separation,
   (d) consenting to a dissolution order being made in relation to a civil partnership on the basis of two years' separation,
   (e) consenting to a child's being placed for adoption by an adoption agency,
   (f) consenting to the making of an adoption order,
   (g) discharging parental responsibilities in matters not relating to a child's property,
   (h) giving a consent under the Human Fertilisation and Embryology Act 1990 (c 37),
   (i) giving a consent under the Human Fertilisation and Embryology Act 2008.
(2) 'Adoption order' means–
   (a) an adoption order within the meaning of the Adoption and Children Act 2002 (c 38) (including a future adoption order), and
   (b) an order under section 84 of that Act (parental responsibility prior to adoption abroad).

Mental Health Act matters
28 (1) Nothing in this Act authorises anyone–
   (a) to give a patient medical treatment for mental disorder, or
   (b) to consent to a patient's being given medical treatment for mental disorder,
   if, at the time when it is proposed to treat the patient, his treatment is regulated by Part 4 of the Mental Health Act.
(1A) Subsection (1) does not apply in relation to any form of treatment to which section 58A of that Act (electro-convulsive therapy, etc) applies if the patient comes within subsection (7) of that section (informal patient under 18 who cannot give consent).
(1B) Section 5 does not apply to an act to which section 64B of the Mental Health Act applies (treatment of community patients not recalled to hospital).
(2) 'Medical treatment', 'mental disorder' and 'patient' have the same meaning as in that Act.

Voting rights
29 (1) Nothing in this Act permits a decision on voting at an election for any public office, or at a referendum, to be made on behalf of a person.
 (2) 'Referendum' has the same meaning as in section 101 of the Political Parties, Elections and Referendums Act 2000 (c 41).

Research

Research
30 (1) Intrusive research carried out on, or in relation to, a person who lacks capacity to consent to it is unlawful unless it is carried out–
 (a) as part of a research project which is for the time being approved by the appropriate body for the purposes of this Act in accordance with section 31, and
 (b) in accordance with sections 32 and 33.
 (2) Research is intrusive if it is of a kind that would be unlawful if it was carried out–
 (a) on or in relation to a person who had capacity to consent to it, but
 (b) without his consent.
 (3) A clinical trial which is subject to the provisions of clinical trials regulations is not to be treated as research for the purposes of this section.
 (3A) Research is not intrusive to the extent that it consists of the use of a person's human cells to bring about the creation *in vitro* of an embryo or human admixed embryo, or the subsequent storage or use of an embryo or human admixed embryo so created.
 (3B) Expressions used in subsection (3A) and in Schedule 3 to the Human Fertilisation and Embryology Act 1990 (consents to use or storage of gametes, embryos or human admixed embryos etc) have the same meaning in that subsection as in that Schedule.
 (4) 'Appropriate body', in relation to a research project, means the person, committee or other body specified in regulations made by the appropriate authority as the appropriate body in relation to a project of the kind in question.
 (5) 'Clinical trials regulations' means–
 (a) the Medicines for Human Use (Clinical Trials) Regulations 2004 (SI No 1031) and any other regulations replacing those regulations or amending them, and
 (b) any other regulations relating to clinical trials and designated by the Secretary of State as clinical trials regulations for the purposes of this section.
 (6) In this section, section 32 and section 34, 'appropriate authority' means–
 (a) in relation to the carrying out of research in England, the Secretary of State, and
 (b) in relation to the carrying out of research in Wales, the National Assembly for Wales.

Requirements for approval
31 (1) The appropriate body may not approve a research project for the purposes of this Act unless satisfied that the following requirements will be met in relation to research carried out as part of the project on, or in relation to, a person who lacks capacity to consent to taking part in the project ('P').

(2) The research must be connected with–
   (a) an impairing condition affecting P, or
   (b) its treatment.
(3) 'Impairing condition' means a condition which is (or may be) attributable to, or which causes or contributes to (or may cause or contribute to), the impairment of, or disturbance in the functioning of, the mind or brain.
(4) There must be reasonable grounds for believing that research of comparable effectiveness cannot be carried out if the project has to be confined to, or relate only to, persons who have capacity to consent to taking part in it.
(5) The research must–
   (a) have the potential to benefit P without imposing on P a burden that is disproportionate to the potential benefit to P, or
   (b) be intended to provide knowledge of the causes or treatment of, or of the care of persons affected by, the same or a similar condition.
(6) If the research falls within paragraph (b) of subsection (5) but not within paragraph (a), there must be reasonable grounds for believing–
   (a) that the risk to P from taking part in the project is likely to be negligible, and
   (b) that anything done to, or in relation to, P will not–
      (i) interfere with P's freedom of action or privacy in a significant way, or
      (ii) be unduly invasive or restrictive.
(7) There must be reasonable arrangements in place for ensuring that the requirements of sections 32 and 33 will be met.

Consulting carers etc

32 (1) This section applies if a person ('R')–
   (a) is conducting an approved research project, and
   (b) wishes to carry out research, as part of the project, on or in relation to a person ('P') who lacks capacity to consent to taking part in the project.
(2) R must take reasonable steps to identify a person who–
   (a) otherwise than in a professional capacity or for remuneration, is engaged in caring for P or is interested in P's welfare, and
   (b) is prepared to be consulted by R under this section.
(3) If R is unable to identify such a person he must, in accordance with guidance issued by the appropriate authority, nominate a person who–
   (a) is prepared to be consulted by R under this section, but
   (b) has no connection with the project.
(4) R must provide the person identified under subsection (2), or nominated under subsection (3), with information about the project and ask him–
   (a) for advice as to whether P should take part in the project, and
   (b) what, in his opinion, P's wishes and feelings about taking part in the project would be likely to be if P had capacity in relation to the matter.
(5) If, at any time, the person consulted advises R that in his opinion P's wishes and feelings would be likely to lead him to decline to take part in the project (or to wish to withdraw from it) if he had capacity in relation to the matter, R must ensure–
   (a) if P is not already taking part in the project, that he does not take part in it;
   (b) if P is taking part in the project, that he is withdrawn from it.

(6) But subsection (5)(b) does not require treatment that P has been receiving as part of the project to be discontinued if R has reasonable grounds for believing that there would be a significant risk to P's health if it were discontinued.
(7) The fact that a person is the donee of a lasting power of attorney given by P, or is P's deputy, does not prevent him from being the person consulted under this section.
(8) Subsection (9) applies if treatment is being, or is about to be, provided for P as a matter of urgency and R considers that, having regard to the nature of the research and of the particular circumstances of the case–
   (a) it is also necessary to take action for the purposes of the research as a matter of urgency, but
   (b) it is not reasonably practicable to consult under the previous provisions of this section.
(9) R may take the action if–
   (a) he has the agreement of a registered medical practitioner who is not involved in the organisation or conduct of the research project, or
   (b) where it is not reasonably practicable in the time available to obtain that agreement, he acts in accordance with a procedure approved by the appropriate body at the time when the research project was approved under section 31.
(10) But R may not continue to act in reliance on subsection (9) if he has reasonable grounds for believing that it is no longer necessary to take the action as a matter of urgency.

Additional safeguards
33 (1) This section applies in relation to a person who is taking part in an approved research project even though he lacks capacity to consent to taking part.
(2) Nothing may be done to, or in relation to, him in the course of the research–
   (a) to which he appears to object (whether by showing signs of resistance or otherwise) except where what is being done is intended to protect him from harm or to reduce or prevent pain or discomfort, or
   (b) which would be contrary to–
      (i) an advance decision of his which has effect, or
      (ii) any other form of statement made by him and not subsequently withdrawn,
   of which R is aware.
(3) The interests of the person must be assumed to outweigh those of science and society.
(4) If he indicates (in any way) that he wishes to be withdrawn from the project he must be withdrawn without delay.
(5) P must be withdrawn from the project, without delay, if at any time the person conducting the research has reasonable grounds for believing that one or more of the requirements set out in section 31(2) to (7) is no longer met in relation to research being carried out on, or in relation to, P.
(6) But neither subsection (4) nor subsection (5) requires treatment that P has been receiving as part of the project to be discontinued if R has reasonable grounds for believing that there would be a significant risk to P's health if it were discontinued.

Loss of capacity during research project

34 (1) This section applies where a person ('P')–
  (a) has consented to take part in a research project begun before the commencement of section 30, but
  (b) before the conclusion of the project, loses capacity to consent to continue to take part in it.
(2) The appropriate authority may by regulations provide that, despite P's loss of capacity, research of a prescribed kind may be carried out on, or in relation to, P if–
  (a) the project satisfies prescribed requirements,
  (b) any information or material relating to P which is used in the research is of a prescribed description and was obtained before P's loss of capacity, and
  (c) the person conducting the project takes in relation to P such steps as may be prescribed for the purpose of protecting him.
(3) The regulations may, in particular,–
  (a) make provision about when, for the purposes of the regulations, a project is to be treated as having begun;
  (b) include provision similar to any made by section 31, 32 or 33.

Independent mental capacity advocate service

Appointment of independent mental capacity advocates

35 (1) The responsible authority must make such arrangements as it considers reasonable to enable persons ('independent mental capacity advocates') to be available to represent and support persons to whom acts or decisions proposed under sections 37, 38 and 39 relate or persons who fall within section 39A, 39C or 39D.
(2) The appropriate authority may make regulations as to the appointment of independent mental capacity advocates.
(3) The regulations may, in particular, provide–
  (a) that a person may act as an independent mental capacity advocate only in such circumstances, or only subject to such conditions, as may be prescribed;
  (b) for the appointment of a person as an independent mental capacity advocate to be subject to approval in accordance with the regulations.
(4) In making arrangements under subsection (1), the responsible authority must have regard to the principle that a person to whom a proposed act or decision relates should, so far as practicable, be represented and supported by a person who is independent of any person who will be responsible for the act or decision.
(5) The arrangements may include provision for payments to be made to, or in relation to, persons carrying out functions in accordance with the arrangements.
(6) For the purpose of enabling him to carry out his functions, an independent mental capacity advocate–
  (a) may interview in private the person whom he has been instructed to represent, and
  (b) may, at all reasonable times, examine and take copies of–

(i) any health record,
(ii) any record of, or held by, a local authority and compiled in connection with a social services function, and
(iii) any record held by a person registered under Part 2 of the Care Standards Act 2000 or Chapter 2 of Part 1 of the Health and Social Care Act 2008,
which the person holding the record considers may be relevant to the independent mental capacity advocate's investigation.
(6A) In subsections (1) and (4), 'the responsible authority' means–
(a) in relation to the provision of the services of independent mental capacity advocates in the area of a local authority in England, that local authority, and
(b) in relation to the provision of the services of independent mental capacity advocates in Wales, the Welsh Ministers.
(6B) In subsection (6A)(a), 'local authority' has the meaning given in section 64(1) except that it does not include the council of a county or county borough in Wales.
(7) In this section, section 36 and section 37, 'the appropriate authority' means–
(a) in relation to the provision of the services of independent mental capacity advocates in England, the Secretary of State, and
(b) in relation to the provision of the services of independent mental capacity advocates in Wales, the National Assembly for Wales.

Functions of independent mental capacity advocates

36 (1) The appropriate authority may make regulations as to the functions of independent mental capacity advocates.
(2) The regulations may, in particular, make provision requiring an advocate to take such steps as may be prescribed for the purpose of–
(a) providing support to the person whom he has been instructed to represent ('P') so that P may participate as fully as possible in any relevant decision;
(b) obtaining and evaluating relevant information;
(c) ascertaining what P's wishes and feelings would be likely to be, and the beliefs and values that would be likely to influence P, if he had capacity;
(d) ascertaining what alternative courses of action are available in relation to P;
(e) obtaining a further medical opinion where treatment is proposed and the advocate thinks that one should be obtained.
(3) The regulations may also make provision as to circumstances in which the advocate may challenge, or provide assistance for the purpose of challenging, any relevant decision.

Provision of serious medical treatment by NHS body

37 (1) This section applies if an NHS body–
(a) is proposing to provide, or secure the provision of, serious medical treatment for a person ('P') who lacks capacity to consent to the treatment, and
(b) is satisfied that there is no person, other than one engaged in providing care or treatment for P in a professional capacity or for remuneration, whom it would be appropriate to consult in determining what would be in P's best interests.

(2) But this section does not apply if P's treatment is regulated by Part 4 or 4A of the Mental Health Act.
(3) Before the treatment is provided, the NHS body must instruct an independent mental capacity advocate to represent P.
(4) If the treatment needs to be provided as a matter of urgency, it may be provided even though the NHS body has not been able to comply with subsection (3).
(5) The NHS body must, in providing or securing the provision of treatment for P, take into account any information given, or submissions made, by the independent mental capacity advocate.
(6) 'Serious medical treatment' means treatment which involves providing, withholding or withdrawing treatment of a kind prescribed by regulations made by the appropriate authority.
(7) 'NHS body' has such meaning as may be prescribed by regulations made for the purposes of this section by–
   (a) the Secretary of State, in relation to bodies in England, or
   (b) the National Assembly for Wales, in relation to bodies in Wales.

Provision of accommodation by NHS body

38 (1) This section applies if an NHS body proposes to make arrangements–
   (a) for the provision of accommodation in a hospital or care home for a person ('P') who lacks capacity to agree to the arrangements, or
   (b) for a change in P's accommodation to another hospital or care home,
and is satisfied that there is no person, other than one engaged in providing care or treatment for P in a professional capacity or for remuneration, whom it would be appropriate for it to consult in determining what would be in P's best interests.
(2) But this section does not apply if P is accommodated as a result of an obligation imposed on him under the Mental Health Act.
(2A) And this section does not apply if–
   (a) an independent mental capacity advocate must be appointed under section 39A or 39C (whether or not by the NHS body) to represent P, and
   (b) the hospital or care home in which P is to be accommodated under the arrangements referred to in this section is the relevant hospital or care home under the authorisation referred to in that section.
(3) Before making the arrangements, the NHS body must instruct an independent mental capacity advocate to represent P unless it is satisfied that–
   (a) the accommodation is likely to be provided for a continuous period which is less than the applicable period, or
   (b) the arrangements need to be made as a matter of urgency.
(4) If the NHS body–
   (a) did not instruct an independent mental capacity advocate to represent P before making the arrangements because it was satisfied that subsection (3)(a) or (b) applied, but
   (b) subsequently has reason to believe that the accommodation is likely to be provided for a continuous period–
      (i) beginning with the day on which accommodation was first provided in accordance with the arrangements, and
      (ii) ending on or after the expiry of the applicable period,
it must instruct an independent mental capacity advocate to represent P.

(5) The NHS body must, in deciding what arrangements to make for P, take into account any information given, or submissions made, by the independent mental capacity advocate.
(6) 'Care home' has the meaning given in section 3 of the Care Standards Act 2000.
(7) 'Hospital' means–
  (a) in relation to England, a hospital as defined by section 275 of the National Health Service Act 2006; and
  (b) in relation to Wales, a health service hospital as defined by section 206 of the National Health Service (Wales) Act 2006 or an independent hospital as defined by section 2 of the Care Standards Act 2000.
(8) 'NHS body' has such meaning as may be prescribed by regulations made for the purposes of this section by–
  (a) the Secretary of State, in relation to bodies in England, or
  (b) the National Assembly for Wales, in relation to bodies in Wales.
(9) 'Applicable period' means–
  (a) in relation to accommodation in a hospital, 28 days, and
  (b) in relation to accommodation in a care home, 8 weeks.
(10) For the purposes of subsection (1), a person appointed under Part 10 of Schedule A1 to be P's representative is not, by virtue of that appointment, engaged in providing care or treatment for P in a professional capacity or for remuneration.

Provision of accommodation by local authority

39 (1) This section applies if a local authority propose to make arrangements–
  (a) for the provision of residential accommodation for a person ('P') who lacks capacity to agree to the arrangements, or
  (b) for a change in P's residential accommodation,
  and are satisfied that there is no person, other than one engaged in providing care or treatment for P in a professional capacity or for remuneration, whom it would be appropriate for them to consult in determining what would be in P's best interests.
(1A) But this section applies only if–
  (a) in the case of a local authority in England, subsection (1B) applies;
  (b) in the case of a local authority in Wales, subsection (2) applies.
(1B) This subsection applies if the accommodation is to be provided in accordance with–
  (a) Part 1 of the Care Act 2014, or
  (b) section 117 of the Mental Health Act.
(2) This subsection applies if the accommodation is to be provided in accordance with–
  (a) Part 4 of the Social Services and Well-being (Wales) Act 2014; or
  (b) section 117 of the Mental Health Act.
(3) This section does not apply if P is accommodated as a result of an obligation imposed on him under the Mental Health Act.
(3A) And this section does not apply if–
  (a) an independent mental capacity advocate must be appointed under section 39A or 39C (whether or not by the local authority) to represent P, and

(b) the place in which P is to be accommodated under the arrangements referred to in this section is the relevant hospital or care home under the authorisation referred to in that section.
(4) Before making the arrangements, the local authority must instruct an independent mental capacity advocate to represent P unless they are satisfied that–
   (a) the accommodation is likely to be provided for a continuous period of less than 8 weeks, or
   (b) the arrangements need to be made as a matter of urgency.
(5) If the local authority–
   (a) did not instruct an independent mental capacity advocate to represent P before making the arrangements because they were satisfied that subsection (4)(a) or (b) applied, but
   (b) subsequently have reason to believe that the accommodation is likely to be provided for a continuous period that will end 8 weeks or more after the day on which accommodation was first provided in accordance with the arrangements,
   they must instruct an independent mental capacity advocate to represent P.
(6) The local authority must, in deciding what arrangements to make for P, take into account any information given, or submissions made, by the independent mental capacity advocate.
(7) For the purposes of subsection (1), a person appointed under Part 10 of Schedule A1 to be P's representative is not, by virtue of that appointment, engaged in providing care or treatment for P in a professional capacity or for remuneration.

Person becomes subject to Schedule A1
39A(1) This section applies if–
   (a) a person ('P') becomes subject to Schedule A1, and
   (b) the managing authority of the relevant hospital or care home are satisfied that there is no person, other than one engaged in providing care or treatment for P in a professional capacity or for remuneration, whom it would be appropriate to consult in determining what would be in P's best interests.
(2) The managing authority must notify the supervisory body that this section applies.
(3) The supervisory body must instruct an independent mental capacity advocate to represent P.
(4) Schedule A1 makes provision about the role of an independent mental capacity advocate appointed under this section.
(5) This section is subject to paragraph 161 of Schedule A1.
(6) For the purposes of subsection (1), a person appointed under Part 10 of Schedule A1 to be P's representative is not, by virtue of that appointment, engaged in providing care or treatment for P in a professional capacity or for remuneration.

Section 39A: supplementary provision
39B(1) This section applies for the purposes of section 39A.
(2) P becomes subject to Schedule A1 in any of the following cases.
(3) The first case is where an urgent authorisation is given in relation to P under

paragraph 76(2) of Schedule A1 (urgent authorisation given before request made for standard authorisation).
(4) The second case is where the following conditions are met.
(5) The first condition is that a request is made under Schedule A1 for a standard authorisation to be given in relation to P ('the requested authorisation').
(6) The second condition is that no urgent authorisation was given under paragraph 76(2) of Schedule A1 before that request was made.
(7) The third condition is that the requested authorisation will not be in force on or before, or immediately after, the expiry of an existing standard authorisation.
(8) The expiry of a standard authorisation is the date when the authorisation is expected to cease to be in force.
(9) The third case is where, under paragraph 69 of Schedule A1, the supervisory body select a person to carry out an assessment of whether or not the relevant person is a detained resident.

Person unrepresented whilst subject to Schedule A1

39C(1) This section applies if–
  (a) an authorisation under Schedule A1 is in force in relation to a person ('P'),
  (b) the appointment of a person as P's representative ends in accordance with regulations made under Part 10 of Schedule A1, and
  (c) the managing authority of the relevant hospital or care home are satisfied that there is no person, other than one engaged in providing care or treatment for P in a professional capacity or for remuneration, whom it would be appropriate to consult in determining what would be in P's best interests.
(2) The managing authority must notify the supervisory body that this section applies.
(3) The supervisory body must instruct an independent mental capacity advocate to represent P.
(4) Paragraph 159 of Schedule A1 makes provision about the role of an independent mental capacity advocate appointed under this section.
(5) The appointment of an independent mental capacity advocate under this section ends when a new appointment of a person as P's representative is made in accordance with Part 10 of Schedule A1.
(6) For the purposes of subsection (1), a person appointed under Part 10 of Schedule A1 to be P's representative is not, by virtue of that appointment, engaged in providing care or treatment for P in a professional capacity or for remuneration.

Person subject to Schedule A1 without paid representative

39D(1) This section applies if–
  (a) an authorisation under Schedule A1 is in force in relation to a person ('P'),
  (b) P has a representative ('R') appointed under Part 10 of Schedule A1, and
  (c) R is not being paid under regulations under Part 10 of Schedule A1 for acting as P's representative.
(2) The supervisory body must instruct an independent mental capacity advocate to represent P in any of the following cases.

(3) The first case is where P makes a request to the supervisory body to instruct an advocate.
(4) The second case is where R makes a request to the supervisory body to instruct an advocate.
(5) The third case is where the supervisory body have reason to believe one or more of the following–
  (a) that, without the help of an advocate, P and R would be unable to exercise one or both of the relevant rights;
  (b) that P and R have each failed to exercise a relevant right when it would have been reasonable to exercise it;
  (c) that P and R are each unlikely to exercise a relevant right when it would be reasonable to exercise it.
(6) The duty in subsection (2) is subject to section 39E.
(7) If an advocate is appointed under this section, the advocate is, in particular, to take such steps as are practicable to help P and R to understand the following matters–
  (a) the effect of the authorisation;
  (b) the purpose of the authorisation;
  (c) the duration of the authorisation;
  (d) any conditions to which the authorisation is subject;
  (e) the reasons why each assessor who carried out an assessment in connection with the request for the authorisation, or in connection with a review of the authorisation, decided that P met the qualifying requirement in question;
  (f) the relevant rights;
  (g) how to exercise the relevant rights.
(8) The advocate is, in particular, to take such steps as are practicable to help P or R–
  (a) to exercise the right to apply to court, if it appears to the advocate that P or R wishes to exercise that right, or
  (b) to exercise the right of review, if it appears to the advocate that P or R wishes to exercise that right.
(9) If the advocate helps P or R to exercise the right of review–
  (a) the advocate may make submissions to the supervisory body on the question of whether a qualifying requirement is reviewable;
  (b) the advocate may give information, or make submissions, to any assessor carrying out a review assessment.
(10) In this section–
  'relevant rights' means–
    (a) the right to apply to court, and
    (b) the right of review;
  'right to apply to court' means the right to make an application to the court to exercise its jurisdiction under section 21A;
  'right of review' means the right under Part 8 of Schedule A1 to request a review.

Limitation on duty to instruct advocate under section 39D
39E (1) This section applies if an advocate is already representing P in accordance with an instruction under section 39D.

616   *Court of Protection Handbook / Appendix A*

(2) Section 39D(2) does not require another advocate to be instructed, unless the following conditions are met.
(3) The first condition is that the existing advocate was instructed–
   (a) because of a request by R, or
   (b) because the supervisory body had reason to believe one or more of the things in section 39D(5).
(4) The second condition is that the other advocate would be instructed because of a request by P.

Exceptions
40 (1) The duty imposed by section 37(3), 38(3) or (4), 39(4) or (5), 39A(3), 39C(3) or 39D(2) does not apply where there is–
   (a) a person nominated by P (in whatever manner) as a person to be consulted on matters to which that duty relates,
   (b) a donee of a lasting power of attorney created by P who is authorised to make decisions in relation to those matters, or
   (c) a deputy appointed by the court for P with power to make decisions in relation to those matters.
(2) A person appointed under Part 10 of Schedule A1 to be P's representative is not, by virtue of that appointment, a person nominated by P as a person to be consulted in matters to which a duty mentioned in subsection (1) relates.

Power to adjust role of independent mental capacity advocate
41 (1) The appropriate authority may make regulations–
   (a) expanding the role of independent mental capacity advocates in relation to persons who lack capacity, and
   (b) adjusting the obligation to make arrangements imposed by section 35.
(2) The regulations may, in particular–
   (a) prescribe circumstances (different to those set out in sections 37, 38 and 39) in which an independent mental capacity advocate must, or circumstances in which one may, be instructed by a person of a prescribed description to represent a person who lacks capacity, and
   (b) include provision similar to any made by section 37, 38, 39 or 40.
(3) 'Appropriate authority' has the same meaning as in section 35.

Miscellaneous and supplementary

Codes of practice
42 (1) The Lord Chancellor must prepare and issue one or more codes of practice–
   (a) for the guidance of persons assessing whether a person has capacity in relation to any matter,
   (b) for the guidance of persons acting in connection with the care or treatment of another person (see section 5),
   (c) for the guidance of donees of lasting powers of attorney,
   (d) for the guidance of deputies appointed by the court,
   (e) for the guidance of persons carrying out research in reliance on any provision made by or under this Act (and otherwise with respect to sections 30 to 34),
   (f) for the guidance of independent mental capacity advocates,
   (fa) for the guidance of persons exercising functions under Schedule A1,
   (fb) for the guidance of representatives appointed under Part 10 of Schedule A1,

(g) with respect to the provisions of sections 24 to 26 (advance decisions and apparent advance decisions), and

(h) with respect to such other matters concerned with this Act as he thinks fit.

(2) The Lord Chancellor may from time to time revise a code.

(3) The Lord Chancellor may delegate the preparation or revision of the whole or any part of a code so far as he considers expedient.

(4) It is the duty of a person to have regard to any relevant code if he is acting in relation to a person who lacks capacity and is doing so in one or more of the following ways–

(a) as the donee of a lasting power of attorney,

(b) as a deputy appointed by the court,

(c) as a person carrying out research in reliance on any provision made by or under this Act (see sections 30 to 34),

(d) as an independent mental capacity advocate,

(da) in the exercise of functions under Schedule A1,

(db) as a representative appointed under Part 10 of Schedule A1,

(e) in a professional capacity,

(f) for remuneration.

(5) If it appears to a court or tribunal conducting any criminal or civil proceedings that–

(a) a provision of a code, or

(b) a failure to comply with a code,

is relevant to a question arising in the proceedings, the provision or failure must be taken into account in deciding the question.

(6) A code under subsection (1)(d) may contain separate guidance for deputies appointed by virtue of paragraph 1(2) of Schedule 5 (functions of deputy conferred on receiver appointed under the Mental Health Act).

(7) In this section and in section 43, 'code' means a code prepared or revised under this section.

Codes of practice: procedure

43 (1) Before preparing or revising a code, the Lord Chancellor must consult–

(a) the National Assembly for Wales, and

(b) such other persons as he considers appropriate.

(2) The Lord Chancellor may not issue a code unless–

(a) a draft of the code has been laid by him before both Houses of Parliament, and

(b) the 40 day period has elapsed without either House resolving not to approve the draft.

(3) The Lord Chancellor must arrange for any code that he has issued to be published in such a way as he considers appropriate for bringing it to the attention of persons likely to be concerned with its provisions.

(4) '40 day period', in relation to the draft of a proposed code, means–

(a) if the draft is laid before one House on a day later than the day on which it is laid before the other House, the period of 40 days beginning with the later of the two days;

(b) in any other case, the period of 40 days beginning with the day on which it is laid before each House.

(5) In calculating the period of 40 days, no account is to be taken of any period during which Parliament is dissolved or prorogued or during which both Houses are adjourned for more than 4 days.

Ill-treatment or neglect

44 (1) Subsection (2) applies if a person ('D')–
  (a) has the care of a person ('P') who lacks, or whom D reasonably believes to lack, capacity,
  (b) is the donee of a lasting power of attorney, or an enduring power of attorney (within the meaning of Schedule 4), created by P, or
  (c) is a deputy appointed by the court for P.
(2) D is guilty of an offence if he ill-treats or wilfully neglects P.
(3) A person guilty of an offence under this section is liable–
  (a) on summary conviction, to imprisonment for a term not exceeding 12 months or a fine not exceeding the statutory maximum or both;
  (b) on conviction on indictment, to imprisonment for a term not exceeding 5 years or a fine or both.

Part 2: The Court of Protection and the Public Guardian

The Court of Protection

The Court of Protection

45 (1) There is to be a superior court of record known as the Court of Protection.
(2) The court is to have an official seal.
(3) The court may sit at any place in England and Wales, on any day and at any time.
(4) The court is to have a central office and registry at a place appointed by the Lord Chancellor, after consulting the Lord Chief Justice.
(5) The Lord Chancellor may, after consulting the Lord Chief Justice, designate as additional registries of the court any district registry of the High Court and any county court office.
(5A) The Lord Chief Justice may nominate any of the following to exercise his functions under this section–
  (a) the President of the Court of Protection;
  (b) a judicial office holder (as defined in section 109(4) of the Constitutional Reform Act 2005).
(6) The office of the Supreme Court called the Court of Protection ceases to exist.

The judges of the Court of Protection

46 (1) Subject to Court of Protection Rules under section 51(2)(d), the jurisdiction of the court is exercisable by a judge nominated for that purpose by–
  (a) the Lord Chief Justice, or
  (b) where nominated by the Lord Chief Justice to act on his behalf under this subsection–
    (i) the President of the Court of Protection; or
    (ii) a judicial office holder (as defined in section 109(4) of the Constitutional Reform Act 2005).
(2) To be nominated, a judge must be–
  (a) the President of the Family Division,
  (b) the Chancellor of the High Court,

(c) a puisne judge of the High Court,
(d) a circuit judge,
(e) a district judge,
(f) a District Judge (Magistrates' Courts),
(g) a judge of the First-tier Tribunal, or of the Upper Tribunal, by virtue of appointment under paragraph 1(1) of Schedule 2 or 3 to the Tribunals, Courts and Enforcement Act 2007,
(h) a transferred-in judge of the First-tier Tribunal or of the Upper Tribunal (see section 31(2) of that Act),
(i) a deputy judge of the Upper Tribunal (whether under paragraph 7 of Schedule 3 to, or section 31(2) of, that Act),
(j) the Chamber President, or Deputy Chamber President, of a chamber of the First-tier Tribunal or of a chamber of the Upper Tribunal,
(k) the Judge Advocate General,
(l) a Recorder,
(m) the holder of an office listed in the first column of the table in section 89(3C) of the Senior Courts Act 1981 (senior High Court Masters etc),
(n) a holder of an office listed in column 1 of Part 2 of Schedule 2 to that Act (High Court Masters etc),
(o) a deputy district judge appointed under section 102 of that Act or under section 8 of the County Courts Act 1984,
(p) a member of a panel of Employment Judges established for England and Wales or for Scotland,
(q) a person appointed under section 30(1)(a) or (b) of the Courts-Martial (Appeals) Act 1951 (assistants to the Judge Advocate General),
(r) a deputy judge of the High Court,
(s) the Senior President of Tribunals,
(t) an ordinary judge of the Court of Appeal (including the vice-president, if any, of either division of that court),
(u) the President of the Queen's Bench Division,
(v) the Master of the Rolls, or
(w) the Lord Chief Justice.

(3) The Lord Chief Justice, after consulting the Lord Chancellor, must—
 (a) appoint one of the judges nominated by virtue of subsection (2)(a) to (c) to be President of the Court of Protection, and
 (b) appoint another of those judges to be Vice-President of the Court of Protection.

(4) The Lord Chief Justice, after consulting the Lord Chancellor, must appoint one of the judges nominated by virtue of subsection (2)(d) to (q) to be Senior Judge of the Court of Protection, having such administrative functions in relation to the court as the Lord Chancellor, after consulting the Lord Chief Justice, may direct.

Supplementary powers

General powers and effect of orders etc

47 (1) The court has in connection with its jurisdiction the same powers, rights, privileges and authority as the High Court.

(2) Section 204 of the Law of Property Act 1925 (orders of High Court conclusive in favour of purchasers) applies in relation to orders and directions of the court as it applies to orders of the High Court.

(3) Office copies of orders made, directions given or other instruments issued by the court and sealed with its official seal are admissible in all legal proceedings as evidence of the originals without any further proof.

Interim orders and directions

48 The court may, pending the determination of an application to it in relation to a person ('P'), make an order or give directions in respect of any matter if—
   (a) there is reason to believe that P lacks capacity in relation to the matter,
   (b) the matter is one to which its powers under this Act extend, and
   (c) it is in P's best interests to make the order, or give the directions, without delay.

Power to call for reports

49 (1) This section applies where, in proceedings brought in respect of a person ('P') under Part 1, the court is considering a question relating to P.
   (2) The court may require a report to be made to it by the Public Guardian or by a Court of Protection Visitor.
   (3) The court may require a local authority, or an NHS body, to arrange for a report to be made—
      (a) by one of its officers or employees, or
      (b) by such other person (other than the Public Guardian or a Court of Protection Visitor) as the authority, or the NHS body, considers appropriate.
   (4) The report must deal with such matters relating to P as the court may direct.
   (5) Court of Protection Rules may specify matters which, unless the court directs otherwise, must also be dealt with in the report.
   (6) The report may be made in writing or orally, as the court may direct.
   (7) In complying with a requirement, the Public Guardian or a Court of Protection Visitor may, at all reasonable times, examine and take copies of—
      (a) any health record,
      (b) any record of, or held by, a local authority and compiled in connection with a social services function, and
      (c) any record held by a person registered under Part 2 of the Care Standards Act 2000 or Chapter 2 of Part 1 of the Health and Social Care Act 2008, so far as the record relates to P.
   (8) If the Public Guardian or a Court of Protection Visitor is making a visit in the course of complying with a requirement, he may interview P in private.
   (9) If a Court of Protection Visitor who is a Special Visitor is making a visit in the course of complying with a requirement, he may if the court so directs carry out in private a medical, psychiatric or psychological examination of P's capacity and condition.
   (10) 'NHS body' has the meaning given in section 148 of the Health and Social Care (Community Health and Standards) Act 2003.
   (11) 'Requirement' means a requirement imposed under subsection (2) or (3).

Practice and procedure

Applications to the Court of Protection

50 (1) No permission is required for an application to the court for the exercise of any of its powers under this Act—

(a) by a person who lacks, or is alleged to lack, capacity,
(b) if such a person has not reached 18, by anyone with parental responsibility for him,
(c) by the donor or a donee of a lasting power of attorney to which the application relates,
(d) by a deputy appointed by the court for a person to whom the application relates, or
(e) by a person named in an existing order of the court, if the application relates to the order.

(1A) Nor is permission required for an application to the court under section 21A by the relevant person's representative.

(2) But, subject to Court of Protection Rules and to paragraph 20(2) of Schedule 3 (declarations relating to private international law), permission is required for any other application to the court.

(3) In deciding whether to grant permission the court must, in particular, have regard to–
(a) the applicant's connection with the person to whom the application relates,
(b) the reasons for the application,
(c) the benefit to the person to whom the application relates of a proposed order or directions, and
(d) whether the benefit can be achieved in any other way.

(4) 'Parental responsibility' has the same meaning as in the Children Act 1989.

Court of Protection Rules

51 (1) Rules of court with respect to the practice and procedure of the court (to be called 'Court of Protection Rules') may be made in accordance with Part 1 of Schedule 1 to the Constitutional Reform Act 2005.

(2) Court of Protection Rules may, in particular, make provision–
(a) as to the manner and form in which proceedings are to be commenced;
(b) as to the persons entitled to be notified of, and be made parties to, the proceedings;
(c) for the allocation, in such circumstances as may be specified, of any specified description of proceedings to a specified judge or to specified descriptions of judges;
(d) for the exercise of the jurisdiction of the court, in such circumstances as may be specified, by its officers or other staff;
(e) for enabling the court to appoint a suitable person (who may, with his consent, be the Official Solicitor) to act in the name of, or on behalf of, or to represent the person to whom the proceedings relate;
(f) for enabling an application to the court to be disposed of without a hearing;
(g) for enabling the court to proceed with, or with any part of, a hearing in the absence of the person to whom the proceedings relate;
(h) for enabling or requiring the proceedings or any part of them to be conducted in private and for enabling the court to determine who is to be admitted when the court sits in private and to exclude specified persons when it sits in public;
(i) as to what may be received as evidence (whether or not admissible apart from the rules) and the manner in which it is to be presented;
(j) for the enforcement of orders made and directions given in the proceedings.

(3) Court of Protection Rules may, instead of providing for any matter, refer to provision made or to be made about that matter by directions.
(4) Court of Protection Rules may make different provision for different areas.

Practice directions

52 (1) Directions as to the practice and procedure of the court may be given in accordance with Part 1 of Schedule 2 to the Constitutional Reform Act 2005.
(2) Practice directions given otherwise than under subsection (1) may not be given without the approval of–
  (a) the Lord Chancellor, and
  (b) the Lord Chief Justice.
(3) The Lord Chief Justice may nominate any of the following to exercise his functions under this section–
  (a) the President of the Court of Protection;
  (b) a judicial office holder (as defined in section 109(4) of the Constitutional Reform Act 2005).

Rights of appeal

53 (1) Subject to the provisions of this section, an appeal lies to the Court of Appeal from any decision of the court.
(2) Court of Protection Rules may provide that, where a decision of the court is made by a specified description of person, an appeal from the decision lies to a specified description of judge of the court and not to the Court of Appeal.
(3) [Repealed.]
(4) Court of Protection Rules may make provision–
  (a) that, in such cases as may be specified, an appeal from a decision of the court may not be made without permission;
  (b) as to the person or persons entitled to grant permission to appeal;
  (c) as to any requirements to be satisfied before permission is granted;
  (d) that where a judge of the court makes a decision on an appeal, no appeal may be made to the Court of Appeal from that decision unless the Court of Appeal considers that–
    (i) the appeal would raise an important point of principle or practice, or
    (ii) there is some other compelling reason for the Court of Appeal to hear it;
  (e) as to any considerations to be taken into account in relation to granting or refusing permission to appeal.

Fees and costs

Fees

54 (1) The Lord Chancellor may with the consent of the Treasury by order prescribe fees payable in respect of anything dealt with by the court.
(2) An order under this section may in particular contain provision as to–
  (a) scales or rates of fees;
  (b) exemptions from and reductions in fees;
  (c) remission of fees in whole or in part.
(3) Before making an order under this section, the Lord Chancellor must consult–
  (a) the President of the Court of Protection,
  (b) the Vice-President of the Court of Protection, and
  (c) the Senior Judge of the Court of Protection.

(4) The Lord Chancellor must take such steps as are reasonably practicable to bring information about fees to the attention of persons likely to have to pay them.

(5) Fees payable under this section are recoverable summarily as a civil debt.

Costs

55 (1) Subject to Court of Protection Rules, the costs of and incidental to all proceedings in the court are in its discretion.

(2) The rules may in particular make provision for regulating matters relating to the costs of those proceedings, including prescribing scales of costs to be paid to legal or other representatives.

(3) The court has full power to determine by whom and to what extent the costs are to be paid.

(4) The court may, in any proceedings–
  (a) disallow, or
  (b) order the legal or other representatives concerned to meet,
  the whole of any wasted costs or such part of them as may be determined in accordance with the rules.

(5) 'Legal or other representative', in relation to a party to proceedings, means any person exercising a right of audience or right to conduct litigation on his behalf.

(6) 'Wasted costs' means any costs incurred by a party–
  (a) as a result of any improper, unreasonable or negligent act or omission on the part of any legal or other representative or any employee of such a representative, or
  (b) which, in the light of any such act or omission occurring after they were incurred, the court considers it is unreasonable to expect that party to pay.

Fees and costs: supplementary

56 (1) Court of Protection Rules may make provision–
  (a) as to the way in which, and funds from which, fees and costs are to be paid;
  (b) for charging fees and costs upon the estate of the person to whom the proceedings relate;
  (c) for the payment of fees and costs within a specified time of the death of the person to whom the proceedings relate or the conclusion of the proceedings.

(2) A charge on the estate of a person created by virtue of subsection (1)(b) does not cause any interest of the person in any property to fail or determine or to be prevented from recommencing.

The Public Guardian

The Public Guardian

57 (1) For the purposes of this Act, there is to be an officer, to be known as the Public Guardian.

(2) The Public Guardian is to be appointed by the Lord Chancellor.

(3) There is to be paid to the Public Guardian out of money provided by Parliament such salary as the Lord Chancellor may determine.

(4) The Lord Chancellor may, after consulting the Public Guardian–
  (a) provide him with such officers and staff, or
  (b) enter into such contracts with other persons for the provision (by them or their sub-contractors) of officers, staff or services,

as the Lord Chancellor thinks necessary for the proper discharge of the Public Guardian's functions.
(5) Any functions of the Public Guardian may, to the extent authorised by him, be performed by any of his officers.

Functions of the Public Guardian
58 (1) The Public Guardian has the following functions–
(a) establishing and maintaining a register of lasting powers of attorney,
(b) establishing and maintaining a register of orders appointing deputies,
(c) supervising deputies appointed by the court,
(d) directing a Court of Protection Visitor to visit–
(i) a donee of a lasting power of attorney,
(ii) a deputy appointed by the court, or
(iii) the person granting the power of attorney or for whom the deputy is appointed ('P'),
and to make a report to the Public Guardian on such matters as he may direct,
(e) receiving security which the court requires a person to give for the discharge of his functions,
(f) receiving reports from donees of lasting powers of attorney and deputies appointed by the court,
(g) reporting to the court on such matters relating to proceedings under this Act as the court requires,
(h) dealing with representations (including complaints) about the way in which a donee of a lasting power of attorney or a deputy appointed by the court is exercising his powers,
(i) publishing, in any manner the Public Guardian thinks appropriate, any information he thinks appropriate about the discharge of his functions.
(2) The functions conferred by subsection (1)(c) and (h) may be discharged in co-operation with any other person who has functions in relation to the care or treatment of P.
(3) The Lord Chancellor may by regulations make provision–
(a) conferring on the Public Guardian other functions in connection with this Act;
(b) in connection with the discharge by the Public Guardian of his functions.
(4) Regulations made under subsection (3)(b) may in particular make provision as to–
(a) the giving of security by deputies appointed by the court and the enforcement and discharge of security so given;
(b) the fees which may be charged by the Public Guardian;
(c) the way in which, and funds from which, such fees are to be paid;
(d) exemptions from and reductions in such fees;
(e) remission of such fees in whole or in part;
(f) the making of reports to the Public Guardian by deputies appointed by the court and others who are directed by the court to carry out any transaction for a person who lacks capacity.
(5) For the purpose of enabling him to carry out his functions, the Public Guardian may, at all reasonable times, examine and take copies of–
(a) any health record,

(b) any record of, or held by, a local authority and compiled in connection with a social services function, and
(c) any record held by a person registered under Part 2 of the Care Standards Act 2000 or Chapter 2 of Part 1 of the Health and Social Care Act 2008, so far as the record relates to P.
(6) The Public Guardian may also for that purpose interview P in private.

59 [Repealed.]

Annual report

60 (1) The Public Guardian must make an annual report to the Lord Chancellor about the discharge of his functions.
(2) The Lord Chancellor must, within one month of receiving the report, lay a copy of it before Parliament.

Court of Protection Visitors

Court of Protection Visitors

61 (1) A Court of Protection Visitor is a person who is appointed by the Lord Chancellor to–
   (a) a panel of Special Visitors, or
   (b) a panel of General Visitors.
(2) A person is not qualified to be a Special Visitor unless he–
   (a) is a registered medical practitioner or appears to the Lord Chancellor to have other suitable qualifications or training, and
   (b) appears to the Lord Chancellor to have special knowledge of and experience in cases of impairment of or disturbance in the functioning of the mind or brain.
(3) A General Visitor need not have a medical qualification.
(4) A Court of Protection Visitor–
   (a) may be appointed for such term and subject to such conditions, and
   (b) may be paid such remuneration and allowances,
   as the Lord Chancellor may determine.
(5) For the purpose of carrying out his functions under this Act in relation to a person who lacks capacity ('P'), a Court of Protection Visitor may, at all reasonable times, examine and take copies of–
   (a) any health record,
   (b) any record of, or held by, a local authority and compiled in connection with a social services function, and
   (c) any record held by a person registered under Part 2 of the Care Standards Act 2000 (c 14) or Chapter 2 of Part 1 of the Health and Social Care Act 2008,
   so far as the record relates to P.
(6) A Court of Protection Visitor may also for that purpose interview P in private.

Part 3: Miscellaneous and General

Declaratory provision

Scope of the Act

62 For the avoidance of doubt, it is hereby declared that nothing in this Act is to be taken to affect the law relating to murder or manslaughter or the operation of section 2 of the Suicide Act 1961 (assisting suicide).

Private international law

International protection of adults

63   Schedule 3–
  (a) gives effect in England and Wales to the Convention on the International Protection of Adults signed at the Hague on 13th January 2000 (Cm 5881) (in so far as this Act does not otherwise do so), and
  (b) makes related provision as to the private international law of England and Wales.

General

Interpretation

64 (1) In this Act–
  'the 1985 Act' means the Enduring Powers of Attorney Act 1985,
  'advance decision' has the meaning given in section 24(1),
  'authorisation under Schedule A1' means either–
    (a) a standard authorisation under that Schedule, or
    (b) an urgent authorisation under that Schedule;
  'the court' means the Court of Protection established by section 45,
  'Court of Protection Rules' has the meaning given in section 51(1),
  'Court of Protection Visitor' has the meaning given in section 61,
  'deputy' has the meaning given in section 16(2)(b),
  'enactment' includes a provision of subordinate legislation (within the meaning of the Interpretation Act 1978),
  'health record' has the meaning given in section 68 of the Data Protection Act 1998 (as read with section 69 of that Act),
  'the Human Rights Convention' has the same meaning as 'the Convention' in the Human Rights Act 1998,
  'independent mental capacity advocate' has the meaning given in section 35(1),
  'lasting power of attorney' has the meaning given in section 9,
  'life-sustaining treatment' has the meaning given in section 4(10),
  'local authority', except in section 35(6A)(a) and Schedule A1, means–
    (a) the council of a county in England in which there are no district councils,
    (b) the council of a district in England,
    (c) the council of a county or county borough in Wales,
    (d) the council of a London borough,
    (e) the Common Council of the City of London, or
    (f) the Council of the Isles of Scilly,
  'Mental Health Act' means the Mental Health Act 1983,
  'prescribed', in relation to regulations made under this Act, means prescribed by those regulations,
  'property' includes any thing in action and any interest in real or personal property,
  'public authority' has the same meaning as in the Human Rights Act 1998,
  'Public Guardian' has the meaning given in section 57,
  'purchaser' and 'purchase' have the meaning given in section 205(1) of the Law of Property Act 1925,

'social services function'–
- (a) in relation to England] has the meaning given in section 1A of the Local Authority Social Services Act 1970,
- (b) in relation to Wales, has the meaning given in section 143 of the Social Services and Well-being (Wales) Act 2014,

'treatment' includes a diagnostic or other procedure,

'trust corporation' has the meaning given in section 68(1) of the Trustee Act 1925, and

'will' includes codicil.

(2) In this Act, references to making decisions, in relation to a donee of a lasting power of attorney or a deputy appointed by the court, include, where appropriate, acting on decisions made.

(3) In this Act, references to the bankruptcy of an individual include a case where a bankruptcy restrictions order under the Insolvency Act 1986 has effect in respect of him.

(3A) In this Act references to a debt relief order (under Part 7A of the Insolvency Act 1986) being made in relation to an individual include a case where a debt relief restrictions order under the Insolvency Act 1986 has effect in respect of him.

(4) 'Bankruptcy restrictions order' includes an interim bankruptcy restrictions order.

(4A) 'Debt relief restrictions order' includes an interim debt relief restrictions order.

(5) In this Act, references to deprivation of a person's liberty have the same meaning as in Article 5(1) of the Human Rights Convention.

(6) For the purposes of such references, it does not matter whether a person is deprived of his liberty by a public authority or not.

Rules, regulations and orders

65 (1) Any power to make rules, regulations or orders under this Act, other than the power in section 21–
- (a) is exercisable by statutory instrument;
- (b) includes power to make supplementary, incidental, consequential, transitional or saving provision;
- (c) includes power to make different provision for different cases.

(2) Any statutory instrument containing rules, regulations or orders made by the Lord Chancellor or the Secretary of State under this Act, other than–
- (a) regulations under section 34 (loss of capacity during research project),
- (b) regulations under section 41 (adjusting role of independent mental capacity advocacy service),
- (c) regulations under paragraph 32(1)(b) of Schedule 3 (private international law relating to the protection of adults),
- (d) an order of the kind mentioned in section 67(6) (consequential amendments of primary legislation), or
- (e) an order under section 68 (commencement),

is subject to annulment in pursuance of a resolution of either House of Parliament.

(3) A statutory instrument containing an Order in Council under paragraph 31 of Schedule 3 (provision to give further effect to Hague Convention) is

subject to annulment in pursuance of a resolution of either House of Parliament.
(4) A statutory instrument containing regulations made by the Secretary of State under section 34 or 41 or by the Lord Chancellor under paragraph 32(1)(b) of Schedule 3 may not be made unless a draft has been laid before and approved by resolution of each House of Parliament.
(4A) Subsection (2) does not apply to a statutory instrument containing regulations made by the Secretary of State under Schedule A1.
(4B) If such a statutory instrument contains regulations under paragraph 42(2)(b), 129, 162 or 164 of Schedule A1 (whether or not it also contains other regulations), the instrument may not be made unless a draft has been laid before and approved by resolution of each House of Parliament.
(4C) Subject to that, such a statutory instrument is subject to annulment in pursuance of a resolution of either House of Parliament.
(5) An order under section 21–
   (a) may include supplementary, incidental, consequential, transitional or saving provision;
   (b) may make different provision for different cases;
   (c) is to be made in the form of a statutory instrument to which the Statutory Instruments Act 1946 applies as if the order were made by a Minister of the Crown; and
   (d) is subject to annulment in pursuance of a resolution of either House of Parliament.

Existing receivers and enduring powers of attorney etc
66 (1) The following provisions cease to have effect–
   (a) Part 7 of the Mental Health Act,
   (b) the Enduring Powers of Attorney Act 1985 (c 29).
(2) No enduring power of attorney within the meaning of the 1985 Act is to be created after the commencement of subsection (1)(b).
(3) Schedule 4 has effect in place of the 1985 Act in relation to any enduring power of attorney created before the commencement of subsection (1)(b).
(4) Schedule 5 contains transitional provisions and savings in relation to Part 7 of the Mental Health Act and the 1985 Act.

Minor and consequential amendments and repeals
67 (1) Schedule 6 contains minor and consequential amendments.
(2) Schedule 7 contains repeals.
(3) The Lord Chancellor may by order make supplementary, incidental, consequential, transitional or saving provision for the purposes of, in consequence of, or for giving full effect to a provision of this Act.
(4) An order under subsection (3) may, in particular–
   (a) provide for a provision of this Act which comes into force before another provision of this Act has come into force to have effect, until the other provision has come into force, with specified modifications;
   (b) amend, repeal or revoke an enactment, other than one contained in an Act or Measure passed in a Session after the one in which this Act is passed.
(5) The amendments that may be made under subsection (4)(b) are in addition to those made by or under any other provision of this Act.

(6) An order under subsection (3) which amends or repeals a provision of an Act or Measure may not be made unless a draft has been laid before and approved by resolution of each House of Parliament.

Commencement and extent

68 (1) This Act, other than sections 30 to 41, comes into force in accordance with provision made by order by the Lord Chancellor.
(2) Sections 30 to 41 come into force in accordance with provision made by order by–
  (a) the Secretary of State, in relation to England, and
  (b) the National Assembly for Wales, in relation to Wales.
(3) An order under this section may appoint different days for different provisions and different purposes.
(4) Subject to subsections (5) and (6), this Act extends to England and Wales only.
(5) The following provisions extend to the United Kingdom–
  (a) paragraph 16(1) of Schedule 1 (evidence of instruments and of registration of lasting powers of attorney),
  (b) paragraph 15(3) of Schedule 4 (evidence of instruments and of registration of enduring powers of attorney).
(6) Subject to any provision made in Schedule 6, the amendments and repeals made by Schedules 6 and 7 have the same extent as the enactments to which they relate.

Short title

69 This Act may be cited as the Mental Capacity Act 2005.

SCHEDULE A1: HOSPITAL AND CARE HOME RESIDENTS: DEPRIVATION OF LIBERTY

Part 1: Authorisation to Deprive Residents of Liberty etc

Application of Part

1 (1) This Part applies if the following conditions are met.
(2) The first condition is that a person ('P') is detained in a hospital or care home–for the purpose of being given care or treatment–in circumstances which amount to deprivation of the person's liberty.
(3) The second condition is that a standard or urgent authorisation is in force.
(4) The third condition is that the standard or urgent authorisation relates–
  (a) to P, and
  (b) to the hospital or care home in which P is detained.

Authorisation to deprive P of liberty

2 The managing authority of the hospital or care home may deprive P of his liberty by detaining him as mentioned in paragraph 1(2).

No liability for acts done for purpose of depriving P of liberty

3 (1) This paragraph applies to any act which a person ('D') does for the purpose of detaining P as mentioned in paragraph 1(2).
(2) D does not incur any liability in relation to the act that he would not have incurred if P–
  (a) had had capacity to consent in relation to D's doing the act, and
  (b) had consented to D's doing the act.

No protection for negligent acts etc

4 (1) Paragraphs 2 and 3 do not exclude a person's civil liability for loss or damage, or his criminal liability, resulting from his negligence in doing any thing.

 (2) Paragraphs 2 and 3 do not authorise a person to do anything otherwise than for the purpose of the standard or urgent authorisation that is in force.

 (3) In a case where a standard authorisation is in force, paragraphs 2 and 3 do not authorise a person to do anything which does not comply with the conditions (if any) included in the authorisation.

Part 2: Interpretation: Main Terms

Introduction

5 This Part applies for the purposes of this Schedule.

Detained resident

6 'Detained resident' means a person detained in a hospital or care home–for the purpose of being given care or treatment–in circumstances which amount to deprivation of the person's liberty.

Relevant person etc

7 In relation to a person who is, or is to be, a detained resident–
'relevant person' means the person in question;
'relevant hospital or care home' means the hospital or care home in question;
'relevant care or treatment' means the care or treatment in question.

Authorisations

8 'Standard authorisation' means an authorisation given under Part 4.
9 'Urgent authorisation' means an authorisation given under Part 5.
10 'Authorisation under this Schedule' means either of the following–
  (a) a standard authorisation;
  (b) an urgent authorisation.
11 (1) The purpose of a standard authorisation is the purpose which is stated in the authorisation in accordance with paragraph 55(1)(d).
 (2) The purpose of an urgent authorisation is the purpose which is stated in the authorisation in accordance with paragraph 80(d).

Part 3: The Qualifying Requirements

The qualifying requirements

12 (1) These are the qualifying requirements referred to in this Schedule–
  (a) the age requirement;
  (b) the mental health requirement;
  (c) the mental capacity requirement;
  (d) the best interests requirement;
  (e) the eligibility requirement;
  (f) the no refusals requirement.
 (2) Any question of whether a person who is, or is to be, a detained resident meets the qualifying requirements is to be determined in accordance with this Part.
 (3) In a case where–
  (a) the question of whether a person meets a particular qualifying requirement arises in relation to the giving of a standard authorisation, and

(b) any circumstances relevant to determining that question are expected to change between the time when the determination is made and the time when the authorisation is expected to come into force,
those circumstances are to be taken into account as they are expected to be at the later time.

The age requirement
13 The relevant person meets the age requirement if he has reached 18.

The mental health requirement
14 (1) The relevant person meets the mental health requirement if he is suffering from mental disorder (within the meaning of the Mental Health Act, but disregarding any exclusion for persons with learning disability).
(2) An exclusion for persons with learning disability is any provision of the Mental Health Act which provides for a person with learning disability not to be regarded as suffering from mental disorder for one or more purposes of that Act.

The mental capacity requirement
15 The relevant person meets the mental capacity requirement if he lacks capacity in relation to the question whether or not he should be accommodated in the relevant hospital or care home for the purpose of being given the relevant care or treatment.

The best interests requirement
16 (1) The relevant person meets the best interests requirement if all of the following conditions are met.
(2) The first condition is that the relevant person is, or is to be, a detained resident.
(3) The second condition is that it is in the best interests of the relevant person for him to be a detained resident.
(4) The third condition is that, in order to prevent harm to the relevant person, it is necessary for him to be a detained resident.
(5) The fourth condition is that it is a proportionate response to–
    (a) the likelihood of the relevant person suffering harm, and
    (b) the seriousness of that harm,
for him to be a detained resident.

The eligibility requirement
17 (1) The relevant person meets the eligibility requirement unless he is ineligible to be deprived of liberty by this Act.
(2) Schedule 1A applies for the purpose of determining whether or not P is ineligible to be deprived of liberty by this Act.

The no refusals requirement
18 The relevant person meets the no refusals requirement unless there is a refusal within the meaning of paragraph 19 or 20.
19 (1) There is a refusal if these conditions are met–
    (a) the relevant person has made an advance decision;
    (b) the advance decision is valid;
    (c) the advance decision is applicable to some or all of the relevant treatment.
(2) Expressions used in this paragraph and any of sections 24, 25 or 26 have the same meaning in this paragraph as in that section.

20 (1) There is a refusal if it would be in conflict with a valid decision of a donee or deputy for the relevant person to be accommodated in the relevant hospital or care home for the purpose of receiving some or all of the relevant care or treatment–
    (a) in circumstances which amount to deprivation of the person's liberty, or
    (b) at all.
(2) A donee is a donee of a lasting power of attorney granted by the relevant person.
(3) A decision of a donee or deputy is valid if it is made–
    (a) within the scope of his authority as donee or deputy, and
    (b) in accordance with Part 1 of this Act.

Part 4: Standard Authorisations

Supervisory body to give authorisation

21 Only the supervisory body may give a standard authorisation.
22 The supervisory body may not give a standard authorisation unless–
    (a) the managing authority of the relevant hospital or care home have requested it, or
    (b) paragraph 71 applies (right of third party to require consideration of whether authorisation needed).
23 The managing authority may not make a request for a standard authorisation unless–
    (a) they are required to do so by paragraph 24 (as read with paragraphs 27 to 29),
    (b) they are required to do so by paragraph 25 (as read with paragraph 28), or
    (c) they are permitted to do so by paragraph 30.

Duty to request authorisation: basic cases

24 (1) The managing authority must request a standard authorisation in any of the following cases.
(2) The first case is where it appears to the managing authority that the relevant person–
    (a) is not yet accommodated in the relevant hospital or care home,
    (b) is likely–at some time within the next 28 days–to be a detained resident in the relevant hospital or care home, and
    (c) is likely–
        (i) at that time, or
        (ii) at some later time within the next 28 days,
    to meet all of the qualifying requirements.
(3) The second case is where it appears to the managing authority that the relevant person–
    (a) is already accommodated in the relevant hospital or care home,
    (b) is likely–at some time within the next 28 days–to be a detained resident in the relevant hospital or care home, and
    (c) is likely–
        (i) at that time, or
        (ii) at some later time within the next 28 days,
    to meet all of the qualifying requirements.
(4) The third case is where it appears to the managing authority that the relevant person–

(a) is a detained resident in the relevant hospital or care home, and
(b) meets all of the qualifying requirements, or is likely to do so at some time within the next 28 days.
(5) This paragraph is subject to paragraphs 27 to 29.

Duty to request authorisation: change in place of detention

25 (1) The relevant managing authority must request a standard authorisation if it appears to them that these conditions are met.
(2) The first condition is that a standard authorisation–
(a) has been given, and
(b) has not ceased to be in force.
(3) The second condition is that there is, or is to be, a change in the place of detention.
(4) This paragraph is subject to paragraph 28.

26 (1) This paragraph applies for the purposes of paragraph 25.
(2) There is a change in the place of detention if the relevant person–
(a) ceases to be a detained resident in the stated hospital or care home, and
(b) becomes a detained resident in a different hospital or care home ('the new hospital or care home').
(3) The stated hospital or care home is the hospital or care home to which the standard authorisation relates.
(4) The relevant managing authority are the managing authority of the new hospital or care home.

Other authority for detention: request for authorisation

27 (1) This paragraph applies if, by virtue of section 4A(3), a decision of the court authorises the relevant person to be a detained resident.
(2) Paragraph 24 does not require a request for a standard authorisation to be made in relation to that detention unless these conditions are met.
(3) The first condition is that the standard authorisation would be in force at a time immediately after the expiry of the other authority.
(4) The second condition is that the standard authorisation would not be in force at any time on or before the expiry of the other authority.
(5) The third condition is that it would, in the managing authority's view, be unreasonable to delay making the request until a time nearer the expiry of the other authority.
(6) In this paragraph–
(a) the other authority is–
(i) the decision mentioned in sub-paragraph (1), or
(ii) any further decision of the court which, by virtue of section 4A(3), authorises, or is expected to authorise, the relevant person to be a detained resident;
(b) the expiry of the other authority is the time when the other authority is expected to cease to authorise the relevant person to be a detained resident.

Request refused: no further request unless change of circumstances

28 (1) This paragraph applies if–
(a) a managing authority request a standard authorisation under paragraph 24 or 25, and

(b) the supervisory body are prohibited by paragraph 50(2) from giving the authorisation.
(2) Paragraph 24 or 25 does not require that managing authority to make a new request for a standard authorisation unless it appears to the managing authority that–
  (a) there has been a change in the relevant person's case, and
  (b) because of that change, the supervisory body are likely to give a standard authorisation if requested.

Authorisation given: request for further authorisation

29 (1) This paragraph applies if a standard authorisation–
  (a) has been given in relation to the detention of the relevant person, and
  (b) that authorisation ('the existing authorisation') has not ceased to be in force.
(2) Paragraph 24 does not require a new request for a standard authorisation ('the new authorisation') to be made unless these conditions are met.
(3) The first condition is that the new authorisation would be in force at a time immediately after the expiry of the existing authorisation.
(4) The second condition is that the new authorisation would not be in force at any time on or before the expiry of the existing authorisation.
(5) The third condition is that it would, in the managing authority's view, be unreasonable to delay making the request until a time nearer the expiry of the existing authorisation.
(6) The expiry of the existing authorisation is the time when it is expected to cease to be in force.

Power to request authorisation

30 (1) This paragraph applies if–
  (a) a standard authorisation has been given in relation to the detention of the relevant person,
  (b) that authorisation ('the existing authorisation') has not ceased to be in force,
  (c) the requirement under paragraph 24 to make a request for a new standard authorisation does not apply, because of paragraph 29, and
  (d) a review of the existing authorisation has been requested, or is being carried out, in accordance with Part 8.
(2) The managing authority may request a new standard authorisation which would be in force on or before the expiry of the existing authorisation; but only if it would also be in force immediately after that expiry.
(3) The expiry of the existing authorisation is the time when it is expected to cease to be in force.
(4) Further provision relating to cases where a request is made under this paragraph can be found in–
  (a) paragraph 62 (effect of decision about request), and
  (b) paragraph 124 (effect of request on Part 8 review).

Information included in request

31 A request for a standard authorisation must include the information (if any) required by regulations.

Records of requests
32 (1) The managing authority of a hospital or care home must keep a written record of–
  (a) each request that they make for a standard authorisation, and
  (b) the reasons for making each request.
(2) A supervisory body must keep a written record of each request for a standard authorisation that is made to them.

Relevant person must be assessed
33 (1) This paragraph applies if the supervisory body are requested to give a standard authorisation.
(2) The supervisory body must secure that all of these assessments are carried out in relation to the relevant person–
  (a) an age assessment;
  (b) a mental health assessment;
  (c) a mental capacity assessment;
  (d) a best interests assessment;
  (e) an eligibility assessment;
  (f) a no refusals assessment.
(3) The person who carries out any such assessment is referred to as the assessor.
(4) Regulations may be made about the period (or periods) within which assessors must carry out assessments.
(5) This paragraph is subject to paragraphs 49 and 133.

Age assessment
34 An age assessment is an assessment of whether the relevant person meets the age requirement.

Mental health assessment
35 A mental health assessment is an assessment of whether the relevant person meets the mental health requirement.
36 When carrying out a mental health assessment, the assessor must also–
  (a) consider how (if at all) the relevant person's mental health is likely to be affected by his being a detained resident, and
  (b) notify the best interests assessor of his conclusions.

Mental capacity assessment
37 A mental capacity assessment is an assessment of whether the relevant person meets the mental capacity requirement.

Best interests assessment
38 A best interests assessment is an assessment of whether the relevant person meets the best interests requirement.
39 (1) In carrying out a best interests assessment, the assessor must comply with the duties in sub-paragraphs (2) and (3).
(2) The assessor must consult the managing authority of the relevant hospital or care home.
(3) The assessor must have regard to all of the following–
  (a) the conclusions which the mental health assessor has notified to the best interests assessor in accordance with paragraph 36(b);
  (b) any relevant needs assessment;
  (c) any relevant care plan.

(4) A relevant needs assessment is an assessment of the relevant person's needs which–
  (a) was carried out in connection with the relevant person being accommodated in the relevant hospital or care home, and
  (b) was carried out by or on behalf of–
    (i) the managing authority of the relevant hospital or care home, or
    (ii) the supervisory body.
(5) A relevant care plan is a care plan which–
  (a) sets out how the relevant person's needs are to be met whilst he is accommodated in the relevant hospital or care home, and
  (b) was drawn up by or on behalf of–
    (i) the managing authority of the relevant hospital or care home, or
    (ii) the supervisory body.
(6) The managing authority must give the assessor a copy of–
  (a) any relevant needs assessment carried out by them or on their behalf, or
  (b) any relevant care plan drawn up by them or on their behalf.
(7) The supervisory body must give the assessor a copy of–
  (a) any relevant needs assessment carried out by them or on their behalf, or
  (b) any relevant care plan drawn up by them or on their behalf.
(8) The duties in sub-paragraphs (2) and (3) do not affect any other duty to consult or to take the views of others into account.

40 (1) This paragraph applies whatever conclusion the best interests assessment comes to.
(2) The assessor must state in the best interests assessment the name and address of every interested person whom he has consulted in carrying out the assessment.

41 Paragraphs 42 and 43 apply if the best interests assessment comes to the conclusion that the relevant person meets the best interests requirement.

42 (1) The assessor must state in the assessment the maximum authorisation period.
(2) The maximum authorisation period is the shorter of these periods–
  (a) the period which, in the assessor's opinion, would be the appropriate maximum period for the relevant person to be a detained resident under the standard authorisation that has been requested;
  (b) 1 year, or such shorter period as may be prescribed in regulations.
(3) Regulations under sub-paragraph (2)(b)–
  (a) need not provide for a shorter period to apply in relation to all standard authorisations;
  (b) may provide for different periods to apply in relation to different kinds of standard authorisations.
(4) Before making regulations under sub-paragraph (2)(b) the Secretary of State must consult all of the following–
  (a) each body required by regulations under paragraph 162 to monitor and report on the operation of this Schedule in relation to England;
  (b) such other persons as the Secretary of State considers it appropriate to consult.
(5) Before making regulations under sub-paragraph (2)(b) the National Assembly for Wales must consult all of the following–

(a) each person or body directed under paragraph 163(2) to carry out any function of the Assembly of monitoring and reporting on the operation of this Schedule in relation to Wales;
(b) such other persons as the Assembly considers it appropriate to consult.

43 The assessor may include in the assessment recommendations about conditions to which the standard authorisation is, or is not, to be subject in accordance with paragraph 53.

44 (1) This paragraph applies if the best interests assessment comes to the conclusion that the relevant person does not meet the best interests requirement.
(2) If, on the basis of the information taken into account in carrying out the assessment, it appears to the assessor that there is an unauthorised deprivation of liberty, he must include a statement to that effect in the assessment.
(3) There is an unauthorised deprivation of liberty if the managing authority of the relevant hospital or care home are already depriving the relevant person of his liberty without authority of the kind mentioned in section 4A.

45 The duties with which the best interests assessor must comply are subject to the provision included in appointment regulations under Part 10 (in particular, provision made under paragraph 146).

Eligibility assessment

46 An eligibility assessment is an assessment of whether the relevant person meets the eligibility requirement.

47 (1) Regulations may–
(a) require an eligibility assessor to request a best interests assessor to provide relevant eligibility information, and
(b) require the best interests assessor, if such a request is made, to provide such relevant eligibility information as he may have.
(2) In this paragraph–
'best interests assessor' means any person who is carrying out, or has carried out, a best interests assessment in relation to the relevant person;
'eligibility assessor' means a person carrying out an eligibility assessment in relation to the relevant person;
'relevant eligibility information' is information relevant to assessing whether or not the relevant person is ineligible by virtue of paragraph 5 of Schedule 1A.

No refusals assessment

48 A no refusals assessment is an assessment of whether the relevant person meets the no refusals requirement.

Equivalent assessment already carried out

49 (1) The supervisory body are not required by paragraph 33 to secure that a particular kind of assessment ('the required assessment') is carried out in relation to the relevant person if the following conditions are met.
(2) The first condition is that the supervisory body have a written copy of an assessment of the relevant person ('the existing assessment') that has already been carried out.
(3) The second condition is that the existing assessment complies with all requirements under this Schedule with which the required assessment would have to comply (if it were carried out).

(4) The third condition is that the existing assessment was carried out within the previous 12 months; but this condition need not be met if the required assessment is an age assessment.
(5) The fourth condition is that the supervisory body are satisfied that there is no reason why the existing assessment may no longer be accurate.
(6) If the required assessment is a best interests assessment, in satisfying themselves as mentioned in sub-paragraph (5), the supervisory body must take into account any information given, or submissions made, by–
   (a) the relevant person's representative,
   (b) any section 39C IMCA, or
   (c) any section 39D IMCA.
(7) It does not matter whether the existing assessment was carried out in connection with a request for a standard authorisation or for some other purpose.
(8) If, because of this paragraph, the supervisory body are not required by paragraph 33 to secure that the required assessment is carried out, the existing assessment is to be treated for the purposes of this Schedule–
   (a) as an assessment of the same kind as the required assessment, and
   (b) as having been carried out under paragraph 33 in connection with the request for the standard authorisation.

Duty to give authorisation

50 (1) The supervisory body must give a standard authorisation if–
   (a) all assessments are positive, and
   (b) the supervisory body have written copies of all those assessments.
(2) The supervisory body must not give a standard authorisation except in accordance with sub-paragraph (1).
(3) All assessments are positive if each assessment carried out under paragraph 33 has come to the conclusion that the relevant person meets the qualifying requirement to which the assessment relates.

Terms of authorisation

51 (1) If the supervisory body are required to give a standard authorisation, they must decide the period during which the authorisation is to be in force.
(2) That period must not exceed the maximum authorisation period stated in the best interests assessment.

52 A standard authorisation may provide for the authorisation to come into force at a time after it is given.

53 (1) A standard authorisation may be given subject to conditions.
(2) Before deciding whether to give the authorisation subject to conditions, the supervisory body must have regard to any recommendations in the best interests assessment about such conditions.
(3) The managing authority of the relevant hospital or care home must ensure that any conditions are complied with.

Form of authorisation

54 A standard authorisation must be in writing.

55 (1) A standard authorisation must state the following things–
   (a) the name of the relevant person;
   (b) the name of the relevant hospital or care home;
   (c) the period during which the authorisation is to be in force;
   (d) the purpose for which the authorisation is given;

(e) any conditions subject to which the authorisation is given;
(f) the reason why each qualifying requirement is met.
(2) The statement of the reason why the eligibility requirement is met must be framed by reference to the cases in the table in paragraph 2 of Schedule 1A.

56 (1) If the name of the relevant hospital or care home changes, the standard authorisation is to be read as if it stated the current name of the hospital or care home.
(2) But sub-paragraph (1) is subject to any provision relating to the change of name which is made in any enactment or in any instrument made under an enactment.

Duty to give information about decision

57 (1) This paragraph applies if–
(a) a request is made for a standard authorisation, and
(b) the supervisory body are required by paragraph 50(1) to give the standard authorisation.
(2) The supervisory body must give a copy of the authorisation to each of the following–
(a) the relevant person's representative;
(b) the managing authority of the relevant hospital or care home;
(c) the relevant person;
(d) any section 39A IMCA;
(e) every interested person consulted by the best interests assessor.
(3) The supervisory body must comply with this paragraph as soon as practicable after they give the standard authorisation.

58 (1) This paragraph applies if–
(a) a request is made for a standard authorisation, and
(b) the supervisory body are prohibited by paragraph 50(2) from giving the standard authorisation.
(2) The supervisory body must give notice, stating that they are prohibited from giving the authorisation, to each of the following–
(a) the managing authority of the relevant hospital or care home;
(b) the relevant person;
(c) any section 39A IMCA;
(d) every interested person consulted by the best interests assessor.
(3) The supervisory body must comply with this paragraph as soon as practicable after it becomes apparent to them that they are prohibited from giving the authorisation.

Duty to give information about effect of authorisation

59 (1) This paragraph applies if a standard authorisation is given.
(2) The managing authority of the relevant hospital or care home must take such steps as are practicable to ensure that the relevant person understands all of the following–
(a) the effect of the authorisation;
(b) the right to make an application to the court to exercise its jurisdiction under section 21A;
(c) the right under Part 8 to request a review;
(d) the right to have a section 39D IMCA appointed;
(e) how to have a section 39D IMCA appointed.

(3) Those steps must be taken as soon as is practicable after the authorisation is given.
(4) Those steps must include the giving of appropriate information both orally and in writing.
(5) Any written information given to the relevant person must also be given by the managing authority to the relevant person's representative.
(6) They must give the information to the representative as soon as is practicable after it is given to the relevant person.
(7) Sub-paragraph (8) applies if the managing authority is notified that a section 39D IMCA has been appointed.
(8) As soon as is practicable after being notified, the managing authority must give the section 39D IMCA a copy of the written information given in accordance with sub-paragraph (4).

Records of authorisations

60 A supervisory body must keep a written record of all of the following information–
   (a) the standard authorisations that they have given;
   (b) the requests for standard authorisations in response to which they have not given an authorisation;
   (c) in relation to each standard authorisation given: the matters stated in the authorisation in accordance with paragraph 55.

Variation of an authorisation

61 (1) A standard authorisation may not be varied except in accordance with Part 7 or 8.
   (2) This paragraph does not affect the powers of the Court of Protection or of any other court.

Effect of decision about request made under paragraph 25 or 30

62 (1) This paragraph applies where the managing authority request a new standard authorisation under either of the following–
   (a) paragraph 25 (change in place of detention);
   (b) paragraph 30 (existing authorisation subject to review).
   (2) If the supervisory body are required by paragraph 50(1) to give the new authorisation, the existing authorisation terminates at the time when the new authorisation comes into force.
   (3) If the supervisory body are prohibited by paragraph 50(2) from giving the new authorisation, there is no effect on the existing authorisation's continuation in force.

When an authorisation is in force

63 (1) A standard authorisation comes into force when it is given.
   (2) But if the authorisation provides for it to come into force at a later time, it comes into force at that time.
64 (1) A standard authorisation ceases to be in force at the end of the period stated in the authorisation in accordance with paragraph 55(1)(c).
   (2) But if the authorisation terminates before then in accordance with paragraph 62(2) or any other provision of this Schedule, it ceases to be in force when the termination takes effect.
   (3) This paragraph does not affect the powers of the Court of Protection or of any other court.

65 (1) This paragraph applies if a standard authorisation ceases to be in force.
  (2) The supervisory body must give notice that the authorisation has ceased to be in force.
  (3) The supervisory body must give that notice to all of the following–
    (a) the managing authority of the relevant hospital or care home;
    (b) the relevant person;
    (c) the relevant person's representative;
    (d) every interested person consulted by the best interests assessor.
  (4) The supervisory body must give that notice as soon as practicable after the authorisation ceases to be in force.

When a request for a standard authorisation is 'disposed of'

66 A request for a standard authorisation is to be regarded for the purposes of this Schedule as disposed of if the supervisory body have given–
    (a) a copy of the authorisation in accordance with paragraph 57, or
    (b) notice in accordance with paragraph 58.

Right of third party to require consideration of whether authorisation needed

67 For the purposes of paragraphs 68 to 73 there is an unauthorised deprivation of liberty if–
    (a) a person is already a detained resident in a hospital or care home, and
    (b) the detention of the person is not authorised as mentioned in section 4A.

68 (1) If the following conditions are met, an eligible person may request the supervisory body to decide whether or not there is an unauthorised deprivation of liberty.
  (2) The first condition is that the eligible person has notified the managing authority of the relevant hospital or care home that it appears to the eligible person that there is an unauthorised deprivation of liberty.
  (3) The second condition is that the eligible person has asked the managing authority to request a standard authorisation in relation to the detention of the relevant person.
  (4) The third condition is that the managing authority has not requested a standard authorisation within a reasonable period after the eligible person asks it to do so.
  (5) In this paragraph 'eligible person' means any person other than the managing authority of the relevant hospital or care home.

69 (1) This paragraph applies if an eligible person requests the supervisory body to decide whether or not there is an unauthorised deprivation of liberty.
  (2) The supervisory body must select and appoint a person to carry out an assessment of whether or not the relevant person is a detained resident.
  (3) But the supervisory body need not select and appoint a person to carry out such an assessment in either of these cases.
  (4) The first case is where it appears to the supervisory body that the request by the eligible person is frivolous or vexatious.
  (5) The second case is where it appears to the supervisory body that–
    (a) the question of whether or not there is an unauthorised deprivation of liberty has already been decided, and
    (b) since that decision, there has been no change of circumstances which would merit the question being decided again.

(6) The supervisory body must not select and appoint a person to carry out an assessment under this paragraph unless it appears to the supervisory body that the person would be–
   (a) suitable to carry out a best interests assessment (if one were obtained in connection with a request for a standard authorisation relating to the relevant person), and
   (b) eligible to carry out such a best interests assessment.
(7) The supervisory body must notify the persons specified in sub-paragraph (8)–
   (a) that the supervisory body have been requested to decide whether or not there is an unauthorised deprivation of liberty;
   (b) of their decision whether or not to select and appoint a person to carry out an assessment under this paragraph;
   (c) if their decision is to select and appoint a person, of the person appointed.
(8) The persons referred to in sub-paragraph (7) are–
   (a) the eligible person who made the request under paragraph 68;
   (b) the person to whom the request relates;
   (c) the managing authority of the relevant hospital or care home;
   (d) any section 39A IMCA.

70 (1) Regulations may be made about the period within which an assessment under paragraph 69 must be carried out.
(2) Regulations made under paragraph 129(3) apply in relation to the selection and appointment of a person under paragraph 69 as they apply to the selection of a person under paragraph 129 to carry out a best interests assessment.
(3) The following provisions apply to an assessment under paragraph 69 as they apply to an assessment carried out in connection with a request for a standard authorisation–
   (a) paragraph 131 (examination and copying of records);
   (b) paragraph 132 (representations);
   (c) paragraphs 134 and 135(1) and (2) (duty to keep records and give copies).
(4) The copies of the assessment which the supervisory body are required to give under paragraph 135(2) must be given as soon as practicable after the supervisory body are themselves given a copy of the assessment.

71 (1) This paragraph applies if–
   (a) the supervisory body obtain an assessment under paragraph 69,
   (b) the assessment comes to the conclusion that the relevant person is a detained resident, and
   (c) it appears to the supervisory body that the detention of the person is not authorised as mentioned in section 4A.
(2) This Schedule (including Part 5) applies as if the managing authority of the relevant hospital or care home had, in accordance with Part 4, requested the supervisory body to give a standard authorisation in relation to the relevant person.
(3) The managing authority of the relevant hospital or care home must supply the supervisory body with the information (if any) which the managing authority would, by virtue of paragraph 31, have had to include in a request for a standard authorisation.
(4) The supervisory body must notify the persons specified in paragraph 69(8)–
   (a) of the outcome of the assessment obtained under paragraph 69, and
   (b) that this Schedule applies as mentioned in sub-paragraph (2).

72 (1) This paragraph applies if—
  (a) the supervisory body obtain an assessment under paragraph 69, and
  (b) the assessment comes to the conclusion that the relevant person is not a detained resident.
(2) The supervisory body must notify the persons specified in paragraph 69(8) of the outcome of the assessment.

73 (1) This paragraph applies if—
  (a) the supervisory body obtain an assessment under paragraph 69,
  (b) the assessment comes to the conclusion that the relevant person is a detained resident, and
  (c) it appears to the supervisory body that the detention of the person is authorised as mentioned in section 4A.
(2) The supervisory body must notify the persons specified in paragraph 69(8)–
  (a) of the outcome of the assessment, and
  (b) that it appears to the supervisory body that the detention is authorised.

Part 5: Urgent Authorisations

Managing authority to give authorisation

74 Only the managing authority of the relevant hospital or care home may give an urgent authorisation.

75 The managing authority may give an urgent authorisation only if they are required to do so by paragraph 76 (as read with paragraph 77).

Duty to give authorisation

76 (1) The managing authority must give an urgent authorisation in either of the following cases.
(2) The first case is where–
  (a) the managing authority are required to make a request under paragraph 24 or 25 for a standard authorisation, and
  (b) they believe that the need for the relevant person to be a detained resident is so urgent that it is appropriate for the detention to begin before they make the request.
(3) The second case is where–
  (a) the managing authority have made a request under paragraph 24 or 25 for a standard authorisation, and
  (b) they believe that the need for the relevant person to be a detained resident is so urgent that it is appropriate for the detention to begin before the request is disposed of.
(4) References in this paragraph to the detention of the relevant person are references to the detention to which paragraph 24 or 25 relates.
(5) This paragraph is subject to paragraph 77.

77 (1) This paragraph applies where the managing authority have given an urgent authorisation ('the original authorisation') in connection with a case where a person is, or is to be, a detained resident ('the existing detention').
(2) No new urgent authorisation is to be given under paragraph 76 in connection with the existing detention.
(3) But the managing authority may request the supervisory body to extend the duration of the original authorisation.

(4) Only one request under sub-paragraph (3) may be made in relation to the original authorisation.
(5) Paragraphs 84 to 86 apply to any request made under sub-paragraph (3).

Terms of authorisation

78 (1) If the managing authority decide to give an urgent authorisation, they must decide the period during which the authorisation is to be in force.
(2) That period must not exceed 7 days.

Form of authorisation

79 An urgent authorisation must be in writing.
80 An urgent authorisation must state the following things–
   (a) the name of the relevant person;
   (b) the name of the relevant hospital or care home;
   (c) the period during which the authorisation is to be in force;
   (d) the purpose for which the authorisation is given.
81 (1) If the name of the relevant hospital or care home changes, the urgent authorisation is to be read as if it stated the current name of the hospital or care home.
   (2) But sub-paragraph (1) is subject to any provision relating to the change of name which is made in any enactment or in any instrument made under an enactment.

Duty to keep records and give copies

82 (1) This paragraph applies if an urgent authorisation is given.
   (2) The managing authority must keep a written record of why they have given the urgent authorisation.
   (3) As soon as practicable after giving the authorisation, the managing authority must give a copy of the authorisation to all of the following–
      (a) the relevant person;
      (b) any section 39A IMCA.

Duty to give information about authorisation

83 (1) This paragraph applies if an urgent authorisation is given.
   (2) The managing authority of the relevant hospital or care home must take such steps as are practicable to ensure that the relevant person understands all of the following–
      (a) the effect of the authorisation;
      (b) the right to make an application to the court to exercise its jurisdiction under section 21A.
   (3) Those steps must be taken as soon as is practicable after the authorisation is given.
   (4) Those steps must include the giving of appropriate information both orally and in writing.

Request for extension of duration

84 (1) This paragraph applies if the managing authority make a request under paragraph 77 for the supervisory body to extend the duration of the original authorisation.
   (2) The managing authority must keep a written record of why they have made the request.
   (3) The managing authority must give the relevant person notice that they have made the request.

(4) The supervisory body may extend the duration of the original authorisation if it appears to them that—
  (a) the managing authority have made the required request for a standard authorisation,
  (b) there are exceptional reasons why it has not yet been possible for that request to be disposed of, and
  (c) it is essential for the existing detention to continue until the request is disposed of.
(5) The supervisory body must keep a written record that the request has been made to them.
(6) In this paragraph and paragraphs 85 and 86—
  (a) 'original authorisation' and 'existing detention' have the same meaning as in paragraph 77;
  (b) the required request for a standard authorisation is the request that is referred to in paragraph 76(2) or (3).

85 (1) This paragraph applies if, under paragraph 84, the supervisory body decide to extend the duration of the original authorisation.
(2) The supervisory body must decide the period of the extension.
(3) That period must not exceed 7 days.
(4) The supervisory body must give the managing authority notice stating the period of the extension.
(5) The managing authority must then vary the original authorisation so that it states the extended duration.
(6) Paragraphs 82(3) and 83 apply (with the necessary modifications) to the variation of the original authorisation as they apply to the giving of an urgent authorisation.
(7) The supervisory body must keep a written record of—
  (a) the outcome of the request, and
  (b) the period of the extension.

86 (1) This paragraph applies if, under paragraph 84, the supervisory body decide not to extend the duration of the original authorisation.
(2) The supervisory body must give the managing authority notice stating—
  (a) the decision, and
  (b) their reasons for making it.
(3) The managing authority must give a copy of that notice to all of the following—
  (a) the relevant person;
  (b) any section 39A IMCA.
(4) The supervisory body must keep a written record of the outcome of the request.

No variation

87 (1) An urgent authorisation may not be varied except in accordance with paragraph 85.
(2) This paragraph does not affect the powers of the Court of Protection or of any other court.

When an authorisation is in force

88 An urgent authorisation comes into force when it is given.

89 (1) An urgent authorisation ceases to be in force at the end of the period stated in the authorisation in accordance with paragraph 80(c) (subject to any variation in accordance with paragraph 85).

(2) But if the required request is disposed of before the end of that period, the urgent authorisation ceases to be in force as follows.
(3) If the supervisory body are required by paragraph 50(1) to give the requested authorisation, the urgent authorisation ceases to be in force when the requested authorisation comes into force.
(4) If the supervisory body are prohibited by paragraph 50(2) from giving the requested authorisation, the urgent authorisation ceases to be in force when the managing authority receive notice under paragraph 58.
(5) In this paragraph–
'required request' means the request referred to in paragraph 76(2) or (3);
'requested authorisation' means the standard authorisation to which the required request relates.
(6) This paragraph does not affect the powers of the Court of Protection or of any other court.

90 (1) This paragraph applies if an urgent authorisation ceases to be in force.
(2) The supervisory body must give notice that the authorisation has ceased to be in force.
(3) The supervisory body must give that notice to all of the following–
  (a) the relevant person;
  (b) any section 39A IMCA.
(4) The supervisory body must give that notice as soon as practicable after the authorisation ceases to be in force.

Part 6: Eligibility Requirement not Met: Suspension of Standard Authorisation

91 (1) This Part applies if the following conditions are met.
(2) The first condition is that a standard authorisation–
  (a) has been given, and
  (b) has not ceased to be in force.
(3) The second condition is that the managing authority of the relevant hospital or care home are satisfied that the relevant person has ceased to meet the eligibility requirement.
(4) But this Part does not apply if the relevant person is ineligible by virtue of paragraph 5 of Schedule 1A (in which case see Part 8).

92 The managing authority of the relevant hospital or care home must give the supervisory body notice that the relevant person has ceased to meet the eligibility requirement.

93 (1) This paragraph applies if the managing authority give the supervisory body notice under paragraph 92.
(2) The standard authorisation is suspended from the time when the notice is given.
(3) The supervisory body must give notice that the standard authorisation has been suspended to the following persons–
  (a) the relevant person;
  (b) the relevant person's representative;
  (c) the managing authority of the relevant hospital or care home.

94 (1) This paragraph applies if, whilst the standard authorisation is suspended, the managing authority are satisfied that the relevant person meets the eligibility requirement again.

(2) The managing authority must give the supervisory body notice that the relevant person meets the eligibility requirement again.

95 (1) This paragraph applies if the managing authority give the supervisory body notice under paragraph 94.

(2) The standard authorisation ceases to be suspended from the time when the notice is given.

(3) The supervisory body must give notice that the standard authorisation has ceased to be suspended to the following persons–
  (a) the relevant person;
  (b) the relevant person's representative;
  (c) any section 39D IMCA;
  (d) the managing authority of the relevant hospital or care home.

(4) The supervisory body must give notice under this paragraph as soon as practicable after they are given notice under paragraph 94.

96 (1) This paragraph applies if no notice is given under paragraph 94 before the end of the relevant 28 day period.

(2) The standard authorisation ceases to have effect at the end of the relevant 28 day period.

(3) The relevant 28 day period is the period of 28 days beginning with the day on which the standard authorisation is suspended under paragraph 93.

97 The effect of suspending the standard authorisation is that Part 1 ceases to apply for as long as the authorisation is suspended.

Part 7: Standard Authorisations: Change in Supervisory Responsibility

Application of this Part

98 (1) This Part applies if these conditions are met.

(2) The first condition is that a standard authorisation–
  (a) has been given, and
  (b) has not ceased to be in force.

(3) The second condition is that there is a change in supervisory responsibility.

(4) The third condition is that there is not a change in the place of detention (within the meaning of paragraph 25).

99 For the purposes of this Part there is a change in supervisory responsibility if–
  (a) one body ('the old supervisory body') have ceased to be supervisory body in relation to the standard authorisation, and
  (b) a different body ('the new supervisory body') have become supervisory body in relation to the standard authorisation.

Effect of change in supervisory responsibility

100 (1) The new supervisory body becomes the supervisory body in relation to the authorisation.

(2) Anything done by or in relation to the old supervisory body in connection with the authorisation has effect, so far as is necessary for continuing its effect after the change, as if done by or in relation to the new supervisory body.

(3) Anything which relates to the authorisation and which is in the process of being done by or in relation to the old supervisory body at the time of the change may be continued by or in relation to the new supervisory body.

(4) But–
(a) the old supervisory body do not, by virtue of this paragraph, cease to be liable for anything done by them in connection with the authorisation before the change; and
(b) the new supervisory body do not, by virtue of this paragraph, become liable for any such thing.

Part 8: Standard Authorisations: Review

Application of this Part

101 (1) This Part applies if a standard authorisation–
(a) has been given, and
(b) has not ceased to be in force.
(2) Paragraphs 102 to 122 are subject to paragraphs 123 to 125.

Review by supervisory body

102 (1) The supervisory body may at any time carry out a review of the standard authorisation in accordance with this Part.
(2) The supervisory body must carry out such a review if they are requested to do so by an eligible person.
(3) Each of the following is an eligible person–
(a) the relevant person;
(b) the relevant person's representative;
(c) the managing authority of the relevant hospital or care home.

Request for review

103 (1) An eligible person may, at any time, request the supervisory body to carry out a review of the standard authorisation in accordance with this Part.
(2) The managing authority of the relevant hospital or care home must make such a request if one or more of the qualifying requirements appear to them to be reviewable.

Grounds for review

104 (1) Paragraphs 105 to 107 set out the grounds on which the qualifying requirements are reviewable.
(2) A qualifying requirement is not reviewable on any other ground.

Non-qualification ground

105 (1) Any of the following qualifying requirements is reviewable on the ground that the relevant person does not meet the requirement–
(a) the age requirement;
(b) the mental health requirement;
(c) the mental capacity requirement;
(d) the best interests requirement;
(e) the no refusals requirement.
(2) The eligibility requirement is reviewable on the ground that the relevant person is ineligible by virtue of paragraph 5 of Schedule 1A.
(3) The ground in sub-paragraph (1) and the ground in sub-paragraph (2) are referred to as the non-qualification ground.

Change of reason ground

106 (1) Any of the following qualifying requirements is reviewable on the ground set out in sub-paragraph (2)–
  (a) the mental health requirement;
  (b) the mental capacity requirement;
  (c) the best interests requirement;
  (d) the eligibility requirement;
  (e) the no refusals requirement.
(2) The ground is that the reason why the relevant person meets the requirement is not the reason stated in the standard authorisation.
(3) This ground is referred to as the change of reason ground.

Variation of conditions ground

107 (1) The best interests requirement is reviewable on the ground that–
  (a) there has been a change in the relevant person's case, and
  (b) because of that change, it would be appropriate to vary the conditions to which the standard authorisation is subject.
(2) This ground is referred to as the variation of conditions ground.
(3) A reference to varying the conditions to which the standard authorisation is subject is a reference to–
  (a) amendment of an existing condition,
  (b) omission of an existing condition, or
  (c) inclusion of a new condition (whether or not there are already any existing conditions).

Notice that review to be carried out

108 (1) If the supervisory body are to carry out a review of the standard authorisation, they must give notice of the review to the following persons–
  (a) the relevant person;
  (b) the relevant person's representative;
  (c) the managing authority of the relevant hospital or care home.
(2) The supervisory body must give the notice–
  (a) before they begin the review, or
  (b) if that is not practicable, as soon as practicable after they have begun it.
(3) This paragraph does not require the supervisory body to give notice to any person who has requested the review.

Starting a review

109 To start a review of the standard authorisation, the supervisory body must decide which, if any, of the qualifying requirements appear to be reviewable.

No reviewable qualifying requirements

110 (1) This paragraph applies if no qualifying requirements appear to be reviewable.
(2) This Part does not require the supervisory body to take any action in respect of the standard authorisation.

One or more reviewable qualifying requirements

111 (1) This paragraph applies if one or more qualifying requirements appear to be reviewable.
(2) The supervisory body must secure that a separate review assessment is carried out in relation to each qualifying requirement which appears to be reviewable.

(3) But sub-paragraph (2) does not require the supervisory body to secure that a best interests review assessment is carried out in a case where the best interests requirement appears to the supervisory body to be non-assessable.
(4) The best interests requirement is non-assessable if–
   (a) the requirement is reviewable only on the variation of conditions ground, and
   (b) the change in the relevant person's case is not significant.
(5) In making any decision whether the change in the relevant person's case is significant, regard must be had to–
   (a) the nature of the change, and
   (b) the period that the change is likely to last for.

Review assessments

112(1) A review assessment is an assessment of whether the relevant person meets a qualifying requirement.
(2) In relation to a review assessment–
   (a) a negative conclusion is a conclusion that the relevant person does not meet the qualifying requirement to which the assessment relates;
   (b) a positive conclusion is a conclusion that the relevant person meets the qualifying requirement to which the assessment relates.
(3) An age review assessment is a review assessment carried out in relation to the age requirement.
(4) A mental health review assessment is a review assessment carried out in relation to the mental health requirement.
(5) A mental capacity review assessment is a review assessment carried out in relation to the mental capacity requirement.
(6) A best interests review assessment is a review assessment carried out in relation to the best interests requirement.
(7) An eligibility review assessment is a review assessment carried out in relation to the eligibility requirement.
(8) A no refusals review assessment is a review assessment carried out in relation to the no refusals requirement.

113(1) In carrying out a review assessment, the assessor must comply with any duties which would be imposed upon him under Part 4 if the assessment were being carried out in connection with a request for a standard authorisation.
(2) But in the case of a best interests review assessment, paragraphs 43 and 44 do not apply.
(3) Instead of what is required by paragraph 43, the best interests review assessment must include recommendations about whether–and, if so, how–it would be appropriate to vary the conditions to which the standard authorisation is subject.

Best interests requirement reviewable but non-assessable

114(1) This paragraph applies in a case where–
   (a) the best interests requirement appears to be reviewable, but
   (b) in accordance with paragraph 111(3), the supervisory body are not required to secure that a best interests review assessment is carried out.
(2) The supervisory body may vary the conditions to which the standard authorisation is subject in such ways (if any) as the supervisory body think are appropriate in the circumstances.

Best interests review assessment positive

115 (1) This paragraph applies in a case where–
  (a) a best interests review assessment is carried out, and
  (b) the assessment comes to a positive conclusion.
(2) The supervisory body must decide the following questions–
  (a) whether or not the best interests requirement is reviewable on the change of reason ground;
  (b) whether or not the best interests requirement is reviewable on the variation of conditions ground;
  (c) if so, whether or not the change in the person's case is significant.
(3) If the supervisory body decide that the best interests requirement is reviewable on the change of reason ground, they must vary the standard authorisation so that it states the reason why the relevant person now meets that requirement.
(4) If the supervisory body decide that–
  (a) the best interests requirement is reviewable on the variation of conditions ground, and
  (b) the change in the relevant person's case is not significant,
they may vary the conditions to which the standard authorisation is subject in such ways (if any) as they think are appropriate in the circumstances.
(5) If the supervisory body decide that–
  (a) the best interests requirement is reviewable on the variation of conditions ground, and
  (b) the change in the relevant person's case is significant,
they must vary the conditions to which the standard authorisation is subject in such ways as they think are appropriate in the circumstances.
(6) If the supervisory body decide that the best interests requirement is not reviewable on–
  (a) the change of reason ground, or
  (b) the variation of conditions ground,
this Part does not require the supervisory body to take any action in respect of the standard authorisation so far as the best interests requirement relates to it.

Mental health, mental capacity, eligibility or no refusals review assessment positive

116 (1) This paragraph applies if the following conditions are met.
(2) The first condition is that one or more of the following are carried out–
  (a) a mental health review assessment;
  (b) a mental capacity review assessment;
  (c) an eligibility review assessment;
  (d) a no refusals review assessment.
(3) The second condition is that each assessment carried out comes to a positive conclusion.
(4) The supervisory body must decide whether or not each of the assessed qualifying requirements is reviewable on the change of reason ground.
(5) If the supervisory body decide that any of the assessed qualifying requirements is reviewable on the change of reason ground, they must vary the standard authorisation so that it states the reason why the relevant person now meets the requirement or requirements in question.

(6) If the supervisory body decide that none of the assessed qualifying requirements are reviewable on the change of reason ground, this Part does not require the supervisory body to take any action in respect of the standard authorisation so far as those requirements relate to it.
(7) An assessed qualifying requirement is a qualifying requirement in relation to which a review assessment is carried out.

One or more review assessments negative
117 (1) This paragraph applies if one or more of the review assessments carried out comes to a negative conclusion.
(2) The supervisory body must terminate the standard authorisation with immediate effect.

Completion of a review
118 (1) The review of the standard authorisation is complete in any of the following cases.
(2) The first case is where paragraph 110 applies.
(3) The second case is where–
  (a) paragraph 111 applies, and
  (b) paragraph 117 requires the supervisory body to terminate the standard authorisation.
(4) In such a case, the supervisory body need not comply with any of the other provisions of paragraphs 114 to 116 which would be applicable to the review (were it not for this sub-paragraph).
(5) The third case is where–
  (a) paragraph 111 applies,
  (b) paragraph 117 does not require the supervisory body to terminate the standard authorisation, and
  (c) the supervisory body comply with all of the provisions of paragraphs 114 to 116 (so far as they are applicable to the review).

Variations under this Part
119 Any variation of the standard authorisation made under this Part must be in writing.

Notice of outcome of review
120 (1) When the review of the standard authorisation is complete, the supervisory body must give notice to all of the following–
  (a) the managing authority of the relevant hospital or care home;
  (b) the relevant person;
  (c) the relevant person's representative;
  (d) any section 39D IMCA.
(2) That notice must state–
  (a) the outcome of the review, and
  (b) what variation (if any) has been made to the authorisation under this Part.

Records
121 A supervisory body must keep a written record of the following information–
  (a) each request for a review that is made to them;
  (b) the outcome of each request;
  (c) each review which they carry out;

(d) the outcome of each review which they carry out;
(e) any variation of an authorisation made in consequence of a review.

Relationship between review and suspension under Part 6

122 (1) This paragraph applies if a standard authorisation is suspended in accordance with Part 6.
(2) No review may be requested under this Part whilst the standard authorisation is suspended.
(3) If a review has already been requested, or is being carried out, when the standard authorisation is suspended, no steps are to be taken in connection with that review whilst the authorisation is suspended.

Relationship between review and request for new authorisation

123 (1) This paragraph applies if, in accordance with paragraph 24 (as read with paragraph 29), the managing authority of the relevant hospital or care home make a request for a new standard authorisation which would be in force after the expiry of the existing authorisation.
(2) No review may be requested under this Part until the request for the new standard authorisation has been disposed of.
(3) If a review has already been requested, or is being carried out, when the new standard authorisation is requested, no steps are to be taken in connection with that review until the request for the new standard authorisation has been disposed of.

124 (1) This paragraph applies if–
(a) a review under this Part has been requested, or is being carried out, and
(b) the managing authority of the relevant hospital or care home make a request under paragraph 30 for a new standard authorisation which would be in force on or before, and after, the expiry of the existing authorisation.
(2) No steps are to be taken in connection with the review under this Part until the request for the new standard authorisation has been disposed of.

125 In paragraphs 123 and 124–
(a) the existing authorisation is the authorisation referred to in paragraph 101;
(b) the expiry of the existing authorisation is the time when it is expected to cease to be in force.

Part 9: Assessments under this Schedule

Introduction

126 This Part contains provision about assessments under this Schedule.

127 An assessment under this Schedule is either of the following–
(a) an assessment carried out in connection with a request for a standard authorisation under Part 4;
(b) a review assessment carried out in connection with a review of a standard authorisation under Part 8.

128 In this Part, in relation to an assessment under this Schedule–
'assessor' means the person carrying out the assessment;
'relevant procedure' means–
(a) the request for the standard authorisation, or
(b) the review of the standard authorisation;
'supervisory body' means the supervisory body responsible for securing that the assessment is carried out.

Supervisory body to select assessor

129 (1) It is for the supervisory body to select a person to carry out an assessment under this Schedule.
  (2) The supervisory body must not select a person to carry out an assessment unless the person–
   (a) appears to the supervisory body to be suitable to carry out the assessment (having regard, in particular, to the type of assessment and the person to be assessed), and
   (b) is eligible to carry out the assessment.
  (3) Regulations may make provision about the selection, and eligibility, of persons to carry out assessments under this Schedule.
  (4) Sub-paragraphs (5) and (6) apply if two or more assessments are to be obtained for the purposes of the relevant procedure.
  (5) In a case where the assessments to be obtained include a mental health assessment and a best interests assessment, the supervisory body must not select the same person to carry out both assessments.
  (6) Except as prohibited by sub-paragraph (5), the supervisory body may select the same person to carry out any number of the assessments which the person appears to be suitable, and is eligible, to carry out.
130 (1) This paragraph applies to regulations under paragraph 129(3).
  (2) The regulations may make provision relating to a person's–
   (a) qualifications,
   (b) skills,
   (c) training,
   (d) experience,
   (e) relationship to, or connection with, the relevant person or any other person,
   (f) involvement in the care or treatment of the relevant person,
   (g) connection with the supervisory body, or
   (h) connection with the relevant hospital or care home, or with any other establishment or undertaking.
  (3) The provision that the regulations may make in relation to a person's training may provide for particular training to be specified by the appropriate authority otherwise than in the regulations.
  (4) In sub-paragraph (3) the 'appropriate authority' means–
   (a) in relation to England: the Secretary of State;
   (b) in relation to Wales: the National Assembly for Wales.
  (5) The regulations may make provision requiring a person to be insured in respect of liabilities that may arise in connection with the carrying out of an assessment.
  (6) In relation to cases where two or more assessments are to be obtained for the purposes of the relevant procedure, the regulations may limit the number, kind or combination of assessments which a particular person is eligible to carry out.
  (7) Sub-paragraphs (2) to (6) do not limit the generality of the provision that may be made in the regulations.

Examination and copying of records

131 An assessor may, at all reasonable times, examine and take copies of–
  (a) any health record,
  (b) any record of, or held by, a local authority and compiled in accordance with a social services function, and

(c) any record held by a person registered under Part 2 of the Care Standards Act 2000 or Chapter 2 of Part 1 of the Health and Social Care Act 2008, which the assessor considers may be relevant to the assessment which is being carried out.

Representations

132 In carrying out an assessment under this Schedule, the assessor must take into account any information given, or submissions made, by any of the following–
(a) the relevant person's representative;
(b) any section 39A IMCA;
(c) any section 39C IMCA;
(d) any section 39D IMCA.

Assessments to stop if any comes to negative conclusion

133 (1) This paragraph applies if an assessment under this Schedule comes to the conclusion that the relevant person does not meet one of the qualifying requirements.
(2) This Schedule does not require the supervisory body to secure that any other assessments under this Schedule are carried out in relation to the relevant procedure.
(3) The supervisory body must give notice to any assessor who is carrying out another assessment in connection with the relevant procedure that they are to cease carrying out that assessment.
(4) If an assessor receives such notice, this Schedule does not require the assessor to continue carrying out that assessment.

Duty to keep records and give copies

134 (1) This paragraph applies if an assessor has carried out an assessment under this Schedule (whatever conclusions the assessment has come to).
(2) The assessor must keep a written record of the assessment.
(3) As soon as practicable after carrying out the assessment, the assessor must give copies of the assessment to the supervisory body.

135 (1) This paragraph applies to the supervisory body if they are given a copy of an assessment under this Schedule.
(2) The supervisory body must give copies of the assessment to all of the following–
(a) the managing authority of the relevant hospital or care home;
(b) the relevant person;
(c) any section 39A IMCA;
(d) the relevant person's representative.
(3) If–
(a) the assessment is obtained in relation to a request for a standard authorisation, and
(b) the supervisory body are required by paragraph 50(1) to give the standard authorisation,
the supervisory body must give the copies of the assessment when they give copies of the authorisation in accordance with paragraph 57.
(4) If–
(a) the assessment is obtained in relation to a request for a standard authorisation, and

(b) the supervisory body are prohibited by paragraph 50(2) from giving the standard authorisation,

the supervisory body must give the copies of the assessment when they give notice in accordance with paragraph 58.

(5) If the assessment is obtained in connection with the review of a standard authorisation, the supervisory body must give the copies of the assessment when they give notice in accordance with paragraph 120.

136(1) This paragraph applies to the supervisory body if–
 (a) they are given a copy of a best interests assessment, and
 (b) the assessment includes, in accordance with paragraph 44(2), a statement that it appears to the assessor that there is an unauthorised deprivation of liberty.

(2) The supervisory body must notify all of the persons listed in sub-paragraph (3) that the assessment includes such a statement.

(3) Those persons are–
 (a) the managing authority of the relevant hospital or care home;
 (b) the relevant person;
 (c) any section 39A IMCA;
 (d) any interested person consulted by the best interests assessor.

(4) The supervisory body must comply with this paragraph when (or at some time before) they comply with paragraph 135.

Part 10: Relevant Person's Representative

The representative

137 In this Schedule the relevant person's representative is the person appointed as such in accordance with this Part.

138(1) Regulations may make provision about the selection and appointment of representatives.

(2) In this Part such regulations are referred to as 'appointment regulations'.

Supervisory body to appoint representative

139(1) The supervisory body must appoint a person to be the relevant person's representative as soon as practicable after a standard authorisation is given.

(2) The supervisory body must appoint a person to be the relevant person's representative if a vacancy arises whilst a standard authorisation is in force.

(3) Where a vacancy arises, the appointment under sub-paragraph (2) is to be made as soon as practicable after the supervisory body becomes aware of the vacancy.

140(1) The selection of a person for appointment under paragraph 139 must not be made unless it appears to the person making the selection that the prospective representative would, if appointed–
 (a) maintain contact with the relevant person,
 (b) represent the relevant person in matters relating to or connected with this Schedule, and
 (c) support the relevant person in matters relating to or connected with this Schedule.

141(1) Any appointment of a representative for a relevant person is in addition to, and does not affect, any appointment of a donee or deputy.

(2) The functions of any representative are in addition to, and do not affect–
   (a) the authority of any donee,
   (b) the powers of any deputy, or
   (c) any powers of the court.

Appointment regulations

142 Appointment regulations may provide that the procedure for appointing a representative may begin at any time after a request for a standard authorisation is made (including a time before the request has been disposed of).

143 (1) Appointment regulations may make provision about who is to select a person for appointment as a representative.
   (2) But regulations under this paragraph may only provide for the following to make a selection–
      (a) the relevant person, if he has capacity in relation to the question of which person should be his representative;
      (b) a donee of a lasting power of attorney granted by the relevant person, if it is within the scope of his authority to select a person;
      (c) a deputy, if it is within the scope of his authority to select a person;
      (d) a best interests assessor;
      (e) the supervisory body.
   (3) Regulations under this paragraph may provide that a selection by the relevant person, a donee or a deputy is subject to approval by a best interests assessor or the supervisory body.
   (4) Regulations under this paragraph may provide that, if more than one selection is necessary in connection with the appointment of a particular representative–
      (a) the same person may make more than one selection;
      (b) different persons may make different selections.
   (5) For the purposes of this paragraph a best interests assessor is a person carrying out a best interests assessment in connection with the standard authorisation in question (including the giving of that authorisation).

144 (1) Appointment regulations may make provision about who may, or may not, be–
      (a) selected for appointment as a representative, or
      (b) appointed as a representative.
   (2) Regulations under this paragraph may relate to any of the following matters–
      (a) a person's age;
      (b) a person's suitability;
      (c) a person's independence;
      (d) a person's willingness;
      (e) a person's qualifications.

145 Appointment regulations may make provision about the formalities of appointing a person as a representative.

146 In a case where a best interests assessor is to select a person to be appointed as a representative, appointment regulations may provide for the variation of the assessor's duties in relation to the assessment which he is carrying out.

Monitoring of representatives

147 Regulations may make provision requiring the managing authority of the relevant hospital or care home to–

(a) monitor, and
(b) report to the supervisory body on,
the extent to which a representative is maintaining contact with the relevant person.

Termination

148 Regulations may make provision about the circumstances in which the appointment of a person as the relevant person's representative ends or may be ended.
149 Regulations may make provision about the formalities of ending the appointment of a person as a representative.

Suspension of representative's functions

150 (1) Regulations may make provision about the circumstances in which functions exercisable by, or in relation to, the relevant person's representative (whether under this Schedule or not) may be–
  (a) suspended, and
  (b) if suspended, revived.
  (2) The regulations may make provision about the formalities for giving effect to the suspension or revival of a function.
  (3) The regulations may make provision about the effect of the suspension or revival of a function.

Payment of representative

151 Regulations may make provision for payments to be made to, or in relation to, persons exercising functions as the relevant person's representative.

Regulations under this Part

152 The provisions of this Part which specify provision that may be made in regulations under this Part do not affect the generality of the power to make such regulations.

Effect of appointment of section 39C IMCA

153 Paragraphs 159 and 160 make provision about the exercise of functions by, or towards, the relevant person's representative during periods when–
  (a) no person is appointed as the relevant person's representative, but
  (b) a person is appointed as a section 39C IMCA.

Part 11: IMCAs

Application of Part

154 This Part applies for the purposes of this Schedule.

The IMCAs

155 A section 39A IMCA is an independent mental capacity advocate appointed under section 39A.
156 A section 39C IMCA is an independent mental capacity advocate appointed under section 39C.
157 A section 39D IMCA is an independent mental capacity advocate appointed under section 39D.
158 An IMCA is a section 39A IMCA or a section 39C IMCA or a section 39D IMCA.

Section 39C IMCA: functions
159(1) This paragraph applies if, and for as long as, there is a section 39C IMCA.
  (2) In the application of the relevant provisions, references to the relevant person's representative are to be read as references to the section 39C IMCA.
  (3) But sub-paragraph (2) does not apply to any function under the relevant provisions for as long as the function is suspended in accordance with provision made under Part 10.
  (4) In this paragraph and paragraph 160 the relevant provisions are–
    (a) paragraph 102(3)(b) (request for review under Part 8);
    (b) paragraph 108(1)(b) (notice of review under Part 8);
    (c) paragraph 120(1)(c) (notice of outcome of review under Part 8).
160(1) This paragraph applies if–
    (a) a person is appointed as the relevant person's representative, and
    (b) a person accordingly ceases to hold an appointment as a section 39C IMCA.
  (2) Where a function under a relevant provision has been exercised by, or towards, the section 39C IMCA, there is no requirement for that function to be exercised again by, or towards, the relevant person's representative.

Section 39A IMCA: restriction of functions
161(1) This paragraph applies if–
    (a) there is a section 39A IMCA, and
    (b) a person is appointed under Part 10 to be the relevant person's representative (whether or not that person, or any person subsequently appointed, is currently the relevant person's representative).
  (2) The duties imposed on, and the powers exercisable by, the section 39A IMCA do not apply.
  (3) The duties imposed on, and the powers exercisable by, any other person do not apply, so far as they fall to be performed or exercised towards the section 39A IMCA.
  (4) But sub-paragraph (2) does not apply to any power of challenge exercisable by the section 39A IMCA.
  (5) And sub-paragraph (3) does not apply to any duty or power of any other person so far as it relates to any power of challenge exercisable by the section 39A IMCA.
  (6) Before exercising any power of challenge, the section 39A IMCA must take the views of the relevant person's representative into account.
  (7) A power of challenge is a power to make an application to the court to exercise its jurisdiction under section 21A in connection with the giving of the standard authorisation.

Part 12: Miscellaneous
Monitoring of operation of Schedule
162(1) Regulations may make provision for, and in connection with, requiring one or more prescribed bodies to monitor, and report on, the operation of this Schedule in relation to England.
  (2) The regulations may, in particular, give a prescribed body authority to do one or more of the following things–
    (a) to visit hospitals and care homes;
    (b) to visit and interview persons accommodated in hospitals and care homes;

(c) to require the production of, and to inspect, records relating to the care or treatment of persons.
(3) 'Prescribed' means prescribed in regulations under this paragraph.
163 (1) Regulations may make provision for, and in connection with, enabling the National Assembly for Wales to monitor, and report on, the operation of this Schedule in relation to Wales.
(2) The National Assembly may direct one or more persons or bodies to carry out the Assembly's functions under regulations under this paragraph.

Disclosure of information

164 (1) Regulations may require either or both of the following to disclose prescribed information to prescribed bodies–
(a) supervisory bodies;
(b) managing authorities of hospitals or care homes.
(2) 'Prescribed' means prescribed in regulations under this paragraph.
(3) Regulations under this paragraph may only prescribe information relating to matters with which this Schedule is concerned.

Directions by National Assembly in relation to supervisory functions

165 (1) The National Assembly for Wales may direct a Local Health Board to exercise in relation to its area any supervisory functions which are specified in the direction.
(2) Directions under this paragraph must not preclude the National Assembly from exercising the functions specified in the directions.
(3) In this paragraph 'supervisory functions' means functions which the National Assembly have as supervisory body, so far as they are exercisable in relation to hospitals (whether NHS or independent hospitals, and whether in Wales or England).
166 (1) This paragraph applies where, under paragraph 165, a Local Health Board ('the specified LHB') is directed to exercise supervisory functions ('delegated functions').
(2) The National Assembly for Wales may give directions to the specified LHB about the Board's exercise of delegated functions.
(3) The National Assembly may give directions for any delegated functions to be exercised, on behalf of the specified LHB, by a committee, sub-committee or officer of that Board.
(4) The National Assembly may give directions providing for any delegated functions to be exercised by the specified LHB jointly with one or more other Local Health Boards.
(5) Where, under sub-paragraph (4), delegated functions are exercisable jointly, the National Assembly may give directions providing for the functions to be exercised, on behalf of the Local Health Boards in question, by a joint committee or joint sub-committee.
167 (1) Directions under paragraph 165 must be given in regulations.
(2) Directions under paragraph 166 may be given–
(a) in regulations, or
(b) by instrument in writing.
168 The power under paragraph 165 or paragraph 166 to give directions includes power to vary or revoke directions given under that paragraph.

Notices

169 Any notice under this Schedule must be in writing.

Regulations

170 (1) This paragraph applies to all regulations under this Schedule, except regulations under paragraph 162, 163, 167 or 183.

(2) It is for the Secretary of State to make such regulations in relation to authorisations under this Schedule which relate to hospitals and care homes situated in England.

(3) It is for the National Assembly for Wales to make such regulations in relation to authorisations under this Schedule which relate to hospitals and care homes situated in Wales.

171 It is for the Secretary of State to make regulations under paragraph 162.

172 It is for the National Assembly for Wales to make regulations under paragraph 163 or 167.

173 (1) This paragraph applies to regulations under paragraph 183.

(2) It is for the Secretary of State to make such regulations in relation to cases where a question as to the ordinary residence of a person is to be determined by the Secretary of State.

(3) It is for the National Assembly for Wales to make such regulations in relation to cases where a question as to the ordinary residence of a person is to be determined by the National Assembly.

Part 13: Interpretation

Introduction

174 This Part applies for the purposes of this Schedule.

Hospitals and their managing authorities

175 (1) 'Hospital' means–
   (a) an NHS hospital, or
   (b) an independent hospital.

(2) 'NHS hospital' means–
   (a) a health service hospital as defined by section 275 of the National Health Service Act 2006 or section 206 of the National Health Service (Wales) Act 2006, or
   (b) a hospital as defined by section 206 of the National Health Service (Wales) Act 2006 vested in a Local Health Board.

(3) Independent hospital'–
   (a) in relation to England, means a hospital as defined by section 275 of the National Health Service Act 2006 that is not an NHS hospital; and
   (b) in relation to Wales, means a hospital as defined by section 2 of the Care Standards Act 2000 that is not an NHS hospital.

176 (1) 'Managing authority', in relation to an NHS hospital, means–
   (a) if the hospital–
      (i) is vested in the appropriate national authority for the purposes of its functions under the National Health Service Act 2006 or of the National Health Service (Wales) Act 2006, or
      (ii) consists of any accommodation provided by a local authority and used as a hospital by or on behalf of the appropriate national authority under either of those Acts,

the Local Health Board or Special Health Authority responsible for the administration of the hospital;
- (aa) in relation to England, if the hospital falls within paragraph (a)(i) or (ii) and no Special Health Authority has responsibility for its administration, the Secretary of State;
- (b) if the hospital is vested in a . . . National Health Service trust or NHS foundation trust, that trust;
- (c) if the hospital is vested in a Local Health Board, that Board.

(2) For this purpose the appropriate national authority is–
- (a) in relation to England: the Secretary of State;
- (b) in relation to Wales: the National Assembly for Wales;
- (c) in relation to England and Wales: the Secretary of State and the National Assembly acting jointly.

177 'Managing authority', in relation to an independent hospital, means–
- (a) in relation to England, the person registered, or required to be registered, under Chapter 2 of Part 1 of the Health and Social Care Act 2008 in respect of regulated activities (within the meaning of that Part) carried on in the hospital, and
- (b) in relation to Wales, the person registered, or required to be registered, under Part 2 of the Care Standards Act 2000 in respect of the hospital.

Care homes and their managing authorities

178 'Care home' has the meaning given by section 3 of the Care Standards Act 2000.
179 'Managing authority', in relation to a care home, means–
- (a) in relation to England, the person registered, or required to be registered, under Chapter 2 of Part 1 of the Health and Social Care Act 2008 in respect of the provision of residential accommodation, together with nursing or personal care, in the care home, and
- (b) in relation to Wales, the person registered, or required to be registered, under Part 2 of the Care Standards Act 2000 in respect of the care home.

Supervisory bodies: hospitals

180(1) The identity of the supervisory body is determined under this paragraph in cases where the relevant hospital is situated in England.

(2) If the relevant person is ordinarily resident in the area of a local authority in England, the supervisory body are that local authority.

(3) If the relevant person is not ordinarily resident in England and the National Assembly for Wales or a Local Health Board commission the relevant care or treatment, the National Assembly are the supervisory body.

(4) In any other case, the supervisory body are the local authority for the area in which the relevant hospital is situated.

(4A) Local authority' means–
- (a) the council of a county;
- (b) the council of a district for which there is no county council;
- (c) the council of a London borough;
- (d) the Common Council of the City of London;
- (e) the Council of the Isles of Scilly.

(5) If a hospital is situated in the areas of two (or more) local authorities, it is to be regarded for the purposes of sub-paragraph (4) as situated in whichever of the areas the greater (or greatest) part of the hospital is situated.

181 (1) The identity of the supervisory body is determined under this paragraph in cases where the relevant hospital is situated in Wales.
  (2) The National Assembly for Wales are the supervisory body.
  (3) But if the relevant person is ordinarily resident in the area of a local authority in England, the supervisory body are that local authority.
  (4) 'Local authority' means–
    (a) the council of a county;
    (b) the council of a district for which there is no county council;
    (c) the council of a London borough;
    (d) the Common Council of the City of London;
    (e) the Council of the Isles of Scilly.

Supervisory bodies: care homes

182 (1) The identity of the supervisory body is determined under this paragraph in cases where the relevant care home is situated in England or in Wales.
  (2) The supervisory body are the local authority for the area in which the relevant person is ordinarily resident.
  (3) But if the relevant person is not ordinarily resident in the area of a local authority, the supervisory body are the local authority for the area in which the care home is situated.
  (4) In relation to England 'local authority' means–
    (a) the council of a county;
    (b) the council of a district for which there is no county council;
    (c) the council of a London borough;
    (d) the Common Council of the City of London;
    (e) the Council of the Isles of Scilly.
  (5) In relation to Wales 'local authority' means the council of a county or county borough.
  (6) If a care home is situated in the areas of two (or more) local authorities, it is to be regarded for the purposes of sub-paragraph (3) as situated in whichever of the areas the greater (or greatest) part of the care home is situated.

Supervisory bodies: determination of place of ordinary residence

183 (1) [Repealed.]
  (2) [Repealed.]
  (2A) Section 39(1), (2) and (4) to (6) of the Care Act 2014 and paragraphs 1(1), 2(1) and 8 of Schedule 1 to that Act apply to any determination of where a person is ordinarily resident for the purposes of paragraphs 180, 181 and 182 as they apply for the purposes of Part 1 of that Act.]
  (2B) Section 194(1), (2), (4) and (5) of the Social Services and Well-being (Wales) Act 2014 apply to a determination of where a person is ordinarily resident for the purposes of paragraphs 180, 181 and 182 as it applies for the purposes of that Act.
  (3) Any question arising as to the ordinary residence of a person is to be determined by the Secretary of State or by the National Assembly for Wales.
  (4) The Secretary of State and the National Assembly must make and publish arrangements for determining which cases are to be dealt with by the Secretary of State and which are to be dealt with by the National Assembly.

(5) Those arrangements may include provision for the Secretary of State and the National Assembly to agree, in relation to any question that has arisen, which of them is to deal with the case.
(6) Regulations may make provision about arrangements that are to have effect before, upon, or after the determination of any question as to the ordinary residence of a person.
(7) The regulations may, in particular, authorise or require a local authority to do any or all of the following things–
   (a) to act as supervisory body even though it may wish to dispute that it is the supervisory body;
   (b) to become the supervisory body in place of another local authority;
   (c) to recover from another local authority expenditure incurred in exercising functions as the supervisory body.

Same body managing authority and supervisory body

184 (1) This paragraph applies if, in connection with a particular person's detention as a resident in a hospital or care home, the same body are both–
   (a) the managing authority of the relevant hospital or care home, and
   (b) the supervisory body.
(2) The fact that a single body are acting in both capacities does not prevent the body from carrying out functions under this Schedule in each capacity.
(3) But, in such a case, this Schedule has effect subject to any modifications contained in regulations that may be made for this purpose.

Interested persons

185 Each of the following is an interested person–
   (a) the relevant person's spouse or civil partner;
   (b) where the relevant person and another person are not married to each other, nor in a civil partnership with each other, but are living together as if they were a married couple: that other person;
   (d) the relevant person's children and step-children;
   (e) the relevant person's parents and step-parents;
   (f) the relevant person's brothers and sisters, half-brothers and half-sisters, and stepbrothers and stepsisters;
   (g) the relevant person's grandparents;
   (h) a deputy appointed for the relevant person by the court;
   (i) a donee of a lasting power of attorney granted by the relevant person.
186 (1) An interested person consulted by the best interests assessor is any person whose name is stated in the relevant best interests assessment in accordance with paragraph 40 (interested persons whom the assessor consulted in carrying out the assessment).
(2) The relevant best interests assessment is the most recent best interests assessment carried out in connection with the standard authorisation in question (whether the assessment was carried out under Part 4 or Part 8).
187 Where this Schedule imposes on a person a duty towards an interested person, the duty does not apply if the person on whom the duty is imposed–
   (a) is not aware of the interested person's identity or of a way of contacting him, and
   (b) cannot reasonably ascertain it.

188 The following table contains an index of provisions defining or otherwise explaining expressions used in this Schedule–

age assessment	paragraph 34
age requirement	paragraph 13
age review assessment	paragraph 112(3)
appointment regulations	paragraph 138
assessment under this Schedule	paragraph 127
assessor (except in Part 8)	paragraph 33
assessor (in Part 8)	paragraphs 33 and 128
authorisation under this Schedule	paragraph 10
best interests (determination of)	section 4
best interests assessment	paragraph 38
best interests requirement	paragraph 16
best interests review assessment	paragraph 112(6)
care home	paragraph 178
change of reason ground	paragraph 106
complete (in relation to a review of a standard authorisation)	paragraph 118
deprivation of a person's liberty	section 64(5) and (6)
deputy	section 16(2)(b)
detained resident	paragraph 6
disposed of (in relation to a request for a standard authorisation)	paragraph 66
eligibility assessment	paragraph 46
eligibility requirement	paragraph 17
eligibility review assessment	paragraph 112(7)
eligible person (in relation to paragraphs 68 to 73)	paragraph 68
eligible person (in relation to Part 8)	paragraph 102(3)
expiry (in relation to an existing authorisation)	paragraph 125(b)
existing authorisation (in Part 8)	paragraph 125(a)
hospital	paragraph 175
IMCA	paragraph 158
in force (in relation to a standard authorisation)	paragraphs 63 and 64
in force (in relation to an urgent authorisation)	paragraphs 88 and 89
ineligible (in relation to the eligibility requirement)	Schedule 1A
interested person	paragraph 185
interested person consulted by the best interests assessor	paragraph 186
lack of capacity	section 2
lasting power of attorney	section 9
managing authority (in relation to a care home)	paragraph 179
managing authority (in relation to a hospital)	paragraph 176 or 177

maximum authorisation period	paragraph 42
mental capacity assessment	paragraph 37
mental capacity requirement	paragraph 15
mental capacity review assessment	paragraph 112(5)
mental health assessment	paragraph 35
mental health requirement	paragraph 14
mental health review assessment	paragraph 112(4)
negative conclusion	paragraph 112(2)(a)
new supervisory body	paragraph 99(b)
no refusals assessment	paragraph 48
no refusals requirement	paragraph 18
no refusals review assessment	paragraph 112(8)
non-qualification ground	paragraph 105
old supervisory body	paragraph 99(a)
positive conclusion	paragraph 112(2)(b)
purpose of a standard authorisation	paragraph 11(1)
purpose of an urgent authorisation	paragraph 11(2)
qualifying requirements	paragraph 12
refusal (for the purposes of the no refusals requirement)	paragraphs 19 and 20
relevant care or treatment	paragraph 7
relevant hospital or care home	paragraph 7
relevant managing authority	paragraph 26(4)
relevant person	paragraph 7
relevant person's representative	paragraph 137
relevant procedure	paragraph 128
review assessment	paragraph 112(1)
reviewable	paragraph 104
section 39A IMCA	paragraph 155
section 39C IMCA	paragraph 156
section 39D IMCA	paragraph 157
standard authorisation	paragraph 8
supervisory body (except in Part 8)	paragraph 180, 181 or 182
supervisory body (in Part 8)	paragraph 128 and paragraph 180, 181 or 182
unauthorised deprivation of liberty (in relation to paragraphs 68 to 73)	paragraph 67
urgent authorisation	paragraph 9
variation of conditions ground	paragraph 107

SCHEDULE 1: LASTING POWERS OF ATTORNEY: FORMALITIES

Section 9

Part 1: Making Instruments

General requirements as to making instruments

1 (1) An instrument is not made in accordance with this Schedule unless–
   (a) it is in the prescribed form,
   (b) it complies with paragraph 2, and
   (c) any prescribed requirements in connection with its execution are satisfied.
(2) Regulations may make different provision according to whether–
   (a) the instrument relates to personal welfare or to property and affairs (or to both);
   (b) only one or more than one donee is to be appointed (and if more than one, whether jointly or jointly and severally).
(3) In this Schedule–
   (a) 'prescribed' means prescribed by regulations, and
   (b) 'regulations' means regulations made for the purposes of this Schedule by the Lord Chancellor.

Requirements as to content of instruments

2 (1) The instrument must include–
   (a) the prescribed information about the purpose of the instrument and the effect of a lasting power of attorney,
   (b) a statement by the donor to the effect that he–
      (i) has read the prescribed information or a prescribed part of it (or has had it read to him), and
      (ii) intends the authority conferred under the instrument to include authority to make decisions on his behalf in circumstances where he no longer has capacity,
   (c) a statement by the donor–
      (i) naming a person or persons whom the donor wishes to be notified of any application for the registration of the instrument, or
      (ii) stating that there are no persons whom he wishes to be notified of any such application,
   (d) a statement by the donee (or, if more than one, each of them) to the effect that he–
      (i) has read the prescribed information or a prescribed part of it (or has had it read to him), and
      (ii) understands the duties imposed on a donee of a lasting power of attorney under sections 1 (the principles) and 4 (best interests), and
   (e) a certificate by a person of a prescribed description that, in his opinion, at the time when the donor executes the instrument–
      (i) the donor understands the purpose of the instrument and the scope of the authority conferred under it,
      (ii) no fraud or undue pressure is being used to induce the donor to create a lasting power of attorney, and
      (iii) there is nothing else which would prevent a lasting power of attorney from being created by the instrument.

(2) Regulations may–
  (a) prescribe a maximum number of named persons;
  (b) provide that, where the instrument includes a statement under sub-paragraph (1)(c)(ii), two persons of a prescribed description must each give a certificate under sub-paragraph (1)(e).
(3) The persons who may be named persons do not include a person who is appointed as donee under the instrument.
(4) In this Schedule, 'named person' means a person named under sub-paragraph (1)(c).
(5) A certificate under sub-paragraph (1)(e)–
  (a) must be made in the prescribed form, and
  (b) must include any prescribed information.
(6) The certificate may not be given by a person appointed as donee under the instrument.

Failure to comply with prescribed form

3 (1) If an instrument differs in an immaterial respect in form or mode of expression from the prescribed form, it is to be treated by the Public Guardian as sufficient in point of form and expression.
(2) The court may declare that an instrument which is not in the prescribed form is to be treated as if it were, if it is satisfied that the persons executing the instrument intended it to create a lasting power of attorney.

Part 2: Registration

Applications and procedure for registration

4 (1) An application to the Public Guardian for the registration of an instrument intended to create a lasting power of attorney–
  (a) must be made in the prescribed form, and
  (b) must include any prescribed information.
(2) The application may be made–
  (a) by the donor,
  (b) by the donee or donees, or
  (c) if the instrument appoints two or more donees to act jointly and severally in respect of any matter, by any of the donees.
(3) The application must be accompanied by–
  (a) the instrument, and
  (b) any fee provided for under section 58(4)(b).
(4) A person who, in an application for registration, makes a statement which he knows to be false in a material particular is guilty of an offence and is liable–
  (a) on summary conviction, to imprisonment for a term not exceeding 12 months or a fine not exceeding the statutory maximum or both;
  (b) on conviction on indictment, to imprisonment for a term not exceeding 2 years or a fine or both.

5 Subject to paragraphs 11 to 14, the Public Guardian must register the instrument as a lasting power of attorney at the end of the prescribed period.

Notification requirements

6 (1) A donor about to make an application under paragraph 4(2)(a) must notify any named persons that he is about to do so.

(2) The donee (or donees) about to make an application under paragraph 4(2)(b) or (c) must notify any named persons that he is (or they are) about to do so.

7 As soon as is practicable after receiving an application by the donor under paragraph 4(2)(a), the Public Guardian must notify the donee (or donees) that the application has been received.

8 (1) As soon as is practicable after receiving an application by a donee (or donees) under paragraph 4(2)(b), the Public Guardian must notify the donor that the application has been received.

(2) As soon as is practicable after receiving an application by a donee under paragraph 4(2)(c), the Public Guardian must notify—
   (a) the donor, and
   (b) the donee or donees who did not join in making the application,
that the application has been received.

9 (1) A notice under paragraph 6 must be made in the prescribed form.
   (2) A notice under paragraph 6, 7 or 8 must include such information, if any, as may be prescribed.

Power to dispense with notification requirements

10 The court may—
   (a) on the application of the donor, dispense with the requirement to notify under paragraph 6(1), or
   (b) on the application of the donee or donees concerned, dispense with the requirement to notify under paragraph 6(2),
if satisfied that no useful purpose would be served by giving the notice.

Instrument not made properly or containing ineffective provision

11 (1) If it appears to the Public Guardian that an instrument accompanying an application under paragraph 4 is not made in accordance with this Schedule, he must not register the instrument unless the court directs him to do so.

(2) Sub-paragraph (3) applies if it appears to the Public Guardian that the instrument contains a provision which—
   (a) would be ineffective as part of a lasting power of attorney, or
   (b) would prevent the instrument from operating as a valid lasting power of attorney.

(3) The Public Guardian—
   (a) must apply to the court for it to determine the matter under section 23(1), and
   (b) pending the determination by the court, must not register the instrument.

(4) Sub-paragraph (5) applies if the court determines under section 23(1) (whether or not on an application by the Public Guardian) that the instrument contains a provision which—
   (a) would be ineffective as part of a lasting power of attorney, or
   (b) would prevent the instrument from operating as a valid lasting power of attorney.

(5) The court must—
   (a) notify the Public Guardian that it has severed the provision, or
   (b) direct him not to register the instrument.

(6) Where the court notifies the Public Guardian that it has severed a provision, he must register the instrument with a note to that effect attached to it.

Deputy already appointed

12 (1) Sub-paragraph (2) applies if it appears to the Public Guardian that–
  (a) there is a deputy appointed by the court for the donor, and
  (b) the powers conferred on the deputy would, if the instrument were registered, to any extent conflict with the powers conferred on the attorney.
(2) The Public Guardian must not register the instrument unless the court directs him to do so.

Objection by donee or named person

13 (1) Sub-paragraph (2) applies if a donee or a named person–
  (a) receives a notice under paragraph 6, 7 or 8 of an application for the registration of an instrument, and
  (b) before the end of the prescribed period, gives notice to the Public Guardian of an objection to the registration on the ground that an event mentioned in section 13(3) or (6)(a) to (d) has occurred which has revoked the instrument.
(2) If the Public Guardian is satisfied that the ground for making the objection is established, he must not register the instrument unless the court, on the application of the person applying for the registration–
  (a) is satisfied that the ground is not established, and
  (b) directs the Public Guardian to register the instrument.
(3) Sub-paragraph (4) applies if a donee or a named person–
  (a) receives a notice under paragraph 6, 7 or 8 of an application for the registration of an instrument, and
  (b) before the end of the prescribed period–
    (i) makes an application to the court objecting to the registration on a prescribed ground, and
    (ii) notifies the Public Guardian of the application.
(4) The Public Guardian must not register the instrument unless the court directs him to do so.

Objection by donor

14 (1) This paragraph applies if the donor–
  (a) receives a notice under paragraph 8 of an application for the registration of an instrument, and
  (b) before the end of the prescribed period, gives notice to the Public Guardian of an objection to the registration.
(2) The Public Guardian must not register the instrument unless the court, on the application of the donee or, if more than one, any of them–
  (a) is satisfied that the donor lacks capacity to object to the registration, and
  (b) directs the Public Guardian to register the instrument.

Notification of registration

15 Where an instrument is registered under this Schedule, the Public Guardian must give notice of the fact in the prescribed form to–
  (a) the donor, and
  (b) the donee or, if more than one, each of them.

Evidence of registration

16 (1) A document purporting to be an office copy of an instrument registered under this Schedule is, in any part of the United Kingdom, evidence of–

(a) the contents of the instrument, and
(b) the fact that it has been registered.
(2) Sub-paragraph (1) is without prejudice to–
(a) section 3 of the Powers of Attorney Act 1971 (proof by certified copy), and
(b) any other method of proof authorised by law.

Part 3: Cancellation of Registration and Notification of Severance

17 (1) The Public Guardian must cancel the registration of an instrument as a lasting power of attorney on being satisfied that the power has been revoked–
(a) as a result of the donor's bankruptcy or a debt relief order (under Part 7A of the Insolvency Act 1986) having been made in respect of the donor, or
(b) on the occurrence of an event mentioned in section 13(6)(a) to (d).
(2) If the Public Guardian cancels the registration of an instrument he must notify–
(a) the donor, and
(b) the donee or, if more than one, each of them.

18 The court must direct the Public Guardian to cancel the registration of an instrument as a lasting power of attorney if it–
(a) determines under section 22(2)(a) that a requirement for creating the power was not met,
(b) determines under section 22(2)(b) that the power has been revoked or has otherwise come to an end, or
(c) revokes the power under section 22(4)(b) (fraud etc).

19 (1) Sub-paragraph (2) applies if the court determines under section 23(1) that a lasting power of attorney contains a provision which–
(a) is ineffective as part of a lasting power of attorney, or
(b) prevents the instrument from operating as a valid lasting power of attorney.
(2) The court must–
(a) notify the Public Guardian that it has severed the provision, or
(b) direct him to cancel the registration of the instrument as a lasting power of attorney.

20 On the cancellation of the registration of an instrument, the instrument and any office copies of it must be delivered up to the Public Guardian to be cancelled.

Part 4: Records of Alterations in Registered Powers

Partial revocation or suspension of power as a result of bankruptcy

21 If in the case of a registered instrument it appears to the Public Guardian that under section 13 a lasting power of attorney is revoked, or suspended, in relation to the donor's property and affairs (but not in relation to other matters), the Public Guardian must attach to the instrument a note to that effect.

Termination of appointment of donee which does not revoke power

22 If in the case of a registered instrument it appears to the Public Guardian that an event has occurred–
(a) which has terminated the appointment of the donee, but
(b) which has not revoked the instrument,
the Public Guardian must attach to the instrument a note to that effect.

Replacement of donee

23 If in the case of a registered instrument it appears to the Public Guardian that the donee has been replaced under the terms of the instrument the Public Guardian must attach to the instrument a note to that effect.

Severance of ineffective provisions

24 If in the case of a registered instrument the court notifies the Public Guardian under paragraph 19(2)(a) that it has severed a provision of the instrument, the Public Guardian must attach to it a note to that effect.

Notification of alterations

25 If the Public Guardian attaches a note to an instrument under paragraph 21, 22, 23 or 24 he must give notice of the note to the donee or donees of the power (or, as the case may be, to the other donee or donees of the power).

SCHEDULE 1A: PERSONS INELIGIBLE TO BE DEPRIVED OF LIBERTY BY THIS ACT

Part 1: Ineligible Persons

Application

1 This Schedule applies for the purposes of–
   (a) section 16A, and
   (b) paragraph 17 of Schedule A1.

Determining ineligibility

2 A person ('P') is ineligible to be deprived of liberty by this Act ('ineligible') if–
   (a) P falls within one of the cases set out in the second column of the following table, and
   (b) the corresponding entry in the third column of the table–or the provision, or one of the provisions, referred to in that entry–provides that he is ineligible.

	Status of P	Determination of ineligibility
Case A	P is– (a) subject to the hospital treatment regime, and (b) detained in a hospital under that regime.	P is ineligible.
Case B	P is– (a) subject to the hospital treatment regime, but (b) not detained in a hospital under that regime.	See paragraphs 3 and 4.
Case C	P is subject to the community treatment regime.	See paragraphs 3 and 4.
Case D	P is subject to the guardianship regime.	See paragraphs 3 and 5.

| Case E | P is–
(a) within the scope of the Mental Health Act, but
(b) not subject to any of the mental health regimes. | See paragraph 5. |

Authorised course of action not in accordance with regime

3 (1) This paragraph applies in cases B, C and D in the table in paragraph 2.
   (2) P is ineligible if the authorised course of action is not in accordance with a requirement which the relevant regime imposes.
   (3) That includes any requirement as to where P is, or is not, to reside.
   (4) The relevant regime is the mental health regime to which P is subject.

Treatment for mental disorder in a hospital

4 (1) This paragraph applies in cases B and C in the table in paragraph 2.
   (2) P is ineligible if the relevant care or treatment consists in whole or in part of medical treatment for mental disorder in a hospital.

P objects to being a mental health patient etc

5 (1) This paragraph applies in cases D and E in the table in paragraph 2.
   (2) P is ineligible if the following conditions are met.
   (3) The first condition is that the relevant instrument authorises P to be a mental health patient.
   (4) The second condition is that P objects–
      (a) to being a mental health patient, or
      (b) to being given some or all of the mental health treatment.
   (5) The third condition is that a donee or deputy has not made a valid decision to consent to each matter to which P objects.
   (6) In determining whether or not P objects to something, regard must be had to all the circumstances (so far as they are reasonably ascertainable), including the following–
      (a) P's behaviour;
      (b) P's wishes and feelings;
      (c) P's views, beliefs and values.
   (7) But regard is to be had to circumstances from the past only so far as it is still appropriate to have regard to them.

Part 2: Interpretation

Application

6   This Part applies for the purposes of this Schedule.

Mental health regimes

7   The mental health regimes are–
     (a) the hospital treatment regime,
     (b) the community treatment regime, and
     (c) the guardianship regime.

Hospital treatment regime

8 (1) P is subject to the hospital treatment regime if he is subject to–
     (a) a hospital treatment obligation under the relevant enactment, or

(b) an obligation under another England and Wales enactment which has the same effect as a hospital treatment obligation.
(2) But where P is subject to any such obligation, he is to be regarded as not subject to the hospital treatment regime during any period when he is subject to the community treatment regime.
(3) A hospital treatment obligation is an application, order or direction of a kind listed in the first column of the following table.
(4) In relation to a hospital treatment obligation, the relevant enactment is the enactment in the Mental Health Act which is referred to in the corresponding entry in the second column of the following table.

Hospital treatment obligation	Relevant enactment
Application for admission for assessment	Section 2
Application for admission for assessment	Section 4
Application for admission for treatment	Section 3
Order for remand to hospital	Section 35
Order for remand to hospital	Section 36
Hospital order	Section 37
Interim hospital order	Section 38
Order for detention in hospital	Section 44
Hospital direction	Section 45A
Transfer direction	Section 47
Transfer direction	Section 48
Hospital order	Section 51

Community treatment regime
9 P is subject to the community treatment regime if he is subject to–
(a) a community treatment order under section 17A of the Mental Health Act, or
(b) an obligation under another England and Wales enactment which has the same effect as a community treatment order.

Guardianship regime
10 P is subject to the guardianship regime if he is subject to–
(a) a guardianship application under section 7 of the Mental Health Act,
(b) a guardianship order under section 37 of the Mental Health Act, or
(c) an obligation under another England and Wales enactment which has the same effect as a guardianship application or guardianship order.

England and Wales enactments
11 (1) An England and Wales enactment is an enactment which extends to England and Wales (whether or not it also extends elsewhere).
(2) It does not matter if the enactment is in the Mental Health Act or not.

P within scope of Mental Health Act
12 (1) P is within the scope of the Mental Health Act if–
(a) an application in respect of P could be made under section 2 or 3 of the Mental Health Act, and
(b) P could be detained in a hospital in pursuance of such an application, were one made.

(2) The following provisions of this paragraph apply when determining whether an application in respect of P could be made under section 2 or 3 of the Mental Health Act.

(3) If the grounds in section 2(2) of the Mental Health Act are met in P's case, it is to be assumed that the recommendations referred to in section 2(3) of that Act have been given.

(4) If the grounds in section 3(2) of the Mental Health Act are met in P's case, it is to be assumed that the recommendations referred to in section 3(3) of that Act have been given.

(5) In determining whether the ground in section 3(2)(c) of the Mental Health Act is met in P's case, it is to be assumed that the treatment referred to in section 3(2)(c) cannot be provided under this Act.

Authorised course of action, relevant care or treatment of relevant instrument

13 In a case where this Schedule applies for the purposes of section 16A–
'authorised course of action' means any course of action amounting to deprivation of liberty which the order under section 16(2)(a) authorises;
'relevant care or treatment' means any care or treatment which–
  (a) comprises, or forms part of, the authorised course of action, or
  (b) is to be given in connection with the authorised course of action;
'relevant instrument' means the order under section 16(2)(a).

14 In a case where this Schedule applies for the purposes of paragraph 17 of Schedule A1–
'authorised course of action' means the accommodation of the relevant person in the relevant hospital or care home for the purpose of being given the relevant care or treatment;
'relevant care or treatment' has the same meaning as in Schedule A1;
'relevant instrument' means the standard authorisation under Schedule A1.

15 (1) This paragraph applies where the question whether a person is ineligible to be deprived of liberty by this Act is relevant to either of these decisions–
  (a) whether or not to include particular provision ('the proposed provision') in an order under section 16(2)(a);
  (b) whether or not to give a standard authorisation under Schedule A1.

(2) A reference in this Schedule to the authorised course of action or the relevant care or treatment is to be read as a reference to that thing as it would be if–
  (a) the proposed provision were included in the order, or
  (b) the standard authorisation were given.

(3) A reference in this Schedule to the relevant instrument is to be read as follows–
  (a) where the relevant instrument is an order under section 16(2)(a): as a reference to the order as it would be if the proposed provision were included in it;
  (b) where the relevant instrument is a standard authorisation: as a reference to the standard authorisation as it would be if it were given.

Expressions used in paragraph 5

16 (1) These expressions have the meanings given–
'donee' means a donee of a lasting power of attorney granted by P;
'mental health patient' means a person accommodated in a hospital for the purpose of being given medical treatment for mental disorder;

'mental health treatment' means the medical treatment for mental disorder referred to in the definition of 'mental health patient'.
(2) A decision of a donee or deputy is valid if it is made–
  (a) within the scope of his authority as donee or deputy, and
  (b) in accordance with Part 1 of this Act.

Expressions with same meaning as in Mental Health Act
17 (1) 'Hospital' has the same meaning as in Part 2 of the Mental Health Act.
  (2) 'Medical treatment' has the same meaning as in the Mental Health Act.
  (3) 'Mental disorder' has the same meaning as in Schedule A1 (see paragraph 14).

SCHEDULE 2: PROPERTY AND AFFAIRS: SUPPLEMENTARY PROVISIONS

Section 18(4)

Wills: general
1   Paragraphs 2 to 4 apply in relation to the execution of a will, by virtue of section 18, on behalf of P.

Provision that may be made in will
2   The will may make any provision (whether by disposing of property or exercising a power or otherwise) which could be made by a will executed by P if he had capacity to make it.

Wills: requirements relating to execution
3 (1) Sub-paragraph (2) applies if under section 16 the court makes an order or gives directions requiring or authorising a person ('the authorised person') to execute a will on behalf of P.
  (2) Any will executed in pursuance of the order or direction–
    (a) must state that it is signed by P acting by the authorised person,
    (b) must be signed by the authorised person with the name of P and his own name, in the presence of two or more witnesses present at the same time,
    (c) must be attested and subscribed by those witnesses in the presence of the authorised person, and
    (d) must be sealed with the official seal of the court.

Wills: effect of execution
4 (1) This paragraph applies where a will is executed in accordance with paragraph 3.
  (2) The Wills Act 1837 has effect in relation to the will as if it were signed by P by his own hand, except that–
    (a) section 9 of the 1837 Act (requirements as to signing and attestation) does not apply, and
    (b) in the subsequent provisions of the 1837 Act any reference to execution in the manner required by the previous provisions is to be read as a reference to execution in accordance with paragraph 3.
  (3) The will has the same effect for all purposes as if–
    (a) P had had the capacity to make a valid will, and
    (b) the will had been executed by him in the manner required by the 1837 Act.

(4) But sub-paragraph (3) does not have effect in relation to the will–
  (a) in so far as it disposes of immovable property outside England and Wales, or
  (b) in so far as it relates to any other property or matter if, when the will is executed–
    (i) P is domiciled outside England and Wales, and
    (ii) the condition in sub-paragraph (5) is met.
(5) The condition is that, under the law of P's domicile, any question of his testamentary capacity would fall to be determined in accordance with the law of a place outside England and Wales.

Vesting orders ancillary to settlement etc

5 (1) If provision is made by virtue of section 18 for–
  (a) the settlement of any property of P, or
  (b) the exercise of a power vested in him of appointing trustees or retiring from a trust,
the court may also make as respects the property settled or the trust property such consequential vesting or other orders as the case may require.
(2) The power under sub-paragraph (1) includes, in the case of the exercise of such a power, any order which could have been made in such a case under Part 4 of the Trustee Act 1925 (c 19).

Variation of settlements

6 (1) If a settlement has been made by virtue of section 18, the court may by order vary or revoke the settlement if–
  (a) the settlement makes provision for its variation or revocation,
  (b) the court is satisfied that a material fact was not disclosed when the settlement was made, or
  (c) the court is satisfied that there has been a substantial change of circumstances.
(2) Any such order may give such consequential directions as the court thinks fit.

Vesting of stock in curator appointed outside England and Wales

7 (1) Sub-paragraph (2) applies if the court is satisfied–
  (a) that under the law prevailing in a place outside England and Wales a person ('M') has been appointed to exercise powers in respect of the property or affairs of P on the ground (however formulated) that P lacks capacity to make decisions with respect to the management and administration of his property and affairs, and
  (b) that, having regard to the nature of the appointment and to the circumstances of the case, it is expedient that the court should exercise its powers under this paragraph.
(2) The court may direct–
  (a) any stocks standing in the name of P, or
  (b) the right to receive dividends from the stocks,
to be transferred into M's name or otherwise dealt with as required by M, and may give such directions as the court thinks fit for dealing with accrued dividends from the stocks.
(3) 'Stocks' includes–
  (a) shares, and

(b) any funds, annuity or security transferable in the books kept by any body corporate or unincorporated company or society or by an instrument of transfer either alone or accompanied by other formalities,
and 'dividends' is to be construed accordingly.

Preservation of interests in property disposed of on behalf of person lacking capacity

8 (1) Sub-paragraphs (2) and (3) apply if–
  (a) P's property has been disposed of by virtue of section 18,
  (b) under P's will or intestacy, or by a gift perfected or nomination taking effect on his death, any other person would have taken an interest in the property but for the disposal, and
  (c) on P's death, any property belonging to P's estate represents the property disposed of.
(2) The person takes the same interest, if and so far as circumstances allow, in the property representing the property disposed of.
(3) If the property disposed of was real property, any property representing it is to be treated, so long as it remains part of P's estate, as if it were real property.
(4) The court may direct that, on a disposal of P's property–
  (a) which is made by virtue of section 18, and
  (b) which would apart from this paragraph result in the conversion of personal property into real property,
property representing the property disposed of is to be treated, so long as it remains P's property or forms part of P's estate, as if it were personal property.
(5) References in sub-paragraphs (1) to (4) to the disposal of property are to–
  (a) the sale, exchange, charging of or other dealing (otherwise than by will) with property other than money;
  (b) the removal of property from one place to another;
  (c) the application of money in acquiring property;
  (d) the transfer of money from one account to another;
and references to property representing property disposed of are to be construed accordingly and as including the result of successive disposals.
(6) The court may give such directions as appear to it necessary or expedient for the purpose of facilitating the operation of sub-paragraphs (1) to (3), including the carrying of money to a separate account and the transfer of property other than money.

9 (1) Sub-paragraph (2) applies if the court has ordered or directed the expenditure of money–
  (a) for carrying out permanent improvements on any of P's property, or
  (b) otherwise for the permanent benefit of any of P's property.
(2) The court may order that–
  (a) the whole of the money expended or to be expended, or
  (b) any part of it,
is to be a charge on the property either without interest or with interest at a specified rate.
(3) An order under sub-paragraph (2) may provide for excluding or restricting the operation of paragraph 8(1) to (3).
(4) A charge under sub-paragraph (2) may be made in favour of such person as may be just and, in particular, where the money charged is paid out of P's general estate, may be made in favour of a person as trustee for P.

(5) No charge under sub-paragraph (2) may confer any right of sale or foreclosure during P's lifetime.

Powers as patron of benefice

10 (1) Any functions which P has as patron of a benefice may be discharged only by a person ('R') appointed by the court.
 (2) R must be an individual capable of appointment under section 8(1)(b) of the 1986 Measure (which provides for an individual able to make a declaration of communicant status, a clerk in Holy Orders, etc to be appointed to discharge a registered patron's functions).
 (3) The 1986 Measure applies to R as it applies to an individual appointed by the registered patron of the benefice under section 8(1)(b) or (3) of that Measure to discharge his functions as patron.
 (4) 'The 1986 Measure' means the Patronage (Benefices) Measure 1986 (No 3).

SCHEDULE 3: INTERNATIONAL PROTECTION OF ADULTS

Section 63

Part 1: Preliminary

Introduction

1 This Part applies for the purposes of this Schedule.

The Convention

2 (1) 'Convention' means the Convention referred to in section 63.
 (2) 'Convention country' means a country in which the Convention is in force.
 (3) A reference to an Article or Chapter is to an Article or Chapter of the Convention.
 (4) An expression which appears in this Schedule and in the Convention is to be construed in accordance with the Convention.

Countries, territories and nationals

3 (1) 'Country' includes a territory which has its own system of law.
 (2) Where a country has more than one territory with its own system of law, a reference to the country, in relation to one of its nationals, is to the territory with which the national has the closer, or the closest, connection.

Adults with incapacity

4 (1) 'Adult' means (subject to sub-paragraph (2) a person who–
 (a) as a result of an impairment or insufficiency of his personal faculties, cannot protect his interests, and
 (b) has reached 16.
 (2) But 'adult' does not include a child to whom either of the following applies–
 (a) the Convention on Jurisdiction, Applicable Law, Recognition, Enforcement and Co-Operation in respect of Parental Responsibility and Measures for the Protection of Children that was signed at The Hague on 19 October 1996;
 (b) Council Regulation (EC) No 2201/2003 concerning jurisdiction and the recognition and enforcement of judgments in matrimonial matters and the matters of parental responsibility.

Protective measures

5 (1) 'Protective measure' means a measure directed to the protection of the person or property of an adult; and it may deal in particular with any of the following–
  (a) the determination of incapacity and the institution of a protective regime,
  (b) placing the adult under the protection of an appropriate authority,
  (c) guardianship, curatorship or any corresponding system,
  (d) the designation and functions of a person having charge of the adult's person or property, or representing or otherwise helping him,
  (e) placing the adult in a place where protection can be provided,
  (f) administering, conserving or disposing of the adult's property,
  (g) authorising a specific intervention for the protection of the person or property of the adult.
(2) Where a measure of like effect to a protective measure has been taken in relation to a person before he reaches 16, this Schedule applies to the measure in so far as it has effect in relation to him once he has reached 16.

Central Authority

6 (1) Any function under the Convention of a Central Authority is exercisable in England and Wales by the Lord Chancellor.
(2) A communication may be sent to the Central Authority in relation to England and Wales by sending it to the Lord Chancellor.

Part 2: Jurisdiction of Competent Authority

Scope of jurisdiction

7 (1) The court may exercise its functions under this Act (in so far as it cannot otherwise do so) in relation to–
  (a) an adult habitually resident in England and Wales,
  (b) an adult's property in England and Wales,
  (c) an adult present in England and Wales or who has property there, if the matter is urgent, or
  (d) an adult present in England and Wales, if a protective measure which is temporary and limited in its effect to England and Wales is proposed in relation to him.
(2) An adult present in England and Wales is to be treated for the purposes of this paragraph as habitually resident there if–
  (a) his habitual residence cannot be ascertained,
  (b) he is a refugee, or
  (c) he has been displaced as a result of disturbance in the country of his habitual residence.

8 (1) The court may also exercise its functions under this Act (in so far as it cannot otherwise do so) in relation to an adult if sub-paragraph (2) or (3) applies in relation to him.
(2) This sub-paragraph applies in relation to an adult if–
  (a) he is a British citizen,
  (b) he has a closer connection with England and Wales than with Scotland or Northern Ireland, and
  (c) Article 7 has, in relation to the matter concerned, been complied with.

(3) This sub-paragraph applies in relation to an adult if the Lord Chancellor, having consulted such persons as he considers appropriate, agrees to a request under Article 8 in relation to the adult.

Exercise of jurisdiction

9 (1) This paragraph applies where jurisdiction is exercisable under this Schedule in connection with a matter which involves a Convention country other than England and Wales.

(2) Any Article on which the jurisdiction is based applies in relation to the matter in so far as it involves the other country (and the court must, accordingly, comply with any duty conferred on it as a result).

(3) Article 12 also applies, so far as its provisions allow, in relation to the matter in so far as it involves the other country.

10 A reference in this Schedule to the exercise of jurisdiction under this Schedule is to the exercise of functions under this Act as a result of this Part of this Schedule.

Part 3: Applicable Law

Applicable law

11 In exercising jurisdiction under this Schedule, the court may, if it thinks that the matter has a substantial connection with a country other than England and Wales, apply the law of that other country.

12 Where a protective measure is taken in one country but implemented in another, the conditions of implementation are governed by the law of the other country.

Lasting powers of attorney, etc

13 (1) If the donor of a lasting power is habitually resident in England and Wales at the time of granting the power, the law applicable to the existence, extent, modification or extinction of the power is—
  (a) the law of England and Wales, or
  (b) if he specifies in writing the law of a connected country for the purpose, that law.

(2) If he is habitually resident in another country at that time, but England and Wales is a connected country, the law applicable in that respect is—
  (a) the law of the other country, or
  (b) if he specifies in writing the law of England and Wales for the purpose, that law.

(3) A country is connected, in relation to the donor, if it is a country—
  (a) of which he is a national,
  (b) in which he was habitually resident, or
  (c) in which he has property.

(4) Where this paragraph applies as a result of sub-paragraph (3)(c), it applies only in relation to the property which the donor has in the connected country.

(5) The law applicable to the manner of the exercise of a lasting power is the law of the country where it is exercised.

(6) In this Part of this Schedule, 'lasting power' means—
  (a) a lasting power of attorney (see section 9),
  (b) an enduring power of attorney within the meaning of Schedule 4, or
  (c) any other power of like effect.

14 (1) Where a lasting power is not exercised in a manner sufficient to guarantee the protection of the person or property of the donor, the court, in exercising jurisdiction under this Schedule, may disapply or modify the power.
   (2) Where, in accordance with this Part of this Schedule, the law applicable to the power is, in one or more respects, that of a country other than England and Wales, the court must, so far as possible, have regard to the law of the other country in that respect (or those respects).
15 Regulations may provide for Schedule 1 (lasting powers of attorney: formalities) to apply with modifications in relation to a lasting power which comes within paragraph 13(6)(c) above.

Protection of third parties

16 (1) This paragraph applies where a person (a 'representative') in purported exercise of an authority to act on behalf of an adult enters into a transaction with a third party.
   (2) The validity of the transaction may not be questioned in proceedings, nor may the third party be held liable, merely because–
      (a) where the representative and third party are in England and Wales when entering into the transaction, sub-paragraph (3) applies;
      (b) where they are in another country at that time, sub-paragraph (4) applies.
   (3) This sub-paragraph applies if–
      (a) the law applicable to the authority in one or more respects is, as a result of this Schedule, the law of a country other than England and Wales, and
      (b) the representative is not entitled to exercise the authority in that respect (or those respects) under the law of that other country.
   (4) This sub-paragraph applies if–
      (a) the law applicable to the authority in one or more respects is, as a result of this Part of this Schedule, the law of England and Wales, and
      (b) the representative is not entitled to exercise the authority in that respect (or those respects) under that law.
   (5) This paragraph does not apply if the third party knew or ought to have known that the applicable law was–
      (a) in a case within sub-paragraph (3), the law of the other country;
      (b) in a case within sub-paragraph (4), the law of England and Wales.

Mandatory rules

17 Where the court is entitled to exercise jurisdiction under this Schedule, the mandatory provisions of the law of England and Wales apply, regardless of any system of law which would otherwise apply in relation to the matter.

Public policy

18 Nothing in this Part of this Schedule requires or enables the application in England and Wales of a provision of the law of another country if its application would be manifestly contrary to public policy.

Part 4: Recognition and Enforcement

Recognition

19 (1) A protective measure taken in relation to an adult under the law of a country other than England and Wales is to be recognised in England and Wales if it was taken on the ground that the adult is habitually resident in the other country.

(2) A protective measure taken in relation to an adult under the law of a Convention country other than England and Wales is to be recognised in England and Wales if it was taken on a ground mentioned in Chapter 2 (jurisdiction).
(3) But the court may disapply this paragraph in relation to a measure if it thinks that–
  (a) the case in which the measure was taken was not urgent,
  (b) the adult was not given an opportunity to be heard, and
  (c) that omission amounted to a breach of natural justice.
(4) It may also disapply this paragraph in relation to a measure if it thinks that–
  (a) recognition of the measure would be manifestly contrary to public policy,
  (b) the measure would be inconsistent with a mandatory provision of the law of England and Wales, or
  (c) the measure is inconsistent with one subsequently taken, or recognised, in England and Wales in relation to the adult.
(5) And the court may disapply this paragraph in relation to a measure taken under the law of a Convention country in a matter to which Article 33 applies, if the court thinks that that Article has not been complied with in connection with that matter.

20 (1) An interested person may apply to the court for a declaration as to whether a protective measure taken under the law of a country other than England and Wales is to be recognised in England and Wales.
(2) No permission is required for an application to the court under this paragraph.

21 For the purposes of paragraphs 19 and 20, any finding of fact relied on when the measure was taken is conclusive.

Enforcement

22 (1) An interested person may apply to the court for a declaration as to whether a protective measure taken under the law of, and enforceable in, a country other than England and Wales is enforceable, or to be registered, in England and Wales in accordance with Court of Protection Rules.
(2) The court must make the declaration if–
  (a) the measure comes within sub-paragraph (1) or (2) of paragraph 19, and
  (b) the paragraph is not disapplied in relation to it as a result of sub-paragraph (3), (4) or (5).
(3) A measure to which a declaration under this paragraph relates is enforceable in England and Wales as if it were a measure of like effect taken by the court.

Measures taken in relation to those aged under 16

23 (1) This paragraph applies where–
  (a) provision giving effect to, or otherwise deriving from, the Convention in a country other than England and Wales applies in relation to a person who has not reached 16, and
  (b) a measure is taken in relation to that person in reliance on that provision.
(2) This Part of this Schedule applies in relation to that measure as it applies in relation to a protective measure taken in relation to an adult under the law of a Convention country other than England and Wales.

Supplementary

24 The court may not review the merits of a measure taken outside England and Wales except to establish whether the measure complies with this Schedule in so far as it is, as a result of this Schedule, required to do so.

25   Court of Protection Rules may make provision about an application under paragraph 20 or 22.

Part 5: Co-operation

Proposal for cross-border placement

26 (1) This paragraph applies where a public authority proposes to place an adult in an establishment in a Convention country other than England and Wales.
  (2) The public authority must consult an appropriate authority in that other country about the proposed placement and, for that purpose, must send it–
    (a) a report on the adult, and
    (b) a statement of its reasons for the proposed placement.
  (3) If the appropriate authority in the other country opposes the proposed placement within a reasonable time, the public authority may not proceed with it.
27   A proposal received by a public authority under Article 33 in relation to an adult is to proceed unless the authority opposes it within a reasonable time.

Adult in danger etc

28 (1) This paragraph applies if a public authority is told that an adult–
    (a) who is in serious danger, and
    (b) in relation to whom the public authority has taken, or is considering taking, protective measures,
    is, or has become resident, in a Convention country other than England and Wales.
  (2) The public authority must tell an appropriate authority in that other country about–
    (a) the danger, and
    (b) the measures taken or under consideration.
29   A public authority may not request from, or send to, an appropriate authority in a Convention country information in accordance with Chapter 5 (co-operation) in relation to an adult if it thinks that doing so–
    (a) would be likely to endanger the adult or his property, or
    (b) would amount to a serious threat to the liberty or life of a member of the adult's family.

Part 6: General

Certificates

30   A certificate given under Article 38 by an authority in a Convention country other than England and Wales is, unless the contrary is shown, proof of the matters contained in it.

Powers to make further provision as to private international law

31   Her Majesty may by Order in Council confer on the Lord Chancellor, the court or another public authority functions for enabling the Convention to be given effect in England and Wales.
32 (1) Regulations may make provision–
    (a) giving further effect to the Convention, or
    (b) otherwise about the private international law of England and Wales in relation to the protection of adults.

(2) The regulations may–
   (a) confer functions on the court or another public authority;
   (b) amend this Schedule;
   (c) provide for this Schedule to apply with specified modifications;
   (d) make provision about countries other than Convention countries.

Exceptions

33 Nothing in this Schedule applies, and no provision made under paragraph 32 is to apply, to any matter to which the Convention, as a result of Article 4, does not apply.

Regulations and orders

34 A reference in this Schedule to regulations or an order (other than an Order in Council) is to regulations or an order made for the purposes of this Schedule by the Lord Chancellor.

Commencement

35 The following provisions of this Schedule have effect only if the Convention is in force in accordance with Article 57–
   (a) paragraph 8,
   (b) paragraph 9,
   (c) paragraph 19(2) and (5),
   (d) Part 5,
   (e) paragraph 30.

SCHEDULE 4: PROVISIONS APPLYING TO EXISTING ENDURING POWERS OF ATTORNEY

Section 66(3)

Part 1: Enduring Powers of Attorney

Enduring power of attorney to survive mental incapacity of donor

1 (1) Where an individual has created a power of attorney which is an enduring power within the meaning of this Schedule–
   (a) the power is not revoked by any subsequent mental incapacity of his,
   (b) upon such incapacity supervening, the donee of the power may not do anything under the authority of the power except as provided by sub-paragraph (2) unless or until the instrument creating the power is registered under paragraph 13, and
   (c) if and so long as paragraph (b) operates to suspend the donee's authority to act under the power, section 5 of the Powers of Attorney Act 1971 (protection of donee and third persons), so far as applicable, applies as if the power had been revoked by the donor's mental incapacity,
   and, accordingly, section 1 of this Act does not apply.
(2) Despite sub-paragraph (1)(b), where the attorney has made an application for registration of the instrument then, until it is registered, the attorney may take action under the power–
   (a) to maintain the donor or prevent loss to his estate, or
   (b) to maintain himself or other persons in so far as paragraph 3(2) permits him to do so.

(3) Where the attorney purports to act as provided by sub-paragraph (2) then, in favour of a person who deals with him without knowledge that the attorney is acting otherwise than in accordance with sub-paragraph (2)(a) or (b), the transaction between them is as valid as if the attorney were acting in accordance with sub-paragraph (2)(a) or (b).

Characteristics of an enduring power of attorney

2 (1) Subject to sub-paragraphs (5) and (6) and paragraph 20, a power of attorney is an enduring power within the meaning of this Schedule if the instrument which creates the power–
(a) is in the prescribed form,
(b) was executed in the prescribed manner by the donor and the attorney, and
(c) incorporated at the time of execution by the donor the prescribed explanatory information.
(2) In this paragraph, 'prescribed' means prescribed by such of the following regulations as applied when the instrument was executed–
(a) the Enduring Powers of Attorney (Prescribed Form) Regulations 1986 (SI 1986/126),
(b) the Enduring Powers of Attorney (Prescribed Form) Regulations 1987 (SI 1987/1612),
(c) the Enduring Powers of Attorney (Prescribed Form) Regulations 1990 (SI 1990/1376),
(d) the Enduring Powers of Attorney (Welsh Language Prescribed Form) Regulations 2000 (SI 2000/289).
(3) An instrument in the prescribed form purporting to have been executed in the prescribed manner is to be taken, in the absence of evidence to the contrary, to be a document which incorporated at the time of execution by the donor the prescribed explanatory information.
(4) If an instrument differs in an immaterial respect in form or mode of expression from the prescribed form it is to be treated as sufficient in point of form and expression.
(5) A power of attorney cannot be an enduring power unless, when he executes the instrument creating it, the attorney is–
(a) an individual who has reached 18 and is not bankrupt or is not subject to a debt relief order (under Part 7A of the Insolvency Act 1986), or
(b) a trust corporation.
(6) A power of attorney which gives the attorney a right to appoint a substitute or successor cannot be an enduring power.
(7) An enduring power is revoked by the bankruptcy of the donor or attorney or the making of a debt relief order (under Part 7A of the Insolvency Act 1986) in respect of the donor or attorney.
(8) But where the donor or attorney is bankrupt merely because an interim bankruptcy restrictions order has effect in respect of him or where the donor or attorney is subject to an interim debt relief restrictions order, the power is suspended for so long as the order has effect.
(9) An enduring power is revoked if the court–
(a) exercises a power under sections 16 to 20 in relation to the donor, and
(b) directs that the enduring power is to be revoked.

(10) No disclaimer of an enduring power, whether by deed or otherwise, is valid unless and until the attorney gives notice of it to the donor or, where paragraph 4(6) or 15(1) applies, to the Public Guardian.

Scope of authority etc of attorney under enduring power

3 (1) If the instrument which creates an enduring power of attorney is expressed to confer general authority on the attorney, the instrument operates to confer, subject to–
   (a) the restriction imposed by sub-paragraph (3), and
   (b) any conditions or restrictions contained in the instrument,
   authority to do on behalf of the donor anything which the donor could lawfully do by an attorney at the time when the donor executed the instrument.
 (2) Subject to any conditions or restrictions contained in the instrument, an attorney under an enduring power, whether general or limited, may (without obtaining any consent) act under the power so as to benefit himself or other persons than the donor to the following extent but no further–
   (a) he may so act in relation to himself or in relation to any other person if the donor might be expected to provide for his or that person's needs respectively, and
   (b) he may do whatever the donor might be expected to do to meet those needs.
 (3) Without prejudice to sub-paragraph (2) but subject to any conditions or restrictions contained in the instrument, an attorney under an enduring power, whether general or limited, may (without obtaining any consent) dispose of the property of the donor by way of gift to the following extent but no further–
   (a) he may make gifts of a seasonal nature or at a time, or on an anniversary, of a birth, a marriage or the formation of a civil partnership, to persons (including himself) who are related to or connected with the donor, and
   (b) he may make gifts to any charity to whom the donor made or might be expected to make gifts,
   provided that the value of each such gift is not unreasonable having regard to all the circumstances and in particular the size of the donor's estate.

Part 2: Action on Actual or Impending Incapacity of Donor

Duties of attorney in event of actual or impending incapacity of donor

4 (1) Sub-paragraphs (2) to (6) apply if the attorney under an enduring power has reason to believe that the donor is or is becoming mentally incapable.
 (2) The attorney must, as soon as practicable, make an application to the Public Guardian for the registration of the instrument creating the power.
 (3) Before making an application for registration the attorney must comply with the provisions as to notice set out in Part 3 of this Schedule.
 (4) An application for registration–
   (a) must be made in the prescribed form, and
   (b) must contain such statements as may be prescribed.
 (5) The attorney–
   (a) may, before making an application for the registration of the instrument, refer to the court for its determination any question as to the validity of the power, and

(b) must comply with any direction given to him by the court on that determination.

(6) No disclaimer of the power is valid unless and until the attorney gives notice of it to the Public Guardian; and the Public Guardian must notify the donor if he receives a notice under this sub-paragraph.

(7) A person who, in an application for registration, makes a statement which he knows to be false in a material particular is guilty of an offence and is liable–
   (a) on summary conviction, to imprisonment for a term not exceeding 12 months or a fine not exceeding the statutory maximum or both;
   (b) on conviction on indictment, to imprisonment for a term not exceeding 2 years or a fine or both.

(8) In this paragraph, 'prescribed' means prescribed by regulations made for the purposes of this Schedule by the Lord Chancellor.

Part 3: Notification Prior to Registration

Duty to give notice to relatives

5   Subject to paragraph 7, before making an application for registration the attorney must give notice of his intention to do so to all those persons (if any) who are entitled to receive notice by virtue of paragraph 6.

6 (1) Subject to sub-paragraphs (2) to (4), persons of the following classes ('relatives') are entitled to receive notice under paragraph 5–
   (a) the donor's spouse or civil partner,
   (b) the donor's children,
   (c) the donor's parents,
   (d) the donor's brothers and sisters, whether of the whole or half blood,
   (e) the widow, widower or surviving civil partner of a child of the donor,
   (f) the donor's grandchildren,
   (g) the children of the donor's brothers and sisters of the whole blood,
   (h) the children of the donor's brothers and sisters of the half blood,
   (i) the donor's uncles and aunts of the whole blood,
   (j) the children of the donor's uncles and aunts of the whole blood.

(2) A person is not entitled to receive notice under paragraph 5 if–
   (a) his name or address is not known to the attorney and cannot be reasonably ascertained by him, or
   (b) the attorney has reason to believe that he has not reached 18 or is mentally incapable.

(3) Except where sub-paragraph (4) applies–
   (a) no more than 3 persons are entitled to receive notice under paragraph 5, and
   (b) in determining the persons who are so entitled, persons falling within the class in sub-paragraph (1)(a) are to be preferred to persons falling within the class in sub-paragraph (1)(b), those falling within the class in sub-paragraph (1)(b) are to be preferred to those falling within the class in sub-paragraph (1)(c), and so on.

(4) Despite the limit of 3 specified in sub-paragraph (3), where–
   (a) there is more than one person falling within any of classes (a) to (j) of sub-paragraph (1), and
   (b) at least one of those persons would be entitled to receive notice under paragraph 5,

then, subject to sub-paragraph (2), all the persons falling within that class are entitled to receive notice under paragraph 5.

7 (1) An attorney is not required to give notice under paragraph 5–
  (a) to himself, or
  (b) to any other attorney under the power who is joining in making the application,
even though he or, as the case may be, the other attorney is entitled to receive notice by virtue of paragraph 6.

  (2) In the case of any person who is entitled to receive notice by virtue of paragraph 6, the attorney, before applying for registration, may make an application to the court to be dispensed from the requirement to give him notice; and the court must grant the application if it is satisfied–
  (a) that it would be undesirable or impracticable for the attorney to give him notice, or
  (b) that no useful purpose is likely to be served by giving him notice.

Duty to give notice to donor

8 (1) Subject to sub-paragraph (2), before making an application for registration the attorney must give notice of his intention to do so to the donor.

  (2) Paragraph 7(2) applies in relation to the donor as it applies in relation to a person who is entitled to receive notice under paragraph 5.

Contents of notices

9 A notice to relatives under this Part of this Schedule must–
  (a) be in the prescribed form,
  (b) state that the attorney proposes to make an application to the Public Guardian for the registration of the instrument creating the enduring power in question,
  (c) inform the person to whom it is given of his right to object to the registration under paragraph 13(4), and
  (d) specify, as the grounds on which an objection to registration may be made, the grounds set out in paragraph 13(9).

10 A notice to the donor under this Part of this Schedule–
  (a) must be in the prescribed form,
  (b) must contain the statement mentioned in paragraph 9(b), and
  (c) must inform the donor that, while the instrument remains registered, any revocation of the power by him will be ineffective unless and until the revocation is confirmed by the court.

Duty to give notice to other attorneys

11 (1) Subject to sub-paragraph (2), before making an application for registration an attorney under a joint and several power must give notice of his intention to do so to any other attorney under the power who is not joining in making the application; and paragraphs 7(2) and 9 apply in relation to attorneys entitled to receive notice by virtue of this paragraph as they apply in relation to persons entitled to receive notice by virtue of paragraph 6.

  (2) An attorney is not entitled to receive notice by virtue of this paragraph if–
  (a) his address is not known to the applying attorney and cannot reasonably be ascertained by him, or
  (b) the applying attorney has reason to believe that he has not reached 18 or is mentally incapable.

Supplementary

12 Despite section 7 of the Interpretation Act 1978 (construction of references to service by post), for the purposes of this Part of this Schedule a notice given by post is to be regarded as given on the date on which it was posted.

Part 4: Registration

Registration of instrument creating power

13 (1) If an application is made in accordance with paragraph 4(3) and (4) the Public Guardian must, subject to the provisions of this paragraph, register the instrument to which the application relates.

(2) If it appears to the Public Guardian that–
   (a) there is a deputy appointed for the donor of the power created by the instrument, and
   (b) the powers conferred on the deputy would, if the instrument were registered, to any extent conflict with the powers conferred on the attorney,
   the Public Guardian must not register the instrument except in accordance with the court's directions.

(3) The court may, on the application of the attorney, direct the Public Guardian to register an instrument even though notice has not been given as required by paragraph 4(3) and Part 3 of this Schedule to a person entitled to receive it, if the court is satisfied–
   (a) that it was undesirable or impracticable for the attorney to give notice to that person, or
   (b) that no useful purpose is likely to be served by giving him notice.

(4) Sub-paragraph (5) applies if, before the end of the period of 5 weeks beginning with the date (or the latest date) on which the attorney gave notice under paragraph 5 of an application for registration, the Public Guardian receives a valid notice of objection to the registration from a person entitled to notice of the application.

(5) The Public Guardian must not register the instrument except in accordance with the court's directions.

(6) Sub-paragraph (7) applies if, in the case of an application for registration–
   (a) it appears from the application that there is no one to whom notice has been given under paragraph 5, or
   (b) the Public Guardian has reason to believe that appropriate inquiries might bring to light evidence on which he could be satisfied that one of the grounds of objection set out in sub-paragraph (9) was established.

(7) The Public Guardian–
   (a) must not register the instrument, and
   (b) must undertake such inquiries as he thinks appropriate in all the circumstances.

(8) If, having complied with sub-paragraph (7)(b), the Public Guardian is satisfied that one of the grounds of objection set out in sub-paragraph (9) is established–
   (a) the attorney may apply to the court for directions, and
   (b) the Public Guardian must not register the instrument except in accordance with the court's directions.

(9) A notice of objection under this paragraph is valid if made on one or more of the following grounds–
  (a) that the power purported to have been created by the instrument was not valid as an enduring power of attorney,
  (b) that the power created by the instrument no longer subsists,
  (c) that the application is premature because the donor is not yet becoming mentally incapable,
  (d) that fraud or undue pressure was used to induce the donor to create the power,
  (e) that, having regard to all the circumstances and in particular the attorney's relationship to or connection with the donor, the attorney is unsuitable to be the donor's attorney.
(10) If any of those grounds is established to the satisfaction of the court it must direct the Public Guardian not to register the instrument, but if not so satisfied it must direct its registration.
(11) If the court directs the Public Guardian not to register an instrument because it is satisfied that the ground in sub-paragraph (9)(d) or (e) is established, it must by order revoke the power created by the instrument.
(12) If the court directs the Public Guardian not to register an instrument because it is satisfied that any ground in sub-paragraph (9) except that in paragraph (c) is established, the instrument must be delivered up to be cancelled unless the court otherwise directs.

Register of enduring powers

14 The Public Guardian has the function of establishing and maintaining a register of enduring powers for the purposes of this Schedule.

Part 5: Legal Position after Registration

Effect and proof of registration

15 (1) The effect of the registration of an instrument under paragraph 13 is that–
  (a) no revocation of the power by the donor is valid unless and until the court confirms the revocation under paragraph 16(3);
  (b) no disclaimer of the power is valid unless and until the attorney gives notice of it to the Public Guardian;
  (c) the donor may not extend or restrict the scope of the authority conferred by the instrument and no instruction or consent given by him after registration, in the case of a consent, confers any right and, in the case of an instruction, imposes or confers any obligation or right on or creates any liability of the attorney or other persons having notice of the instruction or consent.
(2) Sub-paragraph (1) applies for so long as the instrument is registered under paragraph 13 whether or not the donor is for the time being mentally incapable.
(3) A document purporting to be an office copy of an instrument registered under this Schedule is, in any part of the United Kingdom, evidence of–
  (a) the contents of the instrument, and
  (b) the fact that it has been so registered.
(4) Sub-paragraph (3) is without prejudice to section 3 of the Powers of Attorney Act 1971 (c 27) (proof by certified copies) and to any other method of proof authorised by law.

Functions of court with regard to registered power

16 (1) Where an instrument has been registered under paragraph 13, the court has the following functions with respect to the power and the donor of and the attorney appointed to act under the power.

(2) The court may–
  (a) determine any question as to the meaning or effect of the instrument;
  (b) give directions with respect to–
     (i) the management or disposal by the attorney of the property and affairs of the donor;
     (ii) the rendering of accounts by the attorney and the production of the records kept by him for the purpose;
     (iii) the remuneration or expenses of the attorney whether or not in default of or in accordance with any provision made by the instrument, including directions for the repayment of excessive or the payment of additional remuneration;
  (c) require the attorney to supply information or produce documents or things in his possession as attorney;
  (d) give any consent or authorisation to act which the attorney would have to obtain from a mentally capable donor;
  (e) authorise the attorney to act so as to benefit himself or other persons than the donor otherwise than in accordance with paragraph 3(2) and (3) (but subject to any conditions or restrictions contained in the instrument);
  (f) relieve the attorney wholly or partly from any liability which he has or may have incurred on account of a breach of his duties as attorney.

(3) On application made for the purpose by or on behalf of the donor, the court must confirm the revocation of the power if satisfied that the donor–
  (a) has done whatever is necessary in law to effect an express revocation of the power, and
  (b) was mentally capable of revoking a power of attorney when he did so (whether or not he is so when the court considers the application).

(4) The court must direct the Public Guardian to cancel the registration of an instrument registered under paragraph 13 in any of the following circumstances–
  (a) on confirming the revocation of the power under sub-paragraph (3),
  (b) on directing under paragraph 2(9)(b) that the power is to be revoked,
  (c) on being satisfied that the donor is and is likely to remain mentally capable,
  (d) on being satisfied that the power has expired or has been revoked by the mental incapacity of the attorney,
  (e) on being satisfied that the power was not a valid and subsisting enduring power when registration was effected,
  (f) on being satisfied that fraud or undue pressure was used to induce the donor to create the power,
  (g) on being satisfied that, having regard to all the circumstances and in particular the attorney's relationship to or connection with the donor, the attorney is unsuitable to be the donor's attorney.

(5) If the court directs the Public Guardian to cancel the registration of an instrument on being satisfied of the matters specified in sub-paragraph (4)(f) or (g) it must by order revoke the power created by the instrument.

(6) If the court directs the cancellation of the registration of an instrument under sub-paragraph (4) except paragraph (c) the instrument must be delivered up to the Public Guardian to be cancelled, unless the court otherwise directs.

Cancellation of registration by Public Guardian

17 The Public Guardian must cancel the registration of an instrument creating an enduring power of attorney–
   (a) on receipt of a disclaimer signed by the attorney;
   (b) if satisfied that the power has been revoked by the death or bankruptcy of the donor or attorney or the making of a debt relief order (under Part 7A of the Insolvency Act 1986) in respect of the donor or attorney or, if the attorney is a body corporate, by its winding up or dissolution;
   (c) on receipt of notification from the court that the court has revoked the power;
   (d) on confirmation from the court that the donor has revoked the power.

Part 6: Protection of Attorney and Third Parties

Protection of attorney and third persons where power is invalid or revoked

18 (1) Sub-paragraphs (2) and (3) apply where an instrument which did not create a valid power of attorney has been registered under paragraph 13 (whether or not the registration has been cancelled at the time of the act or transaction in question).
   (2) An attorney who acts in pursuance of the power does not incur any liability (either to the donor or to any other person) because of the non-existence of the power unless at the time of acting he knows–
      (a) that the instrument did not create a valid enduring power,
      (b) that an event has occurred which, if the instrument had created a valid enduring power, would have had the effect of revoking the power, or
      (c) that, if the instrument had created a valid enduring power, the power would have expired before that time.
   (3) Any transaction between the attorney and another person is, in favour of that person, as valid as if the power had then been in existence, unless at the time of the transaction that person has knowledge of any of the matters mentioned in sub-paragraph (2).
   (4) If the interest of a purchaser depends on whether a transaction between the attorney and another person was valid by virtue of sub-paragraph (3), it is conclusively presumed in favour of the purchaser that the transaction was valid if–
      (a) the transaction between that person and the attorney was completed within 12 months of the date on which the instrument was registered, or
      (b) that person makes a statutory declaration, before or within 3 months after the completion of the purchase, that he had no reason at the time of the transaction to doubt that the attorney had authority to dispose of the property which was the subject of the transaction.
   (5) For the purposes of section 5 of the Powers of Attorney Act 1971 (protection where power is revoked) in its application to an enduring power the revocation of which by the donor is by virtue of paragraph 15 invalid unless and until confirmed by the court under paragraph 16–

(a) knowledge of the confirmation of the revocation is knowledge of the revocation of the power, but
(b) knowledge of the unconfirmed revocation is not.

Further protection of attorney and third persons

19 (1) If–
  (a) an instrument framed in a form prescribed as mentioned in paragraph 2(2) creates a power which is not a valid enduring power, and
  (b) the power is revoked by the mental incapacity of the donor,
  sub-paragraphs (2) and (3) apply, whether or not the instrument has been registered.
(2) An attorney who acts in pursuance of the power does not, by reason of the revocation, incur any liability (either to the donor or to any other person) unless at the time of acting he knows–
  (a) that the instrument did not create a valid enduring power, and
  (b) that the donor has become mentally incapable.
(3) Any transaction between the attorney and another person is, in favour of that person, as valid as if the power had then been in existence, unless at the time of the transaction that person knows–
  (a) that the instrument did not create a valid enduring power, and
  (b) that the donor has become mentally incapable.
(4) Paragraph 18(4) applies for the purpose of determining whether a transaction was valid by virtue of sub-paragraph (3) as it applies for the purpose or determining whether a transaction was valid by virtue of paragraph 18(3).

Part 7: Joint and Joint and Several Attorneys

Application to joint and joint and several attorneys

20 (1) An instrument which appoints more than one person to be an attorney cannot create an enduring power unless the attorneys are appointed to act–
  (a) jointly, or
  (b) jointly and severally.
(2) This Schedule, in its application to joint attorneys, applies to them collectively as it applies to a single attorney but subject to the modifications specified in paragraph 21.
(3) This Schedule, in its application to joint and several attorneys, applies with the modifications specified in sub-paragraphs (4) to (7) and in paragraph 22.
(4) A failure, as respects any one attorney, to comply with the requirements for the creation of enduring powers–
  (a) prevents the instrument from creating such a power in his case, but
  (b) does not affect its efficacy for that purpose as respects the other or others or its efficacy in his case for the purpose of creating a power of attorney which is not an enduring power.
(5) If one or more but not both or all the attorneys makes or joins in making an application for registration of the instrument–
  (a) an attorney who is not an applicant as well as one who is may act pending the registration of the instrument as provided in paragraph 1(2),
  (b) notice of the application must also be given under Part 3 of this Schedule to the other attorney or attorneys, and

(c) objection may validly be taken to the registration on a ground relating to an attorney or to the power of an attorney who is not an applicant as well as to one or the power of one who is an applicant.

(6) The Public Guardian is not precluded by paragraph 13(5) or (8) from registering an instrument and the court must not direct him not to do so under paragraph 13(10) if an enduring power subsists as respects some attorney who is not affected by the ground or grounds of the objection in question; and where the Public Guardian registers an instrument in that case, he must make against the registration an entry in the prescribed form.

(7) Sub-paragraph (6) does not preclude the court from revoking a power in so far as it confers a power on any other attorney in respect of whom the ground in paragraph 13(9)(d) or (e) is established; and where any ground in paragraph 13(9) affecting any other attorney is established the court must direct the Public Guardian to make against the registration an entry in the prescribed form.

(8) In sub-paragraph (4), 'the requirements for the creation of enduring powers' means the provisions of–
   (a) paragraph 2 other than sub-paragraphs (8) and (9), and
   (b) the regulations mentioned in paragraph 2.

Joint attorneys

21 (1) In paragraph 2(5), the reference to the time when the attorney executes the instrument is to be read as a reference to the time when the second or last attorney executes the instrument.

(2) In paragraph 2(6) to (8), the reference to the attorney is to be read as a reference to any attorney under the power.

(3) Paragraph 13 has effect as if the ground of objection to the registration of the instrument specified in sub-paragraph (9)(e) applied to any attorney under the power.

(4) In paragraph 16(2), references to the attorney are to be read as including references to any attorney under the power.

(5) In paragraph 16(4), references to the attorney are to be read as including references to any attorney under the power.

(6) In paragraph 17, references to the attorney are to be read as including references to any attorney under the power.

Joint and several attorneys

22 (1) In paragraph 2(7), the reference to the bankruptcy of the attorney is to be read as a reference to the bankruptcy of the last remaining attorney under the power; and the bankruptcy of any other attorney under the power causes that person to cease to be an attorney under the power.

(1A) In paragraph 2(7), the reference to the making of a debt relief order (under Part 7A of the Insolvency Act 1986) in respect of the attorney is to be read as a reference to the making of a debt relief order in respect of the last remaining attorney under the power; and the making of a debt relief order in respect of any other attorney under the power causes that person to cease to be an attorney under the power.

(2) In paragraph 2(8), the reference to the suspension of the power is to be read as a reference to its suspension in so far as it relates to the attorney in respect of whom the interim bankruptcy restrictions order has effect.

(2A) In paragraph 2(8), the reference to the suspension of the power is to be read as a reference to its suspension in so far as it relates to the attorney in respect of whom the interim debt relief restrictions order has effect.
 (3) The restriction upon disclaimer imposed by paragraph 4(6) applies only to those attorneys who have reason to believe that the donor is or is becoming mentally incapable.

Part 8: Interpretation

23 (1) In this Schedule–
 'enduring power' is to be construed in accordance with paragraph 2,
 'mentally incapable' or 'mental incapacity', except where it refers to revocation at common law, means in relation to any person, that he is incapable by reason of mental disorder . . . of managing and administering his property and affairs and 'mentally capable' and 'mental capacity' are to be construed accordingly,
 'notice' means notice in writing, and
 'prescribed', except for the purposes of paragraph 2, means prescribed by regulations made for the purposes of this Schedule by the Lord Chancellor.
 (1A) In sub-paragraph (1), 'mental disorder' has the same meaning as in the Mental Health Act but disregarding the amendments made to that Act by the Mental Health Act 2007.
 (2) Any question arising under or for the purposes of this Schedule as to what the donor of the power might at any time be expected to do is to be determined by assuming that he had full mental capacity at the time but otherwise by reference to the circumstances existing at that time.

[SCHEDULES 5–7 are not reproduced here.]

HUMAN RIGHTS ACT 1998 ss3, 6–8 and Sch 1

Legislation

Interpretation of legislation

3 (1) So far as it is possible to do so, primary legislation and subordinate legislation must be read and given effect in a way which is compatible with the Convention rights.

(2) This section–
  (a) applies to primary legislation and subordinate legislation whenever enacted;
  (b) does not affect the validity, continuing operation or enforcement of any incompatible primary legislation; and
  (c) does not affect the validity, continuing operation or enforcement of any incompatible subordinate legislation if (disregarding any possibility of revocation) primary legislation prevents removal of the incompatibility.

Public authorities

Acts of public authorities

6 (1) It is unlawful for a public authority to act in a way which is incompatible with a Convention right.

(2) Subsection (1) does not apply to an act if–
  (a) as the result of one or more provisions of primary legislation, the authority could not have acted differently; or
  (b) in the case of one or more provisions of, or made under, primary legislation which cannot be read or given effect in a way which is compatible with the Convention rights, the authority was acting so as to give effect to or enforce those provisions.

(3) In this section 'public authority' includes–
  (a) a court or tribunal, and
  (b) any person certain of whose functions are functions of a public nature, but does not include either House of Parliament or a person exercising functions in connection with proceedings in Parliament.

(4) [Repealed.]

(5) In relation to a particular act, a person is not a public authority by virtue only of subsection (3)(b) if the nature of the act is private.

(6) 'An act' includes a failure to act but does not include a failure to–
  (a) introduce in, or lay before, Parliament a proposal for legislation; or
  (b) make any primary legislation or remedial order.

Proceedings

7 (1) A person who claims that a public authority has acted (or proposes to act) in a way which is made unlawful by section 6(1) may–
  (a) bring proceedings against the authority under this Act in the appropriate court or tribunal, or
  (b) rely on the Convention right or rights concerned in any legal proceedings, but only if he is (or would be) a victim of the unlawful act.

(2) In subsection (1)(a) 'appropriate court or tribunal' means such court or tribunal as may be determined in accordance with rules; and proceedings against an authority include a counterclaim or similar proceeding.

(3) If the proceedings are brought on an application for judicial review, the applicant is to be taken to have a sufficient interest in relation to the unlawful act only if he is, or would be, a victim of that act.
(4) If the proceedings are made by way of a petition for judicial review in Scotland, the applicant shall be taken to have title and interest to sue in relation to the unlawful act only if he is, or would be, a victim of that act.
(5) Proceedings under subsection (1)(a) must be brought before the end of–
　(a) the period of one year beginning with the date on which the act complained of took place; or
　(b) such longer period as the court or tribunal considers equitable having regard to all the circumstances,
but that is subject to any rule imposing a stricter time limit in relation to the procedure in question.
(6) In subsection (1)(b) 'legal proceedings' includes–
　(a) proceedings brought by or at the instigation of a public authority; and
　(b) an appeal against the decision of a court or tribunal.
(7) For the purposes of this section, a person is a victim of an unlawful act only if he would be a victim for the purposes of Article 34 of the Convention if proceedings were brought in the European Court of Human Rights in respect of that act.
(8) Nothing in this Act creates a criminal offence.
(9) In this section 'rules' means–
　(a) in relation to proceedings before a court or tribunal outside Scotland, rules made by the Lord Chancellor or the Secretary of State for the purposes of this section or rules of court,
　(b) in relation to proceedings before a court or tribunal in Scotland, rules made by the Secretary of State for those purposes,
　(c) in relation to proceedings before a tribunal in Northern Ireland–
　　(i) which deals with transferred matters; and
　　(ii) for which no rules made under paragraph (a) are in force,
　　rules made by a Northern Ireland department for those purposes,
and includes provision made by order under section 1 of the Courts and Legal Services Act 1990.
(10) In making rules, regard must be had to section 9.
(11) The Minister who has power to make rules in relation to a particular tribunal may, to the extent he considers it necessary to ensure that the tribunal can provide an appropriate remedy in relation to an act (or proposed act) of a public authority which is (or would be) unlawful as a result of section 6(1), by order add to–
　(a) the relief or remedies which the tribunal may grant; or
　(b) the grounds on which it may grant any of them.
(12) An order made under subsection (11) may contain such incidental, supplemental, consequential or transitional provision as the Minister making it considers appropriate.
(13) 'The Minister' includes the Northern Ireland department concerned.

Judicial remedies

8 (1) In relation to any act (or proposed act) of a public authority which the court finds is (or would be) unlawful, it may grant such relief or remedy, or make such order, within its powers as it considers just and appropriate.

(2) But damages may be awarded only by a court which has power to award damages, or to order the payment of compensation, in civil proceedings.
(3) No award of damages is to be made unless, taking account of all the circumstances of the case, including–
 (a) any other relief or remedy granted, or order made, in relation to the act in question (by that or any other court), and
 (b) the consequences of any decision (of that or any other court) in respect of that act,
 the court is satisfied that the award is necessary to afford just satisfaction to the person in whose favour it is made.
(4) In determining–
 (a) whether to award damages, or
 (b) the amount of an award,
 the court must take into account the principles applied by the European Court of Human Rights in relation to the award of compensation under Article 41 of the Convention.
(5) A public authority against which damages are awarded is to be treated–
 (a) in Scotland, for the purposes of section 3 of the Law Reform (Miscellaneous Provisions) (Scotland) Act 1940 as if the award were made in an action of damages in which the authority has been found liable in respect of loss or damage to the person to whom the award is made;
 (b) for the purposes of the Civil Liability (Contribution) Act 1978 as liable in respect of damage suffered by the person to whom the award is made.
(6) In this section–
 'court' includes a tribunal;
 'damages' means damages for an unlawful act of a public authority; and
 'unlawful' means unlawful under section 6(1).

SCHEDULE 1: THE ARTICLES

Section 1(3)

Part I: The Convention

Rights and Freedoms

Article 2: Right to life

1 Everyone's right to life shall be protected by law. No one shall be deprived of his life intentionally save in the execution of a sentence of a court following his conviction of a crime for which this penalty is provided by law.
2 Deprivation of life shall not be regarded as inflicted in contravention of this Article when it results from the use of force which is no more than absolutely necessary:
 (a) in defence of any person from unlawful violence;
 (b) in order to effect a lawful arrest or to prevent the escape of a person lawfully detained;
 (c) in action lawfully taken for the purpose of quelling a riot or insurrection.

Article 3: Prohibition of torture

No one shall be subjected to torture or to inhuman or degrading treatment or punishment.

Article 4: Prohibition of slavery and forced labour

1. No one shall be held in slavery or servitude.
2. No one shall be required to perform forced or compulsory labour.
3. For the purpose of this Article the term 'forced or compulsory labour' shall not include:
    (a) any work required to be done in the ordinary course of detention imposed according to the provisions of Article 5 of this Convention or during conditional release from such detention;
    (b) any service of a military character or, in case of conscientious objectors in countries where they are recognised, service exacted instead of compulsory military service;
    (c) any service exacted in case of an emergency or calamity threatening the life or well-being of the community;
    (d) any work or service which forms part of normal civic obligations.

Article 5: Right to liberty and security

1. Everyone has the right to liberty and security of person. No one shall be deprived of his liberty save in the following cases and in accordance with a procedure prescribed by law:
    (a) the lawful detention of a person after conviction by a competent court;
    (b) the lawful arrest or detention of a person for non-compliance with the lawful order of a court or in order to secure the fulfilment of any obligation prescribed by law;
    (c) the lawful arrest or detention of a person effected for the purpose of bringing him before the competent legal authority on reasonable suspicion of having committed an offence or when it is reasonably considered necessary to prevent his committing an offence or fleeing after having done so;
    (d) the detention of a minor by lawful order for the purpose of educational supervision or his lawful detention for the purpose of bringing him before the competent legal authority;
    (e) the lawful detention of persons for the prevention of the spreading of infectious diseases, of persons of unsound mind, alcoholics or drug addicts or vagrants;
    (f) the lawful arrest or detention of a person to prevent his effecting an unauthorised entry into the country or of a person against whom action is being taken with a view to deportation or extradition.
2. Everyone who is arrested shall be informed promptly, in a language which he understands, of the reasons for his arrest and of any charge against him.
3. Everyone arrested or detained in accordance with the provisions of paragraph 1(c) of this Article shall be brought promptly before a judge or other officer authorised by law to exercise judicial power and shall be entitled to trial within a reasonable time or to release pending trial. Release may be conditioned by guarantees to appear for trial.

4 Everyone who is deprived of his liberty by arrest or detention shall be entitled to take proceedings by which the lawfulness of his detention shall be decided speedily by a court and his release ordered if the detention is not lawful.
5 Everyone who has been the victim of arrest or detention in contravention of the provisions of this Article shall have an enforceable right to compensation.

Article 6: Right to a fair trial

1 In the determination of his civil rights and obligations or of any criminal charge against him, everyone is entitled to a fair and public hearing within a reasonable time by an independent and impartial tribunal established by law. Judgment shall be pronounced publicly but the press and public may be excluded from all or part of the trial in the interest of morals, public order or national security in a democratic society, where the interests of juveniles or the protection of the private life of the parties so require, or to the extent strictly necessary in the opinion of the court in special circumstances where publicity would prejudice the interests of justice.
2 Everyone charged with a criminal offence shall be presumed innocent until proved guilty according to law.
3 Everyone charged with a criminal offence has the following minimum rights:
   (a) to be informed promptly, in a language which he understands and in detail, of the nature and cause of the accusation against him;
   (b) to have adequate time and facilities for the preparation of his defence;
   (c) to defend himself in person or through legal assistance of his own choosing or, if he has not sufficient means to pay for legal assistance, to be given it free when the interests of justice so require;
   (d) to examine or have examined witnesses against him and to obtain the attendance and examination of witnesses on his behalf under the same conditions as witnesses against him;
   (e) to have the free assistance of an interpreter if he cannot understand or speak the language used in court.

Article 7: No punishment without law

1 No one shall be held guilty of any criminal offence on account of any act or omission which did not constitute a criminal offence under national or international law at the time when it was committed. Nor shall a heavier penalty be imposed than the one that was applicable at the time the criminal offence was committed.
2 This Article shall not prejudice the trial and punishment of any person for any act or omission which, at the time when it was committed, was criminal according to the general principles of law recognised by civilised nations.

Article 8: Right to respect for private and family life

1 Everyone has the right to respect for his private and family life, his home and his correspondence.
2 There shall be no interference by a public authority with the exercise of this right except such as is in accordance with the law and is necessary in a democratic society in the interests of national security, public safety or the economic well-being of the country, for the prevention of disorder or crime, for the protection of health or morals, or for the protection of the rights and freedoms of others.

Article 9: Freedom of thought, conscience and religion

1 Everyone has the right to freedom of thought, conscience and religion; this right includes freedom to change his religion or belief and freedom, either alone or in community with others and in public or private, to manifest his religion or belief, in worship, teaching, practice and observance.
2 Freedom to manifest one's religion or beliefs shall be subject only to such limitations as are prescribed by law and are necessary in a democratic society in the interests of public safety, for the protection of public order, health or morals, or for the protection of the rights and freedoms of others.

Article 10: Freedom of expression

1 Everyone has the right to freedom of expression. This right shall include freedom to hold opinions and to receive and impart information and ideas without interference by public authority and regardless of frontiers. This Article shall not prevent States from requiring the licensing of broadcasting, television or cinema enterprises.
2 The exercise of these freedoms, since it carries with it duties and responsibilities, may be subject to such formalities, conditions, restrictions or penalties as are prescribed by law and are necessary in a democratic society, in the interests of national security, territorial integrity or public safety, for the prevention of disorder or crime, for the protection of health or morals, for the protection of the reputation or rights of others, for preventing the disclosure of information received in confidence, or for maintaining the authority and impartiality of the judiciary.

Article 11: Freedom of assembly and association

1 Everyone has the right to freedom of peaceful assembly and to freedom of association with others, including the right to form and to join trade unions for the protection of his interests.
2 No restrictions shall be placed on the exercise of these rights other than such as are prescribed by law and are necessary in a democratic society in the interests of national security or public safety, for the prevention of disorder or crime, for the protection of health or morals or for the protection of the rights and freedoms of others. This Article shall not prevent the imposition of lawful restrictions on the exercise of these rights by members of the armed forces, of the police or of the administration of the State.

Article 12: Right to marry

Men and women of marriageable age have the right to marry and to found a family, according to the national laws governing the exercise of this right.

Article 14: Prohibition of discrimination

The enjoyment of the rights and freedoms set forth in this Convention shall be secured without discrimination on any ground such as sex, race, colour, language, religion, political or other opinion, national or social origin, association with a national minority, property, birth or other status.

Article 16: Restrictions on political activity of aliens

Nothing in Articles 10, 11 and 14 shall be regarded as preventing the High Contracting Parties from imposing restrictions on the political activity of aliens.

Article 17: Prohibition of abuse of rights

Nothing in this Convention may be interpreted as implying for any State, group or person any right to engage in any activity or perform any act aimed at the destruction of any of the rights and freedoms set forth herein or at their limitation to a greater extent than is provided for in the Convention.

Article 18: Limitation on use of restrictions on rights

The restrictions permitted under this Convention to the said rights and freedoms shall not be applied for any purpose other than those for which they have been prescribed.

Part II: The First Protocol

Article 1: Protection of property

Every natural or legal person is entitled to the peaceful enjoyment of his possessions. No one shall be deprived of his possessions except in the public interest and subject to the conditions provided for by law and by the general principles of international law.

The preceding provisions shall not, however, in any way impair the right of a State to enforce such laws as it deems necessary to control the use of property in accordance with the general interest or to secure the payment of taxes or other contributions or penalties.

Article 2: Right to education

No person shall be denied the right to education. In the exercise of any functions which it assumes in relation to education and to teaching, the State shall respect the right of parents to ensure such education and teaching in conformity with their own religious and philosophical convictions.

Article 3: Right to free elections

The High Contracting Parties undertake to hold free elections at reasonable intervals by secret ballot, under conditions which will ensure the free expression of the opinion of the people in the choice of the legislature.

Part III: Article 1 of the Thirteenth Protocol

Abolition of the Death Penalty

The death penalty shall be abolished. No one shall be condemned to such penalty or executed.

APPENDIX B

Secondary legislation[1]

Court of Protection Rules 2007   706
Court of Protection Case Management Pilot Rules 2016   772
Mental Capacity Act 2005 (Transfer of Proceedings) Order 2007   792
Court of Protection Fees Order 2007   794

---

1   © Crown Copyright. Reproduced as amended up to date to 1 November 2016.

COURT OF PROTECTION RULES 2007[1]

Part 1: Preliminary

1 Title and commencement
These Rules may be cited as the Court of Protection Rules 2007 and come into force on 1 October 2007.

2 Revocations
The following rules are revoked–
(a) the Court of Protection Rules 2001; and
(b) the Court of Protection (Enduring Powers of Attorney) Rules 2001.

Part 2: The Overriding Objective

3 The overriding objective
(1) These Rules have the overriding objective of enabling the court to deal with a case justly, having regard to the principles contained in the Act.
(2) The court will seek to give effect to the overriding objective when it–
   (a) exercises any power under these Rules; or
   (b) interprets any rule or practice direction.
(3) Dealing with a case justly includes, so far as is practicable–
   (a) ensuring that it is dealt with expeditiously and fairly;
   (b) ensuring that P's interests and position are properly considered;
   (c) dealing with the case in ways which are proportionate to the nature, importance and complexity of the issues;
   (d) ensuring that the parties are on an equal footing;
   (e) saving expense; and
   (f) allotting to it an appropriate share of the court's resources, while taking account of the need to allot resources to other cases.

3A Participation of P
(1) The court shall in each case, on its own initiative or on the application of any person, consider whether it should make one or more of the directions in paragraph (2), having regard to–
   (a) the nature and extent of the information before the court;
   (b) the issues raised in the case;
   (c) whether a matter is contentious; and
   (d) whether P has been notified in accordance with the provisions of Part 7 and what, if anything, P has said or done in response to such notification.
(2) The directions are that–
   (a) P should be joined as a party;
   (b) P's participation should be secured by the appointment of an accredited legal representative to represent P in the proceedings and to discharge such other functions as the court may direct;
   (c) P's participation should be secured by the appointment of a representative whose function shall be to provide the court with information as to the

---

1 © Crown Copyright. SI No 1744. As amended by the Court of Protection (Amendment) Rules 2015 SI No 548. This consolidation silently incorporates the changes to the original Rules without specifically highlighting the amendments.

matters set out in section 4(6) of the Act and to discharge such other functions as the court may direct;
  (d) P should have the opportunity to address (directly or indirectly) the judge determining the application and, if so directed, the circumstances in which that should occur;
  (e) P's interests and position can properly be secured without any direction under sub-paragraphs (a) to (d) being made or by the making of an alternative direction meeting the overriding objective.
(3) Any appointment or directions made pursuant to paragraph (2)(b) to (e) may be made for such period or periods as the court thinks fit.
(4) Unless P has capacity to conduct the proceedings, an order joining P as a party shall only take effect–
  (a) on the appointment of a litigation friend on P's behalf; or
  (b) if the court so directs, on or after the appointment of an accredited legal representative.
(5) If the court has directed that P should be joined as a party but such joinder does not occur because no litigation friend or accredited legal representative is appointed, the court shall record in a judgment or order–
  (a) the fact that no such appointment was made; and
  (b) the reasons given for that appointment not being made.
(6) A practice direction may make additional or supplementary provision in respect of any of the matters set out in this rule.

(The appointment of litigation friends, accredited legal representatives and representatives under paragraph (2)(c) is dealt with under Part 17.)

('Accredited legal representative' is defined in rule 6.)

4 The duty of the parties
(1) The parties are required to help the court to further the overriding objective.
(2) Without prejudice to the generality of paragraph (1), each party is required to–
  (a) co-operate with the other parties and with the court in identifying and narrowing the issues that need to be determined by the court, and the timetable for that determination;
  (b) adhere to the timetable set by these Rules and by the court;
  (c) comply with all directions and orders of the court;
  (d) be full and frank in the disclosure of information and evidence to the court (including any disclosure ordered under Part 16);
  (e) co-operate with the other parties in all aspects of the conduct of the proceedings, including in the preparation of bundles.
(3) If the court determines that any party has failed without reasonable excuse to satisfy the requirements of this rule, it may under rule 159 depart from the general rules about costs in so far as they apply to that party.

(Rule 133(2) deals with the requirements of general disclosure.)

5 Court's duty to manage cases
(1) The court will further the overriding objective by actively managing cases.
(2) Active case management includes–
  (a) encouraging the parties to co-operate with each other in the conduct of the proceedings;

(b) identifying at an early stage–
  (i) the issues; and
  (ii) who should be a party to the proceedings;
(c) deciding promptly–
  (i) which issues need a full investigation and hearing and which do not; and
  (ii) the procedure to be followed in the case;
(d) deciding the order in which issues are to be resolved;
(e) encouraging the parties to use an alternative dispute resolution procedure if the court considers that appropriate;
(f) fixing timetables or otherwise controlling the progress of the case;
(g) considering whether the likely benefits of taking a particular step justify the cost of taking it;
(h) dealing with as many aspects of the case as the court can on the same occasion;
(i) dealing with the case without the parties needing to attend at court;
(j) making use of technology; . . .
(k) giving directions to ensure that the case proceeds quickly and efficiently;
(l) considering whether any hearing should be held in public; and
(m) considering whether any document relating to proceedings should be a public document and, if so, whether and to what extent it should be redacted.

(Rules 91 to 93 make provision about the court's powers to authorise publication of information about proceedings and to order that a hearing be held in public.)

Part 3: Interpretation and General Provisions

6 Interpretation

In these Rules–

'the Act' means the Mental Capacity Act 2005;

'accredited legal representative' means a legal representative authorised pursuant to a scheme of accreditation approved by the President to represent persons meeting the definition of 'P' in this rule in proceedings before the court;

'applicant' means a person who makes, or who seeks permission to make, an application to the court;

'application form' means the document that is to be used to begin proceedings in accordance with Part 9 of these Rules or any other provision of these Rules or the practice directions which requires the use of an application form;

'application notice' means the document that is to be used to make an application in accordance with Part 10 of these Rules or any other provision of these Rules or the practice directions which requires the use of an application notice;

'attorney' means the person appointed as such by an enduring power of attorney created, or purporting to have been created, in accordance with the regulations mentioned in paragraph 2 of Schedule 4 to the Act;

'business day' means a day other than–
- (a) a Saturday, Sunday, Christmas Day or Good Friday; or
- (b) a bank holiday in England and Wales, under the Banking and Financial Dealings Act 1971;

'child' means a person under 18;
'court' means the Court of Protection;
'deputy' means a deputy appointed under the Act;
'donee' means the donee of a lasting power of attorney;
'donor' means the donor of a lasting power of attorney, except where this expression is used in rule 68 or 201(5) (where it means the donor of an enduring power of attorney);
'enduring power of attorney' means an instrument created in accordance with such of the regulations mentioned in paragraph 2 of Schedule 4 to the Act as applied when it was executed;
'filing' in relation to a document means delivering it, by post or otherwise, to the court office;
'hearing' includes a hearing conducted by telephone, video link, or any other method permitted or directed by the court;
'judge' means a judge nominated to be a judge of the court under the Act;
'lasting power of attorney' has the meaning given in section 9 of the Act;
'legal representative' means a–
- (a) barrister,
- (b) solicitor,
- (c) solicitor's employee,
- (d) manager of a body recognised under section 9 of the Administration of Justice Act 1985, or
- (e) person who, for the purposes of the Legal Services Act 2007, is an authorised person in relation to an activity which constitutes the conduct of litigation (within the meaning of that Act),

who has been instructed to act for a party in relation to any application;
'legally aided person' means a person to whom civil legal services (within the meaning of the Legal Aid, Sentencing and Punishment of Offenders Act 2012) have been made available under arrangements made for the purposes of Part 1 of that Act);
'order' includes a declaration made by the court;
'P' means–
- (a) any person (other than a protected party) who lacks or, so far as consistent with the context, is alleged to lack capacity to make a decision or decisions in relation to any matter that is the subject of an application to the court; and
- (b) a relevant person as defined by paragraph 7 of Schedule A1 to the Act,

and references to a person who lacks capacity are to be construed in accordance with the Act;
'party' is to be construed in accordance with rule 73;
'personal welfare' is to be construed in accordance with section 17 of the Act;
'President' and 'Vice-President' refer to those judges appointed as such under section 46(3)(a) and (b) of the Act;
'property and affairs' is to be construed in accordance with section 18 of the Act;

'protected party' means a party or an intended party (other than P or a child) who lacks capacity to conduct the proceedings;
'representative' means a person appointed under rule 3A(2)(c), except where the context otherwise requires;
'respondent' means a person who is named as a respondent in the application form or notice, as the case may be;
'Senior Judge' means the judge who has been nominated to be Senior Judge under section 46(4) of the Act, and references in these Rules to a circuit judge include the Senior Judge;
'Tier 1 Judge' means any judge nominated to act as a judge of the Court of Protection under section 46 of the Act who is neither a Tier 2 Judge nor a Tier 3 Judge;
'Tier 2 Judge' means–
  (a) the Senior Judge; and
  (b) such other judges nominated to act as a judge of the Court of Protection under section 46 of the Act as may be set out in the relevant practice direction;
'Tier 3 Judge' means–
  (a) the President;
  (b) the Vice-President; and
  (c) such other judges nominated to act as a judge of the Court of Protection under section 46 of the Act as may be set out in the relevant practice direction;
'Visitor' means a person appointed as such by the Lord Chancellor under section 61 of the Act.

7 Court officers

(1) Where these Rules permit or require the court to perform an act of a purely formal or administrative character, that act may be performed by a court officer.
(2) A requirement that a court officer carry out any act at the request of any person is subject to the payment of any fee required by a fees order for the carrying out of that act.

7A

(1) The Senior Judge or the President may authorise a court officer to exercise the jurisdiction of the court in such circumstances as set out in the relevant practice direction.
(2) A court officer who has been authorised under paragraph (1)–
  (a) must refer to a judge any application, proceedings or any question arising in any application or proceedings which ought, in the officer's opinion, to be considered by a judge;
  (b) may not deal with any application or proceedings or any question arising in any application or proceedings by way of a hearing; and
  (c) may not deal with an application for the reconsideration of an order made by that court officer or another court officer.

8 Computation of time

(1) This rule shows how to calculate any period of time which is specified–
  (a) by these Rules;
  (b) by a practice direction; or
  (c) in an order or direction of the court.

(2) A period of time expressed as a number of days must be computed as clear days.
(3) In this rule 'clear days' means that in computing the number of days–
  (a) the day on which the period begins; and
  (b) if the end of the period is defined by reference to an event, the day on which that event occurs,
  are not included.
(4) Where the specified period is 7 days or less, and would include a day which is not a business day, that day does not count.
(5) When the specified period for doing any act at the court office ends on a day on which the office is closed, that act will be done in time if done on the next day on which the court office is open.

9 Application of Civil Procedure Rules and Family Procedure Rules

(1) In any case not expressly provided for by these Rules or the practice directions made under them, the court may apply either the Civil Procedure Rules 1998 or the Family Procedure Rules 2010 (including in either case the practice directions made under them) with any necessary modifications, in so far as is necessary to further the overriding objective.
(2) A reference in these Rules to the Civil Procedure Rules 1998 or to the Family Procedure Rules 2010 is to the version of those rules in force at the date specified for the purpose of that reference in the relevant practice direction.

9A Pilot schemes

(1) Practice directions may make provision for the operation of pilot schemes for assessing the use of new practices and procedures in connection with proceedings–
  (a) for specified periods; and
  (b) in relation to proceedings–
    (i) in specified parts of the country; or
    (ii) relating to specified types of application.
(2) Practice directions may modify or disapply any provision of these Rules during the operation of such pilot schemes.

Part 4: Court Documents

10 Documents used in court proceedings

(1) The court will seal or otherwise authenticate with the stamp of the court the following documents on issue–
  (a) [revoked.]
  (b) an application form;
  (c) an application notice;
  (d) an order; and
  (e) any other document which a rule or practice direction requires to be sealed or stamped.
(2) Where these Rules or any practice direction require a document to be signed, that requirement is satisfied if the signature is printed by computer or other mechanical means.
(3) A practice direction may make provision for documents to be filed or sent to the court by–
  (a) facsimile; or
  (b) other means.

11 Documents required to be verified by a statement of truth

(1) The following documents must be verified by a statement of truth–
  (a) an application form, an application notice, an appellant's notice or a respondent's notice, where the applicant seeks to rely upon matters set out in the document as evidence;
  (b) a witness statement;
  (c) a certificate of–
    (i) service or non-service; or
    (ii) notification or non-notification;
  (d) a deputy's declaration; and
  (e) any other document required by a rule or practice direction to be so verified.

(2) Subject to paragraph (3), a statement of truth is a statement that–
  (a) the party putting forward the document;
  (b) in the case of a witness statement, the maker of the witness statement; or
  (c) in the case of a certificate referred to in paragraph (1)(c), the person who signs the certificate,
  believes that the facts stated in the document being verified are true.

(3) If a party is conducting proceedings with a litigation friend, the statement of truth in–
  (a) [revoked.]
  (b) an application form; or
  (c) an application notice;
  (d) an appellant's notice or a respondent's notice,
  is a statement that the litigation friend believes the facts stated in the document being verified are true.

(4) The statement of truth must be signed–
  (a) in the case of an application form, an application notice, an appellant's notice or a respondent's notice–
    (i) by the party or litigation friend; or
    (ii) by the legal representative on behalf of the party or litigation friend; and
  (b) in the case of a witness statement, by the maker of the statement.

(5) A statement of truth which is not contained in the document which it verifies must clearly identify that document.

(6) A statement of truth in an application form, an application notice, an appellant's notice or a respondent's notice may be made by–
  (a) a person who is not a party; or
  (b) two or more parties jointly,
  where this is permitted by a relevant practice direction.

11A Position statement not required to be verified by statement of truth

Nothing in these Rules requires a position statement to be verified by a statement of truth.

12 Failure to verify a document

If an application form, an application notice, an appellant's notice or a respondent's notice is not verified by a statement of truth, the applicant (or respondent as the case may be) may not rely upon the document as evidence of any of the matters set out in it unless the court permits.

13 Failure to verify a witness statement
If a witness statement is not verified by a statement of truth, it shall not be admissible in evidence unless the court permits.

14 False statements
(1) Proceedings for contempt of court may be brought against a person if he makes, or causes to be made, a false statement in a document verified by a statement of truth without an honest belief in its truth.
(2) Proceedings under this rule may be brought only–
  (a) by the Attorney General; or
  (b) with the permission of the court.

15 Personal details
(1) Where a party does not wish to reveal–
  (a) his home address or telephone number;
  (b) P's home address or telephone number;
  (c) the name of the person with whom P is living (if that person is not the applicant); or
  (d) the address or telephone number of his place of business, or the place of business of any of the persons mentioned in sub-paragraphs (b) or (c),
  he must provide those particulars to the court.
(2) Where paragraph (1) applies, the particulars given will not be revealed to any person unless the court so directs.
(3) Where a party changes his home address during the course of the proceedings, he must give notice of the change to the court.
(4) Where a party does not reveal his home address, he must nonetheless provide an address for service which must be within the jurisdiction of the court.

16 Supply of documents to a party from court records
Unless the court orders otherwise, a party to proceedings may inspect or obtain from the records of the court a copy of–
  (a) any document filed by a party to the proceedings; or
  (b) any communication in the proceedings between the court and–
    (i) a party to the proceedings; or
    (ii) another person.

17 Supply of documents to a non-party from court records
(1) Subject to rules 20 and 92(2), a person who is not a party to proceedings may inspect or obtain from the court records a copy of any judgment or order given or made in public.
(2) The court may, on an application made to it, authorise a person who is not a party to proceedings to–
  (a) inspect any other documents in the court records; or
  (b) obtain a copy of any such documents, or extracts from such documents.
(3) A person making an application for an authorisation under paragraph (2) must do so in accordance with Part 10.

(4) Before giving an authorisation under paragraph (2), the court will consider whether any document is to be provided on an edited basis.

18 Subsequent use of court documents

(1) Where a document has been filed or disclosed, a party to whom it was provided may use the document only for the purpose of the proceedings in which it was filed or disclosed, except where–
   (a) the document has been read to or by the court or referred to at a public hearing; or
   (b) the court otherwise permits.
(2) Paragraph (1)(a) is subject to any order of the court made under rule 92(2).

19 Editing information in court documents

(1) A party may apply to the court for an order that a specified part of a document is to be edited prior to the document's service or disclosure.
(2) An order under paragraph (1) may be made at any time.
(3) Where the court makes an order under this rule any subsequent use of that document in the proceedings shall be of the document as edited, unless the court directs otherwise.
(4) An application under this rule must be made in accordance with Part 10.

20 Public Guardian to be supplied with court documents relevant to supervision of deputies

(1) This rule applies in any case where the court makes an order–
   (a) appointing a person to act as a deputy; or
   (b) varying an order under which a deputy has been appointed.
(2) Subject to paragraphs (3) and (6), the Public Guardian is entitled to be supplied with a copy of qualifying documents if he reasonably considers that it is necessary for him to have regard to them in connection with the discharge of his functions under section 58 of the Act in relation to the supervision of deputies.
(3) The court may direct that the right to be supplied with documents under paragraph (2) does not apply in relation to such one or more documents, or descriptions of documents, as the court may specify.
(4) A direction under paragraph (3) or (6) may be given–
   (a) either on the court's own initiative or on an application made to it; and
   (b) either–
      (i) at the same time as the court makes the order which appoints the deputy, or which varies it; or
      (ii) subsequently.
(5) 'Qualifying documents' means documents which–
   (a) are filed in court in connection with the proceedings in which the court makes the order referred to in paragraph (1); and
   (b) are relevant to–
      (i) the decision to appoint the deputy;
      (ii) any powers conferred on him;
      (iii) any duties imposed on him; or
      (iv) any other terms applying to those powers and duties which are contained in the order.
(6) The court may direct that any document is to be provided to the Public Guardian on an edited basis.

21 Provision of court order to Public Guardian
Any order of the court requiring the Public Guardian to do something, or not to do something, will be served by the court on the Public Guardian as soon as practicable and in any event not later than 7 days after the order was made.

22 Amendment of application
(1) The court may allow or direct an applicant, at any stage of the proceedings, to amend his application form or notice.
(2) The amendment may be effected by making in writing the necessary alterations to the application form or notice, but if the amendments are so numerous or of such a nature or length that written alteration would make it difficult or inconvenient to read, a fresh document amended as allowed or directed may be issued.

23 Clerical mistakes or slips
The court may at any time correct any clerical mistakes in an order or direction or any error arising in an order or direction from any accidental slip or omission.

24 Endorsement of amendment
Where an application form or notice, order or direction has been amended under this Part, a note shall be placed on it showing the date on which it was amended and the alteration shall be sealed.

Part 5: General Case Management Powers

25 The court's general powers of case management
(1) The list of powers in this rule is in addition to any powers given to the court by any other rule or practice direction or by any other enactment or any powers it may otherwise have.
(2) The court may–
   (a) extend or shorten the time for compliance with any rule, practice direction, or court order or direction (even if an application for extension is made after the time for compliance has expired);
   (b) adjourn or bring forward a hearing;
   (c) require P, a party, a party's legal representative or litigation friend, to attend court;
   (d) hold a hearing and receive evidence by telephone or any other method of direct oral communication;
   (e) stay the whole or part of any proceedings or judgment either generally or until a specified date or event;
   (f) consolidate proceedings;
   (g) hear two or more applications on the same occasion;
   (h) direct a separate hearing of any issue;
   (i) decide the order in which issues are to be heard;
   (j) exclude an issue from consideration;
   (k) dismiss or give judgment on an application after a decision is made on a preliminary basis;
   (l) direct any party to file and serve an estimate of costs; and
   (m) take any step or give any direction for the purpose of managing the case and furthering the overriding objective.

(3) A judge to whom a matter is allocated may, if he considers that the matter is one which ought properly to be dealt with by another judge, transfer the matter to such a judge.
(4) Where the court gives directions it may take into account whether or not a party has complied with any rule or practice direction.
(5) The court may make any order it considers appropriate even if a party has not sought that order.
(6) A power of the court under these Rules to make an order includes a power to vary or revoke the order;
(7) [revoked.]

26 Court's power to dispense with requirement of any rule
In addition to its general powers and the powers listed in rule 25, the court may dispense with the requirement of any rule.

27 Exercise of powers on the court's own initiative
(1) Except where these Rules or some other enactment make different provision, the court may exercise its powers on its own initiative.
(2) The court may make an order on its own initiative without hearing the parties or giving them the opportunity to make representations.
(3) Where the court proposes to make an order on its own initiative it may give the parties and any person it thinks fit an opportunity to make representations and, where it does so, it will specify the time by which, and the manner in which, the representations must be made.
(4) Where the court proposes–
 (a) to make an order on its own initiative; and
 (b) to hold a hearing to decide whether to make the order,
 it will give the parties and may give any other person it thinks likely to be affected by the order at least 3 days' notice of the hearing.

28 General power of the court to rectify matters where there has been an error of procedure
Where there has been an error of procedure, such as a failure to comply with a rule or practice direction–
 (a) the error does not invalidate any step taken in the proceedings unless the court so orders; and
 (b) the court may waive the error or require it to be remedied or may make such other order as appears to the court to be just.

Part 6: Service of Documents

Service generally

29 Scope
(1) Subject to paragraph (2), the rules in this Part apply to–
 (a) the service of documents; and
 (b) to the requirement under rule 70 for a person to be notified of the issue of an application form,
 and references to 'serve', 'service', 'notice' and 'notify', and kindred expressions shall be construed accordingly.
(2) The rules in this Part do not apply where–

(a) any other enactment, a rule in another Part or a practice direction makes different provision; or
(b) the court directs otherwise.

30 Who is to serve

(1) The general rule is that the following documents will be served by the court–
   (a) an order or judgment of the court;
   (b) an acknowledgment of service or notification; and
   (c) except where the application is for an order for committal, a notice of hearing.
(2) Any other document is to be served by the party seeking to rely upon it, except where–
   (a) a rule or practice direction provides otherwise; or
   (b) the court directs otherwise.
(3) Where the court is to serve a document–
   (a) it is for the court to decide which of the methods of service specified in rule 31 is to be used; and
   (b) if the document is being served on behalf of a party, that party must provide sufficient copies.

31 Methods of service

(1) A document may be served by any of the methods specified in this rule.
(2) Where it is not known whether a solicitor is acting on behalf of a person, the document may be served by–
   (a) delivering it to the person personally;
   (b) delivering it at his home address or last known home address; or
   (c) sending it to that address, or last known address, by first class post (or by an alternative method of service which provides for delivery on the next working day).
(3) Where a solicitor–
   (a) is authorised to accept service on behalf of a person; and
   (b) has informed the person serving the document in writing that he is so authorised,
   the document must be served on the solicitor, unless personal service is required by an enactment, rule, practice direction or court order.
(4) Where it appears to the court that there is a good reason to authorise service by a method other than those specified in paragraphs (2) or (3), the court may direct that service is effected by that method.
(5) A direction that service is effected by an alternative method must specify–
   (a) the method of service; and
   (b) the date when the document will be deemed to be served.
(6) A practice direction may set out how documents are to be served by document exchange, electronic communication or other means.

32 Service of documents on children and protected parties

(1) The following table shows the person on whom a document must be served if it is a document which would otherwise be served on–
   (a) a child; or
   (b) a protected party.

Type of document	Nature of party	Person to be served
Application form	Child	–A person who has parental responsibility for the child within the meaning of the Children Act 1989; or
		–if there is no such person, a person with whom the child resides or in whose care the child is.
Application form	Protected party	–The person who is authorised to conduct the proceedings in the protected party's name or on his behalf; or
		–a person who is a duly appointed attorney, donee or deputy of the protected party; or
		–if there is no such person, a person with whom the protected party lives or in whose care the latter is.
Application for an order appointing a litigation friend, where a child or protected party has no litigation friend	Child or protected party	–See rule 145 (appointment of litigation friend by court order– supplementary).
Any other document	Child or protected party	–The litigation friend or other duly authorised person who is conducting the proceedings on behalf of the child or protected party.

(2) The court may make an order for service on a child or a protected party by permitting the document to be served on some person other than the person specified in the table set out in paragraph (1) above (which may include service on the child or the protected party).
(3) An application for an order under paragraph (2) may be made without notice.
(4) The court may order that, although a document has been served on someone other than the person specified in the table, the document is to be treated as if it had been properly served.
(5) This rule does not apply in relation to the service of documents upon a child in any case where the court has made an order under rule 141(4) permitting the child to conduct proceedings without a litigation friend.

33 Service of documents on P if he becomes a party
(1) If P becomes a party to the proceedings, all documents to be served on him must be served on his litigation friend or as directed by the court on P's behalf.

(2) The court may make an order for service on P by permitting the document to be served on some person other than the person specified in paragraph (1) above (which may include service on P).

(3) An application for an order under paragraph (2) may be made without notice.

(4) The court may order that, although a document has been served on someone other than a person specified in paragraph (1), the document is to be treated as if it had been properly served.

(5) This rule does not apply in relation to the service of documents upon P in any case where the court has made an order under rule 144(1)(b) (power of court to bring to an end the appointment of a litigation friend).

(Rule 41A requires P to be notified where a direction has been made under rule 3A, and of the appointment of a litigation friend, accredited legal representative or representative.)

34 Substituted service

Where it appears to the court that it is impracticable for any reason to serve a document in accordance with any of the methods provided under rule 31, the court may make an order for substituted service of the document by taking such steps as the court may direct to bring it to the notice of the person to be served.

35 Deemed service

(1) A document which is served in accordance with these Rules or any relevant practice direction shall be deemed to be served on the day shown in the following table–

Method of service	Deemed day of service
First class post (or other service for next-day delivery)	The second day after it was posted.
Document exchange	The second day after it was left at the document exchange.
Delivering the document to a permitted address	The day after it was delivered to that address.
Fax	If it is transmitted on a business day before 4pm, on that day; or in any other case, on the business day after the day on which it is transmitted.
Other electronic means	The second day after the day on which it is transmitted.

(2) If a document is served personally–
 (a) after 5pm, on a business day; or
 (b) at any time on a Saturday, Sunday or a Bank Holiday,
it will be treated as being served on the next business day.

36 Certificate of service
(1) Where a rule, practice direction or court order requires a certificate of service for the document, the certificate must state the details set out in the following table–

Method of service	Details to be certified
First class post (or any other service for next-day delivery)	Date of posting
Personal service	Date of personal service
Document exchange	Date when the document was left at the document exchange.
Delivery of document to permitted address	Date when the document was delivered to that address.
Fax	Date of transmission.
Other electronic means	Date of transmission and the means used.
Alternative method permitted by the court	As required by the court.

(2) The certificate must be filed within 7 days after service of the document to which it relates.

37 Certificate of non-service
(1) Where an applicant or other person is unable to serve any document under these Rules or as directed by the court, he must file a certificate of non-service stating the reasons why service has not been effected.
(2) The certificate of non-service must be filed within 7 days of the latest date on which service should have been effected.

38 Power of court to dispense with service
(1) The court may dispense with any requirement to serve a document.
(2) An application for an order to dispense with service may be made without notice.

Service out of the jurisdiction

39 Scope and interpretation
(1) This rule and rules 39A to 39H make provision about–
  (a) service of application forms and other documents out of the jurisdiction; and
  (b) the procedure for service.
(2) In this rule and rules 39A to 39H–
  'application form' includes an application notice;
  'Commonwealth State' means a State listed in Schedule 3 to the British Nationality Act 1981;
  'jurisdiction' means, unless the context otherwise requires, England and Wales and any part of the territorial waters of the United Kingdom adjoining England and Wales;
  'Member State' means a Member State of the European Union;

'the Service Convention' means the Convention on the service abroad of judicial and extra-judicial documents in civil or commercial matters signed at the Hague on November 15, 1965;

'Service Convention country' means a country, not being a Member State, which is a party to the Service Convention; and

'the Service Regulation' means Regulation (EC) No 1393/2007 of the European Parliament and of the Council of 13 November 2007 on the service in the Member States of judicial and extra-judicial documents in civil and commercial matters (service of documents) and repealing Council Regulation (EC) No 1348/2000.

(3) In rules 39A to 39H, a reference to service by a party includes service by a person who is not a party where service by such a person is required under these Rules.

39A Service of application form and other documents out of the jurisdiction

(1) Subject to paragraph (2), any document to be served for the purposes of these Rules may be served out of the jurisdiction without the permission of the court.

(2) An application form may not be served out of the jurisdiction unless the court has power to determine the application to which it relates under the Act.

39B Period for acknowledging service or responding to application where application is served out of the jurisdiction

(1) This rule applies where, under these Rules, a party is required to file–

(a) an acknowledgment of service; or

(b) an answer to an application,

and sets out the time period for doing so where the application is served out of the jurisdiction.

(2) Where the applicant serves an application on a respondent in–

(a) Scotland or Northern Ireland; or

(b) a Member State or Service Convention country within Europe,

the period for filing an acknowledgment of service or an answer to an application is 21 days after service of the application.

(3) Where the applicant serves an application on a respondent in a Service Convention country outside Europe, the period for filing an acknowledgment of service or an answer to an application is 31 days after service of the application.

(4) Where the applicant serves an application on a respondent in a country not referred to in paragraphs (2) and (3), the period for filing an acknowledgment of service or an answer to an application is set out in Practice Direction 6B.

39C Method of service–general provisions

(1) This rule contains general provisions about the method of service of an application form or other document on a party out of the jurisdiction.

Where service is to be effected on a party in Scotland or Northern Ireland

(2) Where a party serves an application form or other document on a party in Scotland or Northern Ireland, it must be served by a method permitted by this Part.

Where service is to be effected out of the United Kingdom
(3) Where an application form or other document is to be served on a person out of the United Kingdom, it may be served by any method–
   (a) provided for by–
      (i) rule 39D (service in accordance with the Service Regulation); or
      (ii) rule 39E (service through foreign governments, judicial authorities and British Consular authorities); or
   (b) permitted by the law of the country in which it is to be served.
(4) Nothing in paragraph (3) or in any court order authorises or requires any person to do anything which is contrary to the law of the country where the application form or other document is to be served.

39D Service in accordance with the Service Regulation
(1) This rule applies where an application form or other document is to be served on a person out of the United Kingdom in accordance with the Service Regulation.
(2) The person wishing to serve must file–
   (a) the application form or other document;
   (b) any translation; and
   (c) any other documents required by the Service Regulation.
(3) When the person wishing to serve files the documents referred to in paragraph (2), the court officer must–
   (a) seal, or otherwise authenticate with the stamp of the court, the copy of the application form; and
   (b) forward the documents to the Senior Master of the Queen's Bench Division.
(4) In addition to the documents referred to in paragraph (2), the person wishing to serve may, if of the view that this would assist in ensuring effective service, file a photograph of the person to be served.

(The Service Regulation is annexed to Practice Direction 6B.)

(Rule 39E makes provision for service on a person in a Service Convention country.)

39E Service through foreign governments, judicial authorities and British Consular authorities
(1) Where an application form or other document is to be served on a person in a Service Convention country, it may be served–
   (a) through the authority designated under the Service Convention in respect of that country; or
   (b) if the law of that country permits, through–
      (i) the judicial authorities of that country; or
      (ii) a British Consular authority in that country.
(2) Where an application form or other document is to be served on a person in a country which is not a Service Convention country, it may be served, if the law of that country so permits, through–
   (a) the government of that country, where that government is willing to serve it; or
   (b) a British Consular authority in that country.
(3) Where an application form or other document is to be served in–
   (a) any Commonwealth State which is not a Service Convention country;

(b) the Isle of Man or the Channel Islands; or
(c) any British Overseas Territory,
the methods of service permitted by paragraphs (1)(b) and (2) are not available and the person wishing to serve, or that person's agent, must effect service direct unless Practice Direction 6B provides otherwise.

(4) This rule does not apply where service is to be effected in accordance with the Service Regulation.

(Rule 39D makes provision for service on a party in a Member State in accordance with the Service Regulation.)

(A list of British Overseas Territories is reproduced in Practice Direction 6B.)

39F Procedure where service is to be through foreign governments, judicial authorities and British Consular authorities

(1) This rule applies where an application form or other document is to be served under rule 39E(1) or (2).
(2) Where this rule applies, the person wishing to serve must file–
   (a) a request for service of the application form or other document, by specifying one or more of the methods in rule 39E(1) or (2);
   (b) a copy of the application form or other document;
   (c) any other documents or copies of documents required by Practice Direction 6B; and
   (d) any translation required under rule 39G.
(3) When the person wishing to serve files the documents specified in paragraph (2), the court officer must–
   (a) seal, or otherwise authenticate with the stamp of the court, the copy of the application form; and
   (b) forward the documents to the Senior Master of the Queen's Bench Division.
(4) The Senior Master shall send documents forwarded under this rule–
   (a) where the application form or other document is being served through the authority designated under the Service Convention, to that authority; or
   (b) in any other case, to the Foreign and Commonwealth Office with a request that it arranges for the application form or other document to be served.
(5) An official certificate which–
   (a) states that the method requested under paragraph (2)(a) has been performed and the date of such performance;
   (b) states, where more than one method is requested under paragraph (2)(a), which method was used; and
   (c) is made by–
      (i) a British Consular authority in the country where the method requested under paragraph (2)(a) was performed;
      (ii) the government or judicial authorities in that country; or
      (iii) the authority designated in respect of that country under the Service Convention,
   is evidence of the facts stated in the certificate.
(6) A document purporting to be an official certificate under paragraph (5) is to be treated as such a certificate unless it is proved not to be.

39G Translation of application form or other document

(1) Except where paragraphs (4) and (5) apply, every copy of the application form or other document filed under rule 39E (service through foreign governments, judicial authorities and British Consular authorities) must be accompanied by a translation of the application form or other document.

(2) The translation must be–
  (a) in the official language of the country in which it is to be served; or
  (b) if there is more than one official language of that country, in any official language which is appropriate to the place in the country where the application form or other document is to be served.

(3) Every translation filed under this rule must be accompanied by a statement by the person making it that it is a correct translation, and the statement must include that person's name, address and qualifications for making the translation.

(4) The applicant is not required to file a translation of the application form or other document filed under rule 39E where it is to be served in a country of which English is an official language.

(5) The applicant is not required to file a translation of the application form or other document filed under rule 39E where–
  (a) the person on whom the document is to be served is able to read and understand English; and
  (b) service of the document is to be effected directly on that person.

(This rule does not apply to service in accordance with the Service Regulation, which contains its own provisions about the translation of documents.)

39H Undertaking to be responsible for expenses of the Foreign and Commonwealth Office

Every request for service under rule 39F (procedure where service is to be through foreign governments, judicial authorities, etc) must contain an undertaking by the person making the request–
  (a) to be responsible for all expenses incurred by the Foreign and Commonwealth Office or foreign judicial authority; and
  (b) to pay those expenses to the Foreign and Commonwealth Office or foreign judicial authority on being informed of the amount.

Part 7: Notifying P

General requirement to notify P

40 General

(1) Subject to paragraphs (2) and (3), the rules in this Part apply where P is to be given notice of any matter or document, or is to be provided with any document, either under the Rules or in accordance with an order or direction of the court.

(2) Except where rule 41A applies, if P becomes a party, the rules in this Part do not apply and service is to be effected in accordance with Part 6 or as directed by the court.

(3) In any case the court may, either on its own initiative or on application, direct that P must not be notified of any matter or document, or provided with any document, whether in accordance with this Part or at all.

(4) Subject to paragraph (5), where P is a child--
   (a) if the person to be notified under this rule is a person with parental responsibility for the child within the meaning of the Children Act 1989 or, if there is no such person, a person with whom the child resides or in whose care the child is;
   (b) all references to 'P' in this Part, except that in paragraph (2), are to be read as referring to the person notified in accordance with sub-paragraph (a).
(5) Paragraph (4) does not apply, and there is no requirement to notify P, where the person referred to in paragraph (4)(a) has already been served or notified of the relevant matter in accordance with another rule or practice direction.

41 Who is to notify P

(1) Where P is to be notified under this Part, notification must be effected by–
   (a) the applicant;
   (b) the appellant (where the matter relates to an appeal);
   (c) an agent duly appointed by the applicant or the appellant; or
   (d) such other person as the court may direct.
(2) The person within paragraph (1) is referred to in this Part as 'the person effecting notification'.

41A Notifying P of appointment of a litigation friend, etc

P must be notified–
   (a) where a direction has been made under rule 3A; and
   (b) of the appointment of a litigation friend, accredited legal representative or representative on P's behalf.

Circumstances in which P must be notified

42 Application forms

(1) P must be notified–
   (a) that an application form has been issued by the court;
   (b) that an application form has been withdrawn; and
   (c) of the date on which a hearing is to be held in relation to the matter, where that hearing is for disposing of the application.
(2) Where P is to be notified that an application form has been issued, the person effecting notification must explain to P–
   (a) who the applicant is;
   (b) that the application raises the question of whether P lacks capacity in relation to a matter or matters, and what that means;
   (c) what will happen if the court makes the order or direction that has been applied for; and
   (d) where the application contains a proposal for the appointment of a person to make decisions on P's behalf in relation to the matter to which the application relates, details of who that person is.
(3) Where P is to be notified that an application form has been withdrawn, the person effecting notification must explain to P–
   (a) that the application form has been withdrawn; and
   (b) the consequences of that withdrawal.
(4) The person effecting notification must also inform P that he may seek advice and assistance in relation to any matter of which he is notified.

43 Appeals
(1) P must be notified–
   (a) that an appellant's notice has been issued by the court;
   (b) that an appellant's notice has been withdrawn; and
   (c) of the date on which a hearing is to be held in relation to the matter, where that hearing is for disposing of the appellant's notice.
(2) Where P is to be notified that an appellant's notice has been issued, the person effecting notification must explain to P–
   (a) who the appellant is;
   (b) the issues raised by the appeal; and
   (c) what will happen if the court makes the order or direction that has been applied for.
(3) Where P is to be notified that an appellant's notice has been withdrawn, the person effecting notification must explain to P–
   (a) that the appellant's notice has been withdrawn; and
   (b) the consequences of that withdrawal.
(4) The person effecting notification must also inform P that he may seek advice and assistance in relation to any matter of which he is notified.

44 Final orders
(1) P must be notified of any decision of the court relating to P except for a case management decision.
(2) Where P is notified in accordance with this rule, the person effecting notification must explain to P the effect of the decision.
(3) The person effecting notification must also inform P that P may seek advice and assistance in relation to any matter of which P is notified.
(4) The person effecting notification must also provide P with a copy of any order relating to a decision of which P must be notified in accordance with paragraph (1).

45 Other matters
(1) This rule applies where the court directs that P is to be notified of any other matter.
(2) The person effecting notification must explain to P such matters as may be directed by the court.
(3) The person effecting notification must also inform P that he may seek advice and assistance in relation to any matter of which he is notified.

Manner of notification, and accompanying documents

46 Manner of notification
(1) Where P is to be notified under this Part, the person effecting notification must provide P with, or arrange for P to be provided with, the information specified in rules 41A to 45 in a way that is appropriate to P's circumstances (for example, using simple language, visual aids or any other appropriate means).
(2) The information referred to in paragraph (1) must be provided to P personally.
(3) P must be provided with the information mentioned in paragraph (1) as soon as practicable and in any event within 14 days of the date on which–
   (a) the application form or appellant's notice was issued or withdrawn;
   (b) the decision was made; . . .

(c) the person effecting notification received the notice of hearing from the court and in any event no later than 14 days before the date specified in the notice of the hearing; and

(d) the order referred to in rule 44(4) was served upon the person who is required to effect notification of P under that rule,

as the case may be.

(4) Where the provisions of rule 40(4) apply, paragraphs (1) and (2) of this rule do not apply and the person effecting notification may provide information and documents of which P must be notified to the person to be notified under rule 40(4), by any method by which service of documents would be permitted under rule 31.

47 Acknowledgment of notification

When P is notified that an application form or an appellant's notice has been issued, he must also be provided with a form for acknowledging notification.

48 Certificate of notification

(1) The person effecting notification must, within 7 days beginning with the date on which notification in accordance with this Part was given, file a certificate of notification which certifies–

(a) the date on which, and how, P was notified; and

(b) that P was notified in accordance with this Part.

(2) Subject to paragraph (3), the person effecting notification in accordance with this Part must in the certificate required by paragraph (1) describe the steps taken to enable P to understand, and the extent to which P appears to have understood, the information.

(3) Where the provisions of rule 40(4) apply, paragraph (2) does not apply.

49 Dispensing with requirement to notify, etc

(1) The applicant, the appellant or other person directed by the court to effect notification may apply to the court seeking an order–

(a) dispensing with the requirement to comply with the provisions in this Part; or

(b) requiring some other person to comply with the provisions in this Part.

(2) An application under this rule must be made in accordance with Part 10.

Part 8: Permission

50 General

Subject to these Rules and to section 50(1) of, and paragraph 20 of Schedule 3 to, the Act, the applicant must apply for permission to start proceedings under the Act.

(Section 50(1) of the Act specifies persons who do not need to apply for permission. Paragraph 20 of Schedule 3 to the Act specifies an application for which permission is not needed.)

51 Where the court's permission is not required

The permission of the court is not required–

(a) where an application is made by–

(i) the Official Solicitor; or

(ii) the Public Guardian;

(b) where the application concerns–
   (i) P's property and affairs;
   (ii) a lasting power of attorney which is, or purports to be, created under the Act; or
   (iii) an instrument which is, or purports to be, an enduring power of attorney;
(c) where an application is made under section 21A of the Act;
(d) where an application is made for an order under section 16(2)(a) of the Act, which is to be relied on to authorise the deprivation of P's liberty pursuant to section 4A(3) of the Act;
(e) where an application is made in accordance with Part 10;
(f) where a person files an acknowledgment of service or notification in accordance with this Part or Part 9, for any order proposed that is different from that sought by the applicant; or
(g) in any other case specified for this purpose in a practice direction.

52 [revoked.]

53 Permission–supplementary
(1) [revoked.]
(2) Where part of the application concerns a matter which requires permission, and part of it does not, permission need only be sought for that part of it which requires permission.

54 Application for permission
Where permission is required, the applicant must apply for permission when making an application.

(Rule 84(1A) explains how the court will deal with an application for permission.)

55 [revoked.]

56 [revoked.]

57 [revoked.]

58 [revoked.]

59 Service of an order giving or refusing permission
The court must serve–
(a) the order granting or refusing permission;
(b) if refusing permission without a hearing, the reasons for its decision in summary form; and
(c) any directions,
on the applicant and on any other person served with or notified of the application form.

60 Appeal against a permission decision following a hearing
Where the court grants or refuses permission following a hearing, any appeal against the permission decision shall be dealt with in accordance with Part 20 (appeals).

(Rule 89 deals with reconsideration of orders and decisions made without a hearing or without notice to any person who is affected by such order or decision.)

Part 9: How to Start Proceedings

Initial steps

61 General

(1) Applications to the court to start proceedings shall be made in accordance with this Part and, as applicable, Part 8 and the relevant practice directions.
(2) The appropriate forms must be used in the cases to which they apply, with such variations as the case requires, but not so as to omit any information or guidance which any form gives to the intended recipient.
(3) [revoked.]

62 When proceedings are started

(1) The general rule is that proceedings are started when the court issues an application form at the request of the applicant.
(2) An application form is issued on the date entered on the application form by the court.

63 Contents of the application form

The application form must–
(a) state the matter which the applicant wants the court to decide;
(b) state the order which the applicant is seeking;
(c) name–
    (i) the applicant;
    (ii) P;
    (iii) as a respondent, any person (other than P) whom the applicant reasonably believes to have an interest which means that he ought to be heard in relation to the application (as opposed to being notified of it in accordance with rule 70); and
    (iv) any person whom the applicant intends to notify in accordance with rule 70; and
(d) if the applicant is applying in a representative capacity, state what that capacity is.

64 Documents to be filed with the application form

When an applicant files his application form with the court, he must also file–
(a) in accordance with the relevant practice direction, any evidence upon which he intends to rely;
(b) [revoked.]
(c) an assessment of capacity form, where this is required by the relevant practice direction;
(d) any other documents referred to in the application form; and
(e) such other information and material as may be set out in a practice direction.

65 What the court will do when an application form is filed

As soon as practicable after an application form is filed the court must issue it and do anything else that may be set out in a practice direction.

Steps following issue of application form

66 Applicant to serve the application form on named respondents

(1) As soon as practicable and in any event within 14 days of the date on which the application form was issued, the applicant must serve a copy of the application form on any person who is named as a respondent in the application form, together with copies of any documents filed in accordance with rule 64 and a form for acknowledging service.

(2) The applicant must file a certificate of service within 7 days beginning with the date on which the documents were served.

67 Applications relating to lasting powers of attorney

(1) Where the application concerns the powers of the court under section 22 or 23 of the Act (powers of the court in relation to the validity and operation of lasting powers of attorney) the applicant must serve a copy of the application form, together with copies of any documents filed in accordance with rule 64 and a form for acknowledging service–
   (a) unless the applicant is the donor or donee of the lasting power of attorney ('the power'), on the donor and every donee of the power;
   (b) if he is the donor, on every donee of the power; and
   (c) if he is a donee, on the donor and any other donee of the power,
but only if the above-mentioned persons have not been served or notified under any other rule.

(2) Where the application is solely in respect of an objection to the registration of a power, the requirements of rules 66 and 70 do not apply to an application made under this rule by–
   (a) a donee of the power; or
   (b) a person named in a statement made by the donor of the power in accordance with paragraph 2(1)(c)(i) of Schedule 1 to the Act.

(3) The applicant must comply with paragraph (1) as soon as practicable and in any event within 14 days of date on which the application form was issued.

(4) The applicant must file a certificate of service within 7 days beginning with the date on which the documents were served.

(5) Where the applicant knows or has reasonable grounds to believe that the donor of the power lacks capacity to make a decision in relation to any matter that is the subject of the application, he must notify the donor in accordance with Part 7.

68 Applications relating to enduring powers of attorney

(1) Where the application concerns the powers of the court under paragraphs 2(9), 4(5)(a) and (b), 7(2), 10(c), 13, or 16(2), (3), (4) and (6) of Schedule 4 to the Act, the applicant must serve a copy of the application form, together with copies of any documents filed in accordance with rule 64 and a form for acknowledging service–
   (a) unless the applicant is the donor or attorney under the enduring power of attorney ('the power'), on the donor and every attorney of the power;
   (b) if he is the donor, on every attorney under the power; or
   (c) if he is an attorney, on the donor and any other attorney under the power,
but only if the above-mentioned persons have not been served or notified under any other rule.

(2) Where the application is solely in respect of an objection to the registration of a power, the requirements of rules 66 and 70 do not apply to an application made under this rule by–
  (a) an attorney under the power; or
  (b) a person listed in paragraph 6(1) of Schedule 4 to the Act.
(3) The applicant must comply with paragraph (1) as soon as practicable and in any event within 14 days of the date on which the application form was issued.
(4) The applicant must file a certificate of service within 7 days beginning with the date on which the documents were served.
(5) Where the applicant knows or has reasonable grounds to believe that the donor of the power lacks capacity to make a decision in relation to any matter that is the subject of the application, he must notify the donor in accordance with Part 7.

69 Applicant to notify P of an application

P must be notified in accordance with Part 7 that an application form has been issued, unless the requirement to do so has been dispensed with under rule 49.

70 Applicant to notify other persons of an application

(1) As soon as practicable and in any event within 14 days of the date on which the application form was issued, the applicant must notify the persons specified in the relevant practice direction–
  (a) that an application form has been issued;
  (b) whether it relates to the exercise of the court's jurisdiction in relation to P's property and affairs, or his personal welfare, or to both; and
  (c) of the order or orders sought.
(2) Notification of the issue of the application form must be accompanied by a form for acknowledging notification.
(3) The applicant must file a certificate of notification within 7 days beginning with the date on which notification was given.

71 Requirements for certain applications

A practice direction may make additional or different provision in relation to specified applications.

Responding to an application

72 Responding to an application

(1) A person who is served with or notified of an application form and who wishes to take part in proceedings must file an acknowledgment of service or notification in accordance with this rule.
(2) The acknowledgment of service or notification must be filed not more than 14 days after the application form was served or notification of the application was given.
(3) The court will serve the acknowledgment of service or notification on the applicant and on any other person who has filed such an acknowledgment.
(4) The acknowledgment of service or notification must–
  (a) state whether the person acknowledging service or notification consents to the application;

(b) state whether he opposes the application and, if so, set out the grounds for doing so;
(c) state whether he seeks a different order from that set out in the application form and, if so, set out what that order is;
(d) provide an address for service, which must be within the jurisdiction of the court; and
(e) be signed by him or his legal representative.
(5) Subject to rules 120 and 123 (restriction on filing an expert's report and court's power to restrict expert evidence), unless the court directs otherwise, where a person who has been served in accordance with rule 66, 67 or 68 opposes the application or seeks a different order, that person must within 28 days of such service file a witness statement containing any evidence upon which that person intends to rely.
(6) In addition to complying with the other requirements of this rule, an acknowledgment of notification filed by a person notified of the application in accordance with rule 67(5), 68(5), 69 or 70 must–
   (a) indicate whether the person wishes to be joined as a party to the proceedings; and
   (b) state the person's interest in the proceedings.
(7) Subject to rules 120 and 123 (restriction on filing an expert's report and court's power to restrict expert evidence), unless the court directs otherwise, where a person has been notified in accordance with rule 67(5), 68(5), 69, 70, that person must within 28 days of such service file a witness statement containing any evidence of his interest in the proceedings and, if he opposes the application or seeks a different order, any evidence upon which he intends to rely.
(8) The court will consider whether to join a person mentioned in paragraph (6) as a party to the proceedings and, if it decides to do so, will make an order to that effect.
(9) Where a person who is notified in accordance with rule 67(5), 68(5), 69 or 70 complies with the requirements of this rule, he need not comply with the requirements of rule 75 (application to be joined as a party).
(10) [revoked.]
(11) A practice direction may make provision about responding to applications.

The parties to the proceedings

73 Parties to the proceedings
(1) Unless the court otherwise directs, the parties to any proceedings are–
   (a) the applicant; and
   (b) any person who is named as a respondent in the application form and who files an acknowledgment of service in respect of the application form.
(2) The court may order a person to be joined as a party if it considers that it is desirable to do so for the purpose of dealing with the application.
(3) The court may at any time direct that any person who is a party to the proceedings is to be removed as a party.
(4) Unless the court orders otherwise, P shall not be named as a respondent to any proceedings.

(5) A party to the proceedings is bound by any order or direction of the court made in the course of those proceedings.

74 Persons to be bound as if parties
(1) The persons mentioned in paragraph (2) shall be bound by any order made or directions given by the court in the same way that a party to the proceedings is so bound.
(2) The persons referred to in paragraph (1) are–
   (a) P; and
   (b) any person who has been served with or notified of an application form in accordance with these Rules.

75 Application to be joined as a party
(1) Any person with sufficient interest may apply to the court to be joined as a party to the proceedings.
(2) An application to be joined as a party must be made by filing an application notice in accordance with Part 10 which must–
   (a) state the full name and address of the person seeking to be joined as a party to the proceedings;
   (b) state his interest in the proceedings;
   (c) state whether he consents to the application;
   (d) state whether he opposes the application and, if so, set out the grounds for doing so;
   (e) state whether he proposes that an order different from that set out in the application form should be made and, if so, set out what that order is;
   (f) provide an address for service, which must be within the jurisdiction of the court; and
   (g) be signed by him or his legal representative.
(3) Subject to rules 120 and 123 (restriction on filing an expert's report and court's power to restrict expert evidence), an application to be joined must be accompanied by–
   (a) a witness statement containing evidence of his interest in the proceedings and, if he proposes that an order different from that set out in the application form should be made, the evidence on which he intends to rely; and
   (b) a sufficient number of copies of the application notice to enable service of the application on every other party to the proceedings.
(4) The court will serve the application notice and any accompanying documents on all parties to the proceedings.
(5) The court will consider whether to join a person applying under this rule as a party to the proceedings and, if it decides to do so, will make an order to that effect.

76 Applications for removal as a party to proceedings
A person who wishes to be removed as a party to the proceedings must apply to the court for an order to that effect in accordance with Part 10.

Part 10: Applications within Proceedings

77 Types of applications for which the Part 10 procedure may be used
(1) The Part 10 procedure is the procedure set out in this Part.
(2) The Part 10 procedure may be used if the application is made by any person–

(a) in the course of existing proceedings; or
(b) as provided for in a rule or practice direction.
(3) The court may grant an interim remedy before an application form has been issued only if–
   (a) the matter is urgent; or
   (b) it is otherwise necessary to do so in the interests of justice.
(4) An application made during the course of existing proceedings includes an application made during appeal proceedings.
(5) Where the application seeks solely to withdraw an existing application–
   (a) the applicant must file a written request for permission setting out succinctly the reasons for the request;
   (b) the request must be in an application notice;
   (c) the court may permit an application to be made orally at a hearing or in such alternative written form as it thinks fit.
(6) Where the court deals with a written request under paragraph (5) without a hearing, rule 89 applies to any order so made.

(Rule 87A requires the court's permission to withdraw proceedings.)

78 Application notice to be filed

(1) Subject to paragraph (5), the applicant must file an application notice to make an application under this Part.
(2) The applicant must, when he files the application notice, file the evidence upon which he relies (unless such evidence has already been filed).
(3) The court will issue the application notice and, if there is to be a hearing, give notice of the date on which the matter is to be heard by the court.
(4) Notice under paragraph (3) must be given to–
   (a) the applicant;
   (b) anyone who is named as a respondent in the application notice (if not otherwise a party to the proceedings);
   (c) every party to the proceedings; and
   (d) any other person, as the court may direct.
(5) An applicant may make an application under this Part without filing an application notice if–
   (a) this is permitted by any rule or practice direction; or
   (b) the court dispenses with the requirement for an application notice.
(6) If the applicant makes an application without giving notice, the evidence in support of the application must state why notice has not been given.

79 What an application notice must include

An application notice must state–
   (a) what order or direction the applicant is seeking;
   (b) briefly, the grounds on which the applicant is seeking the order or direction; and
   (c) such other information as may be required by any rule or a practice direction.

80 Service of an application notice

(1) Subject to paragraphs (4) and (5), the applicant must serve a copy of the application notice on–
   (a) anyone who is named as a respondent in the application notice (if not otherwise a party to the proceedings);

(b) every party to the proceedings; and
(c) any other person, as the court may direct,
as soon as practicable and in any event within 21 days of the date on which it was issued.
(2) The application notice must be accompanied by a copy of the evidence filed in support.
(3) The applicant must file a certificate of service within 7 days beginning with the date on which the documents were served.
(4) This rule does not require a copy of evidence to be served on a person upon whom it has already been served, but the applicant must in such a case give to that person notice of the evidence upon which he intends to rely.
(5) An application may be made without serving a copy of the application notice if this is permitted by–
(a) a rule;
(b) a practice direction; or
(c) the court.

81 Applications without notice

(1) This rule applies where the court has dealt with an application which was made without notice having been given to any person.
(2) Where the court makes an order, whether granting or dismissing the application, the applicant must, as soon as practicable or within such period as the court may direct, serve the documents mentioned in paragraph (3) on–
(a) anyone named as a respondent in the application notice (if not otherwise a party to the proceedings);
(b) every party to the proceedings; and
(c) any other person, as the court may direct.
(3) The documents referred to in paragraph (2) are–
(a) a copy of the application notice;
(b) the court's order; and
(c) any evidence filed in support of the application.

(Rule 89 provides for reconsideration of orders made without a hearing or without notice to a person.)

81A Security for costs

(1) A respondent to any application may apply for security for the respondent's costs of the proceedings.
(2) An application for security for costs must be supported by written evidence.
(3) Where the court makes an order for security for costs, it must–
(a) determine the amount of security; and
(b) direct–
(i) the manner in which; and
(ii) the time within which,
the security must be given.

81B Conditions to be satisfied

(1) The court may make an order for security for costs under rule 81A–
(a) if it is satisfied, having regard to all the circumstances of the case, that it is just to make such an order; and

(b) if—
  (i) one or more of the conditions in paragraph (2) applies; or
  (ii) an enactment permits the court to require security for costs.
(2) The conditions are—
  (a) the applicant is—
    (i) resident out of the jurisdiction; but
    (ii) not resident in a Brussels Contracting State, a State bound by the Lugano Convention or a Regulation State, as defined in section 1(3) of the Civil Jurisdiction and Judgments Act 1982;
  (b) the applicant is a company or other body (whether incorporated inside or outside Great Britain) and there is reason to believe that it will be unable to pay the respondent's costs if ordered to do so;
  (c) the applicant has changed address since proceedings were commenced with a view to avoiding the consequences of the litigation;
  (d) the applicant failed to give an address, or gave an incorrect address, in the application form commencing the proceedings;
  (e) the applicant is acting as a nominal applicant and there is reason to believe that the applicant will be unable to pay the respondent's costs if ordered to do so;
  (f) the applicant has taken steps in relation to the applicant's assets that would make it difficult to enforce an order for costs against the applicant.

81C Security for costs other than from the applicant

(1) The respondent may seek an order against a person other than the applicant, and the court may make an order for security for costs against that person, if—
  (a) it is satisfied, having regard to all the circumstances of the case, that it is just to make such an order; and
  (b) one or more of the conditions in paragraph (2) applies.
(2) The conditions are that the person—
  (a) has assigned the right to the substantive matter to the applicant with a view to avoiding the possibility of a costs order being made against the person; or
  (b) has contributed or agreed to contribute to the applicant's costs in return for a share of any money or property which the applicant may recover or be awarded in the proceedings; and
  is a person against whom a costs order may be made.

  (Rule 166 makes provision about costs orders against non-parties.)

81D Security for costs of an appeal

(1) The court may order security for costs of an appeal against—
  (a) an appellant;
  (b) a respondent who also appeals,
  on the same grounds as it may order security for costs against an applicant under rule 81A.
(2) The court may also make an order under paragraph (1) where the appellant or the respondent who also appeals is a limited company and there is reason to believe it will be unable to pay the costs of the other parties to the appeal should its appeal be unsuccessful.

Interim remedies

82 Orders for interim remedies
(1) The court may grant the following interim remedies–
   (a) an interim injunction;
   (b) an interim declaration; or
   (c) any other interim order it considers appropriate.
(2) Unless the court orders otherwise, a person on whom an application form is served under Part 9, or who is given notice of such an application, may not apply for an interim remedy before he has filed an acknowledgment of service or notification in accordance with Part 9.
(3) This rule does not limit any other power of the court to grant interim relief.

Part 10A: Deprivation of Liberty

82A The practice direction to this Part sets out procedure governing–
   (a) applications to the court for orders relating to the deprivation, or proposed deprivation, of liberty of P; and
   (b) proceedings (for example, relating to costs or appeals) connected with or consequent upon such applications.

Part 11: Human Rights

83 General
(1) A party who seeks to rely upon any provision of or right arising under the Human Rights Act 1998 ('the 1998 Act') or who seeks a remedy available under that Act must inform the court in the manner set out in the relevant practice direction specifying–
   (a) the Convention right (within the meaning of the 1998 Act) which it is alleged has been infringed and details of the alleged infringement; and
   (b) the remedy sought and whether this includes a declaration of incompatibility under section 4 of the 1998 Act.
(2) The court may not make a declaration of incompatibility unless 21 days' notice, or such other period of notice as the court directs, has been given to the Crown.
(3) Where notice has been given to the Crown, a Minister or other person permitted by the 1998 Act will be joined as a party on filing an application in accordance with rule 75 (application to be joined as a party).

Part 12: Dealing with Applications

84 Dealing with the application
(1) As soon as practicable after any application has been issued the court shall consider how to deal with it.
(1A) Where permission to start proceedings is required, and whether or not it has been applied for, the court's consideration under paragraph (1) shall include whether to grant or refuse permission without a hearing, or to direct a hearing to consider whether permission should be granted.
(2) The court may deal with an application or any part of an application at a hearing or without a hearing.
(3) In considering whether it is necessary to hold a hearing, the court shall, as appropriate, have regard to–

(a) the nature of the proceedings and the orders sought;
(b) whether the application is opposed by a person who appears to the court to have an interest in matters relating to P's best interests;
(c) whether the application involves a substantial dispute of fact;
(d) the complexity of the facts and the law;
(e) any wider public interest in the proceedings;
(f) the circumstances of P and of any party, in particular as to whether their rights would be adequately protected if a hearing were not held;
(g) whether the parties agree that the court should dispose of the application without a hearing; and
(h) any other matter specified in the relevant practice direction.
(4) Where the court considers that a hearing is necessary, it will–
  (a) give notice of the hearing date to the parties and to any other person it directs; and
  (b) state what is to be dealt with at the hearing, including whether the matter is to be disposed of at that hearing.
(5) Where the court decides that it can deal with the matter without a hearing it will do so and serve a copy of its order on the parties and on any other person it directs.

85 Directions

(1) The court may–
  (a) give directions in writing; or
  (b) set a date for a directions hearing; and
  (c) do anything else that may be set out in a practice direction.
(2) When giving directions, the court may do any of the following–
  (a) require a report under section 49 of the Act and give directions as to any such report;
  (b) give directions as to any requirements contained in these Rules or a practice direction for the giving of notification to any person or for that person to do anything in response to a notification;
  (c) [revoked.]
  (d) [revoked.]
  (e) if the court considers that any other person or persons should be a party to the proceedings, give directions joining them as a party;
  (f) if the court considers that any party to the proceedings should not be a party, give directions for that person's removal as a party;
  (g) give directions for the management of the case and set a timetable for the steps to be taken between the giving of directions and the hearing;
  (h) subject to rule 86, give directions as to the type of judge who is to hear the case;
  (i) give directions as to whether the proceedings or any part of them are to be heard in public, or as to whether any particular person should be permitted to attend the hearing, or as to whether any publication of the proceedings is to be permitted;
  (j) give directions as to the disclosure of documents, service of witness statements and any expert evidence;
  (k) give directions as to the attendance of witnesses and as to whether, and the extent to which, cross-examination will be permitted at any hearing; and

(l) give such other directions as the court thinks fit.
(3) The court may give directions at any time–
 (a) on its own initiative; or
 (b) on the application of a party.
(4) Subject to paragraphs (5) and (6) and unless these Rules or a practice direction provide otherwise or the court directs otherwise, the time specified by a rule or by the court for a person to do any act may be varied by the written agreement of the parties.
(5) A party must apply to the court if he wishes to vary –
 (a) the date the court has fixed for the final hearing; or
 (b) the period within which the final hearing is to take place.
(6) The time specified by a rule or practice direction or by the court may not be varied by the parties if the variation would make it necessary to vary the date the court has fixed for any hearing or the period within which the final hearing is to take place.

(Participation of P in proceedings is addressed in rule 3A (participation of P) and Part 17 (litigation friends and rule 3A representatives).)

Allocation of proceedings

86 Court's jurisdiction in certain kinds of case to be exercised by certain judges

(1) A practice direction made under this rule may specify certain categories of case to be dealt with by a specific judge or a specific class of judges.
(2) Applications in any matter other than those specified in the practice direction referred to in paragraph (1) may be dealt with by any judge.

Disputing the jurisdiction of the court

87 Procedure for disputing the court's jurisdiction

(1) A person who wishes to–
 (a) dispute the court's jurisdiction to hear an application; or
 (b) argue that the court should not exercise its jurisdiction,
 may apply to the court at any time for an order declaring that it has no such jurisdiction or should not exercise any jurisdiction that it may have.
(2) An application under this rule must be–
 (a) made by using the form specified in the relevant practice direction; and
 (b) supported by evidence.
(3) An order containing a declaration that the court has no jurisdiction or will not exercise its jurisdiction may also make further provision, including–
 (a) setting aside the application;
 (b) discharging any order made;
 (c) staying the proceedings; and
 (d) discharging any litigation friend, accredited legal representative or representative.

87A Permission required to withdraw proceedings

(1) Proceedings may only be withdrawn with the permission of the court.
(2) An application to withdraw proceedings must be made in accordance with Part 10.

Participation in hearings

88 Participation in hearings

(1) The court may hear P on the question of whether or not an order should be made, whether or not he is a party to the proceedings.
(2) The court may proceed with a hearing in the absence of P if it considers that it would be appropriate to do so.
(3) A person other than P who is served with or notified of the application may only take part in a hearing if–
   (a) he files an acknowledgment in accordance with the Rules and is made a party to the proceedings; or
   (b) the court permits.
(Rule 3A deals with participation of P.)

Reconsideration of court orders

89 Orders made without a hearing or without notice to any person

(1) This rule applies where the court makes an order–
   (a) without a hearing; or
   (b) without notice to any person who is affected by it.
(2) Where this rule applies–
   (a) P;
   (b) any party to the proceedings; or
   (c) any other person affected by the order,
   may apply to the court for reconsideration of the order made.
(3) An application under paragraph (2) must be made–
   (a) within 21 days of the order being served or such other period as the court may direct; and
   (b) in accordance with Part 10.
(4) The court will–
   (a) reconsider the order without directing a hearing; or
   (b) fix a date for the matter to be heard, and notify all parties to the proceedings and such other persons as the court may direct, of that date.
(5) Where an application is made in accordance with this rule, the court may affirm, set aside or vary any order made.
(6) An order made by a court officer authorised under rule 7A may be reconsidered by any judge.
(6A) An order made by a Tier 1 Judge may be reconsidered by any judge.
(6B) An order made by a Tier 2 Judge may be reconsidered by any Tier 2 Judge or by a Tier 3 Judge.
(6C) An order made by a Tier 3 Judge may be reconsidered by any Tier 3 Judge.
(6D) In any case to which paragraphs (6A) to (6C) apply the reconsideration may be carried out by the judge who made the order being reconsidered.
(7) No application may be made seeking a reconsideration of–
   (a) an order that has been made under paragraph (5); or
   (b) an order granting or refusing permission to appeal.
(8) An appeal against an order made under paragraph (5) may be made in accordance with Part 20 (appeals).
(9) Any order made without a hearing or without notice to any person, other than one made under paragraph (5) or one granting or refusing permission

to appeal, must contain a statement of the right to apply for a reconsideration of the decision in accordance with this rule.

(10) An application made under this rule may include a request that the court reconsider the matter at a hearing.

(Rule 7A(2)(c) provides that a court officer authorised under that rule may not deal with an application for the reconsideration of an order made by that court officer or another court officer.)

Part 13: Hearings

Private hearings

90 General rule–hearing to be in private

(1) The general rule is that a hearing is to be held in private.
(2) A private hearing is a hearing which only the following persons are entitled to attend–
   (a) the parties;
   (b) P (whether or not a party);
   (c) any person acting in the proceedings as a litigation friend;
   (d) any legal representative of a person specified in any of sub-paragraphs (a) to (c); and
   (e) any court officer.
(3) In relation to a private hearing, the court may make an order–
   (a) authorising any person, or class of persons, to attend the hearing or a part of it; or
   (b) excluding any person, or class of persons, from attending the hearing or a part of it.

91 Court's general power to authorise publication of information about proceedings

(1) For the purposes of the law relating to contempt of court, information relating to proceedings held in private (whether or not contained in a document filed with the court) may be communicated in accordance with paragraph (2) or (2A).
(2) The court may make an order authorising–
   (a) the publication or communication of such information or material relating to the proceedings as it may specify; or
   (b) the publication of the text or a summary of the whole or part of a judgment or order made by the court.
(2A) Subject to any direction of the court, information referred to in paragraph (1) may be communicated in accordance with Practice Direction 13A.
(3) Where the court makes an order under paragraph (2) it may do so on such terms as it thinks fit, and in particular may–
   (a) impose restrictions on the publication of the identity of–
      (i) any party;
      (ii) P (whether or not a party);
      (iii) any witness; or
      (iv) any other person;
   (b) prohibit the publication of any information that may lead to any such person being identified;
   (c) prohibit the further publication of any information relating to the proceedings from such date as the court may specify; or

(d) impose such other restrictions on the publication of information relating to the proceedings as the court may specify.
(4) The court may on its own initiative or upon request authorise communication–
   (a) for the purposes set out in Practice Direction 13A; or
   (b) for such other purposes as it considers appropriate,
   of information held by it.

Power to order a public hearing

92 Court's power to order that a hearing be held in public
(1) The court may make an order–
   (a) for a hearing to be held in public;
   (b) for a part of a hearing to be held in public; or
   (c) excluding any person, or class of persons, from attending a public hearing or a part of it.
(2) Where the court makes an order under paragraph (1), it may in the same order or by a subsequent order–
   (a) impose restrictions on the publication of the identity of–
      (i) any party;
      (ii) P (whether or not a party);
      (iii) any witness; or
      (iv) any other person;
   (b) prohibit the publication of any information that may lead to any such person being identified;
   (c) prohibit the further publication of any information relating to the proceedings from such date as the court may specify; or
   (d) impose such other restrictions on the publication of information relating to the proceedings as the court may specify.

Supplementary

93 Supplementary provisions relating to public or private hearings
(1) An order under rule 90, 91 or 92 may be made–
   (a) only where it appears to the court that there is good reason for making the order;
   (b) at any time; and
   (c) either on the court's own initiative or on an application made by any person in accordance with Part 10.
(2) A practice direction may make further provision in connection with–
   (a) private hearings;
   (b) public hearings; or
   (c) the publication of information about any proceedings.

Part 14: Admissions, Evidence and Depositions

Admissions

94 Making an admission
(1) Without prejudice to the ability to make an admission in any other way, a party may admit the truth of the whole or part of another party's case by giving notice in writing.
(2) The court may allow a party to amend or withdraw an admission.

Evidence

95 Power of court to control evidence

The court may—
(a) control the evidence by giving directions as to—
   (i) the issues on which it requires evidence;
   (ii) the nature of the evidence which it requires to decide those issues; and
   (iii) the way in which the evidence is to be placed before the court;
(b) use its power under this rule to exclude evidence that would otherwise be admissible;
(c) allow or limit cross-examination;
(d) admit such evidence, whether written or oral, as it thinks fit; and
(e) admit, accept and act upon such information, whether oral or written, from P, any protected party or any person who lacks competence to give evidence, as the court considers sufficient, although not given on oath and whether or not it would be admissible in a court of law apart from this rule.

96 Evidence of witnesses—general rule

(1) The general rule is that any fact which needs to be proved by evidence of a witness is to be proved—
   (a) where there is a final hearing, by their oral evidence; or
   (b) at any other hearing, or if there is no hearing, by their evidence in writing.
(2) Where a witness is called to give oral evidence under paragraph (1)(a), his witness statement shall stand as his evidence in chief unless the court directs otherwise.
(3) A witness giving oral evidence at the final hearing may, if the court permits—
   (a) amplify his witness statement; and
   (b) give evidence in relation to new matters which have arisen since the witness statement was made.
(4) The court may so permit only if it considers that there is good reason not to confine the evidence of the witness to the contents of his witness statement.
(5) This rule is subject to—
   (a) any provision to the contrary in these Rules or elsewhere; or
   (b) any order or direction of the court.

97 Written evidence—general rule

A party may not rely upon written evidence unless—
(a) it has been filed in accordance with these Rules or a practice direction;
(b) it is expressly permitted by these Rules or a practice direction; or
(c) the court gives permission.

98 Evidence by video link or other means

The court may allow a witness to give evidence through a video link or by other communication technology.

99 Service of witness statements for use at final hearing

(1) A witness statement is a written statement which contains the evidence which that person would be allowed to give orally.

(2) The court will give directions about the service of any witness statement that a party intends to rely upon at the final hearing.
(3) The court may give directions as to the order in which witness statements are to be served.

(Rules 11 and 100 require witness statements to be verified by a statement of truth.)

100 Form of witness statement
A witness statement must contain a statement of truth and comply with the requirements set out in the relevant practice direction.

101 Witness summaries
(1) A party who wishes to file a witness statement for use at final hearing, but is unable to do so, may apply, without notice, to be permitted to file a witness summary instead.
(2) A witness summary is a summary of–
   (a) the evidence, if known, which would otherwise be included in a witness statement; or
   (b) if the evidence is not known, the matters about which the party filing the witness summary proposes to question the witness.
(3) Unless the court directs otherwise, a witness summary must include the name and address of the intended witness.
(4) Unless the court directs otherwise, a witness summary must be filed within the period in which a witness statement would have had to be filed.
(5) Where a party files a witness summary, so far as practicable, rules 96(3)(a) (amplifying witness statements) and 99 (service of witness statements for use at a final hearing) shall apply to the summary.

102 Affidavit evidence
Evidence must be given by affidavit instead of or in addition to a witness statement if this is required by the court, a provision contained in any rule, a practice direction or any other enactment.

103 Form of affidavit
An affidavit must comply with the requirements set out in the relevant practice direction.

104 Affidavit made outside the jurisdiction
A person may make an affidavit outside the jurisdiction in accordance with–
(a) this Part; or
(b) the law of the place where he makes the affidavit.

105 Notarial acts and instruments
A notarial act or instrument may, without further proof, be received in evidence as duly authenticated in accordance with the requirements of law unless the contrary is proved.

106 Summoning of witnesses
(1) The court may allow or direct any party to issue a witness summons requiring the person named in it to attend before the court and give oral evidence or produce any document to the court.

(2) An application by a party for the issue of a witness summons may be made by filing an application notice which includes–
  (a) the name and address of the applicant and of his solicitor, if any;
  (b) the name, address and occupation of the proposed witness;
  (c) particulars of any document which the proposed witness is to be required to produce; and
  (d) the grounds on which the application is made.
(3) The general rule is that a witness summons is binding if it is served at least 7 days before the date on which the witness is required to attend before the court, and the requirements of paragraph (6) have been complied with.
(4) The court may direct that a witness summons shall be binding although it will be served less than 7 days before the date on which the witness is required to attend before the court.
(5) Unless the court directs otherwise, a witness summons is to be served by the person making the application.
(6) At the time of service the witness must be offered or paid–
  (a) a sum reasonably sufficient to cover his expenses in travelling to and from the court; and
  (b) such sum by way of compensation for loss of time as may be specified in the relevant practice direction.
(7) The court may order that the witness is to be paid such general costs as it considers appropriate.

107 Power of court to direct a party to provide information
(1) Where a party has access to information which is not reasonably available to the other party, the court may direct that party to prepare and file a document recording the information.
(2) The court will give directions about serving a copy of that document on the other parties.

Depositions

108 Evidence by deposition
(1) A party may apply for an order for a person to be examined before the hearing takes place.
(2) A person from whom evidence is to be obtained following an order under this rule is referred to as a 'deponent' and the evidence is referred to as a 'deposition'.
(3) An order under this rule shall be for a deponent to be examined on oath before–
  (a) a circuit judge or a district judge, whether or not nominated as a judge of the court;
  (b) an examiner of the court; or
  (c) such other person as the court appoints.
(4) The order may require the production of any document which the court considers is necessary for the purposes of the examination.
(5) The order will state the date, time and place of the examination.
(6) At the time of service of the order, the deponent must be offered or paid–
  (a) a sum reasonably sufficient to cover his expenses in travelling to and from the place of examination; and

(b) such sum by way of compensation for loss of time as may be specified in the relevant practice direction.
(7) Where the court makes an order for a deposition to be taken, it may also order the party who obtained the order to file a witness statement or witness summary in relation to the evidence to be given by the person to be examined.

109 Conduct of examination
(1) Subject to any directions contained in the order for examination, the examination must be conducted in the same way as if the witness were giving evidence at a final hearing.
(2) If all the parties are present, the examiner may conduct the examination of a person not named in the order for examination if all the parties and the person to be examined consent.
(3) The examiner must ensure that the evidence given by the witness is recorded in full.
(4) The examiner must send a copy of the deposition–
   (a) to the person who obtained the order for the examination of the witness; and
   (b) to the court.
(5) The court will give directions as to the service of a copy of the deposition on the other parties.

110 Fees and expenses of examiners of the court
(1) An examiner of the court may charge a fee for the examination and he need not send the deposition to the court until the fee is paid, unless the court directs otherwise.
(2) The examiner's fees and expenses must be paid by the party who obtained the order for examination.
(3) If the fees and expenses due to an examiner are not paid within a reasonable time, he may report that fact to the court.
(4) The court may order the party who obtained the order for examination to deposit in the court office a specified sum in respect of the examiner's fees and, where it does so, the examiner will not be asked to act until the sum has been deposited.
(5) An order under this rule does not affect any decision as to the person who is ultimately to bear the costs of the examination.

111 Examiners of the court
(1) The Lord Chancellor shall appoint persons to be examiners of the court.
(2) The persons appointed shall be barristers or solicitor-advocates who have been practising for a period of not less than 3 years.
(3) The Lord Chancellor may revoke an appointment at any time.
(4) In addition to appointing persons in accordance with this rule, examiners appointed under rule 34.15 of the Civil Procedure Rules 1998 may act as examiners in the court.

112 Enforcing attendance of a witness
(1) If a person served with an order to attend before an examiner–
   (a) fails to attend; or
   (b) refuses to be sworn for the purpose of the examination or to answer any lawful question or produce any document at the examination,

a certificate of his failure or refusal, signed by the examiner, must be filed by the party requiring the deposition.
(2) On the certificate being filed, the party requiring the deposition may apply to the court for an order requiring that person to attend or to be sworn or to answer any question or produce any document, as the case may be.
(3) An application for an order under this rule may be made without notice.
(4) The court may order the person against whom an order is sought or made under this rule to pay any costs resulting from his failure or refusal.

113 Use of deposition at a hearing

(1) A deposition ordered under rule 108, 115 or 116 may be put in evidence at a hearing unless the court orders otherwise.
(2) A party intending to put a deposition in evidence at a hearing must file notice of his intention to do so on the court and serve the notice on every other party.
(3) Unless the court directs otherwise, he must file the notice at least 14 days before the day fixed for the hearing.
(4) The court may require a deponent to attend the hearing and give evidence orally.

Taking evidence outside the jurisdiction

114 Interpretation

In this Section–
(a) 'Regulation State' has the same meaning as 'Member State' in the Taking of Evidence Regulation, that is all Member States except Denmark; and
(b) 'the Taking of Evidence Regulation' means Council Regulation (EC) No 1206/2001 of 28 May 2001 on co-operation between the courts of Member States in the taking of evidence in civil and commercial matters.

115 Where a person to be examined is in another Regulation State

(1) This rule applies where a party wishes to take a deposition from a person who is–
(a) outside the jurisdiction; and
(b) in a Regulation State.
(2) The court may order the issue of the request to a designated court ('the requested court') in the Regulation State in which the proposed deponent is.
(3) If the court makes an order for the issue of a request, the party who sought the order must file–
(a) a draft Form A as set out in the annex to the Taking of Evidence Regulation (request for the taking of evidence);
(b) except where paragraph (4) applies, a translation of the form;
(c) an undertaking to be responsible for the costs sought by the requested court in relation to–
(i) fees paid to experts and interpreters; and
(ii) where requested by that party, the use of special procedure or communications technology; and
(d) an undertaking to be responsible for the court's expenses.
(4) There is no need to file a translation if–
(a) English is one of the official languages of the Regulation State where the examination is to take place; or

(b) the Regulation State has indicated, in accordance with the Taking of Evidence Regulation, that English is a language which it will accept.
(5) Where article 17 of the Taking of Evidence Regulation (direct taking of evidence by the requested court) allows evidence to be taken directly in another Regulation State, the court may make an order for the submission of a request in accordance with that article.
(6) If the court makes an order for the submission of a request under paragraph (5), the party who sought the order must file–
   (a) draft Form I as set out in the annex to the Taking of Evidence Regulation (request for direct taking of evidence);
   (b) except where paragraph (4) applies, a translation of the form; and
   (c) an undertaking to be responsible for the requested court's expenses.

116 Where a person to be examined is out of the jurisdiction–letter of request

(1) This rule applies where a party wishes to take a deposition from a person who is–
   (a) out of the jurisdiction; and
   (b) not in a Regulation State within the meaning of rule 114.
(2) The court may order the issue of a letter of request to the judicial authorities of the country in which the proposed deponent is.
(3) A letter of request is a request to a judicial authority to take the evidence of that person, or arrange for it to be taken.
(4) If the government of a country permits a person appointed by the court to examine a person in that country, the court may make an order appointing a special examiner for that purpose.
(5) A person may be examined under this rule on oath or affirmation in accordance with any procedure permitted in the country in which the examination is to take place.
(6) If the court makes an order for the issue of a letter of request, the party who sought the order must file–
   (a) the following documents and, except where paragraph (7) applies, a translation of them–
      (i) a draft letter of request;
      (ii) a statement of the issues relevant to the proceedings; and
      (iii) a list of questions or the subject matter of questions to be put to the person to be examined; and
   (b) an undertaking to be responsible for the Secretary of State's expenses.
(7) There is no need to file a translation if–
   (a) English is one of the official languages of the country where the examination is to take place; or
   (b) a practice direction has specified that country is a country where no translation is necessary.

Section 49 reports

117 Reports under section 49 of the Act

(1) This rule applies where the court requires a report to be made to it under section 49 of the Act.
(2) It is the duty of the person who is required to make the report to help the court on the matters within his expertise.

(3) Unless the court directs otherwise, the person making the report must–
   (a) contact or seek to interview such persons as he thinks appropriate or as the court directs;
   (b) to the extent that it is practicable and appropriate to do so, ascertain what P's wishes and feelings are, and the beliefs and values that would be likely to influence P if he had the capacity to make a decision in relation to the matter to which the application relates;
   (c) describe P's circumstances; and
   (d) address such other matters as are required in a practice direction or as the court may direct.
(4) The court will send a copy of the report to the parties and to such persons as the court may direct.
(5) Subject to paragraphs (6) and (7), the person who is required to make the report may examine and take copies of any document in the court records.
(6) The court may direct that the right to inspect documents under this rule does not apply in relation to such documents, or descriptions of documents, as the court may specify.
(7) The court may direct that any information is to be provided to the maker of the report on an edited basis.

118 Written questions to person making a report under section 49
(1) Where a report is made under section 49 the court may, on the application of any party, permit written questions relevant to the issues before the court to be put to the person by whom the report was made.
(2) The questions sought to be put to the maker of the report shall be submitted to the court, and the court may put them to the maker of the report with such amendments (if any) as it thinks fit and the maker of the report shall give his replies in writing to the questions so put.
(3) The court will send a copy of the replies given by the maker of the report under this rule to the parties and to such other persons as the court may direct.

Part 15: Experts

119 References to expert
A reference to an expert in this Part–
   (a) is to an expert who has been instructed to give or prepare evidence for the purpose of court proceedings; but
   (b) does not include any person instructed to make a report under section 49 of the Act.

120 Restriction on filing an expert's report
(1) No person may file expert evidence unless the court or a practice direction permits, or if it is filed with the application form and is evidence–
   (a) that P is a person who lacks capacity to make a decision or decisions in relation to the matter or matters to which the application relates;
   (b) as to P's best interests; or
   (c) that is required by any rule or practice direction to be filed with the application form.
(2) An applicant may only rely upon any expert evidence so filed in support of the application form to the extent and for the purposes that the court allows.

(Rule 64(a) requires the applicant to file any evidence upon which he wishes to rely with the application form)

121 Duty to restrict expert evidence
Expert evidence shall be restricted to that which is reasonably required to resolve the proceedings.

122 Experts–overriding duty to the court
It is the duty of the expert to help the court on the matters within his expertise.

123 Court's power to restrict expert evidence
(1) Subject to rule 120, no party may file or adduce expert evidence unless the court or a practice direction permits.
(2) When a party applies for a direction under this rule he must–
  (a) identify the field in respect of which he wishes to rely upon expert evidence;
  (b) where practicable, identify the expert in that field upon whose evidence he wishes to rely;
  (c) provide any other material information about the expert; and
  (d) provide a draft letter of instruction to the expert.
(3) Where a direction is given under this rule, the court shall specify the field or fields in respect of which the expert evidence is to be provided.
(4) The court may specify the person who is to provide the evidence referred to in paragraph (3).
(5) Where a direction is given under this rule for a party to call an expert or put in evidence an expert's report, the court shall give directions for the service of the report on the parties and on such other persons as the court may direct.
(6) The court may limit the amount of the expert's fees and expenses that the party who wishes to rely upon the expert may recover from any other party.

124 General requirement for expert evidence to be given in a written report
Expert evidence is to be given in a written report unless the court directs otherwise.

125 Written questions to experts
(1) A party may put written questions to–
  (a) an expert instructed by another party; or
  (b) a single joint expert appointed under rule 130,
  about a report prepared by such person.
(2) Written questions under paragraph (1)–
  (a) may be put once only;
  (b) must be put within 28 days beginning with the date on which the expert's report was served; and
  (c) must be for the purpose only of clarification of the report.
(3) Paragraph (2) does not apply in any case where–
  (a) the court permits it to be done on a further occasion;
  (b) the other party or parties agree; or
  (c) any practice direction provides otherwise.
(4) An expert's answers to questions put in accordance with paragraph (1) shall be treated as part of the expert's report.
(5) Paragraph (6) applies where–

(a) a party has put a written question to an expert instructed by another party in accordance with this rule; and
(b) the expert does not answer that question.
(6) The court may make one or both of the following orders in relation to the party who instructed the expert–
(a) that the party may not rely upon the evidence of that expert; or
(b) that the party may not recover the fees and expenses of that expert, or part of them, from any other party.
(7) Unless the court otherwise directs, and subject to any final costs order that may be made, the instructing party is responsible for the payment of the expert's fees and expenses, including the expert's costs of answering questions put by any other party.

126 Contents of expert's report
(1) The court may give directions as to the matters to be covered in an expert's report.
(2) An expert's report must comply with the requirements set out in the relevant practice direction.
(3) At the end of an expert's report there must be a statement that–
(a) the expert understands his duty to the court; and
(b) he has complied with that duty.
(4) The expert's report must state the substance of all material instructions, whether written or oral, on the basis of which the report was written.
(5) The instructions to the expert shall not be privileged against disclosure.

127 Use by one party of expert's report disclosed by another
Where a party has disclosed an expert's report, any party may use that expert's report as evidence at any hearing in the proceedings.

128 Discussions between experts
(1) The court may, at any stage, direct a discussion between experts for the purpose of requiring the experts to–
(a) identify and discuss the expert issues in the proceedings; and
(b) where possible, reach an agreed opinion on those issues.
(2) The court may specify the issues which the experts must discuss.
(3) The court may direct that following a discussion between the experts they must prepare a statement for the court showing–
(a) those issues on which they agree; and
(b) those issues on which they disagree and a summary of their reasons for disagreeing.
(4) Unless the court otherwise directs, the content of the discussions between experts may be referred to at any hearing or at any stage in the proceedings.

129 Expert's right to ask court for directions
(1) An expert may file a written request for directions to assist him in carrying out his function as an expert.
(2) An expert must, unless the court directs otherwise, provide a copy of any proposed request for directions under paragraph (1)–
(a) to the party instructing him, at least 7 days before he files the request; and
(b) to all other parties, at least 4 days before he files it.

(3) The court, when it gives directions, may also direct that a party be served with a copy of the directions.

130 Court's power to direct that evidence is to be given by a single joint expert

(1) Where two or more parties wish to submit expert evidence on a particular issue, the court may direct that the evidence on that issue is to be given by one expert only.
(2) The parties wishing to submit the expert evidence are called 'the instructing parties'.
(3) Where the instructing parties cannot agree who should be the expert, the court may–
   (a) select the expert from a list prepared or identified by the instructing parties; or
   (b) direct the manner by which the expert is to be selected.

131 Instructions to a single joint expert

(1) Where the court gives a direction under rule 130 for a single joint expert to be used, each party may give instructions to the expert.
(2) Unless the court otherwise directs, when an instructing party gives instructions to the expert he must, at the same time, send a copy of the instructions to the other instructing parties.
(3) The court may give directions about–
   (a) the payment of the expert's fees and expenses; and
   (b) any inspection, examination or experiments which the expert wishes to carry out.
(4) The court may, before an expert is instructed, limit the amount that can be paid by way of fees and expenses to the expert.
(5) Unless the court otherwise directs, and subject to any final costs order that may be made, the instructing parties are jointly and severally liable for the payment of the expert's fees and expenses.

Part 16: Disclosure

132 Meaning of disclosure

A party discloses a document by stating that the document exists or has existed.

133 General or specific disclosure

(1) The court may either on its own initiative or on the application of a party make an order to give general or specific disclosure.
(2) General disclosure requires a party to disclose–
   (a) the documents on which he relies; and
   (b) the documents which–
      (i) adversely affect his own case;
      (ii) adversely affect another party's case; or
      (iii) support another party's case.
(3) An order for specific disclosure is an order that a party must do one or more of the following things–
   (a) disclose documents or classes of documents specified in the order;
   (b) carry out a search to the extent stated in the order; or
   (c) disclose any document located as a result of that search.

(4) A party's duty to disclose documents is limited to documents which are or have been in his control.
(5) For the purpose of paragraph (4) a party has or has had a document in his control if–
  (a) it is or was in his physical possession;
  (b) he has or has had possession of it; or
  (c) he has or has had a right to inspect or take copies of it.

134 Procedure for general or specific disclosure
(1) This rule applies where the court makes an order under rule 133 to give general or specific disclosure.
(2) Each party must make, and serve on every other party, a list of documents to be disclosed.
(3) A copy of each list must be filed within 7 days of the date on which it is served.
(4) The list must identify the documents in a convenient order and manner and as concisely as possible.
(5) The list must indicate–
  (a) the documents in respect of which the party claims a right or duty to withhold inspection (see rule 138); and
  (b) the documents that are no longer in his control, stating what has happened to them.

135 Ongoing duty of disclosure
(1) Where the court makes an order to give general or specific disclosure under rule 133, any party to whom the order applies is under a continuing duty to provide such disclosure as is required by the order until the proceedings are concluded.
(2) If a document to which the duty of disclosure imposed by paragraph (1) extends comes to a party's notice at any time during the proceedings, he must immediately notify every other party.

136 Right to inspect documents
(1) A party to whom a document has been disclosed has a right to inspect any document disclosed to him except where–
  (a) the document is no longer in the control of the party who disclosed it; or
  (b) the party disclosing the document has a right or duty to withhold inspection of it.
(2) The right to inspect disclosed documents extends to any document mentioned in–
  (a) a document filed or served in the course of the proceedings by any other party; or
  (b) correspondence sent by any other party.

137 Inspection and copying of documents
(1) Where a party has a right to inspect a document, he–
  (a) must give the party who disclosed the document written notice of his wish to inspect it; and
  (b) may request a copy of the document.
(2) Not more than 14 days after the date on which the party who disclosed the document received the notice under paragraph (1)(a), he must permit inspection of the document at a convenient place and time.

(3) Where a party has requested a copy of the document, the party who disclosed the document must supply him with a copy not more than 14 days after the date on which he received the request.
(4) For the purposes of paragraph (2), the party who disclosed the document must give reasonable notice of the time and place for inspection.
(5) For the purposes of paragraph (3), the party requesting a copy of the document is responsible for the payment of reasonable copying costs, subject to any final costs order that may be made.

138 Claim to withhold inspection or disclosure of document
(1) A party who wishes to claim that he has a right or duty to withhold inspection of a document, or part of a document, must state in writing–
 (a) that he has such a right or duty; and
 (b) the grounds on which he claims that right or duty.
(2) The statement must be made in the list in which the document is disclosed (see rule 134(2)).
(3) A party may, by filing an application notice in accordance with Part 10, apply to the court to decide whether the claim made under paragraph (1) should be upheld.

Part 17: Litigation Friends and Rule 3A Representatives

Section 1–Litigation Friends

140 Who may act as a litigation friend
(1) A person may act as a litigation friend on behalf of a person mentioned in paragraph (2) if that person–
 (a) can fairly and competently conduct proceedings on behalf of that person; and
 (b) has no interests adverse to those of that person.
(2) The persons for whom a litigation friend may act are–
 (a) P;
 (b) a child;
 (c) a protected party.

141 Requirement for a litigation friend
(1) This rule does not apply to P (whether P is an adult or a child).
(2) A protected party (if a party to the proceedings) must have a litigation friend.
(3) A child (if a party to the proceedings) must have a litigation friend to conduct those proceedings on that child's behalf unless the court makes an order under paragraph (4).
(4) The court may make an order permitting a child to conduct proceedings without a litigation friend.
(5) An application for an order under paragraph (4)–
 (a) may be made by the child;
 (b) if the child already has a litigation friend, must be made on notice to the litigation friend; and
 (c) if the child has no litigation friend, may be made without notice.
(6) Where–
 (a) the court has made an order under paragraph (4); and

(b) it subsequently appears to the court that it is desirable for a litigation friend to conduct the proceedings on behalf of the child,
the court may appoint a person to the child's litigation friend.

142 Litigation friend without a court order
(1) This rule does not apply–
    (a) in relation to P;
    (b) where the court has appointed a person under rule 143 or 144; or
    (c) where the Official Solicitor is to act as a litigation friend.
(2) A deputy with the power to conduct legal proceedings in the name of a protected party or on the protected party's behalf is entitled to be a litigation friend of the protected party in any proceedings to which the deputy's power relates.
(3) If no-one has been appointed by the court or, in the case of a protected party, there is no deputy with the power to conduct proceedings, a person who wishes to act as a litigation friend must–
    (a) file a certificate of suitability stating that they satisfy the conditions in rule 140(1); and
    (b) serve the certificate of suitability on–
        (i) the person on whom an application form is to be served in accordance with rule 32 (service on children and protected parties); and
        (ii) every other person who is a party to the proceedings.
(4) If the person referred to in paragraph (2) wishes to act as a litigation friend for the protected party, that person must file and serve on the persons mentioned in paragraph (3)(b) a copy of the court order which appointed that person.

143 Litigation friend by court order
(1) The court may make an order appointing–
    (a) the Official Solicitor; or
    (b) some other person,
    to act as a litigation friend for a protected party, a child or P.
(2) The court may make an order under paragraph (1)–
    (a) either on its own initiative or on the application of any person; but
    (b) only with the consent of the person to be appointed.
(3) An application for an order under paragraph (1) must be supported by evidence.
(4) The court may not appoint a litigation friend under this rule unless it is satisfied that the person to be appointed satisfies the conditions in rule 140(1).
(5) The court may at any stage of the proceedings give directions as to the appointment of a litigation friend.

(Rule 3A requires the court to consider how P should participate in the proceedings, which may be by way of being made a party and the appointment of a litigation friend under this Part.)

144 Court's power to prevent a person from acting as a litigation friend or to bring an end to an appointment of a person as a litigation friend or to appoint another one
(1) The court may either on its own initiative or on the application of any person–
    (a) direct that a person may not act as a litigation friend;

(b) bring to an end a litigation friend's appointment; or
(c) appoint a new litigation friend in place of an existing one.
(2) If an application for an order under paragraph (1) is based on the conduct of the litigation friend, it must be supported by evidence.
(3) The court may not appoint a litigation friend under this rule unless it is satisfied that the person to be appointed satisfies the conditions in rule 140(1).
(4) The appointment of a litigation friend continues until brought to an end by court order.

(Rule 87 applies if P has capacity in relation to the matter or matters to which the application relates.)

145 Appointment of litigation friend by court order–supplementary

The applicant must serve a copy of an application for an order under rule 143 or 144 on–
(a) the person on whom an application form is to be served in accordance with rule 32 (service on children and protected parties);
(b) every other person who is a party to the proceedings;
(c) any person who is the litigation friend, or who is purporting to act as the litigation friend, when the application is made; and
(d) unless that person is the applicant, the person who it is proposed should be the litigation friend,

as soon as practicable and in any event within 14 days of the date on which the application was issued.

145A Procedure where appointment of a litigation friend comes to an end for a child

When a child reaches 18, provided the child is neither–
(a) P; nor
(b) a protected party,

the litigation friend's appointment ends and the child must serve notice on every other party–
 (i) stating that the child has reached full age;
 (ii) stating that the appointment of the litigation friend has ended; and
 (iii) providing an address for service.

146 Practice direction in relation to litigation friends

A practice direction may make additional or supplementary provision in relation to litigation friends.

Section 2–rule 3a Representatives

146A Interpretation

In this Section, references to 'rule 3A representatives' are references to both accredited legal representatives and representatives.

('Accredited legal representative' and 'representative' are defined in rule 6.)

147 Who may act as a rule 3A representative for P

A person may act as an accredited legal representative, or a representative, for P, if that person can fairly and competently discharge his or her functions on behalf of P.

148 Rule 3A representative by court order

(1) The court may make an order appointing a person to act as a representative, or an accredited legal representative, for P.
(2) The court may make an order under paragraph (1)–
   (a) either of its own initiative or on the application of any person; but
   (b) only with the consent of the person to be appointed.
(3) The court may not appoint a representative or an accredited legal representative under this rule unless it is satisfied that the person to be appointed satisfies the conditions in rule 147.
(4) The court may at any stage of the proceedings give directions as to the terms of appointment of a representative or an accredited legal representative.

(Rule 3A requires the court to consider how P should participate in the proceedings, which may be by way of the appointment of a representative or accredited legal representative under this Part.)

148A Application by rule 3A representative or by P for directions

A representative, an accredited legal representative or P may, at any time and without giving notice to the other parties, apply to the court for directions relating to the performance, terms of appointment or continuation of the appointment of the representative or accredited legal representative.

148B Court's power to prevent a person from acting as a rule 3A representative or to bring an end to an appointment of a person as a rule 3A representative or appoint another one

(1) The court may, either of its own initiative or on the application of any person–
   (a) direct that a person may not act as a representative or accredited legal representative;
   (b) bring to an end a representative's or accredited legal representative's appointment;
   (c) appoint a new representative or accredited legal representative in place of an existing one; or
   (d) vary the terms of a representative's or accredited legal representative's appointment.
(2) If an application for an order under paragraph (1) is based on the conduct of the representative or accredited legal representative, it must be supported by evidence.
(3) The court may not appoint a representative or accredited legal representative under this rule unless it is satisfied that the person to be appointed satisfies the conditions in rule 147.
(4) The appointment of a representative or accredited legal representative continues until brought to an end by court order.
(5) The court must bring to an end the appointment of a representative or an accredited legal representative if P has capacity to appoint such a representative and does not wish the appointment by the court to continue.

148C Appointment of rule 3A representative by court order–supplementary

The applicant must serve a copy of an application for an order under rule 148 or rule 148B on–
   (a) the person on whom an application form is to be served in accordance with rule 32 (service on children and protected parties);

(b) every other person who is a party to the proceedings;
(c) any person who is the representative, or accredited legal representative, purporting to act as such representative, when the application is made; and
(d) unless that person is the applicant, the person who it is proposed should be the representative or accredited legal representative,

as soon as practicable and in any event within 14 days of the date on which the application was issued.

149 Practice direction in relation to rule 3A representatives

A practice direction may make additional or supplementary provision in relation to representatives or accredited legal representatives.

Part 18: Change of Solicitor

150 Change of solicitor

(1) This rule applies where a party to proceedings–
   (a) for whom a solicitor is acting wants to change his solicitor or act in person; or
   (b) after having conducted the proceedings in person, appoints a solicitor to act on his behalf (except where the solicitor is appointed only to act as an advocate for a hearing).
(2) The party proposing the change must–
   (a) file a notice of the change with the court; and
   (b) serve the notice of the change on every other party to the proceedings and, if there is one, on the solicitor who will cease to act.
(3) The notice must state the party's address for service.
(4) The notice filed at court must state that it has been served as required by paragraph (2)(b).
(5) Where there is a solicitor who will cease to act, he will continue to be considered the party's solicitor unless and until–
   (a) the notice is filed and served in accordance with paragraphs (2), (3) and (4); or
   (b) the court makes an order under rule 152 and the order is served in accordance with that rule.

151 Legally aided persons

(1) Where the certificate of any person ('A') who is a legally aided person is revoked or withdrawn–
   (a) the solicitor who acted for A will cease to be the solicitor acting in the case as soon as his retainer is determined under regulation 24 or 41 of the Civil Legal Aid (Procedure) Regulations 2012; and
   (b) if A wishes to continue and appoints a solicitor to act on his behalf, rule 150(2), (3) and (4) will apply as if A had previously conducted the application in person.
(2) In this rule, 'certificate' means a certificate issued under the Civil Legal Aid (Procedure) Regulations 2012.

152 Order that a solicitor has ceased to act

(1) A solicitor may apply for an order declaring that he has ceased to be the solicitor acting for a party.

(2) Where an application is made under this rule–
  (a) the solicitor must serve the application notice on the party for whom the solicitor is acting, unless the court directs otherwise; and
  (b) the application must be supported by evidence.
(3) Where the court makes an order that a solicitor has ceased to act, the solicitor must–
  (a) serve a copy of the order on every other party to the proceedings; and
  (b) file a certificate of service.

153 Removal of solicitor who has ceased to act on application of another party

(1) Where–
  (a) a solicitor who has acted for a party–
    (i) has died;
    (ii) has become bankrupt;
    (iii) has ceased to practice; or
    (iv) cannot be found; and
  (b) the party has not served a notice of a change of solicitor or notice of intention to act in person as required by rule 150,
  any other party may apply for an order declaring that the solicitor has ceased to be the solicitor acting for the other party in the case.
(2) Where an application is made under this rule, the applicant must serve the application on the party to whose solicitor the application relates, unless the court directs otherwise.
(3) Where the court makes an order under this rule–
  (a) the court will give directions about serving a copy of the order on every other party to the proceedings; and
  (b) where the order is served by a party, that party must file a certificate of service.

154 Practice direction relating to change of solicitor

A practice direction may make additional or different provision in relation to change of solicitor.

Part 19: Costs

155 Interpretation

(1) In this Part–
  'authorised court officer' means any officer of the Senior Courts Costs Office whom the Lord Chancellor has authorised to assess costs;
  'costs' include fees, charges, disbursements, expenses, remuneration and any reimbursement allowed to a litigant in person;
  'costs judge' means a taxing Master of the Senior Courts;
  'costs officer' means a costs judge or an authorised court officer;
  'detailed assessment' means the procedure by which the amount of costs or remuneration is decided by a costs officer in accordance with Part 47 of the Civil Procedure Rules 1998 (which are applied to proceedings under these Rules, with modifications, by rule 160);
  'fixed costs' are to be construed in accordance with the relevant practice direction;

'fund' includes any estate or property held for the benefit of any person or class of persons, and any fund to which a trustee or personal representative is entitled in that capacity;
'paying party' means a party liable to pay costs;
'pro bono representation' means representation provided free of charge;
'receiving party' means a party entitled to be paid costs;
'summary assessment' means the procedure by which the court, when making an order about costs, orders payment of a sum of money instead of fixed costs or detailed assessment.
  (2) The costs to which the rules in this Part apply include–
    (a) where the costs may be assessed by the court, costs payable by a client to their legal representative; and
    (b) costs which are payable by one party to another party under the terms of a contract, where the court makes an order for an assessment of those costs.
  (3) Where advocacy or litigation services are provided to a client under a conditional fee agreement, costs are recoverable under this Part notwithstanding that the client is liable to pay his legal representative's fees and expenses only to the extent that sums are recovered in respect of the proceedings, whether by way of costs or otherwise.
  (4) In paragraph (3), the reference to a conditional fee agreement means an agreement enforceable under section 58 of the Courts and Legal Services Act 1990.

156 Property and affairs–the general rule
Where the proceedings concern P's property and affairs the general rule is that the costs of the proceedings or of that part of the proceedings that concerns P's property and affairs, shall be paid by P or charged to his estate.

157 Personal welfare–the general rule
Where the proceedings concern P's personal welfare the general rule is that there will be no order as to the costs of the proceedings or of that part of the proceedings that concerns P's personal welfare.

158 Apportioning costs–the general rule
Where the proceedings concern both property and affairs and personal welfare the court, insofar as practicable, will apportion the costs as between the respective issues.

159 Departing from the general rule
  (1) The court may depart from rules 156 to 158 if the circumstances so justify, and in deciding whether departure is justified the court will have regard to all the circumstances, including–
    (a) the conduct of the parties;
    (b) whether a party has succeeded on part of his case, even if he has not been wholly successful; and
    (c) the role of any public body involved in the proceedings.
  (2) The conduct of the parties includes–
    (a) conduct before, as well as during, the proceedings;
    (b) whether it was reasonable for a party to raise, pursue or contest a particular issue;
    (c) the manner in which a party has made or responded to an application or a particular issue;

(d) whether a party who has succeeded in his application or response to an application, in whole or in part, exaggerated any matter contained in his application or response; and
(e) any failure by a party to comply with a rule, practice direction or court order.
(3) Without prejudice to rules 156 to 158 and the foregoing provisions of this rule, the court may permit a party to recover their fixed costs in accordance with the relevant practice direction.

160 Rules about costs in the Civil Procedure Rules to apply
(1) Subject to the provisions of these Rules, Parts 44, 46 and 47 of the Civil Procedure Rules 1998 ('the 1998 Rules') apply with the modifications in this rule and such other modifications as may be appropriate, to costs incurred in relation to proceedings under these Rules as they apply to costs incurred in relation to proceedings in the High Court.
(2) Rules 3.12 to 3.18 of the 1998 Rules and Practice Direction 3E supporting those Rules do not apply in relation to proceedings under these Rules.
(3) The provisions of Part 47 of the 1998 Rules apply with the modifications in this rule and such other modifications as may be appropriate, to a detailed assessment of the remuneration of a deputy under these Rules as they apply to a detailed assessment of costs in proceedings to which the 1998 Rules apply.
(4) Where the definitions in Part 44 (referred to in Parts 44, 46 and 47) of the 1998 Rules are different from the definitions in rule 155 of these Rules, the latter definitions prevail.
(5) Rules 44.2(1) to (5), 44.5, 44.6, 44.9 and 44.13 to 44.18 of the 1998 Rules do not apply.
(6) For rule 46.1(1) of the 1998 Rules there is substituted–
'(1) This paragraph applies where a person applies for an order for specific disclosure before the commencement of proceedings.'.
(7) Rules 46.2, 46.5 and 46.10 to 46.14 of the 1998 Rules do not apply.
(8) In rule 47.3(1)(c) of the 1998 Rules, the words 'unless the costs are being assessed under rule 46.4 (costs where money is payable to a child or protected party)' are omitted.
(9) In rule 47.3(2) of the 1998 Rules, the words 'or a District Judge' are omitted.
(10) Rule 47.4(3) and (4) of the 1998 Rules do not apply.
(11) Rules 47.9(4), 47.10 and 47.11 of the 1998 Rules do not apply where the costs are to be paid by P or charged to P's estate.

161 Detailed assessment of costs
(1) Where the court orders costs to be assessed by way of detailed assessment, the detailed assessment proceedings shall take place in the High Court.
(2) A fee is payable in respect of the detailed assessment of costs and on an appeal against a decision made in a detailed assessment of costs.
(3) Where a detailed assessment of costs has taken place, the amount payable by P is the amount which the court certifies as payable.

162 Employment of a solicitor by two or more persons
Where two or more persons having the same interest in relation to a matter act in relation to the proceedings by separate legal representatives, they shall not be permitted more than one set of costs of the representation unless and

to the extent that the court certifies that the circumstances justify separate representation.

163 Costs of the Official Solicitor
Any costs incurred by the Official Solicitor in relation to proceedings under these Rules or in carrying out any directions given by the court and not provided for by remuneration under rule 167 shall be paid by such persons or out of such funds as the court may direct.

164 Procedure for assessing costs
Where the court orders a party, or P, to pay costs to another party it may either–
(a) make a summary assessment of the costs; or
(b) order a detailed assessment of the costs by a costs officer,
unless any rule, practice direction or other enactment provides otherwise.

165 Costs following P's death
An order or direction that costs incurred during P's lifetime be paid out of or charged on his estate may be made within 6 years after P's death.

166 Costs orders in favour of or against non-parties
(1) Where the court is considering whether to make a costs order in favour of or against a person who is not a party to proceedings, that person must be–
  (a) added as a party to the proceedings for the purposes of costs only;
  (aa) served with such documents as the court may direct; and
  (b) given a reasonable opportunity to attend any hearing at which the court will consider the matter further.
(2) This rule does not apply where the court is considering whether to make an order against the Lord Chancellor in proceedings in which the Lord Chancellor has provided legal aid to a party to the proceedings.

167 Remuneration of a deputy, donee or attorney
(1) Where the court orders that a deputy, donee or attorney is entitled to remuneration out of P's estate for discharging his functions as such, the court may make such order as it thinks fit, including an order that–
  (a) he be paid a fixed amount;
  (b) he be paid at a specified rate; or
  (c) the amount of the remuneration shall be determined in accordance with the schedule of fees set out in the relevant practice direction.
(2) Any amount permitted by the court under paragraph (1) shall constitute a debt due from P's estate.
(3) The court may order a detailed assessment of the remuneration by a costs officer, in accordance with rule 164(b).

168 Practice direction as to costs
A practice direction may make further provision in respect of costs in proceedings.

Part 20: Appeals

169 Scope of this Part
This Part applies to an appeal against any decision of the court.

170 Interpretation

(1) In the following provisions of this Part–
   (a) 'appeal judge' means a judge of the court to whom an appeal is made;
   (b) 'first instance judge' means the judge of the court from whose decision an appeal is brought;
   (c) 'appellant' means the person who brings or seeks to bring an appeal;
   (d) 'respondent' means–
      (i) a person other than the appellant who was a party to the proceedings before the first instance judge and who is affected by the appeal; or
      (ii) a person who is permitted or directed by the first instance judge or the appeal judge to be a party to the appeal; and
   (e) 'a second appeal' means an appeal from a decision of a judge of the court which was itself made on appeal from a judge of the court.
(2) In this Part, where the expression 'permission' is used it means 'permission to appeal' unless otherwise stated.

171 Dealing with appeals

(1) The court may deal with an appeal or any part of an appeal at a hearing or without a hearing.
(2) In considering whether it is necessary to hold a hearing, the court shall have regard to the matters set out in rule 84(3).
(3) Any person bound by an order of the court by virtue of rule 74 (persons to be bound as if parties) may seek permission under this Part.
(4) All parties to an appeal must comply with any relevant practice direction.
(5) Where permission is required, it is to be granted or refused in accordance with this Part.

(Rule 89 provides for reconsideration of orders made without a hearing or without notice to a person.)

171A Destination of appeals

(1) An appeal from a decision of a judge of the court shall lie to the Court of Appeal in the following cases–
   (a) where it is an appeal from a decision of a Tier 3 Judge; or
   (b) where it is a second appeal.
(2) Subject to paragraph (1) and to any alternative provision made by the relevant practice direction–
   (a) where the first instance judge was a Tier 1 Judge, any appeal shall be heard by a Tier 2 Judge;
   (b) where the first instance judge was a Tier 2 Judge, any appeal shall be heard by a Tier 3 Judge.
(3) No appeal may be made against a decision of a court officer authorised under rule 7A.

(A decision of a court officer authorised under rule 7A can be reconsidered by a judge under rule 89.)

171B Permission to appeal–appeals to the Court of Appeal

(1) Subject to rule 172A, an appeal to the Court of Appeal against a decision of a judge of the court may not be made without permission.

(2) Where an appeal to the Court of Appeal is made from a decision of a Tier 3 Judge, permission may be granted by the first instance judge or by the Court of Appeal, unless the appeal is a second appeal.
(3) Where an appeal to the Court of Appeal is a second appeal, permission may only be granted by the Court of Appeal.
(4) No appeal shall lie against–
   (a) the granting or refusal of permission under this rule; or
   (b) an order allowing an extension of time for appealing from an order.

(The procedure for an appeal from a decision of a judge of the court to the Court of Appeal, including requirements for permission, is governed by the Civil Procedure Rules 1998.)

172 Permission to appeal–other cases

(1) Subject to rules 171B and 172A, an appeal against a decision of the court may not be made without permission.
(2) An application for permission to appeal may be made to–
   (a) the first instance judge; or
   (b) another judge who satisfies the relevant condition in paragraph (4) or (5).
(3) Where an application for permission is refused by the first instance judge, a further application for permission may be made to a judge who satisfies the relevant condition in paragraph (4) or (5).
(4) Where the decision sought to be appealed is a decision of a Tier 1 Judge, permission may also be granted or refused by–
   (a) a Tier 2 Judge; or
   (b) a Tier 3 Judge.
(5) Where the decision sought to be appealed is a decision of a Tier 2 Judge, permission may also be granted or refused by a Tier 3 Judge.
(6) Subject to paragraph (7) and except where another rule or a practice direction provides otherwise, where a judge who satisfies the relevant condition in paragraph (4) or (5), without a hearing, refuses permission to appeal against the decision of the first instance judge, the person seeking permission may request the decision to be reconsidered at a hearing.
(7) Where a Tier 3 Judge or the Senior Judge refuses permission to appeal without a hearing and considers that the application is totally without merit, that judge may order that the person seeking permission may not request the decision to be reconsidered at a hearing.
(8) Subject to paragraph (6), no appeal shall lie against–
   (a) the granting or refusal of permission under this rule; or
   (b) an order allowing an extension of time for appealing from an order.

172A Appeal against an order for committal to prison

Permission is not required to appeal against an order for committal to prison.

173 Matters to be taken into account when considering an application for permission

(1) Permission to appeal shall be granted only where–
   (a) the court considers that the appeal would have a real prospect of success; or
   (b) there is some other compelling reason why the appeal should be heard.

(2) An order giving permission may–
  (a) limit the issues to be heard; and
  (b) be made subject to conditions.
(3) Paragraphs (1) and (2) do not apply to second appeals.

174 Power to treat application for permission to appeal as application for reconsideration under rule 89

(1) Where a person seeking permission to appeal a decision would be entitled to seek reconsideration of that decision under rule 89 (or would have been so entitled had the application been made within 21 days of the date of that decision)–
  (a) a practice direction may provide; or
  (b) the court may direct,
  that an application for permission shall be treated as an application for reconsideration under rule 89.
(2) In any case where paragraph (1) applies, the decision in question shall be reconsidered in accordance with the provisions of rule 89.

175 Appellant's notice

(1) Where the appellant seeks permission a judge other than the first instance judge, it must be requested in the appellant's notice.
(2) The appellant must file an appellant's notice at the court within–
  (a) such period as may be directed or specified in the order of the first instance judge; or
  (b) where that judge makes no such direction or order, 21 days after the date of the decision being appealed.
(3) The court will issue the appellant's notice and unless it orders otherwise, the appellant must serve the appellant's notice on each respondent and on such other persons as the court may direct, as soon as practicable and in any event within 21 days of the date on which it was issued.
(4) The appellant must file a certificate of service within 7 days beginning with the date on which he served the appellant's notice.

176 Respondent's notice

(1) A respondent who–
  (a) is seeking permission from a judge other than the first instance judge; or
  (b) wishes to ask the appeal judge to uphold the order of the first instance judge for reasons different from or additional to those given by the first instance judge,
  must file a respondent's notice.
(2) Where the respondent seeks permission from a judge other than the first instance judge, permission must be requested in the respondent's notice.
(3) A respondent's notice must be filed within–
  (a) such period as may be directed by the first instance judge; or
  (b) where the first instance judge makes no such direction, 21 days beginning with the date referred to in paragraph (4).
(4) The date is the soonest of–
  (a) the date on which the respondent is served with the appellant's notice where–
    (i) permission was given by the first instance judge; or
    (ii) permission is not required;

(b) the date on which the respondent is served with notification that a judge other than the first instance judge has given the appellant permission ; or
(c) the date on which the respondent is served with the notification that the application for permission and the appeal itself are to be heard together.
(5) The court will issue a respondent's notice and, unless it orders otherwise, the respondent must serve the respondent's notice on the appellant, any other respondent and on such other parties as the court may direct, as soon as practicable and in any event within 21 days of the date on which it was issued.
(6) The respondent must file a certificate of service within 7 days beginning with the date on which the copy of the respondent's notice was served.

177 Variation of time
(1) [Revoked.]
(2) The parties may not agree to extend any date or time limit for or in respect of an appeal set by–
(a) these Rules;
(b) the relevant practice direction; or
(c) an order of the appeal judge or the first instance judge.

178 Power of appeal judge on appeal
(1) In relation to an appeal, an appeal judge has all the powers of the first instance judge whose decision is being appealed.
(2) In particular, the appeal judge has the power to–
(a) affirm, set aside or vary any order made by the first instance judge;
(b) refer any claim or issue to that judge for determination;
(c) order a new hearing;
(d) make a costs order.
(3) The appeal judge may exercise his powers in relation to the whole or part of an order made by the first instance judge.

179 Determination of appeals
(1) An appeal will be limited to a review of the decision of the first instance judge unless–
(a) a practice direction makes different provision for a particular category of appeal; or
(b) the appeal judge considers that in the circumstances of the appeal it would be in the interests of justice to hold a re-hearing.
(2) Unless he orders otherwise, the appeal judge will not receive–
(a) oral evidence; or
(b) evidence that was not before the first instance judge.
(3) The appeal judge will allow an appeal where the decision of the first instance judge was–
(a) wrong; or
(b) unjust, because of a serious procedural or other irregularity in the proceedings before the first instance judge.
(4) The appeal judge may draw any inference of fact that he considers justified on the evidence.
(5) At the hearing of the appeal a party may not rely upon a matter not contained in his appellant's or respondent's notice unless the appeal judge gives permission.

180 [Revoked.]
181 [Revoked.]
182 [Revoked.]

Part 21: Enforcement

183 Enforcement methods–general
(1) The rules in this Part make provision for the enforcement of judgments and orders.
(2) The relevant practice direction may set out methods of enforcing judgments or orders.
(3) An application for an order for enforcement may be made on application by any person in accordance with Part 10.

184 Application of the Civil Procedure Rules 1998
The following provisions apply, as far as they are relevant and with such modifications as may be necessary, to the enforcement of orders made in proceedings under these Rules–
(a) Parts 70 (General Rules about Enforcement of Judgments and Orders), 71 (Orders to Obtain Information from Judgment Debtors), 72 (Third Party Debt Orders), 73 (Charging Orders, Stop Orders and Stop Notices), 83 (Writs and Warrants–General Provisions) and 84 (Enforcement by Taking Control of Goods) of the Civil Procedure Rules 1998.
(b) [Revoked.]

Orders for committal

185 Contempt of court–generally
An application relating to the committal of a person for contempt of court shall be made to a judge and the power to punish for contempt may be exercised by an order of committal.

186 Application for order of committal
(1) An application for an order of committal must be made by filing an application notice, stating the grounds of the application, and must be supported by an affidavit made in accordance with the relevant practice direction.
(2) Subject to paragraph (3), the application notice, a copy of the affidavit in support thereof and notice of the date of the hearing of the application must be served personally on the person sought to be committed.
(3) Without prejudice to its powers under Part 6, the court may dispense with service under this rule if it thinks it just to do so.

187 Oral evidence
If on the hearing of the application the person sought to be committed expresses a wish to give oral evidence on his own behalf, he shall be entitled to do so.

188 Hearing for committal order
(1) Except where the court permits, no grounds shall be relied upon at the hearing except the grounds set out in the application notice.

(2) Notwithstanding rule 90(1) (general rule–hearing to be in private), when determining an application for committal the court will hold the hearing in public unless it directs otherwise.
(3) If the court hearing an application in private decides that a person has committed a contempt of court, it shall state publicly–
 (a) the name of that person;
 (b) in general terms the nature of the contempt in respect of which the order of committal is being made; and
 (c) any punishment imposed.
(4) If the person sought to be committed does not attend the hearing, the court may fix a date and time for the person to be brought before the court.

189 Power to suspend execution of committal order
(1) A judge who has made an order of committal may direct that the execution of the order of committal shall be suspended for such period or on such terms and conditions as may be specified.
(2) Where an order is suspended under paragraph (1), the applicant for the order of committal must, unless the court otherwise directs, serve on the person against whom it was made a notice informing him of the making and terms of the direction under that paragraph.

190 Warrant for arrest
A warrant for the arrest of a person against whom an order of committal has been made shall not, without further order of the court, be enforced more than 2 years after the date on which the warrant is issued.

191 Discharge of person committed
(1) The court may, on the application of any person committed to prison for contempt of court, discharge him.
(2) Where a person has been committed for failing to comply with a judgment or order requiring him to deliver any thing to some other person or to deposit it in court or elsewhere, and a writ of sequestration has also been issued to enforce that judgment or order, then, if the thing is in the custody or power of the person committed, the commissioners appointed by the writ of sequestration may take possession of it as if it were the property of that person and, without prejudice to the generality of paragraph (1), the court may discharge the person committed and may give such directions for dealing with the thing taken by the commissioners as it thinks fit.

192 Penal notices
(1) The court may direct that a penal notice is to be attached to any order warning the person on whom the copy of the order is served that disobeying the order would be a contempt of court punishable by imprisonment or a fine.
(2) Unless the court gives a direction under paragraph (1), a penal notice may not be attached to any order.
(3) A penal notice is to be in the following terms: 'You must obey this order. If you do not, you may be sent to prison for contempt of court.'.

193 Saving for other powers
The rules in this Part do not limit the power of the court to make an order requiring a person guilty of contempt to pay a fine or give security for his

good behaviour and those rules, so far as applicable, shall apply in relation to an application for such an order as they apply in relation to an application for an order of committal.

194 Power of court to commit on its own initiative
The preceding provisions of these Rules shall not be taken as affecting the power of the court to make an order for committal on its own initiative against a person guilty of contempt of court.

Part 22: Transitory and Transitional Provisions

195 Transitory provision: applications by former receivers
(1) This rule and rule 196–
   (a) apply in any case where a person becomes a deputy by virtue of paragraph 1(2) of Schedule 5 to the Act; but
   (b) shall cease to have effect at the end of the period specified in the relevant practice direction.
(2) The deputy may make an application to the court in connection with–
   (a) any decision in connection with the day-to-day management of P's property and affairs; or
   (b) any supplementary decision which is necessary to give full effect to any order made, or directions given, before 1st October 2007 under Part 7 of the Mental Health Act 1983.
(3) Decisions within paragraph (2) include those that may be specified in the relevant practice direction.
(4) An application–
   (a) may relate only to a particular decision or decisions to be made on P's behalf;
   (b) must specify details of the decision or decisions to be made; and
   (c) must be made using the application form set out in the relevant practice direction.

196 Transitory provision: dealing with applications under rule 195
(1) The court may, in determining an application under rule 195, treat the application as if it were an application to vary the functions of the deputy which is made in accordance with the relevant practice direction made under rule 71, and dispose of it accordingly.
(2) In any other case, an application under rule 195 may be determined by an order made or directions given by–
   (a) the court; or
   (b) a person nominated under paragraph (3).
(3) The Senior Judge or the President may nominate an officer or officers of the court for the purpose of determining applications under rule 195.
(4) Where an officer has been nominated under paragraph (3) to determine an application, he may refer to a judge any proceedings or any question arising in any proceedings which ought, in the officer's opinion, to be considered by a judge.

197 Appeal against a decision of a nominated officer
(1) This rule applies in relation to decisions made under rules 195 and 196 by a nominated officer.

(2) An appeal from a decision to which this rule applies lies to a judge of the court nominated by virtue of section 46(2)(e) of the Act.
(3) No permission is required for an appeal under paragraph (2).
(4) A judge determining an appeal under paragraph (2) has all the powers that an appeal judge on appeal has by virtue of rule 178.
(5) An appeal from a decision made under paragraph (2) ('a second appeal') lies to a judge of the court nominated by virtue of section 46(2)(d) of the Act.
(6) A second appeal may be made from a decision of a nominated officer, and a judge to whom such an appeal is made may, if he considers the matter is one which ought to be heard by a judge of the court nominated by virtue of section 46(2)(a) to (c), transfer the matter to such a judge.
(7) An appeal from a decision made on a second appeal lies to the Court of Appeal.

198 Application of Rules to proceedings within paragraphs 3 and 12 of Schedule 5 to the Act
(1) In this rule, 'pending proceedings' means proceedings on an application within paragraph 3 or 12 of Schedule 5 to the Act.
(2) A practice direction shall make provision for the extent to which these Rules shall apply to pending proceedings.

199 Practice direction
A practice direction may make additional or different provision in relation to transitory and transitional matters.

Part 23: Miscellaneous

200 Order or directions requiring a person to give security for discharge of functions
(1) This rule applies where the court makes an order or gives a direction–
   (a) conferring functions on any person (whether as deputy or otherwise); and
   (b) requiring him to give security for the discharge of those functions.
(2) The person on whom functions are conferred must give the security before he undertakes to discharge his functions, unless the court permits it to be given subsequently.
(3) Paragraphs (4) to (6) apply where the security is required to be given before any action can be taken.
(4) Subject to paragraph (5), the security must be given in accordance with the requirements of regulation 33(2)(a) of the Public Guardian Regulations (which makes provision about the giving of security by means of a bond that is endorsed by an authorised insurance company or deposit-taker).
(5) The court may impose such other requirements in relation to the giving of the security as it considers appropriate (whether in addition to, or instead of, those specified in paragraph (4)).
(6) In specifying the date from which the order or directions referred to in paragraph (1) are to take effect, the court will have regard to the need to postpone that date for such reasonable period as would enable the Public Guardian to be satisfied that–
   (a) if paragraph (4) applies, the requirements of regulation 34 of the Public Guardian Regulations have been met in relation to the security; and

(b) any other requirements imposed by the court under paragraph (5) have been met.
(7) 'The Public Guardian Regulations' means the Lasting Powers of Attorney, Enduring Powers of Attorney and Public Guardian Regulations 2007.

201 Objections to registration of an enduring power of attorney: request for directions
(1) This rule applies in any case where–
  (a) the Public Guardian (having received a notice of objection to the registration of an instrument creating an enduring power of attorney) is prevented by paragraph 13(5) of Schedule 4 to the Act from registering the instrument except in accordance with the court's directions; and
  (b) on or before the relevant day, no application for the court to give such directions has been made under Part 9 (how to start proceedings).
(2) In paragraph (1)(b) the relevant day is the later of–
  (a) the final day of the period specified in paragraph 13(4) of Schedule 4 to the Act; or
  (b) the final day of the period of 14 days beginning with the date on which the Public Guardian receives the notice of objection.
(3) The Public Guardian may seek the court's directions about registering the instrument by filing a request in accordance with the relevant practice direction.
(4) As soon as practicable and in any event within 21 days of the date on which the request was made, the court will notify–
  (a) the person (or persons) who gave the notice of objection; and
  (b) the attorney or, if more than one, each of them.
(5) As soon as practicable and in any event within 21 days of the date on which the request is filed, the Public Guardian must notify the donor of the power that the request has been so filed.
(6) The notice under paragraph (4) must–
  (a) state that the Public Guardian has requested the court's directions about registration;
  (b) state that the court will give directions in response to the request unless an application under Part 9 is made to it before the end of the period of 21 days commencing with the date on which the notice is issued; and
  (c) set out the steps required to make such an application.
(7) 'Notice of objection' means a notice of objection which is made in accordance with paragraph 13(4) of Schedule 4 to the Act.

202 Disposal of property where P ceases to lack capacity
(1) This rule applies where P ceases to lack capacity.
(2) In this rule, 'relevant property' means any property belonging to P and forming part of his estate, and which–
  (a) remains under the control of anyone appointed by order of the court; or
  (b) is held under the direction of the court.
(3) The court may at any time make an order for any relevant property to be transferred to P, or at P's direction, provided that it is satisfied that P has the capacity to make decisions in relation to that property.
(4) An application for an order under this rule is to be made in accordance with Part 10.

COURT OF PROTECTION CASE MANAGEMENT PILOT RULES 2016[1]

Pilot Part 1: The Overriding Objective

1.1 Overriding objective

(1) These Rules have the overriding objective of enabling the court to deal with a case justly and at proportionate cost, having regard to the principles contained in the Act.

(2) The court must seek to give effect to the overriding objective when it–
   (a) exercises any power under the Rules; or
   (b) interprets any rule or practice direction.

(3) Dealing with a case justly and at proportionate cost includes, so far as is practicable–
   (a) ensuring that it is dealt with expeditiously and fairly;
   (b) ensuring that P's interests and position are properly considered;
   (c) dealing with the case in ways which are proportionate to the nature, importance and complexity of the issues;
   (d) ensuring that the parties are on an equal footing;
   (e) saving expense;
   (f) allotting to it an appropriate share of the court's resources, while taking account of the need to allot resources to other cases; and
   (g) enforcing compliance with rules, practice directions and orders.

1.2 Participation of P

(1) The court must in each case, on its own initiative or on the application of any person, consider whether it should make one or more of the directions in paragraph (2), having regard to–
   (a) the nature and extent of the information before the court;
   (b) the issues raised in the case;
   (c) whether a matter is contentious; and
   (d) whether P has been notified in accordance with the provisions of Part 7 and what, if anything, P has said or done in response to such notification.

(2) The directions are that–
   (a) P should be joined as a party;
   (b) P's participation should be secured by the appointment of an accredited legal representative to represent P in the proceedings and to discharge such other functions as the court may direct;
   (c) P's participation should be secured by the appointment of a representative whose function shall be to provide the court with information as to the matters set out in section 4(6) of the Act and to discharge such other functions as the court may direct;
   (d) P should have the opportunity to address (directly or indirectly) the judge determining the application and, if so directed, the circumstances in which that should occur;

---

1 The Case Management Pilot Rules Parts 1–5, and 15 appear in Annex 1 to the Case Management Pilot Practice Direction and are in force as a Pilot pursuant to COPR r9A. The Pilot Scheme started on 1 September 2016 and is expected to run for 12 months to 31 August 2017.

(e) P's interests and position can properly be secured without any direction under sub-paragraphs (a) to (d) being made or by the making of an alternative direction meeting the overriding objective.

(3) Any appointment or directions made pursuant to paragraph (2)(b) to (e) may be made for such period or periods as the court thinks fit.

(4) Unless P has capacity to conduct the proceedings, an order joining P as a party shall only take effect–
 (a) on the appointment of a litigation friend on P's behalf; or
 (b) if the court so directs, on or after the appointment of an accredited legal representative.

(5) If the court has directed that P should be joined as a party but such joinder does not occur because no litigation friend or accredited legal representative is appointed, the court shall record in a judgment or order–
 (a) the fact that no such appointment was made; and
 (b) the reasons given for that appointment not being made.

(6) A practice direction may make additional or supplementary provision in respect of any of the matters set out in this rule.

(The appointment of litigation friends, accredited legal representatives and representatives under paragraph (2)(c) is dealt with under Part 17.)

('Accredited legal representative' is defined in rule 2.1.)

Duties to further the overriding objective

1.3 Court's duty to manage cases

(1) The court must further the overriding objective by actively managing cases.

(2) The court must manage a case at all times and in particular–
 (a) when a case file is referred to a judge;
 (b) at every hearing, whether listed by the court on its own initiative or on application by a party;
 (c) at all stages of a final hearing; and
 (d) when considering enforcement measures including committal.

(3) Active case management includes–
 (a) considering the appropriate case pathway for the case;
 (b) ensuring–
  (i) that the appropriate judge is allocated to the case;
  (ii) judicial continuity, so far as practicable;
 (c) avoiding delay and keeping costs down;
 (d) encouraging the parties to co-operate with each other in the conduct of the proceedings;
 (e) identifying at an early stage–
  (i) the issues; and
  (ii) who should be a party to the proceedings;
 (f) deciding promptly–
  (i) which issues need a full investigation and hearing and which do not; and
  (ii) the procedure to be followed in the case;
 (g) deciding the order in which issues are to be resolved;
 (h) encouraging the parties to use an alternative dispute resolution procedure if the court considers that appropriate;

(i) fixing timetables or otherwise controlling the progress of the case;
(j) considering whether the likely benefits of taking a particular step justify the cost of taking it;
(k) dealing with as many aspects of the case as the court can on the same occasion;
(l) dealing with the case without the parties needing to attend at court;
(m) making use of technology;
(n) giving directions to ensure that the case proceeds quickly and efficiently;
(o) considering whether any hearing should be heard in public; and
(p) considering whether any document relating to proceedings should be a public document and, if so, whether and to what extent it should be redacted.

(Rules 4.2 to 4.4 make provision about the court's powers to authorise publication of information about proceedings and to order that a hearing be held in public.)

1.4 The duty of the parties

(1) The parties are required to help the court to further the overriding objective.
(2) Without prejudice to the generality of paragraph (1), each party is required to–
   (a) ask the court to take steps to manage the case if–
      (i) an order or direction of the court appears not to deal with an issue; or
      (ii) if a matter including any new circumstances, issue or dispute arises of which the court is unaware;
   (b) identify before issue if the case is within the scope of one of case pathways and comply with the requirements of the applicable case pathway;
   (c) co-operate with the other parties and with the court in identifying and narrowing the issues that need to be determined by the court, and the timetable for that determination;
   (d) adhere to the timetable set by these Rules and by the court;
   (e) comply with all directions and orders of the court;
   (f) be full and frank in the disclosure of information and evidence to the court (including any disclosure ordered under Part 16);
   (g) co-operate with the other parties in all aspects of the conduct of the proceedings, including in the preparation of bundles.
(3) If the court determines that any party has failed without reasonable excuse to satisfy the requirements of this rule, it may under rule 159 depart from the general rules about costs in so far as they apply to that party.

(Rule 133(2) deals with the requirements of general disclosure.)

1.5 The duty of legal representatives

(1) Legal representatives of parties are required to help the court to further the overriding objective.
(2) Without prejudice to the generality of paragraph (1), a legal representative of a party must–
   (a) comply with any applicable rules, practice directions or orders of the court;
   (b) follow (where appropriate) the applicable case pathway; and
   (c) address whether the case can be swiftly resolved.

1.6 The duty of unrepresented litigants
(1) Without prejudice to the generality of rule 1.4, unrepresented litigants are required to help the court to further the overriding objective.
(2) This includes–
   (a) engaging with the process applicable in the case and co-operating with the court and the other parties;
   (b) seeking the court's direction if an issue or dispute arises in the case;
   (c) presenting their case fairly; and
   (d) seeking early resolution of any dispute where practicable.

Pilot Part 2: Interpretation and General Provisions

2.1 Interpretation
In these Rules–
'the Act' means the Mental Capacity Act 2005;
'accredited legal representative' means a legal representative authorised pursuant to a scheme of accreditation approved by the President to represent persons meeting the definition of 'P' in this rule in proceedings before the court;
'applicant' means a person who makes, or who seeks permission to make, an application to the court;
'application form' means the document that is to be used to begin proceedings in accordance with Part 9 of these Rules or any other provision of these Rules or the practice directions which requires the use of an application form;
'application notice' means the document that is to be used to make an application in accordance with Part 10 of these Rules or any other provision of these Rules or the practice directions which requires the use of an application notice;
'attorney' means the person appointed as such by an enduring power of attorney created, or purporting to have been created, in accordance with the regulations mentioned in paragraph 2 of Schedule 4 to the Act;
'business day' means a day other than–
   (a) a Saturday, Sunday, Christmas Day or Good Friday; or
   (b) a bank holiday in England and Wales, under the Banking and Financial Dealings Act 1971;
'child' means a person under 18;
'court' means the Court of Protection;
'deputy' means a deputy appointed under the Act;
'donee' means the donee of a lasting power of attorney;
'donor' means the donor of a lasting power of attorney, except where the expression is used in rule 68 or 201(5) (where it means the donor of an enduring power of attorney);
'enduring power of attorney' means an instrument created in accordance with such of the regulations mentioned in paragraph 2 of Schedule 4 to the Act as applied when it was executed;
'filing' in relation to a document means delivering it, by post or otherwise, to the court office;
'hearing' includes a hearing conducted by telephone, video link, or any other method permitted or directed by the court;

'judge' means a judge nominated to be a judge of the court under the Act;
'lasting power of attorney' has the meaning given in section 9 of the Act;
'legal representative' means a–
  (a) barrister;
  (b) solicitor;
  (c) solicitor's employee;
  (d) manager of a body recognised under section 9 of the Administration of Justice Act 1985; or
  (e) person who, for the purposes of the Legal Services Act 2007, is an authorised person in relation to an activity which constitutes the conduct of litigation (within the meaning of that Act),
who has been instructed to act for a party in relation to any application;
'legally aided person' means a person to whom civil legal services (within the meaning of the Legal Aid, Sentencing and Punishment of Offenders Act 2012) have been made available under arrangements made for the purposes of Part 1 of that Act;
'order' includes a declaration made by the court;
'P' means–
  (a) any person (other than a protected party) who lacks or, so far as consistent with the context, is alleged to lack capacity to make a decision or decisions in relation to any matter that is the subject of an application to the court; and
  (b) a relevant person as defined by paragraph 7 of Schedule A1 to the Act,
and references to a person who lacks capacity are to be construed in accordance with the Act;
'party' is to be construed in accordance with rule 73;
'personal welfare' is to be construed in accordance with section 17 of the Act;
'President' and 'Vice-President' refer to those judges appointed as such under section 46(3)(a) and (b) of the Act;
'property and affairs' is to be construed in accordance with section 18 of the Act;
'protected party' means a party or an intended party (other than P or a child) who lacks capacity to conduct the proceedings;
'representative' means a person appointed under rule 1.2(2)(c), except where the context otherwise requires;
'respondent' means a person who is named as a respondent in the application form or notice, as the case may be;
'Senior Judge' means the judge who has been nominated to be Senior Judge under section 46(4) of the Act, and references in these Rules to a circuit judge include the Senior Judge;
'Tier 1 Judge' means any judge nominated to act as a judge of the Court of Protection under section 46 of the Act who is neither a Tier 2 Judge nor a Tier 3 Judge;
'Tier 2 Judge' means–
  (a) the Senior Judge; and
  (b) such other judges nominated to act as a judge of the Court of Protection under section 46 Act as may be set out in the relevant practice direction;

'Tier 3 Judge' means–
- (a) the President;
- (b) the Vice-President; and
- (c) such other judges nominated to act as a judge of the Court of Protection under section 46 Act as may be set out in the relevant practice direction;

'Visitor' means a person appointed as such by the Lord Chancellor under section 61 of the Act.

2.2 Court officers

(1) Where these Rules permit or require the court to perform an act of a purely formal or administrative character, that act may be performed by a court officer.

(2) A requirement that a court officer carry out any act at the request of any person is subject to the payment of any fee required by a fees order for the carrying out of that act.

2.3 Court officers – authorisation

(1) The Senior Judge or the President or Vice-President may authorise a court officer to exercise the jurisdiction of the court in such circumstances as may be set out in the relevant practice direction.

(2) A court officer who has been authorised under paragraph (1)–
- (a) must refer to a judge any application, proceedings or any question arising in any application or proceedings which ought, in the officer's opinion, to be considered by a judge;
- (b) may not deal with any application or proceedings or any question arising in any application or proceedings by way of a hearing; and
- (c) may not deal with an application for the reconsideration of an order made by that court officer or another court officer.

2.4 Computation of time

(1) This rule shows how to calculate any period of time which is specified–
- (a) by these Rules;
- (b) by a practice direction; or
- (c) in an order or direction of the court.

(2) A period of time expressed as a number of days must be computed as clear days.

(3) In this rule, 'clear days' means that in computing the number of days–
- (a) the day on which the period begins; and
- (b) if the end of the period is defined by reference to an event, the day on which that event occurs,

are not included.

(4) Where the specified period is 7 days or less, and would include a day which is not a business day, that day does not count.

(5) When the specified period for doing any act at the court office ends on a day on which the office is closed, that act will be done in time if done on the next day on which the court office is open.

2.5 Application of the Civil Procedure Rules and Family Procedure Rules

(1) In any case not expressly provided for by these Rules or the practice directions made under them, the court may apply either the Civil Procedure Rules

1998 or the Family Procedure Rules 2010 (including in either case the practice directions made under them) with any necessary modifications, in so far as is necessary to further the overriding objective.
(2) A reference in these Rules to the Civil Procedure Rules 1998 or to the Family Procedure Rules 2010 is to the version of those rules in force at the date specified for the purpose of that reference in the relevant practice direction.

2.6 Pilot schemes
(1) Practice directions may make provision for the operation of pilot schemes for assessing the use of new practices and procedures in connection with proceedings–
   (a) for specified periods; and
   (b) in relation to proceedings–
       (i) in specified parts of the country; or
       (ii) relating to specified types of application.
(2) Practice directions may modify or disapply any provision of these Rules during the operation of such pilot schemes.

Pilot Part 3: Managing the Case

3.1 The court's general powers of case management
(1) The list of powers in this rule is in addition to any powers given to the court by any other rule or practice direction or by any other enactment or any powers it may otherwise have.
(2) The court may–
   (a) extend or shorten the time for compliance with any rule, practice direction, or court order or direction (even if an application for extension is made after the time for compliance has expired);
   (b) adjourn or bring forward a hearing;
   (c) require P, a party, a party's legal representative or litigation friend, or P's rule 1.2 representative, to attend court;
   (d) hold a hearing and receive evidence by telephone or any other method of direct oral communication;
   (e) stay the whole or part of any proceedings or judgment either generally or until a specified date or event;
   (f) consolidate proceedings;
   (g) hear two or more applications on the same occasion;
   (h) direct a separate hearing of any issue;
   (i) decide the order in which issues are to be heard;
   (j) exclude an issue from consideration;
   (k) dismiss or give judgment on an application after a decision is made on a preliminary basis;
   (l) direct any party to file and serve an estimate of costs; and
   (m) take any step or give any direction for the purpose of managing the case and furthering the overriding objective.
(3) A judge to whom a matter is allocated may, if the judge considers that the matter is one which ought properly to be dealt with by another judge, transfer the matter to such a judge.
(4) Where the court gives directions it may take into account whether or not a party has complied with any rule or practice direction.

(5) The court may make any order it considers appropriate even if a party has not sought that order.

(6) A power of the court under these Rules to make an order includes a power to vary or revoke the order.

(Rules 1.3 to 1.6 concern the duty of the court to further the overriding objective by actively managing cases, and the duty of parties, legal representatives and unrepresented litigants to assist the court in furthering the overriding objective.)

3.2 Case management – unrepresented parties

(1) This rule applies in any proceedings where at least one party is unrepresented.

(2) When the court is exercising any powers of case management, it must have regard to the fact that at least one party is unrepresented.

(3) The court must adopt such procedure at any hearing as it considers appropriate to further the overriding objective.

(4) At any hearing when the court is taking evidence this may include–
  (a) ascertaining from an unrepresented party the matters about which the witness may be able to give evidence or on which the witness ought to be cross-examined; and
  (b) putting or causing to be put, to the witness such questions as may appear to the court to be proper.

3.3 Court's power to dispense with requirement of any rule

In addition to its general powers and the powers listed in rule 3.1, the court may dispense with the requirements of any rule.

3.4 Exercise of powers on the court's own initiative

(1) Except where these Rules or another enactment make different provision, the court may exercise its powers on its own initiative.

(2) The court may make an order on its own initiative without hearing the parties or giving them the opportunity to make representations.

(3) Where the court proposes to make an order on its own initiative it may give the parties and any other person it thinks fit an opportunity to make representations and, where it does so, must specify the time by which, and the manner in which, the representations must be made.

(4) Where the court proposes–
  (a) to make an order on its own initiative; and
  (b) to hold a hearing to decide whether to make the order,

it must give the parties and may give any other person it thinks likely to be affected by the order at least 3 days' notice of the hearing.

3.5 General power of the court to rectify matters where there has been an error of procedure

Where there has been an error of procedure, such as a failure to comply with a rule or practice direction–
  (a) the error does not invalidate any step taken in the proceedings unless the court so orders; and
  (b) the court may waive the error or require it to be remedied or may make such other order as appears to the court to be just.

3.6 Dealing with the application

(1) This rule and rule 3.7 are subject to any provision made by a practice direction in respect of the case pathway to which the case is allocated.
(2) As soon as practicable after any application has been issued the court shall consider how to deal with it.
(3) Where permission to start proceedings is required, and whether or not it has been applied for, the court's consideration under paragraph (2) shall include whether to grant or refuse permission without a hearing, or to direct a hearing to consider whether permission should be granted.
(4) The court may deal with an application or any part of an application at a hearing or without a hearing.
(5) In considering whether it is necessary to hold a hearing, the court shall, as appropriate, have regard to–
  (a) the nature of the proceedings and the orders sought;
  (b) whether the application is opposed by a person who appears to the court to have an interest in matters relating to P's best interests;
  (c) whether the application involves a substantial dispute of fact;
  (d) the complexity of the facts and the law;
  (e) any wider public interest in the proceedings;
  (f) the circumstances of P and of any party, in particular as to whether their rights would be adequately protected if a hearing were not held;
  (g) whether the parties agree that the court should dispose of the application without a hearing; and
  (h) any other matter specified in the relevant practice direction.
(6) Where the court considers that a hearing is necessary it shall–
  (a) give notice of the hearing date to the parties and to any other person it directs;
  (b) state what is to be dealt with at the hearing, including whether the matter is to be disposed of at that hearing; and
  (c) consider whether it is appropriate–
    (i) for the hearing or any part of it to be in public; and
    (ii) to make any order under rule 4.1, 4.2 or 4.3.

(The practice direction *Practice Direction – Case Management Pilot* makes provision in relation to case management pathways.)

3.7 Directions

(1) The court may–
  (a) give directions in writing; or
  (b) set a date for a directions hearing; and
  (c) do anything else that may be set out in a practice direction.
(2) When giving directions, the court may do any of the following–
  (a) require a report under section 49 of the Act and give directions as to any such report;
  (b) give directions as to any requirements contained in these Rules or a practice direction for the giving of notification to any person or for that person to do anything in response to a notification;
  (c) if the court considers that any other person or persons should be a party to the proceedings, give directions joining them as a party;

(d) if the court considers that any party to the proceedings should not be a party, give directions for that person's removal as a party;
(e) give directions for the management of the case and set a timetable for the steps to be taken between the giving of directions and the hearing;
(f) subject to rule 3.8, give directions as to the type of judge who is to hear the case;
(g) give directions as to whether the proceedings or any part of them are to be heard in public, or as to whether any particular person should be permitted to attend the hearing, or as to whether any publication of the proceedings is to be permitted;
(h) give directions as to the disclosure of documents, service of witness statements and any expert evidence;
(i) give directions as to the attendance of witnesses and as to whether, and the extent to which, cross-examination will be permitted at any hearing; and
(j) give such other directions as the court may think fit.
(3) The court may give directions at any time–
(a) on its own initiative; or
(b) on the application of a party.
(4) Subject to paragraphs (5) and (6) and unless these Rules or a practice direction provide otherwise or the court directs otherwise, the time specified by a rule or by the court for a person to do any act may be varied by the written agreement of the parties.
(5) A party must apply to the court if that party wishes to vary–
(a) the date the court has fixed for the final hearing; or
(b) the period within which the final hearing is to take place.
(6) The time specified by a rule or practice direction or by the court may not be varied by the parties if the variation would make it necessary to vary the date the court has fixed for any hearing or the period within which the final hearing is to take place.

(Participation of P in proceedings is addressed in rule 1.2 (participation of P) and Part 17 (litigation friends and rule 1.2 representatives).)

Allocation of proceedings

3.8 Court's jurisdiction in certain kinds of cases to be exercised by certain judges

(1) A practice direction made under this rule may specify certain categories of case to be dealt with by a specific judge or a specific class of judges.
(2) Applications in any matter other than those specified in the practice direction referred to in paragraph (1) may be dealt with by any judge.

3.9 Allocation of cases to case pathways

(1) This rule provides for the allocation of cases to case pathways.
(2) There are three case pathways–
(a) the Personal Welfare Pathway;
(b) the Property and Affairs Pathway;
(c) the Mixed Welfare and Property Pathway.
(3) Each case shall on issue be allocated to one of the three case pathways unless (subject to paragraph (5)) it is in an excepted class of cases.

(4) Excepted classes of case may be specified in a practice direction.
(5) The court may direct that a case shall be allocated to a case pathway notwithstanding that it is in an excepted class of cases.
(6) A practice direction may make provision for–
   (a) the scope of each case pathway; and
   (b) how cases in each case pathway are to be managed.
   (The practice direction *Practice Direction – Case Management Pilot* makes provision in relation to the case pathways and excepted classes of case.)

Pilot Part 4: Hearings

Private hearings

4.1 General rule – hearing to be held in private
(1) The general rule is that a hearing is to be held in private.
(2) A private hearing is a hearing which only the following persons are entitled to attend–
   (a) the parties;
   (b) P (whether or not a party);
   (c) any person acting in the proceedings as a litigation friend;
   (d) any legal representative of a person specified in any of sub-paragraphs (a) to (c); and
   (e) any court officer.
(3) In relation to a private hearing, the court may make an order–
   (a) authorising any person, or class of persons, to attend the hearing or a part of it; or
   (b) excluding any person, or class of persons, from attending the hearing or a part of it.

4.2 Court's general power to authorise publication of information about proceedings
(1) For the purposes of the law relating to contempt of court, information relating to proceedings held in private (whether or not contained in a document filed with the court) may be communicated in accordance with paragraph (2) or (3).
(2) The court may make an order authorising–
   (a) the publication or communication of such information or material relating to the proceedings as it may specify; or
   (b) the publication of the text or a summary of the whole or part of a judgment or order made by the court.
(3) Subject to any direction of the court, information referred to in paragraph (1) may be communicated in accordance with Practice Direction Pilot 4A.
(4) Where the court makes an order under paragraph (2) it may do so on such terms as it thinks fit, and in particular may–
   (a) impose restrictions on the publication of the identity of–
      (i) any party;
      (ii) P (whether or not a party);
      (iii) any witness; or
      (iv) any other person;
   (b) prohibit the publication of any information that may lead to any such person being identified;

(c) prohibit the further publication of any information relating to the proceedings from such date as the court may specify; or
(d) impose such other restrictions on the publication of information relating to the proceedings as the court may specify.
(5) The court may on its own initiative or upon request authorise communication–
   (a) for the purposes set out in Practice Direction Pilot 4A; or
   (b) for such other purposes as it considers appropriate,
of information held by it.

Power to order a public hearing

4.3 Court's power to order that a hearing be held in public
(1) The court may make an order–
   (a) for a hearing to be held in public;
   (b) for a part of a hearing to be held in public; or
   (c) excluding any person, or class of persons, from attending a public hearing or a part of it.
(2) Where the court makes an order under paragraph (1), it may in the same order or by a subsequent order–
   (a) impose restrictions on the publication of the identity of–
      (i) any party;
      (ii) P (whether or not a party);
      (iii) any witness; or
      (iv) any other person;
   (b) prohibit the publication of any information that may lead to any such person being identified;
   (c) prohibit the further publication of any information relating to the proceedings from such date as the court may specify; or
   (d) impose such other restrictions on the publication of information relating to the proceedings as the court may specify.

Supplementary

4.4 Supplementary provisions relating to public or private hearings
(1) An order under rule 4.1, 4.2 or 4.3 may be made–
   (a) only where it appears to the court that there is good reason for making the order;
   (b) at any time; and
   (c) either on the court's own initiative or on an application made by any person in accordance with Part 10.
(2) A practice direction may make further provision in connection with–
   (a) private hearings;
   (b) public hearings; or
   (c) the publication of information about any proceedings.

Pilot Part 5: Court Documents

5.1 Documents used in court proceedings
(1) The court will seal or otherwise authenticate with the stamp of the court the following documents on issue–
   (a) an application form;
   (b) an application notice;

(c) an order; and
(d) any other document which a rule or practice direction requires to be sealed or stamped.
(2) Where these Rules or any practice direction require a document to be signed, that requirement is satisfied if the signature is printed by computer or other mechanical means.
(3) A practice direction may make provision for documents to be filed or sent to the court by–
(a) facsimile; or
(b) other means.

5.2 Documents required to be verified by a statement of truth
(1) The following documents must be verified by a statement of truth–
(a) an application form, an application notice, an appellant's notice or a respondent's notice, where the applicant seeks to rely upon matters set out in the document as evidence;
(b) a witness statement;
(c) a certificate of–
(i) service or non-service; or
(ii) notification or non-notification;
(d) a deputy's declaration; and
(e) any other document required by a rule or practice direction to be so verified.
(2) Subject to paragraph (3), a statement of truth is a statement that–
(a) the party putting forward the document;
(b) in the case of a witness statement, the maker of the witness statement; or
(c) in the case of a certificate referred to in paragraph (1)(c), the person who signs the certificate,
believes that the facts stated in the document being verified are true.
(3) If a party is conducting proceedings with a litigation friend, the statement of truth in–
(a) an application form;
(b) an application notice; or
(c) an appellant's notice or a respondent's notice,
is a statement that the litigation friend believes that the facts stated in the document being verified are true.
(4) The statement of truth must be signed–
(a) in the case of an application form, an application notice, an appellant's notice or a respondent's notice–
(i) by the party or litigation friend; or
(ii) by the legal representative on behalf of the party or litigation friend; and
(b) in the case of a witness statement, by the maker of the statement.
(5) A statement of truth which is not contained in the document which it verifies must clearly identify that document.
(6) A statement of truth in an application form, an application notice, an appellant's notice or a respondent's notice may be made by–
(a) a person who is not a party; or
(b) two or more parties jointly,
where this is permitted by a relevant practice direction.

5.3 Position statement not required to be verified by statement of truth

Nothing in these Rules requires a position statement to be verified by a statement of truth.

5.4 Failure to verify a document

If an application form, an application notice, an appellant's notice or a respondent's notice is not verified by a statement of truth, the applicant (or appellant or respondent as the case may be) may not rely upon the document as evidence of any of the matters set out in it unless the court permits.

5.5 Failure to verify a witness statement

If a witness statement is not verified by a statement of truth, it shall not be admissible in evidence unless the court permits.

5.6 False statements

(1) Proceedings for contempt of court may be brought against a person if that person makes, or causes to be made, a false statement in a document verified by a statement of truth without an honest belief in its truth.
(2) Proceedings under this rule may be brought only–
   (a) by the Attorney General; or
   (b) with the permission of the court.

5.7 Personal details

(1) Where a party does not wish to reveal–
   (a) his or her home address or telephone number;
   (b) P's home address or telephone number;
   (c) the name of the person with whom P is living (if that person is not the applicant); or
   (d) the address or telephone number of his or her place of business, or the place of business of any of the persons mentioned in sub-paragraphs (b) or (c),
   that party must provide those particulars to the court.
(2) Where paragraph (1) applies, the particulars given will not be revealed to any person unless the court so directs.
(3) Where a party changes home address during the course of the proceedings, that party must give notice in writing of the change to the court.
(4) Where a party does not reveal his or her home address, that party must nonetheless provide an address for service which must be within the jurisdiction of the court.

5.8 Supply of documents to a party from court records

Unless the court orders otherwise, a party to proceedings may inspect or obtain from the records of the court a copy of–
   (a) any document filed by a party to the proceedings; or
   (b) any communication in the proceedings between the court and–
      (i) a party to the proceedings; or
      (ii) another person.

5.9 Supply of documents to a non-party from court records

(1) Subject to rules 5.12 and 4.3(2), a person who is not a party to proceedings may inspect or obtain from the court records a copy of any judgment or order given or made in public.

(2) The court may, on an application made to it, authorise a person who is not a party to proceedings to–
  (a) inspect any other documents in the court records; or
  (b) obtain a copy of any such documents, or extracts from such documents.
(3) A person making an application for an authorisation under paragraph (2) must do so in accordance with Part 10.
(4) Before giving an authorisation under paragraph (2), the court will consider whether any document is to be provided on an edited basis.

5.10 Subsequent use of court documents
(1) Where a document has been filed or disclosed, a party to whom it was provided may use the document only for the purpose of the proceedings in which it was filed or disclosed, except where–
  (a) the document has been read to or by the court or referred to at a public hearing; or
  (b) the court otherwise permits.
(2) Paragraph (1)(a) is subject to any order of the court made under rule 4.3(2).

5.11 Editing information in court documents
(1) A party may apply to the court for an order that a specified part of a document is to be edited prior to the document's service or disclosure.
(2) An order under paragraph (1) may be made at any time.
(3) Where the court makes an order under this rule any subsequent use of that document in the proceedings shall be of the document as edited, unless the court directs otherwise.
(4) An application under this rule must be made in accordance with Part 10.

5.12 Public Guardian to be supplied with court documents relevant to supervision of deputies
(1) This rule applies in any case where the court makes an order–
  (a) appointing a person to act as a deputy; or
  (b) varying an order under which a deputy has been appointed.
(2) Subject to paragraphs (3) and (6), the Public Guardian is entitled to be supplied with a copy of qualifying documents if the Public Guardian reasonably considers that it is necessary to have regard to them in connection with the discharge of the Public Guardian's functions under section 58 of the Act in relation to supervision of deputies.
(3) The court may direct that the right to be supplied with documents under paragraph (2) does not apply in relation to such one or more documents, or descriptions of documents, as the court may specify.
(4) A direction under paragraph (3) or (6) may be given–
  (a) either on the court's own initiative or on an application made to it; and
  (b) either–
    (i) at the same time as the court makes the order which appoints the deputy, or which varies it; or
    (ii) subsequently.
(5) 'Qualifying documents' means documents which–
  (a) are filed in court in connection with the proceedings in which the court makes the order referred to in paragraph (1); and
  (b) are relevant to–

(i) the decision to appoint the deputy;
(ii) any powers conferred on the deputy;
(iii) any duties imposed on the deputy; or
(iv) any other terms applying to those powers and duties which are contained in the order.
(6) The court may direct that any document is to be provided to the Public Guardian on an edited basis.

5.13 Provision of court order to Public Guardian

Any order of the court requiring the Public Guardian to do something, or not to do something, must be served on the Public Guardian as soon as practicable and in any event not later than 7 days after the order was made.

5.14 Amendment of application

(1) The court may allow or direct an applicant, at any stage of the proceedings, to amend the application form or notice.
(2) The amendment may be effected by making in writing the necessary alterations to the application form or notice, but if the amendments are so numerous or of such a nature or length that written alteration would make it difficult or inconvenient to read, a fresh document amended as allowed or directed may be issued.

5.15 Clerical mistakes or slips

The court may at any time correct any clerical mistakes in an order or direction or any error arising in an order or direction from any accidental slip or omission.

5.16 Endorsement of amendment

Where an application form or notice, order or direction has been amended under this Part, a note shall be placed on it showing the date on which it was amended, and the alteration shall be sealed.

Part 15: Experts

119 References to expert

A reference to an expert in this Part–
(a) is to an expert who has been instructed to give or prepare evidence for the purpose of court proceedings; but
(b) does not include any person instructed to make a report under section 49 of the Act.

120 Restriction on filing an expert's report

No person may file expert evidence unless the court or a practice direction permits, or if it is filed with the application form and is evidence–
(a) that P is a person who lacks capacity to make a decision or decisions in relation to the matter or matters to which the application relates;
(b) as to P's best interests; or
(c) that is required by any rule or practice direction to be filed with the application form.
(2) An applicant may only rely on any expert evidence so filed in support of the application form to the extent and for the purposes that the court allows.

(Rule 64(a) requires the applicant to file any evidence upon which the applicant wishes to rely with the application form.)

121 Duty to restrict expert evidence
(1) Expert evidence shall be restricted to that which is necessary to assist the court to resolve the issues in the proceedings.
(2) The court may give permission to file or adduce expert evidence as mentioned in rule 120(1) and 123(1) only if satisfied that the evidence–
   (a) is necessary to assist the court to resolve the issues in the proceedings; and
   (b) cannot otherwise be provided.

122 Experts – overriding duty to the court
(1) It is the duty of the expert to help the court on the matters within the expert's expertise.
(2) This duty overrides any obligation to the person from whom the expert has received instructions or by whom the expert is paid.

123 Court's power to restrict expert evidence
(1) Subject to rule 120, no party may file or adduce expert evidence unless the court or a practice direction permits.
(2) When a party applies for a direction under this rule, that party must–
   (a) identify the field in respect of which that party wishes to rely upon expert evidence, and the issues to which the expert evidence is to relate;
   (b) where practicable, identify the expert in that field upon whose evidence the party wishes to rely;
   (c) provide any other material information about the expert;
   (d) state whether the expert evidence could be obtained from a single joint expert;
   (e) provide any other information or documents required by a practice direction; and
   (f) provide a draft letter of instruction to the expert.
(2A) When deciding whether to give permission as mentioned in paragraph (1), the court is to have regard in particular to–
   (a) the issues to which the expert evidence would relate;
   (b) the questions which the expert would answer;
   (c) the impact which giving permission would be likely to have on the timetable, duration and conduct of the proceedings;
   (d) any failure to comply with any direction of the court about expert evidence; and
   (e) the cost of the expert evidence.
(3) Where a direction is given under this rule, the court shall specify–
   (a) the field or fields in respect of which the expert evidence is to be provided;
   (b) the questions which the expert is required to answer; and
   (c) the date by which the expert is to provide the evidence.
(4) The court may specify the person who is to provide the evidence referred to in paragraph (3).
(5) Where a direction is given under this rule for a party to call an expert or put in evidence an expert's report, the court shall give directions for the service of the report on the parties and on such other persons as the court may direct.

(6) The court may limit the amount of the expert's fees and expenses that the party who wishes to rely upon the expert may recover from any other party.

124 General requirement for expert evidence to be given in a written report
Expert evidence is to be given in a written report unless the court directs otherwise.

125 Written questions to experts
(1) A party may put written questions to–
   (a) an expert instructed by another party; or
   (b) a single joint expert appointed under rule 130.
   about a report prepared by such a person.
(2) Written questions under paragraph (1)–
   (a) may be put once only;
   (b) must be put within 28 days beginning with the date on which the expert's report was served;
   (c) must be for the purpose only of clarification of the report; and
   (d) must be copied and sent to the other parties at the same time as they are sent to the expert.
(3) Paragraph (2) does not apply in any case where–
   (a) the court permits it to be done on a further occasion;
   (b) the other party or parties agree; or
   (c) any practice direction provides otherwise.
(4) An expert's answers to questions put in accordance with paragraph (1) shall be treated as part of the expert's report.
(5) Paragraph (6) applies where–
   (a) a party has put a written question to an expert instructed by another party in accordance with this rule; and
   (b) the expert does not answer that question.
(6) The court may make one or both of the following orders in relation to the party who instructed the expert–
   (a) that the party may not rely upon the evidence of that expert; or
   (b) that the party may not recover the fees and expenses of that expert, or part of them, from any other party.
(7) Unless the court directs otherwise, and subject to any final costs order that may be made, the instructing party is responsible for the payment of the expert's fees and expenses, including the expert's costs of answering questions put by any other party.

126 Contents of expert's report
(1) The court may give directions as to the matters to be covered in an expert's report.
(2) An expert's report must comply with the requirements set out in the relevant practice direction.
(3) At the end of an expert's report there must be a statement that the expert–
   (a) understands his or her duty to the court; and
   (b) has complied with that duty.
(4) The expert's report must state the substance of all material instructions, whether written or oral, on the basis of which the report was written.
(5) The instructions to the expert shall not be privileged against disclosure.

127 Use by one party of expert's report disclosed by another

Where a party has disclosed an expert's report, any party may use that expert's report as evidence at any hearing in the proceedings.

128 Discussions between experts

(1) The court may, at any stage, direct a discussion between experts for the purpose of requiring the experts to–
  (a) identify and discuss the expert issues in the proceedings; and
  (b) where possible, reach an agreed opinion on those issues.
(2) The court may specify the issues which the experts must discuss.
(3) The court may direct that following a discussion between the experts they must prepare a statement for the court showing–
  (a) those issues on which they agree; and
  (b) those issues on which they disagree and a summary of their reasons for disagreeing.
(4) Unless the court directs otherwise, the content of the discussions between experts may be referred to at any hearing or at any stage in the proceedings.

129 Expert's right to ask court for directions

(1) An expert may file a written request for directions to assist in carrying out the expert's functions as an expert.
(2) An expert must, unless the court directs otherwise, provide a copy of any proposed request for directions under paragraph (1)–
  (a) to the party instructing the expert, at least 7 days before filing the request; and
  (b) to all other parties, at least 4 days before filing it.
(3) The court, when it gives directions, may also direct that a party be served with a copy of the directions.

130 Court's power to direct that evidence is to be given by a single joint expert

(1) Where two or more parties wish to submit expert evidence on a particular issue, the court may direct that the evidence on that issue is to be given by one expert only.
(2) The parties wishing to submit the expert evidence are called 'the instructing parties'.
(3) Where the instructing parties cannot agree who should be the expert, the court may–
  (a) select the expert from a list prepared or identified by the instructing parties; or
  (b) direct the manner by which the expert is to be selected.

131 Instructions to a single joint expert

(1) Where the court gives a direction under rule 130 for a single joint expert to be used, the instructions are to be contained in a jointly agreed letter unless the court directs otherwise.
(1A) Where the instructions are to be contained in a jointly agreed letter, in default of agreement the instructions may be determined by the court on the written request of any instructing party copied to the other instructing parties.

(2) Where the court permits the instructing parties to give separate instructions to a single joint expert, unless the court directs otherwise, when an instructing party gives instructions to the expert, that party must at the same time send a copy of the instructions to the other instructing party or parties.
(3) The court may give directions about–
   (a) the payment of the expert's fees and expenses; and
   (b) any inspection, examination or experiments which the expert wishes to carry out.
(4) The court may, before an expert is instructed, limit the amount that can be paid by way of fees and expense to the expert.
(5) Unless the court directs otherwise, and subject to any final costs order that may be made, the instructing parties are jointly and severally liable for the payment of the expert's fees and expenses.

MENTAL CAPACITY ACT 2005 (TRANSFER OF PROCEEDINGS) ORDER 2007
SI No 1899

Citation and commencement

1 (1) This Order may be cited as the Mental Capacity Act 2005 (Transfer of Proceedings) Order 2007.
 (2) This Order shall come into force on 1st October 2007.
 (3) In this Order 'the Children Act' means the Children Act 1989.

Transfers from the Court of Protection to a court having jurisdiction under the Children Act

2 (1) This article applies to any proceedings in the Court of Protection which relate to a person under 18.
 (2) The Court of Protection may direct the transfer of the whole or part of the proceedings to a court having jurisdiction under the Children Act where it considers that in all the circumstances, it is just and convenient to transfer the proceedings.
 (3) In making a determination, the Court of Protection must have regard to–
   (a) whether the proceedings should be heard together with other proceedings that are pending in a court having jurisdiction under the Children Act;
   (b) whether any order that may be made by a court having jurisdiction under that Act is likely to be a more appropriate way of dealing with the proceedings;
   (c) the need to meet any requirements that would apply if the proceedings had been started in a court having jurisdiction under the Children Act; and
   (d) any other matter that the court considers relevant.
 (4) The Court of Protection–
   (a) may exercise the power to make an order under paragraph (2) on an application or on its own initiative; and
   (b) where it orders a transfer, must give reasons for its decision.
 (5) Any proceedings transferred under this article–
   (a) are to be treated for all purposes as if they were proceedings under the Children Act which had been started in a court having jurisdiction under that Act; and
   (b) are to be dealt with after the transfer in accordance with directions given by a court having jurisdiction under that Act.

Transfers from a court having jurisdiction under the Children Act to the Court of Protection

3 (1) This article applies to any proceedings in a court having jurisdiction under the Children Act which relate to a person under 18.
 (2) A court having jurisdiction under the Children Act may direct the transfer of the whole or part of the proceedings to the Court of Protection where it considers that in all circumstances, it is just and convenient to transfer the proceedings.
 (3) In making a determination, the court having jurisdiction under the Children Act must have regard to–

(a) whether the proceedings should be heard together with other proceedings that are pending in the Court of Protection;
(b) whether any order that may be made by the Court of Protection is likely to be a more appropriate way of dealing with the proceedings;
(c) the extent to which any order made as respects a person who lacks capacity is likely to continue to have effect when that person reaches 18; and
(d) any other matter that the court considers relevant.
(4) A court having jurisdiction under the Children Act–
(a) may exercise the power to make an order under paragraph (2) on an application or on its own initiative; and
(b) where it orders a transfer, must give reasons for its decision.
(5) Any proceedings transferred under this article–
(a) are to be treated for all purposes as if they were proceedings under the Mental Capacity Act 2005 which had been started in the Court of Protection; and
(b) are to be dealt with after the transfer in accordance with directions given by the Court of Protection.

Avoidance of double liability for fees

4 Any fee paid for the purpose of starting any proceedings that are transferred under article 2 or 3 is to be treated as if it were the fee that would have been payable if the proceedings had started in the court to which the transfer is made.

COURT OF PROTECTION FEES ORDER 2007
SI No 145 (as amended)[1]

Citation and commencement
1   This Order may be cited as the Court of Protection Fees Order 2007 and comes into force on 1 October 2007.

Interpretation
2   In this Order–
'the Act' means the Mental Capacity Act 2005;
'appellant' means the person who brings or seeks to bring an appeal;
'court' means the Court of Protection;
'P' means any person (other than a protected party) who lacks or, so far as consistent with the context, is alleged to lack capacity to make a decision or decisions in relation to any matter that is the subject of an application to the court and references to a person who lacks capacity are to be construed in accordance with the Act;
'protected party' means a party or an intended party (other than P or a child) who lacks capacity to conduct the proceedings;
'the Regulations' means the Lasting Powers of Attorney, Enduring Powers of Attorney and Public Guardian Regulations 2007; and
'the Rules' means the Court of Protection Rules 2007.

Schedule of fees
3   The fees set out in Schedule 1 to this Order shall apply in accordance with the following provisions of this Order.

Application fee
4 (1) An application fee shall be payable by the applicant on making an application under Part 9 of the Rules (how to start proceedings) in accordance with the following provisions of this article.
  (2) Where permission to start proceedings is required under Part 8 of the Rules (permission), the fee prescribed by paragraph (1) shall be payable on making an application for permission.
  (3) The fee prescribed by paragraph (1) shall not be payable where the application is made under–
    (a) rule 67 of the Rules (applications relating to lasting powers of attorney) by–
      (i) the donee of a lasting power of attorney, or
      (ii) a person named in a statement made by the donor of a lasting power of attorney in accordance with paragraph 2(1)(c)(i) of Part 1 of Schedule 1 to the Act,
    and is solely in respect of an objection to the registration of a lasting power of attorney; or
    (b) rule 68 of the Rules (applications relating to enduring powers of attorney) by–
      (i) a donor of an enduring power of attorney,
      (ii) an attorney under an enduring power of attorney, or
      (iii) a person listed in paragraph 6(1) of Part 3 of Schedule 4 to the Act,

---

1   See also appendix G below.

and is solely in respect of an objection to the registration of an enduring power of attorney.
(4) The fee prescribed by paragraph (1) shall not be payable where the application is made by the Public Guardian.
(5) Where a fee has been paid under paragraph (1) it shall be refunded where P dies within five days of the application being filed.

Appeal fee
5 (1) An appeal fee shall be payable by the appellant on the filing of an appellant's notice under Part 20 of the Rules (appeals) in accordance with the following provisions of this article.
(2) The fee prescribed by paragraph (1) shall not be payable where the appeal is–
   (a) brought by the Public Guardian; or
   (b) an appeal against a decision of a nominated officer made under rule 197 of the Rules (appeal against a decision of a nominated officer).
(3) The fee prescribed by paragraph (1) shall be refunded where P dies within five days of the appellant's notice being filed.

Hearing fees
6 (1) A hearing fee shall be payable by the applicant where the court has–
   (a) held a hearing in order to determine the case; and
   (b) made a final order, declaration or decision.
(2) A hearing fee shall be payable by the appellant in relation to an appeal where the court has–
   (a) held a hearing in order to determine the appeal; and
   (b) made a final order, declaration or decision in relation to the appeal.
(3) The fees prescribed by paragraphs (1) and (2) shall not be payable where the hearing is in respect of an application or appeal brought by the Public Guardian.
(4) The fee prescribed by paragraph (2) shall not be payable where the hearing is in respect of an appeal against a decision of a nominated officer made under rule 197 of the Rules (appeal against a decision of a nominated officer).
(5) The fee prescribed by paragraph (1) shall not be payable where the applicant was not required to pay an application fee under Article 4(1) by virtue of Article 4(3).
(6) The fees prescribed by paragraphs (1) and (2) shall be payable by the applicant or appellant as the case may be within 30 days of the date of the invoice for the fee.

Fee for request for copy of court document
7 (1) A fee for a copy of a court document shall be payable by the person requesting the copy of the document.
(2) . . .
(3) The fee prescribed by paragraph (1) shall be payable at the time the request for the copy is made to the court.

Remissions and part remissions
8 Schedule 2 applies for the purpose of ascertaining whether a party is entitled to a remission or part remission of a fee prescribed by this Order.
9 . . .

Transitional provision

10 (1) In this article 'Court of Protection' means the office of the Supreme Court called the Court of Protection which ceases to exist under section 45(6) of the Act.

(2) Where a hearing that takes place on or after 1 October 2007 was listed by the Court of Protection before 1 October 2007, no hearing fee shall be payable under Article 6.

SCHEDULE 1

Article 3

Column 1	Column 2
Application fee (Article 4)	£400.00
Appeal fee (Article 5)	£400.00
Hearing fees (Article 6)	£500.00
Copy of a document fee (Article 7(1))	£5.00
...	...

SCHEDULE 2: REMISSIONS AND PART REMISSIONS

Interpretation

1 (1) In this Schedule–
'child' means a person–
   (a) whose main residence is with a party and who is aged–
      (i) under 16 years; or
      (ii) 16 to 19 years; and is–
         (aa) not married or in a civil partnership; and
         (bb) enrolled or accepted in full-time education that is not advanced education, or approved training; or
   (b) in respect of whom a party or their partner pays child support maintenance or periodic payments in accordance with a maintenance agreement,
and 'full-time education', 'advanced education' and 'approved training' have the meaning given by the Child Benefit (General) Regulations 2006;
'child support maintenance' has the meaning given in section 3(6) of the Child Support Act 1991;
'couple' has the meaning given in section 3(5A) of the Tax Credits Act 2002;
'disposable capital' has the meaning given in paragraph 5;
'excluded benefits' means any of the following–
   (a) any of the following benefits payable under the Social Security Contributions and Benefits Act 1992 or the corresponding provisions of the Social Security Contributions and Benefits (Northern Ireland) Act 1992–
      (i) attendance allowance under section 64;
      (ii) severe disablement allowance;
      (iii) carer's allowance;
      (iv) disability living allowance;
      (v) constant attendance allowance under section 104 as an increase to a disablement pension;
      (vi) any payment made out of the social fund;

(vii) housing benefit;
(viii) widowed parents allowance;
(b) any of the following benefit payable under the Tax Credits Act 2002–
  (i) any disabled child element or severely disabled child element of the child tax credit;
  (ii) any childcare element of the working tax credit;
(c) any direct payment made under the Community Care, Services for Carers and Children's Services (Direct Payments) (England) Regulations 2009, the Community Care, Services for Carers and Children's Services (Direct Payments) (Wales) Regulations 2011, the Carers and Direct Payments Act (Northern Ireland) 2002, or section 12B(1) of the Social Work (Scotland) Act 1968;
(d) a back to work bonus payable under section 26 of the Jobseekers Act 1995, or article 28 of the Jobseekers (Northern Ireland) Order 1995;
(e) any exceptionally severe disablement allowance paid under the Personal Injuries (Civilians) Scheme 1983;
(f) any payments from the Industrial Injuries Disablement Benefit;
(g) any pension paid under the Naval, Military and Air Forces etc (Disablement and Death) Service Pension Order 2006;
(h) any payment made from the Independent Living Funds;
(i) any payment made from the Bereavement Allowance;
(j) any financial support paid under an agreement for the care of a foster child;
(k) any housing credit element of pension credit;
(l) any armed forces independence payment;
(m) any personal independence payment payable under the Welfare Reform Act 2012;
(n) any payment on account of benefit as defined in the Social Security (Payments on Account of Benefit) Regulations 2013;
(o) any of the following amounts, as defined by the Universal Credit Regulations 2013, that make up an award of universal credit–
  (i) an additional amount to the child element in respect of a disabled child;
  (ii) a housing costs element;
  (iii) a childcare costs element;
  (iv) a carer element;
  (v) a limited capability for work or limited capacity for work and work-related activity element;
'family help (higher)' has the meaning given in paragraph 15(3) of the Civil Legal Aid (Merits Criteria) Regulations 2013;
'family help (lower)' has the meaning given in paragraph 15(2) of the Civil Legal Aid (Merits Criteria) Regulations 2013;
'gross monthly income' has the meaning given in paragraph 13;
'Independent Living Funds' means the funds listed at regulation 20(2)(b) of the Criminal Legal Aid (Financial Resources) Regulations 2013;
'legal representation' has the meaning given in paragraph 18(2) of the Civil Legal Aid (Merits Criteria) Regulations 2013;
'maintenance agreement' has the meaning given in subsection 9(1) of the Child Support Act 1991;

'partner' means a person with whom the party lives as a couple and includes a person with whom the party is not currently living but from whom the party is not living separate and apart;

'party' means the individual who would, but for this Schedule, be liable to pay a fee under this Order;

'restraint order' means–

(a) an order under section 42(1A) of the Senior Courts Act 1981;
(b) an order under section 33 of the Employment Tribunals Act 1996;
(c) a civil restraint order made under rule 3.11 of the Civil Procedure Rules 1998, or a practice direction made under that rule; or
(d) a civil restraint order under rule 4.8 of the Family Procedure Rules 2010, or the practice direction referred to in that rule.

(2) References to remission of a fee are to be read as including references to a part remission of a fee as appropriate and remit and remitted shall be construed accordingly.

Fee remission

2 If a party satisfies the disposable capital test, the amount of any fee remission is calculated by applying the gross monthly income test.

Disposable capital test

Disposable capital test

3 (1) Subject to paragraph 4, a party satisfies the disposable capital test if–
   (a) the fee payable by the party and for which an application for remission is made, falls within a fee band set out in column 1 of Table 1; and
   (b) the party's disposable capital is less than the amount in the corresponding row of column 2.

Table 1	
Column 1 (fee band)	Column 2 (disposable capital)
Up to and including £1,000	£3,000
£1,001 to £1,335	£4,000
£1,336 to £1,665	£5,000
£1,666 to £2,000	£6,000
£2,001 to £2,330	£7,000
£2,331 to £4,000	£8,000
£4,001 to £5,000	£10,000
£5,001 to £6,000	£12,000
£6,001 to £7,000	£14,000
£7,001 or more	£16,000

4 Subject to paragraph 14, if a party or their partner is aged 61 or over, that party satisfies the disposable capital test if that party's disposable capital is less than £16,000.

Disposable capital
5   Subject to paragraph 14, disposable capital is the value of every resource of a capital nature belonging to the party on the date on which the application for remission is made, unless it is treated as income by this Order, or it is disregarded as excluded disposable capital.

Disposable capital–non-money resources
6   The value of a resource of a capital nature that does not consist of money is calculated as the amount which that resource would realise if sold, less–
(a) 10% of the sale value; and
(b) the amount of any borrowing secured against that resource that would be repayable on sale.

Disposable capital–resources held outside the United Kingdom
7 (1) Capital resources in a country outside the United Kingdom count towards disposable capital.
(2) If there is no prohibition in that country against the transfer of a resource into the United Kingdom, the value of that resource is the amount which that resource would realise if sold in that country, in accordance with paragraph 6.
(3) If there is a prohibition in that country against the transfer of a resource into the United Kingdom, the value of that resource is the amount that resource would realise if sold to a buyer in the United Kingdom.

Disposable capital–foreign currency resources
8   Where disposable capital is held in currency other than sterling, the cost of any banking charge or commission that would be payable if that amount were converted into sterling, is deducted from its value.

Disposable capital–jointly owned resources
9   Where any resource of a capital nature is owned jointly or in common, there is a presumption that the resource is owned in equal shares, unless evidence to the contrary is produced.

Excluded disposable capital
10   The following things are excluded disposable capital–
(a) a property which is the main or only dwelling occupied by the party;
(b) the household furniture and effects of the main or only dwelling occupied by the party;
(c) articles of personal clothing;
(d) any vehicle, the sale of which would leave the party, or their partner, without motor transport;
(e) tools and implements of trade, including vehicles used for business purposes;
(f) the capital value of the party's or their partner's business, where the party or their partner is self-employed;
(g) the capital value of any funds or other assets held in trust, where the party or their partner is a beneficiary without entitlement to advances of any trust capital;
(h) a jobseeker's back to work bonus;

(i) a payment made as a result of a determination of unfair dismissal by a court or tribunal, or by way of settlement of a claim for unfair dismissal;
(j) any compensation paid as a result of a determination of medical negligence or in respect of any personal injury by a court, or by way of settlement of a claim for medical negligence or personal injury;
(k) the capital held in any personal or occupational pension scheme;
(l) any cash value payable on surrender of a contract of insurance;
(m) any capital payment made out of the Independent Living Funds;
(n) any bereavement payment;
(o) any capital insurance or endowment lump sum payments that have been paid as a result of illness, disability or death;
(p) any student loan or student grant;
(q) any payments under the criminal injuries compensation scheme.

Gross monthly income test

Remission of fees–gross monthly income

11 (1) If a party satisfies the disposable capital test, no fee is payable under this Order if, at the time when the fee would otherwise be payable, the party or their partner has the number of children specified in column 1 of Table 2 and–
(a) if the party is single, their gross monthly income does not exceed the amount set out in the appropriate row of column 2; or
(b) if the party is one of a couple, the gross monthly income of that couple does not exceed the amount set out in the appropriate row of column 3.

Table 2

Column 1	Column 2	Column 3
Number of children of party	Single	Couple
no children	£1,085	£1,245
1 child	£1,330	£1,490
2 children	£1,575	£1,735

(2) If a party or their partner has more than 2 children, the relevant amount of gross monthly income is the appropriate amount specified in Table 2 for 2 children, plus the sum of £245 for each additional child.
(3) For every £10 of gross monthly income received above the appropriate amount in Table 2, including any additional amount added under sub-paragraph (2), the party must pay £5 towards the fee payable, up to the maximum amount of the fee payable.
(4) This paragraph is subject to paragraph 12.

Gross monthly income cap

12 (1) No remission is available if a party or their partner has the number of children specified in column 1 of Table 3 and–
(a) if the party is single, their gross monthly income exceeds the amount set out in the appropriate row of column 2 of Table 3; or
(b) if the party is one of a couple, the gross monthly income of that couple exceeds the amount set out in the appropriate row of column 3 of Table 3.

Table 3

Column 1	Column 2	Column 3
Number of children of party	Single	Couple
no children	£5,085	£5,245
1 child	£5,330	£5,490
2 children	£5,575	£5,735

(2) If a party or their partner has more than 2 children, the relevant amount of gross monthly income is the appropriate amount specified in Table 3 for 2 children, plus the sum of £245 for each additional child.

Gross monthly income

13 (1) Subject to paragraph 14, gross monthly income means the total monthly income, for the month preceding that in which the application for remission is made, from all sources, other than receipt of any of the excluded benefits.

(2) Income from a trade, business or gainful occupation other than an occupation at a wage or salary is calculated as–
(a) the profits which have accrued or will accrue to the party; and
(b) the drawings of the party;
in the month preceding that in which the application for remission is made.

(3) In calculating profits under sub-paragraph (2)(a), all sums necessarily expended to earn those profits are deducted.

General

Resources and income treated as the party's resources and income

14 (1) Subject to sub-paragraphs (2) to (5), the disposable capital and gross monthly income of a partner is to be treated as disposable capital and gross monthly income of the party.

(2) Where the partner of the party has a contrary interest to the party in the matter to which the fee relates, the disposable capital and gross monthly income of that partner is not treated as the disposable capital and gross monthly income of the party.

(3) Where proceedings are brought concerning the property and affairs of 'P', for the purpose of determining whether a party is entitled to a remission or part remission of a fee in accordance with this Schedule–
(a) the disposable capital and gross monthly income of the person bringing those proceedings is not treated as the disposable capital and gross monthly income of the party;
(b) the disposable capital and gross monthly income of 'P' is to be treated as the disposable capital of the party; and
(c) the disposable capital and gross monthly income of the partner of 'P', if any, is not treated as the disposable capital and gross monthly income of the party.

(4) Where proceedings are brought concerning the personal welfare of 'P', for the purpose of determining whether a party is entitled to a remission or part remission of a fee in accordance with this Schedule, the disposable capital and gross monthly income of a partner, if any, is not treated as the disposable

capital and gross monthly income of the party, where that partner is 'P' who is the subject of those proceedings in which the fee is payable.
(5) Where proceedings concern both the property and affairs of 'P' and their personal welfare, their disposable capital and gross monthly income shall be treated in accordance with sub-paragraph (3).

Application for remission of a fee
15 (1) An application for remission of a fee must be made at the time when the fee would otherwise be payable.
(2) Where an application for remission of a fee is made, the party must–
   (a) indicate the fee to which the application relates;
   (b) declare the amount of their disposable capital; and
   (c) provide documentary evidence of their gross monthly income and the number of children relevant for the purposes of paragraphs 11 and 12.
(3) Where an application for remission of a fee is made on or before the date on which a fee is payable, the date for payment of the fee is disapplied.
(4) Where an application for remission is refused, or if part remission of a fee is granted, the amount of the fee which remains unremitted must be paid within the period notified in writing to the party.

Remission in exceptional circumstances
16 A fee specified in this Order may be remitted where the Lord Chancellor is satisfied that there are exceptional circumstances which justify doing so.

Refunds
17 (1) Subject to sub-paragraph (3), where a party pays a fee at a time when that party would have been entitled to a remission if they had provided the documentary evidence required by paragraph 15, the fee, or the amount by which the fee would have been reduced as the case may be, must be refunded if documentary evidence relating to the time when the fee became payable is provided at a later date.
(2) Subject to sub-paragraph (3), where a fee has been paid at a time when the Lord Chancellor, if all the circumstances had been known, would have remitted the fee under paragraph 15, the fee or the amount by which the fee would have been reduced, as the case may be, must be refunded to the party.
(3) No refund shall be made under this paragraph unless the party who paid the fee applies within 3 months of the date of the order of the court which finally disposed of the proceedings.
(4) The Lord Chancellor may extend the period of 3 months mentioned in sub-paragraph (3) if the Lord Chancellor considers that there is a good reason for a refund being made after the end of the period of 3 months.

Legal aid
18 A party is not entitled to a fee remission if, under Part 1 of the Legal Aid, Sentencing and Punishment of Offenders Act 2012, they are in receipt of the following civil legal services–
   (a) Legal representation; or
   (b) Family help (higher); or
   (c) Family help (lower) in respect of applying for a consent order.

Vexatious litigants

19 (1) This paragraph applies where–
  (a) a restraint order is in force against a party; and
  (b) that party makes an application for permission to–
    (i) issue proceedings or take a step in proceedings as required by the restraint order;
    (ii) apply for amendment or discharge of the order; or
    (iii) appeal the order.
(2) The fee prescribed by this Order for the application is payable in full.
(3) If the party is granted permission, they are to be refunded the difference between–
  (a) the fee paid; and
  (b) the fee that would have been payable if this Schedule had been applied without reference to this paragraph.

Exceptions

20 No remissions or refunds are available in respect of the fee payable for–
  (a) copy or duplicate documents;
  (b) searches.

APPENDIX C

Civil Procedure Rules costs provisions as applied in the Court of Protection[1]

CPR Rule	Title/Description of Rule	Does it apply?
44.1	Interpretation and application	Yes – but see definitions below in accordance with COPR r155(1): '*authorised court officer*' means any officer of the Senior Courts Costs Office whom the Lord Chancellor has authorised to assess costs '*costs*' include fees, charges, disbursements, expenses, remuneration and any reimbursement allowed to a litigant in person '*costs judge*' means a taxing Master of the Senior Courts '*costs officer*' means a costs judge or an authorised court officer '*detailed assessment*' means the procedure by which the amount of costs or remuneration is decided by a costs officer in accordance with Part 47 of the Civil Procedure Rules 1998 (which are applied to proceedings under these Rules, with modifications, by rule 160) '*fixed costs*' are to be construed in accordance with the relevant practice direction

(continued)

---

[1] We are grateful to Hilary O'Keefe, pupil barrister at Doughty Street Chambers, for her work in compiling this table.

CPR Rule	Title/Description of Rule	Does it apply?
		'fund' includes any estate or property held for the benefit of any person or class of persons, and any fund to which a trustee or personal representative is entitled in that capacity
		'paying party' means a party liable to pay costs
		'pro bono representation' means representation provided free of charge
		'receiving party' means a party entitled to be paid costs
		'summary assessment' means the procedure by which the court, when making an order about costs, orders payment of a sum of money instead of fixed costs or detailed assessment.
44.2(1)	Court's discretion as to costs	No
44.2(2)	If the court decides to make an order about costs	No
44.2(3)	Circs where the general rule does not apply	No
44.2(4)	Circs that court will have regard to in deciding what order (if any) to make about costs	No
44.2(5)	Conduct of the parties	No
44.2(6)	Types of orders that are included in the orders which the court may make under this rule	Yes – however the definition of 'costs' in COPR r155(1) applies (see definition above).
44.2(7)	Court will consider whether it is practicable to make an order under paragraph 6	Yes
44.2(8)	Where the court orders a party to pay costs subject to detailed assessment, it will order that party to pay a reasonable sum on account of costs, unless there is a good reason not to do so	Yes – however the definitions of 'costs' and 'detailed assessment' in COPR r155(1) applies (see definition above).

Civil Procedure Rules costs provisions as applied in the Court of Protection

CPR Rule	Title/Description of Rule	Does it apply?
44.3	Basis of assessment	Yes – however the definitions of 'costs', 'detailed assessment', 'summary assessment' and 'paying party' in COPR r155(1) apply
44.4	Factors to be taken into account in deciding the amount of costs	Yes – however the definitions of 'costs' and 'receiving party' in COPR r155(1) apply.
44.5	Amount of costs where costs are payable under a contract	No – and note that COPR r155(2) has specific provision in relation to costs payable under a contract which does not include the presumption in CPR r44.5
44.6	Procedure for assessing costs	No
44.7	Time for complying with an order for costs	Yes – however the definition of 'costs' in COPR r155(1) applies.
44.8	Legal representative's duty to notify the party	Yes
44.9	Cases where costs orders deemed to have been made	No
44.10	Where the court makes no order for costs	Yes – however the definition of 'costs' in COPR r155(1) applies.
44.11	Court's powers in relation to misconduct	Yes – however the definitions of 'summary assessment' and 'detailed assessment' in COPR r155(1) apply.
44.12	Set off	Yes – however the definition of 'costs' in COPR r155(1) applies.
44.13	Qualified one-way costs shifting: scope and interpretation	No
44.14	Effect of qualified one-way costs shifting	No
44.15	Exceptions to qualified one-way costs shifting where permission not required	No
44.16	Exceptions to qualified one-way costs shifting where permission required	No
44.17	Transitional provision	No

CPR Rule	Title/Description of Rule	Does it apply?
44.18	Award of costs where there is a damages based agreement	No
Part 45	Fixed Costs	No – none of this part applies
Part 46	Costs special cases	
46.1(1)	Pre-commencement disclosure and orders for disclosure against a person who is not a party – This part applies but the following wording is substituted; *'This paragraph applies where a person applies for an order for specific disclosure before the commencement of proceedings'*	Yes – with substituted wording
46.2	Costs order in favour of or against non-parties	No
46.3	Limitations on court's power to award costs in favour of trustee or personal representative	Yes – however the definition of 'costs' in COPR r155(1) applies.
46.4	Costs where money is payable by or to a child or protected party	Yes – however the definition of 'costs', and 'detailed assessment' in COPR r155(1) apply Conditional fee agreement means an agreement enforceable under Courts and Legal Services Act 1990 s58 (COPR r155(4))
46.5	Litigants in person	No
46.6	Costs where the court has made a group litigation order	Yes, however the definition of 'costs' in COPR r155(1) applies.
46.7	Orders in respect of pro-bono representation	Yes – however the definitions of 'costs', 'pro bono representation', 'fixed costs', 'detailed assessment', 'paying party' and 'receiving party' in COPR r155(1) apply.

CPR Rule	Title/Description of Rule	Does it apply?
46.8	Personal liability of legal representative for costs – wasted costs orders	Yes – however the definitions of 'costs' and 'costs judge' in COPR r155(1) apply.
46.9	Basis of detailed assessment of solicitor and client costs	Yes – however the definitions of 'costs', 'detailed assessment' and 'conditional fee agreement' in COPR r155(1) apply. Conditional fee agreement means an agreement enforceable under Courts and Legal Services Act 1990 s58 (COPR r155(4))
46.10	Assessment procedure	No
46.11	Costs on the small claims track and fast track	No
46.12	Limitation on amount court may allow where a claim allocated to the fast track settles before trial	No
46.13	Costs following allocation, re-allocation and non-allocation	No
46.14	Costs-only proceedings	No
46.15	Claims for Judicial Review: costs against interveners	Yes – however the definition of 'costs' in COPR r155(1) applies.
Part 47		
47.1	Time when detailed assessment may be carried out	Yes – however the definition of 'costs' and 'detailed assessment' in COPR r155(1) apply.
47.2	No stay of detailed assessment where there is an appeal	Yes – however the definition of 'detailed assessment' in COPR r155(1) applies.
47.3(1)	Powers of an authorised court officer – this section applies but in 47.3(1) (c), the words *'unless the costs are being assessed under rule 64.4 (costs where money is payable to a child or protected party)'* are omitted	Yes, but see note regarding CPR. 47.3(1) (c) The definitions of 'authorised court officer' and 'detailed assessment' in COPR r155(1) apply.

CPR Rule	Title/Description of Rule	Does it apply?
47.3 (2)	Where a party objects to the detailed assessment of costs being made by an authorised court officer, the court may order it to be made by a costs judge or a district judge.	Yes – but the words *'or a district judge'* in 47.3(2) are omitted The definitions of 'authorised court officer' and 'costs judge' in COPR r155(1) apply.
47.4(1)	Venue for detailed assessment proceedings – all applications and requests in detailed assessment proceedings must be made to or filed at the appropriate office	Yes – however the definition of 'detailed assessment' in COPR r155(1) applies.
47.4(2)	The court may direct that the appropriate office is to be the Costs Office	Yes
47.4(3)	In the County Court, a court may direct that another County Court hearing centre is to be the appropriate office	No
47.4(4)	A direction under paragraph (3) may be made without proceedings being transferred to that court	No
47.5	This section of Part 47 applies where a cost officer is to make a detailed assessment of –	Yes – also to a detailed assessment of the remuneration of a deputy
	(a) costs which are payable by one party to another; or	The definitions of 'detailed assessment' and 'costs' in COPR r155(1) apply.
	(b) the sum which is payable by one party to the prescribed charity pursuant to an order under section 194(3) of the 2007 Act	

Civil Procedure Rules costs provisions as applied in the Court of Protection 811

CPR Rule	Title/Description of Rule	Does it apply?
47.6	Commencement of detailed assessment proceedings	Yes – also to a detailed assessment of the remuneration of a deputy
		The definitions of 'detailed assessment', 'paying party', 'receiving party' and 'costs' in COPR r155(1) apply
47.7	Period for commencing detailed assessment proceedings	Yes – also to a detailed assessment of the remuneration of a deputy
		The definition of 'detailed assessment' in COPR r155(1) applies.
47.8	Sanction for delay in bringing detailed assessment proceedings	Yes – also to a detailed assessment of the remuneration of a deputy
		The definitions of 'receiving party', 'detailed assessment', 'paying party' and 'costs' in COPR r155(1) apply.
47.9	Points of dispute and consequences of not serving;

(1) The paying party and any other party to the detailed assessment proceedings may dispute any item in the bill of costs by serving points of dispute on –

(a) the receiving party; and

(b) every other party to the detailed assessment proceedings.

(2) The period for serving points of dispute is 21 days after the date of service of the notice of commencement. | Yes – also to a detailed assessment of the remuneration of a deputy. Paragraph 47.9(4) does not apply where the cost is coming out of P's estate

The definitions of 'paying party', 'detailed assessment' and 'receiving party' in COPR r155(1) apply. |

CPR Rule	Title/Description of Rule	Does it apply?
	(3) If a party serves points of dispute after the period set out in paragraph (2), that party may not be heard further in the detailed assessment proceedings unless the court gives permission.	
	(Practice Direction 47 sets out requirements about the form of points of dispute.)	
	(4) The receiving party may file a request for a default costs certificate if –	
	(a) the period set out in paragraph (2) for serving points of dispute has expired; and	
	(b) the receiving party has not been served with any points of dispute.	
	(5) If any party (including the paying party) serves points of dispute before the issue of a default costs certificate the court may not issue the default costs certificate.	
	(Section IV of this Part sets out the procedure to be followed after points of dispute have been served.)	
47.10	Procedure where costs are agreed	Yes – to a detailed assessment of the remuneration of a deputy also – but not when the costs are to be paid out of P's estate
		The definitions of 'paying party' 'receiving party' and 'costs' in COPR r155(1) apply

Civil Procedure Rules costs provisions as applied in the Court of Protection 813

CPR Rule	Title/Description of Rule	Does it apply?
47.11	Default costs certificate	Yes – also to a detailed assessment of the remuneration of a deputy but not when the costs are to be paid out of P's estate
		The definitions of 'receiving party', and 'detailed assessment' in COPR r155(1) apply.
47.12	Setting aside a costs default certificate	Yes – also to a detailed assessment of the remuneration of a deputy
		The definitions of 'receiving party', and 'detailed assessment' in COPR r155(1) apply.
47.13	Optional reply when party to detailed assessments proceedings	Yes – also to a detailed assessment of the remuneration of a deputy
		The definitions of 'receiving party', and 'detailed assessment' in COPR r155(1) apply.
47.14	Detailed assessment hearing	Yes – also to a detailed assessment of the remuneration of a deputy
		The definitions of 'receiving party', and 'detailed assessment', 'paying party' and 'costs' in COPR r155(1) apply.
47.15	Provisional assessment	Yes – to a detailed assessment of the remuneration of a deputy
		The definitions of 'detailed assessment' and 'receiving party' in COPR r155(1) apply
47.16	Power to issue interim certificate	Yes – also to a detailed assessment of the remuneration of a deputy
		The definitions of 'receiving party', 'costs' and 'detailed assessment' in COPR r155(1) apply.
47.17	Final costs certificate	Yes – also to a detailed assessment of the remuneration of a deputy
		The definitions of 'receiving party', 'costs' and 'detailed assessment' in COPR r155(1) apply.

CPR Rule	Title/Description of Rule	Does it apply?
47.18	Detailed assessment procedure where costs are payable out of the Community Legal Services Fund or by the Lord Chancellor under Part I of the Legal Aid, Sentencing and Punishment of Offenders Act 2012	Yes – however the definitions of 'costs' and 'detailed assessment' in COPR r155(1) apply
47.19	Detailed assessment procedure where costs are payable out of a fund other than the Community Legal Service fund	Yes – however the definitions of 'costs', 'fund', 'detailed assessment' and 'receiving party' in COPR r155(1) apply.
47.20	Liability for costs of detailed assessment proceedings	Yes – however the definitions of 'receiving party', 'detailed assessment', 'pro bono representation', 'costs' and 'paying party' in COPR r155(1) apply
47.21	Right to appeal	Yes, however the definitions of 'detailed assessment', and 'authorised court officer' in COPR r155(1) apply
47.22	Court to hear appeal	Yes – however the definitions of 'authorised court officer' and 'costs judge' in COPR r155(1) apply.
47.23	Appeal procedure	Yes – however the definition of 'detailed assessment' in COPR r155(1) applies
47.24	Powers of the court on appeal	Yes – however the definition of 'authorised court officer' in COPR r155(1) applies.

APPENDIX D

Statements and letters

1 Pre-issue letter   816
2 Position statement   819
3 Witness statement   822
4 Letter of instruction to expert   825
5 Letter of instruction for testamentary capacity assessment from GP   839

1 Pre-issue letter

To: Mrs Jane Smith
[Address]

Legal Services
Any County Council
2 December 2016

Dear Mrs Smith,

Court of Protection – pre-issue letter

Your husband John Smith

I am writing to you about the capacity and best interests of your husband John Smith.

Any County Council has serious concerns about your husband's welfare, and is considering whether an application to the Court of Protection may be necessary. This letter is written as part of what is known as the 'Pre-Issue Stage' in the Court of Protection.

The aim of writing to you is to:
- make sure that you are aware of our intention to start proceedings in the Court of Protection;
- make you aware of the issues that we may ask the Court of Protection to decide, and
- explain to you our proposals as to how we think we could resolve these issues without going to court.

This letter is therefore very important and you should read it carefully. You may wish to take legal advice about the contents.

What is the Court of Protection?

The Court of Protection is part of Her Majesty's Courts and Tribunals Service. Its job is to make decisions in the best interests of those who cannot make the decisions themselves. The Court of Protection sits at Any County Court, High Street, Anytown. You can find out more about the Court of Protection by visiting this website: www.gov.uk/courts-tribunals/court-of-protection.

If we do bring a case in the Court of Protection you will be one of the parties to the case. This means that you will have the right to question witnesses and address the judge, either by yourself or with the help of a lawyer. The court may arrange independent representation for John.

Why are we considering applying to the court?

We are considering making an application to the court because we have not been able to resolve with you important questions about your husband John's welfare.

As you are aware Sarah Kavanagh, John's care manager and a social worker of this council has had several meetings with you to talk about how we can work with you to improve John's care.

At the last meeting with you she discussed the following concerns:

- John appears to have lost a lot of weight since returning to live with you after his injury;
- John often appears disheveled;
- We know that John can become quite challenging when he is confused or upset. Sarah has noticed that you have had several bruises on your face which you have been reluctant to discuss. Sarah is concerned that John may have inadvertently injured you.
- We believe that John needs further help with communication. We have referred John to a speech and language therapist and offered assistance with transport to take him to the appointment. You were unwilling to take him there, telling Sarah that he does not need to see any more doctors.
- John has also missed appointments with the neuro-psychiatrist Dr French who has been overseeing John's rehabilitation.
- John very rarely leaves the house. Sarah as suggested that a day centre would give John a change of scene and provide a break for you. You have refused to consider this.
- Sarah has suggested that it might be a good idea for John to be admitted to a rehabilitation unit as both she and Dr French think this may help him make further improvements. You became very upset at this suggestion and insisted on her leaving the house.
- You have refused to allow John's carers to attend to him and told the care agency that you were sacking them.
- You have been unwilling for Yasmin Rashid, John's Care Act advocate, to see him recently.

We are therefore concerned that it may not be in John's best interests to live with you. We think you are finding it very difficult to care for John and this could put you both at risk.

What will we ask the Court of Protection to do?

We will ask the Court to decide:
- Whether John has capacity for the purpose of the Mental Capacity Act 2005 to make decisions about where he should live and what care he should receive;
- If John cannot make these decisions himself we will ask the court to decide whether it is in his best interests to live with you or to move to a rehabilitation unit for a few months.
- If the judge decides it is in John's best interests to move we will ask the judge to direct that we should move him to the rehabilitation unit. We will give the judge and you details as to how we intend to carry this out.

This decision will be taken by a judge of the Court of Protection after receiving evidence from us and from you, if you wish to provide evidence to the court.

How can we resolve the issues without going to the Court of Protection?

We will only bring a case to court as a last resort.

We would like to attempt to resolve these issues by agreement if possible.

We intend to hold a 'best interests meeting' in two weeks time on 14 December 2016. It will take place at our offices at Any County Council, Town Hall, High Street, Anytown at 3.00 pm. You are invited to the meeting. **Please let me know immediately if you cannot attend and we will see if an alternative date can be arranged. However I will need to know within seven days if the meeting has to be re-arranged; otherwise it will go ahead as planned.**

I have invited the following people to attend the meeting:
- Teresa Harlow, who works for a different team at the Council and has not been involved in the case so far, who will chair the meeting;
- Sarah Kavanagh;
- Dr French;
- a representative of the care agency;
- Yasmin Rashid;
- myself or one of my colleagues from the legal department;
- a minute-taker.

Teresa Harlow will send us all an agenda at least two days before the meeting.

Yasmin Rashid would like to visit John before the meeting and she will contact you to arrange a convenient time. I hope you will be willing to arrange this.

If we are not able to reach agreement at the meeting I will write to you and explain what the next steps will be.

Please confirm safe receipt of this letter.

Yours sincerely

Agnes Brown
Senior Solicitor, Adult Social Care.

2 Position statement

IN THE COURT OF PROTECTION   Case No: 1289256

IN THE MATTER OF THE MENTAL CAPACITY ACT 2005

IN THE MATTER OF JOHN SMITH

BETWEEN:

ANY COUNTY COUNCIL

Applicant

and

JOHN SMITH
(P, by his litigation friend, the Official Solicitor)

first Respondent

and

JANE SMITH

second Respondent

POSITION STATEMENT OF ANY COUNTY COUNCIL FOR DIRECTIONS HEARING   2 APRIL 2017

References in square brackets are to the page numbers in the bundle before the court

Essential re-reading:

(i) Pre-issue correspondence [E1–9]
(ii) Minutes of best interests meeting, 14 December 2016 [E10–15]
(iii) Order of District Judge Bloggs 1 March 2014 [B20–4]
(iv) Report of Dr Williams of 1 February 2014 [G1–9]
(v) Witness statement of Ms Cavanagh, Mr Smith's social worker, dated 15 February 2014 [E1–15]

A   Introduction and dramatis personae

1. This position statement is filed on behalf of Any County Council ('the Council') ahead of the directions hearing listed before District Judge Jones on 2 April 2017. These proceedings concern Mr Smith, who is 33 years old. The medical report of Dr Williams of 1 February 2017 [G1–9] concludes that, as a result of an Acquired Brain Injury sustained on 1 December 2015, he does not have capacity to decide where he should live or as to his care arrangements. Dr Williams also considers that Mr Smith lacks the capacity to make decisions as to contact with his wife, Jane Smith (the Second Respondent), with whom Mr Smith is currently residing.

2. The Council has brought proceedings for (1) declarations as to Mr Smith's capacity to make decisions about his residence and care arrangements and as to contact with his wife; and (2) decisions/declarations as to where Mr

Smith should live and receive care, and as future contact with his wife. The proceedings were initiated as a result of concerns as to quality of care being provided to Mr Smith by his wife, detailed in the statement of Ms Cavanagh at [E1–15], which have led the Council to consider that Mr Smith's interests are best served by his moving into a specialist rehabilitation unit in Anytown. These proceedings were initiated as a last resort by the Council, following the failure of a best interests meeting in December 2016: see minutes [E10-15].

3. Permission was granted to the Council to bring these proceedings by order of District Judge Bloggs on 1 March 2017, at which point John Smith, 'P', was joined as a party and – the Official Solicitor having consented – the Official Solicitor appointed to act as his litigation friend. As at 1 March 2017, Mrs Smith did not have legal representation but indicated that she was intending to seek such representation. District Judge Bloggs therefore made no substantive directions at the hearing on 1 March 2017, instead adjourning matters until the first open date after 1 April 2017 to allow Mrs Smith to obtain such representation.

B Issues for this hearing and the Council's position in respect of each

4. At this hearing, the Court will need to consider:

    (1) What, if any, further evidence as to capacity is required in addition to the report of Dr Williams. The Council will say that there is no requirement for any further such evidence. The Council does not understand that either the Official Solicitor or Mrs Smith disagrees.

    (2) What, if any, evidence is required as to Mr Williams' best interests. The Council understands that the Official Solicitor will invite the Court to agree to the instruction of an independent social worker to report upon Mr Williams' best interests as regards his future residence and care arrangements and contact with his wife. Having regard to the complexities of Mr Smith's condition and the importance of the issues under consideration for both Mr and Mrs Smith the Council considers that the test for necessity is met, and, given the breakdown between Mrs Smith and the statutory bodies involved, a report under MCA 2005 s49 is unlikely to command the confidence of all the parties. In principle, therefore, the Council would not object to such an instruction, but would wish it to be on a joint basis as between the Council, Mr and Mrs Smith.

    (3) Further evidence. Mrs Smith has put in a detailed witness statement addressing matters raised by Ms Cavanagh; the Council would wish the chance to file a short supplemental statement responding to certain points in Mrs Smith's statement. The Council suggests that it would be sensible for this to be done prior to the report of any independent social work expert (if such is permitted) as this will allow the expert to have the complete picture before them.

    (4) Further hearings. It is clear from the witness statement of Mrs Smith that she does not substantially dispute the factual matters outlined in the statement of Ms Cavanagh, but rather would invite the court to put a different interpretation upon those matters than those set out in Ms Cavanagh's statement. In the circumstances, the Council would submit that there is no requirement that a separate fact-finding hearing be listed, but rather

that the court can proceed to list a final hearing to determine where Mr Smith's best interests lie. The Council would envisage that it will be necessary for such a hearing to be listed for two days in order to allow sufficient time for the giving of evidence, the making of submissions, and delivery of judgment.

C Directions order

5. A draft directions order is attached.[1]

---

1 See www.courtofprotectiohandbook.com for an example of a directions order.

3 Witness statement

Statement of the:

Statement no:

Signed:

Filed:

IN THE COURT OF PROTECTION   Case No: 000

IN THE MATTER OF THE MENTAL CAPACITY ACT 2005

AND IN THE MATTER OF JOHN SMITH ('P')

BETWEEN:

ANY COUNTY COUNCIL

Applicant

and

JOHN SMITH ('P')
(by [his/her] litigation friend, the Official Solicitor)

1st Respondent

and

JANE SMITH

2nd Respondent

STATEMENT OF JANE SMITH

I Jane Smith, of [   ] make this statement further to the order of District Judge Bloggs on 1 March 2017. I make this statement knowing and believing the contents to be true and in the knowledge it will be placed before the court.

1. I am the wife of John Smith who is the subject to proceedings by Any County Council. I will refer to him as 'John' in the rest of the statement.

2. I make this statement in order to provide information about my background, my relationship with John and my views as to his best interests.

3. The court will be aware that John is 33 years old and was born on [   ].

4. John and I met when we were both at university. We married when John was 23 and had therefore been together for 10 years. We have had a close and happy marriage until the injury sustained by John on 1 December 2015. Until then John worked as a computer programmer. I am a teacher but have been on compassionate leave since John's accident.

5. I would describe John as an energetic person, who threw himself in to his work and sporting activities, especially swimming which he has always loved.

Neither of us socialise very much and following our marriage we very much enjoyed spending time at home together.

6. Over the past five years we have been trying hard to have a baby. Sadly, up until now, I have not succeeded in becoming pregnant. However this period of time gave both of us an opportunity to reflect upon what we considered to be important. Both of us had concluded that being together and being part of a family was the most important thing for us both.

7. In recent years, we have spent much less time socialising with friends, and more time together, thinking about our future and spending time with our respective families, both of whom live near by. We looked forward to a future as a family, bringing up children together.

8. As the court will know, our lives were turned upside down when John was knocked over by a bus in December 2015. He sustained an acquired brain injury, which has led to a very severe impairment in his functioning. He has largely physically recovered from the physical injuries that he suffered. The problem is his complete change in the way in which he is able to manage and process information.

9. When I learnt of John's accident I was absolutely terrified. I went straight to the hospital where he was treated, and the records will show that I spent the next week by his side, at a time when his prognosis was unclear.

10. I agree that I was very keen for John to be discharged home as soon as possible. John is still able to communicate. I feel that he communicates particularly well with those who he knows well and who are prepared to spend time with him. He has made it very clear to me that he wants to return home and as far as possible resume living with me.

11. I have read the statement of Miss Kavanagh, who sets out a number of concerns about my care for John. I will not deny that looking after John since the accident has been an uphill struggle. Although my own mother has dementia and I have helped support her with personal care, I have never had to be a full time carer before. John needs assistance in many areas, not so much with his physical needs but simply being prompted to do things and to keep him safe. Because John is quite mobile, you have to keep an eye on him all the time.

12. I have tried very hard to manage but I confess that in recent weeks I have felt absolutely exhausted. I accept that I became very upset in a recent meeting with Miss Kavanagh, because I felt that the help I was being offered to look after John was completely inadequate. I was basically being offered 14 hours respite a week. This was just not enough to allow me to get basic household chores done, carry out the shopping and have a breather.

13. I am aware that Miss Kavanagh put forward the possibility of John going to a day centre. I have been to the day centre that she recommended. I found it extremely depressing. Most of the people there appeared to have much more severe disabilities than John and I feel he would just be miserable there and would feel that I am trying to get rid of him.

14. I do not believe that John needs to go in to a specialist rehabilitation unit. I believe that the intensive rehabilitation that Miss Kavanagh believes he needs could be provided to him at home.

15. I am aware that the local hospital has a day unit where there is rehabilitation and I would be very happy for John to attend this as a day patient.
16. In the meantime I would be very happy to accept more support in looking after John, if only it could be offered. I believe that I can manage, but not if I only have a few hours a week additional support. I need to be able to carry out basic household tasks, and occasionally to be able to have a bit of a break, in the knowledge that John is safe, and doing something that he enjoys.
17. For example John has always been a keen swimmer. I have asked for an assessment to see if he could go to the local swimming pool with someone to help him and this has never been carried out. I believe that he would find this very satisfying, and I do not believe that it is impossible to put this in to effect.
18. Rather than move John away from home, where he is happy, I would ask that Miss Kavanagh reconsiders the level of support she is prepared to offer to John. I understand that the council is thinking of having a fact finding hearing which I am advised is rather like a trial of the care that I have provided. Instead of going down this route, I would ask that the council considers giving John more support to remain at home. The court could then review the position and see how things have proceeded.
19. I believe this would be fairer both to me and particularly to John to see if I can manage.
20. I have tried to explain to John what is going on, and he was recently visited by the solicitor instructed by the Official Solicitor. She was very sympathetic and John was able to communicate with her to some extent. However after she left when he realised that he might have to move and go somewhere else, he had tears in his eyes. I do not believe it is necessary or reasonable for John to have leave home at this stage unless all alternatives have been tried.
21. Therefore I ask that the Council think again about how they are prepared to support John and me at home.

The contents of this statement are true to the best of my knowledge and belief

Signed: [   ]

Dated: [   ]

Anyfirm LLP
88–90 Wessex Street
London SE1 7EZ
DX DX 124 XDE
Tel: 020 7123 4567
Fax: 020 7123 4568
E-mail: office@anyfirm.com
Ref: 005808.001
Solicitors for Jane Smith

4 Letter of instruction to expert

[Mr/Ms   ]
Social Care Consultant
Anytown
AN1 5IL

Our ref: /005808.001
Your ref:
Date: 21 April 2017

PROTECT: PERSONAL DATA

Dear [Mr/Ms   ]

Re: Any County Council and (1) John Smith (by his litigation friend the Official Solicitor), (2) Jane Smith/Court of Protection number 000

Thank you for agreeing to prepare a report in this case. You are instructed by the parties below as an expert on an application by the Any County Council for declarations in respect of the best interests of Mr Smith. The Official Solicitor was appointed Mr Smith's litigation friend on 1 March 2017.

By virtue of an order on 2 April 2017 the Court has given permission to the parties to instruct you to produce an independent report in these proceedings. You have permission to see all records and documents filed in these proceedings and to examine Mr Smith and read his social work medical and other records.

Your report must be filed and served by 30 May 2017. If you have any difficulties with that timescale please let me know straight away.

The final hearing has not yet been fixed. There will be a directions hearing at the Court of Protection on the first open date after 6 June 2017. I will keep you informed of any further hearings.

I am the lead solicitor in this case to whom you should look for instructions and information.

1. **The parties**
   (a) The applicant is Any County Council. The Council is represented by Mr James Burton, of Any County Council. Town Hall, Anytown. His direct dial is [   ] and his email address is [   ].
   (b) The 1st respondent is Mr Smith. He currently resides at the address above, which is the matrimonial home he shares with Mrs Smith. He is represented by me instructed by the Official Solicitor as litigation friend. My details appear at the top of this letter.
   (c) The 2nd respondent is Mrs Jane Smith. She resides with Mr Smith at the address above. She is represented by Mr Ian Brightspark, of Brightspark Solicitors LLP, High Street, Anytown. His direct dial is [   ] and his email address is [   ].

Mr Smith has an acquired brain injury, subsequent to a road traffic accident on 3 December 2015.

2. **Documents**

    Please see my letter of today's date which lists the documents which you have been sent. I also attach copies of Mr Smith's records from Any County Council's Adult Social Care Team. Copies of his GP records and records from Anytown Hospital will follow.

3. **Family structure**

    Mr John Albert Smith ('P') [DOB   ]
    Parents: James and Elizabeth Smith, 25 The Lane, Anytown
    Siblings: None
    Wife: Jane Smith [DOB   ]
    Parents-in-law: Janet and Bradley Marriott, 34 Fir Avenue, Anytown

4. **Background history**

    You should note that the court has not made any findings of fact in this case. Mr Smith was born on [   ] and is thus 33 years of age. He achieved well at school and attended Any University where he achieved a degree in mathematics. Whilst at University he met Jane Marriott and they married in 2004. Mr and Mrs Smith have lived at their current address since April 2005. Mr Smith is known to have worked as a computer programmer and Mrs Smith is a teacher. Mrs Smith describes them as a couple who did not socialise much but enjoyed spending time together or with their respective families. Mr and Mrs Smith have no children but are believed to have been trying for a baby. Mr Smith was the victim of a road traffic accident on 3 December 2015, following which he sustained a brain injury which has resulted in a significant impairment. He is said to have made a good recovery from his physical injuries. He currently lives with Mrs Smith who is his main carer, with a care package provided by Any County Council; however following concerns about the quality of the care provided by Mrs Smith (set out in the statement of Ms Cavanagh at C1 in the trial bundle) the Council applied for permission to make an application to the Court of Protection.

5. **Summary of the proceedings to date**

    These proceedings were commenced by the local authority who made an application (form COP1) on 10 March 2017. The application appears at page II 1 of the trial bundle. The local authority asked the court to decide the following questions:

    - Does Mr Smith have capacity to make decisions about where he should live?
    - Does Mr Smith have capacity to make decisions about whom he has contact with?
    - Is it in Mr Smith's best interests to reside at the home he shares with Mrs Smith or at a specialist rehabilitation unit?
    - What should the contact arrangements with Mrs Smith be if Mr Smith moves to the rehabilitation unit?

The local authority set out the orders it sought:
- A declaration that Mr Smith lacks capacity to litigate these proceedings, and to make decisions about residence, care and contact with others.
- A declaration that it is in Mr Smith's best interests to move to a specialist rehabilitation unit for care and treatment.
- A declaration that it is in Mr Smith's best interests to have contact with Mrs Smith by agreement between Mrs Smith and the Unit.

District Judge Bloggs granted permission on 1 March 2017. At the same time he joined Mr Smith as a party and appointed the Official Solicitor to act as his litigation friend, the Official Solicitor having consented to act. Mrs Smith had indicated that she intended to instruct solicitors and you will see that she is now represented.

The first attended hearing took place on 2 April 2017. A copy of the order is with your papers at B30 of the trial bundle. You will see that DJ Jones made interim declarations that Mr Smith lacked capacity to litigate these proceedings and that he lacked capacity to make decisions about residence, care and contact with others. A number of case management orders were made, including provision for your instructions at paragraphs 12 and 13.

6. **Diagnosis**

    The report of Dr Williams of 1 February 2016 contains Dr Williams' view that Mr Smith has an acquired brain injury which has led to an impairment in his cognitive function.

7. **References to Mr Smith's capacity**

    Dr Williams' opinion is that Mr Smith lacks capacity to make decisions about his residence, care and contact, and to litigate these proceedings and that there is no prospect of his recovering such capacity.

    At the hearing on 2 April it became clear that all parties now agree that Mr Smith lacks capacity to make the decisions under consideration and it is likely that final declarations to this effect will be made at the next hearing.

8. **Reference to Mr Smith's views**

    Mr Smith has said consistently that he would prefer to live with Mrs Smith. You are referred to the witness statement of Ms Cavanagh at E13, where she describes her interview with Mr Smith and to my attendance note of my visit to Mr Smith, when he became quiet emotional at the prospect of leaving home.

9. **Assessment of capacity**

    Please note that you are not asked to assess Mr Smith's capacity and this section is for your information only.

    The court is being asked to decide whether Mr Smith has capacity to make the following decision(s):

    i) Where he/she should live (and consequential care arrangements).

    ii) Who he/she should see.

iii) Litigation capacity in connection with the above areas.

The Mental Capacity Act 2005 s2(1) provides that a person lacks capacity if, at the time a decision needs to be made, he or she is unable to make or communicate the decision because of an 'impairment of, or a disturbance in the functioning of, the mind or brain'.

The Act contains a two-stage test of capacity:

1. Is there an impairment of or disturbance in the functioning of, the person's mind or brain?
2. If so, is the impairment or disturbance sufficient that the person lacks the capacity to make a decision in relation to the matter in question (i.e. the matters set out above)?

The assessment of capacity must be based on Mr Smith's ability to make a decision in relation to the relevant matter, and not their ability to make decision in general. It does not matter therefore if the lack of capacity is temporary, or the person retains the capacity to make other decisions, or if the person's capacity fluctuates.

Section 3(1) of the Act provides that a person is regarded as being unable to make a decision if he or she cannot:

- understand information about the decision to be made;
- retain that information;
- use or weigh the information as part of the decision-making process: or
- communicate the decision (by any means).

A lack of capacity cannot be established merely because of a person's age or appearance or his condition or an aspect of his behaviour. Similarly a person is not be treated as being unable to make a decision merely because he or she has made an unwise decision.

Practitioners are required to have regard to the statutory principles set out in section 1 of the Mental Capacity Act 2005 and the Code of Practice when assessing capacity and making decisions on behalf of a person who lacks capacity.

The statutory principles provide that:

s1 (2) A person must be assumed to have capacity unless it is established that he lacks capacity.
   (3) A person is not be treated as unable to make a decision unless all practicable steps to help him to do so have been taken without success.
   (4) A person is not to be treated as unable to make a decision merely because he makes an unwise decision'
   (5) An act done, or decision made, under this Act for or on behalf of a person who lacks capacity must be done, or make , in his best interests
   (6) Before the act is done, or the decision is made, regard must be had to whether the purpose for which it is needed can be as effectively achieved in a way that is less restrictive of the person's rights and freedom of action.

The Code of Practice is available on line at www.publicguardian.gov.uk. [Hard copies are available from The Stationery Office]. A booklet entitled *Making Decisions: a guide for people who work in health and social care* is also available online at www.justice.gov.uk/downloads/protecting-the-vulnerable/mca/opg-603-0409.pdf

Litigation capacity

Paragraph 4.33 of the Code states that the MCA's new definition of capacity is in line with, and does not replace the existing common law tests (including that for capacity to conduct proceedings, i.e. 'litigation capacity'). The common law authorities on capacity to litigate continue to provide a helpful guide when applying the test in sections 2 and 3 in the context of litigation capacity.

The common law approach to litigation capacity has been considered and developed in a number of cases. The leading case is *Masterman-Lister v Brutton & Co* [2003] 3 All ER 162 in which Lord Justice Chadwick stated the following:

> ... *the test to be applied ... is whether the party to legal proceedings is capable of understanding, with the assistance of such proper explanation from legal advisors and experts in other disciplines as the case may require, the issues on which his consent or decision is likely to be necessary in the course of those proceedings. If he has capacity to understand that which he needs to understand in order to pursue or defend a claim, I can see no reason why the law whether substantive or procedure should require the imposition of a next friend or guardian ad litem (or, as such person is now described in the Civil Procedure Rules, a litigation friend ...* (para 75)

> ... *a person should not be held unable to understand the information relevant to a decision if he can understand an explanation of that information in broad terms and simple language; and that he should not be regarded as unable to make a rational decision merely because the decision which he does in fact make is a decision which would not be made by a person of ordinary prudence.* (para 79)

In the same case Lord Justice Kennedy commented as follows (at para 26):

> ... *the mental abilities required include the ability to recognise a problem, obtain and receive, understand and retain relevant information, including advice; the ability to weigh the information (including that derived from advice) in the balance in reaching a decision, and the ability to communicate that decision ...*

He further observed at paragraph 27:

> ... *What, however does seem to me to be of some importance is the issue-specific nature of the test; that is to say the requirement to consider the question of capacity in relation to the particular transaction (its nature and complexity) in respect of which the decisions as to capacity fall to be made ... Of course as Boreham J said in White's case, capacity must be approached in a common sense way, not by reference to each step in the process of litigation, but bearing in mind the basic right of any person to manage his property and*

affairs for himself, a right with which no lawyer and no court should rush to interfere.

The Court of Appeal re-considered the *Masterman-Lister* test in *Bailey v Warren* [2006] EWCA Civ 51. At paragraph 126 of her judgment Lady Justice Arden set out the matters to be considered when assessing a person's capacity to conduct proceedings:

> ... *The assessment of capacity to conduct proceedings depends to some extent on the nature of the proceedings in contemplation. I can only indicate some of the matters to be considered in accessing a client's capacity. The client would need to understand how the proceedings were to be funded. He would need to know about the chances of not succeeding and about the risk of an adverse order as to costs. He would need to have capacity to make the sort of decisions that arise in litigation. Capacity to conduct such proceedings would include the capacity to give proper instructions for and to approve the particulars of claim, and to approve a compromise. For a client to have capacity to approve a compromise, he would need insight into the compromise, an ability to instruct his solicitors to advise him on it, and an understanding of their advice and an ability to weigh their advice ...*

In the case of *The NHS Trust v Ms T* [2004] EWHC 2195 (Fam) Mrs Justice Bracewell when considering the issue of litigation capacity stated the following:

> ... *There is no problem in this case in respect of Miss T's intellectual capacity. She is able to instruct solicitors, articulating well and with an approach which demonstrates that she knows there is a problem. But her difficulties arise in relation to processing information in order to give meaningful instructions to legal advisers. .... her wishes as expressed to her legal advisers are solely driven by a desire to kill herself which arises from mental disorder, that disorder involving a delusional belief that the blood within her body is evil ... Intellectually, she is able to acknowledge that that is a delusional belief, but she is driven by that belief by reason of her mental illness, which prevents her from processing information and giving reasoned instructions on the basis of that which she intellectually knows, but cannot understand by reason of her disability ...* (at para 4)

In considering therefore whether or not a person has capacity to conduct the proceedings it is accordingly important to focus on the particular proceedings in relation to which the issues arise, the complexity of that litigation and the issues to be determined.

Mr Justice Munby stated in *Sheffield CC v E & S* [2005] Fam 236, para 34:

> *The capacity to litigate is not something to be determined in the abstract. One has to focus on a particular piece of litigation in relation to which the issue arises. The question is always whether the litigant has capacity to litigate in relation to particular proceedings in which he is involved ... Someone may have the capacity to litigate in a case where the nature of the dispute and the issues are simple, whilst at the same time lacking the capacity to litigate in a case where either the nature of the dispute or the issues are more complex.*

We draw your attention to the further observations of Mrs Justice Bracewell in her judgment in *The NHS Trust v Ms T* referred to above about the relationship between litigation capacity and decision making capacity where she said at paragraph 2:

> *... capacity to litigate ... is a separate issue from capacity to make decisions about medical treatment, although in many cases ... if there is no capacity to litigate, then by reason of the underlying matrix of factual evidence it would follow that there is no capacity to make decisions about treatment.*

At paragraph 5 of the same judgment she added:

> *... although in some circumstances there may be a different answer to the question of capacity to litigate and capacity to make decisions about medical treatment, this is one of those cases in which the evidence is overwhelming that she lacks capacity to make medical treatment decisions, and it follows that a person who has a very unshakeable delusional belief about the very subject matter of the litigation cannot possess the ability to understand, retain, assimilate or act upon advice received as to the conduct of the litigation ...*

In the case of *Sheffield City Council v (1) E (2) S* [2004] EWHC 2808 (Fam) Mr Justice Munby, having considered the judgment of Mrs Justice Bracewell referred to above, went on to observe:

> *There is no principle either of law or of medical science, which necessarily makes it impossible for someone who has litigation capacity at the same time to lack subject-matter capacity. That said, however, it is much more difficult to imagine a case where someone has litigation capacity whilst lacking subject-matter capacity than it is to imagine a case where someone has subject-matter capacity whilst lacking litigation capacity ... I suspect that cases where someone has litigation capacity whilst lacking subject-matter capacity are likely to be very much more infrequent, indeed pretty rare. Indeed, I would go so far as to say that only in unusual circumstances will it be possible to conclude that someone who lacks subject-matter capacity can nonetheless have litigation capacity ...*

The following factors/questions therefore appear relevant when conducting an assessment of litigation capacity:

(i) The test is contained in sections 2 and 3 of the MCA 2005 but informed by the common law approach to litigation capacity set out in the above cases;

(ii) There is a presumption of capacity to litigate which can only be rebutted by clear evidence to the contrary;

(iii) Capacity to litigate is an issue-specific test so that a person may have capacity to conduct some litigation but not other litigation. Equally a person may have capacity to litigate but not have capacity to deal with (say) the administration of an award of damages;

(iv) The complexity of the particular litigation and the issues to be determined are significant;

(v) All practicable steps must have been taken to help Mr Smith conduct the proceedings without success; it follows that you need to consider the assistance and help that has been given to Mr Smith so far in the litigation and whether there are further practicable steps that could be taken;

(vi) Mr Smith must not be treated as unable to litigate merely because he makes unwise decisions;

(vii) A person can have a temporary lack of capacity and a person's capacity can fluctuate.

The diagnostic test

(1) The question is whether Mr Smith is suffering from an impairment of or disturbance in the functioning of the mind or brain which makes him unable to conduct the litigation.

The functional test

The questions are:

(2) Whether Mr Smith is unable to understand with the assistance of proper explanation and assistance, the issues on which his consent or decision is likely to be necessary during the course of the proceedings? Relevant matters to be understood include the nature of the decision/consent, the reason why the decision/consent is needed and the likely consequences of deciding one way or the other or failing to make a decision.

(3) Whether Mr Smith is unable to understand the issues in the proceedings? It is important to note that a person may have the intellectual capability to instruct solicitors or to act in person, but difficulties in relation to the processing of information may prevent the giving of meaningful or reasoned instructions (which was caused by a delusional belief in the *Ms T* case) or arriving at a meaningful or reasoned decision.

(4) Whether Mr Smith is unable to retain information and advice given to him during the course of these proceedings?

(5) Whether Mr Smith is unable to use or weigh the information in the balance as part of the process of making the decision? The Code notes that a person can understand information but an impairment or disturbance may stop them from using it (para 4.22);

(6) Whether Mr Smith is unable to communicate with any advisors, with the legal representatives or with the court? It is only if a person cannot communicate in any way at all that he or she should be treated as unable to make a decision through inability to communicate (see Code at para 4.23).

10. **Assessment of best interests**

The issue of capacity to make the relevant decision should be determined first. Only if the person is found not to have decision-making capacity will it be necessary to address the best interests issues.

The court is being asked to make a decision in Mr Smith's best interests. You are asked to advise the court and (the parties) on what is in Mr Smith's best interests given the circumstances outlined in this letter, in the documents accompanying this letter and from your own observations.

The term 'best interests' is not defined by the Act. MCA 2005 s4 however provides a statutory checklist of matters which should be taken into account and is set out below.

Best interests

4 *(1) In determining for the purposes of this Act what is in a person's best interests, the person making the determination must not make it merely on the basis of—*
   (a) the person's age or appearance, or
   (b) a condition of his, or an aspect of his behaviour, which might lead others to make unjustified assumptions about what might be in his best interests.
(2) The person making the determination must consider all the relevant circumstances and, in particular, take the following steps.
(3) He must consider—
   (a) whether it is likely that the person will at some time have capacity in relation to the matter in question, and
   (b) if it appears likely that he will, when that is likely to be.
(4) He must, so far as reasonably practicable, permit and encourage the person to participate, or to improve his ability to participate, as fully as possible in any act done for him and any decision affecting him.
(5) Where the determination relates to life-sustaining treatment he must not, in considering whether the treatment is in the best interests of the person concerned, be motivated by a desire to bring about his death.
(6) He must consider, so far as is reasonably ascertainable—
   (a) the person's past and present wishes and feelings (and, in particular, any relevant written statement made by him when he had capacity),
   (b) the beliefs and values that would be likely to influence his decision if he had capacity, and
   (c) the other factors that he would be likely to consider if he were able to do so.
(7) He must take into account, if it is practicable and appropriate to consult them, the views of—
   (a) anyone named by the person as someone to be consulted on the matter in question or on matters of that kind,
   (b) anyone engaged in caring for the person or interested in his welfare,
   (c) any donee of a lasting power of attorney granted by the person, and
   (d) any deputy appointed for the person by the court,
   as to what would be in the person's best interests and, in particular, as to the matters mentioned in subsection (6).
(8) The duties imposed by subsections (1) to (7) also apply in relation to the exercise of any powers which—
   (a) are exercisable under a lasting power of attorney, or
   (b) are exercisable by a person under this Act where he reasonably believes that another person lacks capacity.
(9) In the case of an act done, or a decision made, by a person other than the court, there is sufficient compliance with this section if (having complied with the requirements of subsections (1) to (7)) he reasonably believes that what he does or decides is in the best interests of the person concerned.

(10) 'Life-sustaining treatment' means treatment which in the view of a person providing health care for the person concerned is necessary to sustain life.
(11) 'Relevant circumstances' are those–
   (a) of which the person making the determination is aware, and
   (b) which it would be reasonable to regard as relevant.

Again you are required to have regard to the Principles and provisions of the Act and the Code of Practice when considering and providing your opinion on Mr Smith's best interests (see in particular chapter 5 of the Code).

11. **Your instructions**

I hope the enclosures supply you with all the relevant documents. Please let me know if you need any further information or require clarification on any matters.

Please arrange to see Mr Smith. I am happy to arrange an appointment for you with Mrs Smith if this would assist. You will need to consider his social work and health records. You will need to speak to those responsible for his care. His care manager is Ms Cavanagh who can be contacted via the Council's solicitors.

You will need to meet Mrs Smith and Mr Smith's parents and father-in-law (his mother-in-law herself has dementia and it will not be appropriate for you to interview her). Having regard to section 4(7) in particular you should consider whether there is any other person engaged in caring for Mr Smith or interested in her welfare whom it would be practicable and appropriate for you to consult- for example other family members or social care professionals. If you need assistance in making arrangements to consult any other person please let me know. You should identify in your report all persons whom you have consulted during the course of your assessment.

Please provide a report covering the following areas:

Best interests

Please advise as to Mr Smith's best interests in the following areas.

1. Care

(a) Please set out Mr Smith's care needs. This should include the support needed in the following areas. If you are not able to comment on any of the areas below please say so:
   Mental Health
   Maximising independence
   Daytime activities
   Learning disability
   Physical health
   Cultural

(b) In what kind of setting can the needs you have identified under all the above headings best be met?

2. Residence

(a) What would the benefits be to Mr Smith's physical, mental, psychological, emotional and cultural wellbeing if he remains living with Mrs Smith?

(b) What are the disadvantages to Mr Smith's physical, mental, psychological, emotional and cultural wellbeing if he continues to reside with Mrs Smith.
(c) What would the benefits be to Mr Smith's physical, mental, psychological, emotional and cultural wellbeing if he moves to a specialist rehabilitation unit?
(d) What are the disadvantages to Mr Smith's physical, mental, psychological, emotional and cultural wellbeing if he moves to a specialist rehabilitation unit?
(e) Is it in Mr Smith's best interests to reside with Mrs Smith? If so please advise as to the package of care required to support this.

3. Contact

(a) If it is not in Mr Smith's best interests to live with Mrs Smith, is it in his best interests to have contact with Mrs Smith?
(b) What should the level and frequency of that contact be?
(c) Should there be any restrictions on such contact with Mrs Smith and if so what should these restrictions be?

12. **Role of an expert**

Additional to the documents referred to at (2) above I enclose for your ease of reference Part 15 (Experts) of the Court of Protection Rules 2007 and the supplemental practice direction together with a copy of guidance issued by Mrs Justice Pauffley in December 2010. I draw your attention in particular to rule 122 (paragraph 2 of the practice direction) with regard to the expert's duty to the court and to rule126 (paragraphs 8-11 of the practice direction) with regard to the content of an expert's report, and to paragraphs 8 and 9 of the December 2010 guidance.

13. **Contact with others**

It is essential to both your role as an independent expert and to the parties' perception of your independent status that there are no informal unrecorded discussions or correspondence with anyone involved in the case, particularly when you come to interview others such as the social care staff, etc. If you need further information, please contact me as I am the lead solicitor and I will provide information after consultation with the other solicitors involved. If documents are exchanged with one party, please copy them to all the others. Where possible, communication is best achieved by fax, letter or e-mail copied to all the parties.

Please maintain a careful record of all discussions with all persons with whom you discuss this case in the event that it is necessary to refer to them later.

It will be helpful if you would confirm in writing to me who you would like to have contact with, so that all parties are aware that meetings will be taking place in due course.

14. **Proposed timescale and plan of work**

If you require any help from me in arranging meetings or contacting the other solicitors, please let me know. Otherwise I shall assume that you will go ahead, organise visits and meetings, and will make your own arrangements. If at any time there is a delay in your plan and the timescale has to be altered, please inform me promptly so that I may inform the other parties and the court if appropriate

15. **Factual issues and your report**

    You should express your opinion regarding your findings on the facts of the case, but you must not seek to resolve disputed facts, as this is of course the job of the court at the hearing. Where appropriate, it will be of assistance if you are able to express your opinion on the basis of alternative findings regarding the factual disputes. Your report may be subject to challenge by any of the parties. It is likely that one or more of the parties may put written questions to you following receipt of your report.

    I am under a duty to disclose your report to the court and to the other parties and I will circulate your report on receipt. If you believe, as a rare exception to the general rule, that it should not be disclosed to any party, please let me know and I will seek the court's directions.

16. **Trial date**

    The trial date has not yet been fixed. I will ask you closer to the next hearing to let me have details of your availability so that if a trial is fixed it will be on a date convenient to you.

17. **Fees**

    The following terms and conditions apply:

    The fees for your instruction will be shared, in equal shares between the instructing parties. . Some of the parties are in receipt of public funding and your fees will therefore be met through their public funding certificates.

    Ultimately your fees will therefore be assessed by either the court or the Legal Aid Agency (LAA) at the conclusion of the case as to reasonableness in terms of both hourly rate and time spent. The parties' legal representatives cannot be responsible for any fees over and above those finally assessed and paid by the LAA.

    On receipt of your invoice the legal representatives for the publicly funded parties are entitled to, and should promptly make a claim for payment on account of your fees to the LAA. Promptly upon receipt of such payment on account they should make this payment on account to you.

    Such payments on account may, however, be recouped by the LAA at the end of the case following the final assessment of the bill. Such recoupment will only apply to any sum, paid on account, which exceeds the amount finally allowed on assessment by the Court or LAA. If your fees are reduced on assessment we will notify you within 7 days of receiving notification from the Legal Aid Agency or the court. If you wish us to make representations with regard to the reduction then you should notify us within 7 days, and provide us with the text or those representations, or the supporting documentation as the case may be.

In accepting this instruction you therefore agree that if your fees are subsequently reduced by the court or the LAA you will promptly reimburse the difference between the amount paid on account to you, and the amount finally allowed on assessment, to the parties' legal representatives.

Please bear in mind that although we, as the lead solicitors in instructing you, will do our best to assist you in obtaining prompt payment, we can only be responsible for the share of your fees attributable to our client. The other solicitors involved in this instruction to you are responsible likewise only for the share attributable to their client.

It is also important that during the course of your assessment you inform us immediately if you are likely to exceed your costs estimate. All public funding certificates have a cost limitation and we need to make an application to the LAA for any extension of this if it appears that the aggregate of the fees which are to be incurred in this case is likely to exceed the current costs limitation.. If you exceed your fee estimate without prior notification to us your fees may therefore not be met in full.

In addition, there are terms in the 2010 Unified Contract under which the publicly funded legal representatives must operate. In accordance with these if your fees are to exceed £250 you must keep accurate records of all the time spent on the work for which you have been instructed and of the work done. You must also permit the LAA to audit your records if necessary.

There is also certain work for which the LAA will not pay and limits on certain hourly rates.

The LAA will not pay:

(a) Any separate administration fee including, but not limited to, a fee in respect of offices and consultation rooms, administrative support including typing services, subsistence and couriers.
(b) Any cancellation fee where notice of cancellation is given more than 72 hours before the relevant hearing or appointment.
(c) Any travelling costs in relation to vehicle mileage in excess of 45p per mile.
(d) Any fee for travelling time in excess of £40 per hour.
(e) Any costs or expenses of or relating to the residential assessment of a child.
(f) Any costs or expenses of or relating to treatment, therapy, training or other interventions of an educative or rehabilitative nature.
(g) Any costs and expenses of independent social work provided outside England and Wales.
(h) Any costs and expenses in relation to contact activities including fees, charges and costs of contact centres and any reports or other assessments of contact between children and adults. However, please note that this exclusion does not apply to observation of contact which forms part of a psychological or parenting assessment.

You should therefore ensure that none of these costs are included in your invoice.

This letter of instruction has been agreed between the parties instructing you. I should be grateful if you would acknowledge receipt.

If there is anything at all which is not clear please do not hesitate to contact me.

Yours sincerely

Felicia Anysolicitor

ANYSOLICITORS LLP

5 Letter of instruction for testamentary capacity assessment from GP

Our ref:

Your ref:

Name

Address

Date:

Dear

Re: [Enter client name]

I am the property and affairs deputy for [X]. As deputy for [X] one of my duties is to ensure that appropriate testamentary provisions have been made on behalf of [X]. [X] is at present intestate/[X] has a will which has become outdated and I now wish to apply to the Court of Protection for the authorisation of a statutory will made on behalf of [X].

In order to make an application to the Court I need to obtain evidence that [X] lacks testamentary capacity. The relevant test to apply when assessing testamentary capacity is found in the case of *Banks v Goodfellow* which states that:

> 'It is essential ... that a testator shall understand the nature of the act [of making a will] and its effects; shall understand the extent of the property of which he is disposing; shall be able to comprehend and appreciate the claims to which he ought to give effect, and ... that no disorder of mind shall poison his affections, pervert his sense of right, or prevent the exercise of his natural faculties – that no insane delusion shall influence his will in disposing of his property and bring about a disposal of it which, if his mind had been sound, would not have been made.'

You need only decide on the balance of probabilities whether [X] has or does not have testamentary capacity, in other words, that it is more likely than not. I also request that you pay particular attention to the following points, and indicate whether [X] understands them.

- The nature of the act of making a will. This involves understanding that [s/he] will die and that when [s/he] does the will come into operation. Further, [s/he] can change or revoke the will before his/her death, but only for as long as [s/he] has the mental capacity to do so.

- The effect of making a will. This includes the appointment of executors, deciding who receives what, whether the gifts are outright or limited or conditional in some way, the consequences of a depleted estate, that a beneficiary may pre-decease [him/her], the effect on any previous will, and the reasonably foreseeable consequences of making or not making a will at this time.

- The extent of the estate. This includes the amount of property or money or investments [s/he] holds (although not necessarily the exact value) and the fact that some may be jointly owned, whether [s/he] has any debts, that some benefits may be payable only on [his/her] death irrespective of [his/her] will, and that the estate may change during [his/her] lifetime.
- The possible claims of others. This involves the ability to distinguish between individuals who may have some claim on the estate and to reach some kind of moral judgment in relation to them. Beneficiaries may be left out because they are otherwise well provided for, or because of personal reasons or preferences. [X] must be aware of these reasons and the possibility that these could be challenged.

I attach outline details of [X]'s estate for your reference.

I have requested you prepare this report because [X] informs me that you have been [his/her] doctor for a number of years. If, however, in the course of taking a psychiatric history and conducting a mental state examination you consider a specialist report is required (for example from a psychiatrist or psychologist), please let me know.

If you are of the opinion that [X] has the capacity to make a valid will, I would be grateful if you would confirm this in writing and indicate if you would agree to act as one of the witnesses when the time comes for [him/her] to sign it. If you conclude that [X] lacks testamentary capacity please complete the enclosed Form COP3 'Assessment of Capacity'.

I confirm that we have agreed the sum of £[   ] For the purposes of the examination and preparation of this report. or Please provide me with a note of your fees for providing this opinion. In the unlikely event that you are required to give evidence at court a further fee will be negotiated. Please mark your invoice with the reference stated at the top of this letter.

If you require any further information or clarification on any points please do not hesitate to contact me.

Yours sincerely,

Natasha Molloy

APPENDIX E

Checklists for best interests assessment, care planning and transition planning[1]

A Introduction

1) A common complaint from the court, other parties or the Official Solicitor is that there is insufficient written information about what is proposed for P, why the proposed option is considered to be in P's best interests, and the details of the care plan and transitional arrangements. Often, the relevant issues have in fact been considered by professionals working with P, but the written documentation such as care plans and witness statements does not reflect this adequately.

2) The checklists below list the sort of information and detail that is likely to be required to support an application to the court and within proceedings. They are of particular relevance for local authorities and health bodies considering making an application. They should not, however, simply be applied to every case since not every element will necessarily be relevant.

B Checklist for best interests evidence

1) *Clinical and social work information about P including diagnosis, prognosis, presentation, history*

   Although this information will be contained in the various records, it is helpful to have a summary of relevant details so that anyone unfamiliar with the case can have a picture painted of P and P's care needs.

2) *P's wishes (including IMCA reports if available)*

   P's wishes must be taken into account in making a best interests decision and it is therefore important to make sure that a clear record of P's wishes is kept, whether obtained directly from P, or through reports from third parties such as family members, paid carers, or advocates. This applies whether P expresses consistent or inconsistent wishes – in either case – the information about what P has said will need to be considered, although clearly in the former case it will likely be accorded more weight. Information should also be included about steps that have been taken to improve P's understanding of the issues in dispute, and to assist P in expressing his or her wishes.

---

[1] This is taken from a paper originally drafted by Victoria Butler-Cole and Alex Ruck Keene, both of Thirty Nine Essex Street.

3) *Views of family members*

Careful recording of the views of family members is helpful, including family members who are not parties to proceedings. A record should also be kept of decisions taken as to why particular family members have not been consulted (if relevant).

4) *Details of every option considered for P*

The maxim 'show your working' is vital. If the team working with P have decided that a particular option is in P's best interests, it can be tempting only to explain in detail that preferred option. The other parties and the court need to know what all the possible options are, even if they include options that can immediately be discounted (for example, the option of doing nothing where P faces a serious risk to his or her wellbeing).

Make sure that options proposed by family members are included in the list of possibilities, even though they may not be recommended by the professionals working with P. Where an option proposed by a family member (or indeed by a professional working with P) is not available on funding grounds, this needs clearly to be identified.

5) *Factors for and against each of the options under consideration*

For every option, details of the benefits and risks or disadvantages to P must be set out.[1] It is often easiest to do this in table form, or using bullet points, so that the reader can easily see the issues and can compare the various options under consideration. It is not important not to forget to include practical implications for P as well as less tangible factors such as relationships with family members and care home staff.

---

1 Following the well-established 'balance sheet' approach identified by Thorpe LJ in *Re A* [2000] 1 FLR 549 at 560: 'There can be no doubt in my mind that the evaluation of best interests is akin to a welfare appraisal ... Pending the enactment of a checklist or other statutory direction it seems to me that the first instance judge with the responsibility to make an evaluation of the best interests of a claimant lacking capacity should draw up a balance sheet. The first entry should be of any factor or factors of actual benefit. In the present case the instance would be the acquisition of foolproof contraception. Then on the other sheet the judge should write any counterbalancing dis-benefits to the applicant. An obvious instance in this case would be the apprehension, the risk and the discomfort inherent in the operation. Then the judge should enter on each sheet the potential gains and losses in each instance making some estimate of the extent of the possibility that the gain or loss might accrue. At the end of that exercise the judge should be better placed to strike a balance between the sum of the certain and possible gains against the sum of the certain and possible losses. Obviously, only if the account is in relatively significant credit will the judge conclude that the application is likely to advance the best interests of the claimant'. Whilst this pre-dates the coming into force of the Mental Capacity Act 2005, the Courts have continued to adopt the approach. It is, however, important to note that a balance sheet is not a substitute for applying MCA 2005, s4, simply an 'aide memoire of the key factors and how they match up against each other. [i]t is a route to judgment and not a substitution for the judgment itself': *Cambridge University Hospitals NHS Foundation Trust v BF* [2016] EWCOP 26 at para 29, citing *Re F (A Child) (International Relocation Cases)* [2015] EWCA Civ 882, [2016] Fam Law 565 at para 52.

6) *The likelihood of the pros and cons of each option eventuating*

   Give some indication of whether the risks and benefits identified are likely to occur or not, and this view is taken.

7) *The relative seriousness and/or importance of the pros and cons of each option*

   It may not always be obvious which benefits and disadvantages the professionals place particular importance on and why. A common tension is between avoiding risk and promoting independence: explain why more weight is given to one approach in the particular case.

8) *Reasons for identifying a particular option as being in P's best interests and for rejecting the other options*

   Although it may seem clear in light of the analysis of benefits and disadvantages, it is helpful to set out separately a conclusion about which option is considered to be in P's best interests and why. This is particularly important where there is a dispute and where the proposed option entails significant disadvantages to P, such as a loss of independence, intrusion into a longstanding relationship, or inevitable distress caused by a change of environment.

9) *If proposed option entails risks or disadvantages to P, reasons why these are thought to be outweighed and steps to be taken to minimise them*

   Having decided that certain risks are worth taking in P's best interests, or that certain disadvantages are outweighed by benefits, it is important to show that the professionals have considered what could be done to reduce these risks or disadvantages and set out detailed plans for dealing with them. This might include additional care or staff support for particular periods of time, or the provision of financial assistance to ensure that relationships can continue.

10) *Detailed contingency plans if the proposed option is implemented*

    Where there is the prospect that a proposed option may fail in the short or medium term, there must be thought given to what will happen in those circumstances, to reassure the other parties and the court that hasty and off-the-cuff decisions will not suddenly be required, to the possible detriment of P.

C Checklist for Care Plans

1) Take into account the guidance given by Munby J (as then was) in *R(J) v Caerphilly County Borough Council* [2005] 2 FLR 860, (2005) 8 CCLR 255:

   > 46 ... A care plan is more than a statement of strategic objectives – though all too often even these are expressed in the most vacuous terms. A care plan is – or ought to be – a detailed operational plan. Just how detailed will depend upon the circumstances of the particular case. Sometimes a very high level of detail will be essential. But whatever the level of detail which the individual case may call for, any care plan worth its name ought to set out the operational objectives with sufficient detail – including detail of the 'how, who, what and when' – to enable the care plan itself to be used as a means of checking whether or not those objectives are being met.

2) The assignation of specific responsibilities to individuals is particularly important in the Court of Protection context.

3) Take into account the factors set out in checklist A above wherever the care plan involves the making of decisions for or on behalf of P.

4) Ensure, where appropriate, that consideration is given to the person-centred planning approach.

5) Where the care plan involves any degree of restraint, identify the precise nature of the restraint, the rationale for it, plans to minimise the need for restraint (and contingency plans in case the need for restraint is escalated). If, in the consideration of the need for restraint, it emerges that the requirement goes beyond restraint into a deprivation of the person's liberty then authorisation will be required for that deprivation (how this will be achieved will depend on the setting, and whether the DOLS procedures apply).

6) Be realistic. There is nothing that the Official Solicitor and Court of Protection likes less than to see a care plan founded upon optimism alone: if this means that it is necessary to set a series of apparently limited objectives on the way to a more distant goal, then so be it.

D Checklist for Transition Plans

1) Give details of P's current and proposed care, including full care plans for each setting.

2) Prepare a step-by-step account of how P will be moved from A to B including:
   (a) timing;
   (b) personnel involved;
   (c) who will take responsibility for the transition on the day and subsequently;
   (d) what will happen from P's perspective (eg moving possessions, arrangements for meals on the day etc);
   (e) whether police will be present and if so, details of their involvement (note that unless physical force and/or restraint and/or sedation are essential, it is best to plan on the basis that they will not need to be authorised by the court, and then to return to court in the event the transition does not work and further steps are required); and
   (f) monitoring in days/weeks immediately following move.

3) Where police will be involved in the removal, ensure that the transition plan includes information sufficient to satisfy the guidance given by Coleridge J in Re MP; LBH v GP:[1]

   In the event that it is expected that the assistance of the Police may be required to effect or assist with the removal of a vulnerable/ incapacitated adult ('P') which the Court is being asked to authorise, the following steps should generally be taken:
   (1) the Local Authority/NHS body/other organisation/person (the Applicant) applying to the Court for an authorisation to remove P should, in advance of the hearing of the Application, discuss and, where possible, agree with the Police the way in which it is intended that the removal will be effected, to include, where applicable, the extent to

1 [2009] FD08P01058. (2010) 13 CCLR 171.

which it is expected that restraint and/or force may be used and the nature of any restraint (for example, handcuffs) that may be used;
(2) the Applicant should ensure that information about the way in which it is intended that removal will be effected is provided to the Court and to the litigation friend (in cases where a person has been invited and/or appointed to act as P's litigation friend) before the Court authorises removal. In particular, the Court and the litigation friend should be informed whether there is agreement between the Applicant and the Police and, if there is not, about the nature and extent of any disagreement;
(3) where the Applicant and the Police do not agree about how removal should be effected, the Court should give consideration to inviting/directing the Police to attend the hearing of the Application so that the Court can, where appropriate, determine how it considers removal should be effected and/or ensure that any authorisation for removal is given on a fully informed basis.

APPENDIX F

Court of Protection fees[1]

Fees

At the time of writing, steps have yet to be taken to carry forward the amendments outlined in the Government's response to its consultation on *Court Fees: Proposals for Reform*,[2] which included a number of proposals, including introducing a fee for making an application during the course of proceedings. At present, the fee structure is as set out in the Court of Protection Fees Order 2007 (SI No 145), reproduced in material part in Appendix B. If the fee structure is further updated, news will be reported on at courtofprotectionhandbook.com.

Fee remission

There are provisions for remission of the fees due under the Court of Protection Order[3] which can be summarised thus:

1) Eligibility for remission or part remission of a fee is based on two tests – a disposable capital test and a gross monthly income test. Parties who satisfy the disposable capital test will receive a full fee remission, pay a contribution to the fee or have to pay the fee in full;

2) The gross monthly income test applies a series of thresholds to single people or couples, with an allowance for the number of dependent children they have. Parties with a gross monthly income below a certain threshold will receive a full fee remission. Parties will be required to pay a contribution of £5 towards their fee for every £10 of gross monthly income they earn over the relevant threshold. Parties with income in excess of £4,000 above the relevant threshold will not be eligible for any remission or part remission of a fee;

3) The disposable capital and gross monthly income of a partner is to be treated as disposable capital and gross monthly income of the party. However, where the partner of the party has a contrary interest to the party in the matter to which the fee relates, the disposable capital and gross monthly income of that partner is not treated as the disposable capital and gross monthly income of the party;

---

1 See also the Court of Protection Fees Order 2007, reproduced in appendix B above.
2 See https://consult.justice.gov.uk/digital-communications/court-fees-proposals-for-reform/consult_view/.
3 Under Schedule 2 to the Court of Protection Fees Order 2007 SI No 1745.

4) Where proceedings are brought concerning the property and affairs of 'P', for the purpose of determining whether a party is entitled to a remission or part remission of a fee:
   (a) the disposable capital and gross monthly income of the person bringing those proceedings is not treated as the disposable capital and gross monthly income of the party;
   (b) the disposable capital and gross monthly income of 'P' is to be treated as the disposable capital of the party; and
   (c) the disposable capital and gross monthly income of the partner of 'P', if any, is not treated as the disposable capital and gross monthly income of the party.
5) Where proceedings are brought concerning the personal welfare of 'P', for the purpose of determining whether a party is entitled to a remission or part remission of a fee the disposable capital and gross monthly income of a partner, if any, is not treated as the disposable capital and gross monthly income of the party, where that partner is 'P' who is the subject of those proceedings in which the fee is payable;
6) Where proceedings concern both the property and affairs of 'P' and their personal welfare, their disposable capital and gross monthly income shall be treated in accordance with the rules governing property and affairs proceedings.

Costs proceedings

Special fees apply in relation to the determination in the Senior Court Costs Office by way of detailed assessment of costs incurred in the Court of Protection (by virtue of the Civil Proceedings Fees Order 2008, as amended), as per the table below.

Paragraph of Schedule 1 to the Civil Proceedings Fees Order	Type of case	Fee
6.1(a)	Where the amount of costs does not exceed £3,000	£115
6.1(b)	All other cases	£225
6.2	Appeal (detailed assessment proceedings)	£65
6.3	Request/application to set aside a default costs certificate	£65

APPENDIX G

Useful addresses and resources

Court of Protection	PO Box 70185 First Avenue House 42–49 High Holborn London WC1A 9JA DX 160013 Kingsway 7 Tel: 0300 456 4600 (Monday to Friday, 9am to 5pm) Email: courtofprotectionenquiries@hmcts.gsi.gov.uk
Court of Protection (emergency applications out of office hours)	Tel: 020 7947 6000 (Royal Courts of Justice enquiry number: ask for urgent business officer) or Tel: 020 7947 6260 (Royal Courts of Justice security)
Royal Courts of Justice	The Strand London WC2A 2LL DX 44450 Strand Tel: 020 7936 6000 The Clerk of the Rules (with responsibility for cases before judges of the Family Division sitting in the Court of Protection) 1st Mezzanine Queen's Building Royal Courts of Justice London WC2A 2LL DX 44450 Strand Tel: 020 7947 6543 Email: rcj.familyhighcourt@hmcts.gsi.gov.uk The Chancery Judge's Listing Officer (with responsibility for cases before judges of the Chancery Division sitting in the Court of Protection) Room WG4 Royal Courts of Justice WC2A 2LL DX 44450 Strand Tel: 020 7947 7717

Official Solicitor and Public Trustee	Victory House 30–34 Kingsway London WC2B 6EX DX 141423 Bloomsbury
	Tel: 020 3681 2751 (healthcare and welfare)/ 020 3681 2758 (property and affairs) E-mail: enquiries@offsol.gsi.gov.uk
Office of the Public Guardian	PO Box 16185 Birmingham B12 2WH DX 74424 Birmingham 79 Tel: 0300 456 0300 E-mail: customerservices@publicguardian.gsi.gov.uk
Court Funds Office	Court Funds Office Glasgow G58 1AB DX: 501757 Cowglen Tel: 0300 0200 199 E-mail: enquiries@cfo.gsi.gov.uk

Free legal resources

Website	Contents
www.gov.uk/apply-to-the-court-of-protection	Contains all the Court of Protection forms and current details as to fees
www.judiciary.gov.uk/publication-type/practice-directions/	Contains Practice Directions and Court of Protection Rules
www.bailii.org	British and Irish Legal Information Institute: transcripts of judgments including increasing numbers of decisions of the Court of Protection.
www.mentalhealthlawonline.co.uk	Extensive site containing legislation, case transcripts and other useful material relating to both the Mental Capacity Act 2005 and Mental Health Act 1983. It has transcripts for more Court of Protection cases than any other site (including subscription-only sites).
www.iclr.co.uk	Incorporated Council of Law Reporting website, includes a number of free case summaries and case reports.

Useful addresses and resources

Website	Contents
www.copcasesonline.com	Site maintained by 39 Essex Chambers with searchable database of cases relating to mental capacity law, as well as back issues of newsletter (available for free on a monthly basis. To be added to the mailing list email: marketing@39essex.com)
www.gardensocial.co.uk	Garden Court Chambers has a website and newsletter dedicated to social welfare, including community care, mental health and incapacity issues.
www.courtofprotectionhandbook.com	A free site accompanying *Court of Protection Handbook* with links to relevant statutory material and updates on practice and procedure cross-referenced to the book.
www.legalaidhandbook.com	A free site accompanying the Legal Action Group's *Legal Aid Handbook*, including updates to the handbook and resources relating to legal aid.
www.mhla.co.uk	Mental Health Lawyers Association website including list of members (and associate members) practising in the field of mental health and, increasingly, mental capacity law.
www.lawsociety.org.uk	Law Society website, which includes ability to search for solicitor by area of law.
www.barcouncil.org.uk	The Bar Council maintains a list of all barristers, and a further list of those offering public access, on its website There is also a dedicated telephone number and email address for questions about public access: Tel: 020 7611 1472 E-mail: PAenquiry@barcouncil.org.uk
www.chambersandpartners.com	Legal directory offering information about leading solicitors and barristers, including those specialising in Court of Protection work.

Website	Contents
www.legal500.com	Legal directory offering information about leading solicitors and barristers, including those specialising in Court of Protection work.
www.solicitorsfortheelderly.com	Solicitors for the Elderly (SFE) is an independent, national organisation of lawyers, such as solicitors, barristers and legal executives who provide specialist legal advice for older and vulnerable people, their families and carers. Their website includes a 'find a lawyer' function.
http://pinningtonlaw.co.uk/glossary/	Glossary of legal terms for non-lawyers
www.citizensadvice.org.uk/law-and-rights/	Useful overview of the English legal system and key legal rights

Other useful free resources related to mental capacity law

Website	Contents
www.scie.org.uk	The Social Care Institute for Excellence website includes good practice guidance in a number of areas relating to mental capacity and related law as well as a guide (SCIE Guide 42) to accessing the Court of Protection.
www.mentalcapacitylawandpolicy.org.uk	A website maintained by Alex Ruck Keene dedicated to improving understanding of and practice in the field of mental capacity law, including articles, papers and other resources on the MCA 2005 and discussion forums.
http://thesmallplaces.wordpress.com	Blog site maintained by Lucy Series, socio-legal researcher and expert commentator upon the Court of Protection.
www.communitycare.co.uk	Online magazine dedicated to community care matters, which frequently includes useful stories relating to the MCA 2005.

Website

http://autonomy.essex.ac.uk

Contents

The Essex Autonomy Project is a research and knowledge-exchange initiative based at the University of Essex. It runs a number of projects (and a summer school) relating to the MCA 2005, from a philosophical angle.

Useful books

Practice and procedure

Gordon Ashton OBE (Ed), *Court of Protection Practice*, Jordan Publishing (annual publication)

The Hon Mr Justice Baker, editor-in-chief, *Court of Protection Law Reports*, Jordan Publishing

Christopher Johnston QC and Robert Francis QC (Eds), *Medical Treatment: decisions and the law – the Mental Capacity Act in action*, Bloomsbury Professional, 3rd edition, 2016

Denzil Lush and David Rees, consultant editors, *Heywood & Massey: Court of Protection Practice* (loose-leaf), Sweet & Maxwell

Mental capacity law generally

Caroline Bielanska and Martin Terrell (Eds), *Elderly Client Handbook*, Law Society, 5th edition, 2016

Lawrence Gostin, Jean McHale, Philip Fennell, Ronald D Mackay and Peter Bartlett (Eds), *Principles of Mental Health Law and Policy*, Oxford University Press, 2010

Richard Jones, *Mental Capacity Act Manual*, Sweet & Maxwell, 7th edition, 2016

Penny Letts (Ed), *Assessment of Mental Capacity: a practical guide for doctors and lawyers*, British Medical Association and Law Society, third edition, 2009

Denzil Lush, *Cretney & Lush on Lasting and Enduring Powers of Attorney*, Jordan Publishing, 7th edition, 2013

Alex Ruck Keene (Ed), *Assessment of Mental Capacity: a practical guide for doctors and lawyers*, British Medical Association and Law Society, 4th edition, 2015

publicising matter 5.77
raising matter with elected
representative 5.77
non-contentious personal welfare
matters 5.78–5.84
non-contentious property and
financial matters 5.28–5.75
appointeeships 5.55–5.62
banking arrangements
5.45–5.52
court orders other than
deputyship 5.74–5.75
direct payments 5.69–5.71
enduring power of attorney
5.41
expenditure on person's behalf
5.66–5.68
lasting power of attorney
5.35–5.40
ordinary power of attorney
5.53–5.54
payment for necessary goods
and services 5.6,4 5.65
personal health budgets 5.72
steps to take 5.28–5.34
trusts 5.42–5.44
Appeals 4.122, 18.0–18.60
allowing 18.45
appellant's notice and skeleton
argument 18.26–18.33
evidence given during hearing
18.29
grounds of appeal 18.31
suitable record of judgement
18.27
appellate structure 18.11, 18.12
Court of Appeal, to 18.55–18.60
determination 18.44–18.51
exercise of discretion, against
18.50
fresh evidence 18.46–18.50
permission 18.13–18.25
appeal judge 18.15
conditions 18.25
first instance judge
18.15–18.20
further application 18.23
hearing 18.21
respondents, and 18.21

position between grant of
permission and
determination of appeal 18.43
respondent's notice and skeleton
argument 18.34–18.42
requests 18.35
service 18.39
time for service 18.37
reviews, as 18.46
second 18.52–18.54
Supreme Court, to 18.55–18.60
what can be appealed 18.9
who can appeal 18.10
Applications 5.1–5.84
additional forms 7.15–7.18
appropriateness 5.2
considering evidence 5.4–5.23 see
also Evidence
COP1A form 7.9, 7.10
COP3 form 7.11
dispensing with service 7.28
initial considerations 7.4
jurisdiction 5.2
legal necessity 5.2
maxims 5.3
mixed 7.124–7.128
notifying P 7.30–7.32
permission 5.2
principles 5.3
procedure 7.6–7.35
process 7.19–7.22
property and affairs cases
7.1–7.128
service 7.23–7.27
service abroad 7.29
**Applications in health and welfare
cases** 9.1–9.66
before making 9.2–9.4
Case Management Pilot
4.101–4.103, 9.8–9.14,
10.19–10.28
completing forms 9.21–9.37
confidential matters 9.46–9.47
disputing court's jurisdiction
9.51, 9.52
evidence of capacity 9.38–9.42
form COP3 9.38–9.42
fees 9.45
Form COP1 9.22–9.37

Index

Abuse
  safeguarding, and 23.4–23.7
Accredited legal representatives 11.84–11.114
  appointment 11.86–11.90, 11.93
  definition 11.84, 11.85
  directions 11.101
  duties 11.94–11.100
  good practice guide 11.102–11.114
  requirements for appointment 11.92
  variation or termination of appointment 11.101
Administrative Court 24.1–24.11
  approach of 24.9–24.11
  Court of Protection, and 24.1–24.5
  parallel proceedings 24.6–24.8
Admissions 12.12
Advance decisions 3.102–3.113
  applicability 3.109–3.113
  deputyship, and 3.146
  effect 3.105
  formalities 3.106–3.108
  LPAs, and 3.119–3.120
  refusal of treatment 3.103, 3.104
  validity 3.109–3.113
Advocates' hearing 10.45–10.48
Affidavits 12.28
Alternative dispute resolution 19.1–19.44, *see also* Mediation
  case-law 19.12–19.14
  Code of Practice 19.4–19.8
  COP Rules 19.9– 19.11
  costs, and 16.17
  Select Committee 19.15–19.16

Alternative remedies 5.24–5.84
  banking arrangements 5.45–5.52
    disadvantages 5.50–5.52
    joint accounts and attorneys 5.49
    joint bank accounts 5.47
    limitations 5.50–5.52
    third-party mandates 5.46
  contentious personal welfare matters 5.83, 5.84
    access to health and social care records 5.84
    avenues for complaints and grievances 5.84
    civil applications and proceedings 5.84
    Commissioners 5.84
    complaints about NHS or social services decisions 5.84
    complaints about treatment or care 5.84
    MCA 2005 matters 5.84
    ombudsman 5.84
    possible remedies for incapacitated person 5.84
    possible remedies for public authorities 5.84
    regulatory bodies 5.78, 5.84
  contentious property and financial matters 5.76, 5.77
    civil legal proceedings 5.77
    complaints about NHS or Social Services funding decision 5.77
    criminal legal proceedings 5.77
    MCA 2005 matters 5.77
    ombudsmen 5.77

how to make 9.15–9.20
human rights issues 9.44
issue of proceedings 9.49
notification 9.53
permission 9.50
personal welfare pathway
    9.12–9.14
responding to application 9.54
service 9.48
supporting evidence 9.43
types 9.5–9.7
urgent applications 9.48
Applications under Mental Capacity Act 2005 s21A 21.19–21.55
DOLS regime, and *see* DOLS
making application 21.30–21.32
Appointeeships 5.55–5.62
alternative remedies *see* Alternative remedies
disadvantages 5.61, 5.62
limitations 5.61, 5.62
Authorised court officers 4.20–4.22

Becoming a party 8.13–8.17
Being removed as a party 8.18
Best interests 3.24–3.30, 3.65–3.86
beliefs and values 3.68
care, and 3.78
considerations 3.67
consultation 3.68
future developments 3.68
health, and 3.78
liberty, and 3.79
life-sustaining treatment, and 3.68
matters to consider 3.67–3.71
participation in decision-making 3.68
reasonable belief, and 3.71
safety, and 3.78
serious medical treatment cases, and 22.22–22.25
substituted judgment 3.72–3.77
treatment, and 3.78
weight to be attached to factors 3.70
wishes and feelings 3.68, 3.80–3.83
    balance sheet 3.85
    objectivity, and 3.80–3.86

patient's point of view 3.83
relevant circumstances 3.84
written statements, and 3.68
Bournewood gap 3.172
Bundle preparation 15.14
preliminary documents 15.16–15.17
updating 15.19
witnesses, and 15.21
Bundles 10.32–10.36
agreed 10.33
contents 10.34–10.36
form 10.34, 10.36

Case management 10.7–10.28
applications during proceedings 10.21–10.25
authorised court officers 10.14
directions 10.13
directions hearings 10.13
duty of court 10.9
initial 10.15–10.18
interim hearings 10.26–10.28
overriding objective 10.7–10.11
personal welfare pathway 10.19–10.20
powers of court 10.12–10.14
serious medical treatment cases 22.18
Case Management Pilot 4.101–4.103, 8.26–8.28, 10.19–10.28
Child
litigation friend required by 11.21–11.25
Children 11.21–11.25
Committal proceedings 17.12–17.19
application 17.12
bringing proceedings 17.12–17.16
crucial features 17.15
hearing 17.17–17.19
    evidence 17.16
    private 17.17
    public 17.17
prison, committal to 17.19
vagueness of evidence 17.16
Community treatment order 3.224
Consenting to application 8.9–8.12
Contesting an application 8.19–8.27
flexible approach 8.27

grounds 8.20
property and affairs cases 8.21
Contempt of court 17.20
  continuing *see* Continuing contempt
  publicity, and 13.56, 13.60
Contested facts
  determination of 14.20–14.24
Continuing contempt 17.20–17.24
Convention on the Rights of Persons with Disabilities (CRPD) 25.15–25.21
  aim of 25.15
  arguments, support for 25.21
  best interests, and 25.21
  compliance with 25.20
  lack of capacity, and 25.21
  persuasive authority 25.16
COPR Pr1.2/ COPRA r3A representatives 11.74—11.83
  appointment 11.74, 11.75
  directions 11.81, 11.82
  duties 11.76–11.80
  funding 11.83
  variation or termination of appointment 11.81, 11.82
Copy Direct 13.51, 13.52
Costs 16.1–16.20
  alternative dispute resolution 16.17
  appeals 16.19
  appointment of deputies 16.8
  Civil Procedure Rules, and 16.5, 16.6
  Court of Protection Rules 16.4
  departing from general rule 16.12–16.16
  general rule 16.7–16.11
  mediation 16.17
  Mental Capacity Act 2005 16.2, 16.3
  serious medical treatment cases 16.11
  statutory provisions 16.2–16.6
Court of Appeal
  appeals to 18.55–18.60
Court of Protection 4.1–4.123
  administration 4.15–4.25
  Administrative Court, and 24.1, 24.11
  parallel proceedings 24.6–24.8
  appeals 4.122
  applications under COP Rules r 202 4.92
  applications under MCA 2005 Sch 3 4.93
  appointing deputies under section 16 4.55–4.68
    appointment of successors 4.63
    property and affairs deputyships 4.64
    Public Guardian 4.66
    reimbursement 4.67
    remuneration 4.67
    reports 4.66
    restrictions on deputies 4.65
    revoking 4.68
    security 4.66
    two or more deputies 4.62
    who may be deputy 4.59–4.61
  authorised court officers 4.20–4.22
  budget 4.25
  case-law 4.31–4.33
  case management 4.111–4.123
  children, and 1.9
  circuit judges 4.12
  codes of practice 4.30, 4.37
  contested applications 1.8
  constitution 4.5–4.14
  declarations 4.50, 4.51
  developments 1.7
  district judges 4.12
  duty of parties 4.107
  duty to manage 4.111
  enforcement of orders and declaration 5.123
  EPAs, and 4.79–4.90
    directions concerning operation 4.86
    objections to registration 4.80–4.84
    registered EPA, and 4.85
    registered, objections to 4.88–4.90
    registered, revocation of 4.87
  establishment 4.5–4.14
  European Convention on Human Rights 4.35, 4.39–4.42

habitual residence, and 26.7–26.8
hearings 4.112, 4.113
High Court judge 4.10
history 4.1–4.4
HMCTS 4.15–4.19 *see also* HMCTS
independence of judiciary 4.13, 4.14
interim orders
   reason to believe lack of capacity 4.94–4.99
involvement of person concerned 4.109
jurisdiction 4.7, 4.43–4.48
   exempt matters 4.44
   family matters falling outside MCA 4.46
   limits of 24.3–24.5
   Mental Health Act matters 4.47
   people falling outside MCA 4.45
   voting rights 4.48
law and guidance 4.26–4.42
   lay representation 4.119–4.121
legal aid 4.114
legal textbook opinion 4.34
litigation friends 4.110
LPAs, and 4.69
   best interests, and 4.71–4.73
   determination of existence 4.70
   gifts 4.76
   impropriety, and 4.71–4.73
   powers in relation to operation 4.74–4.75
McKenzie friends 4.116–4.118
Mental Capacity Act 2005, and 4.36
number of applications 4.23, 4.24
orders 4.29, 4.37
orders and decisions under section 16 4.52–4.54
   personal welfare matters 4.53
   property and financial matters 4.54
overriding objective 4.104–4.106
parties to proceedings 4.108
Personal Support Unit 4.115
powers
   advance decisions to refuse treatment 4.77
practice directions 4.30, 4.37
practice guidance 4.30, 4.37
President 4.9
primary legislation 4.28, 4.29
procedures 4.100–4.110
range of applications and orders 4.49–4.99
reform of 1.13
regulations 4.29, 4.37
relevant law and guidance 4.26–4.42
rules 4.29, 4.37
secondary legislation 4.29
Senior Judge 4.9
textbooks 4.38
Vice-President 4.9
workload 4.23, 4.24
Court of Protection Visitor 20.30, 20.37
   evidence, and 12.45, 12.46
   general visit 20.33–20.36
   panels 20.31
   reports 20.37
   routine visits 20.32
Court orders 3.121
Court time
   making effective use of 10.45–10.57
Cross-border matters 26.1–26.15
   basis of jurisdiction 26.6–26.8
   foreign jurisdiction 26.5
   foreign powers of attorney 26.12–26.15
   private international law 26.2
   recognition and enforcement of foreign protective measures 26.9–26.11

Damages
   Human Rights Act 1998 25.6–25.14
Declarations
   Human Rights Act 1998 25.6–25.14
   serious medical treatment cases 22.19–22.21
Deposition 12.39–12.41
Deprivation of liberty 3.166–3.204 *see also* DOLS; DOLS scheme
   authorisation 3.169
   Bournewood gap 3.172
   detention, and 3.200–3.204
   meaning 21.11, 21.12

MHA 1983, and 3.232, 3.233
not permitted 3.169
permitted 3.169
Re X application *see Re X applications*
safeguards 3.175 *see also* DOLS scheme
standard authorisation 3.174
ten commandments 3.198–3.199
three procedures 3.195–3.197
Deputies 3.121–3.148
advance decisions, and 3.146
death of P, and 7.123
duties 3.143–3.145
jointly owned property, and 7.102–7.104
need for 7.36–7.39
panel 21.41, 21.42
personal welfare 3.126–3.138 *see also* Personal welfare deputies
powers 3.125, 3.143–3.145
  court, and 3.148
  donees, and 3.148
recovery of capacity, and 7.120–7.122
register of 20.5–20.15
  searching 20.16–20.22
removal *see* Removal of deputy
restrictions on 3.147
trustee matters, and 7.102–7.104
two or more 3.142
who may be 3.19–3.141
Deputyship applications 7.36–7.83
capacity, and 7.36–7.39
choice of deputy 7.40–7.50
deputy needed, when 7.36–7.39
duties of deputy 7.56–7.59
family care payments 7.64–7.69
gratuitous care 7.64–7.69
investment 7.60–7.63
merits of proposed deputies 7.42–7.45
personal injury award cases 7.70–7.83
  budget 7.75–7.81
  interim payments 7.71
powers of deputy 7.56–7.59
professional deputies 7.49

restrictions 7.54, 7.55
security bond 7.51, 7.52
supervision 7.53
Detention
deprivation of liberty, and 3.200–3.204
Determining application without final hearing 15.3–15.8
Directions
jurisdiction of court 10.4–10.6
Directions hearing 10.50–10.54
powers of court 10.13
Disclosure 12.91–12.119
COP Rules Part 16 12.91, 12.92
general 12.100
issues in practice 12.94–12.101
privilege, and *see* Legal professional privilege
specific categories of documents 12.101
withholding on confidentiality/welfare grounds 12.102–12.111
Documentary evidence 12.29–12.31
DOLS 21.1–21.55
application or review 21.15–21.18
applications under MCA 2005 s21A 21.19–21.55
  after application received 21.40–21.43
  approach of court 21.51–21.55
  making application 21.30–21.32
  preparing application 21.33–21.39
  preparing for first hearing 21.44–21.50
  RPR not bringing challenge 21.25–21.29
  who should make 21.22–21.24
authorisation granted, where 21.13–21.18
challenging in care homes and hospitals 21.9–21.18
no authorisation granted, where 21.9–21.12
reviews 21.13, 21.14
best interests, and 12.67
ECHR article 5, and 12.64

litigation friend, and 12.62–12.68
testing of basis of detention 12.66
DOLS scheme 3.194
  age requirement 3.178
  best interests requirement 3.181, 3.182
  Cheshire West case 3.192
  eligibility requirement 3.187, 3.188
  four mechanisms, and 3.189–3.191
  mental capacity requirement 3.180
  mental health requirement 3.179
  no refusals requirement 3.183–3.186
  Re X 3.194
  six requirements 3.176–3.188
  ten commandments 3.198, 3.199

Enduring power of attorney 5.41
  validity 7.94
Enforcement 17.1–17.24
  contempt of court 17.5
  injunction 17.5
  powers drawn from High Court 17.5, 17.6
  powers of Court of Protection 17.5–17.11
  requirement to take or refrain from actions 17.2
Enforcement of judgments and orders 17.7–17.11
  COP Rules 17.7–17.11
  specific powers contained in COP Rules 17.7–17.11
European Convention on Human Rights
  Court of Protection, and 4.39–4.42, 25.2–25.5
Evidence 5.4–5.23, 12.4–12.90
  admissibility 5.17–5.20
  admissions 12.12
  affidavits 12.28
  analysing 5.16
  applications, and 5.4–5.20
  Court of Protection Visitor, and 12.45, 12.46
  depositions 12.39–12.41
  documentary 12.29–12.31

  documents held by police 12.44
  example 5.11–5.15
  expert *see* Expert evidence
  expert's report 12.82–12.90
    use of 12.85–12.90
  factual 12.13–12.43
  family tensions, and 5.6–58
  hearsay 12.23–12.27
  inquisitorial process, and 12.8
  local authority safeguarding applications 5.9
  meeting 5.23
  notarial acts and instruments 12.32
  powers of court 12.4, 12.5
  Public Guardian, and 12.45, 12.46
  requirements 12.6–12.11
    civil litigation, and 12.8
    costs consequences 12.11
  section 49 reports 12.45–12.53
  standard of proof 5.21–5.22
  weight of 5.17–5.20
  witnesses outside jurisdiction 12.42, 12.43
Expert evidence 12.54–12.90
  access of expert to P 12.80
  capacity, and 12.62–12.63
  duties upon expert 12.81
  expert, meaning 12.56, 12.57
  instructing expert 12.79–12.80, 27.1–27.9
  instructing party 12.74
  letter of instruction 12.80
  permission 12.64–12.78
  public funding, and 12.71–12.75
  single joint experts 12.65, 12.66
  specialist professional witnesses 12.58
  value of 12.55
Experts
  legal aid, and *see* Legal aid

Fact-finding 14.1–14.29
  best interests 14.4
  bundle, and 14.17–14.19
  consequences 14.27–14.29
  determination of contested facts 14.20–14.24
  future risk, and 14.25, 14.26

identification of issues 14.10
interests of adults lacking capacity 14.9
preparing for hearing 14.11–14.19
safeguarding cases, and 14.25
Scott Schedule 14.12–14.14
when necessary 14.3–14.10
Final determination of application 15.1–15.73
Final orders 15.63–15.68
P regaining capacity after 15.69–15.72
Finalising evidence 15.9–15.21
Finalising issues 15.9–15.21
Foreign jurisdiction 26.5
Foreign powers of attorney 26.12–26.15
Funding 6.24–6.89
non-legal aid 6.22
unbundling 6.23

Gifting 7.90–7.92
ability to make 7.90

Habitual residence
meaning 26.7, 26.8
Health and welfare cases
applications in *see* Applications in health and welfare costs
Hearing 15.23–15.59
closing arguments 15.58
day of 15.23, 15.24
negotiations during 15.59
opening speeches 15.26
private or public 15.25
witness evidence 15.27–15.58 *see also* Witnesses
Hearsay evidence 12.23–12.27
HMCTS 4.15–4.19
branches/sections 4.19
functions 4.16
Human Rights Act 1998 25.1–25.15
damages 25.6–25.14
declarations 25.6–25.14
practice points 25.14

Incapacity test 3.40–3.45
unable to make a decision 3.43–3.45

Injunction
power to grant 17.5
Instructing psychiatrists 27.2–27.13
assessment of capacity 27.8, 27.9
evidence of mental disorder 27.6, 27.7
expertise 27.4, 27.5
instructions 27.4–27.12
persuading psychiatrists to get involved 27.2, 27.3
practicalities 27.10–27.12
supporting in court 27.13
Interim hearings 10.26–10.28, 10.58–10.64
undertakings 10.69
Interim injunction 10.61–10.64
Interim orders
jurisdiction of court 10.4–10.6
Interim relief 10.58–10.64
Interpreters 15.48–15.52
Issue of proceedings 9.49

Joining P to proceedings 11.4–11.13
decisions of ECtHR 11.4
Judgment 15.60–15.62
reserved 15.61
Judiciary
independence 4.13, 4.14

Lack of capacity 3.33–3.64
capacity to retain relevant information 3.54
capacity to understand relevant information 3.52, 3.53
capacity to weigh relevant information 3.55–3.63
capacity to communicate decision 3.64
phobia of needles 3.58
serious medical treatment decisions 3.62
correct test 3.39
incapacity test *see* Incapacity test
issue specific approach 3.36, 3.51
relevant information 3.46–3.51
significant transactions 3.50
status approach 3.38
Lasting powers of attorney 3.114–3.120, 7.95–7.101

administrative process 7.97
advance decisions, and 3.119, 3.120
  attorney 3.118
  consent, and 3.116
  donor 3.118
  foreign 26.12–26.15
  personal welfare decision 3.118
  register of 20.5–20.15
    searching 20.16–20.22
  validity 7.76, 7.94
Law Commission
  Mental Capacity Act 2005, and 3.6–3.9
Law reports 4.31–4.33
Lay representation 4.119–4.121
Least restrictive option 3.32
Legal aid 4.114, 6.24–6.89
  advocacy services 6.38
  breaches of ECHR rights 6.40
  contracts 6.30, 6.31
  different levels 6.32
  experts 6.80–6.87
    fees 6.80–6.87
  financial eligibility 6.61–6.89
    evidence of 6.71–6.72
  Help at Court 6.46
  inherent jurisdiction 6.39
  LASPO Act 2012 6.26–6.29
  Lord Chancellor's Guidance 6.59, 6.60
  means test 6.61–6.89
  merits test 6.41–6.58
    cost–benefit 6.52
    Help at Court 6.46
    Legal Help 6.44, 6.45
    Legal Representation 6.47–6.58
    prospects of success 6.53
    standard criteria 6.48
  scope 6.34–6.38
  securing 6.33
  statutory charge 6.76–6.79
  very high costs cases 6.88–6.89
Legal Help
  merits test 6.44, 6.45
Legal professional privilege 12.112–12.119
  legal advice privilege 12.114–12.119

litigation privilege 13.114–12.119
Legal Representation
  merits test 6.47–6.58
Legal representation 6.15–6.23
  barristers 6.18, 6.20, 6.21
  finding a lawyer 6.20, 6.21
  solicitors 6.18, 6.20, 6.21
Litigant in person 6.5–6.14
  legal advice, and 6.7
  overriding objective, and 6.6
  Personal Support Unit 6.8
Litigation friends 4.107, 11.26–11.73
  acting for child or protected party other P 1211.44
  acting for P 11.40–11.43
  appointment 11.27–11.31
    with court order 11.34–11.39
    without court order 11.28–11.33
  child, required by 11.21–11.25
  costs 11.65–11.73
    Official Solicitor 11.65, 11.66
    payable to other parties 11.69–11.73
  duties 11.45–11.52
    deprivation of liberty cases 11.48
    litigation friend acting for child 11.49–11.52
  P, required by 11.40–11.43
  pre-appointment 11.26
  removal by court 11.60–11.64
  terminating appointment 11.53–11.64
    acting on behalf of adult protected party 11.57
    acting on behalf of child 11.58–11.59
    acting on behalf of P 11.53–11.56
    capacity regained 11.53–11.59
  who may be appointed 11.40–11.44
Local authority
  safeguarding, and 23.5–23.12

McKenzie friends 4.116–4.121, 6.9–6.14
  conflict of interest, and 6.11, 6.12
  consultation into role 6.13
  Practice Guidance 6.10
  questions for 6.14

role of 6.9–6.13
Media 13.63–13.85
Mediation 19.26–19.44 *see also*
  Alternative dispute
  resolution
  alternative dispute resolution
    19.26–19.44
  characteristics 19.27
  finding a mediator 19.31, 19.32
  forms 19.27
  mediator, role of 19.28
  practicalities 19.29, 19.30
  preparation for 19.33–19.37
  process 19.38–19.44
  round table meetings
    distinguished 19.22
Medical treatment cases 22.1–22.25
  routine 22.11
  scope of court's jurisdiction 22.3
  serious *see* Serious medical
    treatment cases
  urgent applications 22.13–22.15
Mental Capacity Act 2005 (MCA)
  'acts in connection with a
    person's care or treatment'
    3.149–3.158
    presumed consent 3.150–3.154
  advance decisions *see* Advance
    decisions
  best interests *see* Best interests
  Court of Protection, and 4.36
  court orders 3.121
  deprivation of liberty 3.166–3.204
    see also Deprivation of liberty;
    DOLS
  deputies *see* Deputies
  duty to act in person's best
    interests 3.24–3.30
  duty to consider less restrictive
    options 3.31, 3.32
  duty to help person to make own
    decision where possible
    3.15–3.19
  future developments 3.236
  general framework 3.159–3.165
    advanced dementia example
      3.163–3.165
    personal welfare decisions
      3.159–3.165

withdrawal of artificial support
  example 3.161, 3.162
lack of capacity *see* Lack of
  capacity
lasting powers of attorney (LPA)
  see Lasting powers of
  attorney
Law Commission, and 3.6–3.9
law prior to 3.1–3.5
MHA 1983, and 3.205–3.233
  deprivation of liberty, and
    3.232, 3.233
  mental disorders 3.208–3.231
  physical disorders 3.206, 3.207
  scheme set out in original
    MCA 3.210–3.231
  treating mental disorders
    without consent 3.210–3.231
MHA 2007, and 3.227–3.229
  community treatment order
    3.224
overview 3.1–3.236
presumption of capacity 3.12–3.14
section 5 3.149–3.158
  best interests, and 3.158
  five conditions 3.154
statutory mechanisms 3.90–3.101
  above the line 3.96
  arrangements made after
    capacity lost 3.94
  arrangements made by person
    when they had capacity 3.94
  below the line 3.97
  court application 3.97
  routine care and treatment
    3.100
statutory principles 3.10, 3.11,
  3.87–3.89
United Nations Convention on
  the Rights of Persons with
  Disabilities, and 1.10
unwise decision-making 3.20–3.23
Mental health law
  principles 3.234, 3.235 *see also*
    Principles of mental health
    law

Neary, Steven 2.1–2.15
  accessing Court of Protection 2.6

delay, and 2.8
DOLS, and 2.1, 2.4
DOLS legislation, and 2.14
IMCA, and 2.8, 2.10
legal aid, and 2.6, 2.13
local authority, and 2.3
Magna Carta, and 2.3
Official Solicitor, and 2.12, 2.13
publicity, and 2.15
visits from court-appointed experts 2.12
Nurses 27.14–27.19
family's perspective 27.15
instructing 27.19
nursing report assisting the court 27.14–27.16
P's care needs 27.15
P's current or proposed setting affects care needs 27.15
P's understanding of needs 27.15
potential safeguarding concerns 27.15
registered, types of 27.17, 27.18

Office of the Public Guardian 4.4, 20.1–20.45 *see also* Public Guardian
annual reports 20.27–20.29
investigations 20.38–20.43
nature of 20.1
register of lasting powers of attorney and deputies 20.5–20.15
searching 20.16–20.22
supervision 20.23–20.26
Official Solicitor 11.65, 11.66
litigation friend, as 10.55, 10.57, 11.36, 11.40, 11.41, 12.21

Panel deputies 20.44, 20.45
Participation of P 11.4–11.13
children 11.13
litigation capacity 11.11–11.12
litigation friend 11.10
menu of options 11.6–11.13
practice directions 11.9
recent developments 11.4, 11.5

Permission 9.15, 9.50
test for grant 9.35
Personal injury award cases
deputyship in 7.70–7.83
Personal Support Unit 4.115, 6.8
Personal welfare decision
meaning 3.118
Personal welfare deputies 3.126–3.138
best interest, and 3.138
circumstances in which appropriate 3.127–3.131
donees, and 3.137
ethos of legislation, and 3.134
nearest and dearest 3.133
property and financial deputyship, and 3.135
wishes and feelings, and 3.138
Personal welfare pathway 9.8–9.37
advocates' meetings 10.45–10.48
case management 10.19–10.20
bundles 12.29
interim hearings 10.26–10.28
issue of proceedings 9.49
pre-issue stage 9.12–9.14
urgent applications 9.48
Pilot Practice Direction 4B 10.29–10.44
bundles 10.32–10.36
position statements 10.37–10.44
preliminary documents 10.37–10.44
Police
documents held by 12.44
safeguarding, and 23.22
Position statements 10.37–10.44
Powers of attorney 7.93–7.101
Preliminary documents 10.37–10.44
contents 10.37, 10.38
limited 10.39
lodging 10.44
Presumption of capacity 3.12–3.14
Principles of mental health law 3.234, 3.235
abuse of power, and 3.235
balanced legal structure 3.235
compulsion, use of 3.235

cumulative verifications 3.235
promotion of liberty 3.235
rule of law 3.235
separation of powers 3.235
state intervention 3.235
value judgments 3.235
Private hearings 13.2
Private international law 26.2
Property and affairs application 7.1–7.104
Property and affairs pathway 8.29–8.49
case management on allocation 8.31
costs 8.43, 8.44
dispute resolution hearing 8.32–8.40
final hearing 8.41, 8.42
urgent applications 8.45–8.49
when application becomes contested 8.29, 8.30
Protected parties 11.14–11.20
litigation capacity 11.16–11.20
Protective measures
foreign
recognition and enforcement 26.9–26.11
Psychiatrists
instructing 27.2–27.13 *see also* Instructing psychiatrists
Public Guardian 20.1–20.45
see also Office of the Public Guardian
evidence, and 12.45, 12.46
investigations 20.38–20.43
responsibilities 20.4
Public hearing see Publicity
Publicity
Administration of Justice Act 1960 13.6
Case Management Pilot 13.4
Court of Protection Rules 13.7–13.12
PD Pilot 4A/PD 13A 13.9–13.12
Pilot Order 13.25–13.41
anonymisation of documents 13.37
assessment 13.43
easy read version 13.27

injunctive provision 13.32–13.35
standard order 13.29, 13.30
serious medical treatment cases 13.44–13.55
Transparency Pilot 13.4, 13.13–13.24
application 13.14–13.17
public hearing 13.19

Re X applications 21.56–21.73
ancillary matters 21.67
characteristics 21.62
court can in principle make order 21.67
court consenting to arrangements 21.67
making 21.63–21.73
order 21.67
procedural matters 21.67–21.73
service of order 21.72
Recognition and enforcement of foreign protective measures 26.9–26.11
Reconsideration 18.3–18.8
procedure 18.3–18.8
purpose 18.8
Removal of deputy 7.105–7.116
application 7.107, 7.113–7.115
behaviour to be taken into account 7.108–7.112
redress, and 7.117–7.119
Reports
COP visitor reports 20.37
expert reports, see 'Experts'
section 49 reports 12.45–12.53
Responding to applications 8.1–8.17
becoming a party 8.13–8.17
initial steps 8.4–8.8
Round table meetings 19.17–19.25
advantages 19.22–19.25
disadvantages 19.22–19.25
mediation distinguished 19.19
nature of 19.17
questions to be addressed 19.21

Safeguarding 23.1–23.22
abuse, and 23.4–23.7
Court of Protection, and 23.13–23.18

decision to bring proceedings 23.15
failure to take stock, and 23.16
police involvement 23.22
"voyage of discovery" 23.14
during currency of Court of Protection proceedings 23.19–23.21
local authority, and 23.5–23.12
meaning 23.4–23.12
nature of 23.1, 23.2
obligations 23.3
Scheme of book 1.1–1.5
Serious medical treatment cases 22.4–22.10
allocation 22.16, 22.17
application by organisation providing treatment 22.10
best interests decision 22.22–22.25
case management 22.18
decisions regarded as 22.8, 22.9
declarations 22.19–22.21
definition 22.4–22.10
examples 22.8
pre-action steps 22.12
serious consequences 22.5
urgent applications 22.13–22.15
Service 7.23–7.29
abroad 7.29
dispensing with 7.28
Skeleton arguments 15.22
Skype
evidence by 7.45, 15.57
Standard of proof 5.21–5.22
balance of probability 5.21
Statutory wills 7.84–7.92
medical evidence 7.85
procedure for approval 7.86–7.89

Substituted judgment
best interests, and 3.72–3.77
Supreme Court
appeals to 18.55–18.60

Textbooks 4.38
Timetabling 15.9–15.21
Trusts 5.42–5.44

Unable to make a decision
meaning 3.43–3.45
Urgent applications 10.65–10.72
guiding principle 10.67
order without notice to party 10.69
telephone, by 10.72

Very high costs cases 6.88, 6.89
definition 6.88
Solicitors Information Pack 6.89
Video-links
evidence by 15.52–15.58
Vulnerable witnesses 15.45–15.47

Wasted costs orders 16.18
Witness statements 12.14–12.22
contents 12.14–12.20
formalities 12.14–12.20
timing 12.21–12.22
Witness summons 12.33–12.38
Witnesses 15.27–15.58
evidence 15.22–15.33
handling 15.31
hearing from P 15.34–15.44
interpreters 15.48–15.52
questioning 15.29–15.31
remote evidence giving 15.53–15.58
Skype, evidence by 15.58
video-links 15.53–15.58
vulnerable 15.45–15.47